BYRON: THE CRITICAL HERITAGE

THE CRITICAL HERITAGE SERIES

GENERAL EDITOR: B. C. SOUTHAM, M.A., B.LITT. (OXON.)
Formerly Department of English, Westfield College, University of London

Volumes in the series include

JANE AUSTEN	B. C. Southam
BROWNING	Boyd Litzinger, *St. Bonaventure University* and Donald Smalley, *University of Illinois*
BYRON	Andrew Rutherford, *University of Aberdeen*
COLERIDGE	J. R. de J. Jackson, *Victoria College, Toronto*
DICKENS	Philip Collins, *University of Leicester*
HENRY FIELDING	Ronald Paulson, *The Johns Hopkins University, Baltimore* and Thomas Lockwood, *University of Washington*
THOMAS HARDY	R. G. Cox, *University of Manchester*
HENRY JAMES	Roger Gard, *Queen Mary College, London*
JAMES JOYCE (2 vols)	Robert H. Deming, *University of Miami*
D. H. LAWRENCE	R. P. Draper, *University of Leicester*
MILTON	John T. Shawcross, *University of Wisconsin*
SCOTT	John O. Hayden, *University of California, Davis*
SWIFT	Kathleen Williams, *Rice University, Houston*
SWINBURNE	Clyde K. Hyder
TENNYSON	J. D. Jump, *University of Manchester*
THACKERAY	Geoffrey Tillotson and Donald Hawes, *Birkbeck College, London*
TROLLOPE	Donald Smalley, *University of Illinois*

43945

BYRON

THE CRITICAL HERITAGE

Edited by

ANDREW RUTHERFORD

Regius Professor of English
University of Aberdeen

NEW YORK

BARNES & NOBLE, INC.

Published
in Great Britain 1970
Published in the United States of America 1970
by Barnes & Noble Inc., New York, N.Y., 10003

© Andrew Rutherford 1970

SBN 389-01695-0

Printed in Great Britain

TO MY MOTHER

General Editor's Preface

The reception given to a writer by his contemporaries and near-contemporaries is evidence of considerable value to the student of literature. On one side we learn a great deal about the state of criticism at large and in particular about the development of critical attitudes towards a single writer; at the same time, through private comments in letters, journals or marginalia, we gain an insight upon the tastes and literary thought of individual readers of the period. Evidence of this kind helps us to understand the writer's historical situation, the nature of his immediate reading-public, and his response to these pressures.

The separate volumes in the *Critical Heritage Series* present a record of this early criticism. Clearly for many of the highly productive and lengthily reviewed nineteenth- and twentieth-century writers, there exists an enormous body of material; and in these cases the volume editors have made a selection of the most important views, significant for their intrinsic critical worth or for their representative quality—perhaps even registering incomprehension!

For earlier writers, notably pre-eighteenth century, the materials are much scarcer and the historical period has been extended, sometimes far beyond the writer's lifetime, in order to show the inception and growth of critical views which were initially slow to appear.

In each volume the documents are headed by an Introduction, discussing the material assembled and relating the early stages of the author's reception to what we have come to identify as the critical tradition. The volumes will make available much material which would otherwise be difficult of access and it is hoped that the modern reader will be thereby helped towards an informed understanding of the ways in which literature has been read and judged.

B.C.S.

Contents

CONTENTS

CONTENTS

CONTENTS

I must acknowledge my great debt to Professor S. C. Chew's authoritative survey, *Byron in England: His Fame and After-Fame*, and to Professor W. W. Pratt's excellent account of *Don Juan* criticism in Volume IV of the 'variorum' edition of *Don Juan* edited by W. W. Pratt himself and T. G. Steffan.

I should like to thank the following publishers for permission to quote from the works indicated: The *Atlantic Monthly* (Paul Elmer More, 'The Wholesome Revival of Byron'; J. F. A. Pyre, 'Byron in Our Day'); Ernest Benn, Ltd. (*The Complete Works of Percy Bysshe Shelley*, ed. Roger Ingpen and W. E. Peck); Basil Blackwell and Mott, Ltd. (Friedrich Engels, *The Condition of the Working Class in England*, trans. and ed. W. O. Henderson and W. H. Chaloner); Bowes and Bowes, Ltd. (E. M. Butler, *Byron and Goethe*); The Clarendon Press (*The Letters of Percy Bysshe Shelley*, ed. F. L. Jones; *The Letters of William and Dorothy Wordsworth*, ed. E. de Selincourt; *The Correspondence of Henry Crabb Robinson with the Wordsworth Circle*, ed. Edith J. Morley; *The Letters of Samuel Taylor Coleridge*, ed. E. L. Griggs; *The Letters of Thomas Moore*, ed. W. S. Dowden; *The Poetical Works of John Keats*, ed. H. W. Garrod); Constable and Co. Ltd. and T. M. Raysor (*Coleridge's Miscellaneous Criticism*, ed. T. M. Raysor; *The Letters of Sir Walter Scott*, ed. H. J. C. Grierson, Davidson Cook, W. M. Parker and others); J. M. Dent and Sons, Ltd. (*The Complete Works of William Hazlitt*, ed. P. P. Howe; *Henry Crabb Robinson on Books and their Writers*, ed. Edith J. Morley; *The Letters of Charles and Mary Lamb*, ed. E. V. Lucas); Harvard University Press (*The Letters of John Keats 1814–1821*, ed. H. E. Rollins; *The Keats Circle: Letters and Papers 1814–1879*, ed. H. E. Rollins); Hatchards Booksellers, Ltd. (G. K. Chesterton, *Twelve Types*); Macmillan and Co. Ltd. (George Saintsbury, *A History of Nineteenth Century Literature 1780–1895*); Methuen and Co. Ltd. (*The Letters of Charles and Mary Lamb*, ed. E. V. Lucas); John Murray (Publishers), Ltd. (Lord Broughton, *Recollections of a Long Life*, ed. Lady Dorchester; *Lord Byron's Correspondence*, ed.

ACKNOWLEDGMENTS

John Murray; *Byron. A Self-Portrait. Letters and Diaries, 1798 to 1824*, ed. Peter Quennell; George Paston and Peter Quennell, *To Lord Byron*; L. A. Marchand, *Byron: A Biography; The Works of Lord Byron: Letters and Journals*, ed. R. E. Prothero; *The Works of Lord Byron: Poetry*, ed. E. H. Coleridge); Oklahoma University Press (*John Bull's Letter to Lord Byron*, ed. A. L. Strout; *The Letters of Mary Shelley*, ed. F. L. Jones); Oxford University Press (Jane Austen, *Persuasion*, ed. R. W. Chapman; *The Poetical Works of Leigh Hunt*, ed. H. S. Milford); Yale University Press (*The George Eliot Letters*, ed. Gordon S. Haight). I should also like to thank Mrs. Nona Hill for her permission to quote from Arthur Symons, *The Romantic Movement in English Poetry*.

NOTE ON THE TEXT

The materials printed in this volume follow the original texts in all important respects, and in some typographical conventions which have been retained as characteristic of the period, but the form of reference to titles has been regularized. Wherever possible important studies have been printed in their entirety, or nearly so, but the copious nature of nineteenth-century criticism has necessitated a good deal of cutting. Authorial footnotes have sometimes been omitted, as have line references to the original editions, less essential sections of the critic's argument, and the long summaries of poems with illustrative quotations which were a typical feature of early nineteenth-century reviews. In general, though not invariably, critiques which first appeared as reviews have been reprinted in their original form, whereas critical essays which were subjected to revision have been reprinted in the later version, with the original date given in square brackest. Except in the Introduction, editorial notes are distinguished by square brackets.

The following abbreviations have been used:

Corr   *Lord Byron's Correspondence*, ed. John Murray, 1922.

LJ   *The Works of Lord Byron: Letters and Journals*, ed. R. E. Prothero, 1898–1901.

PW   *The Works of Lord Byron: Poetry*, ed. E. H. Coleridge, 2nd edn., 1904–5.

Introduction

I

Byron was at once the most popular and the most controversial poet of his generation—indeed of the whole English romantic movement. Almost all his publications, therefore, major or minor, failures and successes, were the subject of widespread critical discussion. This could take many different forms. There were short notices or formal reviews in newspapers and periodicals. There were set-piece critical essays (like Hazlitt's in *The Spirit of the Age*), and comments incidental to the discussion of other authors. There were pamphlets, often polemical, on individual works, or on aspects of Byron's writing as a whole; and in due course there were book-length studies, like Sir Samuel Egerton Brydges' *Letters on the Character and Poetical Genius of Lord Byron* (1824). There were tributes, attacks, or parodies in verse (not to mention imitations which, however sincere their flattering appreciation, fall outwith the scope of this collection). There were criticisms by novelists, projected in the form of fiction. There were comments innumerable in private letters and journals, and in conversations which have been preserved by diarists or correspondents, literary gossips or faithful recorders of table-talk like the indefatigable Henry Crabb Robinson. All these varieties are represented in this volume, but the bulk of early nineteenth-century criticism is so great that only a small proportion of the whole can be included.

In selecting material I have avoided an excessive concentration on any single area of Byron's work. Modern critics, like so many of their Victorian predecessors, have seen Byron's *ottava rima* satires as his greatest achievement, but this consensus should not be allowed to distract our attention from other important aspects of his work, or to distort our picture of reactions in the poet's own day. The first half of this volume, therefore, presents examples of contemporary criticism of all the major areas of Byron's poetry, excluding only biographical controversy and comments on certain minor works like *Hebrew Melodies, Heaven and Earth, The Island* and *The Deformed Transformed*. The second half presents major documents of Victorian and Edwardian criticism. The period covered—just over a century—extends from 1808, when the *Edinburgh Review* published its notorious attack on *Hours of Idleness* (No. 1), to 1909, the date of Arthur Symons's interesting critique of Byron (No. 68), which brings us to the very threshold of 'modern' criticism. (This is, for example, the earliest document recommended to historically minded readers in Paul West's collection of *Twentieth Century Views* on Byron,[1] but no extract from it is included in that volume.) Material has been selected on various grounds— for its intrinsic value as criticism, for its historical interest, for the light it throws on other authors through their response to Byron's works, for its impact on Byron himself, and for its representative quality.

The last criterion is, however, an elusive one, since the moral, aesthetic and emotional responses of a generation can hardly be quantified, and the sense in which any individual writer is 'representative' must always be a matter for debate. A literary sociologist might well complain that this collection documents the views of exceptional individuals or of social, educational and literary élites rather than those of the reading public as a whole; but it is of course such individuals and such élites that produce the most interesting and influential criticism. Hence in dealing with periodicals, which provide the majority of texts in the contemporary section of this volume, I have concentrated on the great prestige reviews, the *Edinburgh* and the *Quarterly*, and to a lesser extent on *Blackwood's Edinburgh Magazine*, the most famous—some would say the most infamous—of the literary magazines. Other journals—like the *London Magazine* or the *Examiner*—contain some interesting criticism; and a more sociological investigation of contemporary taste would, of course, involve fuller attention to 'lesser' periodicals—some of which, catering for special sections of the reading public, might have a larger circulation than the prestige reviews, though others again were lesser in sales as well as quality.[2] Such organs of opinion have their proper interest for the historian of periodical criticism, but apart from a very conventional notice of *English Bards* and two notes on *Beppo* (Nos. 2 and 17), I cite from them only some typical comments on *Don Juan*, *Cain* and *The Vision of Judgment*, Byron's most controversial productions. An exhilarating feature of such periodical assessments is their lively rhetoric: one can cull many gems, like the *British Critic*'s denunciation of *Don Juan* Canto I as not 'a history only, but a manual of profligacy'; or the *Literary Gazette*'s description of Canto VI as 'moral vomit', 'the gloating brutality of a wretched debauchee'; or the *Edinburgh Magazine*'s assertion that in this poem Byron 'scatters about ordure like a drunken scavenger; yet he assures us that his organs are endowed with such exquisite sensibility that he could almost "die of a rose in aromatic pain".'³ Such writing, however, brings diminishing returns of interest and amusement, and it is a relief to pass from the fairly predictable judgments of these lesser reviews and magazines—and indeed from the often irresponsible though lively polemic of *Blackwood's*— to the serious, sustained discussions of Byron's poetry in the *Edinburgh* and the *Quarterly*. The traditional accusations of political and literary prejudice cannot be brought against their treatment of Byron, which is characterized over the years by its blend of sympathy and astringency, fairness and rigour, Jeffrey's own contributions being particularly impressive. His judicious assessments, still more his continual endeavour to place particular judgments in an appropriate historical and philosophical framework, make his articles rewarding reading even today— and they document most usefully one exceptionally competent and influential reader's developing response to Byron's poetry.

In citing individuals' opinions from letters, conversations or other sources, I have (while including some miscellaneous items) concentrated on two main groups: firstly, the major writers of the day, whose views are of special interest even when they are misguided or unfair; and secondly, the members of John Murray's 'Synod'—the Albemarle Street circle—many of whom Byron counted as his friends, and who acted to some extent as advisers, whether to the publisher or to the poet. They, together with personal friends like John Cam Hobhouse, constituted a pressure group which he came increasingly to resist, but for much of his career he was acutely conscious of their views on his productions. Byron was never a Shelleyan nightingale, sitting in darkness and singing to cheer his own solitude with sweet sounds: he was always conscious of an audience, whether the inner circle at Albemarle Street or society at large, and his awareness of public response often affected his artistic self-confidence, his creative impulse, and his actual plans for future composition.

II

Byron's sensitivity to criticism was, initially, extreme. *Hours of Idleness* was well received by most reviewers, but his growing self-

3

satisfaction was soon shattered by the *Edinburgh's* attack in February
1808 (No. 1). He had borne some other adverse comments with at
least a pretence of equanimity, noting like a seasoned author that
abuse might help his sales: his very different reaction now was due
partly to the *Edinburgh's* unique prestige among literary periodicals,
and partly to its political importance as an organ of Whig opinion.
'As an author,' he told Hobhouse, 'I am cut to atoms by the E[dinburgh]
Review. It is just out, and has completely demolished my little fabric
of fame. This is rather scurvy treatment from a Whig Review, but
politics and poetry are different things, and I am no adept in either.
I therefore submit in Silence.'⁴ In later years Byron liked to stress his
resilience and combativeness under this attack. 'I . . . read it the day
of its denunciation,' he wrote in his journal of 1813, '—dined and
drank three bottles of claret . . . neither ate nor slept the less, but,
nevertheless, was not easy till I had vented my wrath and my rhyme
. . . against every thing and every body.'⁵ There is reason to suppose,
however, that the immediate effect was more devastating than he
later acknowledged: one of Hobhouse's marginalia in his copy of
Moore's *Life of Byron* indicates that 'he was very near destroying
himself' on this occasion⁶; but his resentment then found expression as
he refashioned his projected *British Bards* to form the satire *English
Bards and Scotch Reviewers*. With new-found caution, he had this
published anonymously in 1809; but when it met with some acclaim
he prepared a second, expanded version, which was published with his
name in the same year. Two further editions appeared while he was
in the East, and on his return he hastened to reinforce success with a
fifth, as well as another work in the same vein. These, however, he
was persuaded to withhold for the time being while *Childe Harold's
Pilgrimage* went through the press; and as he soon became friendly
with Lord and Lady Holland and others whom he had attacked in his
satire, he now suppressed it completely, forbidding even the republication of any of the existing versions.

The triumphant success of *Childe Harold* in March 1812 marks the
beginning of a new phase in Byron's relation with reviewers and
public. Jeffrey's courteous refusal to prolong the *Edinburgh's* quarrel
with him, and his generous review of *Childe Harold* (No. 4), made a
deep impression on Byron, who also valued greatly his subsequent
praise of the verse tales. ('As for Jeffrey,' he wrote to Moore in April
1814, 'it is a very handsome thing of him to speak well of an old
antagonist,—and what a mean mind dared not do. Any one will

revoke praise; but ... very few have strength of mind to unsay their censure, or follow it up with praise of other things.')[7] With the *Quarterly* Byron enjoyed a special relationship. Its publisher, John Murray, was the publisher of his own works from *Childe Harold* onwards; its editor, William Gifford, was his first model as a satirist, his literary mentor, and an admirer of his poetry. The Tory circle which influenced its policies were his friends and acquaintances; and although there were potential conflicts over politics and religion, Byron had in fact the status of a favourite if somewhat prodigal son. Behind the comments of reviews and critics, moreover, rose the great swell of popular approval. *Childe Harold*, as well as being the sensation of the fashionable world when it appeared, ran through some ten editions by 1815, and the popularity of Byron's verse tales can be gauged by the almost incredible rapidity with which edition after edition poured from the press, or more simply by the fact that ten thousand copies of *The Corsair* were sold on the first day of publication. With this kind of success it was easy for him to profess, as he sometimes did, indifference to criticism, or to deplore 'the detestable taste of the day';[8] but he none the less enjoyed the chorus of acclaim that met each new publication; he particularly relished the *Edinburgh*'s approval; and he was gratified in 1814 to find his and Moore's poetic merits being canvassed in a Java gazette which Murray sent him. ('There is *fame* for you at six and twenty!' he commented in 1821. 'Alexander had conquered India at the same age; but I doubt if he was disputed about, or his conquests compared with those of Indian Bacchus, at Java.'[9]) In such circumstances he could disregard any criticism of his poems on moral, political or religious grounds: indeed, he rather enjoyed being the centre of controversy, as long as his genius was freely acknowledged. As Wordsworth shrewdly observed in April 1816, 'It avails nothing to attempt to heap up indignation upon the heads of those whose talents are extolled in the same breath. ... Allow them to be men of high genius, and they have gained their point and will go on triumphing in their iniquity.'[10]

Apart from bridling at accusations of plagiarism, to which he was always very sensitive, Byron went on 'triumphing in his iniquity' until the scandal of his separation from Lady Byron early in 1816. He had already experienced the virulence of newspaper attacks provoked in 1814 by his political verses 'Lines to a Lady Weeping'.[11] Even then he had been somewhat angered and discomposed; but now, with the breakdown of his marriage, he had to face the full fury of popular indignation. The controversy is of small literary as distinct from biographical and social interest, except that it permanently blackened Byron's reputation for some sections of the reading public. Many who had admired his genius while deploring his beliefs, many who had seen him as erring but capable of reformation, now dismissed him as a sinner utterly beyond redemption, a figure of Satanic evil. And henceforward all who wished (like *Blackwood's* first reviewer of *Don Juan*) to condemn the immorality of Byron's writings and denounce what one pamphleteer called his 'deformity . . . as a Christian and as a man',[12] could point to this episode in his life in confirmation of their literary diagnoses. Byron's own friends remained loyal, but his sense of isolation was acute: his gratitude was therefore all the more intense when Leigh Hunt defended him in the *Examiner*, or when Scott and Jeffrey wrote their sympathetic reviews of *Childe Harold* Canto III in the *Quarterly* and *Edinburgh*.[13] Byron himself was never to return to England, and from 1816 onwards his attitude to his public was more ambivalent even than before: still eager, still continually striving for fame and popular success, he felt alienated from, at times antagonistic to, the very readers he was wooing; and he had increasingly a tendency to shock them, to outrage their susceptibilities and beliefs—to exploit the role of exile, rebel and Satanist, which to some extent he had deliberately chosen, and to some extent had forced upon himself.

In spite of the scandal, he was now at the peak of his fame, and Murray, at a booksellers' dinner in December 1816, had no difficulty in selling 7,000 copies of *Childe Harold* Canto III, and 7,000 of *The Prisoner of Chillon*.[14] But after the composition of *Manfred* and *Childe Harold* Canto IV, works which spring obviously from the same kind of inspiration, satisfying the same tastes, Byron's progress was less confident. 'I begin to think I have mined my talent out,' he wrote ruefully in May 1820, 'and proceed in no great phantasy of finding a new vein.'[15] In this long period of experiment, of trial and sometimes error, he felt more dependent in some ways on the advice of his publisher and friends, who were more in touch with public reactions at home. 'If you would tell me exactly,' he wrote to Murray on 17 July 1818, '(for I know nothing and have no correspondents except on business) the state of the reception of our late publications, and the feeling upon them, without consulting any delicacies (I am too seasoned to require them), I should know how and in what manner to proceed.'[16] When, however, adverse opinions did reach him, they were most unwelcome. He was mortified that Gifford did not like his dramas, and indeed their failure with the public was a great disappointment to him, even though he consoled himself with the thought that these works were too good for the taste of the day.[17] He was angered and hurt by Hobhouse's outspoken condemnation of *Cain*;[18] and although this work was deliberately provocative, he resented the outcry which he must have known it would produce. The MS of *Don Juan* Canto I roused consternation in Murray's advisers, and the progress of the poem was undoubtedly affected by the 'nonsensical prudery' of their response. 'I have not yet begun to copy out the second Canto,' Byron wrote on 1 February 1819, '. . . from natural laziness, and the discouragement of the milk and water they have thrown upon the first.'[19] The public outcry too, when Cantos I and II were published, affected his enthusiasm for the project. Yet with Byron disappointment shaded easily into defiance; he refused to accept the validity of the objections urged against the poem; and as time went on he became more and more convinced that his critics were in the wrong. 'You have been careless of this poem,' he told Murray in August 1821, 'because some of your Synod don't approve of it; but I tell you, it will be long before you see any thing half so good as poetry or writing. . . . Your envious little knot of parson-poets may say what they please: time will show that I am not in this instance mistaken.'[20]

In these later years he developed a distaste not merely for the comments of the 'cursed puritanical committee' at Albemarle Street, but for the whole tribe of reviewers, who, like *Blackwood's* men, were 'hyperbolical in their praise, and diabolical in their abuse'.[21] There had been a time when he had relished Reviews 'like Soda-water in an Italian Summer'; but on 8 October 1820 he instructed Murray never to favour him with any periodical publications, 'excepting the *Edinburgh*, *Quarterly*, and an occasional *Blackwood*, or now and then a *Monthly Review*; for the rest I do not feel curiosity enough to look beyond their covers.'[22] He was not wholly consistent about this— consistency was never one of his strong points—and early in 1821 we find him a subscriber to the *Literary Gazette*; but in September of that year he reaffirmed and redefined his position in a series of 'articles' which he presented to John Murray:

4thly [he stipulated] That you send me *no periodical works* whatsoever—*no Edinburgh, Quarterly, Monthly*, nor any Review, Magazine, Newspaper, English or foreign, of any description.

5thly. That you send me *no* opinions whatsoever, either *good, bad*, or *indifferent*, of yourself, or your friends, or others, concerning any work, or works, of mine, past, present, or to come. . . .
Some of these propositions may at first seem strange, but they are founded.
. . . Reviews and Magazines are at the best but ephemeral and superficial reading: *who thinks* of the *grand article* of *last year* in any *given review?* in the next place, if they regard *myself*, they tend to increase *Egotism; if* favourable, I do not deny that the praise *elates*, and if unfavourable, that the abuse *irritates*. . . .
The same applies to opinions, *good, bad*, or *indifferent*, of persons in conversation or correspondence: these do not *interrupt*, but they *soil* the *current* of my *Mind*. . . .
You will say, 'to what tends all this?' I will answer THAT;—to keep my mind *free and unbiassed* by all paltry and personal irritabilities of praise or censure;—to let my Genius take its natural direction, while my feelings are like the dead, who know nothing and feel nothing of all or aught that is said or done in their regard.[23]

This agreement was not strictly kept, but it shows the direction in which Byron's mind was moving. He was by no means indifferent to popular opinion: he still tried, sometimes pathetically, to repeat his former successes; but the feeling that he had lost public favour, that he was, as he told Moore in April 1823, 'as low in popularity and bookselling as any writer can be',[24] had in some ways a salutary effect. 'As to myself,' he wrote to Douglas Kinnaird in May 1822, 'I shall not be deterred by an outcry. They hate me, and I detest them, I mean your present public, but they shall not interrupt the march of my mind, nor prevent me from telling the tyrants who are attempting to trample upon all thought, that their thrones will yet be rocked to their foundation.'[25] It was in this mood that he devoted himself to the later cantos of *Don Juan*. It was in this mood that he turned, with some relief, from literature to action, when he sailed for Greece in 1823.

The attacks which discouraged or angered him by their brutality[26] were directed mainly at the moral, political and religious tendencies of his writings. In the early cantos of *Childe Harold's Pilgrimage* he had dropped the mask of orthodoxy which had served as a useful satiric device in *English Bards and Scotch Reviewers*; and his run of successes had depended (among other things) on the deliciously shocking character of his heroes, the daring scepticism of his metaphysics, and the unconventionality of his political reflections. These had not gone unrebuked, for outrage and delight were fused in the response invited by his poetry, and the balance could easily tip to one extreme or to the other; but from 1816 onwards such criticism was intensified. Jeffrey's charge, in his review of *Childe Harold* Canto III, that Byron with all his genius was guilty of 'not merely errors in taste, but perversions of morality', and Scott's appeal to him, in *his* review of the same poem, to 'submit to the discipline of the soul enjoined by religion, and recommended by philosophy' [27]—these were dignified and sympathetic versions of a rebuke which issued from other pens in terms of strident, virulent denunciation. (The polemic launched by 'Presbyter Anglicanus' against *Beppo* and its predecessors [No. 18] serves as an example.) Byron's attitude to Christianity had also been the subject of continual controversy, which raged over the scepticism of *Childe Harold* and the irreverence of *Don Juan*, but reached its height with the fundamental challenges to orthodoxy in *Cain*, and the blasphemous shock tactics of *The Vision of Judgment*. *Don Juan* also roused a storm of indignation by its personal and political satire, and by what was seen as its profligacy, its lubricity, and its cynical deflation of all moral values. As for the poet's political opinions, these had elicited a protest from the *Quarterly* reviewer in 1812; and Scott, who did not take the poet's 'high strain of . . . Liberalism' very seriously, none the less felt that a firm rebuke was called for in his reviews of *Childe Harold* Cantos III and IV (see Nos. 12 and 20). These are only two examples out of many; but in his later years Byron put himself beyond the pale for a great number of his readers by his revolutionary or republican sympathies, his contempt for the royal family and established order, and his association with such disreputable figures as John and Leigh Hunt in the production of the *Liberal*. In a period of political reaction and repression at home and abroad, a period haunted by the fear of revolution, Byron's activities could be seen as irresponsible, malignant, verging on the diabolical. Indeed, when Wordsworth described the projected *Liberal* as 'a Journal to be directed against everything in religion, in morals and probably in government and literature, which our Forefathers have been accustomed to reverence', [28] he was expressing a widely held view of Byron as not merely a profligate and a blasphemer, but a dangerous force of subversion and corruption, moral, religious and political.

But for all this polemic, Byron remained unrivalled in popularity with English readers. His works ran through edition after edition—the demand indicated by the bibliographies seems to have been almost insatiable; and although his dramas did not catch the public taste, his earlier poems retained their popularity, while both *Don Juan* and *Cain* enjoyed a *succès de scandale*. (When *Don Juan* Cantos III, IV and V were published, we are told, the street outside Murray's premises was filled with booksellers' messengers, while 'parcels of books were given out of the window in answer to their obstreperous demands.')[29] 'Do *not* take it into your head, my dear B.,' Moore wrote on 9 February 1822, 'that the tide is at all turning against you in England. Till I see more symptoms of people *forgetting* you a little, I will not believe that you lose ground. As it is . . . nothing is hardly talked of but you; and though good people sometimes bless themselves when they mention you, it is plain that even *they* think much more about you than, for the good of their souls, they ought. . . .'[30] Nor did Byron lack defenders, advocates prepared to plead his cause in public or private against the charges pressed by hostile critics. These divisions did not necessarily follow party lines, although some periodicals and individuals were so wholly committed to religious or political positions that they could hardly see Byron except in terms of their own stereotypes. Leigh Hunt, with his dogmatic opposition to establishment values, represents one extreme, and Southey, the arch-conservative, the other; but there were many more complicated cases. Hobhouse was a Radical in politics, but he disapproved strongly of *Don Juan* and *Cain*. Croker was a Tory spokesman, but he enjoyed *Don Juan* and thought too much fuss had been made about its offensiveness. Hazlitt's republican enthusiasm could not overcome his literary (and social) distaste for Byron's works; whereas Scott, conservative and pious though he was, felt honoured to appear as the dedicatee of *Cain*, and praised the Shakespearian inclusiveness of *Don Juan*. Personal friendships, mutual respect, could run counter to ideological divisions, as they did with both Scott and Gifford, and indeed the Murray circle generally. Southey was not alone in deploring 'the scandalous silence of the *Quarterly Review* concerning *Don Juan*'[31], and Murray as publisher of both was bound to incur a good deal of odium (such as was expressed in the pamphlet '*Don John*': or *Don Juan Unmasked*, or, after the appearance of *Cain*, in the *Remonstrance Addressed to Mr. John Murray, Respecting a Recent Publication*). A breach with Byron, often threatened by the poet, occurred finally towards the end of 1822, and all subsequent cantos of *Don Juan* were published by John Hunt; but even when their relationship was strained, and Byron's defiance of 'the damned cant and Toryism of the day' made him fair game for most conservative reviewers, the *Quarterly*'s countenance towards him had remained one of sorrow rather than anger. The

tolerance to be found in some powerful Tory circles can be glimpsed
in the earlier correspondence in which Byron sought to procure for
Count Guiccioli a British consulship or vice-consulship at Ravenna,
for the Count's protection in the event of war. 'Will you,' he asked
Murray, 'get a favour done for me. *You* can, by your Government
friends, Croker, Canning, or my old Schoolfellow Peel, and I can't. . . .
Don't you think Croker would do it for us? To be sure, *my interest* is
rare!! but, perhaps a brother-wit in the Tory line might do a good
turn at the request of so harmless and long absent a Whig. . . .'[32] To
which Croker replied with great good-humour in September 1819,
offering advice on the procedure to be followed: 'Vice-Consuls,' he
told Murray, 'are not appointed at home; if they were, I should not
have had the least hesitation in asking Lord Castlereagh, even though
you had published *Don Juan* without an erasure. Tories are placable
people. . . .'[33] Byron was, of course, an exceptional case: his rank,
genius, friendships and social contacts conferred special privileges
and secured special treatment, though these were increasingly eroded
as his own works became more provocative, more outrageous or
extreme. Many of his opponents felt, long before John Hunt was
prosecuted for publishing the anonymous *Vision of Judgment*, that
neither Byron nor his publishers should be exempt from the legal
proceedings brought against humbler purveyors of subversive reading,
like William Hone and Richard Carlile, and his participation in the
Liberal did him incalculable harm. 'Never since I have been a publisher,'
Murray warned him in October 1822, 'did I ever observe such a
universal outcry as this work has occasioned and it is deemed to be no
less dull than wickedly intended. . . . My company used to be courted
for the pleasure of talking about you—it is totally the reverse now—
and by a re-action even your former works are considerably deteriorated
in sale.'[34]

Such variations in individual and group reactions are found also in
periodical criticism. Some journals might praise and others condemn
Byron's works out of hand, but many found them a disturbing or
exciting mixture, variously analysed, of genius and depravity. Judgments could differ, of course, not only from periodical to periodical
but from reviewer to reviewer and from work to work, although
few magazines zig-zagged as wildly as *Blackwood's* did between fierce
denunciation and robust appreciation. None, on the other hand, had
anything to compare with the sustained and near-continuous assessment of Byron's achievement over the years which Jeffrey offered in

the *Edinburgh Review*. But this is to raise the question of the actual critical value of these contemporary comments on Byron's poetry.

This account has stressed the distorting factors which affected criticism, rather than its positive achievements. The validity and lasting value of individual judgments are in any case for readers to assess; but in general contemporary criticism helps us both directly and indirectly to see the objects—Byron's works—as in themselves they really are. Directly, through the often excellent analyses of their appeal, the often perceptive commentaries, formal and thematic, the shrewd technical observations and the individual *aperçus*. Indirectly, since even if we are conscious of critics' bias in one direction or another, we must remember that such bias was assumed and exploited by Byron himself. His works presuppose certain habitual assumptions in his readers—assumptions which he may indulge or outrage, but on which he is deliberately playing. His works are so much part of their historical context—they so much depend on and imply that context—that to see his poetry as it really is, we must, paradoxically, contemplate it for a time at least in the distorting mirrors of contemporary judgment.

III

The news of Byron's death had an effect on readers quite unparalleled in literary history. 'I was told it all at once in a roomful of people,' Jane Welsh wrote to Carlyle. 'My God, if they had said that the sun or the moon had gone out of the heavens, it could not have struck me with the idea of a more awful and dreary blank in the creation than the words "Byron is dead!"' [35] Bulwer-Lytton is only one of many who confirm the typicality of her response:

Never [he wrote in 1833], shall I forget the singular, the stunning sensation, which the intelligence produced. . . . We could not believe that the bright race was run. So much of us died with him, that the notion of his death had something of the unnatural, of the impossible. It was as if a part of the mechanism of the very world stood still;—that we had ever questioned—that we had ever blamed him, was a thought of absolute remorse, and all our worship of his genius was not half so strongly felt as our love for himself.[36]

The circumstances of his death appealed to all the generosity of spirit in his opponents as well as his admirers. 'The voice of just blame', Scott wrote in the *Edinburgh Weekly Journal*, 'and that of malignant censure, are at once silenced; and we feel almost as if the great luminary of Heaven had suddenly disappeared from the sky, at the moment when every telescope was levelled for the examination of the spots which dimmed its brightness.' The Dean of Westminster might refuse him burial in the Abbey, and the fashionable world be reluctant to attend his funeral; but there were few prepared to utter at that moment sentiments as grudging as Lamb's or as venomous as Southey's.[37]

A period of reassessment was, however, bound to follow. The vicissitudes of Byron's reputation in the nineteenth century have been well charted by S. C. Chew and W. W. Pratt; and there is no need for me to summarize the decline in his popularity expressed, for example, by Henry Taylor or Carlyle (whose progressive disillusion makes an interesting case history, and whose ethical imperatives seem to propound an acceptable Victorian solution to Romantic spiritual predicaments). Nor need one comment on the protests registered on Byron's behalf by men like Kingsley (No. 53) or Mazzini (No. 50), or the reassessments which abound from the 1860s onwards. All these speak eloquently and often cogently—at times profoundly—for themselves. It may be useful, however, to consider briefly the main foci, the recurrent themes, of Victorian criticism.

Firstly, there were perennial questions about Byron's personality— about his integrity as an artist and a man. When Goethe said in 1823 that 'a character of such eminence had never existed before, and probably would never come again',[38] he was expressing what many felt in Byron's lifetime. 'He stands alone in our poetical biography,' Sir Samuel Egerton Brydges wrote soon after Byron's death in 1824, 'unlike all other poets in his endowments, his literary boldness and ease, his personal habits, the extraordinary incidents of his adventurous life, the novelty of his poetical career, and the splendour of his original imagination. I have said *our* poetical biography,—I ought to have said the poetical biography of *Europe*.'[39] There were others, however, who felt not only that Byron's character was itself defective, but that his poetry involved a rather corrupt exploitation of personality, the reader being titillated by a near-identification of the poet with his dubious protagonists. 'The personal interest, we believe,' declared the *London Magazine* in January 1821, 'has always been above the poetical in Lord Byron's compositions; and, what is much worse, they seem to have been, in almost every instance, studiously calculated to produce this effect.'[40] The publication of Moore's *Life* in 1830 made possible a more fully documented criticism, of which Macaulay's essay is the first important example. Abundant biographical evidence was now available to supplement the evidence provided by the poems themselves; but such evidence could be variously interpreted, and the differing estimates of Byron's character in life and art provide a major topic of Victorian debate—a debate that focuses particularly on the question of sincerity.

Secondly, related to these problems of personality, there was the question of his pessimism—'the whole eloquence of scorn, misanthropy, and despair',[41] which had held his own generation spell-bound, and which could still fascinate when it did not infuriate Victorian readers. It did not speak to them (or for them) in the same way: John Stuart Mill is not untypical when he tells in his *Autobiography* how little Byron, as opposed to Wordsworth, had to offer him in his time of greatest need. But while Byron's pessimism might be repudiated, it was a literary phenomenon that could not be ignored. Its origins and implications, therefore—its historical, social, psychological and philosophical basis—were discussed with heated partisanship; and we find Byronic gloom attributed variously to conceit, affectation, literary fashion, *Weltschmerz*, the *Zeitgeist*, indigestion, Titanic rebellion, frustrated idealism, disgust at a corrupt society, a consciousness of sin, political disillusion, philosophical inadequacies or profundities, or an ability to voice the spiritual crises of a world in travail.

Thirdly, critics were preoccupied with the truth or falsity of Byron's poetry. There were those like Bagehot (No. 54) who saw him as a mere entertainer, and those who found his poetic vision spurious: 'No genuine productive Thought,' complained Carlyle (No. 46), 'was ever revealed by him to mankind; indeed no clear undistorted vision into anything, or picture of anything; but all had a certain falsehood, or brawling theatrical insincere character.' There were, however, many—especially those who appreciated the comic-satiric achievement of *Don Juan*—who saw Byron as the poet of Truth, a portrayer but not a worshipper of things as they are, an idealist who none the less revealed the realities, sometimes comic, sometimes shocking, sometimes terrible, of human nature, human society, and human experience. '[The] thing wholly new and precious to me in Byron,' Ruskin testified (No. 59), 'was his measured and living *truth*. . . . [Here] at last I had found a man who spoke only of what he had seen, and known; and spoke without exaggeration, without mystery, without enmity, and without mercy. . . . Of all things within range of human thought he felt the facts, and discerned the natures with accurate justice.' Between these extremes lay a wide spectrum of opinion, and much excellent

Victorian criticism results from attempts to define and demonstrate the nature of Byron's truth—or its inadequacy.

Fourthly, discussions of his historical importance and imaginative power often centred on Byronic rebellion. 'Byron's was the genius of revolt,' wrote Henley (No. 61); and the intransigence which had antagonized many of his contemporaries won the admiration of succeeding generations. Mazzini as a Continental liberal hailed him as the poet of 'nationality and liberty'. Swinburne applauded 'his glorious courage, his excellent contempt for things contemptible, and hatred of hateful men' (No. 56). Arnold praised his rebellion against the mental bondage or cant of English society, and noted with approval that 'the falsehood, cynicism, insolence, misgovernment, oppression, with their consequent unfailing crop of human misery, which were produced by this state of things, roused Byron to irreconcilable revolt and battle' (No. 60). Morley sought to trace the relation between Byron's poetry and the spirit of the Revolution itself, to explain why this English aristocrat had become 'the favourite poet of all the most high-minded conspirators and socialists of continental Europe for half a century; of the best of those, that is to say, who have borne the most unsparing testimony against the present ordering of society, and against the theological and moral conceptions which have guided and maintained it' (No. 57). As Macaulay and Kingsley emphasized, Byronic rebellion could easily degenerate to a youthful pose; but its deeper implications and dynamic power were not forgotten by perceptive and historically minded critics.

Finally, there was the question of Byron's poetic art. Some may have been tempted to discuss his personality, his pessimism, his vision or philosophy, his morals and his politics, in isolation from his poetry; but this temptation was resisted by the better critics, who devoted a great deal of attention to the problems raised by Byron's artistry. Few claimed as much for it as Ruskin (who supported his contentions with detailed verbal analyses based on the techniques he had evolved for discussing painting). Few, on the other hand, went as far as Swinburne in 1884, when he accused Byron of almost total poetic incompetence (No. 62). Many, like Swinburne himself, John Addington Symonds (No. 58) and John Churton Collins (No. 66), recognized his supreme mastery in the *ottava rima* mode. (John Nichol, to cite only one of those not represented in this volume, praised in *Don Juan* 'the verbal skill which makes it rank as the *cleverest* of English verse compositions, . . . its shoals of witticisms, telling phrases, and incomparable transitions.'[42]) But in Byron's work as a whole most critics found defective (sometimes seriously defective) artistry. 'Byron is so negligent in his poetic style,' writes Arnold, 'he is often, to say the truth, so slovenly, slipshod, and infelicitous, he is so little haunted by the true artist's fine passion for the correct use and consummate management of words, that he may be described as having for this artistic gift the insensibility of the barbarian. . . .'[43] Yet Arnold, like many who perceived the technical deficiencies of Byron's poetry, also felt in it a greatness which made them rank him far above more perfect but more limited artists. And to reconcile this sense of his poetic greatness with a clear perception of his artistic weaknesses was the dilemma confronting critic after critic. Their attempts to resolve it are a source of detailed analytic and discursive studies of his poetry itself, and thoughtful examinations of their own criteria for poetic greatness.

This list of themes is not exhaustive—Byron's treatment of Nature, for example, might have been included—but it identifies the central issues in Victorian and Edwardian discussions of Byron's poetry. (A new impetus to reassessment was given at the turn of the century by the publication of the great edition of Byron's poetry, letters and journals, edited by E. H. Coleridge and R. E. Prothero; but this did not lead to any major change in critical emphasis.) Such Victorian and Edwardian discussions of his poetry form a sadly neglected portion of our critical heritage, though their interest—and indeed their greatness—seem beyond dispute. A generation has grown up with the Boeotian assumption that twentieth-century views alone merit consideration, and that the true principles of literary criticism were not discovered till the early 1920s. I trust that this volume will help to rectify such errors, compounded as they are of ignorance and prejudice. Each age, no doubt, must write its criticism anew, but this need not involve injustice to the past. Honour should be paid where honour is due; and period interest apart, it seems worth recording that the major issues about Byron's poetry had been discussed, the essential discriminations made, and the most important judgments well substantiated, years before the outbreak of the First World War. Oliver Elton's authoritative chapter on the subject in his *Survey of English Literature 1780–1830* (1912) is no isolated achievement, but the culmination of an important phase of Byron criticism in England.

IV

This collection is concerned with English, not with American and Continental criticism, which would provide enough material for a companion volume. Goethe (Nos. 16, 23, 33, 38, 44) and Mazzini (No. 50) are represented, alone among Continental critics, since they were the two who had most influence on English opinion—the two who were most often cited in the course of English debates on Byron's merits or demerits as a poet. Poe's prosodic analysis of the opening lines of *The Bride of Abydos* (No. 52) is included because of its technical interest; and the critiques by Paul Elmer More (No. 64) and J. F. A. Pyre (No. 67) for their intrinsic excellence, though by this date no useful distinction can be drawn between English and American criticism. Valuable surveys of American and Continental material are provided by W. E. Leonard (*Byron and Byronism in America*, Boston, 1905; reprinted New York, 1964); Edmond Estève (*Byron et le romantisme français*, Paris, 1907); and W. W. Pratt, in his account of *Don Juan* criticism in France, Germany, other European countries, and America (*Byron's 'Don Juan'*, ed T. G. Steffan and W. W. Pratt, Austin [Texas], 1957, IV, 323–340). Further bibliographies are provided by Ian Jack, *English Literature 1815–1832* (1963, pp. 514–15); *The Cambridge Bibliography of English Literature* (III [1940], 17–45, 210–12; V [1957], 568–9); and Robert Escarpit, *Lord Byron: un tempérament littéraire* (Paris, 1955–57, II, 301–13). The following notes do not attempt to cover the same extensive ground, but to suggest some major points of similarity and difference between English and foreign responses to Byron's poetry.

Byron himself was delighted by the spread of interest in his work. A letter written in May 1821 shows his gratification at hearing from Moore that ' "the French had caught the contagion of Byronism to the highest pitch" and . . . that nothing was ever like their "entusymusy" . . . on the subject, even through the "slaver of a prose translation".' [44] He also heard that 'as an author [he was] in great request in Germany', that Goethe was his 'professed patron and protector', and that there were 'frequent translations of several of his works'. [45] He enjoyed occasional visits from travelling Americans, which made him 'feel as if talking with Posterity from the other side of the Styx'; and he was delighted by the flattering reception given him at Leghorn in 1822 by officers of the American Navy, who showed him 'an American edition

of [his] poems, &c. &c., and all kinds of attention and good will.'[46]
'All this,' he reflected, 'is some compensation for your English native
brutality'; and in November 1822 we find him declaring to Murray
that he cares but little for the opinions of the English, as he has long had
both Europe and America for a Public.[47]

Early American notices of his poems were often reprinted or imitated
from British reviews; and when a distinctive note was struck, it was
sometimes rather provincial: 'Mercy on us,' wrote a reviewer of *The
Corsair* in the *Portfolio* (Philadelphia) for July 1814, 'what an amateur
in robbing and throat cutting this young nobleman must be.'[48] The
success of *Childe Harold's Pilgrimage* seems to have been less immediate
in America than in Britain, and one contemporary suggests that this
may have been due to an initial distrust of Byron's rank and social
position. But the vogue, once it gained momentum, was as spectacular
as in other countries, and as independent of moralistic condemnation.
'In vain,' wrote S. G. Goodrich, '. . . the pulpit opened its thunders
against [his poems]; teachers warned their pupils, parents their children.
I remember as late as 1820 that some booksellers refused to sell them,
regarding them as infidel publications. . . . Byron could no more be
kept at bay than the cholera.'[49] As in Britain, the very qualities that
roused indignation contributed to Byron's popularity. Longfellow,
writing anonymously in the *North American Review* for January
1832, deplored the effect that Byron's sullen misanthropy and irreligious
gloom had had on the literary taste and moral principle of America
some years before:

Minds that could not understand his beauties, could imitate his great and glaring
defects. Souls that could not fathom his depths, could grasp the straw and
bubbles that floated upon the agitated surface, until at length every city, town,
and village had its little Byron, its self-tormenting scoffer at morality, its
gloomy misanthropist in song. Happily, this noxious influence has been in some
measure checked and counteracted by the writings of Wordsworth, whose
pure and gentle philosophy has been gradually gaining the ascendancy over the
bold and visionary speculations of an unhealthy imagination.[50]

The political opinions which appeared so controversial in Britain and
Europe caused no scandal to Americans, who had already won their
own war of independence and repudiated monarchy; but the moral and
religious tendencies of Byron's poetry were attacked with no less vigour.
A. H. Everett, for example, in the *North American Review* for January
1825, praised his poetic genius, his depth of thought, his power,
brilliance and felicity of style, while deploring an occasional extrava-

gance of thought and language and a want of care and finish in the versification; but he then went on to condemn the moral tendency as distinct from the literary character of these poems:

It is . . . much to be regretted, that almost the whole mass of Lord Byron's writings is, in one way or another, tainted with immorality, and fitted to produce an unfortunate effect upon the reader's mind. A considerable part of them are disfigured with absolute grossness. . . . But others, which are wholly free from this stain, are infected with faults more dangerous, perhaps, because less obvious to the unsuspecting or uninformed reader; such as the exhibition, under a favorable point of view, of unnatural and vicious characters, and the introduction of false principles in morals and religion. The looseness of Lord Byron's notions upon these subjects, seems to have been one of the principal sources of these, and all the other defects in his poetry.[51]

This puritanical disapproval, sometimes more strongly expressed, is characteristic of early nineteenth-century criticism of Byron in America, and it remained dominant there for longer than in Britain.[52] His admirers and defenders, therefore, were conscious of defying prevailing orthodoxies—which may have added significantly to their pleasure. But such disapproval does not seem to have affected his popularity, and moralists themselves were not always immune to Byron's dangerous appeal. E. P. Whipple, who condemned him in 1845 for robing sin in beauty and conferring dignity on vice, admitted reluctantly that *Manfred* roused 'a kind of shuddering sympathy . . . for the hero'—'a singular fascination from which it is difficult to escape'[53]—and which added therefore to the danger of such reading. As time went on, however, there were many who felt the extremes of either praise or condemnation to be inappropriate. James Russell Lowell, in 1854, described Byron as presenting merely 'an ideal to youth made restless with vague desires not yet regulated by experience nor supplied with motives by the duties of life'[54]; and Charles Eliot Norton, in 1869, dismissed him as 'insincere' in the sense of being 'a rhetorician more than a poet by nature; a man accustomed to make a display of his feelings, and dependent for his satisfaction on the effect produced on other people by the display. . . .'[55]

American responses to Byron may be said, then, to have paralleled with some local variations those of British readers; and his most important British critics throughout the nineteenth century influenced opinion on both sides of the Atlantic. Continental criticism, however, had distinctive features of its own.

There was a time-lag between British and European reactions to Byron's poetry, partly because of the war with Napoleon, which for some years affected cultural communications, and partly because of delays in the production of translations. (The majority of foreign readers was dependent on these, though many could, of course, and did enjoy Byron in the original.) His works, in English, were published in Paris by Galignani in 1818, and further editions appeared in the 1820s. A few individual poems had been published in translation—*The Bride of Abydos* in 1816; extracts from *The Prisoner of Chillon, The Corsair, Lara, The Giaour* and *Childe Harold's Pilgrimage* Canto III, in 1817; *The Lament of Tasso, The Siege of Corinth*, and extracts from *Childe Harold* Canto IV, in 1818. But it was not until the appearance of Pichot's translation of the collected works, from 1819 onwards, that Byron was made generally available to the French reading public. ('The French translation of us!!! *Oime! Oime!* [Alas! Alas!],' lamented Byron, on reading this prose version.[56]) A thirteen-volume edition, in English, was published at Leipzig in 1818–22. The first German translation of his collected works appeared in 1821–8; but individual works had been available before then—*The Corsair* since 1816, *The Siege of Corinth* since 1817, *The Giaour, The Bride of Abydos* and *Manfred* since 1819, *Mazeppa* and the *Hebrew Melodies* since 1820. Similarly, the translations of his collected works into Italian in 1842, into Polish in 1857, into Russian in 1864–6, and into Spanish in 1880, had each been preceded, at varying intervals, by the publication of individual works or selections in translation.[57] The differences of pattern between one country and another are attributable less to geographical distance than to differences in cultural climate and cultural relationships with Britain, while in some cases political censorship seems to have been involved.

The passionate enthusiasm with which Byron's poetry was received on the Continent is attributable in large part to the same causes as his original success in England. Readers were fascinated, abroad as at home, by the Byronic personality, by his experiences, moods and beliefs, by his Titanism and *Weltschmerz*, as these were mediated by his poetry and adumbrated in accounts (often inaccurate in earlier years) of his own life. But on the Continent some special additional factors were involved.

There Byron was acclaimed—or, in some cases, condemned—as a protagonist in the clash between romanticism and classicism. In English literary circles the conflict between old and new poetic movements, if 'movements' they were, had not been formulated in these terms, which Byron himself regarded with amused contempt. This is expressed in an epistle to Goethe, written in October 1820 and intended as a Dedication for *Marino Faliero*:

I perceive [he wrote ironically] that in Germany, as well as in Italy, there is a great struggle about what they call '*Classical*' and '*Romantic*',—terms which were not subjects of classification in England, at least when I left it four or five years ago. Some of the English Scribblers, it is true, abused Pope and Swift, but the reason was that they themselves did not know how to write either prose or verse; but nobody thought them worth making a sect of. Perhaps there may be something of the kind sprung up lately, but I have not heard much about it, and it would be such bad taste that I shall be very sorry to believe it.[58]

Nevertheless, European men of letters were quick to hail him as a leader of the new school (which, in its English manifestations, he had been attacking). Stendhal, for example, declared as early as 1818 that he was himself a tremendous romantic (*un romantique furieux*)—'that is to say that I am for Shakespeare against Racine, and for Lord Byron against Boileau.' This representative significance was soon to be widely acknowledged both by hostile critics and by his admirers—by Victor Hugo, for example, in an essay of 1824 which ranked Byron with Chateaubriand, in spite of their religious and political differences, as the two great leaders of Romanticism.[59] As such, he was an inspiration to two generations of French Romantic poets, to many of the later German Romantics, and indeed to innovating and rebellious writers throughout Europe.

His role as champion of Liberty was another factor in his Continental reputation, in that century of political as well as literary revolution. His polemics against tyranny, his efforts on behalf of oppressed nationalities, above all his death in the cause of Greek independence, appealed to the imagination of thousands of readers, but especially those who themselves yearned or struggled for freedom. 'Byron', declared Mickiewitz, 'is the secret tie which binds the literature of the Slavs with that of the West';[60] and there is symbolic significance in the fact that one Polish translation of *Don Juan* (dated 1863) was issued, according to E. H. Coleridge, 'during the last Polish insurrection, for the benefit of the wounded.'[61] Byron became an ideal, an almost mythical figure in the minds of Continental liberals, for whom Mazzini acts as spokesman:

Surrounded by slaves and their oppressors [he wrote of Byron]; a traveller in countries where even remembrance seemed extinct; never did he desert the cause of the peoples; never was he false to human sympathies. A witness of the progress of the Restoration, and the triumph of the principles of the Holy Alliance, he never swerved from his courageous opposition; he preserved and publicly proclaimed his faith in the rights of the peoples and in the final triumph of liberty. . . . I know no more beautiful symbol of the future destiny and mission of art than the death of Byron in Greece. The holy alliance of poetry with the cause of the peoples; the union—still so rare—of thought and action—which alone completes the human Word, and is destined to emancipate the world; the grand solidarity of all nations in the conquest of the rights ordained by God for all his children . . .;—all that is now the religion and hope of the party of progress throughout Europe, is gloriously typified in this image. . . . The day will come when Democracy will remember all that it owes to Byron.[62]

Finally, in considering Byron's European reputation, we must remember the stature of the writers whom he influenced. Although his works were known to every English and American man of letters, he had virtually no influence on his own great contemporaries, and (apart from the unfortunate John Clare) his imitators on both sides of the Atlantic were near-nonentities. The most important names that Leonard cites, amid a host of poetasters, are those of Fitz-Greene Halleck (whose *Fanny*, published in 1819, satirized New York society in something like the manner of *Don Juan*), Poe in his earliest work, and Joaquin Miller; while the followers or imitators whom Henry Taylor and Kingsley denounced in England are today forgotten. On the Continent, however, Byron influenced to a greater or lesser degree such authors as Hugo, Lamartine, de Musset, de Vigny, Gautier, George Sand, Goethe, Heine, Pushkin, Lermontov, Leopardi and Espronceda, and painters like Delacroix and Géricault, as well as lesser men. Hence, even when the first enthusiasm for his works had waned, he enjoyed an honoured place in literary history: foreign scholars saw him, whatever his faults, as not merely an important English poet, but a European figure, central to their accounts of Romanticism and rebellion in nineteenth-century poetry.

A new factor, therefore, in English reassessments of Byron in the second half of the century was the critics' increasing awareness of Byron's popularity and influence abroad, and of the major status generally accorded to him throughout Europe.

NOTES

1 *Byron: Twentieth Century Views*, ed. Paul West, Englewood Cliffs (N.J.), 1963, p. 175.

2 In 1807, for example, the *Edinburgh Review* had a circulation of 7,000, while the *Methodist Magazine* and *Evangelical Magazine* sold 18,000 to 20,000 copies each. The *Examiner's* circulation in 1808 was 2,200 and the *Quarterly's* in 1810, 5,000. Of course, such figures could vary significantly even over a short period. By 1817–18, the *Quarterly's* sales had risen to 12,000–14,000, while the *Edinburgh's* stood at 12,000 in 1818 (after rising to 13,000 four years previously). *Blackwood's* began in 1817 with sales of 3,700, but these rose to 10,000 with the seventh number, containing the exceptionally scandalous 'Chaldee Manuscript'. (These figures are cited, with a caveat on their reliability, by R. D. Altick, *The English Common Reader*, Chicago, 1957, pp. 391–2.) The maximum circulation figures for reviews and magazines—14,000 is sometimes cited for the *Edinburgh* and the *Quarterly* in 1818–19—do not take account of subsequent republication in bound volumes, which could run through many editions. (See A. L. Strout, *John Bull's Letter to Lord Byron*, Norman [Oklahoma], 1947, pp. 16–17.)

3 *British Critic*, 2nd series, XII (1819), 202; *Literary Gazette*, 1823, p. 451; *Edinburgh Magazine and Literary Miscellany; a New Series of the Scots Magazine*, XIII (1823), 190. A similar vocabulary of abuse is to be found in many of the pamphlets: in *'Don John' or Don Juan Unmasked*, for example, we read of Byron's muse 'grasping with one hand thunderbolts from Olympus, and groping with the other in a filthy jakes.' (*Op. cit.*, 1819, p. 7.)

4 *Byron. A Self-Portrait. Letters and Diaries 1798 to 1824*, ed. Peter Quennell, 1950, I, 40.

5 *LJ*, II, 330. Cf. *LJ*, V, 267, 269–70.

6 L. A. Marchand, *Byron: A Biography*, 1957, I, 148.

7 *LJ*, III, 64. Byron assumed that Brougham's anonymous article on *Hours of Idleness* was by Jeffrey himself, in spite of a hint to the contrary which he had received in 1812 (L. A. Marchand, *op. cit.*, I, 346).

8 *LJ*, II, 344–5; III, 5.

9 *LJ*, V, 175.

10 See below, No. 10.

11 Specimens of these attacks are reprinted in *LJ*, II, 463–92.

12 *Cato to Lord Byron on the Immorality of his Writings*, 1824, p. 4.

13 *LJ*, VI, 2–3; and see below, Nos. 12 and 13.

14 Samuel Smiles, *A Publisher and His Friends*, 1891, I, 369.

15 *LJ*, V, 25.

16 *LJ*, IV, 248.

17 *LJ*, V, 371–2; VI, 67.

18 *Corr*, II, 211.

19 *LJ*, IV, 321, 279.
20 *LJ*, V, 351–2.
21 *LJ*, IV, 279, 384–5.
22 *LJ*, IV, 201; V, 92.
23 *LJ*, V, 374–5.
24 *LJ*, VI, 182.
25 *Corr*, II, 223.
26 *LJ*, V, 467.
27 See below, Nos. 12 and 13.
28 *The Letters of William and Dorothy Wordsworth: The Later Years*, ed. E. de Selincourt, 1939, I, 69.
29 Smiles, *op. cit.*, I, 413.
30 *The Letters of Thomas Moore*, ed. Wilfred S. Dowden, 1964, II, 503.
31 *Selections from the Letters of Robert Southey*, ed. J. W. Warter, 1856, III, 238 (letter of 23 March 1821).
32 *LJ*, IV, 343–4.
33 *The Croker Papers: The Correspondence and Diaries of . . . John Wilson Croker*, ed. L. L. Jennings, 1884, I, 145. Croker refers to the savage attack on Castlereagh in the Dedication to *Don Juan*, which had not in fact been published.
34 L. A. Marchand, *op. cit.*, III, 1040.
35 See below, No. 46.
36 See below, No. 48.
37 *The Prose Works of Sir Walter Scott, Bart.*, 1834–6, IV, 343–4, and see below, No. 42.
38 *The Conversations of Goethe with Eckermann and Soret*, trans. John Oxenford, 1850, I, 73.
39 *Letters on the Character and Poetical Genius of Lord Byron*, 1824, p. 286.
40 *London Magazine*, III, 51.
41 T. B. Macaulay: see below, No. 47.
42 *Byron* (English Men of Letters Series), 1880, p. 174. Nichol (1833–94) was the first Regius Professor of English Language and Literature in the University of Glasgow.
43 See below, No. 60.
44 *LJ*, V, 282–3.
45 *Corr*, II, 225; *LJ*, VI, 73–4.
46 *LJ*, V, 416; *Corr*, II, 225.
47 *LJ*, VI, 74, 138.
48 Quoted by W. E. Leonard, *op. cit.*, p. 23.
49 Quoted by Leonard, *op. cit.*, p. 20.
50 *North American Review*, XXXIV, 76.
51 *North American Review*, XX, 39–40.
52 See Leonard, *op. cit.*, pp. 101–5; and Pratt, *op. cit.*, IV, 335–6.
53 *North American Review*, LX, 80.

54 *Literary Essays*, London, 1890, p. 243.

55 Letter of 17 July 1869, to Ruskin (*The Letters of Charles Eliot Norton*, ed. Sara Norton and M. A. De Wolfe How, 1913, I, 349).

56 *LJ*, V, 96. Full details of French publication of Byron's works in the first half of the century are given by Estève in his *Appendice bibliographique*, *op. cit.*, pp. 525–33.

57 For details, and for similar information on translations into Dutch, Danish, Swedish, Icelandic, Portuguese, Bohemian, Hungarian, Rumanian, Bulgarian, Servian, Armenian, Romaic, Hebrew, and Modern Greek, see E. H. Coleridge's bibliography (*PW*, VII, 89–304).

58 *LJ*, V, 104.

59 See Estève, *op. cit.*, pp. 111, 132 f. It was the verse tales, *Manfred*, and *Childe Harold*, with their melancholy, doubt, rebellion and despair, that made the greatest impact, and Estève gives an amusing account of the consternation which *Don Juan* caused at first among readers who had passionately identified themselves with Byron's 'romantic' persona; but the scepticism, ironies and 'elegant cynicism' of *Don Juan* soon served as inspirations of another kind to a younger generation of poets. (*Op. cit.*, pp. 69–71, 217–18, 228 f.)

60 Quoted by Leonard, *op. cit.*, p. 9.

61 *PW*, VII, 223.

62 See below, No. 50.

HOURS OF IDLENESS

June 1807

1. Henry P. Brougham, unsigned review, *Edinburgh Review*

Dated January 1808, issued February 1808, XI, 285–9

Brougham (1778–1868), the well-known lawyer and politician, was a member of the group that founded the *Edinburgh Review*, to which he was a frequent contributor. For Byron's reaction to this review (which provoked indignant comments from both Scott and Wordsworth), see above, pp. 3–4. The general critical response to *Hours of Idleness, A Series of Poems . . . By George Gordon, Lord Byron, A Minor*, is analysed by W. S. Ward, in his article 'Byron's *Hours of Idleness* and Other than Scotch Reviewers', *Modern Language Notes*, LIX (1944), 547–50.

The poesy of this young lord belongs to the class which neither gods nor men are said to permit.[1] Indeed, we do not recollect to have seen a quantity of verse with so few deviations in either direction from that exact standard. His effusions are spread over a dead flat, and can no more get above or below the level, than if they were so much stagnant water. As an extenuation of this offence, the noble author is peculiarly forward in pleading minority. We have it in the title-page, and on the very back of the volume; it follows his name like a favourite part of his *style*. Much stress is laid upon it in the preface, and the poems are connected with this general statement of his case, by particular dates, substantiating the age at which each was written. Now, the law upon the point of minority, we hold to be perfectly

[1] [An allusion to Horace's *Art of Poetry*, ll. 372–3: 'mediocribus esse poetis/non homines, non di, non concessere columnae.' (Loeb trans.: 'that poets be of middling rank, neither men nor gods nor booksellers ever brooked.')]

27

clear. It is a plea available only to the defendant; no plaintiff can offer it as a supplementary ground of action. Thus, if any suit could be brought against Lord Byron, for the purpose of compelling him to put into court a certain quantity of poetry; and if judgment were given against him, it is highly probable that an exception would be taken, were he to deliver *for poetry*, the contents of this volume. To this he might plead *minority*; but as he now makes voluntary tender of the article, he hath no right to sue, on that ground, for the price in good current praise, should the goods be unmarketable. This is our view of the law on the point, and, we dare to say, so will it be ruled. Perhaps, however, in reality, all that he tells us about his youth, is rather with a view to increase our wonder, than to soften our censures. He possibly means to say, 'See how a minor can write! This poem was actually composed by a young man of eighteen, and this by one of only sixteen!'—But, alas, we all remember the poetry of Cowley at ten, and Pope at twelve; and so far from hearing, with any degree of surprise, that very poor verses were written by a youth from his leaving school to his leaving college, inclusive, we really believe this to be the most common of all occurrences; that it happens in the life of nine men in ten who are educated in England; and that the tenth man writes better verse than Lord Byron.

His other plea of privilege, our author rather brings forward in order to waive it. He certainly, however, does allude frequently to his family and ancestors—sometimes in poetry, sometimes in notes; and while giving up his claim on the score of rank, he takes care to remember us of Dr Johnson's saying, that when a nobleman appears as an author, his merit should be handsomely acknowledged. In truth, it is this consideration only, that induces us to give Lord Byron's poems a place in our review, beside our desire to counsel him, that he do forthwith abandon poetry, and turn his talents, which are considerable, and his opportunities, which are great, to better account.

With this view, we must beg leave seriously to assure him, that the mere rhyming of the final syllable, even when accompanied by the presence of a certain number of feet,—nay, although (which does not always happen) those feet should scan regularly, and have been all counted accurately upon the fingers,—is not the whole art of poetry. We would entreat him to believe, that a certain portion of liveliness, somewhat of fancy, is necessary to constitute a poem; and that a poem in the present day, to be read, must contain at least one thought, either in a little degree different from the ideas of former

writers, or differently expressed. We put it to his candour, whether
there is any thing so deserving the name of poetry in verses like the
following, written in 1806, and whether, if a youth of eighteen could
say any thing so uninteresting to his ancestors, a youth of nineteen
should publish it.

> Shades of heroes, farewell! your descendant, departing
> From the seat of his ancestors, bids you, adieu!
> Abroad, or at home, your remembrance imparting
> New courage, he'll think upon glory, and you.
>
> Though a tear dim his eye, at this sad separation,
> 'Tis nature, not fear, that excites his regret:
> Far distant he goes, with the same emulation;
> The fame of his fathers he ne'er can forget.
>
> That fame, and that memory, still will he cherish,
> He vows that he ne'er will disgrace your renown;
> Like you will he live, or like you will he perish;
> When decay'd, may he mingle his dust with your own.

Now we positively do assert, that there is nothing better than
these stanzas in the whole compass of the noble minor's volume.

Lord Byron should also have a care of attempting what the greatest
poets have done before him, for comparisons (as he must have had
occasion to see at his writing-master's) are odious,—Gray's 'Ode on
Eton College', should really have kept out the ten hobbling stanzas
'on a distant view of the village and school of Harrow.'

> Where fancy, yet, joys to retrace the resemblance
> Of comrades, in friendship and mischief allied;
> How welcome to me, your ne'er fading remembrance,
> Which rests in the bosom, though hope is deny'd!

In like manner the exquisite lines of Mr Rogers, 'On a Tear,'
might have warned the noble author off those premises, and spared
us a whole dozen such stanzas as the following.

> Mild Charity's glow,
> To us mortals below,
> Shows the soul from barbarity clear;
> Compassion will melt,
> Where this virtue is felt,
> And its dew is diffus'd in a Tear.

> The man doom'd to sail,
> With the blast of the gale,
> Through billows Atlantic to steer,
> As he bends o'er the wave,
> Which may soon be his grave,
> The green sparkles bright with a Tear.

And so of instances in which former poets had failed. Thus, we do not think Lord Byron was made for translating, during his non-age, 'Adrian's Address to his Soul', when Pope succeeded so indifferently in the attempt. If our readers, however, are of another opinion, they may look at it.

> Ah! gentle, fleeting, wav'ring sprite,
> Friend and associate of this clay!
> To what unknown region borne,
> Wilt thou now wing thy distant flight?
> No more, with wonted humour gay,
> But pallid, cheerless, and forlorn.

However, be this as it may, we fear his translations and imitations are great favourites with Lord Byron. We have them of all kinds, from Anacreon to Ossian; and, viewing them as school exercises, they may pass. Only, why print them after they have had their day and served their turn? And why call the thing in p. 79 a translation, where *two* words (θελω λεγειν) of the original are expanded into four lines, and the other thing in p. 81, where μεσονυκτιοις ποθ' ὡραις, is rendered by means of six hobbling verses?[1]—As to his Ossianic poesy, we are not very good judges, being, in truth, so moderately skilled in that species of composition, that we should, in all probability, be criticizing some bit of the genuine Macpherson itself, were we to express our opinion of Lord Byron's rhapsodies. *If*, then, the following beginning of a 'Song of bards,' is by his Lordship, we venture to object to it, as far as we can comprehend it. 'What form rises on the roar of clouds, whose dark ghost gleams on the red stream of tempests? His voice rolls on the thunder; 'tis Orla, the brown chief of Otihona. He was,' &c. After detaining this 'brown chief' some time, the bards conclude by giving him their advice to 'raise his fair locks;' then to 'spread them on the arch of the rainbow;' and to 'smile through the tears of the storm.' Of this kind of thing there are no less than *nine*

---

[1] [See *P.W.*, I, 147, 149: *The Poetical Works of Lord Byron*, Oxford Standard Authors, 1960, p. 5.]

pages; and we can so far venture an opinion in their favour, that they look very like Macpherson; and we are positive they are pretty nearly as stupid and tiresome.

It is a sort of privilege of poets to be egotists; but they should 'use it as not abusing it'; and particularly one who piques himself (though indeed at the ripe age of nineteen), of being 'an infant bard'— ('The artless Helicon I boast is youth')—should either not know, or should seem not to know, so much about his own ancestry. Besides a poem above cited on the family seat of the Byrons, we have another of eleven pages on the self-same subject, introduced with an apology, 'he certainly had no intention of inserting it;' but really, 'the particular request of some friends,' &c. &c. It concludes with five stanzas on himself, 'the last and youngest of a noble line.' There is a good deal also about his maternal ancestors, in a poem on Lachin-y-gair, a mountain where he spent part of his youth, and might have learnt that *pibroch* is not a bagpipe, any more than duet means a fiddle.

As the author has dedicated so large a part of his volume to immortalize his employments at school and college, we cannot possibly dismiss it without presenting the reader with a specimen of these ingenious effusions. In an ode with a Greek motto, called Granta, we have the following magnificent stanzas.

> There, in apartments small and damp,
> The candidate for college prizes
> Sits poring by the midnight lamp,
> Goes late to bed, yet early rises.
>
> Who read false quantities in Sele,
> Or puzzles o'er the deep triangle;
> Depriv'd of many a wholesome meal,
> In barbarous Latin doom'd to wrangle.
>
> Renouncing every pleasing page,
> From authors of historic use;
> Preferring to the lettered sage,
> The square of the hypothenuse.
>
> Still harmless are these occupations,
> That hurt none but the hapless student,
> Compar'd with other recreations
> Which bring together the imprudent.

We are sorry to hear so bad an account of the college psalmody as is contained in the following Attic stanzas.

Our choir would scarcely be excus'd,
Even as a band of raw beginners;
All mercy, now, must be refus'd
To such a set of croaking sinners.

If David, when his toils were ended,
Had heard these blockheads sing before him,
To us, his psalms had ne'er descended,
In furious mood he would have tore 'em.

But whatever judgment may be passed on the poems of this noble minor, it seems we must take them as we find them, and be content; for they are the last we shall ever have from him. He is at best, he says, but an intruder into the groves of Parnassus; he never lived in a garret, like thorough-bred poets; and 'though he once roved a careless mountaineer in the Highlands of Scotland,' he has not of late enjoyed this advantage. Moreover, he expects no profit from his publication; and whether it succeeds or not, 'it is highly improbable, from his situation and pursuits hereafter,' that he should again condescend to become an author. Therefore, let us take what we get and be thankful. What right have we poor devils to be nice? We are well off to have got so much from a man of this Lord's station, who does not live in a garret, but 'has the sway' of Newstead Abbey. Again, we say, let us be thankful; and, with honest Sancho, bid God bless the giver, nor look the gift horse in the mouth.

ENGLISH BARDS AND SCOTCH REVIEWERS

March 1809

---

2. From an unsigned review, *Gentleman's Magazine*

March 1809, LXXIX (Part I), 246–9

At length comes forth a poetical work that possesses not only the three avowedly grand recommendations of *time*, *place*, and *circumstance*—of such moment in *all* worldly matters; but, so far as regards Literature, the three no less important, though, alas! far less frequent, recommendations, of defying *enemies*—rendering the favourable sentiments of *friends* superfluous—and the quackery of the *trade* wholly unnecessary. . . .

[Gives brief summary of the poem, with extracts.]

The Poem before us is unquestionably the result of an impassioned yet diligent study of the best masters, grounded on a fine taste and very happy natural endowments. It unites much of the judgment of the *Essay on Criticism*, the playful yet poignant smile and frown of indignation and ridicule of *The Dunciad*, with the versification of the *Epistle to Arbuthnot*, and the acuteness of the *Imitations of Horace* of the same Author; at the same time that we think we have discovered a resemblance of the best epigrammatic points and brilliant turns of the *Love of Fame*. And with all this is it unquestionably an original work. In a word, many years have passed since the English press has given us a performance so replete with mingled genius, good sense, and spirited animadversion.

The concluding passage so beautifully couples and combines the feelings of the Poet and Patriot, the Lover of the Muse with the Lover of his Country, that we cannot resist the pleasure of making it likewise the conclusion of our criticism:

[Quotes passage corresponding to ll. 991–1010 in the final version.]

CHILDE HAROLD'S PILGRIMAGE
CANTOS I AND II

March 1812

---

3. Some contemporary comments

(a) SAMUEL ROGERS (1763-1855), the son of a wealthy banker, enjoyed a considerable reputation as a poet and man of letters. Extract from his *Table-Talk*, published posthumously in 1856: 'Byron sent me *Childe Harold* in the printed sheets before it was published; and I read it to my sister. "This," I said, "in spite of all its beauty, will never please the public: they will dislike the querulous repining tone that pervades it, and the dissolute character of the hero." But I quickly found that I was mistaken. The genius which the poem exhibited, the youth, the rank of the author, his romantic wanderings in Greece,—these combined to make the world stark mad about *Childe Harold* and Byron. I knew two old maids in Buckinghamshire who used to cry over the passage about Harold's "laughing dames" that "long had fed his youthful appetite", &c.' (*Recollections of the Table-Talk of Samuel Rogers*, ed. A. Dyce, 3rd edn., 1856, p. 233.)

(b) ELIZABETH, DUCHESS OF DEVONSHIRE (1758-1824). Extract from undated letter to Augustus Foster: 'The subject of conversation, of curiosity, of enthusiasm almost, one might say, of the moment is not Spain or Portugal, Warriors or Patriots, but Lord Byron! You probably read the *Edinburgh Review*'s criticism of his "Minor Poems", published in 1808, not merely severe, but flippant. They prophesied and entreated never to hear more as a Poet of this young Lord. On this, stung to the quick, he published, without a name, his *English Bards and Scotch Reviewers*. The prodigious success of this made him publish a second edition with his name and additional lines and notes, and, going abroad, said that on his return he would answer to any who called on him. He returned sorry for the severity of some of his lines,

35

and with a new poem, *Childe Harold*, which he published. This poem is on every table, and himself courted, visited, flattered, and praised whenever he appears. He has a pale, sickly, but handsome countenance, a bad figure, animated and amusing conversation, and, in short, he is really the only topic almost of every conversation—the men jealous of him, the women of each other. . . .' (Vere Foster, *The Two Duchesses*, 1898, pp. 375-6.)

(c) SAMUEL TAYLOR COLERIDGE (1772–1834). Extract from letter of 21 April 1812, to his wife: 'Has Southey read *Childe Harold?* All the world is talking of it. I have not; but from what I hear, it is exactly on the plan that I myself had not only conceived six years ago, but have the whole Scheme drawn out in one of my old Memorandum Books.' (*The Letters of Samuel Taylor Coleridge*, ed. E. L. Griggs, 1956–9, III, 387.)

(d) WALTER SCOTT (1771–1832) had resented Byron's attack on him in *English Bards and Scotch Reviewers*, but a correspondence was begun between them in July 1812 through the good offices of John Murray, and Byron apologized for his offensiveness in the early satire. A friendship soon developed, and from this time onwards they expressed consistently high opinions of each other, as men and as authors.

[i] Extract from letter postmarked 4 April 1812, from Scott to Joanna Baillie: 'Have you seen the pilgrimage of Childe Harold, by Lord Byron: it is I think a very clever poem but gives no good symptom of the writers heart or morals. His heroe notwithstanding the affected antiquity of the stile in some parts is a modern man of fashion and fortune worn out and satiated with the pursuits of dissipation and although there is a caution against it in the preface you cannot for your soul avoid concluding that the author as he gives an account of his own travels is also doing so in his own character. Now really this is too bad. Vice ought to be a little more modest and it must require impudence at least equal to the noble lord's other powers to claim sympathy gravely for the ennui arising from his being tired of his wassailers and his paramours. There is a monstrous deal of conceit in it too for it is informing the inferior part of the world that their little old-fashioned scruples and limitation are not worthy of his regard while his fortunes and possessions are such as have put all sorts of

gratification too much in his power to afford him any pleasure. Yet with all this conceit and assurance there is much poetical merit in the book and I wish you would read it.' (*The Letters of Sir Walter Scott*, ed. H. J. C. Grierson, Davidson Cook, W. M. Parker and others, 1932–7, III, 98–9.)

[ii] Extract from letter of 4 May 1812, from Scott to J. B. S. Morritt: 'I agree very much in what you say of *Childe Harold*. Though there is something provoking and insulting both to morality and to feeling in his misanthropical ennui it gives nevertheless an odd poignancy to his descriptions and reflections and upon the whole it is a poem of most extraordinary power and may rank its author with our first poets.' (*Op. cit.*, III, 114–15.)

(*e*) WILLIAM WORDSWORTH (1770–1850), in conversations recorded by Henry Crabb Robinson (1775–1867), in his Diary:
'[24 May 1812] A very interesting day. Rose late; at half-past ten joined Wordsworth in Oxford Road, and we then got into the fields and walked to Hampstead. We talked of Lord Byron. Wordsworth allowed him power, but denied his style to be English. Of his moral qualities we think the same. He adds that there is insanity in Lord Byron's family, and that he believes Lord Byron to be somewhat cracked. I read Wordsworth some of Blake's poems; he was pleased with some of them, and considered Blake as having the elements of poetry a thousand times more than either Byron or Scott. . . .' (*Henry Crabb Robinson on Books and their Writers*, ed. Edith J. Morley, 1938, I, 85.)

'[3 June 1812] He contrasted some fine lines from his verses on the Wye, with a popular passage from Lord Byron on solitude. Lord Byron's is a coarse but palpable assertion of the nature of solitude, with an epigrammatic conclusion. In Wordsworth the feeling is involved and the thought clothed in poetic shapes. It is, therefore, no wonder that Wordsworth's description should be forgotten, and Lord Byron's in general circulation.'[1] (*Op. cit.*, I, 93.)

[1] [For an elaboration of this criticism, to which Wordsworth returned almost obsessively, see below p. 109n.]

4. Francis Jeffrey, from his unsigned review, *Edinburgh Review*

Dated February 1812, issued May 1812, XIX, 466–77

Jeffrey (1773–1850), one of the founders of the *Edinburgh Review*, edited that periodical from 1803 to 1829.

Lord Byron has improved marvellously since his last appearance at our tribunal;—and this, though it bear a very affected title, is really a volume of very considerable power, spirit and originality—which not only atones for the evil works of his nonage, but gives promise of a further excellence hereafter; to which it is quite comfortable to look forward.

The most surprising thing about the present work, indeed, is, that it should please and interest so much as it does, with so few of the ordinary ingredients of interest or poetical delight. There is no story or adventure—and, indeed, no incident of any kind; the whole poem— to give a very short account of it—consisting of a series of reflections made in travelling through a part of Spain and Portugal, and in sailing up the Mediterranean to the shores of Greece. These reflections, too, and the descriptions out of which they arise, are presented without any regular order or connexion—being sometimes strung upon the slender thread of Childe Harold's Pilgrimage, and sometimes held together by the still slighter tie of the author's local situation at the time of writing. As there are no incidents, there cannot well be any characters;—and accordingly, with the exception of a few national sketches, which form part of the landscape of his pilgrimage, that of the hero himself is the only delineation of the kind that is offered to the reader of this volume;—and this hero, we must say, appears to us as oddly chosen as he is imperfectly employed. Childe Harold is a sated epicure—sickened with the very fulness of prosperity—oppressed with ennui, and stung with occasional remorse;—his heart hardened by a long course of sensual indulgence, and his opinion of mankind degraded by his acquaintance with the baser part of them. In this state

38

he wanders over the fairest and most interesting parts of Europe, in the vain hope of stimulating his palsied sensibility by novelty, or at least of occasionally forgetting his mental anguish in the toils and perils of his journey. Like Milton's fiend, however, he 'sees undelighted all delight,' and passes on through the great wilderness of the world with a heart shut to all human sympathy—sullenly despising the stir both of its business and its pleasures—but hating and despising himself most of all, for beholding it with so little emotion.

Lord Byron takes the trouble to caution his readers against supposing that he meant to shadow out his own character under the dark and repulsive traits of that which we have just exhibited; a caution which was surely unnecessary—though it is impossible not to observe, that the mind of the noble author has been so far tinged by his strong conception of this Satanic personage, that the sentiments and reflections which he delivers in his own name, have all received a shade of the same gloomy and misanthropic colouring which invests those of his imaginary hero. The general strain of those sentiments, too, is such as we should have thought very little likely to attract popularity, in the present temper of this country. They are not only complexionally dark and disdainful, but run directly counter to very many of our national passions, and most favoured propensities. Lord Byron speaks with the most unbounded contempt of the Portuguese—with despondence of Spain—and in a very slighting and sarcastic manner of wars, and victories, and military heroes in general. Neither are his religious opinions more orthodox, we apprehend, than his politics; for he not only speaks without any respect of priests, and creeds, and dogmas of all descriptions, but doubts very freely of the immortality of the soul, and other points as fundamental.

Such are some of the disadvantages under which this poem lays claim to the public favour; and it will be readily understood that we think it has no ordinary merit, when we say, that we have little doubt that it will find favour, in spite of these disadvantages. Its chief excellence is a singular freedom and boldness, both of thought and expression, and a great occasional force and felicity of diction, which is the more pleasing that it does not appear to be the result either of long labour or humble imitation. There is, indeed, a tone of self-willed independence and originality about the whole composition—a certain plain manliness and strength of manner, which is infinitely refreshing after the sickly affectations of so many modern writers; and reconciles us not only to the asperity into which it sometimes degenerates, but even in some degree to the unamiableness upon which it constantly borders. We do not know, indeed, whether there is not something *piquant* in the very novelty and singularity of that cast of misanthropy and universal scorn, which we have already noticed as among the repulsive features of the composition. It excites a kind of curiosity, at least, to see how objects, which have been usually presented under so different an aspect, appear through so dark a medium; and undoubtedly gives great effect to the flashes of emotion and suppressed sensibility that occasionally burst through the gloom. The best parts of the poem, accordingly, are those which embody those stern and disdainful reflexions, to which the author seems to recur with unfeigned cordiality and eagerness—and through which we think we can sometimes discern the strugglings of a gentler feeling, to which he is afraid to abandon himself. There is much strength, in short, and some impetuous feeling in this poem—but very little softness; some pity for mankind—but very little affection; and no enthusiasm in the cause of any living men, or admiration of their talents or virtues. The author's inspiration does not appear to have brought him any beatific visions, nor to have peopled his fancy with any forms of loveliness; and though his lays are often both loud and lofty, they neither 'lap us in Elysium,' nor give us any idea that it was in Elysium that they were framed.

The descriptions are often exceedingly good; and the diction, though unequal and frequently faulty, has on the whole a freedom, copiousness and vigour, which we are not sure that we could match in any cotemporary poet. Scott alone, we think, possesses a style equally strong and natural; but Scott's is more made up of imitations, and indeed is frequently a mere cento of other writers—while Lord Byron's has often a nervous simplicity and manly freshness which reminds us of Dryden, and an occasional force and compression, in some of the smaller pieces especially, which afford no unfavourable resemblance of Crabbe.

The versification is in the stanza of Spencer [*sic*]; and none of all the imitators of that venerable bard have availed themselves more extensively of the great range of tones and manners in which his example entitles them to indulge. Lord Byron has accordingly given us descriptions in all their extremes;—sometimes compressing into one stanza the whole characteristic features of a country, and sometimes expanding into twenty the details of a familiar transaction;—condescending, for pages together, to expatiate in minute and ludicrous representations,—and mingling long apostrophes, execrations, and the expression of personal emotion, with the miscellaneous picture which it is his main business to trace on the imagination of his readers. Not satisfied even with this license of variety, he has passed at will, and entirely, from the style of Spencer, to that of his own age—and intermingled various lyrical pieces with the solemn stanza of his general measure. . . .

[Gives outline of poem, with copious extracts.]

The extracts we have now made, will enable our readers to judge of this poem for themselves; nor have we much to add to the general remarks which we took the liberty of offering at the beginning. Its chief fault is the want of story, or object; and the dark, and yet not tender spirit which breathes through almost every part of it. The general strain of the composition, we have already said, appears to us remarkably good; but it is often very diffuse, and not unfrequently tame and prosaic. We can scarcely conceive any thing more mean and flat, for instance, than this encomium on the landscapes of Illyria.

> Yet in fam'd Attica such lovely dales
> Are rarely seen; nor can fair Tempe boast
> A charm they know not; lov'd Parnassus fails,
> Though classic ground and consecrated most,
> To match some spots that lurk within this lowering coast.

Though even this is more tolerable to our taste than such a line as the following—

> Death rides upon the sulphury Siroc;

and several others that might be collected with no great trouble. The work, in short, bears considerable marks of haste and carelessness; and is rather a proof of the author's powers, than an example of their successful exertion. It shows the compass of his instrument, and the power of his hand; though we cannot say that we are very much delighted either with the air he has chosen, or the style in which it is executed. The Notes are written in a flippant, lively, *tranchant* and assuming style—neither very deep nor very witty; though rather entertaining, and containing some curious information as to the character and qualifications of the modern Greeks; of whom, as well as of the Portuguese, Lord Byron seems inclined to speak much more favourably in prose than in verse.

The smaller pieces that conclude the volume, are in general spirited and well versified. . . .

5. George Ellis, from his unsigned review, *Quarterly Review*

Dated March 1812, issued May 1812, VII, 180–200

George Ellis (1753–1815), author, one of the founders of the *Anti-Jacobin*, friend of Scott and Canning, and a frequent contributor to the *Quarterly*.

We have been in general much gratified, and often highly delighted, during our perusal of this volume, which contains, besides the two first cantos of the *Pilgrimage*, and the notes by which they are accompanied, a few smaller poems of considerable merit; together with an Appendix, communicating a good deal of curious information concerning the present state of literature and language in modern Greece. The principal poem is styled 'A Romaunt;' an appellation, perhaps, rather too quaint, but which, inasmuch as it has been always used with a considerable latitude of meaning, and may be considered as applicable to all the anomalous and non-descript classes of poetical composition, is not less suited than any other title to designate the *metrical itinerary* which we are about to examine. . . .

[Gives outline of poem, with copious extracts.]

The foregoing sketch, slight and imperfect as it is, may serve as an introduction to a few general observations on the nature of this work, which we are desirous of submitting to our readers, before we proceed to a minute and particular comment on the sentiments, or language, or versification.

We believe that few books are so extensively read and admired as those which contain the narratives of intelligent travellers. Indeed, the greater part of every community are confined, either by necessity or indolence, to a very narrow space on the globe, and are naturally eager to contemplate, in description at least, that endless variety of new and curious objects which a visit to distant countries and climates is known to furnish, and of which only a very limited portion can be accessible to the most enterprising individual. If, then, this species of information be so attractive when conveyed in prose, and sometimes, it must be confessed, in very dull prose, by what accident has it happened that no English poet before Lord Byron has thought fit to employ his talents on a subject so obviously well suited to their display? This inadvertence, if such it be, is the more extraordinary, because the supposed dearth of epic subjects has been, during many years, the only apparent impediment to the almost infinite multiplication of epic poems. If it be supposed that the followers of the muse have not carelessly overlooked but intentionally rejected the materials offered by a traveller's journal as too anomalous to be employed in a regular and grand composition, we answer that Homer was of a different opinion, and that the *Odyssey* is formed of exactly such materials. It is true that of the two great epic poems which Homer has bequeathed to the world, the *Iliad* is generally preferred as the noblest monument of his genius; but it does not follow that the *Iliad* is therefore the properest model for imitation; because the modern poet does not possess the privilege of conferring sublimity on the squabbles of two rival chiefs, or on the exploits performed during a siege, by calling in the habitual intervention of Heaven;—whereas the magnificent scenery of the *Odyssey* still remains and must ever remain at his disposal.

We do not know whether Lord Byron ever had it in contemplation to write an epic poem; but we conceive that the subject, which he selected, is perfectly suited to such a purpose; that the foundation which he has laid is sufficiently solid, and his materials sufficiently ample for the most magnificent superstructure; but we doubt whether his plan be well conceived, and we are by no means disposed to applaud, in every instance, the selection of his ornaments.

Of the plan indeed we are unable to speak with perfect confidence, because it has not been at all developed in the two cantos which are now given to the public; but it appears to us that the 'Childe Harold,' whom we suppose, in consequence of the author's positive assurance, to be a mere creature of the imagination, is so far from effecting the object for which he is introduced, and 'giving some connection to the piece,' that he only tends to embarrass and obscure it. We are told, however, that 'friends, on whose opinions Lord Byron sets a high value,' have suggested to him that he might be 'suspected' of having sketched in his hero a portrait of real life; a suspicion for which, he says, 'in some very trivial particulars there might be grounds; but in the main points *I hope* none whatever.' Now if he was so anxious to repel a suspicion which had occurred to friends, on whom he set a high value; if he was conscious that the imaginary traveller, whom, from an unwillingness to appear as the hero of his own tale, he had substituted for himself, was so unamiable; we are at a loss to guess at his motives for choosing such a representative. If, for the completion of some design which has not yet appeared, but which is to be effected in the sequel of the poem, it was necessary to unite, in the person of the pilgrim, the eager curiosity of youth with the fastidiousness of a sated libertine, why revert to the rude and simple ages of chivalry in search of a character which can only exist in an age of vicious refinement? Again, if this apparent absurdity was unavoidable; if the 'Childe,' and 'the little page,' and the 'staunch yeoman,' whom the Childe addresses in his farewell to his native land, could not be spared, why is this group of antiques sent on a journey through Portugal and Spain, during the interval between the convention of Cintra and the battle of Talavera?

It may perhaps be said that this anachronism, being convenient, is in some measure pardonable; and that the other inconsistencies which we have pointed out do not, after all, detract much from the general effect of the poem. But we answer that such inconsistencies appear to us to be perfectly needless; that they may be easily removed; and that they are by no means innocent if they have led Lord Byron (as we suspect) to adopt that motley mixture of obsolete and modern phraseology by which the ease and elegance of his verses are often injured, and to degrade the character of his work by the insertion of some passages which will probably give offence to a considerable portion of his readers.

The metre adopted throughout this 'Romaunt' is the stanza of Spencer [*sic*]; and we admit that, for every ancient word employed by the modern poet, the authority of Spencer may be pleaded. But we think that to intersperse such words as 'ee', 'moe', 'feere', 'ne', 'losel', 'eld', &c. amidst the richest decorations of modern language, is to patch embroidery with rags. Even if these words had not been replaced by any substitutes, and if they were always correctly inserted, their uncouth appearance would be displeasing; but Lord Byron is not always correct in his use of them. For instance, when he says,

> Devices quaint, and Frolics ever new,
> Tread on each other's *kibes*, ——

it must be supposed that he did not mean to personify devices and frolics for the purpose of afflicting them with chilblains. When, again, in describing Ali Pacha, he censures,

—— those ne'er forgotten acts of *ruth*
Beseeming all men ill, but most the man
In years, that mark him with a tyger's tooth, &c.

it is plain that the noble lord must have considered 'ruth' as synonymous, not with pity, but with cruelty. In a third instance where we are told that '*Childe* Harold had *a mother*,' the equivocal meaning of the first word has evidently a ludicrous effect, which could not have escaped the attention of our author whilst writing in the language of his own day. On such errors as these, however, which obviously originate, not in any want of genius, but in accidental heedlessness, we do not mean to lay any stress; we complain only of the habitual negligence, of the frequent laxity of expression—of the feeble or dissonant rhymes which almost always disfigure a too close imitation of the language of our early poets, and of which we think that the work before us offers too many examples.

Spencer, it must be observed, is always consistent. He lived at a time when pedantry was the prevailing fault, not of the sedentary and studious, but of the flighty and illiterate; when daily attempts were made to introduce into our vocabulary the mangled elements of the more sonorous languages of Greece and Rome; and when this anomalous jargon was hailed, by many of his contemporaries, as a model of melody and refinement. Anxious to preserve the purity and simplicity of his native tongue, the 'well of English undefiled,' he appealed from the vitiated taste of the court to the good sense of the nation at large: he thought that significant words were not degraded by passing through the lips of the vulgar; his principal aim was to be generally intelligible: he formed his style on the homely models which had been bequeathed to him by preceding writers, and trusted to his own genius for the supply of the necessary embellishments. The extent of that genius is displayed in the extraordinary variety and elegance of the decorations, thus composed from the most common materials. Spencer was in England, as La Fontaine in France, the creator of that style which our neighbours have so aptly denominated *le genre naïf*. The flowers which he scatters over his subject are, indeed, all of *native* growth: and they have a life and fragrance which is not always found in those more gaudy exotics, imported by succeeding poets, with which our language has been enriched and perhaps over-loaded. Hence, though it is easy to catch his manner in short and partial imitations, it is almost impossible to preserve, throughout a long poem, his peculiar exuberance united with his characteristic simplicity. Lord Byron has shewn himself, in some passages, a tolerably successful copyist; but we like him much better in those where he forgets or disdains to copy; and where, without sacrificing the sweetness and variety of pause by which Spencer's stanza is advantageously distinguished from the heroic couplet, he employs a pomp of diction suited to the splendour of the objects which he describes. We rejoice when, dismissing from his memory the wretched scraps of a musty glossary, he exhibits to us, in natural and appropriate language, the rich scenery and golden sunshine of countries which are the

> Boast of the aged, lesson of the young;
> Which sages venerate, and bards adore,
> As Pallas and the Muse unveil their awful lore.

But we have not yet exhausted our complaints against the way-ward hero of the poem, whose character, we think, is most capriciously and uselessly degraded. The moral code of chivalry was not, we admit, quite pure and spotless; but its laxity in some points was redeemed by the noble spirit of gallantry which it inspired; a gallantry which courted personal danger in the defence of the sovereign, because he is the fountain of honour; of women because they are often lovely and always helpless; and of the priesthood because they are at once dis-armed and sanctified by their profession. Now Childe Harold, if not absolutely craven and recreant, is at least a mortal enemy to all martial exertions, a scoffer at the fair sex, and apparently disposed to consider all religions as different modes of superstition.

The reflections which occur to him, when he surveys the preparations for the conflicts between the French and the allied armies, are that these hosts

> Are met (*as if at home they could not die*)
> *To feed the crow* on Talavera's plain.—
> There shall *they rot; ambition's honour'd fools!*
> 'Yes, honour decks the turf that wraps their clay!'
> Vain sophistry! in these behold the tools,
> The broken tools that tyrants cast away, &c.—
> Enough of *battle's minions!—let them play*
> *Their game of lives, and barter breath for fame;*

Fame, that *will scarce reanimate their clay*,
Though thousands fall to deck some single name.
In sooth, 'twere sad to thwart their noble aim,
Who strike, *blest hirelings!* for their country's good,
And die, that *living might have proved her shame.*

—— —— —— —— he would not delight
(Born beneath some *remote* inglorious star)
In themes of bloody fray, or gallant fight,
But loath'd *the bravo's trade*, and *laughed at martial wight.*—

Now surely, it was not worth while to conjure a 'Childe Harold'
out of some old tapestry, and to bring him into the field of Talavera,
for the purpose of indulging in such meditations as these. It is undoubtedly true that the cannon and the musketry must often anticipate the
stroke of time; and carry off, in the vigour of life, many who might
have been reserved at home to a long protracted decay. It is moreover
true that the buried will rot; that the unburied may become food for
crows, and consequently, that the man who has bartered life for fame
has no chance, when once killed, of coming to life again. But these
truths, we apprehend, are so generally admitted that it is needless to
inculcate them. It is certainly untrue that fame is of little value. It is
something to be honoured by those whom we love. It is something to
the soldier when he returns to the arms of a mother, a wife, or a sister,
to see in their eyes the tears of exultation mixing with those of affection,
and of pious gratitude to heaven for his safety. These joys of a triumph,
it may be said, are mere illusions; but for the sake of such illusions is
life chiefly worth having. When we read the preceding sarcasms on
the 'bravo's trade,' we are induced to ask, not without some anxiety
and alarm, whether such are indeed the opinions which a British peer
entertains of a British army.

The second feature in Childe Harold's character, which was introduced, we presume, for the purpose of giving to it an air of originality,
renders it, if not quite unnatural, at least very unpoetical. Of this
indeed the author seems to have been aware; but instead of correcting
what was harsh and exaggerated in his sketch of the woman-hater, he
has only had recourse to the expedient of introducing, under various
pretexts, those delineations of female beauty which a young poet
may be naturally supposed to pen with much complacency. This
we think ill judged. The victim of violent and unrequited passion,
whether crushed into the sullenness of apathy, or irritated into habitual

moroseness, may become, in the hands of an able poet, very generally and deeply interesting; the human heart is certainly disposed to beat in unison with the struggles of strong and concentrated feeling; but the boyish libertine whose imagination is chilled by hit sated appetites, whose frightful gloom is only the result of disappointed selfishness; and 'whose kiss had been pollution,' cannot surely be expected to excite any tender sympathy, and can only be viewed with unmixed disgust. Some softening of such a character would become necessary even if it were distinguished by peculiar acuteness of remark, or by dazzling flashes of wit. But there is not much wit in designating women as 'wanton *things*,' or as 'lovely harmless *things*;' or in describing English women as '*Remoter* females *famed for sickening prate*;' nor is there much acuteness in the observation that

> —— —— Pomp and power alone are woman's care,
> *And where these are, light Eros finds a feere;*
> Maidens, like moths, are ever caught by glare,
> And Mammon wins his way where seraphs might despair.

We utterly dislike the polyglot line compounded of Greek, Saxon, and modern English; and do not much admire the confusion of images in the others; but we wish to abstain from minute criticism, and are only anxious to remonstrate against those blemishes which, in our opinion, detract from the general beauty of the poem.

Having already given our reasons for thinking that the perversity of character attributed to the hero of the piece is far too highly coloured, it is needless to comment on that settled despair,

> *That will not look beyond the tomb,*
> But cannot hope for rest before.

This is the consummation of human misery; and if it had been the author's principal object, in delineating this fictitious personage, to hold him up to his young readers as a dreadful example of early profligacy, such a finishing to the picture might be vindicated as consistent and useful. In that case, however, it would have been doubly essential to divest the 'Childe' of his chivalrous title and attributes; and the attention of the poet and of the reader being engrossed by one dismal object, it would have become necessary to sacrifice a large portion of that elegance and animation by which the present work is confessedly distinguished.

We certainly do not suspect Lord Byron of having made a

pilgrimage to mount Parnassus for the sole purpose of wooing the
muses to assist him in the project of reforming his contemporaries;
but as we are, on the other hand, most unwilling to impute to him
the intention of giving offence to any class of his readers, we much
wish that he had assigned to his imaginary Harold, instead of uttering
as his own, the sentiments contained in the following stanzas. . . .

[Quotes Canto II, stanzas 3 (last 5 ll.), 4, 5, 6, and 7, on death, the
unlikelihood of immortality, and the grave's evidence of bodily
decay.]

The common courtesy of society has, we think, very justly proscribed the intrusive introduction of such topics as these into conversation; and as no reader probably will open *Childe Harold* with
the view of inquiring into the religious tenets of the author, or of
endeavouring to settle his own, we cannot but disapprove, in point
of taste, these protracted meditations, as well as the disgusting objects
by which some of them are suggested. We object to them, also,
because they have the effect of producing some little traces of resemblance between the author and the hero of the piece; a resemblance
which Lord Byron has most sedulously and properly disclaimed in his
preface. . . .

It is now time to take leave—we hope not a long leave—of Childe
Harold's migrations; but we are unwilling to conclude our article
without repeating our thanks to the author for the amusement which
he has afforded us. The applause which he has received has been
very general, and, in our opinion, well deserved. We think that the
poem exhibits some marks of carelessness, many of caprice, but many
also of sterling genius. On the latter we have forborne to expatiate,
because we apprehend that our readers are quite as well qualified as
ourselves to estimate the merits of pleasing versification, of lively
conception, and of accurate expression. Of those errors of carelessness
from which few poems are, in the first instance, wholly exempt, we
have not attempted to form a catalogue, because they can scarcely
fail to be discovered by the author, and may be silently corrected in a
future edition. But it was our duty attentively to search for, and honestly
to point out the faults arising from caprice, or from a disregard of
general opinion; because it is a too common, though a very mischievous prejudice, to suppose that genius and eccentricity are usual
and natural companions; and that, to discourage extravagance is to
check the growth of excellence. Lord Byron has shewn that his confi-

dence in his own powers is not to be subdued by illiberal and unmerited censure; and we are sure that it will not be diminished by our animadversions: we are not sure that we should have better consulted his future fame, or our own character for candour, if we had expressed our sense of his talents in terms of more unqualified panegyric.

THE TURKISH TALES

The Giaour June 1813
The Bride of Abydos December 1813
The Corsair February 1814
Lara August 1814
The Siege of Corinth and *Parisina* February 1816

6. Jeffrey, from his unsigned review of *The Corsair* and *The Bride of Abydos*, *Edinburgh Review*

Dated April 1814, issued July 1814, XXIII, 198–229

Jeffrey had reviewed *The Giaour* in very favourable terms in the *Edinburgh Review* for July 1813, commenting on its fragmentary structure, the quality of the verse, and the character of the hero; but his review of *The Corsair* and *The Bride of Abydos* is a more sustained attempt at analysing the nature of Byron's appeal for contemporary readers. His cyclical theory of taste and his view of romantic primitivism should be contrasted with Thomas Love Peacock's dismissive account in *The Four Ages of Poetry* (1820).

Lord Byron has clear titles to applause, in the spirit and beauty of his diction and versification, and the splendour of many of his descriptions: But it is to his pictures of the stronger passions, that he is indebted for the fulness of his fame. He has delineated, with unequalled force and fidelity, the workings of those deep and powerful emotions which alternately enchant and agonize the minds that are exposed to their inroads; and represented, with a terrible energy, those struggles and sufferings and exaltations, by which the spirit is at once torn and transported, and traits of divine inspiration, or demoniacal possession, thrown across the tamer features of humanity. It is by this spell, chiefly, we think, that he has fixed the admiration of the public; and while other poets delight by their vivacity, or enchant by their sweetness, he alone has been able to *command* the sympathy, even of reluctant readers, by the natural magic of his moral sublimity, and the terrors and attractions of those overpowering feelings, the depths and the heights of which he seems to have so successfully explored. All the considerable poets of the present age have, indeed, possessed this gift in a greater or lesser degree: but there is no man, since the time of Shakespeare himself, in whom it has been made manifest with greater fulness and splendour, than in the noble author before us: and there are various considerations that lead us to believe, that it is chiefly by its means that he has attained the supremacy with which he seems now to be invested.

It must have occurred, we think, to every one who has attended to the general history of poetry, and to its actual condition among ourselves, that it is destined to complete a certain cycle, or great revolution, with respect at least to some of its essential qualities; and that we are now coming round to a taste and tone of composition, more nearly akin to that which distinguished the beginning of its progress, than any that has prevailed in the course of it.

In the rude ages, when such compositions originate, men's passions are violent, and their sensibility dull. Their poetry deals therefore in strong emotions, and displays the agency of powerful passions; both because these are the objects with which they are most familiar in real life, and because nothing of a weaker cast could make any impression on the rugged natures for whose entertainment they are devised.

As civilization advances, men begin to be ashamed of the undisguised vehemence of their primitive emotions; and learn to subdue, or at least to conceal, the fierceness of their natural passions. The first triumph of regulated society, is to be able to protect its members from actual violence; and the first trait of refinement in manners, is to exclude the coarseness and offence of unrestrained and selfish emotions. The complacency however with which these achievements are contemplated, naturally leads to too great an admiration of the principle from which they proceed. All manifestation of strong feeling is soon proscribed as coarse and vulgar; and first a cold and ceremonious politeness, and afterwards a more gay and heartless dissipation, represses, and in part eradicates the warmer affections and generous passions of our nature, along with its more dangerous and turbulent emotions. It is needless to trace the effects of this revolution in the manners and opinions of society upon that branch of literature, which necessarily reflects all its variations. It is enough to say, in general, that, in consequence of this change, poetry becomes first pompous and stately—then affectedly refined and ingenious—and finally gay, witty, discursive and familiar.

There is yet another stage, however, in the history of man and his inventions. When the pleasures of security are no longer new, and the dangers of excessive or intemperate vehemence cease to be thought of in the upper ranks of society, it is natural that the utility of the precautions which had been taken against them should be brought into question, and their severity in a great measure relaxed. There is in the human breast a certain avidity for strong sensation, which cannot be long repressed even by the fear of serious disaster. The consciousness of having subdued and disarmed the natural violence of mankind, is sufficiently lively to gratify this propensity, so long as the triumph is recent, and the hazards still visible from which it has effected our deliverance. In like manner, while it is a new thing, and somewhat of a distinction, to be able to laugh gracefully at all things, the successful derision of affection and enthusiasm is found to do pretty nearly as well as their possession; and hearts comfortably hardened by dissipation, feel little want of gratifications which they have almost lost the capacity of receiving. When these, however, come to be but vulgar accomplishments—when generations have passed away, during which all persons of education have employed themselves in doing the same frivolous things, with the same despair either of interest or glory, it can scarcely fail to happen, that the more powerful spirits will awaken to a sense of their own degradation and unhappiness;—a disdain and impatience of the petty pretensions and joyless elegancies of fashion will gradually arise: and strong and natural sensations will again be sought, without dread of their coarseness, in every scene which promises to supply them. This is the stage of society in which fanaticism has its second birth, and political enthusiasm its first true development—when plans of visionary reform, and schemes of boundless ambition are conceived, and almost realized by the energy with which they are pursued—the era of revolutions and projects—of vast performances, and infinite expectations.

Poetry, of course, reflects and partakes in this great transformation. It becomes more enthusiastic, authoritative and impassioned; and feeling the necessity of dealing in more powerful emotions than suited the tranquil and frivolous age which preceded, naturally goes back to those themes and characters which animated the energetic lays of its first rude inventors. The feats of chivalry, and the loves of romance,[1] are revived with more than their primitive wildness and ardour. For the sake of the natural feeling they contain, the incidents and diction of the old vulgar ballads are once more imitated and surpassed; and poetry does not disdain, in pursuit of her new idol of strong emotion, to descend to the very lowest conditions of society, and to stir up the most revolting dregs of utter wretchedness and depravity.

This is the age to which we are now arrived:—and if we have rightly seized the principle by which we think its peculiarities are to be accounted for, it will not be difficult to show, that the poet who has devoted himself most exclusively, and most successfully, to the delineation of the stronger and deeper passions, is likely to be its reigning favourite. Neither do we think that we can have essentially mistaken that principle:—at least it is a fact, independent of all theory, not only that all the successful poets of the last twenty years have dealt much more in powerful sensations, than those of the century that went before; but that, in order to attain this object, they have employed themselves upon subjects which would have been rejected as vulgar and offensive by the fastidious delicacy of that age of fine writing. Instead of ingenious essays, elegant pieces of gallantry, and witty satires all stuck over with classical allusions, we have, in our popular poetry, the dreams of convicts, and the agonies of Gypsey women,— and the exploits of buccaneers, freebooters, and savages—and pictures to shudder at, of remorse, revenge, and insanity—and the triumph of generous feelings in scenes of anguish and terror—and the heroism of low-born affection and the tragedies of vulgar atrocity. All these various subjects have been found interesting, and have succeeded, in different degrees, in spite of accompaniments which would have disgusted an age more recently escaped from barbarity. And as they agree in nothing but in being the vehicles of strong and natural emotions, and have generally pleased, nearly in proportion to the

The Greek and Roman classics afford no resource in this emergency; partly because by far the greater part of them belong to a period of society as artificial, and as averse to the undisguised exhibition of natural passions, as that which preceded this revulsion; and partly because, at all events, the study of them is associated with the coldest and dullest period of modern literature, and their mythology and other jargon incorporated with the compositions that come now to be looked upon with the greatest derision and disdain.

quantity of that emotion they conveyed, it is difficult not to conclude, that they have pleased only for the sake of that quality—a growing appetite for which may be regarded as the true characteristic of this age of the world.

In selecting subjects and characters for this purpose, it was not only natural, but in a great measure necessary, to go back to the only ages when strong passions were indulged, or at least displayed without controul, by persons in the better ranks of society; in the same way as, in order to get perfect models of muscular force and beauty, we still find that we must go back to the works of those days when men went almost naked, and were raised to the rank of heroes for feats of bodily strength and activity. The savages and barbarians that are still to be found in the world, are, no doubt, very exact likenesses of those whom civilization has driven out of it; and they may be used accordingly for most of the purposes for which their antient prototypes are found serviceable. In poetry, however, it happens again, as in sculpture, that it is safer, at least for a moderate genius, rather to work upon the relics we have of antiquity, than upon what is most nearly akin to it among our own contemporaries; both because there is a certain charm and fascination in what is antient and long remembered, and because those particular modifications of energetic forms and characters, which have already been made the subject of successful art, can be more securely and confidently managed in imitation, than the undefined vastness of a natural condition, however analogous to that from which they were selected.—Mr Southey, accordingly, who has gone in search of strong passions among the savages of America, and the gods and enchanters of India, has had far less success than Mr Scott, who has borrowed his energies from the more familiar scenes of European chivalry, and built his fairy castles with materials already tried and consecrated in the fabric of our old romances. The noble author before us has been obliged, like them, to go out of his own age and country in quest of the same indispensable ingredients; and his lot has fallen among the Turks and Arabs of the Mediterranean:—ruffians and desperadoes, certainly not much more amiable in themselves than the worst subjects of the others,— but capable of great redemption in the hands of a poet of genius, by being placed within the enchanted circle of antient Greece, and preserving among them so many vestiges of Roman pride and magnificence. There is still one general remark, however, to be made, before coming immediately to the merit of the pieces before us.

Although the necessity of finding beings capable of strong passions, thus occasions the revival, in a late stage of civilization, of the characters and adventures which animated the poetry of rude ages, it must not be thought that they are made to act and feel, on this resurrection, exactly as they did in their first natural presentation. They were then produced, not as exotics or creatures of the imagination, but merely as better specimens of the ordinary nature with which their authors were familiar; and the astonishing situations and appalling exploits in which they were engaged, were but a selection from the actual occurrences of the times. Neither the heroes themselves, nor their first celebrators, would have perceived any sublimity in the character itself or the tone of feeling, which such scenes and such exploits indicate to the more reflecting readers of a distant generation; and would still less have thought of analyzing the workings of those emotions, or moralizing on the incidents to which they gave birth. In this primitive poetry, accordingly, we have rather the result than the delineation of strong passions—the events which they produce, rather than the energy that produces them. The character of the agent is unavoidably disclosed indeed in short and impressive glimpses—but it is never made the direct subject of exhibition; and the attention of the reader is always directed to what he does—not to what he feels. A more refined, reflecting, and sensitive generation, indeed, in reading these very legends, supposes what *must* have been felt, both before and after the actions that are so minutely recorded; and thus lends to them, from the stores of its own sensibility, a dignity and an interest which they did not possess in the minds of their own rude composers. When the same scenes and characters, however, are ultimately called back to feed the craving of a race disgusted with heartless occupations, for natural passions and overpowering emotions, it would go near to defeat the very object of their revival, if these passions were still left to indicate themselves only by the giant vestiges of outrageous deeds, or acts of daring and desperation. The passion itself must now be pourtrayed—and all its fearful workings displayed in detail before us. The minds of the great agents must be unmasked for us—and all the anatomy of their throbbing bosoms laid open to our gaze. We must be made to understand what they feel and enjoy and endure;—and all the course and progress of their *possession*, and the crossing and mingling of their opposite affections, must be rendered sensible to our touch; till, without regard to their external circumstances, we can enter into all the motions of their hearts, and read, and shudder as we read, the secret characters which stamp the capacity of unlimited suffering on a nature which we feel to be our own.

It is chiefly by these portraitures of the interior of human nature that the poetry of the present day is distinguished from all that preceded it—and the difference is perhaps most conspicuous when the persons and subjects are borrowed from the poetry of an earlier age. Not only is all this anatomy of the feelings superadded to the primitive legend of exploits, but in many cases feelings are imputed to the agents, of which persons in their condition were certainly incapable, and which no description could have made intelligible to their contemporaries— while, in others, the want of feeling, probably a little exaggerated beyond nature also, is dwelt upon, and made to produce great effect as a trait of singular atrocity, though far too familiar to have excited any sensation either in the readers or spectators of the times to which the adventures naturally belong. Our modern poets, in short, have borrowed little more than the situations and unrestrained passions of the state of society from which they have taken their characters— and have added all the sensibility and delicacy from the stores of their own experience. They have lent their knights and squires of the fifteenth century the deep reflection and considerate delicacy of the nineteenth,—and combined the desperate and reckless valour of a Buccaneer or Corsair of any age, with the refined gallantry and senti- mental generosity of an English gentleman of the present day. The combination we believe to be radically incongruous; but it was almost indispensable to the poetical effect that was in contemplation. The point was, to unite all the fine and strong feelings to which culti- vation and reflection alone can give birth, with those manners and that condition of society, in which passions are uncontrouled, and their natural indications manifested without reserve. It was necessary, therefore, to unite two things that never did exist together in any period of society; and the union, though it may startle sober thinkers a little, is perhaps within the legitimate prerogatives of poetry. The most outrageous, and the least successful attempt of this sort we remember, is that of Mr Southey, who represents a wild Welch chieftain, who goes a buccaneering to America in the twelfth century, with all the softness, decorum, and pretty behaviour of Sir Charles Grandison. But the incongruity itself is universal—from Campbell, who invests a Pennsylvanian farmer with the wisdom and mildness of Socrates, and the dignified manners of an old Croix de St Louis—to Scott, who makes an old, bloodyminded and mercenary ruffian talk like a sentimental hero and poet, in his latter days—or the author before us, who has adorned a merciless corsair on a rock in the Mediterranean, with every virtue under heaven—except common honesty.

Of that noble author, and the peculiarity of his manner, we have not much more to say, before proceeding to give an account of the pieces now before us. His object obviously is, to produce a great effect, partly by the novelty of his situations, but chiefly by the force and energy of his sentiments and expressions; and the themes which he has selected, though perhaps too much resembling each other, are unquestionably well adapted for this purpose. There is something grand and imposing in the unbroken stateliness, courage, and heroic bigotry of a Turk of the higher order; and a certain voluptuous and barbaric pomp about his establishment, that addresses itself very forcibly to the imagination. His climate too, and most of its productions, are magnificent—and glow with a raised and exotic splendour; but the ruins of Grecian art, and of Grecian liberty and glory with which he is surrounded, form by far the finest of his accompaniments. There is nothing, we admit, half so trite in poetry as commonplaces of classical enthusiasm; but it is for this very reason that we admire the force of genius by which Lord Byron has contrived to be original, natural, and pathetic, upon a subject so unpromising, and apparently so long exhausted. How he has managed it, we do not yet exactly understand; though it is partly, we have no doubt, by placing us in the midst of the scene as it actually exists, and superadding the charm of enchanting landscape to that of interesting recollections. Lord Byron, we think, is the only modern poet who has set before our eyes a visible picture of the present aspect of scenes so famous in story; and, instead of feeding us with the unsubstantial food of historical associations, has spread around us the blue waters and dazzling skies—the ruined temples and dusky olives—the desolated cities, and turbaned population, of modern Attica. We scarcely knew before that Greece was still a beautiful country.

He has also made a fine use of the gentleness and submission of the females of these regions, as contrasted with the lordly pride and martial ferocity of the men: and though we suspect he has lent them more *soul* than of right belongs to them, as well as more delicacy and reflection; yet there is something so true to female nature in general, in his representations of this sort, and so much of the Oriental softness and acquiescence in his particular delineations, that it is scarcely possible to refuse the picture the praise of being characteristic and harmonious, as well as eminently sweet and beautiful in itself.

The other merits of his composition are such as his previous publications had already made familiar to the public,—an unparalleled rapidity of narrative, and condensation of thoughts and images—a style always vigorous and original, though sometimes quaint and affected, and more frequently strained, harsh, and abrupt—a diction and versification invariably spirited, and almost always harmonious and emphatic: Nothing diluted in short, or diffused into weakness, but full of life, and nerve, and activity—expanding only in the eloquent expression of strong and favourite affections, and everywhere else concise, energetic, and impetuous—hurrying on with a disdain of little ornaments and accuracies, and not always very solicitous about being comprehended by readers of inferior capacity.

The more considerable of the two poems now before us, entitled *The Corsair*, exhibits all those qualities, perhaps, in a more striking light than any of the author's other publications. It is written in the regular heroic couplet, with a spirit, freedom, and variety of tone, of which, notwithstanding the example of Dryden, we scarcely believed that measure susceptible. In all the descriptive and serious pieces of Dryden, and in all his writings, indeed, except his Political Satires and his immortal Ode, there are innumerable flat, dull, and prosaic passages; —lines without force, spirit, or energy, and in fact without any other merit than that of accurate versification, and easy and natural diction. Nothing can be more exquisite than the couplets of Pope, for the expression of pointed remark, wit, sarcasm, or epigram; but there is nothing in Pope of impetuous passion or enthusiastic vehemence; and his acknowledged mastery in this species of versification had almost brought it to be considered as appropriate to such subjects,—when Goldsmith, and after him Rogers and Campbell, came to show that it was also capable of strains of the deepest tenderness and sweetest simplicity. Still, however, all these were compositions of a measured and uniform structure—and it was yet to be proved that this, the most ponderous and stately verse in our language, could be accommodated to the variations of a tale of passion and of pity, and to all the breaks, starts and transitions of an adventurous and dramatic narration. This experiment Lord Byron has made, with equal boldness and success—and has satisfied us, at least, that the oldest and most respectable measure that is known among us, is at least as flexible as any other —and capable, in the hands of a master, of vibrations as strong and rapid as those of a lighter structure. We shall not be positive that the charm may not be partly at least in the subject—but we certainly never read so many ten-syllabled couplets together before, with so little feeling of heaviness or monotony. . . .

[Gives outline of poem with copious extracts.]

Our readers are now in a condition to judge for themselves of the merits of this singular production—nor are we tempted to interfere with any remarks of our own. The obvious and radical objection, of all the incidents being borrowed from situations that are scarcely *conceivable* by the greater part of his readers, has been already considered in the remarks which we made at the beginning: a more reasonable objection, we think is, that the character of the hero is needlessly loaded in the description with crimes and vices of which his conduct affords no indication. He is spoken of as an abandoned and unfeeling ruffian—and he uniformly comports himself as a perfect pattern of tenderness and humanity. Nay, he even carries his generosity a good deal farther than, we believe, the most moral of his readers would think necessary—for our own part, at least, we do not hesitate to profess that we should have very little scruple about taking the life of any worthy gentleman over night, who had put every thing in order for impaling us in the morning.

The Corsair has detained us so long, that we must make short work with *The Bride of Abydos*—which is a piece indeed of a slighter structure, and more easily despatched. This is a Turkish tale, like *The Giaour*, written in yet more irregular verse, and abounding more in soft and tender scenes, and less in terrors and horrors than any of Lord Byron's other publications. It contains many passages of great interest and beauty—and as many specimens of rich and splendid description as could be selected out of any work of the same extent. The story is wild and tragical—but neither complicated nor horrible. . . .

[Gives outline of poem with copious extracts.]

After these long extracts, we can afford to say but little of Lord Byron's poetical peculiarities. We still wish he would present us with personages with whom we could more entirely sympathize. At present, he will let us admire nothing but adventurous courage in men, and devoted gentleness in women. There is no intellectual dignity or accomplishment about any of his characters; and no very enlightened or equitable principles of morality. We have made the best apology we could for this tribe of heroes, in the remarks we have ventured upon at the beginning; and are aware of the difficulty of exhibiting strong passions in respectable persons. But it belongs to a genius like his, to overcome such difficulties; and he will never be thoroughly nor universally pleasing, till he learns to bespeak our interest for beings a little more like those whom we have been accustomed to love and admire.

We must say a word or two, also, upon the faults of his style and diction—some of which seem to be growing into manner and habit with him. He has a sort of emphatic obscurity, for instance, every now and then, that is always distressing, and sometimes absurd. Speaking of the wild ditty sung by the pirates, for example, he says,

> Such were the sounds that thrilled the rocks among,
> And *unto ears as rugged seemed a song.*

And a little after,

> —— —— she that day had past
> In watching all *that hope proclaimed a mast.*

And again, in the latter poem, with a still more lamentable failure of the intended effect—

> A cup, too, on the board was set,
> That *did not seem to hold sherbet.*

His construction too is often ungrammatical or imperfect—as when giving directions to alter the guard of his sword, he says,

> Last time, it more fatigued my arm than foes.

To *fatigue* foes with a sabre, is at all events a very strange mode of annoyance. In a subsequent passage, it is said,

> He sate him down in silence, and his look
> Resumed the calmness which before forsook.

Forsook what?—The verb is unquestionably active, and not neuter. The whole passage indeed is clumsy in diction, and, we would almost say, vulgar in expression. For example,

> The feast was ushered in; but sumptuous fare,
> He shunned as if some poison mingled there.
> For one so long condemned to toil and fast,
> Methinks he strangely spares the rich repast.
> What ails thee, Dervise?—eat—dost thou suppose
> This feast a Christian's? or my friends thy foes?

The following triplet is heavy, and almost unintelligible—it would be agreeably lightened by striking out the middle line.

> But he has said it—and the jealous well,
> Those tyrants teazing, tempting to rebel,
> Deserve the fate their fretting lips foretell.

There are various imitations of living authors—who would, no doubt, have been proud to have had the noble author acknowledge his obligations—and there is no one certainly who can better afford to acknowledge them. All that we object to however, is, that he sometimes imitates what had better be let alone—as the quaint jingle of Crabbe in such a line as this—

> Or fallen too low, to fear a farther fall.

And the dangerous simplicity and daring pathos of Campbell, in such as this—

> Another—and another—and another.

These are small matters, we allow; and if every one thought as little of them as we do, we doubt whether we should have condescended to take any notice of them. But many who have a good deal to say in awarding poetical glory, consider them as of no light importance; and therefore it becomes us, as professed critics, to admonish the noble author of their existence.—We hope he is not in earnest in meditating even a temporary divorce from his Muse—and would humbly suggest to him to do away the reproach of the age, by producing a tragic drama of the old English school of poetry and pathos. He has all the air, we think, of being the knight for whom the accomplishment of that great adventure is reserved.

7. Ellis from his unsigned review of *The Corsair* and *Lara*, *Quarterly Review*

Dated July 1814, issued Autumn 1814, XI, 428–57

In the course of his review Ellis endorses Jeffrey's views on Byron's heroes, but repudiates his theory of a 'poetical cycle' and a modern preoccupation with the anatomy of feelings (see above, No. 6).

... It is contended that poetry is destined to complete a certain cycle or great revolution, accompanying and dependant on a correspondent cycle of the feelings as well as of the manners of society. That, originating in times of turbulence and anarchy, it was at first coarse and vehement;—then pompous and stately;—then affectedly refined and ingenious—and finally gay, witty, discursive, and familiar. That at this stage of refinement, however, mankind become disgusted with the heartless frivolity of their gratifications, and acquire a longing for strong emotions, so that poetry, following the current of popular opinion, is compelled to seek for subjects in the manners of ruder ages, to revive the feats of chivalry, and the loves of romance; or to wander, in search of unbridled passion, amongst nations yet imperfectly civilized. Lastly, that this is the period at which we are now arrived: that a growing appetite for turbulent emotion is the peculiar characteristic of the age; that we are no longer satisfied with viewing the mere effects of strong passion, but require the passion itself to be dissected before our eyes; and that Lord Byron, having surpassed all his contemporaries in this species of moral anatomy, has, of course, attained the pinnacle of popular favour.

Now we venture to contend that the poetical cycle here described is purely imaginary; and that if any indications of it were, indeed, discoverable in the history of our own poetry, it would not be fair to deduce, from them, a correspondent cycle of the national 'appetite' for any sort of emotions. Language and manners are, from age to age, either progressively improved, or at least changed, and the trace of such changes may be found in the works of contemporary poets; but the passions of mankind are always the same, and always capable of being called out by a proper degree of excitement. If centuries have passed away since the birth of Shakespeare, does it follow that an *appetite* for those emotions, which he alone was able to rouse, lay dormant during the interval, and has only revived within the last twenty years? We greatly doubt the fact, as well as the existence of the symptoms which are adduced in proof of it. The last twenty years have, doubtless, been wonderfully fertile of crimes and miseries, and there have been some persons in this country who have hailed, with joy and praise, every step of that desolating tyranny, which threatened to spread over the world, and awakened in its progress all those strong emotions which are pronounced to be so delectable. But these persons were not very numerous, and certainly not legitimate arbiters of taste, or of poetical talent. In the whole remainder of the nation, we believe that the horrid realities, which passed before their eyes, did not raise any appetite for scenes of mimic terror; and if Mr Scott, Mr Southey, and Lord Byron have transported their readers to the ages of romance, to the wilds of America, or to the shores of Greece, we suspect that they all followed the impulse of their own studies or habits, without dreaming that they thus completed a poetical cycle, or ministered to any taste or appetite peculiar to the present age or country.

Without dwelling any longer on the general objections to this new and fanciful theory, we now proceed to the point immediately at issue. It is contended, on one hand, that for the purpose of suiting the poetical taste of the present times, 'the minds of the great agents must be unmasked for us—and all the anatomy of their throbbing bosoms laid open to our gaze.' We think, on the contrary, that this anatomical operation is essentially unpoetical; and that therefore Lord Byron, who is emphatically styled the 'searcher of dark bosoms,' is least attractive, and least popular, whenever he attempts to execute this special office. We do not mean to question the extent to which the analysis of mind, or of sensation, is capable of being carried, or to vilipend the delight attendant on such researches; we only contend that the pleasures of intellect are materially different from the pleasures of illusion, that the two are incompatible; and that the writer, who seeks to excite any emotion, will never effect this by attempting to analyse its nature and origin, but must content himself with describing its effects, because it is only with these that his readers can be supposed to be conversant. Every passion of the soul has its visible symptoms by which the correspondent feeling of the observer is instantly awakened; and it is only by the delineation of these symptoms, so correct as to be recognized by the simplest reader, and to produce a momentary illusion, and to call out, by means of the pictured image, the same train of sympathies as would have been excited by the reality, that the poet can possess himself of our imagination and become master of our emotions. The secret sensibility which lurks within our bosoms, which pervades the whole animated frame, and transmits through it the indications of joy or grief, of pleasure or pain, but of which the excess is suffocating and unutterable, cannot itself become the subject of description. To attempt such description is, we think, to exceed the legitimate pretensions of poetry, and to invade the province of metaphysics. On this ground we object to some passages in *The Corsair*, which are intended to represent the prison-thoughts of Conrad. On similar grounds we have more strongly objected to *The Giaour*.——But enough of this. We have stated our opinion, and leave the question for the decision of our readers.

8. Some contemporary comments

(*a*) Extracts from the Diary of HENRY CRABB ROBINSON:
'[26 June 1813] . . . Mrs Porden lent me this evening Lord Byron's *Giaour*, a Turkish tale (a fragment only). With a few energetic lines expressing a diseased state of feeling, the thing is as worthless and unmeaning as I should have expected, even from Lord Byron. A man must have a very mistaken notion of the importance of his writings who supposes that a few broken parts of a tale, wanting on that account the gross material interest of a story, and not having the recommendation of teaching any moral truth, or of exhibiting any picture delightful to the imagination or exciting the sympathy, can be in any way worth the attention of cultivated minds. For of the higher objects and views of poetry Lord Byron pretends not to entertain a notion.'

'[5 February 1814] *The Corsair* displeases one less than *The Giaour* and *Childe Harold*, but I doubt whether its principal character does not present an incompatible combination: the "thousand crimes and single virtue" are not so combined as to impress on the reader the necessity or even the probability of their actual union. There are strong passages and a depth of passion which is sure to please those who are more accessible to impressions of strength than of delicacy. But the poem will not stimulate me to a frequent perusal. . . .'

'[11 February 1814] Read part of *The Bride of Abydos*—certainly a pretty poem; that is, full of flashy passages; and [liking] the irregular verse in which it is written, I read it with pleasure, though it has none of the higher excellencies of poetry.'

'[17 February 1816] I went to Mr. Porden's. There I read aloud Lord Byron's *Siege of Corinth*—a story disgusting and horrid in its effects. . . . All is horror throughout, and a description of dogs eating up dead bodies surpasses in filthiness Lord Byron's usual style.' (*Henry Crabb Robinson on Books and their Writers*, ed. Edith J. Morley, 1938, I, 129, 136, 137, 180.)

(*b*) WALTER SCOTT. Extract from letter of 6 November 1813, to Lord Byron: 'I am very much interested in all that concerns your *Giaour*, which is universally approved of among our mountains. I have heard no objection except by one or two geniuses, who run over poetry as a cat does over a harpsichord, and they affect to complain of obscurity. On the contrary, I hold every real lover of the art is obliged to you for condensing the narrative, by giving us only those striking scenes which you have shown to be so susceptible of poetic ornament, and leaving to imagination the says I's and says he's, and all the minutiae of detail which might be proper in giving evidence before a court of justice. The truth is, I think poetry is most striking when the mirror can be held up to the reader, and the same kept constantly before his eyes; it requires most uncommon powers to support a direct and downright narration; nor can I remember many instances of its being successfully maintained even by our greatest bards.' (*The Letters of Sir Walter Scott*, III, 374.)

(c) JOHN MURRAY (1778-1843), the famous publisher, had established what was to be a long connection with Byron by publishing the first two cantos of *Childe Harold*. Extract from his letter of 3 February 1814, telling Byron of the reception of *The Corsair*: 'I am most happy to tell you that your last poem is—what Mr. Southey's is *called*—a *Carmen Triumphale*. Never, in my recollection, has any work, since the *Letter of Burke to the Duke of Bedford*, excited such a ferment—a ferment which I am happy to say will subside into lasting fame. I sold, on the day of publication—a thing perfectly unprecedented—10,000 copies; and I suppose thirty people, who were purchasers (strangers), called to tell the people in the shop how much they had been delighted and satisfied. Mr. Moore says it is masterly—a wonderful performance. Mr. Hammond, Mr. Heber, D'Israeli, every one who comes—and too many call for me to enumerate—declare their unlimited approbation. Mr. Ward was here with Mr. Gifford yesterday, and mingled his admiration with the rest. Mr. Ward is much delighted with the unexpected charge of the Dervis—

"Up rose the Dervis, with that burst of light",

and Gifford did what I never knew him do before—he repeated several passages from memory, particularly the closing stanza,—

"His death yet dubious, deeds too widely known."

Indeed, from what I have observed, from the very general and unvarying sentiment which I have now gathered, the suffrages are decidedly in favour of this poem in preference to *The Bride of Abydos*, and are even now balancing with *The Giaour*. I have heard no one pass without noticing, and without expressing regret at, the idea thrown out by your Lordship of writing no more for a considerable time. I am really marking down, without suppression or extension, literally what I have heard. I was with Mr. Shee this morning, to whom I had presented the poem; and he declared himself to have been delighted, and swore he had long placed you far beyond any contemporary bard; and, indeed, your last poem does, in the opinion of almost all that I have conversed with. I have the highest encomiums in letters from Croker and Mr. Hay; but I rest most upon the warm feeling it has created in Gifford's critical heart. The versification is thought highly of indeed. . . . You have no notion of the sensation which the publication has occasioned; and my only regret is that you were not present to witness it.' (Samuel Smiles, *A Publisher and His Friends*, 1891, I, 223–4.)

(*d*) JOHN CAM HOBHOUSE (1786–1869), politician and close friend of Byron. Extract from Diary, 23 March 1814: 'This evening, after dinner, I read aloud *The Rape of the Lock*, and the "Elegy on the Death of an Unfortunate Lady", also the *Characters of Women*. Nothing will do after Pope. I am convinced that even my friend's poetry would have been thought monstrous and affected in an age still ringing with melody and sense of that great writer. Indeed, the great success of *Childe Harold* is due chiefly to Byron's having dared to give utterance to certain feelings which every one must have encouraged in the melancholy and therefore morbid hours of his existence, and also by the intimate knowledge which he has shown of the turns taken by the passions of women. He says himself that his poems are of that sort, which will, like everything of the kind in these days, pass away, and give place to the ancient reading, but that he esteems himself fortunate in getting all that can now be got by such a passing reputation, for which there are so many competitors.'
(Lord Broughton [John Cam Hobhouse], *Recollections of a Long Life*, ed. Lady Dorchester, 1909–11, I, 99–100.)

(*e*) WILLIAM GIFFORD (1756–1826), editor of the *Anti-Jacobin* (1797–8) and first editor of the *Quarterly Review*. Byron had a high respect for him as poet, critic and satirist, and allowed many of his own works to be submitted to him for comment. Note from Gifford to John Murray on *The Siege of Corinth*: 'It is a dreadful picture: Caravaggio outdone in his own way. I have hinted at the removal of one couplet: if its sense be wanted, it may be compressed into one of the other lines. Its powers are unquestionable; but can any human being deserve such a delineation? I keep my old opinion of Lord Byron. He may be what he will. Why will he not *will* to be the first of poets and of men. I lament bitterly to see a great mind run to seed, and waste itself in rank growth.' (Smiles, *op. cit.*, I, 357-8.)

(*f*) ISAAC D'ISRAELI (1766-1848), author, and father of Benjamin Disraeli. Letter of December 1815, to John Murray, on *The Siege of Corinth*: 'I am anxious to tell you, that I find myself, this morning, so strangely affected by the perusal of the poem last night, that I feel that it is one which stands quite by itself. I know of nothing of the kind which is worthy of comparison with it. There is no scene, no incident, nothing so marvellous in pathos and terror in Homer, or any bard of antiquity. It impresses one with such a complete feeling of utter desolation, mental and scenical, that when Minotti touched that last spark which scattered its little world into air, he did not make it more desolate than the terrible and affecting energy of the poet's imagination. But Homer had not such a sort of spirit as the mistress of Alp—he had wolves, and vultures, and dogs; but Homer has never conveyed his reader into a vast Golgotha, nor harrowed us with the vulture flapping the back of the gorged wolf, nor the dogs: the terror, the truth, and the loneliness of that spot will never be erased from my memory. Alp by the side of the besieged wall; that ghost-like manner of giving him a minute's reflection by showing one of the phenomena of nature—that is a stroke of a spirit's character never before imagined, and can never be surpassed. And after the most sublime incident that ever poet invented, still to have the power to agitate the mind, by that eagle who flies nearer the sun, mistaking the cloud of destruction for night; in a word, I could not abstain from assuring you, that I never read any poem that exceeded in power this, to me, most extraordinary production. I do not know where I am to find any which can excite the same degree of emotion.' (Smiles, *op. cit.*, I, 358.)

(*g*) Extract from a 'Critique on *Lara*' in the anonymous *Byroniana: Bozzies and Piozzies*, 1825, p. 44: 'Perhaps it may with truth be said, the tendency of this Poem is, by its seductive brilliancy, to allow human beings to yield "too much to grief," and finally, become either misanthropes or madmen. The power which this species of sentimental

writing has over the susceptible mind of ardent youth, is inconceivable.'
(*Note:* This is given out of chronological sequence because its diagnosis
of the effect of Byron's poetry is relevant to the Jane Austen passage
which follows.)

(*h*) JANE AUSTEN (1775–1817), extract from *Persuasion* (1818):
'While Captains Wentworth and Harville led the talk on one side
of the room, and, by recurring to former days, supplied anecdotes
in abundance to occupy and entertain the others, it fell to Anne's
lot to be placed rather apart with Captain Benwick; and a very
good impulse of her nature obliged her to begin an acquaintance
with him. He was shy, and disposed to abstraction; but the engaging
mildness of her countenance, and gentleness of her manners, soon had
their effect; and Anne was well repaid the first trouble of exertion.
He was evidently a young man of considerable taste in reading, though
principally in poetry; and besides the persuasion of having given him at
least an evening's indulgence in the discussion of subjects, which his
usual companions had probably no concern in, she had the hope of
being of real use to him in some suggestions as to the duty and benefit
of struggling against affliction, which had naturally grown out of their
conversation. For, though shy, he did not seem reserved; it had
rather the appearance of feelings glad to burst their usual restraints;
and having talked of poetry, the richness of the present age, and gone
through a brief comparison of opinion as to the first-rate poets, trying
to ascertain whether *Marmion* or *The Lady of the Lake* were to be
preferred, and how ranked *The Giaour* and *The Bride of Abydos*;
and moreover, how *The Giaour* was to be pronounced, he shewed
himself so intimately acquainted with all the tenderest songs of the one
poet, and all the impassioned descriptions of hopeless agony of the
other; he repeated, with such tremulous feeling, the various lines which
imaged a broken heart, or a mind destroyed by wretchedness, and
looked so entirely as if he meant to be understood, that she ventured
to hope he did not always read only poetry; and to say, that she thought
it was the misfortune of poetry, to be seldom safely enjoyed by those
who enjoyed it completely; and that the strong feelings which alone
could estimate it truly, were the very feelings which ought to taste it
but sparingly.

His looks shewing him not pained, but pleased with this allusion
to his situation, she was emboldened to go on; and feeling in herself
the right of seniority of mind, she ventured to recommend a larger

allowance of prose in his daily study; and on being requested to particularize, mentioned such works of our best moralists, such collections of the finest letters, such memoirs of characters of worth and suffering, as occurred to her at the moment as calculated to rouse and fortify the mind by the highest precepts, and the strongest examples of moral and religious endurances.' (*Northanger Abbey and Persuasion*, ed. R. W. Chapman, 3rd edn., 1933, pp. 100-1.)

9. Verse commentaries on Byron's poetry

1812–1815

(a) Extract (omitting stanzas IV, VII, VIII, XI, XII) from *Rejected Addresses: or The New Theatrum Poetarum*, 1812. Drury Lane Theatre, which had been destroyed by fire in February 1809, was reopened in October 1812. The committee of management had invited entries for 'a fair and free competition for an Address, to be spoken upon the opening of the Theatre'; but all the resulting entries were rejected, and the Committee invited Byron to compose the Address instead. This provided the occasion for *Rejected Addresses*, published anonymously by the brothers James Smith (1775–1839) and Horace Smith (1779–1849). It consisted of a series of parodies of contemporary poets, purporting to be their entries for the competition. Byron himself enjoyed the joke: 'I like the volume of *"rejected A."* better and better', he told John Murray on 23 October (*LJ*, II, 180).

CUI BONO? [1]

By Lord B.

I

Sated with home, of wife, of children tired,
The restless soul is driven abroad to roam;
Sated abroad, all seen, yet nought admired,
The restless soul is driven to ramble home;
Sated with both, beneath new Drury's dome
The fiend Ennui awhile consents to pine,
There growls, and curses, like a deadly Gnome,
Scorning to view fantastic Columbine,
Viewing with scorn and hate the nonsense of the Nine.

II

Ye reckless dupes, who hither wend your way,
To gaze on puppets in a painted dome,
Pursuing pastimes glittering to betray,
Like falling stars in life's eternal gloom,

[1] ['For whose advantage?']

74

What seek ye here? Joy's evanescent bloom?
Woe's me! the brightest wreaths she ever gave
Are but as flowers that decorate a tomb.
Man's heart, the mournful urn o'er which they wave,
Is sacred to despair, its pedestal the grave.

III

Has life so little store of real woes,
That here ye wend to taste fictitious grief?
Or is it that from truth such anguish flows,
Ye court the lying drama for relief?
Long shall ye find the pang, the respite brief,
Or if one tolerable page appears
In folly's volume, 'tis the actor's leaf,
Who dries his own by drawing others' tears,
And raising present mirth, makes glad his future years.....

V

This goodly pile, upheav'd by Wyatt's toil,
Perchance than Holland's edifice more fleet,
Again red Lemnos' artizan may spoil;
The fire alarm, and midnight drum may beat,
And all be strew'd ysmoking at your feet.
Start ye? Perchance Death's angel may be sent
Ere from the flaming temple ye retreat,
And ye who met on revel idlesse bent
May find in pleasure's fane your grave and monument.

VI

Your debts mount high—ye plunge in deeper waste,
The tradesman calls—no warning voice ye hear;
The plaintiff sues—to public shews ye haste;
The bailiff threats—ye feel no idle fear;
Who can arrest your prodigal career?
Who can keep down the levity of youth?
What sound can startle age's stubborn ear?
Who can redeem from wretchedness and ruth
Men true to falsehood's voice, false to the voice of truth? . . .

IX

Sons of Parnassus! whom I view above,
Not laurel-crown'd, but clad in rusty black,
Not spurring Pegasus through Tempè's grove,
But pacing Grub-street on a jaded hack;

What reams of foolscap, while your brains ye rack,
Ye mar to make again! for sure, ere long,
Condemn'd to tread the bard's time-sanction'd track,
Ye all shall join the bailiff-haunted throng,
And reproduce in rags the rags ye blot in song.

x

So fares the follower in the Muses' train,
He toils to starve, and only lives in death;
We slight him till our patronage is vain,
Then round his skeleton a garland wreathe,
And o'er his bones an empty requiem breathe—
Oh! with what tragic horror would he start
(Could he be conjur'd from the grave beneath)
To find the stage again a Thespian cart,
And elephants and colts down trampl[ing] Shakespear's art . . .
            (*Rejected Addresses*, 2nd edn., 1812, pp. 14–19.)

(b) Extract from *The Modern Dunciad, A Satire*, 1814. This poem appeared anonymously, but is known to be the work of George Daniel, the writer, book-collector, and Elizabethan scholar:

The town is pleas'd when BYRON will rehearse,
And finds a thousand beauties in his verse;
So fix'd his fame—that write whate'er he will,
The patient public must admire it still;
Yes,—though bereft of half his force and fire,
They still must read,—and, dozing, must admire;
While you and I, who stick to common sense,
To genius, taste, and wit, have no pretence.
Throughout the whole we toil to understand;
Where'er we tread—'tis strange, 'tis foreign land;
Nay, half the thoughts and language of the strain
Require a glossary to make them plain.
Beauties there are, which candour bids me own,
Atone for these—for more than these atone:—
Beauties—which e'en the coldest must admire—
Quick, high-wrought passion—true poetic fire—
Bold, energetic language—thoughts sublime—
And all the artful cadences of rhyme.
            (*The Modern Dunciad*, 2nd edn., 1815, pp. 58–9.)

(c) JOHN KEATS (1795–1821), 'To Lord Byron' (written December 1814):

Byron! how sweetly sad thy melody!
 Attuning still the soul to tenderness,
 As if soft Pity, with unusual stress,
Had touch'd her plaintive lute, and thou, being by,
Hadst caught the tones, nor suffer'd them to die.
 O'ershading sorrow doth not make thee less
 Delightful: thou thy griefs dost dress
With a bright halo, shining beamily,
As when a cloud the golden moon doth veil,
 Its sides are ting'd with a resplendent glow,
Through the dark robe oft amber rays prevail,
 And like fair veins in sable marble flow;
Still warble, dying swan! still tell the tale,
 The enchanting tale, the tale of pleasing woe.
     (*The Poetical Works of John Keats*,
      ed. H. W. Garrod, 1939, p. 477)

(*d*) JAMES HOGG (1770–1835), 'the Ettrick Shepherd', dedicated his *Pilgrims of the Sun* (1815) 'To the Right Hon. Lord Byron':

Not for thy crabbed state-creed, wayward wight,
Thy noble lineage, nor thy virtues high,
(God bless the mark!) do I this homage plight;
No—'tis thy bold and native energy;
Thy soul that dares each bound to overfly,
Ranging through Nature on erratic wing—
These do I honour—and would fondly try
With thee a wild aërial strain to sing:
Then O! round Shepherd's head thy charmed mantle fling.
   (*The Poetical Works of James Hogg. In Four Volumes*,
      1822, II, iii.)

(*e*) JAMES HENRY LEIGH HUNT (1784–1859), extract from *The Feast of the Poets*, 1815. Byron had visited Hunt in Surrey County Gaol in May 1813, and renewed his acquaintanceship with him in December. He saw some faults in Hunt, but admired his political integrity. In *The Feast of the Poets*, published in book-form in 1814, Hunt chooses Scott, Campbell, Moore and Southey as the only modern poets fit to dine with Apollo, but he added a complimentary note on Byron, and the following passage was inserted in the 1815 edition:

 . . . Byron relieved him [Moore] by taking his place,
 Which he did with so kind yet unconscious a face,

So ardent a frankness, yet modest an ease,
As much as to say 'Now for me, if you please',—
That Apollo took *his* hand, and earnestly said,
'Pray how came misanthropy into *your* head?
I suspect (it is true), that in all which you tell us
Of robbers, and rakes, and such terrible fellows,
There's something mere scorn could have never devised,
And a sorrow-wise charity roughly disguised;
But you must not be always indulging this tone;
You owe some relief to our hearts and your own;
For poets, earth's heav'n-linking spirits, were born,
What they can, to amend—what they can't, to adorn;
And you hide the best proof of your office and right,
If you make not as I do a contrast with night,
And help to shed round you a gladness and light.
So remember; and as to the style of your song,
And to straight-forward speaking, 'twill come before long:
But the fact is, that what with your courts and your purses,
I've never done well with you lords who write verses:
I speak not of people like Sheffield or Lansdowne,
Whom some silly Body of Poetry hands down—,
But Rochester raked himself into his grave;
A poor sceptred scoundrel slew Surrey the brave;
And Sackville stopped short of his better ambition,
And lost a great name in the *shrewd* politician.
I wouldn't divorce, mind, the muse from the state;
Great poets have been politicians as great;
Let both be combined as becomes a true Briton,
And laurels add weight to the bench that you sit on;
I love a free spirit; its fancy is free;
But so much the more you and I must agree.
      (*The Poetical Works of Leigh Hunt*, ed. H. S. Milford,
               1923, pp. 150-1.)

10. Wordsworth on Byron's lack of genius

April 1816

From a letter of 18 April 1816 to John Scott. (*The Letters of William and Dorothy Wordsworth: The Middle Years*, ed. E. de Selincourt, 1937, II, 734–5.)

You yourself, appear to me to labour under some delusion as to the merits of Lord B's Poetry, and treat those wretched verses, 'The Farewell', with far too much respect. They are disgusting in sentiment, and in execution contemptible. 'Though my many faults deface me' etc. Can worse doggrel be written than such a stanza? One verse is commendable, 'All my madness none can know,' '*Sine dementia nullus Phoebus*'[1]; but what a difference between the *amabilis insania* of inspiration, and the fiend-like exasperation of these wretched productions. It avails nothing to attempt to heap up indignation upon the heads of those whose talents are extolled in the same breath. The true way of dealing with these men is to show that they want genuine power. That talents they have, but that these talents are of a *mean* order; and that their productions have no solid basis to rest upon. Allow them to be men of high genius, and they have gained their point and will go on triumphing in their iniquity; demonstrate them to be what in truth they are, in all essentials, Dunces, and I will not say that you will reform them; but by abating their pride you will strip their wickedness of the principal charm in their own eyes.

[1] ['There is no Apollo (i.e. inspiration) without madness.']

CHILDE HAROLD'S PILGRIMAGE
CANTO III
November 1816

11. Some first reactions

(*a*) JOHN CAM HOBHOUSE. Extract from Diary for 1 September 1816:
'Byron has given me another canto of *Childe Harold* to read. It is
very fine in parts, but I don't know whether I like it so much as his
first cantos. There is an air of mystery and metaphysics about it. . . .'
(*Recollections of a Long Life*, ed. Lady Dorchester, 1909–11, II, 11.)

(*b*) Extract from letter of 12 September 1816, from John Murray to
Byron, telling him of Gifford's reaction to this canto: 'I have rarely
addressed you with more pleasure than upon the present occasion. I
was thrilled with delight yesterday by the announcement of Mr.
Shelley with the MS. of *Childe Harold*. I had no sooner got the quiet
possession of it than, trembling with auspicious hope about it, I carried
it direct to Mr. Gifford. He has been exceedingly ill with jaundice,
and unable to write or do anything. He was much pleased by my
attention. I called upon him to-day. He said he was unable to leave off
last night, and that he had sat up until he had finished every line of
the canto. It had actually agitated him into a fever, and he was much
worse when I called. He had persisted this morning in finishing the
volume, and he pronounced himself infinitely more delighted than
when he first wrote to me. He says that what you have heretofore
published is nothing to this effort. He says also, besides its being the
most original and interesting, it is the most finished of your writings;
and he has undertaken to correct the press for you.

Never, since my intimacy with Mr. Gifford, did I see him so heartily
pleased, or give one-fiftieth part of the praise, with one-thousandth
part of the warmth. He speaks in ecstasy of "The Dream"—the whole
volume beams with genius. I am sure he loves you in his heart; and

when he called upon me some time ago, and I told him that you were gone, he instantly exclaimed in a full room, "Well! he has not left his equal behind him—that I will say!" . . .' (Samuel Smiles, *A Publisher and his Friends*, 1891, I, 365–6.)

(*c*) JOHN WILSON CROKER (1780–1857), Tory politician, Secretary to the Admiralty, and contributor to the *Quarterly Review*. Extract from letter of 18 September 1816, to John Murray: 'I have read with great pleasure the poem you lent me. It is written with great vigour, and all the descriptive part is peculiarly to my taste, for I am fond of realities, even to the extent of being fond of localities. A spot of ground a yard square, a rock, a hillock, on which some great achievement has been performed, or to which any recollections of interest attach, excite my feelings more than all the monuments of art. Pictures fade, and statues moulder, and forests decay, and cities perish, but the sod of Marathon is immortal, and he who has had the good fortune to stand on that sacred spot has identified himself with Athenian story in a way which all the historians, painters, and poets of the world could not have accomplished for him. Shakespeare, whom nothing escaped, very justly hints that one of the highest offices of good poetry is to connect our ideas with some "local habitation." It is an old and highly absurd phrase to say that poetry deals in fiction; alas, *history*, I fear, deals in fiction, but good poetry is concerned only with *realities*, either of visible or moral nature; and so much for local poetry. But I did not read with equal pleasure a note or two which reflects on the Bourbon family. What has a poet who writes for immortality, to do with the little temporary passions of political parties? Such notes are like Pope's "flies in amber." I wish you could persuade Lord Byron to leave out these two or three lines of prose, which will make thousands dissatisfied with his glorious poetry. For my own part I am not a man of rank and family, and have not, therefore, such motives for respecting rank and family as Lord Byron has, yet I own (however I may disapprove and lament much of what is going on in France) that I could not bring myself to speak irreverently of the children of St. Louis, of assuredly the most ancient and splendid family of the civilised world, of a house which is connected with the whole system of European policy, European literature, European refinement, and, I will add, European glory. . . . No; pray use your influence on this point. As to the poem itself, except a word or two suggested by Mr. Giffard [*sic*], I do not think anything can be altered for the better.' (*The*

Croker Papers. The Correspondence and Diaries of . . . John Wilson Croker, ed. L. L. Jennings, 1884, I, 94–5.)

(*d*) ELIZABETH, DUCHESS OF DEVONSHIRE. Extract from letter of 16 December 1816, to Augustus Foster: 'I hear from England that Lord Byron's third canto of *Childe Harold* is beautiful, but Lord Cowper don't like it so much, and Lady Bessborough is sending it to me, and I long for it, as, however odious his character, he is a great Poet.' (Vere Foster, *The Two Duchesses*, 1898, pp. 424–5.)

12. Scott, from his unsigned review, *Quarterly Review*

Dated October 1816, issued February 1817, XVI, 172–208

Scott was grieved by the scandal of Byron's separation from his wife, and disturbed as well as impressed by his poetry of the summer of 1816. 'The last part of *Childe Harold*,' he wrote to Joanna Baillie on 26 November, 'intimates a terrible state of mind and with all the power and genius which characterized his former productions the present seems to indicate a more serious and desperate degree of misanthropy. . . . On my word of honour I should expect it to end either in actual insanity or something equally frightful.' (*The Letters of Sir Walter Scott*, IV, 300.) In this review he aimed at paying full tribute to Byron's genius, while rebuking his political aberrations, and giving sound counsel, personal and moral, if this could be done without offence. (See his letters of 10 January 1817, to John Murray and Croker— *Letters*, IV, 363–5, 366.) Byron was delighted by the review: 'You will agree,' he wrote to Thomas Moore on 10 March 1817, 'that such an article is still more honourable to him than to myself'; while to Scott himself he expressed, much later, his gratitude for 'the extraordinary good-heartedness of the whole proceeding'. (*LJ*, IV, 72; VI, 2.)

We have felt ourselves very much affected by the perusal of these poems, nor can we suppose that we are singular in our feelings. Other poets have given us their literary productions as the subject of criticism, impersonally as it were, and generally speaking, abstracted from their ordinary habits and feelings; and all, or almost all, might apply to their poetical effusions, though in somewhat a different sense, the *l'envoy* of Ovid.

Sine me, Liber, ibis in urbem.[1]

[1] ['You will go, my book, without me to the city.' Ovid was alluding to his own exile from Rome.]

84

The work of the poet is indeed before the public, but the character, the habits of the author, the events of his life and the motives of his writing, are known but to the small circle of literary gossips, for whose curiosity no food is too insipid. . . . The time therefore appeared to be passed when the mere sin of having been dipped in rhyme was supposed to exclude the poet from the usual business and habits of life, and to single him out from the herd as a marked deer expected to make sport by his solitary exertions for escape. Whether this has arisen from the diminished irritability of the rhyming generation, or from the peculiar habits of those who have been distinguished in our time, or from their mental efforts having been early directed to modify and to restrain the excess of their enthusiasm, we do not pretend to conjecture; but it is certain, that for many years past, though the number of our successful poets may be as great as at any period of our literary history, we have heard little comparatively of their eccentricities, their adventures, or their distresses. The wretched Dermody is not worth mentioning as an exception, and the misfortunes of Burns arose from circumstances not much connected with his powerful poetical genius.

It has been, however, reserved for our own time to produce one distinguished example of the Muse having descended upon a bard of a wounded spirit, and lent her lyre to tell, and we trust to soothe, afflictions of no ordinary description, afflictions originating probably in that singular combination of feeling which has been called the poetical temperament, and which has so often saddened the days of those on whom it has been conferred. If ever a man could lay claim to that character in all its strength and all its weakness, with its unbounded range of enjoyment, and its exquisite sensibility of pleasure and of pain, it must certainly be granted to Lord Byron. Nor does it require much time or a deep acquaintance with human nature to discover why these extraordinary powers should in many cases have contributed more to the wretchedness than to the happiness of their possessor.

The 'imagination all compact,' which the greatest poet who ever lived has assigned as the distinguishing badge of his brethren, is in every case a dangerous gift. It exaggerates, indeed, our expectations, and can often bid its possessor hope, where hope is lost to reason: but the delusive pleasure arising from these visions of imagination, resembles that of a child whose notice is attracted by a fragment of glass to which a sun-beam has given momentary splendour. He hastens to the spot with breathless impatience, and finds the object of his curiosity and expectation is equally vulgar and worthless. Such is the man of quick and exalted powers of imagination. His fancy over-estimates the object of his wishes, and pleasure, fame, distinction, are alternately pursued, attained, and despised when in his power. Like the enchanted fruit in the palace of a sorcerer, the objects of his admiration lose their attraction and value as soon as they are grasped by the adventurer's hand, and all that remains is regret for the time lost in the chase, and astonishment at the hallucination under the influence of which it was undertaken. The disproportion between hope and possession which is felt by all men, is thus doubled to those whom nature has endowed with the power of gilding a distant prospect by the rays of imagination. These reflexions, though trite and obvious, are in a manner forced from us by the poetry of Lord Byron, by the sentiments of weariness of life and enmity with the world which they so frequently express—and by the singular analogy which such sentiments hold with incidents of his life so recently before the public. The works before us contain so many direct allusions to the author's personal feelings and private history, that it becomes impossible for us to divide Lord Byron from his poetry, or to offer our criticism upon the continuation of *Childe Harold*, without reverting to the circumstances in which the commencement of that singular and original work first appeared. . . .

[After a long, appreciative account of Byron's literary career up to this date, Scott defends him against the charge of over-production.]

This rapidity of composition and publication we have heard blamed as endangering the fame of the author, while it gave such proofs of talent. We are inclined to dispute the proposition, at least in the present instance.

We are sometimes tempted to blame the timidity of those poets, who, possessing powers to arrest the admiration of the public, are yet too much afraid of censure to come frequently forward, and thus defraud themselves of their fame, and the public of the delight which they might afford us. Where success has been unexpectedly, and perhaps undeservedly, obtained by the capricious vote of fashion, it may be well for the adventurer to draw his stake and leave the game, as every succeeding hazard will diminish the chance of his rising a winner. But they cater ill for the public, and give indifferent advice to the poet, supposing him possessed of the highest qualities of his art, who do not advise him to labour while the laurel around his brows yet retains its freshness. Sketches from Lord Byron are more valuable than finished pictures from others; nor are we at all sure that any labour which he might bestow in revisal would not rather efface than refine those outlines of striking and powerful originality which they exhibit, when flung rough from the hand of the master. No one would have wished to condemn Michel Angelo to work upon a single block of marble, until he had satisfied, in every point, the petty criticism of that Pope, who, neglecting the sublime and magnificent character and attitude of his Moses, descended to blame a wrinkle in the fold of the garment. Should it be urged, that in thus stimulating genius to unsparing exertion, we encourage carelessness and hurry in the youthful candidates for literary distinction, we answer, it is not the learner to whom our remarks apply; they refer to him only, who, gifted by nature with the higher power of poetry, an art as difficult as it is enchanting; has made himself master, by application and study, of the mechanical process, and in whom, we believe, frequent exertions upon new works awaken and stimulate that genius, which might be cramped and rendered tame, by long and minute attention to finish to the highest possible degree any one of the number. If we look at our poetical library we shall find, generally speaking, the most distinguished poets have been the most voluminous, and that those who, like Gray, limited their productions to a few poems, anxiously and sedulously corrected and revised, have given them a stiff and artificial character, which, far from disarming criticism, has rather embittered its violence. . . . [We] cannot but repeat our conviction that poetry being, in its higher classes, an art which has for its elements sublimity and unaffected beauty, is more liable than any other to suffer from the labour of polishing, or from the elaborate and composite style of ornament, and alternate affectation of simplicity, and artifice, which characterize the works, even of the first poets, when they have been over-anxious to secure public applause, by long and reiterated correction. It must be remembered that we speak of the higher tones of composition; there are others of a subordinate character, where extreme art and labour are not bestowed in vain. But we cannot consider over-anxious correction as likely to be employed with advantage upon poems like those of Lord Byron, which have for their object to rouse the imagination, and awaken the passions.

It is certain, to return to the subject from which we have gone somewhat astray, that the rapidity with which Lord Byron's poems succeeded each other, during four years, served to arrest as well as to dazzle and delight the public; nor did there appear room to apply to him, in the height of his fame and the flower of his age, the caution which we might whisper to other bards of popular celebrity. *The Giaour, The Bride of Abydos, The Corsair, Lara, The Siege of Corinth*, followed each other with a celerity, which was only rivalled by their success; and if at times the author seemed to pause in his poetic career, with the threat of forbearing further adventure for a time, the public eagerly pardoned the breach of a promise by keeping which they must have been sufferers. Exquisitely beautiful in themselves, these tales received a new charm from the romantic climes into which they introduced us, and from the oriental costume so strictly preserved and so picturesquely exhibited. Greece, the cradle of the poetry with which our earliest studies are familiar, was presented to us among her ruins and her sorrows. Her delightful scenery, once dedicated to those deities who, though dethroned from their own Olympus, still preserve a poetical empire, was spread before us in Lord Byron's poetry, varied by all the moral effect derived from what Greece is and what she has been, while it was doubled by comparisons, perpetually excited, between the philosophers and heroes who formerly inhabited that romantic country, and their descendants, who either stoop to their Scythian conquerors, or maintain, among the recesses of their classical mountains, an independence as wild and savage as it is precarious. The oriental manners also and diction, so peculiar in their picturesque effect that they can cast a charm even over the absurdities of an eastern tale, had here the more honourable occupation of decorating that which in itself was beautiful, and enhancing by novelty what would have been captivating without its aid. The powerful impression produced by this peculiar species of poetry confirmed us in a principle, which, though it will hardly be challenged when stated as an axiom, is very rarely complied with in practice. It is, that every author should, like Lord Byron, form to himself, and communicate to the reader, a precise, defined and distinct view of the landscape, sentiment, or action which he intends to describe to the reader. This simple proposition has been so often neglected that we feel warranted in giving it a little more consideration and illustration than plain men may at first sight think necessary.

An author occasionally forgets that it is his business rather to excite than to satiate the imagination of his readers; rather to place before him such a distinct and intelligible sketch as his own imagination can fill up, than, by attempting to exhaust all that can be said on the subject, to confuse the apprehension and weary the attention. There should be, even in poetical description, that *keeping* and *perspective* which is demanded in the sister art of painting, and which alone can render the scenes presented by either distinct, clear and intelligible. Here the painter has, in some degree, the advantage of the poet, for *perspective* is the very foundation of his art. The most stupid bungler that ever took brush in hand is aware that his objects must diminish as they withdraw from the eye, that he is not entitled to render the rocks of his distance too distinct, and that the knowledge that such things do actually exist will not justify him in painting with minuteness the lichens and shrubs, which grow on their surface and in their crevices, at a distance from which these minute objects cannot be discovered by the eye. Yet suppose such a novice a follower of the Muses, and he will not hesitate a moment to transgress this wholesome rule. Every thing which he knows to exist in fact, he will, with the confused minuteness of a Chinese painter, labour to introduce into his description, and, by confounding that which is important to his purpose with that which is subordinate, he will produce a mass of images more or less splendid, according to the vivacity of his imagination, but perplexing, incongruous and unsatisfactory, in all respects, to the reader, who, in vain, endeavours to reduce them in his own mind into one distinct landscape whose parts shall bear a just proportion to each other. Such a poet has assembled, perhaps, excellent materials for composition, but he does not present them in intelligible arrangement to the reader, and he fails to produce upon the mind of others the desired effect, probably because the picture has never been presented to his own with sufficient accuracy.

This is more particularly the case with such authors as, lacking the erudition of Southey or the personal experience of Lord Byron, attempt to lay their scene in countries or ages with the costume and manners of which they are but imperfectly acquainted. Such adventurers are compelled to draw heavily on their slender stock of knowledge on every occasion, and to parade, as fully as they can, before the eye of the reader, whatsoever their reading has gleaned concerning their subject. Without Chatterton's genius, they fall into Chatterton's error, who, not considering that in the most ancient authors scarcely one word in ten has become obsolete, wrote a set of poems in which every second word was taken from a glossary, and necessarily remitted to one, under the idea that he was imitating the language of the ancients. Thus, when a poet deals in materials of which he is not fully master, he is obliged, at the risk of outraging both taste and nature, to produce as frequently, and detain before the reader as long as possible, those distinctive marks by which he means to impress him with the reality of his story; and the outrage is committed in vain; for it is not enough for the representation of an eastern landscape, that the foreground should be encumbered with turbans and sabres, and the fantastic architecture of the kiosk or the mosque, if the distance be not marked by those slight but discriminating touches which mark the reality of the scene, the lightly indicated palm-tree, which overhangs the distant fountain, or the shadowy and obscure delineation of the long column of the caravan retreating through the distance; or the watchman who rests on his lance while his tribe slumber around him, as in the following exquisite picture taken from one of the poems before us.

[Quotes 'The Dream', ll. 106–25.]

This is true *keeping*—an Eastern picture perfect in its foreground, and distance, and sky, and no part of which is so dwelt upon or laboured as to obscure the principal figure. It is often in the slight and almost imperceptible touches that the hand of the master is shewn, and that a single spark, struck from his fancy, lightens with a long train of illumination that of the reader.

[Scott then discusses the similarity of all Byron's heroes, and concludes:]

The versatility of authors who have been able to draw and support characters as different from each other as from their own, has given to their productions the inexpressible charm of variety, and has often secured them against that neglect which in general attends what is technically called mannerism. But it was reserved to Lord Byron to present the same character on the public stage again and again, varied only by the exertions of that powerful genius, which searching the springs of passion and of feeling in their innermost recesses, knew how to combine their operations, so that the interest was eternally varying, and never abated, although the most important personage of the drama retained the same lineaments. It will one day be considered as not the least remarkable literary phenomenon of this age, that during a period of four years, notwithstanding the quantity of distinguished poetical talent of which we may be permitted to boast, a single author, and he managing his pen with the careless and negligent ease of a man of quality, and chusing for his theme subjects so very similar, and personages bearing so close a resemblance to each other,—did, in despite of these circumstances, of the unamiable attributes with which he usually invested his heroes, and of the proverbial fickleness of the public, maintain the ascendency in their favour, which he had acquired by his first matured production. So however it indisputably has been; and those comparatively small circles of admirers excepted, which assemble naturally around individual poets of eminence, Lord Byron has been for that time, and may for some time continue to be, the Champion of the English Parnassus. . . .

The family misfortunes which have for a time lost Lord Byron to his native land have neither chilled his poetical fire, nor deprived England of its benefit. The Third Canto of *Childe Harold* exhibits, in all its strength and in all its peculiarity, the wild, powerful and original vein of poetry which, in the preceding cantos, first fixed the public attention upon the author. If there is any difference, the former seem to us to have been rather more sedulously corrected and revised for publication, and the present work to have been dashed from the author's pen with less regard to the subordinate points of expression and versification. Yet such is the deep and powerful strain of passion, such the original tone and colouring of description, that the want of polish in some of its minute parts rather adds to than deprives the poem of its energy. It seems, occasionally, as if the consideration of mere grace was beneath the care of the poet, in his ardour to hurry upon the reader the 'thoughts that glow and words that burn;' and that the occasional roughness of the verse corresponded with the stern tone of thought, and of mental suffering which it expresses. We have remarked the same effect produced by the action of Mrs. Siddons, when, to give emphasis to some passage of overwhelming passion, she has seemed wilfully to assume a position constrained, stiffened, violent, diametrically contrary to the rules of grace, in order, as it were, to concentrate herself for the utterance of grief, or passion which disdained embellishment. In the same manner, versification, in the hands of a master-bard, is as frequently correspondent to the thoughts it expresses as to the action it describes, and the 'line labours and the words move slow' under the heavy and painful thought; wrung, as it were, from the bosom, as when Ajax is heaving his massy rock. . . .

[Gives summary of poem, with extracts and comments: I cite only the passage on Byron's treatment of Waterloo.]

He [the Pilgrim] arrives on Waterloo,—a scene where all men, where a poet especially, and a poet such as Lord Byron, must needs pause, and amid the quiet simplicity of whose scenery is excited a moral interest, deeper and more potent even than that which is produced by gazing upon the sublimest efforts of Nature in her most romantic recesses.

That Lord Byron's sentiments do not correspond with ours is obvious, and we are sorry for both our sakes. For our own—because we have lost that note of triumph with which his harp would otherwise have rung over a field of glory such as Britain never reaped before; and on Lord Byron's account,—because it is melancholy to see a man of genius duped by the mere cant of words and phrases, even when facts are most broadly confronted with them. If the poet has mixed with original, wild, and magnificent creations of his imagination, prejudices which he could only have caught by the contagion which he most professes to despise, it is he himself must be the loser. If his lofty muse has soared in all her brilliancy over the field of Waterloo without dropping even one leaf of laurel on the head of Wellington, his merit can dispense even with the praise of Lord Byron. And as, when the images of Brutus were excluded from the triumphal procession, his memory became only the more powerfully imprinted on the souls of the Romans,—the name of the British hero will be but more eagerly recalled to remembrance by the very lines in which his praise is forgotten.

We would willingly avoid mention of the political opinions hinted at by Childe Harold, and more distinctly expressed in other poems of Lord Byron;—the more willingly, as we strongly suspect that these effusions are rather the sport of whim and singularity, or at best the suggestion of sudden starts of feeling and passion, than the expressions of any serious or fixed opinion. . . . For to compare Waterloo to the battle of Cannæ, and speak of the blood which flowed on the side of the vanquished as lost in the cause of freedom, is contrary not only to plain sense and general opinion, but to Lord Byron's own experience, and to the testimony of that experience which he has laid before the public. Childe Harold, in his former Pilgrimage, beheld in Spain the course of the 'tyrant and of the tyrant's slaves'. He saw 'Gaul's vulture with her wings unfurled',

and indignantly expostulated with Fate on the impending destruction
of the patriotic Spaniards.

> And must they fall,—the young, the proud, the brave,
>   To swell one bloated Chief's unwholesome reign,
> No step between submission and a grave,
>   The rise of rapine, and the fall of Spain!

Childe Harold saw the scenes which he celebrates,—and does he
now compare to the field of Cannæ the plain of Waterloo, and
mourn over the fall of the tyrant and the military satraps and slaves
whose arms built his power, as over the fall of the cause of liberty?
We know the ready answer which will be offered by the few who
soothe their own prejudices, or seek to carry their own purposes
by maintaining this extravagant proposition. They take a distinction:
Buonaparte, according to their creed, fell a tyrant in 1814, and revived
a deliverer in 1815. A few months' residence in the Isle of Elba had
given him time for better thoughts, and had mortified within his
mind that gorging ambition for which Russia was not too great, nor
Hamburgh too small a morsel; which neither evaporated under the
burning sun of Egypt nor was chilled by the polar snows; which
survived the loss of millions of soldiers and an incalculable tract of
territory, and burned as fiercely during the conferences of Chatillon,
when the despot's fate was trembling in the scales, as at those of Tilsit,
when that of his adversary had kicked the beam. All the experience
which Europe had bought by oceans of blood and years of degradation
ought, according to these gentlemen, to have been forgotten upon the
empty professions of one whose word, whensoever or wheresoever
pledged, never bound him an instant when interest or ambition required
a breach of it. Buonaparte assured the world he was changed in
temper, mind and disposition; and his old agent and minister (Fouché
of Nantes) was as ready to give his security as Bardolph was to engage
for Falstaff. When Gil Blas found his old comrades in knavery, Don
Raphael and Ambrose de Lamela, administrating the revenues of a
Carthusian convent, he shrewdly conjectured that the treasure of the
holy fathers was in no small danger, and grounded his suspicion on
the old adage *Il ne faut pas mettre à la cave un ivrogne qui à renoncé
au vin.*[1] But Europe—when France had given the strongest proof of
her desire to recover what she termed her glory, by expelling a king

[1] ['You must not put a reformed drunkard in the wine-cellar.']

whose reign was incompatible with foreign wars, and recalling Napoleon to whom conquest was as the very breath of his nostrils— Europe, most deserving, had she yielded to such arguments, to have been crowned with 'the diadem, hight foolscap', is censured for having exerted her strength to fix her security, and confuting with her own warlike weapons those whose only law was arms, and only argument battle. We do not believe there lives any one who can seriously doubt the truth of what we have said. If, however, there were any simple enough to expect to hail Freedom restored by the victorious arms of Buonaparte, their mistake (had Lord Wellington not saved them from its consequences) would have resembled that of poor Slender, who, rushing to the embraces of Anne Page, found himself unexpectedly in the gripe of a lubberly post-master's boy. But probably no one was foolish enough to nourish such hopes, though there are some—their number is few—whose general opinions concerning the policy of Europe are so closely and habitually linked with their party prejudices at home, that they see in the victory of Waterloo only the triumph of Lord Castlereagh; and could the event have been reversed, would have thought rather of the possible change of seats in St. Stephen's, than of the probable subjugation of Europe. Such were those who, hiding perhaps secret hopes with affected despondence, lamented the madness which endeavoured to make a stand against the Irresistible whose military calculations were formed on plans far beyond the comprehension of all other minds; and such are they who, confuted by stubborn facts, now affect to mourn over the consequences of a victory which they had pronounced impossible. But, as we have already hinted, we cannot trace in Lord Byron's writings any systematic attachment to a particular creed of politics, and he appears to us to seize the subjects of public interest upon the side in which they happen to present themselves for the moment, with this qualification, that he usually paints them on the shaded aspect, perhaps that their tints may harmonize with the sombre colours of his landscape. Dangerous as prophecies are, we could almost hazard a prediction that, if Lord Byron enjoys that length of life which we desire for his sake and our own, his future writings may probably shew that he thinks better of the morals, religion, and constitution of his country, than his poems have hitherto indicated. Should we fail in a hope which we cherish fondly, the disgrace of false prophecy must rest with us, but the loss will be with Lord Byron himself.

[Scott's discussion of *The Prisoner of Chillon,* and other poems in the same volume, is followed by an exhortation to Byron himself:]

. . . With kinder feelings to Lord Byron in person and reputation no one could approach him than ourselves: we owe it to the pleasure which he has bestowed upon us, and to the honour he has done to our literature. We have paid our warmest tribute to his talents—it is their due. We will touch on the uses for which he was invested with them—it is our duty; and happy, most happy, should we be, if, in discharging it, we could render this distinguished author a real service. We do not assume the office of harsh censors;—we are entitled at no time to do so towards genius, least of all in its hour of adversity; and we are prepared to make full allowance for the natural effect of misfortune upon a bold and haughty spirit.

> ———— When the splitting wind
> Makes flexible the knee of knotted oaks,
> And flies fled under shade, the Thing of Courage
> As roused with rage, with rage doth sympathise,
> And, with an accent tuned in self-same key,
> Returns to chiding fortune. ————

But this mode of defiance may last too long, and hurry him who indulges it into further evils; and to this point our observations tend. The advice ought not to be contemned on account of the obscurity of those by whom it is given:—the roughest fisherman is an useful pilot when a gallant vessel is near the breakers; the meanest shepherd may be a sure guide over a pathless heath, and the admonition which is given in well meant kindness should not be despised, even were it tendered with a frankness which may resemble a want of courtesy.

If the conclusion of Lord Byron's literary career were to be such as these mournful verses have anticipated—if this darkness of the spirit, this scepticism concerning the existence of worth, of friendship, of sincerity, were really and permanently to sink like a gulph between this distinguished poet and society, another name will be added to the illustrious list to whom Preston's caution refers.

> Still wouldst thou write?—to tame thy youthful fire
> Recall to life the masters of the lyre;
> Lo every brow the shade of sorrow wears,
> And every wreath is stained with dropping tears!

But this is an unfair picture. It is not the temper and talents of the poet, but the use to which he puts them, on which his happiness or misery is grounded. A powerful and unbridled imagination is, we have already said, the author and architect of its own disappointments. Its fascinations, its exaggerated pictures of good and evil, and the mental distress to which they give rise, are the natural and necessary evils attending on that quick susceptibility of feeling and fancy incident to the poetical temperament. But the Giver of all talents, while he has qualified them each with its separate and peculiar alloy, has endowed the owner with the power of purifying and refining them. But, as if to moderate the arrogance of genius, it is justly and wisely made requisite, that he must regulate and tame the fire of his fancy, and descend from the heights to which she exalts him, in order to obtain ease of mind and tranquillity. The materials of happiness, that is of such degree of happiness as is consistent with our present state, lie around us in profusion. But the man of talents must stoop to gather them, otherwise they would be beyond the reach of the mass of society, for whose benefit, as well as for his, Providence has created them. There is no royal and no poetical path to contentment and heart's-ease: that by which they are attained is open to all classes of mankind, and lies within the most limited range of intellect. To narrow our wishes and desires within the scope of our powers of attainment; to consider our misfortunes, however peculiar in their character, as our inevitable share in the patrimony of Adam; to bridle those irritable feelings, which ungoverned are sure to become governors; to shun that intensity of galling and self-wounding reflection which our poet has so forcibly described in his own burning language:

> ——————— I have thought
> Too long and darkly, till my brain became,
> In its own eddy, boiling and o'erwrought,
> A whirling gulf of phantasy and flame—

—to stoop, in short, to the realities of life; repent if we have offended, and pardon if we have been trespassed against; to look on the world less as our foe than as a doubtful and capricious friend, whose applause we ought as far as possible to deserve, but neither to court nor contemn —such seem the most obvious and certain means of keeping or regaining mental tranquillity. . . .

We are compelled to dwell upon this subject: for future ages, while our language is remembered, will demand of this why Lord

Byron was unhappy? We retort this query on the noble poet himself while it is called 'to-day'. He does injustice to the world, if he imagines he has left it exclusively filled with those who rejoice in his sufferings. If the voice of consolation be in cases like his less loudly heard than that of reproach or upbraiding, it is because those who long to conciliate, to advise, to mediate, to console, are timid in thrusting forward their sentiments, and fear to exasperate where they most seek to soothe; while the busy and officious intrude, without shame or sympathy, and embitter the privacy of affliction by their rude gaze and importunate clamour. But the pain which such insects can give only lasts while the wound is raw. Let the patient submit to the discipline of the soul enjoined by religion, and recommended by philosophy, and the scar will become speedily insensible to their stings. Lord Byron may not have loved the world, but the world has loved him, not perhaps with a wise or discriminating affection, but as well as it is capable of loving any one. And many who do not belong to the world, as the word is generally understood, have their thoughts fixed on Lord Byron, with the anxious wish and eager hope that he will bring his powerful understanding to combat with his irritated feelings, and that his next efforts will shew that he has acquired the peace of mind necessary for the free and useful exercise of his splendid talents.

I decus, i nostrum, melioribus utere fatis.[1]

[1] ['Go, glory of our race, and enjoy a happier fate.']

13. Jeffrey, from his unsigned review, *Edinburgh Review*

Dated December 1816, issued February 1817, XXVII, 277–310

Byron expressed his appreciation of this review as well as Scott's: 'I am perfectly pleased with Jeffrey's also, which I wish you to tell him', he wrote in a letter of 10 March 1817 to Thomas Moore. '. . . I wish you would also add, what you know, that I was not, and, indeed, am not even *now*, the misanthropical and gloomy gentleman he takes me for, but a facetious companion, well to do with those with whom I am intimate, and as loquacious and laughing as if I were a much cleverer fellow. I suppose now I shall never be able to shake off my sables in public imagination. . . .' (*LJ*, IV, 72–4.)

If the finest poetry be that which leaves the deepest impression on the minds of its readers—and this is not the worst test of its excellence—Lord Byron, we think, must be allowed to take precedence of all his distinguished contemporaries. He has not the variety of Scott—nor the delicacy of Campbell—nor the absolute truth of Crabbe—nor the polished sparkling of Moore; but in force of diction, and inextinguishable energy of sentiment, he clearly surpasses them all. 'Words that breathe, and thoughts that burn,' are not merely the ornaments, but the common staple of his poetry; and he is not inspired or impressive only in some happy passages, but through the whole body and tissue of his composition. It was an unavoidable condition, perhaps, of this higher excellence, that his scene should be narrow, and his persons few. To compass such ends as he had in view, it was necessary to reject all ordinary agents, and all trivial combinations. He could not possibly be amusing, or ingenious, or playful; or hope to maintain the requisite pitch of interest by the recitation of sprightly adventures, or the opposition of common characters. To produce great effects, he felt that it was necessary to deal only with the greater passions—with the exaltations of a daring fancy, and the errors of a lofty intellect

98

—with the pride, the terrors, and the agonies of strong emotion—the fire and air alone of our human elements.

In this respect, and in his general notion of the end and the elements of poetry, we have sometimes thought that his views fell more in with those of the Lake poets, than of any other party in the poetical commonwealth; and, in some of his later productions especially, it is impossible not to be struck with his occasional approaches to the style and manner of this class of writers. Lord Byron, however, it should be observed, like all other persons of a quick sense of beauty, and sure enough of their own originality to be in no fear of paltry imputations, is a great mimic of styles and manners, and a great borrower of external character. He and Mr Scott are full of imitations of all the writers from whom they have ever derived gratification; and the two most original writers of the age might appear, to superficial observers, to be the most deeply indebted to their predecessors. In this particular instance, we have no fault to find with Lord Byron: for undoubtedly the finer passages of Wordsworth and Southey have in them where-withal to give an impulse to the utmost ambition of rival genius; and their diction and manner of writing is frequently both striking and original. But we must say, that it would afford us still greater pleasure to find these tuneful gentlemen returning the compliment which Lord Byron has here paid to their talents, and forming themselves on the model rather of his imitations, than of their own originals. In these imitations they will find that, though he is sometimes abundantly mystical, he never, or at least very rarely, indulges in absolute nonsense—never takes his lofty flights upon mean or ridiculous occasions—and, above all, never dilutes his strong conceptions and magnificent imaginations with a flood of oppressive verbosity. On the contrary, he is, of all living writers, the most concise and condensed; and, we would fain hope, may go far, by his example, to redeem the great reproach of our modern literature—its intolerable prolixity and redundance. In his nervous and manly lines, we find no elaborate amplification of common sentiments—no ostentatious polishing of pretty expressions; and we really think that the brilliant success which has rewarded his disdain of these paltry artifices, should put to shame for ever that puling and self-admiring race, who can live through half a volume on the stock of a single thought, and expatiate over diverse fair quarto pages with the details of one tedious description.—In Lord Byron, on the contrary, we have a perpetual stream of thick-coming fancies—an eternal spring of fresh-blown images, which seem called into existence by the sudden flash of those glowing thoughts and overwhelming emotions, that struggle for expression through the whole flow of his poetry—and impart to a diction that is often abrupt and irregular, a force and a charm which seem frequently to realize all that is said of inspiration.

With all these undoubted claims to our admiration, however, it is impossible to deny that the Noble author before us has still something to learn, and a good deal to correct. He is frequently abrupt and careless, and sometimes obscure. There are marks, occasionally, of effort and straining after an emphasis which is generally spontaneous;—and, above all, there is far too great a monotony in the moral colouring of his pictures, and too much repetition of the same sentiments and maxims. He delights too exclusively in the delineation of a certain morbid exaltation of character and of feeling,—a sort of demoniacal sublimity, not without some traits of the ruined Archangel. He is haunted almost perpetually with the image of a being feeding and fed upon by violent passions, and the recollections of the catastrophes they have occasioned: And, though worn out by their past indulgence, unable to sustain the burden of an existence which they do not continue to animate—full of pride and revenge and obduracy—disdaining life and death, and mankind and himself—and trampling, in his scorn, not only upon the falsehood and formality of polished life, but upon its tame virtues and slavish devotion: Yet envying, by fits, the selfish beings he despises, and melting into mere softness and compassion when the helplessness of childhood or the frailty of woman make an appeal to his generosity. Such is the person with whom we are called upon almost exclusively to sympathize in all the greater productions of this distinguished writer:—In *Childe Harold*—in *The Corsair*—in *Lara*—in *The Siege of Corinth*—in *Parisina*, and in most of the smaller pieces.

It is impossible to represent such a character better than Lord Byron has done in all these productions,—or indeed to represent anything more terrible in its anger, or more attractive in its relenting. In point of effect, we readily admit, that no one character can be more poetical or impressive.—But it is really too much to find the scene perpetually filled by one character—not only in all the acts, but in all the different pieces;—and, grand and impressive as it is, we feel at last that these very qualities make some relief more indispensable, and oppress the spirits of ordinary mortals with too deep an impression of awe and repulsion. There is too much guilt in short, and too much gloom, in the leading character;—and though it be a fine thing to gaze, now and then, on stormy seas, and thunder-shaken mountains, we should prefer passing our days in sheltered vallies, and by the murmur of calmer waters. We are aware that these metaphors may be turned against us—and that, without metaphor, it may be said that men do not *pass their days* in reading poetry,—and that, as they may look into Lord Byron only about as often as they look abroad upon tempests, they have no more reason to complain of him for being grand and gloomy, than to complain of the same qualities in the Glaciers and Volcanoes which they go so far to visit. Painters have often gained great reputation by their representations of tygers and other ferocious animals, or of caverns and banditti,—and poets should be allowed, without reproach, to indulge in analogous exercises. We are far from thinking that there is no weight in these considerations; and feel how plausibly it may be said, that we have no better reason for a great part of our complaint, than that an author, to whom we are already very greatly indebted, has chosen rather to please himself than us in the use he makes of his talents. This, no doubt, seems both unreasonable and ungrateful; but it is nevertheless true, that a public benefactor becomes a debtor to the public; and is, in some degree, responsible for the employment of those gifts which seem to be conferred upon him, not merely for his own delight, but for the delight and improvement of his fellows through all generations. Independent of this, however, we think there is a reply to the apology. A great living poet is not like a distant volcano, or an occasional tempest. He is a volcano in the heart of our land, and a cloud that hangs over our dwellings; and we have some cause to complain, if, instead of genial warmth and grateful shade, he darkens and inflames our atmosphere with perpetual explosions of fiery torrents and pitchy vapours. Lord Byron's poetry, in short, is too attractive and too famous to lie dormant or inoperative; and therefore, if it produce any painful or pernicious effects, there will be murmurs, and ought to be suggestions of alteration. Now, though an artist may draw fighting tygers and hungry lions in as lively and natural a way as he can, without giving any encouragement to human ferocity, or even much alarm to human fear, the case is somewhat different, when a poet represents men with tygerlike dispositions—and yet more so, when he exhausts the resources of his genius to make this terrible being interesting and attractive, and to represent all the lofty virtues as the natural allies of their ferocity. It is still worse when he proceeds to show, that all these precious gifts of dauntless courage, strong affection, and high imagination, are not only akin to Guilt, but the parents of Misery;—and that those only have any chance of tranquillity or happiness in this world, whom it is the object of his poetry to make us shun and despise.

These, it appears to us, are not merely errors in taste, but perversions of morality; and, as a great poet is necessarily a Moral Teacher, and gives forth his ethical lessons, in general, with far more effect and authority than any of his graver brethren, he is peculiarly liable to the censures reserved for those who turn the means of improvement to purposes of corruption.

It may no doubt be said, that poetry in general tends less to the useful than the splendid qualities of our nature—that a character poetically good has long been distinguished from one that is morally so—and that, ever since the time of Achilles, our sympathies, on such occasions, have been chiefly engrossed by persons whose deportment is by no means exemplary, and who in many points approach to the temperament of Lord Byron's ideal hero. There is some truth in this suggestion also. But other poets, in the *first* place, do not allow their favourites so outrageous a monopoly of the glory and interest of the piece—and sin less therefore against the laws either of poetical or distributive justice. In the *second* place, their heroes are neither so bad nor so good as Lord Byron's—and do not indeed very much exceed the standard of truth and nature in either of the extremes. His, however, are as monstrous and unnatural as centaurs and hippogriffs—and must ever figure in the eye of sober reason as so many bright and hateful impossibilities. But the most important distinction is, that the other poets who deal in peccant heroes, neither feel nor express that ardent affection for them, which is visible in the whole of this author's delineations, but merely make use of them as necessary agents in the extraordinary adventures they have to detail, and persons whose mingled vices and virtues are requisite to bring about the catastrophe of their story. In Lord Byron, however, the interest of the story, where there happens to be one, which is not always the case, is uniformly postponed to that of the character itself—into which he enters so deeply, and with so extraordinary a fondness, that he generally continues to speak in its language, after it has been dismissed from the stage; and to inculcate, on his own authority, the same sentiments which had been previously recommended by its example. We do not consider it as unfair, therefore, to say that Lord Byron appears to us to be the zealous apostle of a certain fierce and magnificent misanthropy, which has already saddened his poetry with too deep a shade, and not only led to a great misapplication of great talents, but contributed to render popular some very false estimates of the constituents of human happiness and merit. . . .

[There follows a retrospective account of Byron's poetical productions since *The Corsair*, with copious extracts.]

. . . Of the verses entitled 'Fare thee well',—and some others of a similar character, we shall say nothing but that, in spite of their beauty, it is painful to read them—and infinitely to be regretted that they should have been given to the public. It would be a piece of idle affectation to consider them as mere effusions of fancy, or to pretend ignorance of the subjects to which they relate—and with the knowledge which all the world has of these subjects, we must say, that not even the example of Lord Byron can persuade us that they are fit for public discussion. We come, therefore, to the consideration of the Noble author's most recent publications.

The most considerable of these, is the Third Canto of *Childe Harold*, a work which has the disadvantage of all continuations in admitting of little absolute novelty in the plan of the work, or the cast of its character, and must, besides, remind all Lord Byron's readers of the extraordinary effect produced by the sudden blazing forth of his genius upon their first introduction to that title. In spite of all this, however, we are persuaded that this Third Part of the poem will not be pronounced inferior to either of the former; and, we think, will probably be ranked above them by those who have been most delighted with the whole. The great success of this singular production, indeed, has always appeared to us an extraordinary proof of its merits; for, with all its genius, it does not belong to a sort of poetry that rises easily to popularity.—It has no story or action—very little variety of character—and a great deal of reasoning and reflection of no very attractive tenor. It is substantially a contemplative and ethical work, diversified with fine description, and adorned or overshaded by one emphatic person, who is sometimes the author, and sometimes the object of the reflections on which the interest is chiefly rested. It required, no doubt, great force of writing, and a decided tone of originality to recommend a performance of this sort so powerfully as this has been recommended to public notice and admiration—and those high characteristics belong perhaps still more eminently to the part that is now before us, than to any of the former. There is the same stern and lofty disdain of mankind, and their ordinary pursuits and enjoyments, with the same bright gaze on nature, and the same magic power of giving interest and effect to her delineations—but mixed up, we think, with deeper and more matured reflections, and a more intense sensibility to all that is grand or lovely in the external world.— Harold, in short, is somewhat older since he last appeared upon the scene—and while the vigour of his intellect has been confirmed, and his confidence in his own opinions increased, his mind has also become more sensitive; and his misanthropy, thus softened over by habits of calmer contemplation, appears less active and impatient, even although more deeply rooted than before. Undoubtedly the finest parts of the poem before us are those which thus embody the weight of his moral sentiments, or disclose the lofty sympathy which binds the despiser of Man to the glorious aspects of Nature. It is in these, we think, that the great attractions of the work consist, and the strength of the author's genius is seen. The narrative and description are of far inferior interest. With reference to the sentiments and opinions, however, which thus give its distinguishing character to the piece, we must say, that it seems no longer possible to ascribe them to the ideal person whose name it bears, or to any other than the author himself.—Lord Byron, we think, has formerly complained of those who identified him with his hero, or supposed that Harold was but the expositor of his own feelings and opinions;—and in noticing the former portions of the work, we thought it unbecoming to give any countenance to such a supposition.—In this last part, however, it is really impracticable to distinguish them.—Not only do the author and his hero travel and reflect together—but, in truth, we scarcely ever have any notice to which of them the sentiments so energetically expressed are to be ascribed; and in those which are unequivocally given as those of the Noble author himself, there is the very same tone of misanthropy, sadness and scorn, which we were formerly willing to regard as a part of the assumed costume of the Childe. We are far from supposing, indeed, that Lord Byron would disavow any of these sentiments; and though there are some which we must ever think it most unfortunate to entertain, and others which it appears improper to have published, the greater part are admirable, and cannot be perused without emotion even by those to whom they may appear erroneous.

[Gives outline of poem with copious extracts, and comments of which I cite three examples.]

(a) ... There is a richness and energy in the following passage which is peculiar to Lord Byron, among all modern poets—a throng of glowing images, poured forth at once, with a facility and profusion which must appear mere wastefulness to more economical writers, and a certain negligence and harshness of diction which can belong only to an author who is oppressed with the exuberance and rapidity of his conceptions.

> The Archangel's trump, not Glory's, must awake
> Those whom they thirst for; though the sound of Fame
> May for a moment sooth, it cannot slake
> The fever of vain longing, and the name
> So honoured but assumes a stronger, bitterer claim.

> They mourn, but smile at length; and, smiling, mourn;
> The tree will wither long before it fall;
> The hull drives on, though mast and sail be torn;
> The roof-tree sinks, but moulders on the hall
> In massy hoariness; the ruined wall
> Stands when its wind-worn battlements are gone;
> The bars survive the captive they enthral;
> The day drags through though storms keep out the sun;
> And thus the heart will break, yet brokenly live on;

> Even as a broken mirror, which the glass
> In every fragment multiplies; and makes
> A thousand images of one that was,
> The same, and still the more, the more it breaks;
> And thus the heart will do which not forsakes,
> Living in shattered guise, and still, and cold,
> And bloodless, with its sleepless sorrow aches,
> Yet withers on till all without is old,
> Showing no visible sign,—for such things are untold.

(b) [Quotes stanzas 42–5 on the restlessness and wretchedness of great men, and comments:]

This is splendidly written, no doubt—but we trust it is not true; and as it is delivered with much more than poetical earnestness, and recurs, indeed, in other forms in various parts of the volume, we must really be allowed to enter our dissent somewhat at large. With regard to conquerors, we wish with all our hearts that the case were as the Noble author represents it: But we greatly fear they are neither half so unhappy, nor half so much hated as they should be. On the contrary, it seems plain enough that they are very commonly idolized and admired, even by those on whom they trample; and we suspect, moreover, that in general they pass their time rather agreeably, and derive considerable satisfaction from the ruin and desolation of the world. From Macedonia's Madman to the Swede—from Nimrod to Bonaparte, the hunters of men have pursued their sport with as much gaiety, and as little remorse, as the hunters of other animals—and have lived as cheerily in their days of action, and as comfortably in their repose, as the followers of better pursuits. For this, and for the fame which they have generally enjoyed, they are obviously indebted to the great interests connected with their employment, and the mental excitement which belongs to its hopes and hazards. It would be strange, therefore, if the other active, but more innocent spirits whom Lord Byron has here placed in the same predicament, and who share all their sources of enjoyment, without the guilt and the hardness which they cannot fail of contracting, should be more miserable or more unfriended than those splendid curses of their kind—and it would be *passing strange*, and pitiful, if the most precious gifts of Providence should produce only unhappiness, and mankind regard with hostility their greatest benefactors. We do not believe in any such prodigies. Great vanity and ambition may indeed lead to feverish and restless efforts—to jealousies, to hate and to mortification—but these are only their effects when united to inferior abilities. It is not those, in short, who actually surpass mankind, that are unhappy, but those who struggle in vain to surpass them; and this moody temper, which eats into itself from within, and provokes fair and unfair opposition from without, is generally the result of pretensions which outgo the merits by which they are supported—and disappointments, that may be clearly traced, not to the excess of genius, but its defect.

It will be found, we believe, accordingly, that the master spirits of their age have always escaped the unhappiness which is here supposed to be the inevitable lot of extraordinary talents; and that this strange tax upon genius has only been levied upon those who held the secondary shares of it. Men of truly great powers of mind have generally been cheerful, social, and indulgent;—while a tendency to sentimental whining, or fierce intolerance, may be ranked among the surest symptoms of little souls and inferior intellects. In the whole list of our English poets, we can only remember Shenstone and Savage—two, certainly, of the lowest—who were querulous and discontented. Cowley, indeed, used to call himself melancholy,—but he was full of conceits and affectations, and has nothing to make us proud of him. Shakespeare, the greatest of them all, was evidently of a free and joyous temperament,—and so was Chaucer, their common master. The same disposition appears to have predominated in Fletcher, Johnson, and their great contemporaries. The genius of Milton partook something of the austerity of the party to which he belonged, and of the controversies in which he was involved; but even when fallen on evil days and evil tongues, his spirit seems to have retained its serenity as well as its dignity;—and in his private life, as well as in his poetry, the majesty of a high character is tempered with great sweetness and practical wisdom. In the succeeding age, our poets were but too gay; and though we forbear to speak of living authors, we know enough of them to say with confidence, that to be miserable or to be hated is not now, any more than heretofore, the common lot of those who excel.

If this, however, be the case with poets, confessedly the most irritable and fantastic of all men of genius—and of poets, too, bred and born in the gloomy climate of England, it is not likely that those who have surpassed their fellows in other ways, or in other regions, have been more distinguished for unhappiness. Were Socrates and Plato, the greatest philosophers of antiquity, remarkable for unsocial or gloomy tempers? Was Bacon, the greatest in modern times? Was Sir Thomas More, or Erasmus, or Hume, or Voltaire? Was Newton, or Fenelon? Was Henry IV, the paragon of kings and conquerors? Was Fox, the most ardent, and, in the vulgar sense, the least successful of statesmen? These, and men like these, are undoubtedly the lights and the boast of the world. Yet there was no alloy of misanthropy or gloom in their genius. They did not disdain the men they had surpassed; and neither feared nor experienced their hostility. Some detractors they might have, from envy or misapprehension; but, beyond all doubt, the prevailing sentiments in respect to them have always been those of gratitude and admiration; and the error of public judgment, where it has erred, has much oftener been to overrate than to undervalue the merits of those who had claims on their good opinion. On the whole, we are far from thinking that eminent men are happier than those who glide through life in peaceful obscurity; but it is their eminence, and the consequences of it, rather than the mental superiority by which it is obtained, that interferes with their enjoyment. Distinction, however won, usually leads to a passion for more distinction;

and is apt to engage us in laborious efforts and anxious undertakings: and those, even when successful, seldom repay, in our judgment at least, the ease, the leisure and tranquillity, of which they require the sacrifice. But it really passes our imagination to conceive, that the very highest degrees of intellectual vigour, or fancy, or sensibility, should of themselves be productive either of unhappiness or general dislike. . . .

(c) The closing stanzas of the poem are extremely beautiful; but we are immoveable in the resolution that no statement of ours shall ever give additional publicity to the subjects of which they treat.

We have not left room now to notice the faults of this performance. We hinted, at the outset, that the Noble author seemed to lean rather too kindly to the peculiarities of the Lake school; and in some of the passages we have already quoted, there are traces enough perhaps of this partiality. The following, however, will more completely justify that observation.

> I live not in myself, but I become
> Portion of that around me; and to me,
> High mountains are a feeling, but the hum
> Of human cities torture, . . .

> Ye stars! which are the poetry of heaven!
> If in your bright leaves we would read the fate
> Of men and empires,—'tis to be forgiven,
> That in our aspirations to be great,
> Our destinies o'erleap their mortal state,
> And claim a kindred with you; for ye are
> A beauty and a mystery, and create
> In us such love and reverence from afar,
> That fortune, fame, power, life, have named themselves a star.

These are mystical enough, we think; but what follows is nearly as unintelligible as some of the sublimities of Wordsworth himself.

> Could I embody and unbosom now
> That which is most within me,—could I wreak
> My thoughts upon expression, and thus throw
> Soul, heart, mind, passions, feelings, strong or weak,
> All that I would have sought, and all I seek,
> Bear, know, feel, and yet breathe—into *one* word,
> And that one word were Lightning, I would speak;

> But as it is, I live and die unheard,
> With a most voiceless thought, sheathing it as a sword.[1]

[Goes on to give summary of *The Prisoner of Chillon*, with extracts, and to discuss more briefly the shorter poems ('Darkness', 'The Dream', etc.) in the same volume.]

Beautiful as this poetry is, it is a relief at last to close the volume. We cannot maintain our accustomed tone of levity, or even speak like calm literary judges, in the midst of these agonizing traces of a wounded and distempered spirit. Even our admiration is at last swallowed up in a most painful feeling of pity and of wonder. It is impossible to mistake these for fictitious sorrows, conjured up for the purpose of poetical effect. There is a dreadful tone of sincerity, and an energy that cannot be counterfeited in the expression of wretchedness and alienation from human kind, which occurs in every page of this publication; and as the author has at last spoken out in his own person, and unbosomed his griefs a great deal too freely to his readers, the offence now would be to entertain a doubt of their reality. We certainly have no hope of preaching him into philanthropy and cheerfulness; but it is impossible not to mourn over such a catastrophe of such a mind, or to see the prodigal gifts of Nature, Fortune, and Fame, thus turned to bitterness, without an oppressive feeling of impatience, mortification and surprise. Where there are such elements, however, it is equally impossible to despair that they may yet enter into happier combinations,—or not to hope that 'this puissant spirit'

> yet shall reascend
> Self-raised, and repossess its native seat.

[1] [On 1 December 1816 Crabb Robinson noted that Lord Byron 'has grossly and palpably imitated Wordsworth in his latter works, but his imitations are by no means happy'. (*Henry Crabb Robinson on Books and their Writers*, ed. Edith J. Morley, 1938, I, 199.) Wordsworth himself took the same view. Moore tells of a visit which the older poet paid to him in October 1820: Wordsworth 'spoke of Byron's plagiarisms from him; the whole third canto of *Childe Harold* founded on his style and sentiments. The feeling of natural objects which is there expressed, not caught by B. from nature herself, but from him [Wordsworth] and spoiled in the transmission. "Tintern Abbey" the source of it all; from which same poem too the celebrated passage about Solitude, in the first canto of *Childe Harold*, is (he said) taken, with this difference, that what is naturally expressed by him, has been worked by Byron into a laboured and antithetical sort of declamation.' (*Memoirs, Journal and Correspondence of Thomas Moore*, ed. Lord John Russell, 1853–6, III, 161. Cf. *The Letters of William and Dorothy Wordsworth*, ed. E. de Selincourt: *The Middle Years*, 1937, II, 790; *The Later Years*, 1939, I, 130.) And see above, p. 37.]

MANFRED

June 1817

---

14. John Wilson, from his unsigned review, *Blackwood's Magazine*

June 1817, I, 289–95

John Wilson (1785–1854), journalist and, from 1820, Professor of Moral Philosophy at Edinburgh University. He was a member of the editorial staff of *Blackwood's*, a frequent contributor, and author of most of the *Noctes Ambrosianae* (in which he figures as 'Christopher North'). Of this review Byron wrote to John Murray on 12 October 1817: 'The review in the Magazine you say was written by Wilson? it had all the air of being a poet's, and was a very good one.' (*LJ*, IV, 175.)

Lord Byron has been elected by acclamation to the throne of poetical supremacy; nor are we disposed to question his title to the crown. There breathes over all his genius an air of kingly dignity; strength, vigour, energy, are his attributes; and he wields his faculties with a proud consciousness of their power, and a confident anticipation of their effect. Living poets perhaps there are, who have taken a wider range, but none who have achieved such complete, such perfect, triumphs. In no great attempt has he ever failed; and, soon as he begins his flight, we feel that he is to soar upon unflagging wings; that when he has reached the black and tempestuous elevation of his favourite atmosphere, he will, eagle-like, sail on undisturbed through the heart of clouds, storms, and darkness.

To no poet was there ever given so awful a revelation of the passions of the human soul. He surveys, with a stern delight, that tumult and conflict of terrible thoughts from which other highly-gifted and powerful minds have involuntarily recoiled; he calmly and fearlessly stands upon the brink of that abyss from which the soul would seem to shrink with horror; and he looks down upon, and listens to, the ever-lasting agitation of the howling waters. There are in his poetry feelings, thoughts, sentiments, and passions, that we at once recognize to be human, though we know not whence they come: they break upon us like the sudden flash of a returning dream, like some wild cry from another world. And even those whose lives have had little experience of the wilder passions, for a moment feel that an unknown region of their own souls has been revealed to them, and that there are indeed fearful mysteries in our human nature.

When this dark and powerful spirit for a while withdraws from the contemplation of his own wild world, and condescends to look upon the ordinary shews and spectacles of life, he often seems unexpectedly to participate in the feelings and emotions of beings with whom it might be thought he could claim no kindred; and thus many passages are to be found in his poetry, of the most irresistible and overpowering pathos, in which the depth of his sympathy with common sorrows and common sufferers, seems as profound as if his nature knew nothing more mournful than sighs and tears.

We have no intention of drawing Lord Byron's poetical character, and have been led, we know not how, into these very general and imperfect observations. But perhaps the little we have said may in some degree shew, why hitherto this great poet has dealt so seldom with the forms of the external world. He has so deeply looked into the soul of man, and so intensely sympathized with all the struggles there,—that he has had no feelings or passions to fling away on the mere earth he inhabits. But it is evident that the same powers, which he has so gloriously exerted upon man as their subject, would kindle up and enlighten, or darken and disturb, the features of external nature; and that, if he so willed it, his poetry, instead of being rife with wrath, despair, remorse, and all other agitating passions, might present an equally sublime assemblage of woods, glens, and mountains,—of lakes and rivers, cataracts and oceans. In the third canto of *Childe Harold*, accordingly, he has delivered up his soul to the impulses of Nature, and we have seen how that high communion has elevated and sublimed it. He instantly penetrated into her heart, as he had before into the heart of Man; and, in a few months of solitary wandering among the Alps, his soul became as deeply imbued with her glory and magnificence, as if, from youth, he had dedicated himself to no other power, and had for ever devoutly worshipped at her altar. He leapt at once into the first rank of descriptive poets. He came into competition with Wordsworth upon his own ground, and with his own weapons; and in the first encounter he vanquished and overthrew him. His description of the stormy night among the Alps—of the blending,—the mingling,—the fusion of his own soul, with the raging elements around him,—is alone worth all the dull metaphysics of *The Excursion*, and shews that he might enlarge the limits of human consciousness regarding the operations of matter upon mind, as widely as he has enlarged them regarding the operations of mind upon itself.

In the very singular, and, we suspect, very imperfect poem, of which we are about to give a short account, Lord Byron has pursued the same course as in the third canto of *Childe Harold*, and put out his strength upon the same objects. The action is laid among the mountains of the Alps—the characters are all, more or less, formed and swayed by the operations of the magnificent scenery around them, and every page of the poem teems with imagery and passion, though, at the same time, the mind of the poet is often overborne, as it were, by the strength and novelty of its own conceptions; and thus the composition, as a whole, is liable to many and fatal objections.

But there is a still more novel exhibition of Lord Byron's powers in this extraordinary drama. He has here burst into the world of spirits; and, in the wild delight with which the elements of nature seem to have inspired him, he has endeavoured to embody and call up before him their ministering agents, and to employ these wild Personifications, as he formerly employed the feelings and passions of man. We are not prepared to say, that, in this daring attempt, he has completely succeeded. We are inclined to think, that the plan he has conceived, and the principal Character which he has wished to delineate, would require a fuller development than is here given to them; and accordingly, a sense of imperfection, incompleteness, and confusion, accompanies the mind throughout the perusal of the poem, owing either to some failure on the part of the poet, or to the inherent mystery of the subject. But though on that account it is difficult to comprehend distinctly the drift of the composition, and almost impossible to give any thing like a distinct account of it, it unquestionably exhibits many noble delineations of mountain scenery,—many impressive and terrible pictures of passion,—and many wild and awful visions of imaginary horror.

[Gives summary of the poem, with extracts.]

We had intended making some observations upon this extraordinary production, but, to be intelligible, we could not confine them within the limits which necessity imposes. On some other occasion we may enter at length into the philosophy of the subject; but we have given such an account as will enable our readers to comprehend its general character. One remark we must make on the versification. Though generally flowing, vigorous, and sonorous, it is too often slovenly and careless to a great degree; and there are in the very finest passages, so many violations of the plainest rules of blank verse, that we suspect Lord Byron has a very imperfect knowledge of that finest of all music, and has yet much to learn before his language can be well adapted to dramatic compositions.

15. Jeffrey, from his unsigned review, *Edinburgh Review*

Dated August 1817, issued September 1817, XXVIII, 418–31

'Many thanks', Byron wrote to Murray in a letter of 12 October, 'for the *Edinburgh Review* which is very kind about *Manfred*, and defends its originality, which I did not know that any body had attacked. I *never read*, and do not know that I ever saw, the *Faustus* of Marlow . . ., but I heard Mr Lewis translate verbally some scenes of Goethe's *Faust* (which were some good, and some bad) last summer;—which is all I know of the history of that magical personage; and as to the germs of *Manfred*, they may be found in the Journal which I sent to Mrs. Leigh. . . . The *Prometheus*, if not exactly in my plan, has always been so much in my head, that I can easily conceive its influence over all or every thing that I have written;—but I deny Marlow and his progeny. . . .' (*LJ*, IV, 173–5.)

This is a very strange—not a very pleasing—but unquestionably a very powerful and most poetical production. The noble author, we find, still deals with that dark and overawing Spirit, by whose aid he has so often subdued the minds of his readers, and in whose might he has wrought so many wonders. In Manfred, we recognize at once the gloom and potency of that soul which burned and blasted and fed upon itself in Harold, and Conrad, and Lara—and which comes again in this piece, more in sorrow than in anger—more proud, perhaps, and more awful than ever—but with the fiercer traits of its misanthropy subdued, as it were, and quenched in the gloom of a deeper despondency. Manfred does not, like Conrad and Lara, wreak the anguish of his burning heart in the dangers and daring of desperate and predatory war—nor seek to drown bitter thoughts in the tumult of perpetual contention—nor yet, like Harold, does he sweep over the peopled scenes of the earth with high disdain and aversion, and make his survey of the business and pleasures and studies of man, an occasion for taunts and sarcasms, and the food of an unmeasurable spleen. He is fixed by the genius of the poet in the majestic solitudes of the central Alps—where, from his youth up, he has lived in proud but calm seclusion from the ways of men, conversing only with the magnificent forms and aspects of nature by which he is surrounded, and with the Spirits of the Elements over whom he has acquired dominion, by the secret and unhallowed studies of Sorcery and Magic. He is averse indeed from mankind, and scorns the low and frivolous nature to which he belongs; but he cherishes no animosity or hostility to that feeble race. Their concerns excite no interest—their pursuits no sympathy—their joys no envy. It is irksome and vexatious for him to be crossed by them in his melancholy musings, —but he treats them with gentleness and pity; and, except when stung to impatience by too importunate an intrusion, is kind and considerate of the comforts of all around him.

This piece is properly entitled a dramatic Poem—for it is merely poetical, and is not at all a drama or play in the modern acceptation of the term. It has no action; no plot—and no characters; Manfred merely muses and suffers from the beginning to the end. His distresses are the same at the opening of the scene and at its closing—and the temper in which they are borne is the same. A hunter and a priest, and some domestics, are indeed introduced; but they have no connexion with the passions or sufferings on which the interest depends; and Manfred is substantially alone throughout the whole piece. He holds no communion but with the memory of the Being he had loved; and the immortal Spirits whom he evokes to reproach with his misery, and their inability to relieve it. These unearthly beings approach nearer to the character of persons of the drama—but still they are but choral accompaniments to the performance; and Manfred is, in reality, the only actor and sufferer on the scene. To delineate his character indeed—to render conceivable his feelings—is plainly the whole scope and design of the poem; and the conception and execution are, in this respect, equally admirable. It is a grand and terrific vision of a being invested with superhuman attributes, in order that he may be capable of more than human sufferings, and be sustained under them by more than human force and pride. To object to the improbability of the fiction is, we think, to mistake the end and aim of the author. Probabilities, we apprehend, did not enter at all into his consideration—his object was, to produce effect—to exalt and dilate the character through whom he was to interest or appal us—and to raise our conception of it, by all the helps that could be derived from the majesty of nature, or the dread of superstition. It is enough, therefore, if the situation in which he has placed him is *conceivable*—and if the supposition of its reality enhances our emotions and kindles our imagination;—for it is Manfred only that we are required to fear, to pity, or admire. If we can once conceive of him as a real existence, and enter into the depth and the height of his pride and his sorrows, we may deal as we please with the means that have been used to furnish us with this impression, or to enable us to attain to this conception. We may regard them but as types, or metaphors, or allegories: But *he* is the thing to be expressed, and the feeling and the intellect of which all these are but shadows.

[Gives summary of poem, with extracts. Comments include a criticism of the incongruity of a speech by Nemesis ('I was detain'd repairing shattered thrones, Marrying fools, restoring dynasties,' etc.). 'This', writes Jeffrey, 'we think is out of place at least, if we must not say out of character; and though the author may tell us that human calamities are naturally subjects of derision to the Ministers of Vengeance, yet we cannot be persuaded that satirical and political allusions are at all compatible with the feelings and impressions which it was here his business to maintain.']

There are great faults, it must be admitted, in this poem;—but it is undoubtedly a work of genius and originality. Its worst fault, perhaps, is, that it fatigues and overawes us by the uniformity of its terror and solemnity. Another is the painful and offensive nature of the circumstances on which its distress is ultimately founded. It all springs from the disappointment or fatal issue of an incestuous passion; and incest, according to our modern ideas—for it was otherwise in antiquity—is not a thing to be at all brought before the imagination. The lyrical songs of the Spirits are too long, and not all excellent. There is something of pedantry in them now and then; and even Manfred deals in classical allusions a little too much. If we were to consider it as a proper drama, or even as a finished poem, we should be obliged to add, that it is far too indistinct and unsatisfactory. But this we take to be according to the design and conception of the author. He contemplated but a dim and magnificent sketch of a subject which did not admit of more accurate drawing, or more brilliant colouring. Its obscurity is a part of its grandeur; and the darkness that rests upon it, and the smoky distance in which it is lost, are all devices to increase its majesty, to stimulate our curiosity, and to impress us with deeper awe.

It is suggested, in an ingenious paper, in a late Number of the

Edinburgh Magazine that the general conception of this piece, and much of what is excellent in the manner of its execution, have been borrowed from *The Tragical History of Dr Faustus* of Marlow [*sic*]; and a variety of passages are quoted, which the author considers as similar, and, in many respects, superior to others in the poem before us. We cannot agree in the general terms of this conclusion;—but there is, no doubt, a certain resemblance, both in some of the topics that are suggested, and in the cast of the diction in which they are expressed. . . .

[Cites examples of Marlowe's poetry.]

But these, and many other smooth and fanciful verses in this curious old drama, prove nothing, we think, against the originality of *Manfred*; for there is nothing to be found there of the pride, the abstraction, and the heartrooted misery in which that originality consists. Faustus is a vulgar sorcerer, tempted to sell his soul to the Devil for the ordinary price of sensual pleasure, and earthly power and glory—and who shrinks and shudders in agony when the forfeit comes to be exacted. The style, too, of Marlow, though elegant and scholarlike, is weak and childish compared with the depth and force of much of what we have quoted from Lord Byron; and the disgusting buffoonery and low farce of which his piece is principally made up, place it much more in contrast, than in any terms of comparison, with that of his noble successor. In the tone and pitch of the composition, as well as in the character of the diction in the more solemn parts, the piece before us reminds us much more of the *Prometheus* of Aeschylus, than of any more modern performance. The tremendous solitude of the principal person, the supernatural beings with whom alone he holds communion, the guilt, the firmness, the misery, are all points of resemblance to which the grandeur of the poetic imagery only gives a more striking effect. The chief differences are, that the subject of the Greek poet was sanctified and exalted by the established belief of his country, and that his terrors are nowhere tempered with the sweetness which breathes from so many passages of his English rival.

16. Goethe on *Manfred*

[1817] 1820

Johann Wolfgang von Goethe (1749–1832) wrote a review of
Manfred in 1817, which was not published until 1820. It was
translated for Byron, at his eager request, by R. B. Hoppner, the
British Consul at Venice. The following extract from his version
is reprinted from *LJ*, V, 506. Byron was delighted by the favourable opinon of the 'Greatest man of Germany—perhaps of
Europe' (*LJ*, V, 36), although he was amused by the 'Florentine
husband-killing story' (*op. cit.*, p. 113) which illustrates the wildly
inaccurate accounts of Byron current in Europe before the publication of Moore's *Life*. For a detailed account of Goethe's views
on Byron, and Byron's on Goethe, see E. M. Butler, *Byron and
Goethe*, 1956.

Byron's tragedy, *Manfred*, was to me a wonderful phenomenon, and
one that closely touched me. This singular intellectual poet has taken
my *Faustus* to himself, and extracted from it the strangest nourishment
for his hypochondriac humour. He has made use of the impelling
principles in his own way, for his own purposes, so that no one of them
remains the same; and it is particularly on this account that I cannot
enough admire his genius. The whole is in this way so completely
formed anew that it would be an interesting task for the critic to point
out, not only the alterations he has made, but their degree of resemblance with, or dissimilarity to, the original; in the course of which
I cannot deny that the gloomy heat of an unbounded and exuberant
despair becomes at last oppressive to us. Yet is the dissatisfaction we
feel always connected with esteem and admiration.

We find thus in this tragedy the quintessence of the most astonishing
talent born to be its own tormentor. The character of Lord Byron's life
and poetry hardly permits a just and equitable appreciation. He has
often enough confessed what it is that torments him. He has repeatedly
pourtrayed it; and scarcely any one feels compassion for this intolerable
suffering, over which he is ever laboriously ruminating. There are,

properly speaking, two females whose phantoms for ever haunt him, and which, in this piece also, perform principal parts—one under the name of Astarte; the other without form or actual presence, and merely a voice. Of the horrid occurrence which took place with the former the following is related: When a bold and enterprising young man, he won the affections of a Florentine lady. Her husband discovered the amour, and murdered his wife; but the murderer was the same night found dead in the street, and there was no one on whom any suspicion could be attached. Lord Byron removed from Florence, and these spirits haunted him all his life after.

This romantic incident is rendered highly probable by innumerable allusions to it in his poems. . . .

BEPPO

February 1818

---

17. Some early opinions

(*a*) Extract from letter of 16 June 1818, from John Murray to Byron. ('Mr. Frere' was John Hookham Frere, author of *Whistlecraft*, which provided Byron with his immediate model for *Beppo*.) 'Mr. Frere is at length satisfied that you are the author of *Beppo*. He had no conception that you possessed the protean talent of Shakespeare, thus to assume at will so different a character. He, and every one, continues in the same very high opinion of its great beauties. I am glad to find that you are disposed to pursue this strain, which has occasioned so much delight. Do you never think of prose? . . . I have just put forth two more cantos of *Whistlecraft*—which the knowing ones think excellent, and of which the public think nothing, for they cannot see the drift of it. I have not sold 500 copies of the first parts yet; and of *Beppo*, I have sold six times that quantity in a sixth part of the time, and before, indeed, it is generally known to be yours. . . .' (Samuel Smiles, *A Publisher and his Friends*, 1891, I, 393–4.)

(*b*) Extract from unsigned notice in the *Monthly Review* for March 1818: 'His satire, though at times a little tinged with vulgarity, is usually good-humoured and often well pointed: he throws about his observations in a lively strain; and it is very amusing to remark how every thing, of which he speaks or thinks, becomes the immediate thesis of a new episode of playful moralizing.' (*Monthly Review*, LXXXV, 287.)

(*c*) Extract from unsigned notice in the *Eclectic Review* for June 1818: 'The poem is of the burlesque kind, and were it not that it is licentious in its moral, occasionally vulgar and profane in its expressions, and rather tedious in its narrative, it might serve very well to laugh through after dinner. There is a happy whimsicality in some of the rhymes, and now and then a stroke of humour and of satire, which will succeed with the good natured reader, who has not adventured to read the poem aloud, nor set himself to read it through.' (*Eclectic Review*, N.S., IX, 555.)

(*d*) Extract from unsigned review by Jeffrey in the *Edinburgh Review* for February 1818 (issued Spring 1818): 'Though there is as little serious meaning or interest in this extraordinary performance, as can easily be imagined, we think it well entitled to a place in our fastidious Journal—and that, not merely because it is extremely clever and amusing, but because it affords a very curious and complete specimen of a kind of diction and composition of which our English literature has hitherto afforded very few examples. It is, in itself, absolutely a thing of nothing—without story, characters, sentiments, or intelligible object—a mere piece of lively and loquacious prattling, in short, upon all kinds of frivolous subjects,—a sort of gay and desultory babbling about Italy and England, Turks, balls, literature and fish sauces. But still there is something very engaging in the uniform gayety, politeness, and good humour of the author—and something still more striking and admirable in the matchless facility with which he has cast into regular, and even difficult versification, the unmingled, unconstrained, and unselected language of the most light, familiar, and ordinary conversation. The French have always had a great deal of this sort of poetry—though with a very severe regard to the purity of the diction—and the Italians also, in a looser and more extravagant tone; but, in England, it seems never to have been naturalized. The nearest approach to it is to be found in some of the tales and lighter pieces of Prior—a few stanzas here and there among the trash and burlesque of Peter Pindar—and in several passages of Mr Moore, and the author of the facetious miscellany, entitled, *The Twopenny Post Bag*. Chaucer and Shakespeare had ease and gayety enough for the style of which we are speaking—but it belongs intrinsically to the silver, and not to the golden age of poetry; and implies the existence of certain habits of dissipation, derision, and intelligence in general society, and of a sort of conventional language, for the expression of those things, which were still to be formed in the days of these great masters.—It is scarcely necessary to add, except for our duller readers, that this same familiar, lively, conversational poetry is perfectly distinct both from the witty, epigrammatic and satirical vein in which Pope will never be surpassed—or equalled; and from the burlesque, humorous and distorted style which attained its greatest height in *Hudibras*, and has been copied abundantly enough by humbler imitators. The style of which we are speaking is, no doubt, occasionally satirical and witty and humorous—but it is, on the whole, far more gay than poignant, and is characterized, exactly as good conversation is, rather by its constant ease and amenity, than by any traits either of extraordinary brilliancy, or of strong and ludicrous effect. There must be a certain allowance of sense and sagacity—and little flying traits of picturesque description—and small flights of imagination —and sallies of naïveté and humour—but nothing very powerful, and nothing very long. The great charm is in the simplicity and naturalness of the language,—the free but guarded use of all polite idioms, and even of all phrases of temporary currency that have the stamp of good company upon them,—with the exclusion of all scholastic or ambitious eloquence, all profound views, and all deep emotions.

The unknown writer before us has accomplished all these objects with great skill and felicity; and, in particular, has furnished us with an example, unique we rather think in our language, of about one hundred stanzas of good verse, entirely composed of common words, in their common places; never presenting us with one sprig of what is called poetical diction, or even making use of a single inversion, either to raise the style or assist the rhyme—but running on in an inexhaustible series of good easy colloquial phrases, and finding them fall into verse by some unaccountable and happy fatality. In this great and characteristic quality it is almost invariably excellent. In some other respects it is more unequal. About one half is as good as possible, in the style to which it belongs; the other half bears perhaps too many marks of that haste with which we take it for granted that such a work must necessarily be written. Some passages are rather too foolish, some too snappish, and some run too much on the cheap and rather plebeian humour of out-of-the-way rhymes and strange sounding words and epithets. But the greater part is very pleasant, amiable, and gentlemanlike.

It is not perhaps worth while to give any account of the subject of a work which almost professes to have no subject. But as it has a name, and a sort of apology for a story, we shall proceed, according to our laudable custom, to teach our gentle readers all we know . . .

[Gives brief summary of plot.]

This story, such as it is, occupies about twenty stanzas, we think, out of the ninety-five of which the poem consists. The rest is made up of digressions and dissertations at the author's discretion; and these form unquestionably by far the most lively and interesting part of the work, of which we must now give our readers a few specimens—to explain and make amends for our critical disquisitions. . . .

[Gives extracts, with comments. Stanza 45 ('I like the women too' etc.) is criticized as follows:]

In these last lines, it will be observed, that the author rises above the usual and appropriate pitch of his composition, and is betrayed into something too like enthusiasm and deep feeling for the light and fantastic strain of his poetry. Neither does the fit go off immediately; for he rises quite into rapture in the succeeding stanza—in which he seems to have caught a spark from the ardent genius of Byron. . . .

This, however, is the only slip of the kind in the whole work—the only passage in which the author betrays the secret—which might however have been suspected—of his own genius, and his affinity to a higher order of poets than those to whom he has here been pleased to hold out a model. . . .' (*Edinburgh Review*, XXIX, 302–4, 306–7.)

18. 'Presbyter Anglicanus', from a 'Letter to the Author of *Beppo*', *Blackwood's Magazine*

June 1818, III, 323–9

In his 'Note to the Editor', the anonymous author protests at the excessive indulgence shown to Byron by reviewers in *Blackwood's*, and expresses his wonder at 'the conduct of the ingenious critic [Jeffrey], who, in the last number of the *Edinburgh Review*, entertained us with a little, lively, flimsy dissertation on ludicrous poetry in general, and with many expressions of admiration for the ease, grace, and vivacity of this Venetian Story, without thinking himself bound to express a single feeling of indignation at the wickedness of those topics on which so much of all this ease, grace, and vivacity has been wasted.' Byron later protested (*LJ*, IV, 475) at the reviewer's identification of him with his heroes.

. . . Your predecessors, in one word, my Lord, have been the friends— you are the enemy of your species. You have transferred into the higher departments of poetry (or you have at least endeavoured to transfer) that spirit of mockery, misanthropy, and contempt, which the great bards of elder times left to preside over the humbler walk of the satirist and the cynic. The calm respect which these men felt for themselves inspired them with sympathetic reverence for their brethren. They perceived, indeed, the foibles and the frailties of humanity, and they depicted, at least as well as you have ever done, the madness of the senses and the waywardness of the passions; but they took care to vindicate the original dignity of their nature, and contrasted their representations of the vice and weakness, which they observed in some, with the more cheering spectacle of the strength and the virtue, whose stirrings they felt within themselves, and whose workings they contemplated in others. Conscious of the glorious union of intellectual grandeur and moral purity within, they pitied the errors of other men; but they were not shaken from their reverence for the general character of man. Instead of raving with demoniacal satisfaction about the worthlessness of our motives and the nothingness of our attainments, they strove, by shewing us what we might be and what we had been, to make us what we should be. They drew the portraits of wrath, jealousy, and hatred, only that we might appreciate more justly the kindly feelings which these fierce passions expel from the rightful possession of our bosoms. They took our nature as it is, but it was for the purpose of improving it. . . .

In all your writings, how little is there whose object it is to make us reverence virtue, or love our country! You never teach us to despise earthly sufferings, in the hope of eternal happiness. With respect to all that is best and greatest in the nature and fate of man, you preserve not merely a sorrowful, but a sullen silence. Your poetry need not have been greatly different from what it is, although you had lived and died in the midst of a generation of heartless, vicious, and unbelieving demons. With you, heroism is lunacy, philosophy folly, virtue a cheat, and religion a bubble. Your Man is a stern, cruel, jealous, revengeful, contemptuous, hopeless, solitary savage. Your Woman is a blind, devoted, heedless, beautiful minister and victim of lust. The past is a vain record, and the present a fleeting theatre, of misery and madness: the future one blank of horrid darkness, whereon your mind floats and fluctuates in a cheerless uncertainty, between annihilation and despair.

The interest which you have found means to excite for the dismal creations of your poetry, is proof abundant of the vigour of your genius, but should afford small consolation to your conscience-stricken mind. You are a skilful swordsman; but you have made use of poisoned weapons, and the deadliness of your wound gives no addition to your valour. You have done what greater and better men despised to do. You have brought yourself down to the level of that part of our erring and corrupted nature, which it was their pride and privilege to banish from the recollection and the sympathy of those to whom they spake. In the great struggle between the good and the evil principle, you have taken the wrong side, and you enjoy the worthless popularity of a daring rebel. But hope not that the calm judgment of posterity will ratify the hasty honours which you have extorted from the passions of your contemporaries. Believe me, Men are not upon the whole quite so unprincipled,—nor Women quite so foolish,—nor Virtue so useless, —nor Religion so absurd,—nor Deception so lasting,—nor Hypocrisy so triumphant, as your Lordship has been pleased to fancy. A day of terrible retribution will arrive, and the punishment inflicted may not

improbably consist of things the most unwelcome to a poet's view—
the scorn of many, and the neglect of all. Even now, among the serious
and reflective part of the Men and the Women of England, your poetry
is read, indeed, and admired, but you yourself are never talked of except
with mingled emotions of anger and pity. With what pain do the high
spirits of your virtuous and heroic ancestors contemplate the degradation of their descendant. Alas! that the genius which might have ennobled any name, should have only assisted you to stamp a more lasting
stain upon the pure, the generous, the patriotic, the English name of
Byron.

Any other poet might complain with justice, should he see remarks
of a personal nature mixed up with a criticism upon his writings. You,
my Lord, can scarcely flatter yourself that you have any right to expect
such forbearance. If the scrutiny of the world be disagreeable to you,
either in its operation or in its effects, you need blame no one but yourself. We were well enough disposed to treat you with distant respect,
but you have courted and demanded our gaze. You have bared your
bosom when no man entreated you; it is your own fault if we have
seen there not the scars of honourable wounds, but the festering
blackness of a loathsome disease. You have been the vainest and the
most egotistical of poets. You have made yourself your only theme;
shall we not dare to dissect the hero, because, forsooth, he and his poet
are the same? You have debased your nobility by strutting upon the
stage; shall we still be expected to talk of you as of a private and un-
obtrusive individual? You must share the fate of your brethren, and
abide the judgment of the spectators. . . .

You made your debut in the utmost dignity and sadness of the
Cothurnus. You were the most lugubrious of mortals; it was the main
ambition of your vanity to attract to your matchless sorrows the overflowing sympathies of the world. We gave you credit for being sincere
in your affliction. We looked upon you as the victim of more than
human misery, and sympathized with the extravagance of your public
and uncontrollable lamentations. It is true that no one knew whence
your sorrow had sprung, but we were generous in our compassion, and
asked few questions. In time, however, we have become less credulous
and more inquisitive; the farce was so often renewed, that we became
weary of its wonders; we have come to suspect at last, that whatever
sorrows you may have, they are all of your own creating; and that,
whencesoever they may be, they are at least neither of so uniform nor of
so majestic a character as you would fain have had us to suppose. . . .

Under pretence of making us partakers in a fictitious or exaggerated grief, you have striven to make us sympathize with all the sickly whims and phantasies of a self-dissatisfied and self-accusing spirit. That you were, as you have yourself told us, a dissipated, a sceptical, and therefore, for there was no other cause, a wretched man, was no reason why you should wish to make your readers devoid of religion, virtue, and happiness. You had no right to taint the pure atmosphere of the English mind with the infectious phrenzies of the fever of debauch. Your misery was the punishment of your folly and your wickedness; why did you come to rack the eyes of the wise, the good, and the tranquil, with the loathsome spectacle of your merited torments? Could genius, a thousand times more splendid than yours, entitle the poor, giddy, restless victim of remorse, to make his art the instrument of evil,—to abuse the gifts of his God, by rendering them the engines of corruption and ruin among his fellow-men? For shame! my Lord, for shame upon your manhood! . . .

Visible, however, as was your apostacy, and mean your vengeance, there was still something about you to create respect, even in those who comprehended the best your vices and your errors. If you were an immoral and an unchristian, you were at least a serious, poet. Your pictures of depravity were sketched with such a sombre magnificence, that the eye of vulgar observers could gain little from surveying their lineaments. The harp of the mighty was still in your hands; and when you dashed your fingers over its loosened strings, faded as was the harmony, and harsh the execution, the notes were still made for their listening, who had loved the solemn music of the departed.

The last lingering talisman which secured to you the pity, and almost the pardon, even of those that abhorred your guilt,—with the giddiness of a lunatic, or the resolution of a suicide,—you have tossed away. You have lost the mournful and melancholy harp which lent a protecting charm even to the accents of pollution; and bought, in its stead, a gaudy viol, fit for the fingers of eunuchs, and the ears of courtezans. You have parted

> With what permissive glory, since that fall,
> Was left—

You have flung off the last remains of the 'regal port;' you are no longer one of 'the great seraphic lords,' that sat even in Pandemonium, 'in their own dimensions like themselves.' You have grown weary of your fallen grandeur, and dwarfed your stature, that you might gain easier access, and work paltrier mischief. You may resume, if you will, your giant-height, but we shall not fail to recognize, in spite of all your elevation, the swollen features of the same pigmy imp whom we have once learned—a lasting lesson—not to abhor merely, and execrate, but to *despise*. You may wish, as heretofore, to haunt our imaginations in the shadowy semblance of Harold, Conrad, Lara, or Manfred: you may retain their vice, and their unbelief, and their restlessness; but you have parted irretrievably with the majesty of their despair. We see you in a shape less sentimental and mysterious. We look below the disguise which has once been lifted, and claim acquaintance, not with the sadness of the princely masque, but with the scoffing and sardonic merriment of the ill-dissembling reveller beneath it. In evil hour did you step from your vantage-ground, and teach us that Harold, Byron, and the Count of *Beppo* are the same.[1]

---

[1] [See Byron's comment, *LJ*, IV, 475: 'the conclusion drawn was, that "Childe Harold, Byron, and the Count in *Beppo*, were one and the same person"; thereby making me turn out to be, as Mrs. Malaprop says, "*like Cerberus, three gentlemen at once*".'

CHILDE HAROLD'S PILGRIMAGE
CANTO IV
April 1818

---

19. Hazlitt, from his unsigned review,
Yellow Dwarf
2 May 1818

William Hazlitt (1778–1830), critic, essayist and journalist, combined radical politics with an admiration for Napoleon. This review from the *Yellow Dwarf* is reprinted in *The Complete Works of William Hazlitt*, Centenary Edn., ed. P. P. Howe, 1930–4, XIX, 35–43.

I do perceive a fury in your words, but nothing wherefore.

The fourth and last canto of *Childe Harold* has disappointed us. It is a falling off from the three former ones. We have read it carefully through, but it has left only the same impression on our minds that a troubled dream does—as disturbed, as confused, as disjointed, as harassing, and as unprofitable. It is an indigestion of the mind. It is the lassitude or feverish tossing and tumbling of the imagination, after having taken a surfeit of pleasure, and fed upon the fumes of pride. Childe Harold is a spoiled child of the Muses—and of Fortune. He looks down upon human life, not more with the superiority of intellect than with the arrogance of birth. The poet translates the lord into high sounding and supercilious verse. It is Agamemnon and Thersites in one person. The common events and calamities of the world afford matter for the effusions of his spleen, while they seem resented as affronts to his personal dignity.

And as the soldiers bore dead bodies by,
He called them untaught knaves, unmannerly,
To bring a slovenly, unhandsome corse
Betwixt the wind and his nobility.

So when 'the very age and body of the time' comes between his Lord-ship's speculative notions and hereditary prejudices, he stops the nose at it, and plays some very fantastic tricks before the public, who are lookers-on. In general, the idle wants, the naughty airs, the ill humours and *ennui*, the contempt for others, and disgust at themselves, common to exalted birth and station, are suffered to corrupt and stagnate in the blood that inherits them;—they are a disease in the flesh, an obstinate tumour in the mind, a cloud upon the brow, a venom that vents itself in hateful looks and peevish words to those about them; but in this poem and this author they have acquired 'an understanding and a tongue,'—are sublimed by imagination, systematised by sophistry—mount the steps of the Capitol, fulmine over Greece, and are poured in torrents of abuse on the world. It is well if the world like it—we are tired of the monotony of his Lordship's griefs, of which we can perceive neither beginning nor end. 'They are begot of nothing, born of nothing.' He volunteers his own Pilgrimage,—appoints his own penance,—makes his own confession,—and all—for nothing. He is in despair, because he has nothing to complain of—miserable, because he is in want of nothing. 'He has tasted of all earth's bliss, both living and loving,' and therefore he describes himself as suffering the tortures of the damned. He is in love with misery, because he has possessed every enjoyment; and because he has had his will in every thing, is inconsolable because he cannot have impossibilities. His Lordship, in fact, makes out his own hard case to be, that he has attained all those objects that the rest of the world admire; that he has met with none of those disasters which embitter their lives; and he calls upon us to sympathise with his griefs and his despair.

This will never do. It is more intolerable than even Mr. Words-worth's arbitrary egotism and pampered self-sufficiency. *He* creates a factitious interest out of nothing: Lord Byron would destroy our interest in all that is. Mr. Wordsworth, to salve his own self-love, makes the merest toy of his own mind,—the most insignificant object he can meet with,—of as much importance as the universe: Lord Byron would persuade us that the universe itself is not worth his or our notice; and yet he would expect us to be occupied with him.

———— The man whose eye
Is ever on himself doth look on one,
The least of Nature's works, one who might move
The wise man to that scorn which wisdom holds
Unlawful ever.[1]

These lines, written by one of these two poets, might be addressed to both of them with equal propriety.

Lord Byron, in this the fourth and last Canto of *Childe Harold's Pilgrimage*, seems to have worn out the glowing fervour of his genius to a *calx*, and to have exhausted the intense enthusiasm of his favourite topics of invective. There is little about himself, historically speaking— there is no plot, no story, no interest excited, no catastrophe. The general reflections are connected together merely by the accidental occurrence of different objects—the Venus of Medici, or the statue of Pompey,—the Capitol at Rome, or the Bridge of Sighs at Venice,— Shakespear, and Mrs. Radcliffe,—Bonaparte, and his Lordship in person, are brought together as in a phantasmagoria, and with as little attention to keeping or perspective, as in Hogarth's famous print for reversing the laws of vision. The judgments pronounced are often more dogmatical than profound, and with all their extravagance of expression, common-place. His Lordship does not understand the Apollo Belvidere or the Venus de Medicis, any more than Bonaparte. He cants about the one and against the other, and in doing the last, cuts his own throat. We are not without hopes that his friend Mr. Hobhouse will set this matter right in his 'Historical Illustrations'; and shew that, however it may suit his Noble Friend's poetical cross-purposes, politically and practically speaking, a house divided against itself cannot stand. He first, in his disdain of modern times, finds nothing to compare with the grandeur of antiquity but Bonaparte; and then 'as 'twere in spite of scorn' goes on to disdain this idol, which he had himself gratuitously set up, in a strain of effeminate and rancorous abuse worthy of Mr. Wordsworth's pastoral, place-hunting Muse. Suppose what is here said of 'the child and champion of Jacobinism' to be true, are there not venal tongues and venal pens enough to echo it, without his Lordship's joining in the cry? Will 'the High Legitimates, the Holy Band' be displeased with these captious efforts to level the object of their hate to the groveling standard of royalty? Is there not a division of labour even on Mount Parnassus? The other writers of prose and verse, who enter the Temple of Fame by Mr. Murray's door in Albemarle-street,

[1] [From Wordsworth's 'Lines left upon a Seat in a Yew-tree. . . .']

have their cues. Mr. Southey, for instance, never sings or says, or dreams of singing or saying, that the Prince Regent is not so great a man as Julius Cæsar. Why then should Lord Byron force the comparison between the modern and the ancient hero? It is because the slaves of power mind the cause they have to serve, because their own interest is concerned; but the friends of liberty always sacrifice their cause, which is *only* the cause of humanity, to their own spleen, vanity, and self-opinion. The league between tyrants and slaves is a chain of adamant; the bond between poets and the people is a rope of sand. Is this a truth, or is it not? If it is not, let Lord Byron write no more on this subject, which is beyond his height and his depth. Let him not trample on the mighty or the fallen! Bonaparte is not Beppo.

The versification and style of this poem are as perverse and capricious as the method or the sentiments. One stanza perpetually runs on into the next, making the exception the rule, merely because it properly ends in itself; and there is a strange mixture of stately phraseology and far-fetched metaphor, with the most affected and bald simplicity of expression and uncouthness in the rhymes. It is well his Lordship is born so high, or all Grub-street would set him down as a plebeian for such lines as the following:

> I lov'd her from my boyhood—she to me
> Was as a fairy city of the heart,
> Rising like water-columns from the sea,
> Of joy the sojourn, and of wealth the mart;
> And Otway, Ratcliff, Schiller, Shakspeare's art,
> Had stamp'd her image in me, and even so,
> Although I found her thus, we did not part,
> Perchance even dearer in her day of woe,
> Than when she was a boast, a marvel, and a show.

> I can repeople with the past—*and of*
> The present there is still for eye and thought,
> And meditation chasten'd down, *enough*;
> And more, it may be, than I hop'd or sought.

What will the Critics of the Cockney School of Poetry say to this? Lie on, and swear that it is high patrician poetry, and of very noble birth.[1]

[1] [Cf. Rogers' comment (*Recollections of the Table Talk of Samuel Rogers*, ed. A. Dyce, 3rd edn., 1856, p. 245): 'There is a great deal of incorrect and hasty writing in Byron's works; but it is overlooked in this age of hasty readers. For instance,

... From these recollections the poet proceeds to describe the fall of
the Velino, 'a hell of waters'. We cannot say but that we think his
powers better suited to express the human passions than to reflect the
forms of nature. In the present instance, however, the poet has not in-
voked the genius of the place in vain: it represents, in some measure,
the workings of his own spirit,—disturbed, restless, labouring, foaming, sparkling, and now hid in labyrinths and plunging into the gloom
of night. The following description is obscure, tortuous, perplexed,
and abortive; yet who can say that it is not beautiful, striking, and impassioned?—

> How profound
> The gulf! and how the giant element
> From rock to rock leaps with delirious bound,
> Crushing the cliffs, which, downward worn and rent,
> With his fierce footsteps, yield in chasms a fearful vent!
>
> To the broad column which rolls on, and shows
> More like the fountain of an infant sea
> Torn from the womb of mountains by the throes
> Of a new world, than only thus to be
> Parent of rivers, which flow gushingly,
> With many windings through the vale:—Look back!
> Lo! where it comes like an eternity
> As if to sweep down all things in its track,
> Charming the eye with dread,—a matchless cataract,
>
> Horribly beautiful! but on the verge,
> From side to side, beneath the glittering morn,
> An Iris sits, amidst the infernal surge,
> Like Hope upon a death-bed, and, unworn
> Its steady dyes, while all around is torn
> By the distracted waters, bears serene
> Its brilliant hues with all their beams unshorn:
> Resembling, 'mid the torture of the scene,
> Love watching Madness with unalterable mien.

We'll look no more: such kind of writing is enough to turn the
brain of the reader or the author. The repetitions in the last stanza are

---

> I stood in Venice, on the Bridge of Sighs,
> A palace and a prison *on each hand*.

He meant to say, that on one hand was a palace, on the other a prison. And what
think you of—

> And dashest him again to earth:—there let him *lay*?']

like interlineations in an imperfect manuscript, left for after-selection; such as, 'Hope upon a death-bed'—'Love watching madness'—'Unworn its steady dies'–'Serene its brilliant hues'—'the distracted waters' —'the torture of the scene', &c. There is here in every line an effort at brilliancy, and a successful effort; and yet, in the next, as if nothing had been done, the same thing is attempted to be expressed again with the same labour as before, the same success, and with as little appearance of repose or satisfaction of mind.

It is in vain to attempt a regular account of the remainder of this poem, which is a mass of discordant things, incoherent, not gross, seen 'now in glimmer and now in gloom', and 'moving wild laughter in the throat of death'. . . .

20. Scott, from his unsigned review, *Quarterly Review*

Dated April 1818, issued September 1818, XIX, 215–32

Byron's comment on this review and the next is to be found in a letter of 24 November 1818, to John Murray: 'You ask me of the two reviews—I will tell you. Scott's is the review of one poet on another—his friend; and Wilson's the review of a poet, too, on another—his *idol*; for he likes me better than he chooses to avow to the public, with all his eulogy. I speak, judging only from the article, for I don't know him personally.' (*LJ*, IV, 274–5.)

. . . Originality, as it is the highest and rarest property of genius, is also that which has most charms for the public. Not that originality is always necessary, for the world will be contented, in the poverty of its mental resources, with mere novelty or singularity, and must therefore be enchanted with a work that exhibits both qualities. The vulgar author is usually distinguished by his treading, or attempting to tread, in the steps of the reigning favourite of the day. He is didactic, sentimental, romantic, epic, pastoral, according to the taste of the moment, and his 'fancies and delights', like those of Master Justice Shallow, are sure to be adapted to the tunes *which the carmen whistle*. The consequence is, not that the herd of imitators gain their object, but that the melody which they have profaned becomes degraded in the sated ears of the public—its original richness, wildness and novelty are forgotten when it is made manifest how easily the leading notes can be caught and parodied, and whatever its intrinsic merit may have been, it becomes, for the time, stale and fulsome. If the composition which has been thus hunted down possesses intrinsic merit, it may—indeed it will—eventually revive and claim its proper place amid the poetical galaxy; deprived, indeed, of the adventitious value which it may at first have acquired from its novelty, but at the same time no longer over-shaded and incumbered by the croud of satellites now consigned to chaos and primaeval night. When the success of Burns, writing in his native dialect with unequalled vigour and sweetness, had called from their flails an hundred peasants to cudgel their brains for rhymes, we can well remember that even the bard of Coila was somewhat injured in the common estimation—as a masterpiece of painting is degraded by being placed amid the flaring colours and ill-drawn figures of imitative daubers. The true poet attempts the very reverse of the imitator. He plunges into the stream of public opinion even when its tide is running strongest, crosses its direction, and bears his crown of laurel as Caesar did his imperial mantle, triumphant above the waves. Such a phenomenon seldom fails at first to divide and at length to alter the reigning taste of the period, and if the bold adventurer has successfully buffeted the ebbing tide which bore up his competitor, he soon has the benefit of the flood in his own favour.

In applying these general remarks to Lord Byron's gravest and most serious performance, we must recall to the reader's recollection that since the time of Cowper he has been the first poet who, either in his own person, or covered by no very thick disguise, has directly appeared before the public, an actual living man expressing his own sentiments, thoughts, hopes and fears. Almost all the poets of our day, who have possessed a considerable portion of public attention, are personally little known to the reader, and can only be judged from the passions and feelings assigned by them to persons totally fictitious. Childe Harold appeared—we must not say in the character of *the* author—but certainly in that of a real existing person, with whose feelings as such the public were disposed to associate those of Lord Byron. Whether the reader acted right or otherwise in persisting to neglect the shades of distinction which the author endeavoured to point out betwixt his pilgrim and himself, it is certain that no little power over the public attention was gained from their being identified. Childe Harold may not be, nor do we believe he is, Lord Byron's very self, but he is Lord Byron's picture, sketched by Lord Byron himself, arrayed in a fancy dress, and disguised perhaps by some extrinsic attributes, but still bearing a sufficient resemblance to the original to warrant the conclusion that we have drawn. . . .

But besides the pleasing novelty of a traveller and a poet, throwing before the reader his reflections and opinions, his loves and his hates, his raptures and his sorrows; besides the novelty and pride which the public felt, upon being called as it were into familiarity with a mind so powerful, and invited to witness and partake of its deep emotions; the feelings themselves were of a character which struck with awe those to whom the noble pilgrim thus exposed the sanctuary of his bosom. They were introduced into no Teian paradise of lutes and maidens, were placed in no hall resounding with music and dazzling with many-coloured lights, and called upon to gaze on those gay forms that flutter in the muse's beam. The banquet had ceased, and it was the pleasure of its melancholy lord that his guests should witness that gloominess, which seems most dismal when it succeeds to exuberant and unre-strained gaiety. The emptied wine-cup lay on the ground, the withered garland was flung aside and trodden under foot, the instruments of music were silent, or waked but those few and emphatic chords which express sorrow; while, amid the ruins of what had once been the palace of pleasure, the stern pilgrim stalked from desolation to desolation, spurning from him the implements of former luxury, and repelling with equal scorn the more valuable substitutes which wisdom and philosophy offered to supply their place. The reader felt as it were in the presence of a superior being, when, instead of his judgment being consulted, his imagination excited or soothed, his taste flattered or con-ciliated in order to bespeak his applause, he was told, in strains of the most sublime poetry, that neither he, the courteous reader, nor aught the earth had to shew, was worthy the attention of the noble traveller. —All countries he traversed with a heart for entertaining the beauties of nature, and an eye for observing the crimes and follies of mankind; and from all he drew subjects of sorrow, of indignation, of contempt. From Dan to Beersheba all was barrenness. To despise the ordinary sources of happiness, to turn with scorn from the pleasures which captivate others, and to endure, as it were voluntarily, evils which others are most anxious to shun, is a path to ambition; for the monarch is scarcely more respected for possessing, than the anchoret for con-temning the means of power and of pleasure. A mind like that of Harold, apparently indifferent to the usual enjoyments of life, and which entertains, or at least exhibits, such contempt for its usual pursuits, has the same ready road to the respect of the mass of mankind, who judge that to be superior to humanity which can look down upon its common habits, tastes, and pleasures.

This fashion of thinking and writing of course had its imitators, and those right many. But the humorous sadness which sat so gracefully on the original made but a poor and awkward appearance on those who

—— wrapp'd themselves in Harold's inky cloak,
To show the world how 'Byron' did *not* 'write.'

Their affected melancholy shewed like the cynicism of Apemantus contrasted with the real misanthropy of Timon. And, to say the truth, we are not sorry that the fashion has latterly lost ground. This species of general contempt of intellectual pleasures, and worldly employment, is more closely connected with the Epicurean philosophy than may be at first supposed. If philosophy be but a pursuit of words, and the revolutions of empires inevitable returns of the same cycle of fearful transitions; if our earliest and best affections 'run to waste, and water but the desert', the want of worthier motives to action gives a tremendous and destructive impulse to the dangerous *Carpe diem* of the Garden—that most seductive argument of sensual pleasure. This doctrine of the nothingness of human pursuits, not as contrasted with those of religion and virtue, (to which they are indeed as nothing,) but absolutely and in themselves, is too apt to send its pupils in despair to those pleasures which promise a real gratification, however short and gross. Thus do thoughts and opinions, in themselves the most melancholy, become incitements to the pursuit of the most degrading pleasures; as the Egyptians placed skulls upon their banqueting tables, and as the fools of Holy Writ made the daring and fearful association of imminent fate and present revelling—*Let us eat and drink, for to-morrow we die.* . . .

But it was not merely to the novelty of an author speaking in his own person, and in a tone which arrogated a contempt of all the ordinary pursuits of life, that *Childe Harold* owed its extensive popularity: these formed but the point or sharp edge of the wedge by which the work was enabled to insinuate its way into that venerable block, the British public. The high claims inferred at once in the direct appeal to general attention, and scorn of general feeling, were supported by powers equal to such pretensions. He who despised the world intimated that he had the talents and genius necessary to win it if he had thought it worth while. There was a strain of poetry in which the sense predominated over the sound; there was the eye keen to behold nature, and the pen powerful to trace her varied graces of beauty or terror; there was the heart ardent at the call of freedom or of generous feeling, and belying every moment the frozen shrine in which false philosophy had incased it, glowing like the intense and concentrated alcohol, which remains one single but burning drop in the centre of the ice which its more watery particles have formed. In despite of the character which he had assumed, it was impossible not to see in the Pilgrim what nature designed him to be, and what, in spite of bad metaphysics and worse politics, he may yet be, a person whose high talents the wise and virtuous may enjoy without a qualifying sigh or frown. Should that day arrive, and if time be granted, it will arrive, we who have ventured upon the precarious task of prophecy—we who have been censured for not mingling the faults of genius with its talents —we shall claim our hour of heartfelt exultation. . . .

For ourselves, amid the various attendants on the triumph of genius, we would far rather be the soldier who, pacing by the side of his general, mixes, with military frankness, censure amid his songs of praise, than the slave in the chariot to flatter his vanity by low adulation, or exasperate his feelings by virulent invective. In entering our protest therefore against the justice and the moral tendency of that strain of dissatisfaction and despondency, that cold and sceptical philosophy which clouds our prospects on earth, and closes those beyond it, we willingly render to this extraordinary poem the full praise that genius in its happiest efforts can demand from us.

The plan, if it can be termed so, hovers between that of a descriptive and a philosophical poem. The Pilgrim passes from land to land, alternately describing, musing, meditating, exclaiming, and moralizing; and the reader, partaking of his enthusiasm, becomes almost the partner of his journey. . . .

[Gives outline of the poem, with extracts.]

From the copious specimens which we have given, the reader will be enabled to judge how well the last part of this great poem has sustained Lord Byron's high reputation. Yet we think it possible to trace a marked difference, though none in the tone of thought and expression, betwixt this canto and the first three. There is less of passion, more of deep thought and sentiment, at once collected and general. The stream which in its earlier course bounds over cataracts and rages through narrow and rocky defiles, deepens, expands, and becomes less turbid as it rolls on, losing the aspect of terror and gaining that of sublimity. Eight years have passed between the appearance of the first volume and the present which concludes the work, a lapse of time which, joined with other circumstances, may have contributed somewhat to moderate the tone of Childe Harold's quarrel with the world, and, if not to reconcile him to his lot, to give him, at least, the firmness which endures it without loud complaint.—To return, however, to the proposition with which we opened our criticism, certain it is, that whether as Harold or as Lord Byron no author has ever fixed upon himself personally so intense a share of the public attention. His descriptions of present and existing scenes however striking and beautiful, his recurrence to past actions however important and however powerfully described, become interesting chiefly from the tincture which they receive from the mind of the author. The grot of Egeria, the ruins of the Palatine, are but a theme for his musings, always deep and powerful though sometimes gloomy even to sullenness. This cast of solemnity may not perhaps be justly attributed to the native disposition of the author, which is reported to be as lively as, judging from this single poem at least, we might pronounce it to be grave. But our ideas of happiness are chiefly caught by reflection from the minds of others, and hence it may be observed that those enjoy the most uniform train of good spirits who are thinking much of others and little of themselves. The contemplation of our minds, however salutary for the purposes of self-examination and humiliation, must always be a solemn task, since the best will find enough for remorse, the wisest for regret, the most fortunate for sorrow. And to this influence more than to any natural disposition to melancholy, to the pain which necessarily follows this anatomizing of his own thoughts and feelings which is so decidedly and peculiarly the characteristic of the Pilgrimage, we are disposed in a great measure to ascribe that sombre tint which pervades the poem. The poetry which treats of the actions and sentiments of others may be grave or gay according to the light in which the author chuses to view his subject, but he who shall mine long and deeply for materials in his own bosom will encounter abysses at the depth of which he must necessarily tremble. This moral truth appears to us to afford, in a great measure, a key to the peculiar tone of Lord Byron. How then, will the reader ask, is our proposition to be reconciled to that which preceded it? If the necessary result of an inquiry into our own thoughts be the conviction that all is vanity and vexation of spirit, why should we object to a style of writing, whatever its consequences may be, which involves in it truths as certain as they are melancholy? If the study of our own enjoyments leads us to doubt the reality of all except the indisputable pleasures of sense, and inclines us therefore towards the Epicurean system,—it is nature, it may be said, and not the poet which urges us upon the fatal conclusion. But this is not so. Nature, when she created man a social being, gave him the capacity of drawing that happiness from his relations with the rest of his race, which he is doomed to seek in vain in his own bosom. These relations cannot be the source of happiness to us if we despise or hate the kind with whom it is their office to unite us more closely. If the earth be a den of fools and knaves, from whom the man of genius differs by the more mercurial and exalted character of his intellect, it is natural that he should look down with pitiless scorn on creatures so inferior. But if, as we believe, each man, in his own degree, possesses a portion of the ethereal flame, however smothered by unfavourable circumstances, it is or should be enough to secure the most mean from the scorn of genius as well as from the oppression of power, and such being the case, the relations which we hold with society through all their gradations are channels through which the better affections of the loftiest may, without degradation, extend themselves to the lowest. Farther, it is not only our social connections which are assigned us in order to qualify that contempt of mankind, which too deeply indulged tends only to intense selfishness; we have other and higher motives for enduring the lot of humanity—sorrow, and pain, and trouble—with patience of our own griefs and commiseration for those of others. The wisest and the best of all ages have agreed that our present life is a state of trial, not of enjoyment, and that we now suffer sorrow that we may hereafter be partakers of happiness. If this be true, and it has seldom been long, or at least ultimately, doubted by those who have turned their attention to so serious an investigation, other and worthier motives of action and endurance must necessarily occur to the mind than philosophy can teach or human pride supply. . . .

Our task respecting Lord Byron's poetry is finished, when we have mentioned the subject, quoted passages of superior merit, or which their position renders most capable of being detached from the body of the poem. For the character of his style and versification once distinctly traced, (and we have had repeated occasion to consider it,) cannot again be dwelt on without repetition. The harmony of verse, and the power of numbers, nay, the selection and arrangement of expressions, are all so subordinate to the thought and sentiment, as to become comparatively light in the scale. His poetry is like the oratory which hurries the hearers along without permitting them to pause on its solecisms or singularities. Its general structure is bold, severe, and as it were Doric, admitting few ornaments but those immediately suggested by the glowing imagination of the author, rising and sinking with the tones of his enthusiasm, roughening into argument, or softening into the melody of feeling and sentiment, as if the language fit for either were alike at the command of the poet, and the numbers not only came un-called, but arranged themselves with little care on his part into the varied modulation which the subject requires. Many of the stanzas, considered separately from the rest, might be objected to as involved, harsh, and overflowing into each other beyond the usual license of the Spenserian stanza. But considering the various matter of which the poet had to treat—considering the monotony of a long-continued smoothness of sound, and accurate division of the sense according to the stanzas—considering also that the effect of the general harmony is, as in music, improved by the judicious introduction of discords wherewith it is contrasted, we cannot join with those who state this occasional harshness as an objection to Lord Byron's poetry. If the line sometimes 'labours and the words move slow,' it is in passages where the sense is correspondent to these laborious movements. A highly finished strain of versification resembles a dressed pleasure ground, elegant—even beautiful—but tame and insipid compared to the majesty and interest of a woodland chase, where scenes of natural loveliness are rendered sweeter and more interesting by the contrast of irregularity and wildness.

We have done with the poem; we have, however, yet a few words to say before we finally close our strictures.

To this canto, as to the former, notes are added, illustrative of the contents; and these, we are informed, are written by Mr. Hobhouse, the author of that facetious account of Buonaparte's reign of an hundred days, which it was our office last year to review. They are distinct and classical illustrations of the text, but contain of course many political sentiments of a class which have ceased to excite anger, or any feeling stronger than pity, and a sense of the weakness of humanity which, in all ages, has inclined even men of talents and cultivation to disgrace themselves, by the adoption of sentiments of which it is impossible they can have examined either the grounds or the consequences—whence the doctrines come, or whither they are tending. The mob of a corrupt metropolis, who vindicate the freedom of election by knocking out the brains of the candidate of whom they disapprove, act upon obvious and tangible principles; so do the Spenceans, Spar-fieldians and Nottingham conspirators. That 'seven halfpenny loaves should be sold for a penny', that 'the three-hooped pot should have ten hoops',—and that 'the realm should be all in common',—have been the watch-words of insurrection among the vulgar, from Jack Straw's time to the present, and, if neither honest nor praiseworthy, are at least sufficiently plain and intelligible. But the frenzy which makes individuals of birth and education hold a language as if they could be willing to risk the destruction of their native country, and all the horrors of a civil war, is not so easily accounted for. To believe that these persons would accelerate a desolation in which they themselves directly, or through their nearest and dearest connections, must widely share, merely to remove an obnoxious minister, would be to form a hasty and perhaps a false judgment of them. The truth seems to be, that the English, even those from whom better things might be expected, are born to be the dupes of jugglers and mountebanks in all professions. It is not only in physic that the names of our nobility and gentry decorate occasionally the list of cures to which the empiric appeals as attesting the force of his remedy. Religion, in the last age, and politics in the present, have had their quacks, who substituted words for sense, and theoretical dogmata for the practice of every duty.—But whether in religion, or politics, or physic, one general mark distinguishes the empiric; the patient is to be cured without interruption of business, or pleasure—the proselyte to be saved without reformation of the future, or repentance of the past—the country to be made happy by an alteration in its political system; and all the vice and misery which luxury and poor's rates, a crouded population, and decayed morality can introduce into the community, to be removed by extending farther political rights to those who daily show that they require to be taught the purpose for which those they already enjoy were entrusted to them. That any one above the rank of an interested demagogue should teach this is wonderful—that any should believe it except the lowest of the vulgar is more so—but vanity makes as many dupes as folly.

If, however, these gentlemen will needs identify their own cause with that of their country's enemies, we can forgive them as losers, who have proverbial leave to pout. And when, in bitterness of spirit, they term the great, the glorious victory of Waterloo the 'carnage of Saint Jean',[1] we can forgive that too, since, trained in the school of revolutionary France, they must necessarily abhor those

> ———— whose art was of such power
> It could controul their dam's God Setebos,
> And make a vassal of him.

From the dismal denunciations which Lord Byron, acting more upon his feeling than his judgment, has made against our country, although

> Were ne'er prophetic sounds so full of woe,

we entertain no fears—none whatever.

[1] [Quotation from Byron's dedication of this Canto to Hobhouse.]

At home, the noble author may hear of better things than 'a permanent army and a suspended Habeas Corpus'[1]—he may hear of an improving revenue and increasing public prosperity. And while he continues abroad he may haply call to mind that the Pilgrim, whom, eight years since, the universal domination of France compelled to wander into distant and barbarous countries, is *now* at liberty to travel where he pleases, certain that there is not a corner of the civilized world where his title of Englishman will not ensure him a favourable and respectful reception.

---

[1] [Another quotation from Byron's dedication to Hobhouse.]

21. John Wilson, from his unsigned review, *Edinburgh Review*

Dated June 1818, issued September 1818, XXX, 87–120

For Byron's comment see above p. 137. Wilson also reviewed this canto anonymously for *Blackwood's Magazine*, May 1818. Later, in his 'Detached Thoughts' (15 October 1821), Byron repudiated the comparison between Rousseau and himself: 'I can't see any point of resemblance: he wrote prose, I verse: he was of the people, I of the Aristocracy: he was a philosopher, I am none . . .', etc. (*LJ*, V, 408 f.)

There are two writers, in modern literature, whose extraordinary power over the minds of men, it may be truly said, has existed less in their works than in themselves—Rousseau and Lord Byron. They have other points of resemblance. Both are distinguished by the most ardent and vivid delineations of intense conception, and by an intense sensibility of passion, rather than of affection. Both, too, by this double power, have held a dominion over the sympathy of their readers, far beyond the range of those ordinary feelings which are usually excited by the mere efforts of genius. The impression of this interest still accompanies the perusal of their writings: But there is another interest of more lasting, and far stronger power, which the one has possessed, and the other now possesses,—which lies in the continual embodying of the individual character—it might almost be said, of the very person of the writer. When we speak or think of Rousseau or Byron, we are not conscious of speaking or thinking of an author. We have a vague but empassioned remembrance of men of surpassing genius, eloquence and power,—of prodigious capacity both of misery and happiness. We feel as if we had transiently met such beings in real life, or had known them in the dim and dark communion of a dream. Each of their works presents, in succession, a fresh idea of themselves; and, while the productions of other great men stand out from them, like something they have created, theirs, on the contrary, are images, pictures, busts of their living selves,—clothed, no doubt, at different times in different drapery, and prominent from a different background,—but uniformly impressed with the same form, and mien, and lineaments, and not to be mistaken for the representations of any other of the children of men.

But this view of the subject, though universally felt to be a true one, requires perhaps a little explanation. The personal character of which we have spoken, it should be understood, is not, altogether, that on which the seal of life has been set,—and to which, therefore, moral approval or condemnation is necessarily annexed, as to the language or conduct of actual existence. It is the character, so to speak, which is prior to conduct, and yet open to good and to ill,—the constitution of the being, in body and in soul. Each of those illustrious writers has, in this light, filled his works with expressions of his own character,—has unveiled to the world the secrets of his own being,—the mysteries of the framing of man. They have gone down into those depths which every man may sound for himself, though not for another; and they have made disclosures to the world of what they beheld and knew there—disclosures that have commanded and enforced a profound and universal sympathy, by proving that all mankind, the troubled and the untroubled, the lofty and the low, the strongest and the frailest, are linked together by the bonds of a common but inscrutable nature.

Thus, each of these wayward and richly-gifted spirits has made himself the object of profound interest to the world,—and that too, during periods of society when ample food was everywhere spread abroad for the meditations and passions of men. What love and desire,—what longing and passionate expectation hung upon the voice of Rousseau, the idol of his day!—That spell is broken. We now can regard his works in themselves, in great measure free from all the delusions and illusions that, like the glories of a bright and vapoury atmosphere, were for ever rising up and encircling the image of their wonderful creator. Still is the impression of his works vivid and strong. The charm which cannot pass away is there,—life breathing in dead words,—the pulses of passion,—the thrilling of the frame,—the sweet pleasure stealing from senses touched with ecstasy into sounds which the tongue frames, and the lips utter with delight. All these still are there,—the fresh beauty, the undimmed lustre,—the immortal bloom and verdure and fragrance of life. These, light and vision-like as they seem, endure as in marble. But that which made the spirits of men, from one end of Europe to the other, turn to the name of Rousseau,—that idolizing enthusiasm which we can now hardly conceive, was the illusion of one generation, and has not survived to another. And what was the spell of that illusion? Was it merely that bewitching strain of dreaming melancholy which lent to moral declamation the tenderness of romance? Or that fiery impress of burning sensibility which threw over abstract and subtle disquisitions all the colours of a lover's tale? These undoubtedly—but not these alone. It was that continual impersonation of himself in his writings, by which he was for ever kept brightly present before the eyes of men. There was in him a strange and unsated desire of de-picturing himself, throughout all the changes of his being. His wild temper only found ease in tracing out, in laying bare to the universal gaze, the very groundwork, the most secret paths, the darkest coverts of one of the most wayward and unimaginable minds ever framed by nature. From the moment that his first literary success had wedded him to the public, this was his history,—and such his strange, contradictory, divided life. Shy, and shunning the faces of men in his daily walks, yet searching and rending up the inmost recesses of his heart for the in-spection of that race which he feared or hated. As a man, turning from the light, as from something unsupportably loathsome, and plunging into the thickest shades. Yet, in that other existence which he held from imagination, living only in the presence of men,—in the full broad glare of the world's eye,—and eagerly, impetuously, passionately, un-sparingly seizing on all his own most hidden thoughts—his loneliest moods,—his most sacred feelings,—which had been cherished for the seclusion in which they sprung,—for their own still deep peace,—and for their breathings of unbeheld communions—seizing upon all these, and flinging them out into the open air, that they might feed the curiosity of that eager, idle, frivolous world from which he had fled in misanthropical disgust—that he might array an exhibition to their greedy gaze,—and that he, the morbid and melancholy lover of soli-tude, might act a conspicuous and applauded part on the crowded theatre of public fame.

It might, on a hasty consideration, seem to us, that such undisguised revelation of feelings and passions, which the becoming pride of human nature, jealous of its own dignity, would, in general, desire to hold in unviolated silence, could produce in the public mind only pity, sorrow, or repugnance. But, in the case of men of real genius, like Rousseau or Byron, it is otherwise. Each of us must have been aware in himself of a singular illusion, by which these disclosures, when read with that tender or high interest which attaches to poetry, seem to have something of the nature of private and confidential communications.

They are not felt, while we read, as declarations published to the world,—but almost as secrets whispered to chosen ears. Who is there that feels, for a moment, that the voice which reaches the inmost recesses of his heart is speaking to the careless multitudes around him? Or, if we do so remember, the words seem to pass by others like air, and to find their way to the hearts for whom they were intended,—kindred and sympathizing spirits, who discern and own that secret language, of which the privacy is not violated, though spoken in hearing of the uninitiated,—because it is not understood. There is an unobserved beauty that smiles on us alone; and the more beautiful to us, because we feel as if chosen out from a crowd of lovers. Something analogous to this is felt in the grandest scenes of Nature and of Art. Let a hundred persons look from a hill-top over some transcendent landscape. Each will select from the wide-spread glory at his feet, for his more special love and delight, some different glimpse of sunshine,—or solemn grove,—or embowered spire,—or brown-mouldering ruin,—or castellated cloud. During their contemplation, the soul of each man is amidst its own creations, and in the heart of his own solitude;—nor is the depths of that solitude broken, though it lies open to the sunshine, and before the eyes of unnumbered spectators. It is the same in great and impressive scenes of art,—for example, in a theatre. The tenderest tones of acted tragedy reach our hearts with a feeling as if that inmost soul which they disclose revealed itself to us alone. The audience of a theatre forms a sublime unity to the actor; but each person sees and feels with the same incommunicated intensity, as if all passed only before his own gifted sight. The publicity which is before our eyes is not acknowledged by our minds; and each heart feels itself to be the sole agitated witness of the pageant of misery.

But there are other reasons why we read with complacency writings which, by the most public declaration of most secret feelings, ought, it might seem, to shock and revolt our sympathy. A great poet may address the whole world in the language of intensest passion, concerning objects of which, rather than speak, face to face, with any one human being on earth, he would perish in his misery. For it is in solitude that he utters what is to be wafted by all the winds of heaven. There are, during his inspiration, present with him only the shadows of men. He is not daunted, or perplexed, or disturbed, or repelled by real living breathing features. He can updraw just as much as he chuses of the curtain that hangs between his own solitude and the world of life. He thus pours his soul out, partly to himself alone,—partly to the ideal abstractions, and impersonated images that float round him at his own conjuration,—and partly to human beings like himself, moving in the dark distance of the every-day world. He confesses himself, not before men, but before the Spirit of Humanity. And he thus fearlessly lays open his heart,—assured that nature never prompted unto genius that which will not triumphantly force its wide way into the human heart. We can thus easily imagine the poet whom, in real life, the countenances and voices of his fellowmen might silence into shame, or fastidiousness, or timidity, or aversion or disdain,—yet kindling in his solitude into irrepressible passion and enthusiasm towards human nature and all its transitory concerns,—anxiously moulding himself into the object of men's most engrossing and vehement love or aversion,—identifying his own existence with all their strongest and profoundest passions,—claiming kindred with them, not in their virtues alone, but in their darkest vices and most fatal errors; yet, in the midst of all this, proudly guarding his own prevailing character, so that it shall not merge in the waves of a common nature, but stand 'in shape and gesture proudly eminent', contemplated with still-increasing interest by the millions that, in spite of themselves, feel and acknowledge its strange and unaccountable ascendency.

The reasons then are obvious, why a writer of very vivid sensibilities may, by empassioned self-delineation, hold a wondrous power over the entranced minds of his readers. But this power is in his living hands; and, like the wand of the magician, it loses its virtue on its master's death. We feel chiefly the influence of such a writer, while he lives— our cotemporary—going with us a fellow-voyager on the stream of life, and from time to time flashing towards us the emanations of his spirit. Our love—our expectation follow the courses of his mind, and, if his life repel us not, the courses of his life. It was the strange madness of Rousseau to pour the blaze of his reputation over the scandals of his life. But this was later in his career; and his name for a long time in Europe was that of an hermit-sage,—a martyr of liberty and virtue,— a persecuted good man loving a race unworthy of him, and suffering alike from their injustice and from the excess of his own spirit. He made a character for himself;—and whatever he had made it, it might have been believed. It was an assumed ideal impersonation of a character of literary and philosophical romance. At last, indeed, he broke up his own spell. But if he could have left the delusion behind him, he could not have left the power;—for the power hangs round the living man: it does not rest upon the grave.

When death removes such a writer from our sight, the magical influence of which we have spoken gradually fades away; and a new generation, free from all personal feelings towards the idol of a former age, may perhaps be wearied with that perpetual self-reference which to them seems merely the querulousness or the folly of unhappy or diseased egoism. It is even probable, that they may perversely withhold a portion of just admiration and delight from him who was once the undisputed sovereign of the soul, and that they may show their surprise at the subjection of their predecessors beneath the tyrannical despotism of genius, by scorning themselves to bow before its power, or acknowledge its legitimacy. It is at least certain, that by the darkness of death such luminaries, if not eclipsed, are shorn of their beams. So much, even in their works of most general interest, derives its beauty and fascination from a vivid feeling, in the reader's mind, of its being a portraiture of one with whom he has formed a kind of strange, wild and disturbed friendship, that they who come after, and have never felt the sorcery of the living man, instead of being kindled up by such pictures into impassioned wonder and delight, may gaze on them with no stronger emotion than curiosity, and even turn from them with indifference. Such must be more or less the fate of all works of genius, however splendid and powerful, of which the chief interest is not in universal truth, so much as in the intensity of individual feeling, and the impersonation of individual character.

It would, indeed, be in most violent contradiction to all we have formerly written of Lord Byron, were we to say that he stands in this predicament. Yet, there is a certain applicability of our observations even to him, as well as to Rousseau, with whom, perhaps too fancifully, we have now associated his nature and his name. Posterity may make fewer allowances for much in himself and his writings, than his contemporaries are willing to do; nor will they, with the same passionate and impetuous zeal, follow the wild voice that too often leads into a haunted wilderness of doubt and darkness. To them, as to us, there will always be something majestic in his misery—something sublime in his despair. But they will not, like us, be withheld from sterner and severer feelings, and from the more frequent visitings of moral condemnation, by that awful commiseration and sympathy which a great poet breathes at will into all hearts, from his living agonies,—nor, by that restless, and watchful, and longing anxiety, to see again and again the princely sufferer rising up with fresh confessions of a still more magnificent sorrow,—nor, by that succession of affecting appeals to the frailties and troubles of our own hearts, which now keeps him vividly, and brightly, in our remembrance, wherever his soul, tempest-like, may have driven him over earth and sea,—nor, above all, by the cheering and lofty hope now felt by them who wish to see genius the inseparable companion of virtue,—that he whose inspiration holds us always in wonder, and so often in delight, may come ere long to breath a serener atmosphere of thought,—and, after all his wanderings, and all his woes,—with sub-sided passions, and invigorated intellect, calmly rest at last in the collected majesty of his power.

We are not now writing a formal critique on the genius of Byron, but rather expressing our notions of the relation in which he stands with the lovers of poetry. There is felt to be between him and the public mind, a stronger personal bond than ever linked its movements to any other living poet. And we think that this bond will in future be still more closely rivetted. During the composition of the first cantos of *Childe Harold*, he had but a confused idea of the character he wished to delineate,—nor did he perhaps very distinctly comprehend the scope and tendencies of his own genius. Two conceptions, distinct from each other, seem therein to be often blended,—one, of ideal human beings, made up of certain troubled powers and passions,—and one, of himself ranging the world of Nature and Man in wonder and delight and agitation, in his capacity of a poet. These conceptions, which frequently jostled and interfered with each other, he has since more distinctly un-folded in separate poems. His troubled imaginary beings,—possessing much of himself, and far more not of himself, he has made into Giaours, Conrads, Laras and Alps,—and his conception of himself has been expanded into Childe Harold, as we now behold him on that splendid pilgrimage. It is not enough to say that the veil is at last thrown off. It is a nobler creature who is before us. The ill-sustained mis-anthropy, and disdain of the two first Cantos, more faintly glimmer throughout the third, and may be said to disappear wholly from the fourth, which reflects the high and disturbed visions of earthly glory, as a dark swollen tide images the splendours of the sky in portentous colouring, and broken magnificence.

We have admitted, that much of himself is depicted in all his heroes; but when we seem to see the poet shadowed out in all those states of disordered being which such heroes exhibit, we are far from believing that his own mind has gone through those states of disorder, in its own experience of life. We merely conceive of it as having felt within itself the capacity of such disorders, and therefore exhibiting itself before us in possibility. This is not general—it is rare with great poets. Neither Homer, nor Shakspeare, nor Milton, ever so show themselves in the characters which they portray. Their poetical personages have no reference to themselves; but are distinct, independent creatures of their minds, produced in the full freedom of intellectual power. In Byron, there does not seem this freedom of power. There is little appropriation of character to events. Character is first, and all in all. It is dictated— compelled by some force in his own mind necessitating him,—and the events obey. These poems, therefore, with all their beauty and vigour, are not, like Scott's poems, full and complete narrations of some one definite story, containing within itself a picture of human life. They are merely bold, confused, and turbulent exemplifications of certain sweeping energies and irresistible passions. They are fragments of a poet's dark dream of life. . . .

22. Percy Bysshe Shelley and Thomas Love Peacock on Byronic misanthropy

1818

(a) In his Preface to *The Revolt of Islam* (January 1818) Shelley (1792–1822) had already given his diagnosis of the causes of melancholy and misanthropy in contemporary literature: '. . . Methinks, those who now live have survived an age of despair.

The French Revolution may be considered as one of those manifestations of a general state of feeling among civilized mankind, produced by a defect of correspondence between the knowledge existing in society and the improvement or gradual abolition of political institutions. The year 1788 may be assumed as the epoch of one of the most important crises produced by this feeling. The sympathies connected with that event extended to every bosom. The most generous and amiable natures were those which participated the most extensively in these sympathies. But such a degree of unmingled good was expected, as it was impossible to realize. If the Revolution had been in every respect prosperous, then misrule and superstition would lose half their claims to our abhorrence, as fetters which the captive can unlock with the slightest motion of his fingers, and which do not eat with poisonous rust into the soul. The revulsion occasioned by the atrocities of the demagogues and the re-establishment of successive tyrannies in France was terrible, and felt in the remotest corner of the civilized world. Could they listen to the plea of reason who had groaned under the calamities of a social state, according to the provisions of which, one man riots in luxury while another famishes for want of bread? Can he who the day before was a trampled slave, suddenly become liberal-minded, forbearing, and independent? This is the consequence of the habits of a state of society to be produced by resolute perseverance and indefatigable hope, and long-suffering and long believing courage, and the systematic efforts of generations of men of intellect and virtue. Such is the lesson which experience teaches now. But, on the first reverses of hope in the progress of French liberty, the sanguine eagerness for good overleapt the solution of these questions, and for a time extinguished itself in the unexpectedness of their result.

Thus many of the most ardent and tender-hearted of the worshippers of public good have been morally ruined by what a partial glimpse of the events they deplored, appeared to show as the melancholy desolation of all their cherished hopes. Hence gloom and misanthropy have become the characteristics of the age in which we live, the solace of a disappointment that unconsciously finds relief only in the wilful exaggeration of its own despair. This influence has tainted the literature of the age with the hopelessness of the minds from which it flows. Metaphysics, and enquiries into moral and political science, have become little else than vain attempts to revive exploded superstitions, or sophisms like those of Mr. Malthus, calculated to lull the oppressors of mankind into a security of everlasting triumph. Our works of fiction and poetry have been overshadowed by the same infectious gloom. But mankind appear to me to be emerging from their trance. I am aware, methinks, of a slow, gradual, silent change.' (*The Complete Works of Percy Bysshe Shelley*, ed. Roger Ingpen and W. E. Peck, 1965, I, 241–2.)

(*b*) Shelley's admiration for Byron's genius was clouded for a time by disillusion at his way of life, and when Peacock (1785–1866) criticized the wilful misanthropy and gloom of *Childe Harold's Pilgrimage* Canto IV, Shelley replied in a letter of 17 or 18 December 1818: 'I entirely agree with what you say about *Childe Harold*. The spirit in which it is written is, if insane, the most wicked & mischievous insanity that ever was given forth. It is a kind of obstinate & selfwilled folly in which he hardens himself. I remonstrated with him in vain on the tone of mind from which such a view of things alone arises. For its real root is very different from its apparent one, & nothing can be less sublime than the true source of these expressions of contempt & desperation. The fact is, that first, the Italian women are perhaps the most contemptible of all who exist under the moon; the most ignorant, the most disgusting, the most bigotted, the most filthy. Countesses smell so of garlick that an ordinary Englishman cannot approach them. Well, L[ord] B[yron] is familiar with the lowest sort of these women, the people his *gondolieri* pick up in the streets. He allows fathers & mothers to bargain with him for their daughters, & though this is common enough in Italy, yet for an Englishman to encourage such sickening vice is a melancholy thing. He associates with wretches who seem almost to have lost the gait & phisiognomy of man, & who do not scruple to avow practices which are not only not named but I believe seldom even conceived in England. He says he dissapproves [*sic*], but he endures. He is not yet an Italian &

is heartily & deeply discontented with himself, & contemplating in the distorted mirror of his own thoughts, the nature & the destiny of man, what can he behold but objects of contempt & despair? But that he is a great poet, I think the address to Occan proves.' (*The Letters of Percy Bysshe Shelley*, ed. F. L. Jones, 1964, II, 57–8.)

(c) In *Nightmare Abbey* (1818), Peacock's object, he told Shelley in a letter of 15 September, was 'to bring to a sort of philosophical focus a few of the morbidities of modern literature, and to let in a little day-light on its atrabilarious complexion.' (*Letters of Percy Bysshe Shelley*, II, 30n.) Byron figures as Mr. Cypress, whose utterances consist largely of parodic quotations from *Childe Harold* Canto IV; but the satire extends, as the following extracts suggest, to the whole fashion for melancholy and misanthropy in poetry:

[i]   MR. FLOSKY

It is very certain ... that our literature is hag-ridden. Tea has shattered our nerves; late dinners make us slaves of indigestion; the French Revolution has made us shrink from the name of philosophy, and has destroyed, in the more refined part of the community, (of which number I am one,) all enthusiasm for political liberty. That part of the *reading public* which shuns the solid food of reason for the light diet of fiction, requires a perpetual adhibition of *sauce piquante* to the palate of its depraved imagination. It lived upon ghosts, goblins, and skeletons ... till even the devil himself, though magnified to the size of Mount Athos, became too base, common, and popular, for its sur-feited appetite. The ghosts have therefore been laid, and the devil has been cast into outer darkness, and now the delight of our spirits is to dwell on all the vices and blackest passions of our nature, tricked out in a masquerade dress of heroism and disappointed benevolence: the whole secret of which lies in forming combinations that contradict all our experience, and affixing the purple shred of some particular virtue to that precise character, in which we should be most certain not to find it in the living world; and making this single virtue not only redeem all the real and manifest vices of the character, but make them actually pass for necessary adjuncts, and indispensable accompaniments and characteristics of the said virtue. ...

                         MARIONETTA

I do not precisely enter into your meaning, Mr. Flosky, and should be glad if you would make it a little more plain to me.

MR. FLOSKY

One or two examples will do it, Miss O'Carroll. If I were to take all the mean and sordid qualities of a little Jew broker, and tack on to them, as with a nail, the quality of extreme benevolence, I should have a very decent hero for a modern novel, and should contribute my quota to the fashionable method of administering a mass of vice, under a thin and unnatural covering of virtue, like a spider wrapt in a bit of gold leaf, and administered as a wholesome pill. On the same principle, if a man knocks me down, and takes my purse and watch by main force, I turn him to account, and set him forth in a tragedy as a dashing young fellow, disinherited for his romantic generosity, and full of a most amiable hatred of the world in general and his own country in particular, and of a most enlightened and chivalrous affection for himself: then, with the addition of a wild girl to fall in love with him, and a series of adventures in which they break all the Ten Commandments in succession, (always, you will observe, for some sublime motive, which must be carefully analysed in its progress,) I have as amiable a pair of tragic characters as ever issued from that new region of the belles lettres which I have called the Morbid Anatomy of Black Bile, and which is greatly to be admired and rejoiced at, as affording a fine scope for the exhibition of mental power.' (*Nightmare Abbey*, 1818, pp. 76—80.)

[ii]   #### THE HONORABLE MR. LISTLESS
You are pleased to be severe upon our fashionable belles lettres.

MR. ASTERIAS

Surely not without reason, when pirates, highwaymen, and other varieties of the extensive genus Marauder, are the only *beau idéal* of the active, as splenetic and railing misanthropy is of the speculative energy. A gloomy brow and a tragical voice seem to have been, of late, the characteristics of fashionable manners; and a morbid, withering, deadly, antisocial sirocco, loaded with moral and political despair, breathes through all the groves and valleys of the modern Parnassus. . . .

MR. HILARY

. . . Misanthropy is sometimes the product of disappointed benevolence; but it is more frequently the offspring of overweening and mortified vanity, quarrelling with the world for not being better treated than it deserves. (*op. cit.*, pp. 98—9, 105.)

DON JUAN

Cantos I and II	July 1819
Cantos III, IV and V	August 1821
Cantos VI, VII and VIII	July 1823
Cantos IX, X and XI	August 1823
Cantos XII, XIII and XIV	December 1823
Cantos XV and XVI	March 1824

23. Some reactions to Cantos I and II

1818–21

(a) JOHN CAM HOBHOUSE, extracts from Diary (*Recollections of a Long Life*, ed. Lady Dorchester, London, 1909–11, II, 107, 109–11):

'[27 December 1818] S. B. Davies breakfasted with me. We read the poems. I have my doubts about *Don Juan*; the blasphemy and bawdry and the domestic facts overpower even the great genius it displays. Of *Mazeppa* and the "Ode" [on Venice], I do not think much. Murray called and wanted to advertise at once. I told him I was not sure about the publication.'

'[29 December 1818] I called on Hookham Frere, and had a long conversation with him about Byron's *Don Juan*. He was decisively against publication, and gave some excellent reasons. First, "A friend of freedom should be a friend to morality." Second, there was preparing a convulsion between the religionists and free-thinkers. The first would triumph and the latter be extirpated with their works. ... He said that Byron should not attack his wife, because she and her family forbore all attack as he could witness. ...'

'[8 January 1819] I wrote a long letter to Byron advising him not to publish *Don Juan*. Sent it on Tuesday, having read it to Murray and to Kinnaird, and part to Davies. All agree with me, and Frere said stronger things to Murray than he did to me. The attacks on the wife, the bawdry and the blasphemy, as it is called, are the reasons. I trust he will listen to me. It is a very ticklish affair, and most likely Byron will refer to Rogers or to Moore, who, being bepraised therein, will advise publication.'

'[1 February 1819] Tom Moore breakfasted with me and read *Don Juan*. He perfectly agreed with me it could not be published, and told me to tell Byron his opinion.'

'[21 April 1819] Byron has written to Murray resolving on publication, and to me; also a second canto of *Don Juan* sent.'

'[1 May 1819] *Don Juan* going through the press. I do not think it so bad or so good as I did, not so indecent or so clever.'

(*b*) PERCY BYSSHE SHELLEY. Extracts from letters:
(i) 8 October 1818, to Thomas Love Peacock: 'He [Byron] read me the first canto of his *Don Juan* a thing in the style of *Beppo*, but infinitely better, & dedicated to Southey in ten or a dozen stanzas more like a mixture of wormwood & verdigrease than satire. The poor wretch will writhe under the lash.' (*The Letters of Percy Bysshe Shelley*, ed. F. L. Jones, 1964, II, 42.)

(ii) 26 May 1820, to Lord Byron: 'I have read your *Don Juan* in print, and I observe that the *murrain* has killed some of the finest of the flock, i.e. that your bookseller has omitted certain passages. The personal ones, however, though I thought them wonderfully strong, I do not regret. What a strange and terrible storm is that at sea, and the two fathers, how true, yet how strong a contrast! Dante hardly exceeds it. With what flashes of divine beauty have you not illuminated the familiarity of your subject towards the end! The love letter, and the account of its being written, is altogether a masterpiece of portraiture; of human nature laid with the eternal colours of the feeling of humanity. Where did you learn all these secrets? I should like to go to school there. I cannot say I equally approve of the service to which this letter was appropriated; or that I altogether think the bitter mocking of our common nature, of which this is one of the expressions, quite worthy of your genius. The power and the beauty and the wit, indeed, redeem all this—chiefly because they belie and refute it. Perhaps it is foolish to wish that there had been nothing to redeem.' (*Op. cit.*, II, 198.)

(*c*) A glimpse of fashionable opinion is provided by the Hon. Mrs. George Lamb, in a letter of 31 July 1819, to Augustus Foster: 'The Noels and Lady Byron are my only acquaintances here, but as I am very fond of the latter, it satisfies me. She has been very much abused in Lord Byron's new poem of *Don Juan* under the name of Donna Inez. It is very bad in him, and the whole poem is in a very bad style, improper, and flippant, and very odious, but it is reckoned clever.' (Vere Foster, *The Two Duchesses*, 1898, p. 430.)

(*d*) WILLIAM GIFFORD. Extracts from letters (Samuel Smiles, *A Publisher and his Friends*, 1891, I, 403–4):

(i) 1 July 1819, to John Murray: 'Lord B.'s letter is shockingly amusing. He must be mad; but then there's method in his madness. I dread however, the end. He is, or rather might be, the most extraordinary character of his age. I have lived to see three great men—men to whom none come near in their respective provinces—Pitt, Nelson, Wellington. Morality and religion would have placed our friend among them as the fourth boast of the time; even a decent respect for the good opinion of mankind might have done much now; but all is tending to displace him.'

(ii) [?] July 1819, to John Murray: 'How goes on, or rather how goes off, the Don? I read the second canto this morning, and lost all patience at seeing so much beauty so wantonly and perversely disfigured. A little care, and a little wish to do right, would have made this a superlative thing. As it is, it is better than any other could have done; but this is poor praise for Lord Byron. What a store of shame and sorrow is he laying up for himself! I never much admired the vaunt of Draconianism, "And all this I dare do, because I dare," yet what but this is Lord Byron's plea!'

(*e*) JOHN WILSON CROKER. Extracts from letters (*The Croker Papers. The Correspondence and Diaries of . . . John Wilson Croker*, ed. L. L. Jennings, 1884, I, 145–6):

(i) 18 July 1819, to John Murray: 'I am agreeably disappointed at finding *Don Juan* very little offensive. It is by no means worse than *Childe Harold*, which it resembles as comedy does tragedy. There is a prodigious power of versification in it, and a great deal of very good pleasantry. There is also some magnificent poetry, and the shipwreck, though too long, and in parts very disgusting, is on the whole finely described. In short, I think it will not lose him any character as a poet, and, on the score of morality, I confess it seems to me a more innocent production than *Childe Harold*. What *Don Juan* may become by-and-bye I cannot foresee, but at present I had rather a son of mine

were Don Juan than, I think, any other of Lord Byron's heroes.
Heaven grant he may never resemble any of them.'
(ii) 15 September 1819, to John Murray: 'I told you from the first
moment that I read *Don Juan*, that your fears had exaggerated its
danger. I say nothing about what may have been suppressed; but if
you had published *Don Juan* without hesitation or asterisks, nobody
would ever have thought worse of it than as a larger *Beppo*, gay and
lively and a little loose. Some persons would have seen a strain of
satire running beneath the gay surface, and might have been vexed or
pleased according to their temper; but there would have been no
outcry either against the publisher or author.'

(*f*) A view from the *demi-monde* is provided by Harriette Wilson
(1786–1846), the famous Regency courtesan, who wrote to Byron
from Paris in a letter of 1820, dated 'exactly 20 minutes past 12 o'clock
at night': '. . . Strange to tell, I never heard of *Don Juan* till I found it
on Galignani's table yesterday and took it to bed with me, where
I contrived to keep my large *quiet* good-looking brown eyes
open (now, you *know*, they are very handsome) till I had finished
it.

Dear *Adorable* Lord Byron, *don't* make a mere *coarse* old libertine of
yourself. When everybody advised you not to publish your *English
Bards*, you would mind nobody. *I am nobody*: therefore attend to me.
What harm did the Commandments (no matter by whom composed,
whether god or mortal) ever do you or anybody else, and what
catch-penny ballad writer could not make a parody on them? When
you don't feel quite up to a spirit of benevolence, the encouragement
of which you are pretty sure contributes more to one's earthly happiness
than anything else, in *gratitude* for the talent which, after all, must have
caused you exquisite moments in your time, throw away your pen,
my love, and take a little *calomel*. I wish the Deuce had all the paper,
pens and ink burning, frizzling and drying up in the very hottest place
in his dominions, rather than *you* should use them to wilfully destroy
the respect and admiration of those who deserve to love you and all
the fine illusions with which my mind was filled. Ecoutez, mon Ange.[1]
It is not in my power or in my nature to forget any kindness shown
me (supposing I had not half loved you before) but I would not, even
to *you*, who in a wrong-headed moment wrote it, lie under the
imputation of such bad taste as to admire what in your cool moments,

[1] ['Listen, my angel.']

I am sure, you must feel to be *vulgar* at least. . . .' (George Paston and Peter Quennell, *To Lord Byron*, 1939, pp. 159–60.)

(*g*) Keats had referred to *Don Juan*, in a letter of 18 September 1819, as 'Lord Byron's last flash poem': this was on hearing extracts from it read from a magazine. (*The Letters of John Keats*, ed. H. E. Rollins, Cambridge [Mass.] 1958, II, 192.) His comments of October 1820 were reported, possibly with some distortion, by Joseph Severn in 1845: 'When we had passed the bay of Biscay where we had been in danger & great fright from a storm of three days—Keats took up Ld Byrons *Don Juan* accidentally as one of the books he had brought from England & singular enough he opened on the description of the Storm, which is evidently taken from the Medusa frigate & which the taste of Byron tryes to make a jest of—Keats threw down the book & exclaimed, "this gives me the most horrid idea of human nature, that a man like Byron should have exhausted all the pleasures of the world so compleatly that there was nothing left for him but to laugh & gloat over the most solemn & heart-rending since [i.e. scenes] of human misery this storm of his is one of the most diabolical attempts ever made upon our sympathies, and I have no doubt it will fascenate thousands into extreem obduracy of heart—the tendency of Byrons poetry is based on a paltry originality, that of being new by making solemn things gay & gay things solemn. . . ." ' (*The Keats Circle: Letters and Papers 1814–1879*, ed. H. E. Rollins, 2nd edn., Cambridge [Mass.], 1965, II, 134.)

(*h*) Extract from letter from Wordsworth, probably to Henry Crabb Robinson. Sir Charles Firth argues from internal evidence that this letter was written in January 1820. (The *Quarterly*'s 'hunting down' of Shelley had taken the form of a severe review of *The Revolt of Islam* in the number for April 1819.) '. . . You will probably see Gifford, the Editor of the *Quarterly Review*; tell him from me, if you think proper, that every true-born Englishman will regard the pretensions of the Review to the character of a faithful defender of the institutions of the country, as *hollow*, while it leaves that infamous publication *Don Juan* unbranded; I do not mean by a formal Critique, for it is not worth it; it would also tend to keep it in memory; but by some decisive words of reprobation, both as to the damnable tendency of such works, and as to [the] despicable quality of the powers requisite for their production. What avails it to hunt down Shelley, whom few read, and leave Byron untouched?

I am persuaded that *Don Juan* will do more harm to the English character, than anything of our time; not so much as a *Book*;—But thousands who would be afraid to have it in that shape, will batten upon choice bits of it, in the shape of Extracts. . . .' (*The Correspondence of Henry Crabb Robinson with the Wordsworth Circle*, ed. Edith J. Morley, 1927, II, 850-1.)

(*i*) WILLIAM BLACKWOOD (1776-1834), the Edinburgh publisher (and proprietor of *Blackwood's Edinburgh Magazine.*) Extract from letter of 19 June 1821, to 'Ralph Tuckett Scott' [i.e. William Maginn]: '. . . I do most cordially agree with you that *I* deserve quizzing for refusing to sell *Don Juan*. . . . The only apology I have to offer *you* is this, that it proceeded partly from pique and partly from principle. When the book was published by Murray, I was just on the point of breaking with him. I had not had a letter from him for some months. He sent me copies of the book per mail, without either letter or invoice, so that when I received them I was not disposed to read it with a favourable eye. I did read it, and I declare solemnly to you, much as I admired the talent and genius displayed in it, I never in my life was so filled with utter disgust. It was not the grossness or blackguardism which struck me, but it was the vile, heartless, and cold-blooded way in which this fiend attempted to degrade every tender and sacred feeling of the human heart. I felt such a revolting at the whole book after I had finished it, that I was glad of the excuse I had, from Mr. Murray not writing me, for refusing to sell it. I was terribly laughed at by my friends here, and I daresay you will laugh as much still at my prudery and pique.' (Mrs. Oliphant, *Annals of a Publishing House: William Blackwood and his Sons*, 1897, I, 380-1.)

(*j*) GOETHE. Extract from review of *Don Juan* written in 1819 but not published until 1821: '*Don Juan* is a work of boundless genius, manifesting the bitterest and most savage hatred of humanity, and then again penetrated with the deepest and tenderest love for mankind. And as we already know and esteem the author and would not have him other than he is, we gratefully enjoy what with excessive licence, nay with audacity, he dares to set before us. The technical handling of the verse is quite in harmony with the strange, wild, ruthless content; the poet spares his language as little as he spares humanity; and as we approach closer we become aware that English poetry is already in possession of something we Germans totally lack: a cultured comic language.' (*Goethes Werke*, Weimar, 1888–1919, XLI.I, 245–9. Passage translated by E. M. Butler, *Byron and Goethe*, 1956, p. 49.)

24. *Blackwood's Magazine*'s 'Remarks on Don Juan'

August 1819, V, 512–18

In its number for July 1819 *Blackwood's* noted the receipt of a copy of *Don Juan*, with the comment: 'It is indeed truly pitiable to think that one of the greatest Poets of the age should have written a Poem that no respectable Bookseller could have published without disgracing himself—but a Work so atrocious must not be suffered to pass into oblivion without the infliction of that punishment on its guilty author due to such a wanton outrage on all most dear to human nature.' (*Blackwood's Magazine*, V, 483.) The 'Remarks' in the August number, which fulfil this threat, have been tentatively ascribed to John Wilson or John Gibson Lockhart (*John Bull's Letter to Lord Byron*, ed. A. L. Strout, Norman [Oklahoma], 1947, p. 118; A. L. Strout, *A Bibliography of Articles in Blackwood's Magazine 1817–1825*, Lubbock [Texas], 1959, p. 42). Byron was much annoyed by the review: 'I like and admire Wilson,' he told Murray, 'and *he* should not have indulged himself in such outrageous licence: it is overdone and defeats itself. What would he say to the grossness without passion, and the misanthropy without feeling, of *Gulliver's Travels*? When he talks of Lady Byron's business, he talks of what he knows nothing about. . . .' (*LJ*, IV, 384–5.) The attack provoked him to write his own defence, 'Some Observations upon an Article in *Blackwood's Magazine*,' dated 15 March 1820, and circulated in MS or proof by Murray, but not published in Byron's lifetime. (*LJ*, IV, 474–95.)

It has not been without much reflection and overcoming many reluctancies, that we have at last resolved to say a few words more to our readers concerning this very extraordinary poem. The nature and causes of our difficulties will be easily understood by those of them who have read any part of *Don Juan*—but we despair of standing justified as to the conclusion at which we have arrived, in the opinion of any but those who have read and understood the whole of a work, in the composition of which there is unquestionably a more thorough and intense infusion of genius and vice—power and profligacy—than in any poem which had ever before been written in the English, or indeed in any other modern language. Had the wickedness been less inextricably mingled with the beauty and the grace, and the strength of a most inimitable and incomprehensible muse, our task would have been easy: But SILENCE would be a very poor and a very useless chastisement to be inflicted by us, or by any one, on a production, whose corruptions have been so effectually embalmed—which, in spite of all that critics can do or refrain from doing, nothing can possibly prevent from taking a high place in the literature of our country, and remaining to all ages a perpetual monument of the exalted intellect, and the depraved heart, of one of the most remarkable men to whom that country has had the honour and the disgrace of giving birth.

That Lord Byron has never written any thing more decisively and triumphantly expressive of the greatness of his genius, will be allowed by all who have read this poem. That (laying all its manifold and grievous offences for a moment out of our view) it is by far the most admirable specimen of the mixture of ease, strength, gayety, and seriousness extant in the whole body of English poetry, is a proposition to which, we are almost as well persuaded, very few of them will refuse their assent. With sorrow and humiliation do we speak it—the poet has devoted his powers to the worst of purposes and passions; and it increases his guilt and our sorrow, that he has devoted them entire. What the immediate effect of the poem may be on contemporary literature, we cannot pretend to guess—too happy could we hope that its lessons of boldness and vigour in language, and versification, and conception, might be attended to, as they deserve to be—without any stain being suffered to fall on the purity of those who minister to the general shape and culture of the public mind, from the mischievous insults against all good principle and all good feeling, which have been unworthily embodied in so many elements of fascination.

The moral strain of the whole poem is pitched in the lowest key—and if the genius of the author lifts him now and then out of his pollution, it seems as if he regretted the elevation, and made all haste to descend again. To particularize the offences committed in its pages would be worse than vain—because the great genius of the man seems to have been throughout exerted to its utmost strength, in devising every possible method of pouring scorn upon every element of good or noble nature in the hearts of his readers. Love—honour—patriotism—religion, are mentioned only to be scoffed at and derided, as if their sole resting-place were, or ought to be, in the bosoms of fools. It appears, in short, as if this miserable man, having exhausted every species of sensual gratification—having drained the cup of sin even to its bitterest dregs, were resolved to shew us that he is no longer a human being, even in his frailties,—but a cool unconcerned fiend, laughing with a detestable glee over the whole of the better and worse elements of which human life is composed—treating well nigh with equal derision the most pure of virtues, and the most odious of vices—dead alike to the beauty of the one, and the deformity of the other—a mere heartless despiser of that frail but noble humanity, whose type was never exhibited in a shape of more deplorable degradation than in his own contemptuously distinct delineation of himself. To confess in secret to his Maker, and weep over in secret agonies the wildest and most phantastic transgressions of heart and mind, is the part of a conscious sinner, in whom sin has not become the sole principle of life and action—of a soul for which there is yet hope. But to lay bare to the eye of man and of *woman* all the hidden convulsions of a wicked spirit—thoughts too abominable, we would hope, to have been imagined by any but him that has expressed them—and to do all this without one symptom of pain, contrition, remorse, or hesitation, with a calm careless ferociousness of contented and satisfied depravity—this was an insult which no wicked man of genius had ever before dared to put upon his Creator or his Species. This highest of all possible exhibitions of self-abandonment has been set forth in mirth and gladness, by one whose name was once pronounced with pride and veneration by every English voice. This atrocious consummation was reserved for Byron.

It has long been sufficiently manifest, that this man is devoid of religion. At times, indeed, the power and presence of the Deity, as speaking in the sterner workings of the elements, seems to force some momentary consciousness of their existence into his labouring breast;—a spirit in which there breathes so much of the divine, cannot always resist the majesty of its Maker. But of true religion terror is a small part—and of all religion, that founded on mere terror, is the least worthy of such a man as Byron. We may look in vain through all his works for the slightest evidence that his soul had ever listened to the *gentle voice* of the oracles. His understanding has been subdued into conviction by some passing cloud; but his heart has never been touched. He has never written one line that savours of the spirit of meekness. His faith is but for a moment—'he believes and trembles,' and relapses again into his gloom of unbelief—a gloom in which he is at least as devoid of Hope and Charity as he is of Faith.—The same proud hardness of heart which makes the author of *Don Juan* a despiser of the Faith for which his fathers bled, has rendered him a scorner of the better part of woman; and therefore it is that his love poetry is a continual insult to the beauty that inspires it. The earthy part of the passion is all that has found a resting place within his breast—His idol is all of clay—and he dashes her to pieces almost in the moment of his worship. Impiously railing against his God—madly and meanly disloyal to his Sovereign and his country,—and brutally outraging all the best feelings of female honour, affection, and confidence—How small a part of chivalry is that which remains to the descendant of the Byrons—a gloomy vizor, and a deadly weapon!

Of these offences, however, or of such as these, Lord Byron had been guilty abundantly before, and for such he has before been rebuked in our own, and in other more authoritative pages. There are other and newer sins with which the author of *Don Juan* has stained himself— sins of a class, if possible, even more despicable than any he had before committed; and in regard to which it is matter of regret to us, that as yet our periodical critics have not appeared to express themselves with any seemly measure of manly and candid indignation.

Those who are acquainted, (as who is not?) with the main incidents in the private life of Lord Byron,—and who have not seen this production, (and we are aware, that very few of our Northern readers have seen it),—will scarcely believe, that the odious malignity of this man's bosom should have carried him so far, as to make him commence a filthy and impious poem, with an elaborate satire on the character and manners of his wife—from whom, even by his own confession, he has been separated only in consequence of his own cruel and heartless misconduct. It is in vain for Lord Byron to attempt in any way to justify his own behaviour in that affair; and, now that he has so openly and audaciously invited inquiry and reproach, we do not see any good reason why he should not be plainly told so by the general voice of his countrymen. It would not be an easy matter to persuade any Man who has any knowledge of the nature of Woman, that a female such as Lord Byron has himself described his wife to be, would rashly, or hastily, or lightly separate herself, from the love which she had once been inspired for such a man as he is, or was. Had he not heaped insult upon insult, and scorn upon scorn—had he not forced the iron of his contempt into her very soul—there is no woman of delicacy and virtue, as he *admitted* Lady Byron to be, who would not have hoped all things and suffered all things from one, her love of whom must have been inwoven with so many exalting elements of delicious pride, and more delicious humility. To offend the love of such a woman was wrong—but it might be forgiven; to desert her was unmanly—but he might have returned and wiped for ever from her eyes the tears of her desertion;—but to injure, and to desert, and then to turn back and wound her widowed privacy with unhallowed strains of cold-blooded mockery—was brutally, fiendishly, inexpiably mean. For impurities there might be some possibility of pardon, were they supposed to spring only from the reckless buoyancy of young blood and fiery passions,—for impiety there might at least be pity, were it visible that the misery of the impious soul were as great as its darkness;—but for offences such as this, which cannot proceed either from the madness of sudden impulse, or the bewildered agonies of self-perplexing and self-despairing doubt—but which speak the wilful and determined spite of an unrepenting, unsoftened, smiling, sarcastic, joyous sinner—for such diabolical, such slavish vice, there can be neither pity nor pardon. Our knowledge that it is committed by one of the most powerful intellects our island ever has produced, lends intensity a thousand fold to the bitterness of our indignation. Every high thought that was ever kindled in our breasts by the muse of Byron—every pure and lofty feeling that ever responded from within us to the sweep of his majestic inspirations—every remembered moment of admiration and enthusiasm is up in arms against him. We look back with a mixture of wrath and scorn to the delight with which we suffered ourselves to be filled by one who, all the while he was furnishing us with delight, must, we cannot doubt it, have been mocking us with a cruel mockery—less cruel only, because less peculiar, than that with which he has now turned him from the lurking-place of his selfish and polluted exile, to pour the pitiful chalice of his contumely on the surrendered devotion of a virgin-bosom, and the holy hopes of the mother of his child. The consciousness of the insulting deceit which has been practised upon us, mingles with the nobler pain arising from the contemplation of perverted degraded genius—to make us wish that no such being as Byron ever had existed. It is indeed a sad and an humiliating thing to know, that in the same year there proceeded from the same pen two productions, in all things so different, as the Fourth Canto of *Childe Harold* and this loathsome *Don Juan*.

Lady Byron, however, has one consolation still remaining, and yet we fear she will think it but a poor one. She shares the scornful satire of her husband, not only with all that is good, and pure, and high, in human nature,—its principles and its feelings; but with every individual also, in whose character the predominance of these blessed elements has been sufficient to excite the envy, or exacerbate the despair of this guilty man. We shall not needlessly widen the wound by detailing its cruelty; we have mentioned one, and, all will admit, the worst instance of the private malignity which has been embodied in so many passages of *Don Juan*; and we are quite sure, the lofty-minded and virtuous men whom Lord Byron has debased himself by insulting, will close the volume which contains their own injuries, with no feelings save those of pity for Him that has inflicted them, and for Her who partakes so largely in the same injuries; and whose hard destiny has deprived her for ever of that proud and pure privilege, which enables themselves to despise them. As to the rest of the world, we know not that Lord Byron could have invented any more certain means of bringing down contempt inexpiable on his own head, than by turning the weapons of his spleen against men whose virtues few indeed can equal, but still fewer are so lost and unworthy as not to love and admire.

The mode in which we have now expressed ourselves, might be a sufficient apology for making no extracts from this poem itself. But our indignation, in regard to the morality of the poem, has not blinded us to its manifold beauties; and we are the more willing to quote a few of the passages which can be read without a blush, because the comparative rarity of such passages will, in all probability, operate to the complete exclusion of the work itself from the libraries of the greater part of our readers. As it is out of the question for us to think of analyzing the story, we must quote at the hazard of some of our quotations being very imperfectly understood.

[Quotes extensively from Canto I, with occasional comments. E.g., 'Thinking her lover effectually concealed, Donna Julia rates her Lord in a style of volubility in which, it must be granted, there is abundance of the true *vis comica*.']

Perhaps there are not a few women who may profit from seeing in what a style of contemptuous coldness the sufferings to which licentious love exposes them are talked of by such people as the author of *Don Juan*. The many fine eyes that have wept dangerous tears over his descriptions of the Gulnares and Medoras cannot be the worse for seeing the true side of *his* picture.

[Quotes Canto II, stanzas 199–201.]

The amour with this Spanish lady is succeeded by a shipwreck, in which Juan alone escapes. He is dashed on the shore of the Cyclades, where he is found by a beautiful and innocent girl, the daughter of an old Greek pirate,—with whom, as might be supposed, the same game of guilt and abandonment is played over again. There is, however, a very superior kind of poetry in the conception of this amour—the desolate isles—the utter loneliness of the maiden, who is as ignorant as she is innocent—the helpless condition of the youth—every thing conspires to render it a true romance. How easy for Lord Byron to have kept it free from any stain of pollution! What cruel barbarity, in creating so much of beauty only to mar and ruin it! This is really the very suicide of genius.

[Further quotations from Canto II.]

But the best and the worst part of the whole is without doubt the description of the shipwreck. As a piece of terrible painting, it is as much superior as can be to every description of the kind—not even excepting that in the *Aeneid*—that ever was created. In comparison with the fearful and intense reality of its horrors, every thing that any former poet had thrown together to depict the agonies of that awful scene, appears chill and tame.

> Then rose from sea to sky the wild farewell,
>   Then shrieked the timid—and stood still the brave—
> Then some leaped overboard with dreadful yell,
>   As eager to anticipate their grave:
> And the sea yawned around her like a hell,
>   And down she sucked with her the whirling wave—
> Like one who grapples with his enemy,
> And strives to strangle him before he die.
>
> And first one universal shriek there rushed,
>   Louder than the loud ocean, like a crash
> Of echoing thunder. And then all was hushed
>   Save the wild wind, and the remorseless dash

Of billows; but at intervals there gushed,
  Accompanied with a convulsive splash,
A solitary shriek, the bubbling cry
Of some strong swimmer in his agony.

But even here the demon of his depravity does not desert him. We dare not stain our pages with quoting any specimens of the disgusting merriment with which he has interspersed his picture of human suffering. He paints it well, only to shew that he scorns it the more effectually; and of all the fearful sounds which ring in the ears of the dying, the most horrible is the demoniacal laugh with which this unpitying brother exults over the contemplation of their despair. Will our readers believe that the most innocent of all his odious sarcasms is contained in these two lines?

They grieved for those that perished in the cutter.
And also for the biscuit casks, and butter.

25. Leigh Hunt, from his unsigned review of Cantos I and II, *Examiner*

31 October 1819, pp. 700–2

Seeing Byron as an ally in the struggle against political and religious reaction, Hunt gave him partisan support in the *Examiner*. Praise from such a source, however, tended to discredit Byron still further in the eyes of many conservative reviewers, as did his later, ill-fated co-operation with Hunt in the production of the *Liberal*. (See below, pp. 193–4, 249–51, 253–4.)

Some persons consider this the finest work of Lord Byron,—or at least that in which he displays most power. It is at all events the most extraordinary that he has yet published. His other poems, with the exception of that amusing satire *Beppo*, are written for the most part with one sustained serious feeling throughout,—either of pathos, or grandeur, or passion, or all united. But *Don Juan* contains specimens of all the author's modes of writing, which are mingled together and push one another about in a strange way. The ground-work (if we may so speak of a stile) is the satirical and humourous; but you are sometimes surprised and moved by a touching piece of human nature, and again startled and pained by the sudden transition from loveliness or grandeur to ridicule or the mock-heroic. The delicious and deep descriptions of love, and youth, and hope, come upon us like the 'young beams' of the sun breaking through the morning dew, and the terrific pictures of the misery of man and his most appalling sensations, like awful flashes of lightning;—but when the author reverses this change, he trifles too much with our feelings, and occasionally goes on, turning to ridicule or hopelessness all the fine ideas he has excited, with a recklessness that becomes extremely unpleasant and mortifying. What, for instance, can be more beautiful and at the same time true to nature than where,—just after a very anti-pathetic description of the confusion of *Julia* at her husband's sudden appearance, and her contrivances and lovers' falsehoods to elude his search for the beloved youth, he says (speaking of their alarm at the expected return of the old gentleman)—

> Julia did not speak,
> But pressed her bloodless lip to Juan's cheek.

> He turn'd his lip to hers, and with his hand
>   Call'd back the tangles of her wandering hair;
> Even then their love they could not all command,
>   And half forgot their danger and despair.

What more calculated to 'harrow up one's soul' than the following stanzas, which come in the very midst of some careless jests on the abstract ludicrousness of the wretched shifts of starving sailors in a becalmed boat, surrounded by a boundless prospect of the ocean? The Italics are our own.

> The seventh day, and no wind—the burning sun
>   Blister'd and scorch'd; and, stagnant on the sea,
> They lay like carcases! and hope was none,
>   Save in the breeze which came not: *savagely*
> *They glared upon each other*—all was done,
>   Water, and wine, and food,—and you might see
> The *longings of the cannibal arise*,
> (*Although they spoke not*) in their *wolfish* eyes.

> At length one whispered his companion, who
>   Whispered another, and thus it went round
> And then into a *hoarser murmur* grew,
>   An ominous and wild and desperate sound;
> And when his comrade's thought each sufferer knew,
>   'Twas but his own, suppress'd till now, he found:
> And *out they spoke* of lots for flesh and blood,
> And who should die to be his fellow's food.

Then, immediately following this awful passage, comes an affected delicacy at the tearing up of *Julia*'s letter to *Juan* to make the lots ('material which must shock the muse'), and a *sang froid* account of the division of the body: shortly after follow some terrific lines relating the dreadful consequences of this gorging of human flesh; and a little farther on there is a laughable description of *Juan*'s dislike to feed on 'poor Pedrillo', and his preference for 'chewing a piece of bamboo and some lead', the stanza ending with the irresistible fact, that

> At length they caught two boobies and a noddy,
> And then they left off eating the dead body.

It is not difficult to account for this heterogeneous mixture,—for the bard has furnished us with the key to his own mind. His early hopes were blighted, and his disappointment vents itself in satirizing absurdities which rouse his indignation; and indeed a good deal of bitterness may be found at the bottom of much of this satire. But his genius is not naturally satirical; he breaks out therefore into those frequent veins of passion and true feeling of which we have just given specimens, and goes on with them till his memory is no longer able to bear the images conjured up by his fine genius; and it is to get rid of such painful and 'thick-coming' recollections, that he dashes away and relieves himself by getting into another train of ideas, however incongruous or violently contrasted with the former. This solution will, we think, be borne out by the following affecting description of the poet's feelings. Observe in particular the remarkable parenthesis after the first line, whose pregnant meaning seems to have compelled him to take refuge in a lighter and more humorous idea:

> But now at thirty years my hair is grey—
>   (I wonder what it will be like at forty?
> I thought of a peruke the other day)—
>   My heart is not much greener; and, in short, I
> Have squandered my whole summer while 'twas May,
>   And feel no more the spirit to retort; I
> Have spent my life, both interest and principal,
> And deem not, what I deem'd, my soul invincible.
>
> No more—no more—Oh! never more on me
>   The freshness of the heart can fall like dew,
> Which out of all the lovely things we see
>   Extracts emotions beautiful and new,
> Hived in our bosoms like the bag o' the bee:
>   Think'st thou the honey with those objects grew?
> Alas! 'twas not in them, but in thy power
> To double even the sweetness of a flower.
>
> No more—no more—Oh! never more, my heart,
>   Canst thou be my sole world—my universe!
> Once all in all, but now a thing apart
>   Thou canst not be my blessing or my curse.

Here is some evidence that the poet is not without the milk of human kindness, and to our minds there is much more in the rest of the volume. His bent is not, as we have said, satirical, nor is he naturally disposed to be ill-natured with respect to the faults and vices of his fellow-creatures. There is an evident struggle throughout these two cantos in the feelings of the writer, and it is very fine to see him, as he gets on, growing more interested in his fiction, and pouring out at the conclusion in a much less interrupted strain of rich and deep beauty. . . .

Don Juan is accused of being an 'immoral' work, which we cannot at all discover. We suppose that this charge more particularly alludes to the first canto. Let us see then on what foundation it rests. The son of a Spanish patrician, educated in the most prudish manner by a licentious, yet affectedly virtuous mother, falls in love with the young wife of an old man. She returns his affection, and their passion being favoured by opportunity, she gives way to her natural feelings, and is unfaithful to her marriage vows, the example (observe) being set her by this very husband's intrigues with *Juan*'s mother. Now Lord Byron speaks lightly of the effect of any scruples of conscience upon her, and of her infidelity; and this, it is said, has tendency to corrupt the minds of 'us youth', and to make us *think* lightly of breaking the matrimonial contract. But if to do this be immoral, we can only say that Nature is immoral. Lord Byron does no more than relate the consequences of certain absurdities. If he speaks slightingly of the ties between a girl and a husband old enough for her father, it is because the ties them-selves *are* slight. He does not ridicule the bonds of marriage generally, or where they are formed as they should be: he merely shows the folly and wickedness of setting forms and opinions against nature. If stupid and selfish parents will make up matches between persons whom difference of age or disposition disqualifies for mutual affection, they must take the consequences;—but we do not think it fair that a poet should be exclaimed against as a promoter of nuptial infidelity because he tells them what those consequences are. In this particular case, too, the author does not omit some painful consequences to those who have sinned according to 'nature's law'. *Julia*, the victim of selfishness and 'damned custom', is shut up in a convent, where no consolation remains to her but the remembrance of her entire and hapless love; but even that was perhaps pleasanter to her than living in the constant irksomeness of feigning an affection she could not feel.

There are a set of prudish and very suspicious moralists who endeavour to make vice appear to inexperienced eyes much more hateful than it really is. They would correct Nature;—and they always over-reach themselves. Nature has made vice to a certain degree pleasurable, though its painful consequences outweigh its present gratification. Now the said prudes, in their lectures and sermons and moral discourses (for they are chiefly priests) are constantly declaiming on the *deformity* of vice, and its almost total want of attraction. The consequence is, that when they are found to have deceived (as they always are), and immoral indulgence is discovered to be not without its charms,—the minds of young persons are apt to confound their true with their false maxims, and to think the threats of future pain and repentance mere fables invented to deter them from their rightful enjoyments. Which then, we would ask, are the immoral writings,—those which, by misrepresenting the laws of nature, lead to false views of morality and consequent licentiousness?—or those, which ridicule and point out the effects of absurd contradictions of human feelings and passions, and help to bring about a reformation of such practices.

Of the story in the second canto it is unnecessary to say much, for these remarks will apply to both. We suppose there has been some sermonizing on the description of the delight arising from the 'illicit intercourse' of *Juan* and *Haidee*. People who talk in this way can perceive no distinctions. It certainly is not to be inculcated, that every handsome young man and woman will find their account in giving way to all their impulses, because the very violent breaking through the habits and forms of society would create a great deal of unhappiness, both to the individuals, and to others. But what is there to blame in a beautiful and affectionate girl who gives way to a passion for a young shipwrecked human creature, bound to her by gratitude as well as love? She exacts no promises, says the bard, because she fears no inconstancy. Her father had exposed her to the first temptation that comes across her, because he had not provided against it by allowing her to know more of mankind. And does she not receive, as well as bestow, more real pleasure (for that is the question) in the enjoyment of a first and deep passion, than in becoming the wife of some brother in iniquity to whom her pirating father would have trucked her for lucre?

The fact is, at the bottom of all these questions, that many things are made vicious, which are not so by nature; and many things made virtuous, which are only so by calling and agreement: and it is on the horns of this self-created dilemma, that society is continually writhing and getting desperate. . . .

26. Robert Southey on *Don Juan* and the Satanic School of Poetry

1820-1

(*a*) Extract from letter of 20 February 1820, from Robert Southey (1774–1843) to Walter Savage Landor: 'A fashion of poetry has been imported which has had a great run, and is in a fair way of being worn out. It is of Italian growth,—an adaptation of the manner of Pulci, Berni, and Ariosto in his sportive mood. Frere began it. What he produced was too good in itself and too inoffensive to become popular; for it attacked nothing and nobody; and it had the fault of his Italian models, that the transition from what is serious to what is burlesque was capricious. Lord Byron immediately followed; first with his *Beppo*, which implied the profligacy of the writer, and, lastly, with his *Don Juan*, which is a foul blot on the literature of his country, an act of high treason on English poetry. The manner has had a host of imitators. The use of Hudibrastic rhymes (the only thing in which it differs from the Italian) makes it very easy.' (*The Life and Correspondence of the late Robert Southey*, ed. C. C. Southey, 1849–50, V, 21.)

(*b*) Extract from Southey's Preface to his *Vision of Judgement* (published April 1821). Having explained the principles on which his metrical experiments were based in that poem, Southey goes on (pp. xvii–xxii): '. . . I am well aware that the public are peculiarly intolerant of such innovations; not less so than the populace are of any foreign fashion, whether of foppery or convenience. Would that this literary intolerance were under the influence of a saner judgement, and regarded the morals more than the manner of a composition; the spirit rather than the form! Would that it were directed against those monstrous combinations of horrors and mockery, lewdness and impiety, with which English poetry has, in our days, first been polluted! For more than half a century English literature had been distinguished by its moral purity, the effect, and, in its turn, the cause of an improvement in national manners. A father might, without apprehension of evil, have put into the hands of his children any book which issued from the press, if it did not bear, either in its title-page or frontispiece, manifest signs that it was intended as furniture for the brothel. There was no danger in any work which bore the name of a respectable publisher, or was to be procured at any respectable booksellers. This was particularly the case with regard to our poetry. It is now no longer so; and woe to those by whom the offence cometh! The greater the talents of the offender, the greater is his guilt, and the more enduring will be his shame. Whether it be that the laws are in themselves unable to abate an evil of this magnitude, or whether it be that they are remissly administered, and with such injustice that the celebrity of an offender serves as a privilege whereby he obtains impunity, individuals are bound to consider that such pernicious works would neither be published nor written, if they were discouraged as they might, and ought to be, by public feeling; every person, therefore, who purchases such books, or admits them into his house, promotes the mischief, and thereby, as far as in him lies, becomes an aider and abettor of the crime.

The publication of a lascivious book is one of the worst offences which can be committed against the well-being of society. It is a sin, to the consequences of which no limits can be assigned, and those consequences no after repentance in the writer can counteract. Whatever remorse of conscience he may feel when his hour comes (and come it must!) will be of no avail. The poignancy of a death-bed repentance cannot cancel one copy of the thousands which are sent abroad; and as long as it continues to be read, so long is he the pander of posterity, and so long is he heaping up guilt upon his soul in perpetual accumulation.

These remarks are not more severe than the offence deserves, even when applied to those immoral writers who have not been conscious of any evil intention in their writings, who would acknowledge a little levity, a little warmth of colouring, and so forth, in that sort of language with which men gloss over their favourite vices, and deceive themselves. What then should be said of those for whom the thoughtlessness and inebriety of wanton youth can no longer be pleaded, but who have written in sober manhood and with deliberate purpose? Men of diseased hearts and depraved imaginations, who, forming a system of opinions to suit their own unhappy course of conduct, have rebelled against the holiest ordinances of human society, and hating that revealed religion which, with all their efforts and bravadoes, they are unable entirely to disbelieve, labour to make others as miserable as themselves, by infecting them with a moral virus that eats into the soul! The school which they have set up may properly be called the Satanic school; for though their productions breathe the spirit of Belial in their lascivious parts, and the spirit of Moloch in those loathsome images of atrocities and horrors which they delight to represent, they are more especially characterized by a Satanic spirit of pride and audacious impiety, which still betrays the wretched feeling of hopelessness wherewith it is allied.

This evil is political as well as moral, for indeed moral and political evils are inseparably connected. Truly has it been affirmed by one of our ablest and clearest reasoners[1], that "the destruction of governments may be proved and deduced from the general corruption of the subjects' manners, as a direct and natural cause thereof, by a demonstration as certain as any in the mathematics." There is no maxim more frequently enforced by Machiavelli, than that where the manners of a people are generally corrupted, there the government cannot long subsist,—a truth which all history exemplifies; and there is no means whereby that corruption can be so surely and rapidly diffused, as by poisoning the waters of literature.

Let rulers of the state look to this, in time! But, to use the words of South, if "our physicians think the best way of *curing* a disease is to *pamper* it, the Lord in mercy prepare the kingdom to suffer, what He by miracle only can prevent!"

No apology is offered for these remarks. The subject led to them; and the occasion of introducing them was willingly taken, because it is the duty of every one, whose opinion may have any influence, to expose the drift and aim of those writers who are labouring to subvert the foundations of human virtue, and of human happiness. . . .'

[1] South [i.e. Robert South, D.D. (1634-1716), a famous Anglican controversialist and preacher].

27. From John Gibson Lockhart's anonymous *Letter to the Right Hon. Lord Byron. By John Bull*[1]

April/May 1821

John Gibson Lockhart (1794–1854), Scott's son-in-law and biographer, and editor of the *Quarterly Review* from 1825 to 1853, was one of the main contributors to *Blackwood's* in its early years. His authorship of *John Bull's Letter* has been established by A. L. Strout, from whose edition the following extract is reprinted. (*John Bull's Letter to Lord Byron*, ed. A. L. Strout Norman [Oklahoma], 1947, pp. 80–8, 90–100.) Byron enjoyed the pamphlet: 'I have just read "John Bull's letter", ' he wrote to Murray on 29 June 1821, 'it is diabolically *well* written, and full of fun and ferocity. I must forgive the dog, whoever he is.' (*LJ*, V, 315–6.)

... You are a great poet, but even with your poetry you mix too much of that at present very saleable article against which I am now bestirring myself [i.e. humbug]. The whole of your misanthropy, for example, is humbug. You do not hate men, 'no, nor woman neither', but you thought it would be a fine, interesting thing for a handsome young Lord to depict himself as a dark-souled, melancholy, morbid being, and you have done so, it must be admitted, with exceeding cleverness. In spite of all your pranks, (*Beppo*, &c. *Don Juan* included,) every boarding-school in the empire still contains many devout believers in the amazing misery of the black-haired, high-browed, blue-eyed, bare-throated, Lord Byron. How melancholy you look in the prints! Oh! yes, this is the true cast of face. Now, tell me, Mrs. Goddard, now tell me, Miss Price, now tell me, dear Harriet Smith, and dear, dear Mrs. Elton, do tell me, is not this just the very

[1] [From *John Bull's Letter to Lord Byron*, edited by Alan Lang Strout. Copyright 1947 by the University of Oklahoma Press.]

look, that one would have fancied for Childe Harold? Oh! what eyes and eyebrows!—Oh! what a chin!—well, after all, who knows what may have happened. One can never know the truth of such stories. Perhaps her *Ladyship* was in the wrong after all.—I am sure if I had married such a man, I would have borne with all his little eccentricities—a man so evidently unhappy.—Poor Lord Byron! who can say how much he may have been to be pitied? I am sure I would; I bear with all Mr. E.'s eccentricities, and I am sure any woman of real sense would have done so to Lord Byron's: poor Lord Byron!— well, say what they will, I shall always pity him;—do you remember these dear lines of his—

> It is that settled ceaseless gloom,
> The fabled Hebrew wanderer bore,
> That will not look beyond the tomb,
> But cannot hope for rest before.

—Oh! beautiful! and how beautifully you repeat them! You always repeat Lord Byron's fine passages so beautifully. What think you of that other we were talking of on Saturday evening at Miss Bates's?

> Nay, smile not at my sullen brow,
> Alas! I cannot smile again.

I forget the rest;—but nobody has such a memory as Mrs. E. Don't you think Captain Brown has a look of Lord Byron?

How you laugh in your sleeve when you imagine to yourself (which you have done any one half-hour these seven years) such beautiful scenes as these:—they are the triumphs of humbug: but you are not a Bowles: you ought to be (as you might well afford to be) ashamed of them. You ought to put a stop to them, if you are able; and the only plan I can point out is, that of making a vow and sticking to it, as I have done, and ever, I hope, shall do, of never writing a line more except upon the anti-humbug principle. You say you admire Pope, and I believe you: well, in this respect, I should really be at a loss to suggest a better model; do you also, my Lord, 'stoop to truth, and ⟨de⟩ moralize your song.' Stick to *Don Juan*: it is the only sincere thing you have ever written; and it will live many years after all your humbug Harolds have ceased to be, in your own words,

> A school-*girl's* tale—the wonder of an hour.

Perhaps you will stare at this last piece of my advice: but, neverthe- less, upon honour, it is as sincere as possible. I consider *Don Juan* as out of all sight the best of your works; it is by far the most spirited, the most straightforward, the most interesting, and the most poetical; and everybody thinks as I do of it, although they have not the heart to say so. Old Gifford's brow relaxed as he gloated over it; Mr. Croker chuckled; Dr. Whitaker smirked; Mr. Milman sighed; Mr. Coleridge (I mean not the madman, but the madman's idiot nephew) took it to his bed with him. The whole band of the *Quarterly* were delighted; each man in his own *penetralia*, (I except, indeed, Mr. Southey, who read the beginning very placidly, but threw the Don behind the fire when he came to the cut at himself, in the parody on the ten commandments); but who should dare to say a word about such a thing in the *Quarterly*? Poor Mr. Shelley cannot publish a wicked poem which nobody ever read, or was likely to read, but the whole band were up in arms against him: one throwing in his face his having set fire to a rotten tree when he was a boy at Eton; and another, turning over the leaves of his own travelling memorandum book to discover the very date at which Mr. Shelley wrote himself '*Αθεος*' [Atheist] in a Swiss album; and the whole of these precious materials handed forthwith to——I know whom. But not so with the noble Don. Every body poring over the wicked, smiling face of Don Juan,—pirated duodecimo competing it all over the island with furtive quarto; but the devil a word of warning in the high-spirited, most ethical, most impartial *Quarterly Review*. No; never a word—because—because—the wicked book contained one line ending with

My grand-dad's narrative.

—and its publisher was—no it was not—Mr. John Murray.

Firstly, They would not speak of it at all, because it would never have done to speak of it without abusing you; and that was the *vetitum nefas*,[1] through which it is only real sons of the *Japeti genus*[2] (like me) that dare run. Secondly, They could not speak of it without praising it, and that would have been doing something against themselves—it would have amounted to little less than coming in as accessories to the crime of *lèse majesté* against the liege Lord of the Quarterly Reviewers, and of all other reviewers who print their Reviews—Humbug.—But even this is nothing to the story that is told (God knows with what truth!) of Blackwood—I mean the *man* Blackwood, not the *thing* Blackwood,—the bibliopole, not the magazine. This

[1] ['Forbidden sin.']

[2] ['Race of Iapetus' (the father of Prometheus).]

worthy bibliopole, it is said, actually refused to have *Don Juan* seen in his shop; '*procul, procul, esto profane*,'[1] was the language of the indignant Master William Blackwood to the intrusive Don Juan. Now, had Lord Byron, (forgive the supposition,) had Lord Byron sent *Don Juan*, with five hundred thousand million times more of the devil about him than he really has exhibited, to that well-known character Christopher North, Esq. with a request to have the Don inserted in his Magazine,—lives there that being with wit enough to keep him from putrefying, who doubts the great KIT would have smiled a sweet smile, and desired the right honourable guest to ascend into the most honourable place of his upper chamber of immortality? This is clear enough; and then came the redoubted Magazine itself,— (why, by the way, have you delayed so long publishing that letter upon it which many have seen, and of which all have heard?)—what could it do? could it refuse to row in the wake of the admiral? could the clay rebel against the potter? No, no; a set of obsequious moralists meet in a tavern, and after being thoroughly maddened with tobacco smoke and whiskey punch, they cry out—'Well, then, so be it; have at *Don Juan*.' Upon a table all round in a roar of blasphemy, and by men hot from ——'s, and breathing nothing but pollution, furious paragraph after furious paragraph is written against a book of which the whole knot would have been happy to club their brains to write one stanza,—a book which they had all got by heart ere they set about reviewing it, and which thousands will get by heart after all the reviews they ever wrote shall have sunk into the 'melodious wave' of the same Lake, where now slumber gently side by side, the fallen and fettered angel of the *Isle of Palms*, and the thrice rueful ghost of the late 'much and justly regretted' Dr. Peter Morris.[2]

From the pure *Quarterly*, and its disowned, if not discarded, Cloaca, the leap is not 'Wilsonian' to the *Edinburgh*. *Don Juan* was not reviewed there neither; but Little's poems were; 'aye, there's the rub.' It was very right to rebuke Tom Moore for his filth; but what was his filth to the filth of *Don Juan*? Why, not much more than his poetry was (and is) to the poetry of *Don Juan*. This, indeed, was straining at the shrimp, and swallowing the lobster; and what was the reason for it?

[1] ['Stand back, stand back, uninitiated'; but Lockhart is punning here on the English sense of profane. For William Blackwood's reaction to *Don Juan*, see above, p. 164.]
[2] [*The Isle of Palms* (1812) was a poem by John Wilson; 'Peter Morris' was Lockhart's own pseudonym in *Peter's Letters to his Kinsfolk* (1819).]

Your Lordship knows very well it is to be found in a certain wicked page of a certain wicked little book of yours called *English Bards and Scotch Reviewers*,—the suppression of which, by the way, is another egregious piece of humbug on the part of your Lordship. Had you never written that little book, (I wish you would write a better on the same subject—now that you are a man)—Mr. Francis Jeffrey, that grave doctor of morality, would have flourished his thong and laid on with all his might, and Don Juan would have scratched his back, for he would have thought a flea had skipped within his linens. The thong was not flourished, the healing stripe was withheld, and the Don slumbered undisturbed. The Review, however, has really ventured to allude to him since; yes, in an article on some verses of Mr. Procter, commonly called (*Euphoniae causa*)[1] by the romantic and soul-melting name of Barry Cornwall, among many other excellent things there is a timely and comfortable remark that the style of the said Mr. Procter does not bear so much resemblance to that of *Don Juan* as it does to that of *Parisina*. It would have been just as proper to inform the world that the parlour in which Mr. Procter writes (I have no doubt it is very neatly papered and contains some good *prints*) does not bear so much resemblance to Westminster Abbey as it does to the Parthenon of Athens: or that Mr. Procter himself, (if he were turned into stone and stuck up upon a pedestal) would bear more resemblance to the Antinous than to the Farnese Hercules; or that Mr. Francis Jeffrey, were he to go upon the stage, would do better in the part of Jack the Giant-killer than in that of the Giant.

Enough, however, for the present, of these gentlemen: for their hour is not yet come, and I meant no more than to give them a jog in passing. . . .

I will not insult *Don Juan* by saying that his style is *not* like that of Signior Penseroso di Cornuaglia; in truth, I think the great charm of its style is, that it is not much like the style of any other poem in the world. It is utter humbug to say, that it is borrowed from the style of the Italian weavers of merry *rima ottava;* their merriment is nothing, because they have nothing but their merriment; yours is every thing, because it is delightfully intermingled with and contrasted by all manner of serious things—murder and lust included. It is also mere *humbug* to accuse you of having plagiarized it from Mr. Frere's pretty and graceful little *Whistlecrafts*. The measure to be sure is the same, but then the measure is as old as the hills. But the spirit of the two

[1] ['For the sake of euphony.']

poets is as different as can be. Mr Frere writes elegantly, playfully, very like a gentleman, and a scholar, and a respectable man, and his poems never sold, nor ever will sell. Your *Don Juan* again, is written strongly, lasciviously, fiercely, laughingly—every body sees in a moment, that nobody could have written it but a man of the first order both in genius and in dissipation;—a real master of all his tools— a profligate, pernicious, irresistible, charming Devil—and, accordingly, the *Don* sells, and will sell to the end of time, whether our good friend Mr. John Murray honours it with his *imprimatur* or doth not so honour it. I will mention a book, however, from which I do think you have taken a great many hints—nay, a great many pretty full sketches for your Juan. It is one which (with a few more) one never sees mentioned in reviews, because it is a book written on the anti-humbug principle. It is—you know it excellently well—it is no other than FAUBLAS, [1] a book which contains as much good fun as *Gil Blas*, or Molière—as much good luscious description as the *Heloise;* as much fancy and imagination as all the Comedies in the English language put together— and less humbug than any one given romance that has been written since *Don Quixote*—a book which is to be found on the tables of Roués, and in the desks of divines and under the pillows of spinsters— a book, in a word, which is read universally—I wish I could add,— in the original. Your fine Spanish lady, with her black hair lying on the pillow, and the curly-headed little Juan couched under the coverlid— she is taken—every inch of her—from the *Marquise de B——;* your Greek girl (sweet creature!) is *La petite Contesse,* but she is the better, because of her wanting even the semblance of being married. You have also taken some warm touches from *Peregrine Proteus,* [2] and if you read *Peregrine* over again you will find there is still more well worth the taking.

But all this has nothing to do with the charming *style* of *Don Juan,* which is entirely and inimitably your own—the sweet, fiery, rapid, easy—beautifully easy, anti-humbug style of *Don Juan.* Ten stanzas of it are worth all your *Manfred*—and yet your *Manfred* is a noble poem too in its way; and Meinherr von Goëthe has exhibited no more palpable symptom of dotage than in his attempt to persuade his *lesende publicum* [3] that you stole it from his *Faustus*; for it is, as I have said, a noble and an original poem, and not in the least like either

[1] [Jean Baptiste Louvet de Couvray, *Les Amours du chevalier de Faublas,* 1787-9.]
[2] [A work by Christoph Martin Wieland, published in 1791.]
[3] ['Reading public.']

Don Juan or *Faust*, and quite inferior to both of them. I had really no idea what a very clever fellow you were till I read *Don Juan*. In my humble opinion, there is very little in the literature of the present day that will really stand the test of half a century, except the *Scotch* novels of Sir Walter Scott and *Don Juan*. *They* will do so because they are written with perfect facility and nature—because their materials are all drawn from nature—in other words, because they are neither made up of cant, like Wordsworth and Shelley, nor of humbug like *Childe Harold* and *The City of the Plague*,[1] nor of Brunswick Mum, like the *Rime of the Ancient Mariner*, nor of milk and water like Mr. Barry Cornwall.

The truth is, that the Baron and the Baronet stand quite by themselves: all the rest of the literati are little better than *canaille* compared to you. You are good friends, I am told, and I have no doubt you will continue so to the end of the chapter;—first, because you never can be rivals; and, secondly, because if you were rivals tomorrow, you are both men of the world and men of sense. Your ages are very different; yet, talking of you as authors go, you may both be said to be still young men. Some years ago there was a good deal of humbug about the Baronet's productions, and now I see scarcely a trace of it; and a few years hence, I don't know what should prevent you from exhibiting a reformation quite as complete. If you mean to do so, it must be by adhering to the key of *Don Juan*; and, if he means not to relapse, his plan is to stick to the key of *Guy Mannering*. Take my advice, both of you, and 'know when you are well.' Sir Walter has Scotland all to himself; and as for exhausting that or any other field of true nature—he and you are both quite aware that it is humbug to speak of it. War, love, life, death, mirth, sorrow, imagination, observation—who beyond the calibre of 'my grandmother'[2] ever thought or spoke of exhausting these things? And as for rivals in *his* field—who are they I pray you, or who are they ever likely to be? Mr. James Hogg, who represents haughty kings as stupid lairds, and lairds as drunken ploughmen, and ladies like haycock-wenches,—who turns Dundee into a highland sergeant—and highland sergeants into covenanters. No, no, *Blackwood's* Brownie will never do, nor Mr. Allan Cunningham, whose mouth is so full of butter that it has no room for bread. These are both of them clever fellows, indeed, and either of them worth all

[1] [*The City of the Plague* (1816) was by John Wilson.]
[2] [The *British Review*—an allusion to Byron's joke in *Don Juan* about having bribed 'my grandmother's review—the British' to secure a favourable notice.]

the Clares that ever trod upon hobnails: but Scottish poetry numbers just three true geniuses, (and it is enough in all conscience,) and their names are Dunbar, Burns, Scott,—and they are all of them enemies to humbug, at least I would have said so without hesitation, but for the sickening remembrance of the Ayrshire Ploughman's Sentimental Letters, which, upon my honour, I think are as nauseous as any thing even in Southey's *Pilgrimage to Waterloo*, or your own imitations of Ossian, or in Macpherson himself. As for *Marriage*,[1] that is indeed a much superior book to any that Hogg or Cunningham, or any of that sort will ever write—but then who does not remember the History of Triermaine? . . . Scotland, therefore, is and will remain Sir Walter's. And what, you will say, is mine? I will tell you, Lord Byron: England is yours, if you choose to make it so.—I do not speak of the England of days past, or of the England of days to come, but of the England of the day that now is, with which, if you be not contented, you are about as difficult to please as a Buonaparte. There is nobody but yourself who has any chance of conveying to posterity a true idea of the *spirit* of England in the days of his Majesty George IV. Mr. Wordsworth may write fifty years about his 'dalesmen;' if he paints them truly, it is very well; if untruly, it is no matter: but you know what neither Mr. Wordsworth nor any Cumberland stamp-master ever can know. You know the society of England,—you know what English gentlemen are made of, and you very well know what English ladies are made of; and, I promise you, that *knowledge* is a much more precious thing, whatever you at present may think or say, than any *notion* you or any other Englishman ever can acquire either of Italians, or Spaniards, or Greeks. Do you really suppose, for a moment, (laying aside humbug), that you know any thing at all about either Venice or Ravenna worthy of being compared either as to extent or as to accuracy with what you know of London?—I mean of the true London, for as to the London east of Temple Bar, God knows there are enough of rhymsters, and prosers too, (whereof more anon,) who know, or ought to know, more about it than you ever can know, or ought to know; for no gentleman ought to know more of the polite Cockneys than may be learnt from reading one number of the *Examiner*, nor more of the unpolite Cockneys than may be picked up from one evening of Mr. Mathews's 'At Home.'

[1] [By Susan Ferrier, published anonymously 1818. Scott's *Bridal of Triermain*, referred to in the next sentence, was not originally acknowledged as his. Lockhart implies that Scott may have been the author of *Marriage* also.]

I believe the thing will bear looking into, that nothing worth much has ever been done either in literature, or in any of the sister arts, except by taking things as they are, or representing them as they are. Compare Homer's description of the old savage heroes with the descriptions of the same heroes even in Aeschylus—far more with those in Sophocles, or Euripides, or Virgil, or any of all his imitators. Compare Tacitus, or Petronius, or Juvenal, with Seneca or Lucan. Compare Aristophanes with Xenophon. Compare Lucian, or Swift, or Montaigne, or Le Sage, or Cervantes, with any of their contemporaries—except the last of them, by the way, for he was the contemporary of Shakespeare, and died (odd enough!) on the same day with him, and I doubt if two such fine fellows ever died on the same day before or since. Compare Boccaccio's novels with Petrarch's sonnets. Compare Goëthe's life of himself with his *Sorrows of Werther*. Compare Horace with Ovid, or with any body but Pope. Compare Hogarth with Sir Joshua, or Wilkie with Fuseli, or Baillie Jarvie with the goblin-groom, or Flittertigibbet, or Mrs. Mucklebacket, junior, with Mrs. Mucklebacket, senior,—or Lord Byron in the letter on the Reverend William Lisle Bowles with Lord Byron on the field of Talavera, (where your English heart burned within you, although you had humbug enough to deny it.) Compare Lord Byron when he is describing a beautiful woman, or when he is quizzing Southey or Sotheby with Lord Byron when he is puffing old Samuel Rogers, the banker, and pretending (what vile humbug!) to class him among the great poets of England, who has only written a very, very few lukewarm verses in his day; albeit it may be most true that he hath given a great many piping hot dinners—or still worse, perhaps, with the same Lord Byron, when he is writing down Wordsworth an ass, who, (with all his foibles,) he well knows, has put more genius (now and then) into ten lines, than all the poetical bankers in Christendom will ever be able to comprehend—and this for no earthly reason, except that he, (Lord Byron,) and the stamp-master did not take kindly to each other when they met, and that he, (Lord Byron,) knows the stamp-master is wrapped round in vanity, fold above fold, like one of Belzoni's mummies, and that the least touch of sarcasm from one who really can be sarcastic will probably put the stamp-master's swaddling-bands into such a flutter, that he, the stamp-master, shan't be able to compose himself for a single 'Mood of my mind' during the rest of the season. Wherever you find them in short, compare reality with vision, sincerity with insincerity, honesty with humbug,—and there you will see what I mean when I advise you to continue the Don—on, through all his cantos, (observe I don't mean to continue it as wickedly as it is begun, but as sincerely)—to bring the Don forthwith into England—to put him to school at Harrow, and to college at Cambridge,—to lodge him at the Clarendon, and make him see the world,—as you yourself have seen it,—and describe it as Sir Walter Scott has described Captain Clutterbuck.

I know very well what a great many very knowing people, very shrewd people, very superior, very deep-thinking 'earnest' people will say, when they read what I have just written. They will say, 'Here now is a fellow that thinks himself a judge of literature, and yet, it is evident, he has only an eye and a relish for one particular species of literary excellence. He enjoys what is coarse, comic, obvious to every capacity,—but he has neither heart nor soul for the grand, the sublime, the pathetic, the truly *imaginative*.' You will say no such thing: you have discovered, many pages ago, that I am *up to trap*: and you know quite well that nobody *can* enjoy in a rational manner any one species of literary excellence, without being able to enjoy many kinds of it. But fine words are the very essence of humbug; and men-tailors and women-tailors are made to be taken in by them. None of these worthy people have ever read Longinus, but you and I have; and we know full well that what he considers as the true point of ambition in writing, his famous 'ὕψος' [sublime] has nothing whatever to do with what 'the fine spirits of the earth' talk about under the fine names of 'the sublime' and so forth. The sublime of Longinus means nothing whatever but the '*energetic*'. . . . Wherever energetic thoughts are expressed in energetic language, there I see the sublime: and there I am sure you see it. . . .

28. Croker on Cantos III and IV

March 1820

Croker read Cantos III and IV in manuscript, and his letter of 26 March to John Murray illustrates the kind of pressures brought to bear on both poet and publisher by the latter's advisers. (Samuel Smiles, *A Publisher and his Friends*, 1891, I, 413–16.)

Dear Murray,

I have to thank you for letting me see your two new cantos [the 3rd and 4th], which I return. What sublimity! what levity! what boldness! what tenderness! what majesty! what trifling! what variety! what *tediousness!*—for tedious to a strange degree, it must be confessed that whole passages are, particularly the earlier stanzas of the fourth canto. I know no man of such general powers of intellect as Brougham, yet I think *him* insufferably tedious; and I fancy the reason to be that he has such *facility* of expression that he is never recalled to a *selection* of his thoughts. A more costive orator would be obliged to choose, and a man of his talents could not fail to choose the best; but the power of uttering all and everything which passes across his mind, tempts him to say all. He goes on without thought—I should rather say, without pause. His speeches are poor from their richness, and dull from their infinite variety. An impediment in his speech would make him a perfect Demosthenes. Something of the same kind, and with something of the same effect, is Lord Byron's wonderful fertility of thought and facility of expression; and the Protean style of *Don Juan*, instead of checking (as the fetters of rhythm generally do) his natural activity, not only gives him wider limits to range in, but even generates a more roving disposition. I dare swear, if the truth were known, that his digressions and repetitions generate one another, and that the happy jingle of some of his comical rhymes has led him on to episodes of which he never originally thought; and thus it is that, with the most extraordinary merit, *merit of all kinds*, these two cantos have been to *me*, in several points, tedious and even obscure.

As to the PRINCIPLES, all the world, and you, Mr. Murray, *first of all*, have done this poem great injustice. There are levities here and there, more than good taste approves, but nothing to make such a terrible rout about—nothing so bad as *Tom Jones*, nor within a hundred degrees of *Count Fathom*. I know that it is no justification of one fault to produce a greater, neither am I justifying Lord Byron. I have acquaintance none, or next to none, with him, and of course no interest beyond what we must all take in a poet who, on the whole, is one of the first, if not the very first, of our age; but I direct my observations against you and those whom you deferred to. If you print and sell *Tom Jones* and *Peregrine Pickle*, why did you start at *Don Juan*? Why smuggle it into the world and, as it were, pronounce it illegitimate in its birth, and induce so many of the learned rabble, when they could find so little specific offence in it, to refer to its supposed original state as one of original sin? If instead of this you had touched the right string and in the right place, Lord Byron's own good taste and good nature would have revised and corrected some phrases in his poem which in reality disparage it more than its imputed looseness of principle; I mean some expressions of political and personal feelings which, I believe, he, in fact, never felt, and threw in wantonly and *de gaieté de cœur*, and which he would have omitted, advisedly and *de bonté de cœur*,[1] if he had not been goaded by indiscreet, contradictory, and urgent *criticisms*, which, in some cases, were dark enough to be called *calumnies*. But these are blowing over, if not blown over; and I cannot but think that if Mr. Gifford, or some friend in whose taste and disinterestedness Lord Byron could rely, were to point out to him the cruelty to individuals, the injury to the national character, the offence to public taste, and the injury to his own reputation, of such passages as those about Southey and Waterloo and the British Government and the head of that Government, I cannot but hope and believe that these blemishes in the first cantos would be wiped away in the next edition; and that some that occur in the two cantos (which you sent me) would never see the light. What interest can Lord Byron have in being the poet of a party in politics, or of a party in morals, or of a party in religion? Why should he wish to throw away the suffrages (you see the times infect my dialect) of more than half the nation? He has no interest in that direction, and, I believe, has no feeling of that kind. In politics, he cannot be what he appears, or rather what Messrs. Hobhouse and Leigh Hunt wish to make him appear. A man of his birth, a man of his taste,

[1] ['From joyousness of heart' / 'from goodness of heart.']

a man of his talents, a man of his habits, can have nothing in common with such miserable creatures as we now call *Radicals*, of whom I know not that I can better express the illiterate and blind ignorance and vulgarity than by saying that the best informed of them have probably never heard of Lord Byron. No, no, Lord Byron may be indulgent to these jackal followers of his; he may connive at their use of his name—nay, it is not to be denied that he has given them too, too much countenance—but he never can, I should think, now that he sees not only the road but the rate they are going, continue to take a part so contrary to all his own interests and feelings, and to the feelings and interests of all the respectable part of his country. And yet it was only yesterday at dinner that somebody said that he had read or seen a letter of Lord Byron's to somebody, saying that if the Radicals only made a little progress and showed some real force, he would hasten over and get on horseback to head them. This is evidently either a gross lie altogether, or a grosser misconstruction of some epistolary pleasantry; because if the proposition were serious, the letter never would have been shown. Yet see how a bad name is given. We were twelve at dinner, all (except myself) people of note, and yet (except Walter Scott and myself again) every human being will repeat the story to twelve others—and so on. But what is to be the end of all this rigmarole of mine? To conclude, this—to advise you, for your own sake as a tradesman, for Lord Byron's sake as a poet, for the sake of good literature and good principles, which ought to be united, to take such measures as you may be able to venture upon to get Lord Byron to revise these two cantos, and not to make another step in the odious path which Hobhouse beckons him to pursue. There is little, very little, of this offensive nature in these cantos; the omission, I think, of five stanzas out of 215, would do all I should ask on this point; but I confess that I think it would be much better for his fame and your profit if the two cantos were thrown into one, and brought to a proper length by the retrenchment of the many careless, obscure, and idle passages which *incuria fudit*.[1] I think Tacitus says that the Germans formed their plans when drunk and matured them when sober. I know not how this might answer in public affairs, but in poetry I should think it an excellent plan—to pour out, as Lord Byron says, his whole mind in the intoxication of the moment, but to revise and condense in the sobriety of the morrow. One word more: experience shows that the Pulcian style is very easily written. Frere, Blackwood's Magaziners, Rose,

[1] ['Carelessness has scattered.']

Cornwall, all write it with ease and success; it therefore behoves Lord Byron to distinguish his use of this measure by superior and peculiar beauties. He should refine and polish; and by the *limae labor et mora*,[1] attain the perfection of ease. A vulgar epigram says that '*easy writing is damned hard reading;*' and it is one of the eternal and general rules by which heaven warns us, at every step and at every look, that this is a mere transitory life; that what costs no trouble soon perishes; that what grows freely dies early; and that nothing endures but in some degree of proportion with the time and labour it has cost to create. Use these hints if you can, but not my name.

Yours ever,

J. W. Croker.

[1] ['Delaying toil of the file.']

29. Shelley on Cantos III, IV and V.

1821

(a) Extract from letter of 17 April 1821, to Byron: '. . . You have now arrived about at the age at which those eternal poets, of whom we have authentic accounts, have ever begun their supreme poems; considering all their others, however transcendent, as the steps, the scaffolding, the exercise which may sustain and conduct them to their great work. If you are inferior to these, it is not in genius, but industry and resolution. Oh, that you would subdue yourself to the great task of building up a poem containing within itself the germs of a permanent relation to the present, and to all succeeding ages! . . .' (*The Letters of Percy Bysshe Shelley*, ed. F. L. Jones, 1964, II, 283–4.)

(b) Extract from letter of 10 August 1821, to Mary Shelley: '. . . He has read to me one of the unpublished cantos of *Don Juan* [i.e. Canto V, see below], which is astonishingly fine.—It sets him not above but far above all the poets of the day: every word has the stamp of immortality.—I despair of rivalling Lord Byron, as well I may: and there is no other with whom it is worth contending. This canto is in style, but totally, & sustained with incredible ease & power, like the end of the second canto: there is not a word which the most rigid assertor of the dignity of human nature could desire to be cancelled: it fulfills in a certain degree what I have long preached of producing something wholly new & relative to the age—and yet surpassingly beautiful. It may be vanity, but I think I see the trace of my earnest exhortations to him to create something wholly new. . . .' (*Op. cit.*, II, 323.)

(c) Extract from letter of [?10] August 1821, to Thomas Love Peacock: '. . . . Lord Byron is in excellent cue both of health and spirits. He has got rid of all those melancholy and degrading habits which he indulged at Venice. He lives with one woman, a lady of rank here, to whom he is attached, and who is attached to him, and is in every respect an altered man. He has written three more cantos of *Don Juan*. I have yet only heard the fifth, and I think that every word of it is pregnant with immortality. I have not seen his late plays except *Marino Faliero*, which is very well, but not so transcendently fine as the *Don Juan*. . . .' (*Op. cit.*, II, 330.)

(*d*) Extract from letter of 14 September 1821, to Byron: '. . . The poetry of this piece [*The Prophecy of Dante*] is indeed sublime; and if it have not general admiration you ought still to be contented; because the subject, no less than the style, is addressed to the few, and, like some of the highest passages in *Childe Harold*, will only be *fully* appreciated by the select readers of many generations. But *Don Juan* is your greatest victory over the alleged inflexibility of your powers. . . .' (*Op. cit.*, II, 347.)

(*e*) Extract from letter of 21 October 1821, to Byron: '. . . Many thanks for *Don Juan* [i.e. Cantos III, IV and V]—It is a poem totally of its own species, & my wonder and delight at the grace of the composition no less than the free & grand vigour of the conception of it perpetually increase.—The few passages which any one might desire to be cancelled in the 1st & 2nd Cantos are here reduced almost to nothing. This poem carries with it at once the stamp of originality and a defiance of imitation. Nothing has ever been written like it in English—nor if I may venture to prophesy, will there be; without carrying upon it the mark of a secondary and borrowed light.—You unveil & present in its true deformity what is worst in human nature, & this is what the witlings of the age murmur at, conscious of their want of power to endure the scrutiny of such a light.—We are damned to the knowledge of good & evil, and it is well for us to know what we should avoid no less than what we should seek.—The character of Lambro—his return—the merriment of his daughters guests made as it were in celebration of his funeral—the meeting with the lovers—and the death of Haidée—are circumstances combined & developed in a manner that I seek elsewhere in vain. The fifth canto, which some of your pet Zoili in Albemarle St. said was *dull*, gathers instead of loses, splendour & energy—the language in which the whole is clothed—a sort of c[h]ameleon under the changing sky of the spirit that kindles it— is such as these lisping days could not have expected,—and are, believe me, in spite of the approbation which you wrest from them, little pleased to hear. One can hardly judge from recitation and it was not until I read it in print that I have been able to do it justice.—This sort of writing only on a great plan & perhaps in a more compact form is what I wished you to do when I made my vows for an epic.—But I am content—You are building up a drama, such as England has not yet seen, and the task is sufficiently noble & worthy of you. . . .' (*Op. cit.*, II, 357–8.)

30. Jeffrey on *Don Juan*

1822

Extract from unsigned review of *Sardanapalus, The Two Foscari*
and *Cain*, in the *Edinburgh Review* for February 1822 (see below
No. 36). *Edinburgh Review*, xxxvi, 446–52.

. . . We have a word or two to say on the griefs of Lord Byron himself. He complains bitterly of the detraction by which he has been
assailed—and intimates that his works have been received by the public
with far less cordiality and favour than he was entitled to expect. We
are constrained to say that this appears to us a very extraordinary
mistake. In the whole course of our experience, we cannot recollect a
single author who has had so little reason to complain of his reception—
to whose genius the public has been so early and so constantly just—to
whose faults they have been so long and so signally indulgent. From
the very first, he must have been aware that he offended the principles
and shocked the prejudices of the majority, by his sentiments, as much
as he delighted them by his talents. Yet there never was an author so
universally and warmly applauded, so gently admonished—so kindly
entreated to look more heedfully to his opinions. He took the praise, as
usual, and rejected the advice. As he grew in fame and authority, he
aggravated all his offences—clung more fondly to all he had been
reproached with—and only took leave of Childe Harold to ally himself
to Don Juan! That he has since been talked of, in public and in private,
with less unmingled admiration—that his name is now mentioned as
often for censure as for praise—and that the exultation with which his
countrymen once hailed the greatest of our living poets, is now alloyed
by the recollection of the tendency of his writings—is matter of
notoriety to all the world; but matter of surprise, we should imagine,
to nobody but Lord B. himself.

He would fain persuade himself, indeed, that this decline of his
popularity—or rather this stain upon its lustre—for he is still popular
beyond all other example—and it is only because he is so that we feel
any interest in this discussion;—he wishes to believe, that he is

indebted for the censures that have reached him, not to any actual demerits of his own, but to the jealousy of those he has supplanted, the envy of those he has outshone, or the party rancour of those against whose corruptions he has testified;—while, at other times, he seems inclined to insinuate, that it is chiefly because he is a *Gentleman* and a *Nobleman* that plebeian censors have conspired to bear him down! We scarcely think, however, that these theories will pass with Lord B. himself—we are sure they will pass with no other person. They are so manifestly inconsistent as mutually to destroy each other—and so weak, as to be quite insufficient to account for the fact, even if they could be effectually combined for that purpose. *The party* that Lord B. has offended, bears no malice to Lords and Gentlemen. Against its rancour, on the contrary, these qualities have undoubtedly been his best protection; and had it not been for them, he may be assured that he would, long ere now, have been shown up in the pages of the *Quarterly*, with the same candour and liberality that has there been exercised towards his friend Lady Morgan. That the base and the bigotted—those whom he has darkened by his glory, spited by his talent, or mortified by his neglect—have taken advantage of the prevailing disaffection, to vent their puny malice in silly nicknames and vulgar scurrility, is natural and true. But Lord B. may depend upon it, that the dissatisfaction is not confined to them,—and, indeed, that they would never have had the courage to assail one so immeasurably their superior, if he had not at once made himself vulnerable by his errors, and alienated his natural defenders by his obstinate adherence to them. We are not bigots, nor rival poets. We have not been detractors from Lord Byron's fame, nor the friends of his detractors; and *we* tell him—far more in sorrow than in anger—that we verily believe the great body of the English nation—the religious, the moral, and the candid part of it—consider the tendency of his writings to be immoral and pernicious—and look upon his perseverance in that strain of composition with regret and reprehension. We ourselves are not easily startled, either by levity of temper, or boldness, or even rashness of remark; we are, moreover, most sincere admirers of Lord Byron's genius—and have always felt a pride and an interest in his fame. But we cannot dissent from the censure to which we have alluded; and shall endeavour to explain, in as few and as temperate words as possible, the grounds upon which we rest our concurrence.

He has no priestlike cant or priestlike reviling to apprehend from us. We do not charge him with being either a disciple or an apostle of

Satan; nor do we describe his poetry as a mere compound of blasphemy and obscenity. On the contrary, we are inclined to believe that he wishes well to the happiness of mankind—and are glad to testify, that his poems abound with sentiments of great dignity and tenderness, as well as passages of infinite sublimity and beauty. But their general tendency we believe to be in the highest degree pernicious; and we even think that it is chiefly by means of the fine and lofty sentiments they contain, that they acquire their most fatal power of corruption. This may sound at first, perhaps, like a paradox; but we are mistaken if we shall not make it intelligible enough in the end.

We think there are indecencies and indelicacies, seductive descriptions and profligate representations, which are extremely reprehensible; and also audacious speculations, and erroneous and uncharitable assertions, equally indefensible. But if these had stood alone, and if the whole body of his works had been made up of gaudy ribaldry and flashy scepticism, the mischief, we think, would have been much less than it is. He is not more obscene, perhaps, than Dryden or Prior, and other classical and pardoned writers; nor is there any passage in the history even of Don Juan, so degrading as Tom Jones's affair with Lady Bellaston. It is no doubt a wretched apology for the indecencies of a man of genius, that equal indecencies have been forgiven to his predecessors: But the precedent of lenity might have been followed; and we might have passed both the levity and the voluptuousness—the dangerous warmth of his romantic situations, and the scandal of his cold-blooded dissipation. It might not have been so easy to get over his dogmatic scepticism—his hard-hearted maxims of misanthropy— his cold-blooded and eager expositions of the non-existence of virtue and honour. Even this, however, might have been comparatively harmless, if it had not been accompanied by that which may look, at first sight, as a palliation—the frequent presentment of the most touching pictures of tenderness, generosity, and faith.

The charge we bring against Lord B. in short is, that his writings have a tendency to destroy all belief in the reality of virtue—and to make all enthusiasm and constancy of affection ridiculous; and that this is effected, not merely by direct maxims and examples, of an imposing or seducing kind, but by the constant exhibition of the most profligate heartlessness in the persons of those who had been transiently represented as actuated by the purest and most exalted emotions—and in the lessons of that very teacher who had been, but a moment before, so beautifully pathetic in the expression of the loftiest conceptions. When a rash and gay voluptuary descants, somewhat too freely, on the intoxications of love and wine, we ascribe his excesses to the effervescence of youthful spirits, and do not consider him as seriously impeaching either the value or the reality of the severer virtues; and in the same way, when the satirist deals out his sarcasms against the sincerity of human professions, and unmasks the secret infirmities of our bosoms, we consider this as aimed at hypocrisy, and not at mankind: or, at all events, and in either case, we consider the Sensualist and the Misanthrope as wandering, each in his own delusion—and pity those who have never known the charms of a tender or generous affection. The true antidote to such seductive or revolting views of human nature, is to turn to the scenes of its nobleness and attraction; and to reconcile ourselves again to our kind, by listening to the accents of pure affection and incorruptible honour. But if those accents have flowed, in all their sweetness, from the very lips that instantly open again to mock and blaspheme them, the antidote is mingled with the poison, and the draught is the more deadly for the mixture!

The reveller may pursue his orgies, and the wanton display her enchantments with comparative safety to those around them, while they know or believe that there are purer and higher enjoyments, and teachers and followers of a happier way. But if the priest pass from the altar, with persuasive exhortations to peace and purity still trembling on his tongue, to join familiarly in the grossest and most profane debauchery—if the matron, who has charmed all hearts by the lovely sanctimonies of her conjugal and maternal endearments, glides out from the circle of her children, and gives bold and shameless way to the most abandoned and degrading vices—our notions of right and wrong are at once confounded—our confidence in virtue shaken to the foundations—and our reliance on truth and fidelity at an end for ever.

This is the charge which we bring against Lord Byron. We say that, under some strange misapprehension as to the truth, and the duty of proclaiming it, he has exerted all the powers of his powerful mind to convince his readers, both directly and indirectly, that all ennobling pursuits, and disinterested virtues, are mere deceits or illusions—hollow and despicable mockeries for the most part, and, at best, but laborious follies. Love, patriotism, valour, devotion, constancy, ambition—all are to be laughed at, disbelieved in, and despised!—and nothing is really good, so far as we can gather, but a succession of dangers to stir the blood, and of banquets and intrigues to sooth it again! If this doctrine stood alone, with its examples, it would revolt, we believe, more than it would seduce:—but the author of it has the unlucky gift of personating all those sweet and lofty illusions, and that with such grace and force and truth to nature, that it is impossible not to suppose, for the time, that he is among the most devoted of their votaries—till he casts off the character with a jerk—and, the moment after he has moved and exalted us to the very height of our conception, resumes his mockery at all things serious or sublime—and lets us down at once on some coarse joke, hard-hearted sarcasm, or fierce and relentless personality—as if on purpose to show

Whoe'er was edified, himself was not—

or to demonstrate practically as it were, and by example, how possible it is to have all fine and noble feelings, or their appearance, for a moment, and yet retain no particle of respect for them—or of belief in their intrinsic worth or permanent reality. Thus, we have an indelicate but very clever scene of the young Juan's concealment in the bed of an amorous matron, and of the torrent of 'rattling and audacious eloquence' with which she repels the too just suspicions of her jealous lord. All this is merely comic, and a little coarse:—But then the poet chuses to make this shameless and abandoned woman address to her young gallant, an epistle breathing the very spirit of warm, devoted, pure and unalterable love—thus profaning the holiest language of the heart, and indirectly associating it with the most hateful and degrading sensuality. In like manner, the sublime and terrific description of the Shipwreck is strangely and disgustingly broken by traits of low humour and buffoonery;—and we pass immediately from the moans of an agonizing father fainting over his famished son, to facetious stories of Juan's begging a paw of his father's dog—and refusing a slice of his tutor!—as if it were a fine thing to be hard-hearted—and pity and compassion were fit only to be laughed at. In the same spirit, the glorious Ode on the aspirations of Greece after Liberty, is instantly followed up by a strain of dull and cold-blooded ribaldry;—and we are hurried on from the distraction and death of Haidee to merry scenes of intrigue and masquerading in the seraglio. Thus all good feelings are excited only to accustom us to their speedy and complete extinction; and we are brought back, from their transient and theatrical exhibition, to the staple and substantial doctrine of the work—the non-existence of constancy in women or honour in men, and the folly of expecting to meet with any such virtues, or of cultivating them, for an undeserving world;—and all this mixed up with so much wit and cleverness, and knowledge of human nature, as to make it irresistibly pleasant and plausible—while there is not only no antidote supplied, but everything that might have operated in that way has been anticipated, and presented already in as strong and engaging a form as possible—but under such associations as to rob it of all efficacy, or even turn it into an auxiliary of the poison.

This is our sincere opinion of much of Lord B.'s most splendid poetry—a little exaggerated perhaps in the expression, from a desire to make our exposition clear and impressive—but, in substance, we think merited and correct. We have already said, and we deliberately repeat, that we have no notion that Lord B. had any mischievous intention in these publications—and readily acquit him of any wish to corrupt the morals, or impair the happiness of his readers. Such a wish, indeed, is in itself altogether inconceivable; but it is our duty, nevertheless, to say, that much of what he has published appears to us to have this tendency —and that we are acquainted with no writings so well calculated to extinguish in young minds all generous enthusiasm and gentle affection —all respect for themselves, and all love for their kind—to make them practise and profess hardily what it teaches them to suspect in others— and actually to persuade them that it is wise and manly and knowing, to laugh, not only at self-denial and restraint, but at all aspiring ambition, and all warm and constant affection.

How opposite to this is the system, or the temper, of the great author of *Waverley*—the only living individual to whom Lord Byron must submit to be ranked as inferior in genius—and still more deplorably inferior in all that makes genius either amiable in itself, or useful to society! With all his unrivalled power of invention and judgment, of pathos and pleasantry, the tenor of his sentiments is uniformly generous, indulgent, and good-humoured; and so remote from the bitterness of misanthropy, that he never indulges in sarcasm, and scarcely, in any case, carries his merriment so far as derision. But the peculiarity by which he stands most broadly and proudly distinguished from Lord Byron is, that, beginning, as he frequently does, with some ludicrous or satirical theme, he never fails to raise out of it some feelings of a generous or gentle kind, and to end by exciting our tender pity, or deep respect for those very individuals or classes of persons who seemed at first to be brought on the stage for our mere sport and amusement—thus making the ludicrous itself subservient to the cause of benevolence—and inculcating, at every turn, and as the true end and result of all his trials and experiments, the love of our kind, and the duty and delight of a cordial and genuine sympathy, with the joys and sorrows of every condition of men. It seems to be Lord Byron's way, on the contrary, never to excite a kind or a noble sentiment, without making haste to obliterate it by a torrent of unfeeling mockery or relentless abuse, and taking pains to show how well those passing fantasies may be reconciled to a system of resolute misanthropy, or so managed as even to enhance its merits, or confirm its truth. With what different sensations, accordingly, do we read the works of these two great writers!—With the one, we seem to share a gay and gorgeous banquet—with the other, a wild and dangerous intoxication. Let Lord Byron bethink him of this contrast—and its causes and effects. Though he scorns the precepts, and defies the censure of ordinary men, he may yet be moved by *the example* of his only superior!—In the mean time, we have endeavoured to point out the canker that stains the splendid flowers of his poetry—or, rather, the serpent that lurks beneath them. If it will not listen to the voice of the charmer, that brilliant garden, gay and glorious as it is, must be deserted, and its existence deplored, as a snare to the unwary.

There is a minor blemish, of which we meant to say something also—but it is scarcely worth while—we mean the outrageous, and, till he set the example, the unprecedented *personalities* in which this noble author indulges. We have already noticed the ferocity of his attacks on Mr. Southey. The Laureate had railed at him indeed before; but he had railed 'in good set terms;'—and, if we recollect right, had not even mentioned his Lordship's name. It was all, in his exquisite way, by innuendo. In spite of this, we do not mean to deny that Lord B. had a right to name Mr. Southey—but he had no right to say any thing of Mr. Southey's wife; and the mention of her, and of many other people, is cruel, coarse, and unhandsome. If his Lordship's sense of propriety does not cure him of his propensity, we hope his pride may. For the practice has gone down to such imitators, as can do him no honour in pointing to him as their original. We rather think it would be better after all, to be called the founder of the Satanic School, than the Master of the John Bulls, Beacons, and Sentinels.

THE DRAMAS

Marino Faliero, Doge of Venice. An Historical Tragedy April 1821
Sardanapalus, a Tragedy
The Two Foscari, a Tragedy } December 1821
Cain, a Mystery

---

31. Hazlitt, from his unsigned review of *Marino Faliero, London Magazine*

May 1821

Quoted from *The Complete Works of William Hazlitt*, ed. P. P. Howe, 1930–4, XIX, 44–6.

We cannot speak in terms of very enthusiastic praise of this historical play. Indeed, it hardly corresponds to its title. It has little of a local or circumstantial air about it. We are not violently transported to the time or scene of action. We know not much about the plot, about the characters, about the motives of the persons introduced, but we know a good deal about their sentiments and opinions on matters in general, and hear some very fine descriptions from their mouths; which would, however, have become the mouth of any other individual in the play equally well, and the mouth of the noble poet better than that of any of his characters. We have, indeed, a previous theory, that Lord Byron's genius is not dramatic, and the present performance is not one that makes it absolutely necessary for us to give up that theory. It is very inferior to *Manfred*, both in beauty and interest. The characters and situations there were of a romantic and poetical cast, mere creatures of the imagination; and the sentiments such as the author might easily conjure up by fancying himself on enchanted ground, and adorn with all the illusions that hover round the poet's pen, 'prouder than when blue Iris bends.' The more the writer indulged himself in following out the phantoms of a morbid sensibility, or lapt himself in the voluptuous dream of his own existence, the nearer he would approach to the truth of nature, the more he would be identified with the airy and preternatural personages he represented. But here he descends to the ground of fact and history; and we cannot say that in that circle he treads with the same firmness of step that he has displayed boldness and smoothness of wing in soaring above it. He paints the cloud, or the rainbow in the cloud; or dives into the secret and subterraneous workings of his own breast; but he does not, with equal facility or earnestness, wind into the march of human affairs upon the earth, or mingle in the throng and daily conflict of human passions. There is neither action nor reaction in his poetry; both which are of the very essence of the Drama. He does not commit himself in the common arena of man; but looks down, from the high tower of his rank, nay, of his genius, on the ignobler interests of humanity, and describes them either as a dim and distant phantasmagoria or a paltry fantoccini exhibition, scarce worth his scorn. He fixes on some point of imagination or of brooding thought as a resting-place for his own pride and irritability, instead of seeking to borrow a new and unnecessary stimulus from the busy exploits and over-wrought feelings of others. His Lordship's genius is a spirit of necromancy or of misanthropy, not of humanity. He is governed by antipathies more than by sympathies; but the genius of dramatic poetry is like charity which 'endureth much, is patient, and by humbling itself, is exalted.' Lord Byron, for instance, sympathizes readily with Dante, who was a poet, a patriot, a noble Florentine, and exile from his country: he can describe the feelings of Dante, for in so doing, he does little more than describe his own: he makes nothing out of Marino Faliero, Doge of Venice, and cares nothing about him, for he himself is neither a warrior, a statesman, nor a conspirator. Lord Byron can gaze with swimming eyes upon any of the great lights of Italy, and view them through the misty, widespread glory of lengthening centuries: that is, he can take a high and romantic interest in them, as they appear to us and to him; but he cannot take an historical event in her annals, transport us to the time and place of action, give us a real, living interest in the scene, and by filling the mind with the agonizing hopes, and panic-fears, and incorrigible will, and sudden projects of the authentic actors in the world's volume, charm us out of ourselves, and make us forget that there are such half-faced fellows as readers, authors, or critics in existence. Lord Byron's page has not this effect; it is modern, smooth, fresh from Mr. Murray's, and does not smack of the olden time. It is not rough, Gothic, pregnant with past events, unacquainted with the present time, glowing with the spirit of that dark and fiery age: but strewn with the flowers of poetry and the tropes of rhetoric. The author does not try to make us *overhear* what old Faliero, and his young wife, and his wily, infuriated accomplices would say, but makes them his proxies to discuss the topics of love and marriage, the claims of rank and common justice, or to describe a scene by moonlight, with a running allusion to the pending controversy between his Lordship, Mr. Bowles, and Mr. Campbell, on the merits of the natural and artificial style in poetry. 'That was not the way' of our first tragic writers, nor is it (thank God) that of some of the last. 'One touch of nature makes the whole world kin:'—one line of Webster, Decker, or Ford (to say nothing of Shakspeare), is worth all the didactic and descriptive paraphrases of what would neither be seen nor felt by men in a state of strong agitation as they occur in this play. We cannot call to mind, after reading it, a single electric shock of passion; nor a spark of genius struck out of the immediate occasion, like fire out of the flint; not one revelation of our inmost nature, forced from the rack of restless circumstance. But this is all that is truly dramatic in any tragedy or poem: the rest is but a form of words, an imposing display of ingenuity, or understanding, or fancy, which the writer (however excellent he may be in any of these respects) might as well or much better make in his own person. We think most highly of Lord Byron's powers 'on this side of idolatry'; but we do not think those powers are dramatic, nor can we regard the present work as a splendid exception to that general opinion. But enough of prefatory remark.

Marino Faliero is without a plot, without characters, without fluctuating interest, and without the spirit of dialogue. . . .

32. Jeffrey, from his unsigned review of *Marino Faliero, Edinburgh Review*

Dated July 1821, issued September 1821, XXXV, 271-85

This piece has undoubtedly considerable beauties, both dramatic and poetical; and might have made the fortune of any young aspirant after fame. But the name of Byron raises expectations which are not so easily satisfied; and, judging of it by the lofty standard which he himself has established, we are compelled to say, that we cannot but regard it as a failure, both as a Poem and a Play. This may be partly accounted for, from the inherent difficulty of uniting these two sorts of excellence —of confining the daring and digressive genius of poetry within the forms and limits of a regular drama, and, at the same time, imparting its warm and vivifying spirit to the practical preparation and necessary details of a complete theatrical action. These, however, are difficulties with which dramatic adventurers have long had to struggle; and over which, though they are incomparably most formidable to the most powerful spirits, there is no reason to doubt that the powers of Lord Byron would have triumphed.

The true history of his failure, therefore, we conceive, and the actual cause of his miscarriage on the present occasion, is to be found in the bad choice of his subject—his selection of a story which not only gives no scope to the peculiar and commanding graces of his genius, but runs continually counter to the master currents of his fancy. His great gifts, as all the world knows, are exquisite tenderness and demoniacal sublimity—the power of conjuring up at pleasure those delicious visions of love and beauty, and pity and purity, which melt our hearts within us with a thrilling and etherial softness—and of wielding, at the same time, that infernal fire which blasts and overthrows all things with the dark and capricious fulminations of its scorn, rancour, and revenge. With the consciousness of these great powers, and as if in wilful perversity to their suggestions, he has here chosen a story which, in a great measure, excludes the agency of either; and resolutely conducted it, so as to secure himself against their intrusion;—a story without love or hatred—misanthropy or pity—containing nothing voluptuous and

210

nothing terrific—but depending, for its grandeur, on the anger of a very old and irritable man—and, for its attraction, on the elaborate representations of conjugal dignity and domestic honour,—the sober and austere triumphs of cold and untempted chastity, and the noble propriety of a pure and disciplined understanding. These, we think, are not the most promising themes for any writer whose business is to raise powerful emotions—nor very likely, in any hands, to redeem the modern drama from the imputation of want of spirit, interest and excitement. But for Lord Byron to select them for a grand dramatic effort, is as if a swift-footed racer were to tie his feet together at the starting, or a valiant knight to enter the lists without his arms. No mortal prowess could succeed under such disadvantages. Amadis himself, when he laid aside his enchanted sword and his helmet of proof, was only a very strong man, and no way fit for the encounter of giants and dragons; and Lord Byron, without his bitters and his sweets, his softness and horrors, is only a very bold and clever writer—withal somewhat clumsy and verbose.

The story, in so far as it is original in our drama, is extremely improbable; though, like most other very improbable stories, derived from authentic sources: But, in the main, it is [un]original—being indeed merely another *Venice Preserved*, and continually recalling, though certainly without eclipsing, the memory of the first. Except that Jaffier is driven to join the conspirators by the natural impulse of love and misery, and the Doge by a resentment so outrageous as to exclude all sympathy—and that the disclosure, which is produced by love in the old play, is here ascribed to mere friendship, the general action and catastrophe of the two pieces are almost identical—while, with regard to the writing and management, it must be owned that, if Lord Byron has most sense and vigour, Otway has by far the most passion and pathos; and that, though his conspirators are better orators and reasoners than the gang of Pierre and Reynault, the tenderness of Belvidera is as much more touching, as it is more natural than the stoical and self-satisfied decorum of Angiolina. But lest some of our readers may not have read the play through, it may be as well to preface the rest of our remarks with a short abstract of it. . . .

This naked outline, we confess, gives no great information as to the merits of the piece; and it is fair, therefore, to let the reader a little more into its details. The first scenes represent, rather tediously, the Doge waiting impatiently for the sentence of the Senate, and raving very extravagantly at its lenity. We think all this part very heavily and even unskilfully executed; nor can it be at all surprising that ordinary readers should not enter into his Highness's fury; when it appears that even his nephew does not at first understand it. This dutiful person comments thus calmly on the matter, in a speech which, though set down by Lord Byron in lines of ten syllables, we shall take the liberty to print as prose—which it undoubtedly is—and very ordinary and homely prose too.

> *Ber. Fal.* I cannot but agree with you, the sentence is too slight for the offence. It is not honourable in the Forty to affix so slight a penalty to that which was a foul affront to you, and even to them, as being your subjects; but 'tis not yet without remedy: you can appeal to them once more, or to the Avogadori, who, seeing that true justice is withheld, will now take up the cause they once declined, and do you right upon the bold delinquent. Think you not thus, good uncle? why do you stand so fixed?

[Gives summary of play, with copious quotations.]

It will not now be difficult to estimate the character of this work.— As a play, it is deficient in the attractive passions, in probability, and in depth and variety of interest; and revolts throughout, by the extravagant disproportion which the injury bears to the unmeasured resentment with which it is pursued. As a poem, though it occasionally displays great force and elevation, it obviously wants both grace and facility. The diction is often heavy and cumbrous, and the versification without sweetness or elasticity. It is generally very verbose, and sometimes exceedingly dull. Altogether, it gives us the impression of a thing worked out against the grain, and not poured forth from the fulness of the heart or the fancy—the ambitious and elaborate work of a powerful mind engaged with an unsuitable task—not the spontaneous effusion of an exuberant imagination, sporting in the fulness of its strength. Every thing is heightened and enforced with visible effort and design; and the noble author is often contented to be emphatic by dint of exaggeration, and eloquent by the common topics of declamation. Lord Byron is, undoubtedly, a poet of the very first order—and has talents to reach the very highest honours of the drama. But he must not again disdain love and ambition and jealousy—he must not substitute what is merely *bizarre* and extraordinary, for what is naturally and universally interesting—nor expect, by any exaggerations, so to rouse and rule our sympathies by the senseless anger of an old man, and the prudish proprieties of an untempted woman, as by the agency of the great and simple passions with which, in some of their degrees, all men are familiar, and by which alone the Dramatic Muse has hitherto wrought her miracles.

To this very long play there is subjoined, in the volume before us, four short Cantos of a larger projected poem, called *The Prophecy of Dante*, which seems to be written far more from the impulse of the author's soul, and with ten times more good will to the work, than the tragedy which stands before it. It is a very grand, fervid, turbulent, and somewhat mystical composition—full of the highest sentiments, and the highest poetry;—but disfigured by many faults of precipitation, and overclouded with many obscurities. Its great fault with common readers will be, that it is not sufficiently intelligible, either in its general drift or in particular passages;—and even those who are qualified to enter into its spirit, and can raise themselves to the height of the temper in which it is conceived, will be entitled to complain of the interminable periods and endless interlacings of the diction, and of the general crudity and imperfect concoction of the bulk of the composition. It is however, beyond all question, the work of a man of great genius; and if he would only digest his matter a little more carefully, and somewhat concentrate the potent spirit of poetry which he has here poured abroad so lavishly in its unrectified state, we have no doubt that he might produce something that would command universal admiration, and not merely confirm, but extend the great fame he has already acquired.

33. Some reactions to *Cain*

1821, 1822, 1824

(*a*) JOHN CAM HOBHOUSE. Extracts from Diary. (*Recollections of a Long Life*, ed. Lady Dorchester, 1909–11, II, 172–3):
'[28 October 1821] Return to Murray, the publisher, the proofs of *Cain*, a poem by Lord Byron. Burdett and I read this poem. I think it has scarce one specimen of real poetry or even musical numbers in it. He says in a letter to Kinnaird that it is written in his purest metaphysical manner. Some will call it blasphemous, and I think the whole world will finally agree in thinking it unworthy. Yet I hear T. Moore says it is the best thing Byron ever wrote.'
'[17 November 1821] I lately wrote a letter to Lord Byron remonstrating in the strongest terms against his publishing *Cain*, which appears to me a complete failure.'

(*b*) THOMAS MOORE (1779–1852), the Irish poet, had taken offence at Byron's treatment of his duel with Jeffrey in *English Bards and Scotch Reviewers*, but the quarrel was soon made up, and the two poets became close friends. Extract from letter of 30 September 1821, to Byron:
'. . . I have read *Foscari* and *Cain*. The former does not please me so highly as *Sardanapalus*. It has the fault of all those violent Venetian stories, being unnatural and improbable, and therefore, in spite of all your fine management of them, appealing but remotely to one's sympathies. But *Cain* is wonderful—terrible—never to be forgotten. If I am not mistaken, it will sink deep into the world's heart; and while many will shudder at its blasphemy, all must fall prostrate before its grandeur. Talk of Aeschylus and his Prometheus!—here is the true spirit both of the Poet—and the Devil.' (*The Letters of Thomas Moore*, ed. Wilfred S. Dowden, 1964, II, 494–5.)

(*c*) SIR WALTER SCOTT. Extract from letter of 17 December 1821, to John Murray, accepting Byron's proposal to dedicate *Cain* to him:
'My Dear Sir,—I accept with feelings of great obligation the flattering proposal of Lord Byron to prefix my name to the very grand and tremendous drama of *Cain*. I may be partial to it, and you will allow I

have cause; but I do not know that his Muse has ever taken so lofty a flight amid her former soarings. He has certainly matched Milton on his own ground. Some part of the language is bold, and may shock one class of readers, whose tone will be adopted by others out of affectation or envy. But then they must condemn the *Paradise Lost*, if they have a mind to be consistent. The fiend-like reasoning and bold blasphemy of the fiend and of his pupil, lead exactly to the point which was to be expected—the commission of the first murder, and the ruin and despair of the perpetrator.

I do not see how any one can accuse the author himself of Manicheism. The devil takes the language of that sect, doubtless; because, not being able to deny the existence of the Good Principle, he endeavours to exalt himself—the Evil Principle—to a seeming equality with the Good; but such arguments, in the mouth of such a being, can only be used to deceive and to betray. Lord Byron might have made this more evident, by placing in the mouth of Adam, or of some good and protecting spirit, the reasons which render the existence of moral evil consistent with the general benevolence of the Deity. The great key to the mystery is, perhaps, the imperfection of our own faculties, which see and feel strongly the partial evils which press upon us, but know too little of the general system of the universe, to be aware how the existence of these is to be reconciled with the benevolence of the great Creator. . . .' (*The Letters of Sir Walter Scott*, VII, 37–8.)

(*d*) MARY SHELLEY and PERCY BYSSHE SHELLEY.
(i) Mary Shelley (1797–1851). Extract from letter of 20 December 1821, to Maria Gisborne: 'My Lord is now living very sociably, giving dinners to his male acquaintance and writing divinely; perhaps by this time you have seen *Cain* and will agree with us in thinking it his finest production—To me it sounds like a revelation—of some works one says—one has thought of such things though one could not have expressed it so well—It is not this with *Cain*—one has perhaps stood on the extreme verge of such ideas and from the midst of the darkness which has surrounded us the voice of the Poet now is heard telling a wondrous tale.' (From *The Letters of Mary Shelley*, edited by Frederick L. Jones. Copyright 1944 by the University of Oklahoma Press. Vol. I, p. 153, ll. 13–20.)

(ii) Percy Bysshe Shelley. Extracts from letters to John Gisborne:
12 January 1822: 'What think you of Lord Byron now? Space

wondered less at the swift and fair creations of God, when he grew weary of vacancy, than I at the late works of this spirit of an angel in the mortal paradise of a decaying body. So I think—let the world envy while it admires, as it may.' *The Letters of Percy Bysshe Shelley*, ed. F. L. Jones, 1964, II, 376.)

26 January 1822: 'What think you of Lord Byron's last Volume? In my opinion it contains finer poetry than has appeared in England since the publication of *Paradise Regained.—Cain* is apocalyptic—it is a revelation not before communicated to man.' (*Op. cit.*, II, 388.)

18 June 1822: 'I write little now. It is impossible to compose except under the strong excitement of an assurance of finding sympathy in what you write. Imagine Demosthenes reciting a Philippic to the waves of the Atlantic! Lord Byron is in this respect fortunate. He touched a chord to which a million hearts responded, and the coarse music which he produced to please them disciplined him to the perfection which he now approaches.' (*Op. cit.*, II, 436. This comment refers, no doubt, to *Don Juan* as well as to *Cain*.)

(e) HENRY CRABB ROBINSON. Extract from Diary for 1 March 1822: '. . . I called at Aders's and came home early to read *Cain*, which I finished the next day. *Cain* has not advanced any novelties in the author's speculations on the origin of evil, but he has stated one or two points with great effect. The book is calculated to spread infidelity by furnishing a ready expression to difficulties which must occur to every one, more or less, and which are passed over by those who confine themselves to scriptural representations. The second act is full of poetic energy, and there is some truth of passion in the scenes between Cain's wife and himself. It is certainly a mischievous work calculated to do nothing but harm.' (*Henry Crabb Robinson on Books and their Writers*, ed. E. J. Morley, 1938, I, 281.)

(f) JOHN GIBSON LOCKHART. Extract from unsigned review of *Sardanapalus, The Two Foscari* and *Cain*, in *Blackwood's Magazine* for January 1822: '. . . It would be highly ridiculous to enter, at this time of day, into any thing like a formal review, *here*, of Lord Byron's new volume. We have not happened to meet with any two individuals who expressed two different opinions about it and its contents. There is a great deal of power in *Sardanapalus* . . . but as a play, it is an utter failure; and, in God's name, why call a thing a tragedy, unless it be meant to be a play? What would people say to a new song of Tom Moore's, prefaced with an earnest injunction on man, woman, and child, never to think of singing it? A tragedy, *not meant to be acted*, seems to us to be just about as reasonable an affair as a song not meant to be sung. But even as *a poem*, *Sardanapalus* is *not* quite worthy of its author. Let any one just think, for a moment, of the magnificent story of Sardanapalus, and then imagine what a thing Lord Byron might have made of it, had he chosen the fiery narrative-pace of *Lara*, or *The Giaour*—instead of this lumbering, and lax, and highly *undramatic* blank-verse dialogue.—The *Foscari* is totally inferior to the *Sardanapalus*. It is a ridiculous caricature of some historical situations, in themselves beautiful and interesting. The true tragedy of the Foscari is to be read in the notes at the end of Lord Byron's tragedy bearing that name; and the public is much obliged to him, and so is M. Simonde de Sismondi, for these very pretty extracts. *Cain* contains, perhaps, five or six passages of as fine poetry as Lord Byron ever wrote or will write; but, taken altogether, it is a wicked and blasphemous performance, destitute of any merit sufficient to overshadow essential defects of the most abominable nature. The three plays, bound up together, we repeat, constitute a dullish volume—perhaps one of the heaviest that has appeared in the poetical world since the days of *Ricciarda, Tragedia*.[1] (*Blackwood's Magazine*, XI, 90–1.)

(g) EGERTON BRYDGES [see below, p. 262], *Letters on the Character and Genius of Lord Byron*, 1824, pp. 264–5: '. . . There is another extraordinary poem of which I have not spoken hitherto; because, I will confess, that I know not how to speak of it properly, yet something must be said of it.—*Cain* is a poem much too striking to be passed in silence. But its impiety is so frightful that it is impossible to praise it, while its genius and beauty of composition would demand all the notice which mere literary merit can claim. It is scarcely necessary to repeat the answer to the very futile defence which has been made for it, against the charge of its attack on the goodness of Province. It must be obvious to every intelligent reader that the example of *Milton* does not apply to the manner in which Lord Byron has executed his poem of *Cain*. Milton puts rebellious and blasphemous speeches into the mouth of *Satan*; but Milton never leaves those speeches unanswered: on the contrary, he always brings forward a *good angel* to controvert triumphantly all the daring assertions and arguments of the EVIL SPIRIT. Lord Byron leaves all which he ascribes to *Cain* and *Lucifer*

[1] [Ugo Foscolo's drama, *Ricciarda, Tragedia*, was published in 1820.]

in their full force on the reader's mind, without even an attempt to repel them.

It seems to me, that of all Lord Byron's poems this is that of which the ill tendency is most unequivocal, and for which no plausible excuse can be made;—and it is the more dangerous, because it is one of the best written. . . .'

(*h*) Goethe's praise of *Cain* in February 1824 is reported by J. P. Eckermann: 'Goethe then showed me a short critique, which he had written on Byron's *Cain*, and which I read with great interest.

"We see," he said, "how the inadequate dogmas of the church work upon a free mind like Byron's, and how by such a piece he struggles to get rid of a doctrine which has been forced upon him. The English clergy will not thank him; but I shall be surprised if he does not go on treating biblical subjects of similar import, and if he lets slip a subject like the destruction of Sodom and Gomorrah."' (*Conversations of Goethe with Eckermann and Soret*, trans. John Oxenford, 1850, I, 129–30.)

The short critique was a eulogistic review of *Cain*, written in 1824: 'This poet [it declares at one point], whose burning spiritual vision penetrates beyond all comprehension into the past and the present and, in their train, also into the future, has now conquered new worlds for his boundless talent; and no human being can foresee what he will achieve with them. . . .' (*Goethes Werke*, Weimar, 1888–1919, XLI. II, 9; trans. E. M. Butler, *Byron and Goethe*, 1956, p. 183.)

This high estimate of *Cain* was reasserted in a conversation with Eckermann in June 1827: '"It is, indeed, admirable," said Goethe. "Its beauty is such as we shall not see a second time in the world."' (*Conversations*, trans. Oxenford, I, 419.)

34. Three orthodox attacks on *Cain*

1821, 1822

(*a*) Extract from an anonymous review in the Supplement to the *Gentleman's Magazine* for July–December 1821 (XCI[ii], 613–15), in which the reviewer takes his leave of Lord Byron's *Cain* 'with feelings of the most unqualified disgust and disapprobation', after presenting extracts under the twin headings 'Hideous Blasphemy', 'Twaddle and Nonsense': 'This [he begins] is unquestionably one of the most pernicious productions that ever proceeded from the pen of a man of genius. It is in fact neither more nor less than a series of wanton libels upon the Supreme Being and His attributes. If the slanderer of a fellow mortal deserve reprobation and punishment, what ought to be the penalty of the calumniator of his omnipotent Maker, the miserable traducer of his God. If any additional fame can attach to Lord Byron from this odious "Mystery", it can be none other than an immortality of infamy. . . .'

(*b*) Extract from an anonymous review of *Cain* and Southey's *Vision of Judgement* in the *Eclectic Review* for May 1822 (N. S., XVII, 418–27). This reviewer speaks of 'the irretrievable infamy which, as the Author of *Don Juan* and *Cain*, [Lord Byron] has purchased;' he finds in him a notable example of the 'morbid love of impurity . . . strikingly manifested in alliance with impiety;' and he deplores this latest production: 'He has summoned both fiction and falsehood to aggravate the philosophical difficulties which he, in this poem, has laboured to embalm in verse; difficulties new to a large proportion of his readers, and with which the young and inexperienced are ill able to grapple. These, this new apostle of infidelity has endeavoured to propagate in a shape the most adapted to make an impression on the imagination. In the very spirit of the fabled Sphinx, he propounds these dark enigmas, that those who fail to unravel them, may perish.

That this is a heinous offence against society, who will dare deny? It is an offence of the deepest dye. . . .' (*Op. cit.*, p. 426.)

(*c*) Extract from *A Remonstrance addressed to Mr. John Murray, respecting a Recent Publication*, by 'Oxoniensis' [the Rev. H. J. Todd, 1763–1845], 1822, pp. 9–10, 18–19: '. . . As a bookseller, I conclude you have but one standard of poetic excellence;—the extent of your sale. Without assuming any thing beyond the bounds of ordinary foresight, I venture to foretell, that in this case you will be mistaken; the book will disappoint your cupidity, as much as it discredits your feeling and discretion. Your noble employer has deceived you, Mr. Murray; he has profited by the celebrity of his name to palm upon you obsolete trash, the very off-scourings of Bayle and Voltaire, which he has made you pay for, as though it were first rate poetry and sound metaphysics. But I tell you (and if you doubt it, you may consult any of the literary gentlemen who frequent your reading room) that this poem, this Mystery with which you have insulted us, is nothing more than a Cento from Voltaire's novels and the most objectionable articles in Bayle's Dictionary, served up in clumsy cuttings of ten syllables, for the purpose of giving it the guise of poetry. . . .'

'. . . He seems to have been possessed of all the gifts of nature and fortune, only that he might prove how vain such possessions are to those who know not how to use them rightly.

He was gifted with the highest intellectual talents, but he has "profaned this God-given strength" to the worst purposes: he was born a Briton, and inherited the honours and privileges of a class to which the proudest might have been proud to belong, yet when does he allude to his country or her institutions, without an expression of scorn or hatred? He did not scruple to contract the most solemn obligations which society can impose, and which usually call into exercise the tenderest feelings of our nature; those feelings he has wilfully thrown from him, and trampled on the ties from which they sprung: and now at last he quarrels with the very conditions of humanity, rebels against that Providence which guides and governs all things, and dares to adopt the language which had never before been attributed to any being but one, "Evil be thou my good." Such as far as we can judge is Lord Byron.'

35. Leigh Hunt, *Examiner*

2 June 1822, pp. 338–41

From a letter on *Cain* to the readers of the *Examiner*.

You must have been much edified by the sensation which this poem
has made. The civil authorities would rather say nothing about it: the
religious cannot say anything fairly; and the critical are exceedingly
hampered betwixt the two. . . .

The truth is simply this: The Jews, like many other nations, in endeavouring to account for the difficulties in the government of the
world, put forth some apologues; and because these apologues have
been incorporated with the books which the Christians account
sacred, the latter, though the very essence of their religion consists in
going counter to the Jews, think it their business to uphold them in
every particular, and to find in them nothing but morality, right
reason, and perfection. When I speak thus of the apologues in question,
I do not mean to undervalue them in some respects. On the contrary,
some of them appear to me very beautiful, as a sort of imperfect
illustration, particularly the account of the Fall of Man, of that loss of a
sense of innocence, which is generated by the subtle and wise absurdity
of finding guilt where there is none. There is a very deep sentiment in
it. But the worst of this and of other apologues is, that they are not
complete in all their members. They give the Supreme Being a part in
them: *the God of the apologue becomes in time identified with the Great
First Cause of all things*; and, at last, even in ages of extreme civilization,
if you do not take the letter of the story for the very essence of the
Divine Spirit and its intentions, you are thought guilty of a daring
impiety. Whereas it may be your very piety that prevents you. For
instance; the Goths were of opinion that God drank mead with you in
heaven out of the sculls of your enemies. Now though the Divine
Principle includes small as well as great in its operations, yet if the
Goths were extant still in any other shape than those of the Allied
Governments, and I could go among them with my present opinions,
I could never be brought to think that it would concentrate and

221

infinitely diminish itself into the likeness of a Vandal Chieftain, and sit at table with me over the above liquor. If this is thought an irreverend instance, it is the fault of those who force one to bring such incompatible ideas together. I mean no irreverence, or I could have put the thing in a much more ridiculous light. By the same rule, if I were a Turk or a Persian, nothing could induce me to persuade myself that the Divine Principle had had those personal conferences with Mahomet, and given him a written license to have more wives than any one else. If I were a Hindoo, I should more than doubt the celestial origin of the injunctions about paring my nails, cooking my rice, and turning to the south-east when I put on my clothes. And to return to the Jews, if I were a Jew, I should have an exceeding scepticism about the trouble which the Great First Cause took to regulate the ornaments of the ark and temple, settling how many knobs there should be on this and that piece of furniture, and taking other strange delights in the borders. All this, I grant, may have had its uses. The Great Being in question (if we must use human terms in speaking of its mode of action) has at all events permitted it. It has taken place. But so have thousands of other things and trifles. So has the Pagan religion: so have the bishops' wigs; but we are not bound to have faith in either. I once more deprecate the idea of willingly bringing together two such incompatible subjects of contemplation, as the Divine Mystery of the Universe, and these toys of priestly invention. And again I say it is not my fault. Not that I presume to judge of the Divine feelings by those of the petty authorities of this earth, and conclude, that because a king or a clergyman cannot put up with a jest, the Supreme Being is equally unable to afford it. There are other reasons, and much more reverential ones, why they should not drive us upon these ludicrous inconsistencies. But let the anti-judaical defenders of judaism, and the believers in eternal punishment, think as they may, no man is more inclined than myself to be grave on the subject of that mighty and beneficent Power, which has been so much degraded by the self-love and bad passions of creeds and sects under the title of God; so much so indeed, that one wishes one could give it some other name without hurting the feelings of the truly pious. If I cannot help smiling, and if others cannot help a movement of indignation, when people attribute to it all their little fugitive tastes and their more pernicious bigotries, a third time I say the fault belongs solely to the latter. Men of my way of thinking would identify with it nothing but love and joy, and the beauties of nature, and the bringing of good out of stubborn materials, and the great principle (whatever it

be) of universal motion, and those energies of the better part of mankind, which, for aught we know to the contrary, are only so many
experiments of its very self, trying how far it can extend itself, and take
our nature along with it. Why are these aspirations to be diverted by
the petty dogmas of theologians and critics, who, under pretence of
enlarging and settling one's notions of the Divinity, only narrow, and
confuse, and barbarize them?

Why murder and other evils came into the world to disturb the
otherwise beneficent results of our passions, is a great mystery. But if
philosophy cannot explain it, otherwise than as a portion of the stubborn materials above mentioned, our passions themselves can still less
explain it; and yet it was with nothing better that the Jews undertook
to do so. Fontenelle, in one of those apparently profane speeches which
have often more piety at bottom than some of our most orthodox
sentiments, said, that if God had made man in his own likeness, man
had returned the compliment by making him in his. Yet nothing can
be more true. Nations have made their gods according to their own
tempers: individuals continue to do the same. If we were suffered to
regard the account of Cain and Abel as a mere apologue, or as one of
those poetical traditions which might mingle with the early history of
all nations, or even as what it really appears to be, a semi-barbarous,
semi-philosophical attempt to account for part of the origin of evil, it
would be all very well; but by confounding the God of an eastern
fable with the God of the Universe, and attributing to him the half-
reasoning passions and the crude notions of morality and punishment
which belong to the first stages of civilization, we do a number of very
foolish things. In the first place, we give no real explanation of the
mystery at all, but merely make passions account for passions: secondly,
we make God the merest of men, even in his notions of justice: thirdly,
we encourage ourselves in our own false notions of it; and fourthly,
when better opinions arise by dint of experience and enquiry, we
enable the bigoted to oppose us, and hinder the timid from siding with
us, by making piety itself appear impious;—that is to say, by making it
appear an impious thing to shew the wide difference between the vulgar
idea of God, and the nobler one.

If the Jews, in the story of Cain and Abel, merely intended to shew
the unhappy consequences of envy and murder, they made a very
affecting apologue; imperfect, it is true, as far as they introduced the
Divine Being, but very touching nevertheless; and, if you could keep
the imperfect part of it out of sight, very useful. But this is impossible

as men grow wiser, and require more complete and consistent lessons of justice: and it becomes worse than impossible, if they are then to be told, that they are impious for not liking to see modes of jurisprudence attributed to God, which their experience and knowledge have taught them to consider as unworthy of men. If they are to have no medium between considering the God of the apologue and the Great Principle of all things as the same being, their next step is to ask how he could be perfectly omnipotent and perfectly good, and yet permit all these evils which he so heavily punished: and again, how he could partake of so many human passions himself: and again, why he did not mend Cain rather than perpetuate his misery, and confirm him in his sullen temper;—how he knew so little of human nature, as not to be aware that extreme punishment went counter to the only utility of punishment, which is improvement. I omit other questions equally obvious but they are all questions which it is impossible to get over, as long as the Deity is thus set on a level with ourselves: nay, they bring us round, in its blankest sense, to the most godless feeling of Atheism, tending to prove that there is no other Deity than what we find in our human nature, the bad parts as well as the good:—whereas, by not playing the hypocrite with those terms of Invisible and Incomprehensible, which we are so fond of using and contradicting, and by sincerely leaving the Divine Nature its mystery, its universality, and its tendency to make the most of the stubborn materials it has to work upon, we leave it in possession of all that renders it truly adorable, and at the same time keep ourselves in that patient and all-endeavouring frame of mind, which, as I observed before, is, for aught we know to the contrary, necessary to the divinest of its own operations among us, and made to carry us along with its very self into ages of we know not what divine improvement. If it is so, how do we not encumber ourselves with these old and half-informed beggings of the question? If it is not so, the belief is at least a good, kind, and patient one; unperplexed with all that worries other systems of religion; quite compatible with the goodness we all wish to believe in; and a promoter of that very spirit of endeavour, which is at all events one of the best principles of human action.

The history of Cain has furnished matter of very perplexing consideration to a variety of persons in modern times. . . . [A remarkable instance in Bayle of the effect which this story had upon men's minds] is that of the Cainites, a sect who sprung up in the second century merely out of the perplexities of this single story, and who found it so contradictory to their ideas of justice, that they ran, out of resentment, into a great absurdity. They supposed the God of the Old Testament to be a real malignant principle, who had sown discord in the world, and subjected our nature to a thousand calamities; upon which they concluded, that it was their business to oppose him in every one of his injunctions; which must have brought them into some very ridiculous dilemmas. To 'commit adultery' out of resentment, is bad enough; but how they could have contrived to dishonour their father and mother upon a moral principle,—to steal, out of a virtuous preference,—and to bear false witness against their neighbour, from charity to all mankind, —are difficulties which I leave to those who can reconcile anything,— the theologians. However, it has been well observed, that the instincts of mankind soon contrive to elude the literal injunctions of their respective faiths, except where they are turned into a handle of worldliness. The Cainite, like his neighbour, would soon discover that the natural interests of society, as well as the orders of a religion which he opposed, required him not to be dishonest; and the sect would speedily have fallen to nothing at any time, not only (as it did then) because it ran so diametrically opposite to all the received opinions, and certainly not because it was hostile to evil, but because not knowing how to separate the evil from the good, and acting in the very spirit to which it objected, it made its inconsistencies appear the greater by holding them up as opposed to inconsistency.

The only real fault to be found with productions like the one before us, is that the poet either compliments or disregards the understandings of his readers a little too much; and by leaving them to gather his actual opinions on the subject for themselves, gives occasion to the weak and the hypocritical to charge him with something of this Cainite spirit. People are led to imagine that he has no other ideas of the Divine Being than the one which his drama puts in so disadvantageous a light; and not being able to take the real meaning of his hint, and work out his conclusion for themselves, they pay their unlucky faith the most unfortunate compliments, and complain bitterly of the atrocious and fiend-like person, who after all only lays before them a vigorous statement of their own proposition. Doubtless, if the ruling Deity were such a being as the advocates of unjust systems and eternal punishment represent him, it would be the duty of every humane disposition and decent mind to be in the most glorious and most awful of all minorities. Their very consciousness of the existence of something nobler in their own hearts would be their warrant and their strength;

that itself would be a diviner, if not a more powerful, Deity; and who should tell them, if a Heavenly Sovereign is thus to be made out of common despotic matter, that his sovereignty did not in like manner depend upon opinion; and that, in the process of time, the homage fading away, the lonely tyranny must cease? It would be a similar case in one respect, if the Deity were nothing but an imagination of men's minds, and depended entirely upon them for the greater or less divinity with which they invested it. But as the amount of good in the world, that is to say, of ordinary and pleasurable excitement, is much greater than the reverse, (though if it were not, it would take more than bigotry's absurdities to prove that good was not ultimately regarded)— and as it seems impossible for the human mind to get rid of a consciousness of something superior to matter and impulsive of motion, however theologians degrade it and deists are puzzled to define it,—it is desirable in those who would do away false notions of things human and super-human, not that they should let people fancy them more perplexed on these points than they are, nor that in every instance they should let them draw their own conclusions (which a variety of circumstances may long prevent them from drawing to any good purpose); but that they should frankly state the amount of the common opinion and their own, contrast the two as forcibly and sincerely as possible, and then leave the reader to draw the united conclusions of his heart and understanding. One or two more of Lord Byron's pithy prefatory sentences would have done away every objection on this score, and left to his drama all the effect which it is so well calculated to produce. It is true, he may say that this is not his humour,—not the turn of his genius. I do not think the answer unanswerable; though genius may say a great deal for being left to its impulses. But at all events, if the genius is worth having its omissions supplied by others, others (*ecce signum*)[1] will most likely be found to supply them.

And now to refresh ourselves after these polemics with a little of his Lordship's poetry. Oh the beauty and the benignity of poetry! How it survives all circumstance of discussion, and subject, and contingency, and remains lovely and divine for its own sake! The noble-mindedness which flashes through the darkest and most mistakable parts of this drama, and the character of Adah alone, who makes a god of her affection, would be sufficient to lead thinking and sensitive minds to higher notions of the Deity, than those furnished by an uncivilized people. Although the author's genius is not dramatic in the true sense

[1] ['Behold the proof.']

of the word, that is to say, although he does not so much go out of himself to describe others, as furnish others out of himself, yet this is the most dramatic of all his productions. . . . The magnificent melancholy of the description of Lucifer, when Cain sees him first coming, is worthy of Milton. . . .

36. Jeffrey, from his unsigned review of *Sardanapalus, The Two Foscari* and *Cain, Edinburgh Review*

Dated February 1822, issued April 1822, XXXVI, 413–52

Jeffrey's condemnation of *Don Juan* (see above, pp. 199–205) forms part of this review. Byron came on it in *Galignani's Messenger*, and his letters show some regret at Jeffrey's attacking him (*LJ*, VI, 80–1, 89).

It must be a more difficult thing to write a good play—or even a good dramatic poem—than we had imagined. Not that we should, *a priori*, have imagined it to be very easy; but it is impossible not to be struck with the fact, that, in comparatively rude times, when the resources of the art had been less carefully considered, and Poetry certainly had not collected all her materials, success seems to have been more frequently, and far more easily obtained. From the middle of Elizabeth's reign till the end of James's, the drama formed by far the most brilliant and beautiful part of our poetry,—and indeed of our literature in general. From that period to the Revolution, it lost a part of its splendour and originality; but still continued to occupy the most conspicuous and considerable place in our literary annals. For the last century, it has been quite otherwise—our poetry has ceased almost entirely to be dramatic; and, though men of great name and great talent have occasionally adventured into this once fertile field, they have reaped no laurels, and left no trophies behind them. . . .

[After a brief survey of the decline in English drama, and some discussion of the reasons for the inferiority of modern playwrights, Jeffrey passes to Byron's most recent works.]

. . . we think it is certain that his late dramatic efforts have not been made carelessly, or without anxiety. To us, at least, they seem very elaborate and hardwrought compositions; and this indeed we take to be their leading characteristic, and the key to most of their peculiarities.

Considered as Poems, we confess they appear to us to be rather heavy, verbose, and inelegant—deficient in the passion and energy which belongs to the other writings of the noble author—and still more in the richness of imagery, the originality of thought, and the sweetness of versification for which he used to be distinguished. They are for the most part solemn, prolix, and ostentatious—lengthened out by large preparations for catastrophes that never arrive, and tantalizing us with slight specimens and glimpses of a higher interest scattered thinly up and down many weary pages of pompous declamation. Along with the concentrated pathos and homestruck sentiments of his former poetry, the noble author seems also, we cannot imagine why, to have discarded the spirited and melodious versification in which they were embodied, and to have formed to himself a measure equally remote from the spring and vigour of his former compositions, and from the softness and inflexibility of the ancient masters of the drama. There are some sweet lines, and many of great weight and energy; but the general march of the verse is cumbrous and unmusical. His lines do not vibrate like polished lances, at once strong and light, in the hands of his persons, but are wielded like clumsy batons in a bloodless affray. Instead of the graceful familiarity and idiomatical melodies of Shakespeare, it is apt, too, to fall into clumsy prose, in its approaches to the easy and collo-quial style; and, in the loftier passages, is occasionally deformed by low and common images that harmonize but ill with the general solemnity of the diction.

As Plays, we are afraid we must also say that the pieces before us are wanting in interest, character, and action:—at least we must say this of the two last of them—for *there is* interest in *Sardanapalus*—and beauties besides, that make us blind to its other defects. There is, however, throughout, a want of dramatic effect and variety; and we suspect there is something in the character or habit of Lord B.'s genius which will render this unattainable. He has too little sympathy with the ordinary feelings and frailties of humanity, to succeed well in their representa-tion—'His soul is like a star, and dwells apart.' It does not 'hold the mirror up to nature,' nor catch the hues of surrounding objects; but, like a kindled furnace, throws out its intense glare and gloomy grandeur on the narrow scene which it irradiates. He has given us, in his other works, some glorious pictures of nature—some magnificent reflections, and some inimitable delineations of character: But the same feelings prevail in them all; and his portraits in particular, though a little varied in the drapery and attitude, seem all copied from the same original.

His Childe Harold, his Giaour, Conrad, Lara, Manfred, Cain, and Lucifer,—are all one individual. There is the same varnish of voluptuousness on the surface—the same canker of misanthropy at the core, of all he touches. He cannot draw the changes of many-coloured life, nor transport himself into the condition of the infinitely diversified characters by whom a stage should be peopled. The very intensity of his feelings—the loftiness of his views—the pride of his nature or his genius, withhold him from this identification; so that in personating the heroes of the scene, he does little but repeat himself. It would be better for him, we think, if it were otherwise. We are sure it would be better for his readers. He would get more fame, and things of far more worth than fame, if he would condescend to a more extended and cordial sympathy with his fellow-creatures; and we should have more variety of fine poetry, and, at all events, better tragedies. We have no business to read him a homily on the sinfulness of pride and uncharity; but we have a right to say, that it argues a poorness of genius to keep always to the same topics and persons; and that the world will weary at last of the most energetic pictures of misanthropes and madmen—outlaws and their mistresses!

A man gifted as he is, when he aspires at dramatic fame, should emulate the greatest of dramatists. Let Lord B. then think of Shakespeare—and consider what a noble range of character, what a freedom from mannerism and egotism, there is in him! How much he seems to have studied nature; how little to have thought about himself; how seldom to have repeated or glanced back at his own most successful inventions! Why indeed should he? Nature was still open before him, and inexhaustible; and the freshness and variety that still delight his readers, must have had constant attractions for himself. Take his Hamlet, for instance. What a character is there!—how full of thought and refinement, and fancy and individuality! 'How infinite in faculties! In form and motion how express and admirable! The beauty of the universe, the paragon of animals!' Yet close the play, and we meet with him no more—neither in the author's other works, nor any where else! A common author, who had hit upon such a character, would have dragged it in at every turn, and worn it to very tatters. Sir John Falstaff, again, is a world of wit and humour in himself. But except in the two parts of *Henry IV* there would have been no trace of such a being, had not the author been 'ordered to continue him' in *The Merry Wives of Windsor*. He is not the least like Benedick, or Mercutio, or Sir Toby Belch, or any of the other witty personages of the same author,—nor are they like each other. Othello is one of the most striking and powerful inventions on the stage. But when the play closes, we hear no more of him! The poet's creation comes no more to life again under a fictitious name, than the real man would have done. Lord Byron, in Shakespeare's place, would have peopled the world with black Othellos! What indications are there of *Lear* in any of his earlier plays? What traces of it in any that he wrote afterwards? None. It might have been written by any other man, he is so little conscious of it. He never once returns to that huge sea of sorrow; but has left it standing by itself, shoreless and unapproachable. Who else could have afforded not to have 'drowned the stage with tears' from such a source? But we must break away from Shakespeare, and come at last to the work before us.

In a very brief preface, Lord B. renews his protest against looking upon any of his plays, as having been composed 'with the most remote view to the stage'—and, at the same time, testifies in behalf of the *Unities*, as essential to the existence of the drama—according to what 'was, till lately, the law of literature throughout the world, and is still so, in the more civilized parts of it.' We do not think those opinions very consistent; and we think that neither of them could possibly find favour with a person whose genius had a truly dramatic character. We should as soon expect an orator to compose a speech altogether unfit to be spoken. A drama is not merely a dialogue, but *an action:* and necessarily supposes that something is to pass before the eyes of assembled spectators. Whatever is peculiar to its written part, should derive its peculiarity from this consideration. Its style should be an accompaniment to action—and should be calculated to excite the emotions, and keep alive the attention, of gazing multitudes. If an author does not bear this continually in his mind, and does not write in the ideal presence of an eager and diversified assemblage, he may be a poet perhaps, but assuredly he never will be a dramatist. If Lord B. really does not wish to impregnate his elaborate scenes with the living spirit of the drama—if he has no hankering after stage-effect—if he is not haunted with the visible presentment of the persons he has created —if, in setting down a vehement invective, he does not fancy the tone in which Mr Kean would deliver it, and anticipate the long applauses of the pit, then he may be sure that neither his feelings nor his genius are in unison with the stage at all. Why, then, should he affect the form, without the power of tragedy? He may, indeed, produce a mystery like *Cain*, or a far sweeter vision like *Manfred*, without subjecting himself to the censure of legitimate criticism; but if, with a regular subject before him, capable of all the strength and graces of the drama, he does not feel himself able or willing to draw forth its resources so as to affect an audience with terror and delight, he is not the man we want—and his time and talents are wasted here. Didactic reasoning and eloquent description, will not compensate, in a play, for a dearth of dramatic spirit and invention: and besides, sterling sense and poetry, as such, ought to stand by themselves, without the unmeaning mockery of a *dramatis personae*.

As to Lord Byron's pretending to set up the *Unities* at this time of day, as 'the law of literature throughout the world', it is mere caprice and contradiction. He, if ever man was, is *a law to himself*—'a chartered libertine;'—and now, when he is tired of this unbridled license, he wants to do penance within the *Unities!* This certainly looks very like affectation; or, if there is any thing sincere in it, the motive must be, that, by getting rid of so much story and action, in order to simplify the plot and bring it within the prescribed limits, he may fill up the blank spaces with long discussions, and have nearly all the talk to himself! For ourselves, we will confess that we have had a considerable contempt for these same *Unities*, ever since we read Dennis's *Criticism on Cato* in our boyhood—except indeed the unity of action, which Lord Byron does not appear to set much store by. Dr Johnson, we conceive, has pretty well settled this question: and if Lord Byron chuses to grapple with him, he will find that it requires a stronger arm than that with which he puts down our Laureates. We shall only add, that when the moderns tie themselves down to write tragedies of the same length, and on the same simple plan, in other respects, with those of Sophocles and Aeschylus, we shall not object to their adhering to the Unities; for there can, in that case, be no sufficient inducement for violating them. But, in the mean time, we hold that English dramatic poetry soars above the *Unities*, just as the imagination does. The only pretence for insisting on them is, that we suppose the stage itself to be, actually and really, the very spot on which a given action is performed; and, if so, this space cannot be removed to another. But the supposition is manifestly quite contrary to truth and experience. The stage is considered merely as a place in which any given action *ad libitum* may be performed; and accordingly may be shifted, and is so in imagination, as often as the action requires it. That any writer should ever have insisted on such an unity as this, must appear sufficiently preposterous; but, that the defence of it should be taken up by an author whose plays are never to be acted at all, and which, therefore, have nothing more than a nominal reference to any stage or locality whatever, must strike one as absolutely incredible.

It so happens, however, that the disadvantage, and, in truth, absurdity, of sacrificing higher objects to a formality of this kind, is strikingly displayed in one of these dramas—*The Two Foscari*. The whole interest here turns upon the younger of them having returned from banishment, in defiance of the law and its consequences, from an unconquerable longing after his own country. Now, the only way to have made this sentiment palpable, the practicable foundation of stupendous suffering, would have been, to have presented him to the audience wearing out his heart in exile—and forming his resolution to return, at a distance from his country, or hovering, in excruciating suspense, within sight of its borders. We might then have caught some glimpse of the nature of his motives, and of so extraordinary a character. But as this would have been contrary to one of the unities, we first meet with him led from 'the Question,' and afterwards taken back to it in the Ducal Palace, or clinging to the dungeon-walls of his native city, and expiring from his dread of leaving them; and therefore feel more wonder than sympathy, when we are told, in a Jeremiad of wilful lamentations, that these agonizing consequences have resulted not from guilt or disaster, but merely from the intensity of his love for his country. . . .

[After a long account of *Sardanapalus* and a shorter one of *The Two Foscari*, Jeffrey gives the following critique of *Cain*.]

Of *Cain, a Mystery* we are constrained to say, that, though it abounds in beautiful passages, and shows more *power* perhaps than any of the author's dramatical compositions, we regret very much that it should ever have been published. It will give great scandal and offence to pious persons in general—and may be the means of suggesting the most painful doubts and distressing perplexities, to hundreds of minds that might never otherwise have been exposed to such dangerous disturbance. It is nothing less than absurd, in such a case, to observe, that Lucifer cannot well be expected to talk like an orthodox divine—and that the conversation of the first Rebel and the first Murderer was not likely to be very unexceptionable—or to plead the authority of Milton, or the authors of the old mysteries, for such offensive colloquies. The fact is, that here *the whole argument*—and a very elaborate and specious argument it is—is directed against the goodness or the power of the

Deity, and against the reasonableness of religion in general; and there is no answer so much as attempted to the offensive doctrines that are so strenuously inculcated. The Devil and his pupil have the field entirely to themselves—and are encountered with nothing but feeble obtestations and unreasoning horrors. Nor is this argumentative blasphemy a mere incidental deformity that arises in the course of an action directed to the common sympathies of our nature. It forms, on the contrary, the great staple of the piece—and occupies, we should think, not less than two-thirds of it;—so that it is really difficult to believe that it was written for any other purpose than to inculcate these doctrines—or at least to discuss the question upon which they bear. Now, we can certainly have no objection to Lord Byron writing an Essay on the Origin of Evil—and sifting the whole of that vast and perplexing subject with the force and the freedom that would be expected and allowed in a fair philosophical discussion. But we do not think it fair, thus to argue it partially and *con amore*, in the name of Lucifer and Cain; without the responsibility or the liability to answer that would attach to a philosophical disputant—and in a form which both doubles the danger, if the sentiments are pernicious, and almost precludes his opponents from the possibility of a reply.

Philosophy and Poetry are both very good things in their way; but, in our opinion, they do not go very well together. It is but a poor and pedantic sort of poetry that seeks to embody nothing but metaphysical subtleties and abstract deductions of reason—and a very suspicious philosophy that aims at establishing its doctrines by appeals to the passions and the fancy. Though such arguments, however, are worth little in the schools, it does not follow that their effect is inconsiderable in the world. On the contrary, it is the mischief of all poetical paradoxes, that, from the very limits and end of poetry, which deals only in obvious and glancing views, they are never brought to the fair test of argument. An allusion to a doubtful topic will often pass for a definitive conclusion on it; and, clothed in beautiful language, may leave the most pernicious impressions behind. We therefore think that poets ought fairly to be confined to the established creed and morality of their country, or to the *actual* passions and sentiments of mankind; and that poetical dreamers and sophists who pretend to *theorise* according to their feverish fancies, without a warrant from authority or reason, ought to be banished the commonwealth of letters. In the courts of morality, poets are unexceptionable *witnesses*; they may give in the evidence, and depose to facts whether good or ill; but we demur to their arbitrary and self-pleasing summing up; they are suspected *judges*, and not very often safe advocates, where great questions are concerned, and universal principles brought to issue. But we shall not press this point farther at present. We do not doubt that Lord Byron has written conscientiously, and that he is of opinion that the publication of his sentiments will not be disadvantageous to mankind. Upon this, and upon other matters, we confess we think otherwise—and we too think it our duty to make public our dissent.

As to the question of the Origin of Evil, which is the burden of this misdirected verse, he has neither thrown any new light upon it, nor darkened the previous knowledge which we possessed. It remains just where it was, in its mighty, unfathomed obscurity. His Lordship may, it is true, have recapitulated some of the arguments with a more concise and cavalier air, than the old schoolmen or fathers; but the result is the same. There is no poetical road to metaphysics. In one view, however, which our rhapsodist has taken of the subject, we conceive he has done well. He represents the temptations held out to Cain by Satan as constantly succeeding and corresponding to some previous discontent and gloomy disposition in his own mind; so that Lucifer is little more than the personified demon of his imagination: And farther, the acts of guilt and folly into which Cain is hurried are not treated as accidental, or as occasioned by passing causes, but as springing from an internal fury, a morbid state akin to phrensy, a mind dissatisfied with itself and all things, and haunted by an insatiable, stubborn longing after knowledge rather than happiness, and a fatal proneness to dwell on the evil side of things, rather than the good. We here see the dreadful consequences of not curbing this disposition (which is, after all, perhaps the sin that most easily besets humanity), exemplified in a striking point of view; and we so far think, it is but fair to say, that the moral to be derived from a perusal of this MYSTERY is a valuable one. . . .

37. Reginald Heber, from his unsigned review of *Marino Faliero, Sardanapalus, The Two Foscari* and *Cain, Quarterly Review*

Dated July 1822, issued November (?) 1822, XXVII, 476–524

Reginald Heber (1783–1826), clergyman and man of letters, was appointed Bishop of Calcutta late in 1822. He had already rebuked Byron for 'a strange predilection for the worser half of manicheism', in a review of Henry Hart Milman's *Fall of Jerusalem* (*Quarterly Review* [May 1820], XXIII, 225). His condemnation of *Don Juan* ends the *Quarterly's* much criticized silence on this publication. Byron sent back 'uncut and unopened' the copy of this *Quarterly* which Murray sent him; but he then came on the first half of the review in *Galignani's Messenger*. He was favourably surprised by its tone, finding it on the whole 'extremely handsome, and any thing but unkind or unfair. As I take the good in good part [he went on], I must not . . . quarrel with the bad: what the Writer says of *Don Juan* is harsh, but it is inevitable. . . . *Don Juan* will be known by and bye, for what it is intended,—a *Satire* on *abuses* of the present states of Society, and not an eulogy of vice. . . .' (*LJ*, VI, 143, 155.)

Several years have passed away since we undertook the review of any of Lord Byron's Poetry. Not that we have been inattentive observers of that genius whose fertility is, perhaps, not the least extraordinary of its characteristics, of whose earlier fruits we were among the first and warmest eulogists, and whose later productions—though hardly answering the expectation which he once excited—would have been, of themselves, sufficient to establish the renown of many scores of ordinary writers. Far less have we been able to witness, without deep regret and disappointment, the systematic and increasing prostitution of those splendid talents to the expression of feelings, and the promulgation of opinions, which, as Christians, as Englishmen, and even as men, we were constrained to regard with abhorrence. But it was from this very conflict of admiration and regret;—this recollection of former merits and sense of present degradation;—this reverence for talent and scorn of sophistry, that we remained silent. The little effect which our advice had, on former occasions, produced, still further tended to confirm us in our silence,—a silence of which the meaning could hardly, as we conceived, be misunderstood, and which we wished Lord Byron himself to regard as an appeal, of not the least impressive kind,—to his better sense and taste and feelings. We trusted that he would himself, ere long, discover that wickedness was not strength, nor impiety courage, nor licentiousness warmheartedness, nor an aversion to his own country philosophy; and that riper years, and a longer experience, and a deeper knowledge of his own heart, and a more familiar acquaintance with that affliction to which all are heirs, and those religious principles by which affliction is turned into a blessing, would render him not only almost but altogether such a poet as virgins might read, and Christians praise, and Englishmen take pride in.

With these feelings we have altogether abstained from noticing those strange, though often beautiful productions, which, since the appearance of the Third part of his *Childe Harold*, have flowed on, wave after wave, redundant as that ocean which Lord Byron loves to describe, but with few exceptions, little less monotonous,—and stained, in succession, with deeper and yet deeper tokens of those pollutions, which, even in the full tide of genius, announce that its ebb is near. We knew not any severity of criticism which could reach the faults or purify the taste of *Don Juan*, and we trusted that its author would himself, ere long, discover, that if he continued to write such works as these, he would lose the power of producing any thing better, and that his pride, at least, if not his principle, would recall him from the island of Acrasia.

In this hope we have not been disappointed. Whatever may be the other merits of his tragedies, on the score of morals they are unimpeachable. His females, universally, are painted in truer and worthier colours than we have been accustomed to witness from his pencil, and the qualities which he holds up, in his other characters, to admiration and to pity, are entirely unmingled with those darker and disgusting tints, from which even *Childe Harold* was not free, and which he appears to have thought necessary to excite an interest in such characters as Manfred, Lara, Alp, and the Giaour. Even the *Mystery of Cain*, wicked as it may be, is the work of a nobler and more daring wickedness

237

than that which delights in insulting the miseries, and stimulating the evil passions, and casting a cold-blooded ridicule over all the lofty and generous feelings of our nature: and it is better that Lord Byron should be a manichee, or a deist,—nay, we would almost say, if the thing were possible, it is better that he should be a moral and argumentative atheist, than the professed and systematic poet of seduction, adultery and incest; the contemner of patriotism, the insulter of piety, the raker into every sink of vice and wretchedness to disgust and degrade and harden the hearts of his fellow-creatures. The speculations of a Hume and a D'Alembert may be the objects of respectful regret and pity, while the *Pucelle* is regarded with unmingled contempt and detestation. The infidel *may* be, the adversary of good morals *cannot* be, under a mistake as to the tendency of his doctrines.

Nor is this our only motive for returning at length to the examination of Lord Byron's writings. In his *Cain* he professes to reason, (with how much or how little success is nothing to the purpose,) but his appeal is made to the reason as well as to the passions of his readers. To remove, in his own instance, the difficulties by which he is perplexed, would indeed be a triumph beyond our expectations, but now that, by circumstances which Lord Byron himself could not foresee,—those speculations which he designed for the educated ranks alone, are thrown open to the gaze of the persons most likely to be influenced by them, and disseminated, with remorseless activity, among the young, the ignorant, and the poor,—by the efforts of the basest and most wicked faction that ever infested a christian country,—we are not only justified but compelled by every sense of duty and of charity, to unmask the sophisms which lurk under his poetical language; and to show how irrelevant to the truths of natural and revealed religion are those apparent irregularities in the present course of things, which he makes his objection to the being or the benignity of the Creator. With these feelings,—very different from each other, but either of which would be sufficient to warrant an interruption of our late silence,—we undertake the review of his Tragedies and his *Cain*. . . .

[After a long discussion of Byron's theories of drama, 'regularity,' the unities, etc., Heber passes to the individual plays.]

Marino Faliero has, we believe, been pretty generally pronounced a failure by the public voice, and we see no reason to call for a revision of their sentence. It contains, beyond all doubt, many passages of commanding eloquence and some of genuine poetry, and the scenes, more particularly, in which Lord Byron has neglected the absurd creed of his pseudo-Hellenic writers, are conceived and elaborated with great tragic effect and dexterity. But the subject is decidedly ill-chosen. In the main tissue of the plot and in all the busiest and most interesting parts of it, it is, in fact, no more than another *Venice Preserved*, in which the author has had to contend (nor has he contended successfully) with our recollections of a former and deservedly popular play on the same subject. And the only respect in which it differs is, that the Jaffier of Lord Byron's plot is drawn in to join the conspirators, not by the natural and intelligible motives of poverty, aggravated by the sufferings of a beloved wife, and a deep and well-grounded resentment of oppression, but by his outrageous anger for a private wrong of no very atrocious nature. The Doge of Venice, to chastize the vulgar libel of a foolish boy, attempts to overturn that republic of which he is the first and most trusted servant; to massacre all his ancient friends and fellow-soldiers, the magistracy and nobility of the land. With such a resentment as this, thus simply stated and taken singly, who ever sympathized, or who but Lord Byron would have expected in such a cause to be able to awaken sympathy? It is little to the purpose to say that this is all historically true. A thing may be true without being probable, and such a case of idiosyncrasy as is implied in a resentment so sudden and extravagant, is no more a fitting subject for the poet than an animal with two heads would be for an artist of a different description. . . .

[More might have been made of the story, Heber argues, if the development of character, situation and emotion had been shown over a considerable period of time; but this was precluded by 'Lord Byron's passion for the unities'.]

Nor is it in the plot only, thus curtailed and crippled of what would have been its due proportions, that we think we can trace the injurious effects of Lord Byron's continental prejudices and his choice of injudicious models. We trace them in the uniform and unbending severity of his diction, no less than in the abruptness of his verse, which has all the harshness though not all the vigour of Alfieri, and which, instead of that richness and variety of cadence which distinguishes even the most careless of our elder dramatists, is often only distinguishable from prose by the unrelenting uniformity with which it is divided into decasyllabic portions. The sentence of the College of Justice, in the first act, was likely indeed to be prosaic; and Shakspeare and our other elder tragedians would have given it as bona fide prose, without that affectation (for which however Lord Byron has many precedents in modern times) which condemns letters, proclamations, the speeches of the vulgar, and the outcries of the rabble and the soldiery, to strut in the same precise measure with the lofty musings and dignified resentment of the powerful and the wise. But Bertuccio Faliero might as well have spoken poetry; and it might have been hoped and expected that the Doge himself, in the full flood-tide of his passion and his wrongs, should express himself in more vigorous terms than these:

> I sought not, *wished* not, *dreamed* not the election,
> Which reached me first at Rome, and I obeyed,—
> But found on my arrival, that, besides
> The jealous vigilance which always led you
> To mock and mar your sovereign's best intents,
> You had, even in the interregnum of
> My journey to the capital, curtail'd
> And mutilated the few privileges
> Yet left the Duke.————

One source of feebleness in the foregoing passage, and it is one of frequent occurrence in all Lord Byron's plays, is his practice of ending his lines with insignificant monosyllables. 'Of,' 'to,' 'and,' 'till,' 'but,' 'from,' all occur in the course of a very few pages, in situations where, had the harmony or vigour of the line been consulted, the voice would have been allowed to pause, and the energy of the sentiment would have been carried to its highest tone of elevation. This we should have set down to the account of carelessness, had it not been so frequent, and had not the stiffness and labour of the author's general style almost tempted us to believe it systematic. A more inharmonious system of versification, or one more necessarily tending to weight and feebleness, could hardly have been invented. . . .

On the whole the *Doge of Venice* is the effect of a powerful and cultivated mind. It has all the requisites of tragedy, sublimity, terror and pathos—all but that without which the rest are unavailing, interest! With many detached passages which neither derogate from Lord Byron's former fame, nor would have derogated from the reputation of our best ancient tragedians, it is, as a whole, neither sustained nor impressive. The poet, except in the soliloquy of Leoni, scarcely ever seems to have written with his own thorough good liking. He may be suspected throughout to have had in his eye some other model than nature; and we rise from his work with the same feeling as if we had been reading a translation. For this want of interest the subject itself is doubtless in some measure to blame, though, if the same subject had been differently treated, we are inclined to believe a very different effect would have been produced. But for the constraint and stiffness of the poetry, we have nothing to blame but the apparent resolution of its author to set (at whatever risk) an example of classical correctness to his uncivilized countrymen, and rather to forego success than to succeed after the manner of Shakspeare.

[A discussion of *Sardanapalus* and *The Two Foscari* is followed by Heber's critique of *Cain*.]

The drama of *Cain*, Lord Byron himself has thought proper to call a 'Mystery,'—the name which, as is well known, was given in our own country, before the reformation, to those scenic representations of the mysterious events of our religion, which, indecent and unedifying as they seem to ourselves, were, perhaps, the principal means by which a knowledge of those events was conveyed to our rude and uninstructed ancestors. But, except in the topics on which it is employed, Lord Byron's Mystery has no resemblance to those which it claims as its prototypes. These last, however absurd and indecorous in their execution, were, at least, intended reverently. The composition now before us, is, unhappily, already too famous for its contrary character; a character to which we fear it is, in no small degree, indebted for the celebrity which it has attained, and which, though it certainly is marked with much of Lord Byron's peculiar talent, its inherent merits would hardly have secured for it. Of this our readers will judge from the following sketch on the plot, and from some of the finest and least offensive specimens which we have been able to select of the poetry and the argument.

[Gives summary, with quotations.]

To apply the severe rules of criticism to a composition of this kind would be little better than lost labour. Yet it can hardly fail to strike the reader as a defect in poetry no less than a departure from history, that the event which is the catastrophe of the drama is no otherwise than incidentally, we may say, accidentally, produced by those which precede it. Cain, whose whole character is represented in scripture as envious and malicious rather than impious;—this Cain, as painted by Lord Byron, has no quarrel with his brother whatever, nor, except in a single word, does he intimate any jealousy of him. Two acts and half the third are passed without our advancing a single step towards the conclusion; and Abel, at length, falls by a random blow given in a struggle of which the object is not *his* destruction but the overthrow of Jehovah's altar. If we could suppose a reader to sit down to a perusal of the drama in ignorance of its catastrophe, he would scarcely be less surprized by its termination in such a stroke of chance-medley, than if Abel had been made to drop down in an apoplexy, and Cain to die of grief over his body.

Nor is it easy to perceive what natural or rational object the Devil proposes to himself in carrying his disciple through the abyss of space, to show him that repository, of which we remember hearing something in our infant days, 'where the old moons are hung up to dry.' To prove that there is a life beyond the grave was surely no part of his business when he was engaged in fostering the indignation of one who repined at the necessity of dying. And, though it would seem that entire Hades is, in Lord Byron's picture, a place of suffering, yet, when Lucifer himself had premised that these sufferings were the lot of those spirits who sided with him against Jehovah, is it likely that a more accurate knowledge of them would increase Cain's eagerness for the alliance, or that he would not rather have inquired whether a better fortune did not await the adherents of the triumphant side? At all events, the spectacle of many ruined worlds was more likely to awe a mortal into submission than to rouse him to hopeless resistance; and even if it made him a hater of God, had no natural tendency to render him furious against a brother who was to be his fellow-sufferer.

We do not think, indeed, that there is much vigour or poetical propriety in any of the characters of Lord Byron's Mystery. Eve on one occasion and one only expresses herself with energy, and not even then with any great depth of that maternal feeling which the death of her favourite son was likely to excite in her. Adam moralizes without dignity. Abel is as dull as he is pious. Lucifer, though his first appearance is well conceived, is as sententious and sarcastic as a Scotch metaphysician, and the gravamina which drive Cain into impiety are circumstances which could only produce a similar effect on a weak and sluggish mind, the necessity of exertion and the fear of death! Yet, in the happiest climate of earth and amid the early vigour of nature, it would be absurd to describe (nor has Lord Byron so described it) the toil to which Cain can have been subject, as excessive or burthensome. And he is made too happy in his love, too extravagantly fond of his wife and his child to have much leisure for those gloomy thoughts which belong to disappointed ambition and jaded licentiousness.

Nor, though there are, as we have already shown, some passages in this drama of no common power, is the general tone of its poetry so excellent as to atone for these imperfections of design. The dialogue is cold and constrained. The descriptions are like the shadows of a phantasmagoria, at once indistinct and artificial. Except Adah, there is no person in whose fortunes we are interested; and we close the book with no distinct or clinging recollection of any single passage in it, and with the general impression only that Lucifer has said much and done little, and that Cain has been unhappy without grounds and wicked without an object.

But if, as a poem, *Cain* is little qualified to add to Lord Byron's reputation; we are unfortunately constrained to observe that its poetical defects are the very smallest of its demerits. It is not, indeed, as some both of its admirers and its enemies appear to have supposed, a direct attack on Scripture and on the authority of Moses. The expressions of Cain and Lucifer are not more offensive to the ears of piety than such discourses must necessarily be, or than Milton, without offence, has put into the mouths of beings similarly situated. And though the intention is evident which has led the Atheists and Jacobins (the terms are convertible) of our metropolis, to circulate the work in a cheap form, among the populace, we are not ourselves of opinion that it possesses much power of active mischief, or that many persons will be very deeply or lastingly impressed by insinuations which lead to no practical result, and difficulties which so obviously transcend the range of human experience. But it is unhappily certain that, if Lord Byron has not attacked Moses, it is only because his ambition soars higher than to assail any particular creed. The sarcasms of Lucifer and the murmurs of Cain are directed against Providence in general; and proceed to the subversion of every system of theology, except that (if theology it may be called) which holds out God to the abhorrence of his creatures as a capricious tyrant, and which regards the Devil (or under whatever name Lord Byron may chuse to embody the principle of resistance to the Supreme) as the champion of all which is energetic and interesting and noble; the spirit of free thought and stern endurance, unbrokenly contending against the bondage which makes nature miserable.

This deification of vice; this crazy attachment to the worser half of Manicheism, we long since lamented to find (as it even then was tolerably conspicuous) in some of the most powerful lines which have proceeded from Lord Byron's pen; and he has thought proper to express, though in a tone of good tempered expostulation, a degree of

243

displeasure at the freedom with which we then gave vent to our feelings.[1] We certainly, therefore, did not expect, and were still further removed from *hoping* or *desiring* that he would himself, at length, so unequivocally express those sentiments of which he so much disliked the reputation: but, if we had been anxious to justify the language which we then employed, no further justification could be required than *Cain* has now afforded.

In one respect, it is true, Lord Byron misunderstood us. He supposed that we accused him of '*worshipping* the Devil.' We certainly had, at the time, no particular reason for apprehending that he *worshipped* any thing; and he has himself now taught us, on the best authority which the case admits of, how, by neglecting exterior service to *one* of the rival principles, the other may be virtually honoured. But seriously, if to represent, through three long acts, the Devil as sympathizing with the miseries of mankind and moralizing on the injustice of Providence; if to represent God as the unrelenting tyrant of nature; the capricious destroyer of worlds which he has himself created; the object of open flattery and of secret horror even to the celestial ministers of his will and minstrels of his glory; if this be not to transfer, from God to Satan and from Satan to God, the qualities by which, in the general estimation of mankind, they are most distinguished from each other, we must own ourselves very little skilled in the usual topics of praise or censure.

We should have done an essential wrong, however, to the most celebrated of ancient heretics, if we had designated this system as more than the worser half of the system of Manes. His followers,—though they imputed the prevalence of evil in the world to the inveterate and invincible obstinacy of that principle of darkness, which they supposed to share with God the empire of things, and to pervade and govern all material existence,—confessed, nevertheless, that the superior and supreme Intelligence was transcendantly wise and benevolent. They anticipated, in fullness of faith, the ultimate victory of this last over his malignant enemy, and looked forward to a future state of happiness and glory, where the souls of the good were to be delivered from the God of this world and the bondage of their corporeal prisons. But the

---

[1] [See Byron's *Letter* of February 1821 on the Bowles controversy (*LJ*, V, 563); and cf. his private letter of 17 July 1820, to John Murray: '. . . I should be glad to know why your Quartering Reviewers, at the close of *the Fall of Jerusalem*, accuse me of Manicheism? . . . I am not a Manichean, nor an *Any*-chean. I should like to know what harm my "poeshies" have done: I can't tell what your people mean by making me a hobgoblin.' (*LJ*, V, 54.)]

theology of *Cain* is altogether gloomy and hopeless. His evil God is *the supreme:* his Hades exclusively a state of misery; the body of man is, on his system, ordained to nothing more than to labour, disease and death, and the soul is immortal only to be wretched.

It is idle to say that this statement is put into the mouth of one who is described in scripture as an evil being, and whose assertions are to be only understood as the ex-parte statement of an insidious enemy.

Of Lucifer, as drawn by Lord Byron, we absolutely know no evil: and, on the contrary, the impression which we receive of him is, from his first introduction, most favourable. He is indued not only with all the beauty, the wisdom and the unconquerable daring which Milton has assigned him, and which may reasonably be supposed to belong to a spirit of so exalted a nature, but he is represented as unhappy without a crime and as pitying our unhappiness. Even before he appears, we are prepared (so far as the poet has had skill to prepare us) to sympathize with any spiritual being who is opposed to the government of Jehovah. The conversations, the exhibitions which ensue are all conducive to the same conclusions, that whatever is is *evil*, and that, had the Devil been the Creator, he would have made his creatures happier. Above all, his arguments and insinuations are allowed to pass uncontradicted, or are answered only by overbearing force, and punishment inflicted not on himself but on his disciple. Nor is the intention less apparent nor the poison less subtle, because the language employed is not indecorous, and the accuser of the Almighty does not descend to ribaldry or scurrilous invective.

That the monstrous creed thus inculcated is really the creed of Lord Byron himself, we, certainly, have some difficulty in believing. As little are we inclined to assert that this frightful caricature of Deism is intended as a covert recommendation of that further stage to which the scepticism of modern philosophers has sometimes conducted them. We are willing to suppose, that he has, after all, no further view than the fantastic glory of supporting a paradox ably; of showing his powers of argument and poetry at the expense of all the religious and natural feelings of the world, and of ascertaining how much will be forgiven him by the unwearied devotion of his admirers. But we cannot, with some of our contemporaries, give him the credit of 'writing conscientiously.' We respect his understanding too highly to apprehend that he intended a benefit to mankind in doing his best to make them vicious and discontented; and we tell him, '*even more in anger than in sorrow,*' that the great talents which he has received are ill employed in writing a libel on his Maker, and that the dexterity which flings about fire-brands in sport is no object of ambition to any but a mind perverted by self-opinion and flattery.

We return, however, to *Cain*, and it is some comfort to find that the argument, however plausibly put together, is as infirm and disjointed as poetic arguments are apt to be. It depends on the admitted fact that evil exists, and on the presumption that a wise and benevolent Deity would not have permitted its existence. And it is, consequently, levelled (as we have already observed, and as we must intreat the reader to bear in mind) not against the Mosaic account of the manner in which evil first appeared on earth, (for whenever and however evil manifested itself, the same objection would apply,) but against the God by whom the present frame of things was constituted. It is not the Jehovah only, of the Christian or the Jew, against whom it may be alleged that he has created men to toil, to sicken and to die. If we admit a Creator at all, we must admit that he sends us into the world under this necessity; and any man, with whatever religious opinions, who dislikes these accompaniments of life more than he likes life with its countervailing advantages, may plead with Cain,—

> I was unborn;
> I sought not to be born, nor love the state
> To which that birth has brought me!

To cut this knot, as the ancient Stoics attempted to do, by denying the existence of evil, was a measure of which the success was not likely to be equal to its hardiness or its motive. But, before we proceed with Lord Byron, from the mixture of evil and sorrow which the world presents, to infer a malevolent Creator, it may be well to inquire, first, whether *more* good than evil, *more* happiness than misery is not found, after all, in the world with which we are so much displeased; and, secondly, whether the good which exists is not, apparently, the result of direct *design*, while the evil is *incidental* only.

Both these positions have, we think, been proved by Paley, in a work too sensible, too philosophical, too accordant with the general feelings and general experience of our species, to be in much danger of overturn from a few well-pointed sarcasms, a few daring assertions, and a little poetic phantasmagoria of former worlds created and ruined. . . .

[After elaborating this argument, and confuting Byron's view that the Old Testament evidences no belief in the immortality of the soul and a life after death, Heber concludes:]

The origin of evil itself is among those secrets of Providence which, if they do not surpass our present faculties, are, at least, not as yet communicated to us. It is one of the many vulgar errors by which the subject has been encumbered, to suppose that such a communication is found in the Book of Genesis. All which Moses relates is the first *appearance* of that evil which must have previously existed, the first demonstration of those hateful passions and that aspiring pride which have made labour and death no more than necessary to the well-being of nature. Of the causes which may have induced the Almighty to create man peccable, to expose him to temptations, and to try him by suffering, our reason may conjecture, but our faith is uninformed; and it is a fact which may be advantageously recollected by those who, on these accounts, insult Christianity, that the difficulties of which they complain belong not to Christianity alone, but to every creed which admits the responsibility of man, and the power and goodness of his Maker. But though Christianity does not tell us the *cause* of our calamities, she has not failed to point out their *cure;* in fostering those amiable affections which enable us to bear our own sorrows best while they most dispose us to alleviate the sorrows of others, and in holding out to us a clearer and brighter prospect of that life where Love shall reap his harvest of enjoyment, and where the happy and benevolent inhabitant of a better world shall neither feel nor witness affliction! . . .

THE VISION OF JUDGMENT

October 1822

38. Contemporary comments

(a) Extract from unsigned review of the first number of the *Liberal* (in which this poem appeared), in the *Literary Gazette* for 19 October 1822: Byron's every energy, says the reviewer, 'is directed to deteriorate and degrade humanity. It is truly shocking to contemplate this constant aim at debasing every sentiment which elevates man above the brute. Heaven has no sanctity, earth no refuge, which is not invaded in order to reduce the whole to one abominable equality;—the body, the soul, life, death, eternity, are, in all their fearful changes or awful elements, but themes for the buffoon jest, the depreciating satire. And the individuals guilty of these attacks upon all that constitutes the superiority and happiness of human nature, are, forsooth, Liberals, Philosophers, Advocates for our abstract Dignity. . . .'

On Byron's satirical attacks on George III, the reviewer comments: 'If we do not express our abhorrence of such heartless and beastly ribaldry, it is because we know no language strong enough to declare the disgust and contempt which it inspires. We affect no cant, we speak the sentiments of no party, but we are as confident as that "day is day, and night, night," that we deliver the judgment of Britain when we assert, that these passages are so revolting to every good feeling, there is not a gentleman in the country who will not hold their author in contempt as unworthy of the character of a gentleman—nor a man of common sense in the country who will not think him a posthumous libeller and assassin—nor a person of common humanity in the country who will not deem him a callous violator of every natural and ennobling sympathy—nor a Christian in the country who will not pity and pray for him. Even had wit and genius gilded the odious thoughts, and had they been clothed in admirable language, as they are, on the contrary, feebly and stupidly expressed, we believe, for the honour of England, that there are very few of its people who would not have despised and detested the cold-blooded posthumous libeller.' (*Literary Gazette*, 1822, pp. 655-6.)

(*b*) Extract from *A Critique on 'The Liberal'*, 1822, pp. 6-7, 14-15: 'The first article in the work is called *The Vision of Judgment*, supposed to be written by Lord Byron. . . . Had his Lordship's wit been limited by his judgment to the ridicule of Mr. Southey *only*, we should, perhaps, rather have admired his talent than condemn [*sic*] his severity; but in this production every thing we revere as sacred—every thing we hope for, or fear—every thing we regard with awe or dread, is treated with ridicule and contempt. The inhabitants of heaven and hell are alike, with the most impious ribaldry, burlesqued, and then offered for the amusement of Christians.

> Can such things be
> And overcome us like a summer's cloud
> Without our special wonder?

Surely men owe some respect to the laws and established faith of the land that gave them birth—that shelters their persons and property! . . .'

'We have now gone through this poem, which every reader must see to be very poorly written. Waiving the blasphemy, it contains nothing but abuse. The author has melted a pearl in the cup of intemperance, and then thrown it on a dunghill—he has bartered his reputation for the liberty of writing this book; and then has not made the most of it. Instead of politics we find railing. Satan's only particular accusations are, the being old; blind, helpless, and a mad bedlam bigot.

And this they call *Liberalism*, the essentials of which are candour and moderation! if Liberalism seals the heart to every tender sensation of loyalty and patriotism—if it teaches us to despise that great captain who has been Heaven's instrument to save Europe from the grasp of a despot—if it would lead us to spurn at the memory of the venerable George III and above all if it would teach us to think prayer and praise to God a superfluous trouble—to make morality a toy, and to treat future judgment as a meer bugbear—to throw off all check, and bring society to a chaos of wickedness, let us banish it as a traitor, and avoid it as a pestilence.'

This critic regards the description of Satan (stanza 24) as 'the only part of this poem that bears the signature of Byron; it is a departing gleam of Childe Harold, such as he was once, before the fogs of scepticism and Liberalism obscured the bright star of his genius. It is almost the only passage deserving the name of poetry.' (*Op. cit.*, p. 9.)

(*c*) Extracts from the Diary of Henry Crabb Robinson (*Henry Crabb Robinson on Books and their Writers*, ed. Edith J. Morley, 1938, I, 286, 367, 447): '[20 October 1822] . . . I read *The Liberal*. This worthless work will scarcely reach a second, certainly not a third number. Lord Byron's blasphemies will cease to excite curiosity. His *Vision of Judgment* is as dull as it is profligate. He offends the moral feelings of men and does not bribe their taste. He introduces George III at heaven's gate. St. Peter hears it is a king, and asks whether he has a head. The last one had one under his arm. He got in only by flinging it at us. Junius and Wilkes are heard as witnesses against the king; the trial is suspended by the devil bringing Southey, who begins to read his hexameters, and the court breaks up; but the poet at last sees the king in heaven and hears him singing the hundredth psalm. The trash is not redeemed by a single passage of poetry, sense, or wit. The book has also epigrams treating Lord Castlereagh's death with ridicule.'

'[2 August 1829] . . . We spoke of Lord Byron and I mentioned the *Vision of Judgment*. He [Goethe] called it sublime and laughed while he referred to the summoning of Junius and Wilkes as witnesses and to the letting the king slip into heaven, etc., as admirable hits. He said: "*Es sind keine Flickwörter im Gedichte*",[1] and he compared the brilliancy and clearness of his style to a metal wire drawn through a steel plate!'

'[16 September 1834] . . . I read the beginning and the end of Lord Byron's *Vision of Judgment*. I was again as much as ever impressed with the dashing impudence and overflowing wit of Byron and the spirit of derision with which the vulgar notions of the other world are met. . . .'

(*d*) Extract from the *Conversations of Goethe with Eckermann and Soret* (trans. John Oxenford, London, 1850, I, 172): '[18 May 1824] . . . "However," continued [Goethe], "although Byron has died so young, literature has not suffered an essential loss, through a hindrance to its further extension. Byron could, in a

[1] ['There is no padding in the poem.']

certain sense, go no further. He had reached the summit of his creative power, and whatever he might have done in the future, he would have been unable to extend the boundaries of his talent. In the incomprehensible poem, *The Vision of Judgment*, he has done the utmost of which he was capable." '

Blackwood's comments on *Don Juan* alternate between moral outrage and robust appreciation—sometimes expressed by the same writers on different occasions. Cantos VI, VII and VIII were attacked by 'Timothy Tickler' in a letter to 'Christopher North' in the number for July 1823 (*Blackwood's Magazine*, XIV, 88 f.) This review was written by William Maginn (1793–1842) and revised by Lockhart. ('I really have not read the poem,' he wrote to Blackwood, 'but dipping here and there it seems worthy of all that Maginn says.') Cantos IX, X and XI were more sympathetically reviewed in the September number by Lockhart himself under the pseudonym of 'Odoherty' (*Blackwood's Magazine*, XIV, 282 f.) On these attributions see A. L. Strout, *John Bull's Letter to Lord Byron*, Norman (Oklahoma), 1947, pp. 127–8.

(*a*) Extract from 'Tickler' on Cantos VI–VIII:
'. . . Well, I have read the three new Cantos.

ALAS! POOR BYRON!

Not ten times a-day, dear Christopher, but ten times a-page, as I wandered over the intense and incredible stupidities of this duodecimo, was the departed spirit of the genius of *Childe Harold* saluted with this exclamation. Alas! that one so gifted—one whose soul gave such appearance of being deeply imbued with the genuine spirit of poetry—one, to whom we all looked as an ornament of our literature, and who indeed has contributed in no small degree towards spreading a strain of higher mood over our poetry—should descend to the composition of heartless, heavy, dull, anti-British garbage, to be printed by the Cockneys, and puffed in the *Examiner.*—Alas! alas! that he should stoop to the miserable degradation of being extolled by Hunt!—that he who we hoped would be the Samson of our poetical day, should suffer himself to be so enervated by the unworthy Delilahs which have enslaved his imagination, as to be reduced to the foul office of displaying blind buffooneries before the Philistines of Cockaigne.

But so it is. Here we have three cantos of some hundred verses, from which it would be impossible to extract twenty, distinguished by any readable quality. Cant I never speak, and, with the blessing of God, never will speak—especially to *you*; and accordingly, though I was thoroughly disgusted with the scope and tendency of the former cantos of the Don—though there were passages in them which, in common with all other men of upright minds and true feelings, I looked on with indignation—yet I, for one, never permitted my moral or political antipathies so to master my critical judgment, as to make me whiningly decry the talent which they often wickedly, sometimes properly, exhibited. But here we are in a lower deep—we are wallowing in a sty of mere filth. Page after page presents us with a monotonous unmusical drawl, decrying chastity, sneering at matrimony, cursing wives, abusing monarchy, deprecating lawful government, lisping dull double-entendres, hymning Jacobinism, in a style and manner so little unrelieved by any indication of poetic power, that I feel a moral conviction that his lordship must have taken the *Examiner*, the *Liberal*, the *Rimini*, the *Round Table*, as his model, and endeavoured to write himself down to the level of the capacities and the swinish tastes of those with whom he has the misfortune, originally, I believe, from charitable motives, to associate. This is the most charitable hypothesis which I can frame. Indeed there are some verses which have all the appearance of having been interpolated by the King of the Cockneys. At least I hope so—I hope that there is but one set capable of writing anything so leering and impotent, as the loinless drivelling (if I may venture a translation of the strong expression of the Stoic satirist) which floats on the slaver of too many of these pages. I allude, for instance, to the attempt at wit, where the poet (the *poet!*) is facetious at the state of females during the sack of a town;[1] the greatest part of the seraglio scene; and other places to which I must decline making any farther reference. . . .'

[1] [Quotes in a footnote Canto VIII, stanzas 128–34, with the comment, 'It is a pity to reprint such things, but a single specimen here may do good, by the disgust for the whole which it must create.']

(*b*) Extract from 'Odoherty's' reply, in his review of Cantos IX–XI:

'Dear North,—I have a great respect both for Old Tickler and yourself, but now and then you both disquiet me with little occasional bits
of lapses into the crying sin of the age—*humbug*! What could possess
him to write, and you to publish, that absurd critique—if indeed it be
worthy of any such name—upon the penult batch of *Don Juan*? The
ancient scribe must have read those cantos when he was crop-sick, and
had snapped his fiddle-string. You must never have read them at all.

Call things wicked, base, vile, obscene, blasphemous; run your
tackle to its last inch upon these scores, but never say that they are
stupid when they are not. I cannot suffer this sort of cant from YOU.
Leave it to Wordsworth to call Voltaire "a dull scoffer." Leave it to the
British Review to talk of "the dotage" of Lord Byron. Depend upon it,
your chief claim to merit as a critic has always been *your justice to*
INTELLECT. I cannot bear to see you parting with a shred of this high
reputation. It was you "that first praised Shelley as he deserved to be
praised." Mr. Tickler himself said so in his last admirable letter to you.
It was in your pages that justice was first done to Lamb and to Coleridge
—greatest of all, it was through and by you that the public opinion
was first turned in regard to the poetry of Wordsworth himself.—
These are things which never can be forgotten; these are your true and
your most honourable triumphs. Do not, I beseech you, allow your
claim to this noble distinction to be called in question. Do not let it be
said, that even in one instance you have suffered any prejudices
whatever, no matter on what proper feelings they may have been
bottomed, to interfere with your candour as a judge of *intellectual*
exertion.—Distinguish as you please: brand with the mark of your
indignation whatever offends your feelings, moral, political, or
religious—but "nothing extenuate." If you mention a book at all,
say what it really is. Blame *Don Juan*; blame *Faublas*; blame *Candide*;
but blame them for what really is deserving of blame. Stick to your
own good old rule—abuse Wickedness, but acknowledge Wit.

In regard to such a man as Byron, this, it must be evident, is absolutely necessary—that is, if you really wish, which you have always said
you do, to be of any use to him. Good heavens! Do you imagine that
people will believe three cantos of *Don Juan* to be unredeemedly and
uniformly DULL, merely upon your saying so, without proving what
you say by quotation? No such things need be expected by you,
North, far less by any of your coadjutors.

I maintain, and have always maintained, that *Don Juan* is, without exception, the first of Lord Byron's works. It is by far the most original in point of *conception*. It is decidedly original in point of *tone*, (for to talk of the tone of Berni, &c. being in the least like this, is pitiable stuff: Any old Italian of the 15th or 16th century write in the same tone with Lord Byron! Stuff! Stuff!)—It contains the finest specimens of serious poetry he has ever written; and it contains the finest specimens of ludicrous poetry that our age has witnessed. Frere may have written the stanza earlier; he may have written it more carefully, more musically if you will; but what is he to Byron? Where is the sweep, the pith, the soaring pinion, the lavish luxury, of genius revelling in strength? No, sir; *Don Juan*, say the canting world what it will, is destined to hold a permanent rank in the literature of our country. It will always be referred to as furnishing the most powerful picture of that vein of thought, (no matter how false and bad,) which distinguishes *a great portion of the thinking people of our time*. You and I disagree with them—we do not think so; we apprehend that to think so, is to think greenly, rashly, and wickedly; but who can deny, that many, many thousands, do think so? Who can deny, that that is valuable in a certain way which paints the prevailing sentiment of a large proportion of the people of any given age in the world? Or, who, that admits these things, can honestly hesitate to admit that *Don Juan* is a great work— a work that must last? I cannot.

And, after all, say the worst of *Don Juan*, that can with fairness be said of it, what does the thing amount to? Is it *more* obscene than *Tom Jones*?—Is it *more* blasphemous than Voltaire's novels? In point of fact, it is not within fifty miles of either of them: and as to obscenity, there is more of that in the pious Richardson's pious *Pamela*, than in all the novels and poems that have been written since.

The whole that can with justice be said of Byron, *as to these two great charges*, is, that he has practised in this age something of the licence of the age of our grandfathers. In doing so, he has acted egregiously amiss. The things were bad, nobody can doubt that, and we had got rid of them; and it did not become a man of Byron's genius to try to make his age retrograde in anything, least of all in such things as these. He also has acted most unwisely and imprudently in regard to himself. By offending the feelings of his age, in regard to points of this nature, he has undone himself as a popular writer.—I don't mean to say that he has done so for ever—Mercy and Repentance forbid! but he has done so most effectually for the present. . . . But,— and here I come back to my question—Is he no longer a great author?

Has his genius deserted him along with his prudence? Is his Hippocrene lazy as well as impure? Has he ceased, in other words, to be Byron, or is he only Byron playing mad tricks?

The latter is my opinion. . . .'

40. Some minor reviewers on *Don Juan*

1819–23

(*a*) In an anonymous review of *Mazeppa* in the *Eclectic Review* for August 1819, the writer comments on 'a subsequent publication of notorious character'—*Don Juan*, Cantos I and II: 'Poetry which it is impossible not to read without admiration, yet, which it is equally impossible to admire without losing some degree of self-respect; such as no brother could read aloud to his sister, no husband to his wife;—poetry in which the deliberate purpose of the Author is to corrupt by inflaming the mind, to seduce to the love of evil which he has himself chosen as his good; can be safely dealt with only in one way, by passing it over in silence. There are cases in which it is equally impossible to relax into laughter or to soften into pity, without feeling that an immoral concession is made to vice. . . .

He writes like a man who has that clear perception of the truth of things, which is the result of the guilty knowledge of good and evil, and who by the light of that knowledge, has deliberately preferred the evil, with a proud malignity of purpose which would seem to leave little for the last consummating change to accomplish. When he calculates that the reader is on the verge of pitying him, he takes care to throw him back the defiance of laughter, as if to let him know that all the Poet's pathos is but the sentimentalism of the drunkard between his cups, or the relenting softness of the courtesan, who the next moment resumes the bad boldness of her degraded character. With such a man who would wish either to laugh or to weep? And yet, who that reads him, can refrain alternately from either? . . .' (*Eclectic Review*, N. S., XII, 149–50.)

(*b*) [i] Extract from anonymous review of *Don Juan*, Cantos I and II, in the *British Critic* for August 1819. The reviewer denounces the 'shameless indecency' of Canto I, expresses disgust at 'so flippant, dull and disgraceful a publication', and denies its claim to rank as satire: '. . . If *Don Juan* then be not a satire—what is it? A more perplexing question could not be put to the critical squad. Of the four hundred and odd stanzas which the two Cantos contain, not a tittle could, even in the utmost latitude of interpretation, be dignified by the name of poetry. It has not wit enough to be comic; it has not spirit enough to make it lyric; nor is it didactic of any thing but mischief. The versification and morality are about upon a par; as far therefore as we are enabled to give it any character at all, we should pronounce it a narrative of degrading debauchery in doggerel rhyme. . . .' (*British Critic*, 2nd series, XII, 197.)

[ii] The anonymous reviewer of Cantos III, IV and V in the *British Critic* for September 1821 comments on the anonymity of author and publisher: '. . . The Poem before us is . . . not only begotten but spawned in filth and darkness. Every accoucheur of literature has refused his obstetric aid to the obscure and ditch-delivered foundling; and even its father, though he unblushingly has stamped upon it an image of himself which cannot be mistaken, forbears to give it the full title of avowed legitimacy. . . .' (*Op. cit.*, XVI, 252.)

[iii] Extract from review of Cantos IX, X and XI in the *British Critic* for November 1823. The reviewer describes the muse ('that nondescript goddess') who seems to have presided over the composition of *Don Juan*: '. . . In the first canto we saw her elegant, highly talented, and graceful, and lamented her deflection from virtue. We can trace her subsequently through each stage of deterioration, till we find her a camp-follower at Ismail, still possessing allurements of a coarse and sensual sort, and though thoroughly depraved, full of anecdote and adventurous spirit. In the present three cantos we behold her a reckless and desperate outcast from society, smarting under the sense of universal neglect, and venting it in the roar of scurrilous defiance against every one who comes in her way: her conversation a mixture of metaphysical scraps picked up in the course of her former education, with broader slang, and more unblushing indecency, than she had as yet ventured upon. Such is the history of the rise and progress, the decline and fall, of the tenth, or Juanic muse. . . .' (*Op. cit.*, XX, 529–30.)

(*c*) Extract from anonymous review of *Don Juan*, Cantos IX, X and XI, in the *Literary Gazette* for 6 September 1823. Lord Byron, argues the reviewer, must have been insane when he composed these cantos: '. . . The whole composition is so utterly contemptible and incoherent, so disgustingly vulgar and obscene, so wandering in a metaphysical cloud of scepticism, and so destitute of any thing like a comprehensive or correct idea, so pointless and unpoetical, that it seems impossible that Lord Byron, fallen as we have seen him, can be at the same time in his senses and the author. . . .' (*Literary Gazette*, 1823, p. 652.)

On 6 December, however, the reviewer of Cantos XII, XIII and XIV for the *Literary Gazette* found more to be said in their favour: these cantos, he admitted, 'certainly exhibit a knowledge of life and nature, and are written in a sportive satirical vain which renders them very entertaining. Without comparing this sort of trifling badinage with the higher efforts of Lord Byron, we are free to say that it is long since we have read any production of his with more amusement and less regret. . . .' (*Op. cit.*, 1823, p. 771.)

(*d*) [i] Extract from anonymous review of *Don Juan*, Cantos III, IV and V, in the *Edinburgh Magazine and Literary Miscellany; a New Series of the Scots Magazine*, for August 1821: '. . . Here is my Lord Byron, doubtless one of the most extraordinarily gifted intellectual men of the day, again enacting the part of DON JUAN again, and with impunity, poisoning the current of fine poetry, by the intermixture of ribaldry and blasphemy such as no man of pure taste can read a *second* time, and such as no woman of correct principles can read the *first*. Why is this ridiculous and disgusting farce to go on, unnoticed by the more powerful critical journals of the day ?. . .' (*Op. cit.*, IX,* 105–6.)

[ii] Extract from anonymous review of Cantos VI, VII and VIII, in the *Edinburgh Magazine* for August 1823: '. . . The first of these three additional Cantos is a piece of unredeemed and unrelieved sensuality and indecency; the second and third, which are filled with the details of the siege, contain some very powerful description, and occasional passages of great beauty and strength, followed close at the heels, however, by that incessant mockery of human feelings and human sufferings for which this poem as well as most others of the noble bard, are remarkable: nay, when he succeeds in touching a higher string, and calling up nobler emotions than usual, he is sure to turn his own effort, however successful, into ridicule,—so that mockery is the *omne in uno*,[1] the beginning, the middle, and the end of the poem. . . .' (*Op. cit.*, XIII, 193.)

[iii] Extract from anonymous review of Cantos IX, X and XI, in the *Edinburgh Magazine* for September 1823: '. . . These cantos are, in fact, nothing but measured prose, replete with bad puns, stale jests, small wit, indecency, and irreligion, and exhibiting none of those

[1] ['The whole essence', 'the one all-embracing aim'.]

redeeming bursts of true poetical inspiration for which their predecessors were remarkable. . . .' In them, says the reviewer, we can perceive
'many indications of labour and effort, as well as of a spirit generally
at war with the world and itself, and apparently susceptible of delight
only when it dwells on the follies, miseries, or crimes of mankind. . . .
His Lordship plainly affects to become the modern Juvenal; and he is
certainly a keen, and sometimes a powerful satirist; but he will never
equal the terseness and vigour of the great original, however much he
may surpass it in grossness and obscenity. . . .' (*Op. cit.*, XIII, 357.)

41. Sir Samuel Egerton Brydges on *Don Juan*

1824

Sir Samuel Egerton Brydges (1762–1837), man of letters, bibliographer, genealogist, and editor (especially of Elizabethan texts), began his *Letters on the Character and Poetical Genius of Lord Byron* in May 1824 on hearing of Byron's death, and completed the work in July of the same year. The following extracts contain some of his most interesting comments on *Don Juan*.

(*a*) '. . . [*Don Juan*] is, no doubt, very licentious in parts, which renders it dangerous to praise it very much; and makes it improper for those who have not a cool and correct judgment, and cannot separate the objectionable parts from the numerous beautiful passages intermixed. But no where is the poet's mind more elastic, free, and vigorous, and his knowledge of human nature more surprising' (p. 185).

(*b*) 'It may be difficult to assign a satisfactory reason, but it is surely a fact, that WIT almost always appears *heartless.* . . .

Ridicule produces a feeling not congenial with those feelings which it is the end of the best poetry to awaken. Ridicule begets contempt for the object on which it is thrown, whereas it is the noblest and highest purpose of poetry to make us admire or love what is represented. Contempt is a chilling, ungenerous passion, and less poetical even than hatred, because hatred is at least energetic.

Humour does not deal so much in ridicule: there is oftener much gravity in humour.

Lord Byron had both wit and humour; and it seems to me, notwithstanding a few instances may be found which may seem to contradict me, that these qualities had in him more of gravity and earnestness than of ridicule and laughter; and I think that, notwithstanding all his affected gaiety, we can discover that the same sombre and deep emotions as belong to his more serious poetry, give rise to the colours of scorn or absurdity in which he paints his comic subjects. To *me* this is an attraction, not a fault; it rouses sympathy, not fear and distrust . . .' (pp. 255, 256–7).

(c) '. . . After all, *Don Juan*, the principal comic production of Lord Byron, is a very strange medley. It has all sorts of faults, many of which cannot be defended, and some of which are disgusting; but it has, also, almost every sort of poetical merit: there are in it some of the finest passages which Lord Byron ever wrote; there is amazing knowledge of human nature in it; there is exquisite humour; there is freedom, and bound, and vigour of narrative, imagery, sentiment, and style, which are admirable; there is a vast fertility of deep, extensive, and original thought; and, at the same time, there is the profusion of a prompt and most richly-stored memory. The invention is lively and poetical; the descriptions are brilliant and glowing, yet not over-wrought, but fresh from nature, and faithful to her colours; and the prevalent character of the whole, (bating too many dark spots,) not dispiriting, though gloomy; not misanthropic, though bitter; and not repulsive to the visions of poetical enthusiasm, though indignant and resentful' (pp. 262–3).

(d) '. . . His powers grew to the last: the two last cantos of *Don Juan* (XV, XVI) were perhaps the best written of any of that poem,—though his incidents might have been supposed to have been exhausted, and his subject worn out! I am astonished at his ease, his point, his humour, his freshness, the admirable sagacity of his understanding, his intimate insight into the diversities of the human character, the keenness with which he dissects, the brilliancy with which he discovers, the smiles and good humour with which he delineates and exposes, and the irresistible fidelity and truth with which he marks out the features of his innumerable *personae dramatis*. Here all is comic without extra-vagance; and ridiculous without anger or scorn. Nor is there a single hereditary subject of satire; no transmitted images; no hackneyed formularies of contempt or indignation; no borrowed portraits; no obsolete absurdities;—all comes new and direct from life; and this poem, perhaps, affords a greater novelty, as well as freedom, in the combination of words, than can elsewhere be found: with such an extraordinary lucidness; such a prevalence of the thought over the language; and such an utter rejection of all artifice and common-place ornament, as to hold the attention, and carry forward the reader by an inexhaustible charm' (pp. 283–4).

(e) '. . . A mind of intuitive perception, like Lord Byron's, a heart of quick and strong emotion, and a frankness and force of language to give vent to his impressions, were almost inevitably led to many of those scornful ebullitions of overwhelming ridicule with which he has covered his political adversaries. The misfortune is, that wit and ridicule know no bounds; and the line between things which are fair game, and those which ought not to be touched, was never yet duly observed. There is something fatal in the stroke of ridicule, which puts esteem and respect at once to flight,—even when it falls on what ought to be held most sacred. . . .

But I know not how to wish he had never written *Don Juan*, in defiance of all its faults and intermingled mischief and poison! There are parts in it which are among the most brilliant proofs of his genius; and, what is even yet better, there are parts which throw a blaze of light upon the knowledge of human life . . .' (pp. 356–7).

42. Dismissive comments on Byron, by Keats, Coleridge, Lamb, Southey and Wordsworth

1819–33

(*a*) KEATS.

[i] Extract from letter of 19 February 1819, to George and Georgiana Keats: '. . . A Man's life of any worth is a continual allegory—and very few eyes can see the Mystery of his life—a life like the scriptures, figurative—which such people can no more make out than they can the hebrew Bible. Lord Byron cuts a figure—but he is not figurative—Shakespeare led a life of Allegory; his works are the comments on it. . . .' (*The Letters of John Keats, 1814–1821,* ed. H. E. Rollins, Cambridge [Mass.], 1958, II, 67.)

[ii] Extract from letter of 20 September, 1819, to the same: '. . . You speak of Lord Byron and me—There is this great difference between us. He describes what he sees—I describe what I imagine—Mine is the hardest task. You see the immense difference. . . .' (*Op. cit.,* II, 200.)

(*b*) COLERIDGE.

[i] Extract from *Table Talk* (1835) on 29 December 1822: 'It seems, to my ear, that there is a sad want of harmony in Lord Byron's verses. Is it not unnatural to be always connecting very great intellectual power with utter depravity? Does such a combination often really exist *in rerum naturâ*?[1] (*Coleridge's Miscellaneous Criticism,* ed. T. M. Raysor, 1936, p. 401.)

[ii] Extract from *Table Talk* on 7 June 1824: 'How lamentably the *art* of versification is neglected by most of the poets of the present day!— by Lord Byron, as it strikes me, in particular, among those of eminence for other qualities. Upon the whole, I think the part of *Don Juan* in which Lambro's return to his home, and Lambro himself, are described, is the best, that is, the most individual, thing in all I know of Lord B.'s works. The festal abandonment puts one in mind of Nicholas Poussin's pictures.' (*Op. cit.,* p. 402.)

[iii] From Coleridge's marginalia in Pepys's *Memoirs,* ed. Lord

[1] ['In the nature of things.']

Braybrooke, 1825: 'W. Wordsworth calls Lord Byron the mocking bird of our Parnassian ornithology, but the mocking bird, they say, has a very sweet song of his own, in true notes proper to himself. Now I cannot say I have ever heard any such in his Lordship's volumes of warbles: and [in] spite of Sir W. Scott, I dare predict that in less than a century, the Baronet's and the Baron's Poems will lie on the same shelf of oblivion, Scott be read and remembered as a novelist and the founder of a new race of novels, and Byron not remembered at all, except as a wicked lord who, from morbid and restless vanity, pretended to be ten times more wicked than he was.' (*Op. cit.*, p. 285.)

(*c*) CHARLES LAMB (1775–1834).
[i] Extract from letter of 26 May 1820, to Joseph Cottle: '. . . It was quite a mistake that I could dislike anything you should write against Ld Byron, for I have a thorough aversion to his character, and a very moderate admiration of his genius—he is great in so little a way—To be a Poet is to be the Man, the whole Man—not a petty portion of occasional low passion worked up into a permanent form of Humanity. Shakspeare has thrust such rubbishly feelings into a corner, the dark dusty heart of Don John in the *Much Ado*. . . .' (*The Letters of Charles and Mary Lamb*, ed. E. V. Lucas, 1935, II, 279.)

[ii] Extract from letter of 15 May 1824, to Bernard Barton: '. . . So we have lost another Poet. I never much relished his Lordship's mind, and shall be sorry if the Greeks have cause to miss him. He was to me offensive, and I never can make out his great *power*, which his admirers talk of. Why, a line of Wordsworth's is a lever to lift the immortal spirit! Byron can only move the Spleen. He was at best a Satyrist,—in any other way he was mean enough. I dare say I do him an injustice; but I cannot love him, nor squeeze a tear to his memory. . .' (*Op. cit.*, II, 426.)

(*d*) SOUTHEY. Extract from letter of 26 May 1824, to Henry Taylor: '. . . . I am sorry Lord Byron is dead, because some harm will arise from his death, and none was to be apprehended while he was living; for all the mischief which he was capable of doing he had done. Had he lived some years longer, he would either have continued in the same course, pandering to the basest passions and proclaiming the most flagitious principles, or he would have seen his errors and sung his palinodia,—perhaps have passed from the extreme of profligacy to some extreme of superstition. In the one case he would have been smothered in his own evil deeds. In the other he might have made some atonement for his offences.

We shall now hear his praises from all quarters. I dare say he will be held up as a martyr to the cause of liberty, as having sacrificed his life by his exertions in behalf of the Greeks. Upon this score the liberals will beatify him; and even the better part of the public will for some time think it becoming in them to write those evil deeds of his in water, which he himself has written in something more durable than brass. I am sorry for his death therefore, because it comes in aid of a pernicious reputation which was stinking in the snuff. . . .' (*The Life and Correspondence of the late Robert Southey*, ed. C. C. Southey, 1849–50, V, 178–9.)

(*e*) WORDSWORTH. Extract from letter of 30 January 1833, to Miss Kinnaird: '. . . What a monster is a Man of Genius whose heart is perverted. . . .' (*The Letters of William and Dorothy Wordsworth: The Later Years*, ed. E. de Selincourt, 1939, II, 640.)

43. Hazlitt on Byron

1825

Essay on 'Lord Byron' in *The Spirit of the Age*, 1825. (*The Complete Works of William Hazlitt*, Centenary Edn., ed. P. P. Howe, 1930–4, XI, 69–78.)

Lord Byron and Sir Walter Scott are among writers now living[1] the two, who would carry away a majority of suffrages as the greatest geniuses of the age. The former would, perhaps, obtain the preference with the fine gentlemen and ladies (squeamishness apart)—the latter with the critics and the vulgar. We shall treat of them in the same connection, partly on account of their distinguished pre-eminence, and partly because they afford a complete contrast to each other. In their poetry, in their prose, in their politics, and in their tempers, no two men can be more unlike.

If Sir Walter Scott may be thought by some to have been

> Born universal heir to all humanity,

it is plain Lord Byron can set up no such pretension. He is, in a striking degree, the creature of his own will. He holds no communion with his kind; but stands alone, without mate or fellow—

> As if a man were author of himself,
> And owned no other kin.

He is like a solitary peak, all access to which is cut off not more by elevation than distance. He is seated on a lofty eminence, 'cloud-capt,' or reflecting the last rays of setting suns; and in his poetical moods, reminds us of the fabled Titans, retired to a ridgy steep, playing on their Pan's-pipes, and taking up ordinary men and things in their hands with haughty indifference. He raises his subject to himself, or tramples on it; he neither stoops to, nor loses himself in it. He exists not by sympathy, but by antipathy. He scorns all things,

---

[1] This Essay was written just before Lord Byron's death.

268

even himself. Nature must come to him to sit for her picture—he does not go to her. She must consult his time, his convenience, and his humour; and wear a *sombre* or a fantastic garb, or his Lordship turns his back upon her. There is no ease, no unaffected simplicity of manner, no 'golden mean.' All is strained, or petulant in the extreme. His thoughts are sphered and crystalline; his style 'prouder than when blue Iris bends'; his spirit fiery, impatient, wayward, indefatigable. Instead of taking his impressions from without, in entire and almost unimpaired masses, he moulds them according to his own temperament, and heats the materials of his imagination in the furnace of his passions.—Lord Byron's verse glows like a flame, consuming every thing in its way; Sir Walter Scott's glides like a river, clear, gentle, harmless. The poetry of the first scorches, that of the last scarcely warms. The light of the one proceeds from an internal source, ensanguined, sullen, fixed; the other reflects the hues of Heaven, or the face of nature, glancing vivid and various. The productions of the Northern Bard have the rust and the freshness of antiquity about them; those of the Noble Poet cease to startle from their extreme ambition of novelty, both in style and matter. Sir Walter's rhymes are 'silly sooth'—

> And dally with the innocence of thought,
> Like the old age—

his Lordship's Muse spurns *the olden time*, and affects all the supercilious airs of a modern fine lady and an upstart. The object of the one writer is to restore us to truth and nature: the other chiefly thinks how he shall display his own power, or vent his spleen, or astonish the reader either by starting new subjects and trains of speculation, or by expressing old ones in a more striking and emphatic manner than they have been expressed before. He cares little what it is he says, so that he can say it differently from others. This may account for the charges of plagiarism which have been repeatedly brought against the Noble Poet—if he can borrow an image or sentiment from another, and heighten it by an epithet or an allusion of greater force and beauty than is to be found in the original passage, he thinks he shows his superiority of execution in this in a more marked manner than if the first suggestion had been his own. It is not the value of the observation itself he is solicitous about; but he wishes to shine by contrast—even nature only serves as a foil to set off his style. He therefore takes the thoughts of others (whether contemporaries or not) out of their mouths, and is content to make them his own, to set his stamp upon them, by imparting to them a more meretricious gloss, a higher relief, a greater loftiness of tone, and a characteristic inveteracy of purpose. Even in those collateral ornaments of modern style, slovenliness, abruptness, and eccentricity (as well as in terseness and significance), Lord Byron, when he pleases, defies competition and surpasses all his contemporaries. Whatever he does, he must do in a more decided and daring manner than any one else—he lounges with extravagance, and yawns so as to alarm the reader! Self-will, passion, the love of singularity, a disdain of himself and of others (with a conscious sense that this is among the ways and means of procuring admiration) are the proper categories of his mind: he is a lordly writer, is above his own reputation, and condescends to the Muses with a scornful grace!

Lord Byron, who in his politics is a *liberal*, in his genius is haughty and aristocratic: Walter Scott, who is an aristocrat in principle, is popular in his writings, and is (as it were) equally *servile* to nature and to opinion. The genius of Sir Walter is essentially imitative, or 'denotes a foregone conclusion': that of Lord Byron is self-dependent; or at least requires no aid, is governed by no law, but the impulses of its own will. We confess, however much we may admire independence of feeling and erectness of spirit in general or practical questions, yet in works of genius we prefer him who bows to the authority of nature, who appeals to actual objects, to mouldering superstitions, to history, observation, and tradition, before him who only consults the pragmatical and restless workings of his own breast, and gives them out as oracles to the world. We like a writer (whether poet or prose-writer) who takes in (or is willing to take in) the range of half the universe in feeling, character, description, much better than we do one who obstinately and invariably shuts himself up in the Bastile of his own ruling passions. In short, we had rather be Sir Walter Scott (meaning thereby the Author of *Waverley*) than Lord Byron, a hundred times over. And for the reason just given, namely, that he casts his descriptions in the mould of nature, ever-varying, never tiresome, always interesting and always instructive, instead of casting them constantly in the mould of his own individual impressions. He gives us man as he is, or as he was, in almost every variety of situation, action, and feeling. Lord Byron makes man after his own image, woman after his own heart; the one is a capricious tyrant, the other a yielding slave; he gives us the misanthrope and the voluptuary by turns; and with these two characters, burning or melting in their own fires, he makes out everlasting centos of himself. He hangs the cloud, the film of his existence over all outward things—sits in the centre of his thoughts, and enjoys dark night, bright day, the glitter and the gloom 'in cell monastic'—we see the mournful pall, the crucifix, the death's heads, the faded chaplet of flowers, the gleaming tapers, the agonized brow of genius, the wasted form of beauty—but we are still imprisoned in a dungeon, a curtain intercepts our view, we do not breathe freely the air of nature or of our own thoughts—the other admired author draws aside the curtain, and the veil of egotism is rent, and he shows us the crowd of living men and women, the endless groups, the landscape back-ground, the cloud and the rainbow, and enriches our imaginations and relieves one passion by another, and expands and lightens reflection, and takes away that tightness at the breast which arises from thinking or wishing to think that there is nothing in the world out of a man's self!—In this point of view, the Author of *Waverley* is one of the greatest teachers of morality that ever lived, by emancipating the mind from petty, narrow, and bigotted prejudices: Lord Byron is the greatest pamperer of those prejudices, by seeming to think there is nothing else worth encouraging but the seeds or the full luxuriant growth of dogmatism and self-conceit. In reading the Scotch Novels, we never think about the author, except from a feeling of curiosity respecting our unknown benefactor: in reading Lord Byron's works, he himself is never absent from our minds. The colouring of Lord Byron's style, however rich and dipped in Tyrian dyes, is nevertheless opaque, is in itself an object of delight and wonder: Sir Walter Scott's is perfectly transparent. In studying the one, you seem to gaze at the figures cut in stained glass, which exclude the view beyond, and where the pure light of Heaven is only a means of setting off the gorgeousness of art: in reading the other, you look through a noble window at the clear and varied landscape without. Or to sum up the distinction in one word, Sir Walter Scott is the most *dramatic* writer now living; and Lord Byron is the least so. It would be difficult to imagine that the Author of *Waverley* is in the smallest degree a pedant; as it would be hard to persuade ourselves that the author of *Childe Harold* and *Don Juan* is not a coxcomb, though a provoking and sublime one. In this decided preference given to Sir Walter Scott over Lord Byron, we distinctly include the prose-works of the former; for we do not think his poetry alone by any means entitles him to that precedence. Sir Walter in his poetry, though pleasing and natural, is a comparative trifler:

it is in his anonymous productions that he has shown himself for what he is!—

Intensity is the great and prominent distinction of Lord Byron's writings. He seldom gets beyond force of style, nor has he produced any regular work or masterly whole. He does not prepare any plan beforehand, nor revise and retouch what he has written with polished accuracy. His only object seems to be to stimulate himself and his readers for the moment—to keep both alive, to drive away *ennui*, to substitute a feverish and irritable state of excitement for listless indolence or even calm enjoyment. For this purpose he pitches on any subject at random without much thought or delicacy—he is only impatient to begin—and takes care to adorn and enrich it as he proceeds with 'thoughts that breathe and words that burn.' He composes (as he himself has said) whether he is in the bath, in his study, or on horseback—he writes as habitually as others talk or think—and whether we have the inspiration of the Muse or not, we always find the spirit of the man of genius breathing from his verse. He grapples with his subject, and moves, penetrates, and animates it by the electric force of his own feelings. He is often monotonous, extravagant, offensive; but he is never dull, or tedious, but when he writes prose. Lord Byron does not exhibit a new view of nature, or raise insignificant objects into importance by the romantic associations with which he surrounds them; but generally (at least) takes commonplace thoughts and events, and endeavours to express them in stronger and statelier language than others. His poetry stands like a Martello tower by the side of his subject. He does not, like Mr. Wordsworth, lift poetry from the ground, or create a sentiment out of nothing. He does not describe a daisy or a periwinkle, but the cedar or the cypress: not 'poor men's cottages, but princes' palaces.' His *Childe Harold* contains a lofty and impassioned review of the great events of history, of the mighty objects left as wrecks of time, but he dwells chiefly on what is familiar to the mind of every schoolboy; has brought out few new traits of feeling or thought; and has done no more than justice to the reader's preconceptions by the sustained force and brilliancy of his style and imagery.

Lord Byron's earlier productions, *Lara*, *The Corsair*, &c. were wild and gloomy romances, put into rapid and shining verse. They discover the madness of poetry, together with the inspiration: sullen, moody, capricious, fierce, inexorable, gloating on beauty, thirsting for revenge, hurrying from the extremes of pleasure to pain, but with nothing permanent, nothing healthy or natural. The gaudy decorations and the morbid sentiments remind one of flowers strewed over the face of death! In his *Childe Harold* (as has been just observed) he assumes a lofty and philosophic tone, and 'reasons high of providence, fore-knowledge, will, and fate.' He takes the highest points in the history of the world, and comments on them from a more commanding eminence: he shows us the crumbling monuments of time, he invokes the great names, the mighty spirit of antiquity. The universe is changed into a stately mausoleum:—in solemn measures he chaunts a hymn to fame. Lord Byron has strength and elevation enough to fill up the moulds of our classical and time-hallowed recollections, and to rekindle the earliest aspirations of the mind after greatness and true glory with a pen of fire. The names of Tasso, of Ariosto, of Dante, of Cincinnatus, of Caesar, of Scipio, lose nothing of their pomp or their lustre in his hands, and when he begins and continues a strain of panegyric on such subjects, we indeed sit down with him to a banquet of rich praise, brooding over imperishable glories,

> Till Contemplation has her fill.

Lord Byron seems to cast himself indignantly from 'this bank and shoal of time,' or the frail tottering bark that bears up modern reputation, into the huge sea of ancient renown, and to revel there with untired, outspread plume. Even this in him is spleen—his contempt of his contemporaries makes him turn back to the lustrous past, or project himself forward to the dim future!—Lord Byron's tragedies, *Faliero*,[1] *Sardanapalus*, &c. are not equal to his other works. They want the essence of the drama. They abound in speeches and descriptions, such as he himself might make either to himself or others, lolling on his couch of a morning, but do not carry the reader out of the poet's mind to the scenes and events recorded. They have neither action, character, nor interest, but are a sort of *gossamer* tragedies, spun out, and glittering, and spreading a flimsy veil over the face of nature. Yet he spins them on. Of all that he has done in this way the *Heaven and Earth* (the same subject as Mr. Moore's *Loves of the Angels*) is the best. We prefer it even to *Manfred*. *Manfred* is merely himself, with a fancy-drapery on: but in the dramatic

[1] Don Juan was my Moscow, and Faliero
My Leipsic, and my Mont St. Jean seems Cain.
Don Juan, Canto XI.

fragment published in the *Liberal*, the space between Heaven and Earth, the stage on which his characters have to pass to and fro, seems to fill his Lordship's imagination; and the Deluge, which he has so finely described, may be said to have drowned all his own idle humours.

We must say we think little of our author's turn for satire. His *English Bards and Scotch Reviewers* is dogmatical and insolent, but without refinement or point. He calls people names, and tries to transfix a character with an epithet, which does not stick, because it has no other foundation than his own petulance and spite; or he endeavours to degrade by alluding to some circumstance of external situation. He says of Mr. Wordsworth's poetry, that 'it is his aversion.' That may be: but whose fault is it? This is the satire of a lord, who is accustomed to have all his whims or dislikes taken for gospel, and who cannot be at the pains to do more than signify his contempt or displeasure. If a great man meets with a rebuff which he does not like, he turns on his heel, and this passes for a repartee. The Noble Author says of a celebrated barrister and critic, that he was 'born in a garret sixteen stories high.' The insinuation is not true; or if it were, it is low. The allusion degrades the person who makes, not him to whom it is applied. This is also the satire of a person of birth and quality, who measures all merit by external rank, that is, by his own standard. So his Lordship, in a 'Letter to the Editor of My Grandmother's Review,' addresses him fifty times as '*my dear Robarts*'; nor is there any other wit in the article. This is surely a mere assumption of superiority from his Lordship's rank, and is the sort of *quizzing* he might use to a person who came to hire himself as a valet to him at *Long's*—the waiters might laugh, the public will not. In like manner, in the controversy about Pope, he claps Mr. Bowles on the back with a coarse facetious familiarity, as if he were his chaplain whom he had invited to dine with him, or was about to present to a benefice. The reverend divine might submit to the obligation, but he has no occasion to subscribe to the jest. If it is a jest that Mr. Bowles should be a parson, and Lord Byron a peer, the world knew this before; there was no need to write a pamphlet to prove it.

The *Don Juan* indeed has great power; but its power is owing to the force of the serious writing, and to the oddity of the contrast between that and the flashy passages with which it is interlarded. From the sublime to the ridiculous there is but one step. You laugh and are surprised that any one should turn round and *travestie* himself: the drollery is in the utter discontinuity of ideas and feelings. He makes virtue serve as a foil to vice; *dandyism* is (for want of any other) a variety of genius. A classical intoxication is followed by the splashing of soda-water, by frothy effusions of ordinary bile. After the lightning and the hurricane, we are introduced to the interior of the cabin and the contents of wash-hand basins. The solemn hero of tragedy plays *Scrub* in the farce. This is 'very tolerable and not to be endured.' The Noble Lord is almost the only writer who has prostituted his talents in this way. He hallows in order to desecrate; takes a pleasure in defacing the images of beauty his hands have wrought; and raises our hopes and our belief in goodness to Heaven only to dash them to the earth again, and break them in pieces the more effectually from the very height they have fallen. Our enthusiasm for genius or virtue is thus turned into a jest by the very person who has kindled it, and who thus fatally quenches the sparks of both. It is not that Lord Byron is sometimes serious and sometimes trifling, sometimes profligate, and sometimes moral— but when he is most serious and most moral, he is only preparing to mortify the unsuspecting reader by putting a pitiful *hoax* upon him. This is a most unaccountable anomaly. It is as if the eagle were to build its eyry in a common sewer, or the owl were seen soaring to the mid-day sun. Such a sight might make one laugh, but one would not wish or expect it to occur more than once.[1]

In fact, Lord Byron is the spoiled child of fame as well as fortune. He has taken a surfeit of popularity, and is not contented to delight, unless he can shock the public. He would force them to admire in spite of decency and common sense—he would have them read what they would read in no one but himself, or he would not give a rush for their applause. He is to be 'a chartered libertine,' from whom insults are favours, whose contempt is to be a new incentive to admiration. His Lordship is hard to please: he is equally averse to notice or neglect, enraged at censure and scorning praise. He tries the patience of the town to the very utmost, and when they show signs of weariness or disgust, threatens to *discard* them. He says he will write on, whether he is read or not. He would never write another page, if it were not to court popular applause, or to affect a superiority over it. In this respect also, Lord Byron presents a striking

[1] This censure applies to the first Cantos of *Don Juan* much more than to the last. It has been called a *Tristram Shandy* in rhyme: it is rather a poem written about itself.

contrast to Sir Walter Scott. The latter takes what part of the public favour falls to his share, without grumbling (to be sure he has no reason to complain); the former is always quarrelling with the world about his *modicum* of applause, the *spolia opima*[1] of vanity, and ungraciously throwing the offerings of incense heaped on his shrine back in the faces of his admirers. Again, there is no taint in the writings of the Author of *Waverley*, all is fair and natural and *above-board*: he never outrages the public mind. He introduces no anomalous character: broaches no staggering opinion. If he goes back to old prejudices and superstitions as a relief to the modern reader, while Lord Byron floats on swelling paradoxes—

> Like proud seas under him;

if the one defers too much to the spirit of antiquity, the other panders to the spirit of the age, goes to the very edge of extreme and licentious speculation, and breaks his neck over it. Grossness and levity are the playthings of his pen. It is a ludicrous circumstance that he should have dedicated his *Cain* to the worthy Baronet! Did the latter ever acknowledge the obligation? We are not nice, not very nice; but we do not particularly approve those subjects that shine chiefly from their rottenness: nor do we wish to see the Muses drest out in the flounces of a false or questionable philosophy, like *Portia* and *Nerissa* in the garb of Doctors of Law. We like metaphysics as well as Lord Byron; but not to see them making flowery speeches, nor dancing a measure in the fetters of verse. We have as good as hinted, that his Lordship's poetry consists mostly of a tissue of superb commonplaces; even his paradoxes are *common-place*. They are familiar in the schools: they are only new and striking in his dramas and stanzas, by being out of place. In a word, we think that poetry moves best within the circle of nature and received opinion: speculative theory and subtle casuistry are forbidden ground to it. But Lord Byron often wanders into this ground wantonly, wilfully, and unwarrantably. The only apology we can conceive for the spirit of some of Lord Byron's writings, is the spirit of some of those opposed to him. They would provoke a man to write anything. 'Farthest from them is best.' The extravagance and license of the one seems a proper antidote to the bigotry and narrowness of the other. The first *Vision of Judgment* was a set-off to the second, though

> None but itself could be its parallel.

[1] ['Spoils of honour.']

Perhaps the chief cause of most of Lord Byron's errors is, that he is that anomaly in letters and in society, a Noble Poet. It is a double privilege, almost too much for humanity. He has all the pride of birth and genius. The strength of his imagination leads him to indulge in fantastic opinions; the elevation of his rank sets censure at defiance. He becomes a pampered egotist. He has a seat in the House of Lords, a niche in the Temple of Fame. Every-day mortals, opinions, things are not good enough for him to touch or think of. A mere nobleman is, in his estimation, but 'the tenth transmitter of a foolish face': a mere man of genius is no better than a worm. His Muse is also a lady of quality. The people are not polite enough for him: the Court not sufficiently intellectual. He hates the one and despises the other. By hating and despising others, he does not learn to be satisfied with himself. A fastidious man soon grows querulous and splenetic. If there is nobody but ourselves to come up to our idea of fancied perfection, we easily get tired of our idol. When a man is tired of what he is, by a natural perversity he sets up for what he is not. If he is a poet, he pretends to be a metaphysician: if he is a patrician in rank and feeling, he would fain be one of the people. His ruling motive is not the love of the people, but of distinction; not of truth, but of singularity. He patronizes men of letters out of vanity, and deserts them from caprice, or from the advice of friends. He embarks in an obnoxious publication to provoke censure, and leaves it to shift for itself for fear of scandal. We do not like Sir Walter's gratuitous servility: we like Lord Byron's preposterous *liberalism* little better. He may affect the principles of equality, but he resumes his privilege of peerage, upon occasion. His Lordship has made great offers of service to the Greeks—money and horses. He is at present in Cephalonia, waiting the event!

★   ★   ★   ★   ★   ★   ★

We had written thus far when news came of the death of Lord Byron, and put an end at once to a strain of somewhat peevish invective, which was intended to meet his eye, not to insult his memory. Had we known that we were writing his epitaph, we must have done it with a different feeling. As it is, we think it better and more like himself, to let what we had written stand, than to take up our leaden shafts, and try to melt them into 'tears of sensibility,' or mould them into dull praise, and an affected show of candour. We were not silent during the author's life-time, either for his reproof or encouragement (such as we could give, and *he* did not disdain to accept) nor can we now turn undertakers' men to fix the glittering plate upon his coffin, or fall into the procession of popular woe.—Death cancels every thing but truth; and strips a man of every thing but genius and virtue. It is a sort of natural canonization. It makes the meanest of us sacred—it installs the poet in his immortality, and lifts him to the skies. Death is the great assayer of the sterling ore of talent. At his touch the drossy particles fall off, the irritable, the personal, the gross, and mingle with the dust—the finer and more ethereal part mounts with the winged spirit to watch over our latest memory, and protect our bones from insult. We consign the least worthy qualities to oblivion, and cherish the nobler and imperishable nature with double pride and fondness. Nothing could show the real superiority of genius in a more striking point of view than the idle contests and the public indifference about the place of Lord Byron's interment, whether in Westminster Abbey or his own family-vault. A king must have a coronation—a nobleman a funeral-procession.—The man is nothing without the pageant. The poet's cemetery is the human mind, in which he sows the seeds of never-ending thought—his monument is to be found in his works:

> Nothing can cover his high fame but Heaven;
> No pyramids set off his memory,
> But the eternal substance of his greatness.

Lord Byron is dead: he also died a martyr to his zeal in the cause of freedom, for the last, best hopes of man. Let that be his excuse and his epitaph!

44. Newman and Goethe: *Don Juan* unpoetical?

[1829] 1871; [1827] 1850

(*a*) JOHN HENRY NEWMAN (1801–90), the famous churchman and theologian, published his essay on 'Poetry, With Reference to Aristotle's Poetics' in the first number of the *London Review* in 1829. It was reprinted in his *Essays Critical and Historical* in 1871, with (he explained) the original readings restored at points where alterations had been imposed by the editor. The following extract (*Essays Critical and Historical*, pp. 10–12) deals with the unpoetical in poetry: '. . . It follows that the poetical mind is one full of the eternal forms of beauty and perfection; these are its material of thought, its instrument and medium of observation,—these colour each object to which it directs its view. It is called imaginative or creative, from the originality and independence of its modes of thinking, compared with the commonplace and matter-of-fact conceptions of ordinary minds, which are fettered down to the particular and individual. At the same time it feels a natural sympathy with everything great and splendid in the physical and moral world; and selecting such from the mass of common phenomena, incorporates them, as it were, into the substance of its own creations. From living thus in a world of its own, it speaks the language of dignity, emotion, and refinement. Figure is its necessary medium of communication with man; for in the feebleness of ordinary words to express its ideas, and in the absence of terms of abstract perfection, the adoption of metaphorical language is the only poor means allowed it for imparting to others its intense feelings. A metrical garb has, in all languages, been appropriated to poetry—it is but the outward development of the music and harmony within. The verse, far from being a restraint on the true poet, is the suitable index of his sense, and is adopted by his free and deliberate choice. . . . Let not our notion be thought arbitrarily to limit the number of poets, generally considered such. It will be found to lower particular works, or parts of works, rather than the authors themselves; sometimes to disparage only the vehicle in which the poetry is conveyed. There is an ambiguity in the word "poetry", which is taken to signify both the gift itself, and the written composition which is the result of it. Thus there is an apparent, but no real contradiction, in saying a poem may be but partially poetical; in some passages more so than in others; and sometimes not poetical at all. We only maintain, not that the writers forfeit the name of poet who fail at times to answer to our requisitions, but that they are poets only so far forth, and inasmuch as they do answer to them. We may grant, for instance, that the vulgarities of old Phoenix in the ninth *Iliad*, or of the nurse of Orestes in the *Choephoroe*, are in themselves unworthy of their respective authors, and refer them to the wantonness of exuberant genius; and yet maintain that the scenes in question contain much incidental poetry. Now and then the lustre of the true metal catches the eye, redeeming whatever is unseemly and worthless in the rude ore; still the ore is not the metal. Nay, sometimes, and not unfrequently in Shakspeare, the introduction of unpoetical matter may be necessary for the sake of relief, or as a vivid expression of recondite conceptions, and, as it were, to make friends with the reader's imagination. This necessity, however, cannot make the additions in themselves beautiful and pleasing. Sometimes, on the other hand, while we do not deny the incidental beauty of a poem, we are ashamed and indignant on witnessing the unworthy substance in which that beauty is imbedded. This remark applies strongly to the immoral compositions to which Lord Byron devoted his last years.'

(*b*) Such a conception of the poetical had been challenged by Goethe in a conversation of July 1827, reported by Eckermann (*Conversations of Goethe with Eckermann and Soret*, trans. John Oxenford, 1850, I, 423–4): ' "In Lord Byron," said I, "I frequently find passages which merely bring objects before us, without affecting our feelings otherwise than the drawing of a good painter. *Don Juan* is, especially, rich in such passages."

"Yes," said Goethe, "here Lord Byron was great; his pictures have an air of reality, as lightly thrown off as if they were improvised. I know but little of *Don Juan*, but I remember passages from his other poems, especially sea scenes, with a sail peeping out here and there, which are quite invaluable, for they make us seem to feel the sea-breeze blowing."

"In his *Don Juan*," said I, "I have particularly admired the representation of London, which his careless verses bring before our very eyes. He is not very scrupulous whether an object is poetical or not; but he seizes and uses all just as they come before him, down to the wigs in the haircutter's window, and the men who fill the street-lamps with oil."

"Our German aesthetical people," said Goethe, "are always talking about poetical and unpoetical objects; and, in one respect, they are not quite wrong; yet, at bottom, no real object is unpoetical, if the poet knows how to use it properly." '

45. Galt, Moore and Northcote on *Don Juan*

1830

(*a*) JOHN GALT (1779–1839), the Scottish novelist and man of letters, had travelled on the same ship as Byron from Gibraltar to Malta in 1809. This limited acquaintanceship encouraged him to produce a *Life of Lord Byron*, which was published in 1830. The following quotation is taken from the third edition, 1830, pp. 261–4: 'Hitherto I have not noticed *Don Juan* otherwise than incidentally. It was commenced in Venice, and afterwards continued at intervals to the end of the sixteenth canto, until the author left Pisa, when it was not resumed, at least no more has been published. Strong objections have been made to its moral tendency, but, in the opinion of many, it is the poet's masterpiece, and undoubtedly it displays all the variety of his powers, combined with a quaint playfulness not found to an equal degree in any other of his works. The serious and pathetic portions are exquisitely beautiful; the descriptive have all the distinctness of the best pictures in *Childe Harold*, and are, moreover, generally drawn from nature, while the satire is for the most part curiously associated and sparklingly witty. The characters are sketched with amazing firmness and freedom, and though sometimes grotesque, are yet not often overcharged. It is professedly an epic poem, but it may be more properly described as a poetical novel. Nor can it be said to inculcate any particular moral, or to do more than unmantle the decorum of society. Bold and buoyant throughout, it exhibits a free irreverent knowledge of the world, laughing or mocking as the thought serves, in the most unexpected antitheses to the proprieties of time, place, and circumstance. . . . It is generally supposed to contain much of the author's own experience, but still, with all its riant knowledge of bowers and boudoirs, it is deficient as a true limning of the world, by showing man as if he were always ruled by one predominant appetite. . . . But it is not my intention to analyze this eccentric and meandering poem; a composition which cannot be well estimated by extracts. Without, therefore, dwelling at greater length on its variety and merits, I would only observe that the general accuracy of the poet's descriptions is verified by that of the scenes in which Juan is placed in England, a point the reader may determine for himself; while the vagueness of the parts derived from books, or sketched from fancy, as contrasted with them, justify the opinion, that invention was not the most eminent faculty of Byron, either in scenes or in characters. Of the demerits of the poem it is only necessary to remark, that it has been proscribed on account of its immorality; perhaps, however, there was more of prudery than of equity in the decision, at least it is liable to be so considered, so long as reprints are permitted of the older dramatists, with all their unpruned licentiousness. . . .'

(b) THOMAS MOORE's biography of Byron is a notable achievement, but he had little critical insight, and the following remarks on *Don Juan* are of interest mainly as echoing widely held opinions (*Letters and Journals of Lord Byron: with Notices of his Life*, 1830, II, 189, 786): 'It was at this time . . . that he conceived, and wrote some part of, his Poem of *Don Juan*;—and never did pages more faithfully and, in many respects, lamentably reflect every variety of feeling, and whim, and passion that, like the rack of autumn, swept across the author's mind in writing them. Nothing less, indeed, than that singular combination of attributes, which existed and were in full activity in his mind at this moment, could have suggested, or been capable of, the execution of such a work. The cool shrewdness of age with the vivacity and glowing temperament of youth,—the wit of a Voltaire, with the sensibility of a Rousseau,—the minute, practical knowledge of the man of society, with the abstract and self-contemplative spirit of the poet,— a susceptibility of all that is grandest and most affecting in human virtue, with a deep, withering experience of all that is most fatal to it,— the two extremes, in short, of man's mixed and inconsistent nature, now rankly smelling of earth, now breathing of heaven,—such was the strange assemblage of contrary elements, all meeting together in the same mind, and all brought to bear, in turn, upon the same task, from which alone could have sprung this extraordinary Poem,— the most powerful and, in many respects, painful display of the versatility of genius that has ever been left for succeeding ages to wonder at and deplore. . . .'

'It must be perceived by all endowed with quick powers of association how constantly, when any particular thought or sentiment presents itself to their minds, its very opposite, at the same moment, springs up there also:—if any thing sublime occurs, its neighbour, the ridiculous, is by its side;—with a bright view of the present or the future, a dark one mixes also its shadow;—and, even in questions respecting morals and conduct, all the reasonings and consequences that may suggest themselves on the side of one of two opposite courses will, in such minds, be instantly confronted by an array just as cogent on the other. A mind of this structure,—and such, more or less, are all those in which the reasoning is made subservient to the imaginative faculty,—though enabled, by such rapid powers of association to multiply its resources without end, has need of the constant exercise of a controlling judgment to keep its perceptions pure and undisturbed between the contrasts it thus simultaneously calls up; the obvious danger being that, where matters of taste are concerned, the habit of forming such incongruous juxtapositions—as that, for example, between the burlesque and sublime—should at last vitiate the mind's relish for the nobler and higher quality; and that, on the yet more important subject of morals, a facility in finding reasons for every side of a question may end, if not in the choice of the worst, at least in a sceptical indifference to all.

In picturing to oneself so awful an event as a shipwreck, its many horrors and perils are what alone offer themselves to ordinary fancies. But the keen, versatile imagination of Byron could detect in it far other details, and, at the same moment with all that is fearful and appalling in such a scene, could bring together all that is most ludicrous and low. That in this painful mixture he was but too true to human nature, the testimony of De Retz (himself an eye-witness of such an event) attests: —"*Vous ne pouvez vous imaginer* (says the Cardinal) *l'horreur d'une grande tempête;—vous en pouvez imaginer aussi peu le ridicule.*"[1] But, assuredly, a poet less wantoning in the variety of his power, and less proud of displaying it, would have paused ere he mixed up, thus mockingly, the degradation of humanity with its sufferings, and, content to probe us to the core with the miseries of our fellow-men, would have forborne to wring from us, the next moment, a bitter smile at their baseness. . . .'

(c) JAMES NORTHCOTE (1746–1831), painter and author, a pupil and friend of Sir Joshua Reynolds, won fame mainly as a portrait painter, though he also treated historical subjects. Hazlitt's *Conversations of James Northcote, Esq., R.A.* were published in book form in 1830. Most of the items had already appeared, between 1826 and 1830, in the

---

[1] ['You cannot picture to yourself the horror of a great storm: it is as difficult to imagine its absurdity.']

following periodicals: the *New Monthly Magazine*, the *Court Journal*, the *London Weekly Review*, and the *Atlas*. It is impossible to determine the extent to which these are an accurate record of Northcote's actual conversations on which they were based, as Hazlitt makes it clear that much of the work is his own composition. (See *The Complete Works of William Hazlitt*, ed. P. P. Howe, 1930–4, XI, 350–1.) The following comments on *Don Juan* are from the Sixteenth Conversation, first published in the *Atlas*, April 1829. (*Complete Works*, ed. Howe, XI, 279–80):

'N.— . . . I cannot help thinking there are essences in Lord Byron that are not to be surpassed. He is on a par with Dryden. All the other modern poets appear to me vulgar in the comparison. . . . I do not mean to vindicate the immorality or misanthropy in that poem [*Don Juan*]—perhaps his lameness was to blame for this defect—but surely no one can deny the force, the spirit of it; and there is such a fund of drollery mixed up with the serious part. Nobody understood the tragi-comedy of poetry so well. People find fault with this mixture in general, because it is not well managed; there is a comic story and a tragic story going on at the same time, without their having any thing to do with one another. But in Lord Byron they are brought together, just as they are in nature. In like manner, if you go to an execution at the very moment when the criminal is going to be turned off, and all eyes are fixed upon him, an old apple-woman and her stall are over-turned, and all the spectators fall a-laughing. In real life the most ludicrous incidents border on the most affecting and shocking. How fine that is of the cask of butter in the storm! Some critics have objected to it as turning the whole into burlesque; on the contrary, it is that which stamps the character of the scene more than any thing else. What did the people in the boat care about the rainbow, which he has described in such vivid colours; or even about their fellow-passengers who were thrown overboard, when they only wanted to eat them? No, it was the loss of the firkin of butter that affected them more than all the rest; and it is the mention of this circumstance that adds a hardened levity and a sort of ghastly horror to the scene. It shows the master-hand—there is such a boldness and sagacity and superiority to ordinary rules in it! . . .'

46. Carlyle on Byron and Byronism

1824–43

Thomas Carlyle (1795–1881), an eminent Victorian born in the
same year as Keats, wrote no formal critique of Byron's work,
but incidental comments in his letters, essays and other writings
enable us to chart his changing views. (For a discussion of these
see Charles R. Sanders, 'The Byron Closed in *Sartor Resartus*',
Studies in Romanticism, III [1963–4], 77–108.)

(*a*) On 20 May 1824 Jane Baillie Welsh (1801–66) wrote to her future
husband: 'And Byron is dead! I was told it all at once in a roomful
of people. My God, if they had said that the sun or the moon had gone
out of the heavens, it could not have struck me with the idea of a more
awful and dreary blank in the creation than the words, "Byron is
dead!" I have felt quite cold and dejected ever since: all my thoughts
have been fearful and dismal.'

On the previous day Carlyle had written to her on the same subject:
'Poor Byron! Alas poor Byron! The news of his death came down
upon my heart like a mass of lead; and yet, the thought of it sends a
painful twinge thro' all my being, as if I had lost a Brother! O God!
That so many sons of mud and clay should fill up their base existence
to its utmost bound, and this, the noblest spirit in Europe, should
sink before half his course was run! Late so full of fire and generous
passion, and proud purposes, and now forever dumb and cold! Poor
Byron! And but a young man; still struggling among the perplexities,
and sorrows and aberrations of a mind not arrived at maturity or settled
in its proper place in life. Had he been spared to the age of three score
and ten, what might he not have done, what might he not have been!
But we shall hear his voice no more: I dreamed of seeing him and
knowing him; but the curtain of everlasting night has hid him from
our eyes. We shall go to him, he shall not return to us.—Adieu, my
dear Jane! There is a blank in your heart and a blank in mine, since
this man passed away.' (*The Love Letters of Thomas Carlyle and Jane
Welsh*, ed. Alexander Carlyle, 1909, I, 369, 366–7.)

(b) Extract from 'The State of German Literature' (*Edinburgh Review*, October, 1827), quoted here from *The Works of Thomas Carlyle*, Centenary Edn., ed. H. D. Traill, 1896–9, XXVI: *Critical and Miscellaneous Essays*, I, 68–9: 'Poetry arose again, and in a new and singular shape. The *Sorrows of Werter*, *Götz von Berlichingen*, and the *Robbers*, may stand as patriarchs and representatives of three separate classes, which, commingled in various proportions, or separately co-existing, now with the preponderance of this, now of that, occupied the whole popular literature of Germany till near the end of the last century. These were the Sentimentalists, the Chivalry-play writers, and other gorgeous and outrageous persons; as a whole, now pleasantly denominated the *Kraftmänner*, literally, Power-men. They dealt in sceptical lamentation, mysterious enthusiasm, frenzy and suicide: they recurred with fondness to the Feudal Ages, delineating many a battlemented keep, and swart buff-belted man-at-arms; for in reflection, as in action, they studied to be strong, vehement, rapidly effective; of battle-tumult, love-madness, heroism and despair, there was no end. This literary period is called the *Sturm- und Drang-Zeit*, the Storm- and Stress-Period; for great indeed was the woe and fury of these Power-men. Beauty, to their mind, seemed synonymous with Strength. All passion was poetical, so it were but fierce enough. Their head moral virtue was pride; their *beau idéal* of manhood was some transcript of Milton's Devil. Often they inverted Bolingbroke's plan, and instead of "patronising Providence", did directly the opposite; raging with extreme animation against Fate in general, because it enthralled free virtue; and with clenched hands, or sounding shields, hurling defiance towards the vault of heaven.

These Power-men are gone too; and, with few exceptions, save the three originals above named, their works have already followed them. The application of all this to our own literature is too obvious to require much exposition. Have not we also had our Power-men? And will not, as in Germany, to us likewise a milder, a clearer, and a truer time come round? Our Byron was in his youth but what Schiller and Goethe had been in theirs: yet the author of *Werter* wrote *Iphigenie* and *Torquato Tasso*; and he who began with the *Robbers* ended with *Wilhelm Tell*. With longer life, all things were to have been hoped for from Byron: for he loved truth in his inmost heart, and would have discovered at last that his Corsairs and Harolds were not true. It was otherwise appointed. But with one man all hope does not die. If this way is the right one, we too shall find it.'

(c) Extract from 'Goethe' (*Foreign Review*, July 1828), quoted here from *Critical and Miscellaneous Essays*, ed. Traill, I, 217-19: 'The poet, says Schiller, is a citizen not only of his country, but of his time. Whatever occupies and interests men in general, will interest him still more. That nameless Unrest, the blind struggle of a soul in bondage, that high, sad, longing Discontent, which was agitating every bosom, had driven Goethe almost to despair. All felt it; he alone could give it voice. And here lies the secret of his popularity; in his deep, susceptive heart, he felt a thousand times more keenly what every one was feeling; with the creative gift which belonged to him as a poet, he bodied it forth into visible shape, gave it a local habitation and a name; and so made himself the spokesman of his generation. *Werter* is but the cry of that dim, rooted pain, under which all thoughtful men of a certain age were languishing: it paints the misery, it passionately utters the complaint; and heart and voice, all over Europe, loudly and at once respond to it. True, it prescribes no remedy; for that was a far different, far harder enterprise, to which other years and a higher culture were required; but even this utterance of the pain, even this little, for the present, is ardently grasped at, and with eager sympathy appropriated in every bosom. If Byron's life-weariness, his moody melancholy, and mad stormful indignation, borne on the tones of a wild and quite artless melody, could pierce so deep into many a British heart, now that the whole matter is no longer new,—is indeed old and trite,—we may judge with what vehement acceptance this *Werter* must have been welcomed, coming as it did like a voice from unknown regions; the first thrilling peal of that impassioned dirge, which, in country after country, men's ears have listened to, till they were deaf to all else. For *Werter*, infusing itself into the core and whole spirit of Literature, gave birth to a race of Sentimentalists, who have raged and wailed in every part of the world; till better light dawned on them, or at worst, exhausted Nature laid herself to sleep, and it was discovered that lamenting was an unproductive labour. These funereal choristers, in Germany a loud, haggard, tumultuous, as well as tearful class, were named the *Kraftmänner*, or Power-men; but have all long since, like sick children, cried themselves to rest.

Byron was our English Sentimentalist and Power-man; the strongest of his kind in Europe; the wildest, the gloomiest, and it may be hoped the last. For what good is it to "whine, put finger i' the eye, and sob," in such a case? Still more, to snarl and snap in malignant wise, "like dog distract, or monkey sick"? Why should we quarrel with our existence, here as it lies before us, our field and inheritance, to make or to mar, for better or for worse; in which, too, so many noblest men have, ever from the beginning, warring with the very evils we war with, both made and been what will be venerated to all time?

> What shapest thou here at the World? 'Tis shapen long ago;
> The Maker shaped it, *he* thought it best even *so*.
> Thy lot is appointed, go follow its hest;
> Thy journey's begun, thou must move and not rest;
> For sorrow and care cannot alter thy case,
> And running, not raging, will win thee the race.[1]

(*d*) Extract from 'Burns' (*Edinburgh Review*, December 1828), quoted here from *Critical and Miscellaneous Essays*, ed. Traill, I, 267-9: 'The excellence of Burns is, indeed, among the rarest, whether in poetry or prose; but, at the same time, it is plain and easily recognised: his *Sincerity*, his indisputable air of Truth. Here are no fabulous woes or joys; no hollow fantastic sentimentalities; no wiredrawn refinings, either in thought or feeling: the passion that is traced before us has glowed in a living heart; the opinion he utters has risen in his own understanding, and been a light to his own steps. He does not write from hearsay, but from sight and experience; it is the scenes that he has lived and laboured amidst, that he describes: those scenes, rude and humble as they are, have kindled beautiful emotions in his soul, noble thoughts, and definite resolves; and he speaks forth what is in him, not from any outward call of vanity or interest, but because his heart is too full to be silent. He speaks it with such melody and modulation as he can; "in homely rustic jingle"; but it is his own, and genuine. This is the grand secret for finding readers and retaining them: let him who would move and convince others, be first moved and convinced himself. Horace's rule, *Si vis me flere*,[2] is applicable in a wider sense than the literal one. To every poet, to every writer, we might say: Be true, if you would be believed. Let a man but speak forth with genuine earnestness the thought, the emotion, the actual condition of his own heart; and other men, so strangely are we all knit together by the tie of sympathy, must and will give heed to him. In culture, in extent of view, we may stand above the speaker, or below him; but in either case, his words, if they are earnest and sincere, will find some

[1] [A free translation of some verses by Goethe.]
[2] [See the *Art of Poetry*, ll. 102-3: 'If you would have me weep, you must first feel grief yourself' (Loeb trans.).]

response within us; for in spite of all casual varieties in outward rank or inward, as face answers to face, so does the heart of man to man. This may appear a very simple principle, and one which Burns had little merit in discovering. True, the discovery is easy enough: but the practical appliance is not easy; is indeed the fundamental difficulty which all poets have to strive with, and which scarcely one in the hundred ever fairly surmounts. A head too dull to discriminate the true from the false; a heart too dull to love the one at all risks, and to hate the other in spite of all temptations, are alike fatal to a writer. With either, or as more commonly happens, with both of these deficiencies combine a love of distinction, a wish to be original, which is seldom wanting, and we have Affectation, the bane of literature, as Cant, its elder brother, is of morals. How often does the one and the other front us, in poetry, as in life! Great poets themselves are not always free of this vice; nay, it is precisely on a certain sort and degree of greatness that it is most commonly ingrafted. A strong effort after excellence will sometimes solace itself with a mere shadow of success; he who has much to unfold, will sometimes unfold it imperfectly. Byron, for instance, was no common man: yet if we examine his poetry with this view, we shall find it far enough from faultless. Generally speaking, we should say that it is not true. He refreshes us, not with the divine fountain, but too often with vulgar strong waters, stimulating indeed to the taste, but soon ending in dislike, or even nausea. Are his Harolds and Giaours, we would ask, real men; we mean, poetically consistent and conceivable men? Do not these characters, does not the character of their author, which more or less shines through them all, rather appear a thing put on for the occasion; no natural or possible mode of being, but something intended to look much grander than nature? Surely, all these stormful agonies, this volcanic heroism, superhuman contempt and moody desperation, with so much scowling, and teeth-gnashing, and other sulphurous humour, is more like the brawling of a player in some paltry tragedy, which is to last three hours, than the bearing of a man in the business of life, which is to last three-score and ten years. To our minds there is a taint of this sort, something which we should call theatrical, false, affected, in every one of these otherwise so powerful pieces. Perhaps *Don Juan*, especially the latter parts of it, is the only thing approaching to a *sincere* work, he ever wrote; the only work where he showed himself, in any measure, as he was; and seemed so intent on his subject as, for moments, to forget himself. Yet Byron hated this vice; we believe, heartily detested it: nay he had declared formal war against it in words. So difficult is it even for the strongest to make this primary attainment, which might seem the simplest of all: to *read its own consciousness without mistakes, without errors involuntary or wilful!*'

(*e*) Extract from letter of 28 April 1832, to Macvey Napier, editor of the *Edinburgh Review*: 'In my mind, Byron has been sinking at an accelerated rate, for the last ten years, and has now reached a very low level: I should say *too* low, were there not a *Hibernicism* involved in the expression. His fame has been very great, but I see not how it is to endure; neither does that make *him* great. No genuine productive Thought was ever revealed by him to mankind; indeed no clear undistorted vision into anything, or picture of anything; but all had a certain falsehood, a brawling theatrical insincere character. The man's moral nature too was bad, his demeanor, as a man, was bad. What was he, in short, but a huge *sulky Dandy*; of giant dimensions, to be sure, yet still a Dandy; who sulked, as poor Mrs. Hunt expressed it "like a schoolboy that had got a plain bunn given him instead of a plum one"? His Bunn was nevertheless God's Universe with what Tasks are there; and it had served better men than he. I love him not; I *owe* him nothing; only pity, and forgiveness: he taught me nothing that I had not again to forget.' (R. H. Shepherd and C. N. Williamson, *Memoirs of the Life and Writings of Thomas Carlyle*, 1881, I, 104–5; C. R. Sanders, *op. cit., Studies in Romanticism*, III [1963–4], 79–80.)

(*f*) Extract from 'Goethe's Works' (*Foreign Quarterly Review*, August 1832), quoted here from *Works*, ed. Traill, XXVII: *Critical and Miscellaneous Essays*, II, 435–6: 'The greatness of his [Goethe's] Endowment, manifested in such a work, has long been plain to all men. That it belongs to the highest class of human endowments, entitling the wearer thereof, who so nobly used it, to the appellation, in its strictest sense, of Great Man,—is also becoming plain. A giant strength of Character is to be traced here; mild and kindly and calm, even as strength ever is. In the midst of so much spasmodic Byronism, bellowing till its windpipe is cracked, how very different looks *this* symptom of strength: "He appeared to aim at pushing away from him everything that did not hang upon his individual will." "In his own imperturbable firmness of character, he had grown into the habit of never contradicting any one. On the contrary, he listened with a friendly air to every one's opinion, and would himself elucidate and strengthen it by instances and reasons of his own. All who did not know him fancied that he thought as they did; for he was possessed of a preponderating intellect, and could transport himself into the mental state of any man, and imitate his manner of conceiving." Beloved brethren, who wish to be strong! Had not the man, who could take this smooth method of it, more strength in him than any teeth-grinding, glass-eyed "lone Caloyer" you have yet fallen-in with? Consider your ways; consider, first, whether you cannot do with being *weak*! If the answer still prove negative, consider, secondly, what strength actually is, and where you are to try for it. A certain strong man, of former time, fought stoutly at Lepanto; worked stoutly as Algerine slave; stoutly delivered himself from such working; with stout cheerfulness endured famine and nakedness and the world's ingratitude; and, sitting in jail, with the one arm left him, wrote our joyfulest, and all but our deepest, modern book, and named it *Don Quixote*: this was a genuine strong man. A strong man, of recent time, fights little for any good cause anywhere; works weakly as an English lord; weakly delivers himself from such working; with weak despondency endures the cackling of plucked geese at St. James's; and, sitting in sunny Italy, in his coach-and-four, at a distance of two thousand miles from them, writes, over many reams of paper, the following sentence, with variations: *Saw ever the world one greater or unhappier?* This was a sham strong man. Choose ye.—'

(*g*) Extracts from *Sartor Resartus* (*Fraser's Magazine*, 1833-4; in book form, Boston 1836). Quoted here from *Works*, ed. Traill, I, 125-6, 127-8, 153.

The soul-sickness of the protagonist, Professor Teufelsdröckh, which Carlyle diagnoses and for which he prescribes a remedy, is closely akin to Byronism, though Byronism itself is seen by Carlyle as only one manifestation of a general spiritual crisis of that age.

[i] 'If we ask now, not indeed with what ulterior Purpose, for there was none, yet with what immediate outlooks; at all events, in what mood of mind, the Professor undertook and prosecuted this world-pilgrimage,—the answer is more distinct than favourable. "A nameless Unrest," says he, "urged me forward; to which the outward motion was some momentary lying solace. Whither should I go? My Loadstars were blotted out; in that canopy of grim fire shone no star. Yet forward must I; the ground burnt under me; there was no rest for the

sole of my foot. I was alone, alone! Ever too the strong inward longing shaped Fantasms for itself: towards these, one after the other, must I fruitlessly wander. A feeling I had, that for my fever-thirst there was and must be somewhere a healing Fountain. To many fondly imagined Fountains, the Saints' Wells of these days, did I pilgrim; to great Men, to great Cities, to great Events: but found there no healing. In strange countries, as in the well-known; in savage deserts, as in the press of corrupt civilisation, it was ever the same: how could your Wanderer escape from—*his own Shadow*? Nevertheless still Forward! I felt as if in great haste; to do I saw not what. From the depths of my own heart, it called to me, Forwards! The winds and the streams, and all Nature sounded to me, Forwards! *Ach Gott*, I was even, once for all, a Son of Time."

From which is it not clear that the internal Satanic School was still active enough? He says elsewhere: "The *Enchiridion of Epictetus* I had ever with me, often as my sole rational companion; and regret to mention that the nourishment it yielded was trifling." Thou foolish Teufelsdröckh! How could it else? Hadst thou not Greek enough to understand thus much: *The End of Man is an Action, and not a Thought*, though it were the noblest?. . . .

Poor Teufelsdröckh! Flying with Hunger always parallel to him; and a whole Internal Chase in his rear; so that the countenance of Hunger is comparatively a friend's! Thus must he, in the temper of ancient Cain, or of the modern Wandering Jew,—save only that he feels himself not guilty and but suffering the pains of guilt,—wend to and fro with aimless speed. Thus must he, over the whole surface of the Earth (by footprints), write his *Sorrows of Teufelsdröckh;* even as the great Goethe, in passionate words, had to write his *Sorrows of Werter*, before the spirit freed herself, and he could become a Man. Vain truly is the hope of your swiftest Runner to escape "from his own Shadow"! Nevertheless, in these sick days, when the Born of Heaven first descries himself (about the age of twenty) in a world such as ours, richer than usual in two things, in Truths grown obsolete, and Trades grown obsolete,—what can the fool think but that it is all a Den of Lies, wherein whoso will not speak Lies and act Lies, must stand idle and despair? Whereby it happens that, for your nobler minds, the publishing of some such Work of Art, in one or the other dialect, becomes almost a necessity. For what is it properly but an Altercation with the Devil, before you begin honestly Fighting him? Your Byron publishes his *Sorrows of Lord George*, in verse and in prose, and copiously otherwise: your Bonaparte represents his *Sorrows of Napoleon* Opera, in an all-too stupendous style; with music of cannon-volleys, and murder-shrieks of a world; his stage-lights are the fires of Conflagration; his rhyme and recitative are the tramp of embattled Hosts and the sound of falling Cities.—Happier is he who, like our Clothes-Philosopher, can write such matter, since it must be written, on the insensible Earth, with his shoe-soles only; and also survive the writing thereof!'

(ii) [The protagonist describes his own recovery:] ' "I asked myself: What is this that, ever since earliest years, thou hast been fretting and fuming, and lamenting and self-tormenting, on account of? Say it in a word: is it not because thou art not HAPPY? Because the THOU (sweet gentleman) is not sufficiently honoured, nourished, soft-bedded, and lovingly cared-for? Foolish soul! What Act of Legislature was there that *thou* shouldst be Happy? A little while ago thou hadst no right to *be* at all. What if thou wert born and predestined not to be Happy, but to be Unhappy! Art thou nothing other than a Vulture, then, that fliest through the Universe seeking after somewhat to *eat*; and shrieking dolefully because carrion enough is not given thee? Close thy *Byron*; open thy *Goethe*." '

(h) Extract from *Past and Present* (1843). Quoted here from *Works*, ed. Traill, X, 196: 'The latest Gospel in this world is, Know thy work and do it. "Know thyself:" long enough has that poor "self" of thine tormented thee; thou wilt never get to "know" it, I believe! Think it not thy business, this of knowing thyself; thou art an unknowable individual: know what thou canst work at; and work at it, like a Hercules! That will be thy better plan.

It has been written, "an endless significance lies in Work;" a man perfects himself by working. Foul jungles are cleared away, fair seedfields rise instead, and stately cities; and withal the man himself first ceases to be a jungle and foul unwholesome desert thereby. Consider how, even in the meanest sorts of Labour, the whole soul of a man is composed into a kind of real harmony, the instant he sets himself to work! Doubt, Desire, Sorrow, Remorse, Indignation, Despair itself, all these like helldogs lie beleaguering the soul of the poor dayworker, as of every man: but he bends himself with free valour against his task, and all these are stilled, all these shrink murmuring far off into their caves. The man is now a man.'

47. Macaulay on Byron

1831

Thomas Babington Macaulay (1800–59), essayist, historian, and politician. Review (here given almost in its entirety) of Thomas Moore's *Letters and Journals of Lord Byron: with Notices of his Life* (1830), *Edinburgh Review*, June 1831, LIII, 544–72. (The essay was reprinted with minor revisions in Macaulay's *Critical and Historical Essays*, 1843, which ran through many editions.)

We have read this book with the greatest pleasure. Considered merely as a composition, it deserves to be classed among the best specimens of English prose which our age has produced. It contains, indeed, no single passage equal to two or three, which we could select from the *Life of Sheridan*. But, as a whole, it is immeasurably superior to that work. The style is agreeable, clear, and manly; and, when it rises into eloquence, rises without effort or ostentation. Nor is the matter inferior to the manner.

It would be difficult to name a book which exhibits more of kindness, fairness, and modesty. It has evidently been written, not for the purpose of showing, what, however, it often shows, how well its author can write; but for the purpose of vindicating, as far as truth will permit, the memory of a celebrated man who can no longer vindicate himself. Mr Moore never thrusts himself between Lord Byron and the public. With the strongest temptations to egotism, he has said no more about himself than the subject absolutely required. A great part—indeed the greater part of these volumes, consists of extracts from the Letters and Journals of Lord Byron; and it is difficult to speak too highly of the skill which has been shown in the selection and arrangement. We will not say that we have not occasionally remarked in these two large quartos an anecdote which should have been omitted, a letter which should have been suppressed, a name which should have been concealed by asterisks; or asterisks which do not answer the purpose of concealing the name. But it is impossible, on a general survey, to deny that the task has been executed with great judgment and great humanity. When we consider the life which Lord Byron had led, his petulance, his irritability, and his communicativeness, we cannot but admire the dexterity with which Mr Moore has contrived to exhibit so much of the character and opinions of his friend, with so little pain to the feelings of the living.

The extracts from the journals and correspondence of Lord Byron, are in the highest degree valuable—not merely on account of the information which they contain respecting the distinguished man by whom they were written, but on account, also, of their rare merit as compositions. The Letters—at least those which were sent from Italy—are among the best in our language. They are less affected than those of Pope and Walpole;—they have more matter in them than those of Cowper. Knowing that many of them were not written merely for the person to whom they were directed, but were general epistles, meant to be read by a large circle, we expected to find them clever and spirited, but deficient in ease. We looked with vigilance for instances of stiffness in the language, and awkwardness in the transitions. We have been agreeably disappointed; and we must confess, that if the epistolary style of Lord Byron was artificial, it was a rare and admirable instance of that highest art, which cannot be distinguished from nature.

Of the deep and painful interest which this book excites, no abstract can give a just notion. So sad and dark a story is scarcely to be found in any work of fiction; and we are little disposed to envy the moralist who can read it without being softened.

The pretty fable by which the Duchess of Orleans illustrates the character of her son the regent, might, with little change, be applied to Byron. All the fairies, save one, had been bidden to his cradle. All the gossips had been profuse of their gifts. One had bestowed nobility, another genius, a third beauty. The malignant elf who had been uninvited, came last, and, unable to reverse what her sisters had done for their favourite, had mixed up a curse with every blessing. In the rank of Lord Byron, in his understanding, in his character, in his very person, there was a strange union of opposite extremes. He was born to all that men covet and admire. But in every one of those eminent advantages which he possessed over others, there was mingled something of misery and debasement. He was sprung from a house, ancient indeed and noble, but degraded and impoverished by a series of crimes and follies, which had attained a scandalous publicity. The kinsman whom he succeeded had died poor, and, but for merciful judges, would have died upon the gallows. The young peer had great intellectual powers;

yet there was an unsound part in his mind. He had naturally a generous and tender heart; but his temper was wayward and irritable. He had a head which statuaries loved to copy, and a foot, the deformity of which the beggars in the streets mimicked. Distinguished at once by the strength and by the weakness of his intellect, affectionate yet perverse, a poor lord, and a handsome cripple, he required, if ever man required, the firmest and the most judicious training. But, capriciously as nature had dealt with him, the relative to whom the office of forming his character was intrusted, was more capricious still. She passed from paroxysms of rage to paroxysms of fondness. At one time she stifled him with her caresses—at another time she insulted his deformity. He came into the world, and the world treated him as his mother treated him—sometimes with kindness, sometimes with severity, never with justice. It indulged him without discrimination, and punished him without discrimination. He was truly a spoiled child,—not merely the spoiled child of his parent, but the spoiled child of nature, the spoiled child of fortune, the spoiled child of fame, the spoiled child of society. His first poems were received with a contempt which, feeble as they were, they did not absolutely deserve. The poem which he published on his return from his travels, was, on the other hand, extolled far above its merit. At twenty-four he found himself on the highest pinnacle of literary fame, with Scott, Wordsworth, Southey, and a crowd of other distinguished writers, beneath his feet. There is scarcely an instance in history of so sudden a rise to so dizzy an eminence.

Every thing that could stimulate, and every thing that could gratify the strongest propensities of our nature—the gaze of a hundred drawingrooms, the acclamations of the whole nation, the applause of applauded men, the love of the loveliest women—all this world, and all the glory of it, were at once offered to a young man to whom nature had given violent passions, and whom education had never taught to control them. He lived as many men live who have no similar excuses to plead for their faults. But his countrymen and his countrywomen would love him and admire him. They were resolved to see in his excesses only the flash and outbreak of that same fiery mind which glowed in his poetry. He attacked religion; yet in religious circles his name was mentioned with fondness, and in many religious publications his works were censured with singular tenderness. He lampooned the prince regent; yet he could not alienate the Tories. Every thing, it seemed, was to be forgiven to youth, rank, and genius.

Then came the reaction. Society, capricious in its indignation as it had been capricious in its fondness, flew into a rage with its froward and petted darling. He had been worshipped with an irrational idolatry. He was persecuted with an irrational fury. Much has been written about those unhappy domestic occurrences which decided the fate of his life. Yet nothing is, nothing ever was positively known to the public, but this,—that he quarrelled with his lady, and that she refused to live with him. There have been hints in abundance, and shrugs and shakings of the head, and 'Well, well, we know,' and 'We could an if we would,' and 'If we list to speak,' and 'There be that might an they list.' But we are not aware that there is before the world, substantiated by credible, or even by tangible evidence, a single fact indicating that Lord Byron was more to blame than any other man who is on bad terms with his wife. The professional men whom Lady Byron consulted, were undoubtedly of opinion that she ought not to live with her husband. But it is to be remembered that they formed that opinion without hearing both sides. We do not say, we do not mean to insinuate, that Lady Byron was in any respect to blame. We think that those who condemn her on the evidence which is now before the public, are as rash as those who condemn her husband. We will not pronounce any judgment; we cannot, even in our own minds, form any judgment on a transaction which is so imperfectly known to us. It would have been well if, at the time of the separation, all those who knew as little about the matter then as we know about it now, had shown that forbearance, which, under such circumstances, is but common justice.

We know no spectacle so ridiculous as the British public in one of its periodical fits of morality. In general, elopements, divorces, and family quarrels, pass with little notice. We read the scandal, talk about it for a day, and forget it. But once in six or seven years, our virtue becomes outrageous. We cannot suffer the laws of religion and decency to be violated. We must make a stand against vice. We must teach libertines, that the English people appreciate the importance of domestic ties. Accordingly, some unfortunate man, in no respect more depraved than hundreds whose offences have been treated with lenity, is singled out as an expiatory sacrifice. If he has children, they are to be taken from him. If he has a profession, he is to be driven from it. He is cut by the higher orders, and hissed by the lower. He is, in truth, a sort of whipping-boy, by whose vicarious agonies, all the other transgressors of the same class are, it is supposed, sufficiently chastised. We reflect very complacently on our own severity, and compare with great pride the high standard of morals established in England, with the Parisian laxity. At length our anger is satiated. Our victim is ruined and heart-broken. And our virtue goes quietly to sleep for seven years more. . . .

The obloquy which Byron had to endure, was such as might well have shaken a more constant mind. The newspapers were filled with lampoons. The theatres shook with execrations. He was excluded from circles where he had lately been the observed of all observers. All those creeping things that riot in the decay of nobler natures, hastened to their repast; and they were right;—they did after their kind. It is not every day that the savage envy of aspiring dunces is gratified by the agonies of such a spirit, and the degradation of such a name.

The unhappy man left his country for ever. The howl of contumely followed him across the sea, up the Rhine, over the Alps; it gradually waxed fainter; it died away. Those who had raised it began to ask each other, what, after all, was the matter about which they had been so clamorous; and wished to invite back the criminal whom they had just chased from them. His poetry became more popular than it had ever been; and his complaints were read with tears by thousands and tens of thousands who had never seen his face.

He had fixed his home on the shores of the Adriatic, in the most picturesque and interesting of cities, beneath the brightest of skies, and by the brightest of seas. Censoriousness was not the vice of the neigh-bours whom he had chosen. They were a race corrupted by a bad government and a bad religion; long renowned for skill in the arts of voluptuousness, and tolerant of all the caprices of sensuality. From the public opinion of the country of his adoption, he had nothing to dread. With the public opinion of the country of his birth, he was at open war. He plunged into wild and desperate excesses, ennobled by no generous or tender sentiment. From his Venetian haram he sent forth volume after volume, full of eloquence, of wit, of pathos, of ribaldry, and of bitter disdain. His health sank under the effects of his intemperance. His hair turned grey. His food ceased to nourish him. A hectic fever withered him up. It seemed that his body and mind were about to perish together.

From this wretched degradation he was in some measure rescued by an attachment, culpable indeed, yet such as, judged by the standard of morality established in the country where he lived, might be called virtuous. But an imagination polluted by vice, a temper embittered by misfortune, and a frame habituated to the fatal excitement of intoxica-tion, prevented him from fully enjoying the happiness which he might

have derived from the purest and most tranquil of his many attach-
ments. Midnight draughts of ardent spirits and Rhenish wines had
begun to work the ruin of his fine intellect. His verse lost much of the
energy and condensation which had distinguished it. But he would not
resign, without a struggle, the empire which he had exercised over the
men of his generation. A new dream of ambition arose before him—to
be the centre of a literary party; the great mover of an intellectual
revolution;—to guide the public mind of England from his Italian
retreat, as Voltaire had guided the public mind of France from the villa
of Ferney. With this hope, as it should seem, he established the *Liberal*.
But, powerfully as he had affected the imaginations of his contemporaries, he mistook his own powers, if he hoped to direct their
opinions; and he still more grossly mistook his own disposition, if he
thought that he could long act in concert with other men of letters.
The plan failed, and failed ignominiously: Angry with himself, angry
with his coadjutors, he relinquished it; and turned to another project,
the last and the noblest of his life.

A nation, once the first among the nations, pre-eminent in knowledge, pre-eminent in military glory, the cradle of philosophy, of
eloquence, and of the fine arts, had been for ages bowed down under
a cruel yoke. All the vices which tyranny generates—the abject vices
which it generates in those who submit to it—the ferocious vices which
it generates in those who struggle against it—had deformed the
character of that miserable race. The valour which had won the great
battle of human civilisation,—which had saved Europe, and subjugated Asia, lingered only among pirates and robbers. The ingenuity,
once so conspicuously displayed in every department of physical and
moral science, had been depraved into a timid and servile cunning. On
a sudden this degraded people had risen on their oppressors. Discoun-
tenanced or betrayed by the surrounding potentates, they had found in
themselves something of that which might well supply the place of all
foreign assistance,—something of the energy of their fathers.

As a man of letters, Lord Byron could not but be interested in the
event of this contest. His political opinions, though, like all his opinions,
unsettled, leaned strongly towards the side of liberty. He had assisted
the Italian insurgents with his purse; and if their struggle against the
Austrian government had been prolonged, would probably have
assisted them with his sword. But to Greece he was attached by peculiar
ties. He had, when young, resided in that country. Much of his most
splendid and popular poetry had been inspired by its scenery and by its

history. Sick of inaction,—degraded in his own eyes by his private vices, and by his literary failures,—pining for untried excitement and honourable distinction,—he carried his exhausted body and his wounded spirit to the Grecian camp.

His conduct in his new situation showed so much vigour and good sense as to justify us in believing, that, if his life had been prolonged, he might have distinguished himself as a soldier and a politician. But pleasure and sorrow had done the work of seventy years upon his delicate frame. The hand of death was on him: he knew it; and the only wish which he uttered was that he might die sword in hand.

This was denied to him. Anxiety, exertion, exposure, and those fatal stimulants which had become indispensable to him, soon stretched him on a sickbed, in a strange land, amidst strange faces, without one human being that he loved near him. There, at thirty-six, the most celebrated Englishman of the nineteenth century closed his brilliant and miserable career.

We cannot even now retrace those events without feeling something of what was felt by the nation, when it was first known that the grave had closed over so much sorrow and so much glory;—something of what was felt by those who saw the hearse, with its long train of coaches, turn slowly northward, leaving behind it that cemetery, which had been consecrated by the dust of so many great poets, but of which the doors were closed against all that remained of Byron. We well remember that, on that day, rigid moralists could not refrain from weeping for one so young, so illustrious, so unhappy, gifted with such rare gifts, and tried by such strong temptations. It is unnecessary to make any reflections. The history carries its moral with it. Our age has indeed been fruitful of warnings to the eminent, and of consolations to the obscure. Two men have died within our recollection, who, at a time of life at which few people have completed their education, had raised themselves, each in his own department, to the height of glory. One of them died at Longwood,[1] the other at Missolonghi.

It is always difficult to separate the literary character of a man who lives in our own time from his personal character. It is peculiarly difficult to make this separation in the case of Lord Byron. For it is scarcely too much to say, that Lord Byron never wrote without some reference, direct or indirect, to himself. The interest excited by the events of his life, mingles itself in our minds, and probably in the minds of almost all our readers, with the interest which properly belongs to

[1] [I.e. Napoleon.]

his works. A generation must pass away before it will be possible to form a fair judgment of his books, considered merely as books. At present they are not only books, but relics. We will, however, venture, though with unfeigned diffidence, to offer some desultory remarks on his poetry.

His lot was cast in the time of a great literary revolution. That poetical dynasty which had dethroned the successors of Shakspeare and Spenser was, in its turn, dethroned by a race who represented themselves as heirs of the ancient line, so long dispossessed by usurpers. The real nature of this revolution has not, we think, been comprehended by the great majority of those who concurred in it.

If this question were proposed—wherein especially does the poetry of our times differ from that of the last century?—ninety-nine persons out of a hundred would answer that the poetry of the last century was correct, but cold and mechanical, and that the poetry of our time, though wild and irregular, presented far more vivid images, and excited the passions far more strongly than that of Parnell, of Addison, or of Pope. In the same manner we constantly hear it said, that the poets of the age of Elizabeth had far more genius, but far less correctness, than those of the age of Anne. It seems to be taken for granted, that there is some necessary incompatibility, some antithesis between correctness and creative power. We rather suspect that this notion arises merely from an abuse of words; and that it has been the parent of many of the fallacies which perplex the science of criticism.

What is meant by correctness in poetry? If by correctness be meant the conforming to rules which have their foundation in truth, and in the principles of human nature, then correctness is only another name for excellence. If by correctness be meant the conforming to rules purely arbitrary, correctness may be another name for dulness and absurdity.

[Elaborates case against arbitrary and irrational 'rules' as opposed to the 'eternal and immutable principles' of poetry.]

Poetry is, as that most acute of human beings Aristotle said, more than two thousand years ago, imitation. It is an art analogous in many respects to the arts of painting, sculpture, and acting. The imitations of the painter, the sculptor, and the actor, are, indeed, within certain limits, more perfect than those of the poet. The machinery which the poet employs, consists merely of words; and words cannot, even when employed by such an artist as Homer or Dante, present to the mind images of visible objects quite so lively and exact as those which we carry away from looking on the works of the brush and the chisel. But, on the other hand, the range of poetry is infinitely wider than that of any other imitative art, or than that of all the other imitative arts together. The sculptor can imitate only form; the painter only form and colour; the actor, until the poet supplies him with words, only form, colour, and motion. Poetry holds the outer world in common with the other arts. The heart of man is the province of poetry, and of poetry alone. The painter, the sculptor, and the actor, when the actor is unassisted by the poet, can exhibit no more of human passion and character than that small portion which overflows into the gesture and the face—always an imperfect, often a deceitful sign—of that which is within. The deeper and more complex parts of human nature can be exhibited by means of words alone. Thus the objects of the imitation of poetry are the whole external and the whole internal universe, the face of nature, the vicissitudes of fortune, man as he is in himself, man as he appears in society, all things of which we can form an image in our minds, by combining together parts of things which really exist. The domain of this imperial art is commensurate with the imaginative faculty.

An art essentially imitative ought not surely to be subjected to rules which tend to make its imitations less perfect than they would otherwise be; and those who obey such rules ought to be called, not correct, but incorrect artists. The true way to judge of the rules by which English poetry was governed during the last century, is to look at the effects which they produced.

It was in 1780 that Johnson completed his *Lives of the Poets*. He tells us in that work, that since the time of Dryden, English poetry had shown no tendency to relapse into its original savageness; that its language had been refined, its numbers tuned, and its sentiments improved. It may, perhaps, be doubted whether the nation had any great reason to exult in the refinements and improvements, which gave it *Douglas* for *Othello*, and the *Triumphs of Temper* for the *Fairy Queen*.

It was during the thirty years which preceded the appearance of Johnson's *Lives*, that the diction and versification of English poetry were, in the sense in which the word is commonly used, most correct. Those thirty years form the most deplorable part of our literary history. They have bequeathed to us scarcely any poetry which deserves to be remembered. Two or three hundred lines of Gray, twice as many of Goldsmith, a few stanzas of Beattie and Collins, a few strophes of

Mason, and a few clever prologues and satires, were the masterpieces of this age of consummate excellence. They may all be printed in one volume, and that volume would be by no means a volume of extraordinary merit. It would contain no poetry of the highest class, and little which could be placed very high in the second class. The *Paradise Regained*, or *Comus*, would outweigh it all.

At last, when poetry had fallen into such utter decay that Mr Hayley was thought a great poet, it began to appear that the excess of the evil was about to work the cure. Men became tired of an insipid conformity to a standard which derived no authority from nature or reason. A shallow criticism had taught them to ascribe a superstitious value to the spurious correctness of poetasters. A deeper criticism brought them back to the free correctness of the first great masters. The eternal laws of poetry regained their power, and the temporary fashions which had superseded those laws went after the wig of Lovelace and the hoop of Clarissa.

It was in a cold and barren season that the seeds of that rich harvest which we have reaped, were first sown. While poetry was every year becoming more feeble and more mechanical,—while the monotonous versification which Pope had introduced, no longer redeemed by his brilliant wit and his compactness of expression, palled on the ear of the public,—the great works of the dead were every day attracting more and more of the admiration which they deserved. The plays of Shakspeare were better acted, better edited, and better known than they had ever been. Our noble old ballads were again read with pleasure, and it became a fashion to imitate them. Many of the imitations were altogether contemptible. But they showed that men had at least begun to admire the excellence which they could not rival. A literary revolution was evidently at hand. There was a ferment in the minds of men,—a vague craving for something new; a disposition to hail with delight any thing which might at first sight wear the appearance of originality. A reforming age is always fertile of impostors. The same excited state of public feeling which produced the great separation from the see of Rome, produced also the excesses of the Anabaptists. The same stir in the public mind of Europe, which overthrew the abuses of the old French government, produced the Jacobins and Theophilanthropists: Macpherson and the Della Cruscas were to the true reformers of English poetry, what Knipperdolling was to Luther, or what Clootz was to Turgot. The public was never more disposed to believe stories without evidence, and to admire books without merit. Any thing which could break the dull monotony of the correct school was acceptable.

The forerunner of the great restoration of our literature was Cowper. His literary career began and ended at nearly the same time with that of Alfieri. A parallel between Alfieri and Cowper may, at first sight, seem as unpromising as that which a loyal Presbyterian minister is said to have drawn, in 1745, between George the Second and Enoch. It may seem that the gentle, shy, melancholy Calvinist, whose spirit had been broken by fagging at school,—who had not courage to earn a livelihood by reading the titles of bills in the House of Lords,—and whose favourite associates were a blind old lady and an evangelical divine, could have nothing in common with the haughty, ardent, and voluptuous nobleman,—the horse-jockey, the libertine, who fought Lord Ligonier in Hyde Park, and robbed the Pretender of his queen. But though the private lives of these remarkable men present scarcely any points of resemblance, their literary lives bear a close analogy to each other. They both found poetry in its lowest state of degradation,— feeble, artificial, and altogether nerveless. They both possessed precisely the talents which fitted them for the task of raising it from that deep abasement. They cannot, in strictness, be called great poets. They had not in any very high degree the creative power,

The vision and the faculty divine;

but they had great vigour of thought, great warmth of feeling,—and what, in their circumstances, was above all things important, a manliness of taste which approached to roughness. They did not deal in mechanical versification and conventional phrases. They wrote concerning things, the thought of which set their hearts on fire; and thus what they wrote, even when it wanted every other grace, had that inimitable grace which sincerity and strong passion impart to the rudest and most homely compositions. Each of them sought for inspiration in a noble and affecting subject, fertile of images, which had not yet been hackneyed. Liberty was the muse of Alfieri,—Religion was the muse of Cowper. The same truth is found in their lighter pieces. They were not among those who deprecated the severity, or deplored the absence, of an unreal mistress in melodious commonplaces. Instead of raving about imaginary Chloes and Sylvias, Cowper wrote of Mrs Unwin's knitting-needles. The only love verses of Alfieri were addressed to one whom he truly and passionately loved. . . .

These great men were not free from affectation. But their affectation was directly opposed to the affectation which generally prevailed. Each of them has expressed, in strong and bitter language, the contempt which he felt for the effeminate poetasters who were in fashion both in England and in Italy. Cowper complains that

> Manner is all in all, whate'er is writ,
> The substitute for genius, taste, and wit.

He praised Pope; yet he regretted that Pope had

> Made poetry a mere mechanic art,
> And every warbler had his tune by heart.

Alfieri speaks with similar scorn of the tragedies of his predecessors. . . .

To men thus sick of the languid manner of their contemporaries, ruggedness seemed a venial fault, or rather a positive merit. In their hatred of meretricious ornament, and of what Cowper calls 'creamy smoothness,' they erred on the opposite side. Their style was too austere, their versification too harsh. It is not easy, however, to overrate the service which they rendered to literature. Their merit is rather that of demolition than that of construction. The intrinsic value of their poems is considerable. But the example which they set of mutiny against an absurd system was invaluable. The part which they performed was rather that of Moses than that of Joshua. They opened the house of bondage;—but they did not enter the promised land.

During the twenty years which followed the death of Cowper, the revolution in English poetry was fully consummated. None of the writers of this period, not even Sir Walter Scott, contributed so much to the consummation as Lord Byron. Yet he, Lord Byron, contributed to it unwillingly, and with constant self-reproach and shame. All his tastes and inclinations led him to take part with the school of poetry which was going out, against the school which was coming in. Of Pope himself he spoke with extravagant admiration. He did not venture directly to say that the little man of Twickenham was a greater poet than Shakspeare or Milton. But he hinted pretty clearly that he thought so. Of his contemporaries, scarcely any had so much of his admiration as Mr Gifford, who, considered as a poet, was merely Pope, without Pope's wit and fancy; and whose satires are decidedly inferior in vigour and poignancy to the very imperfect juvenile performance of Lord Byron himself. He now and then praised Mr Wordsworth and Mr Coleridge; but ungraciously, and without cordiality. When he attacked them, he brought his whole soul to the work. Of the most elaborate of Mr Wordsworth's poems he could find nothing to say, but that it was 'clumsy, and frowsy, and his aversion.' 'Peter Bell' excited his spleen to such a degree, that he apostrophized the shades of Pope and Dryden, and demanded of them whether it were possible that such trash could evade contempt? In his heart, he thought his own Pilgrimage of Harold inferior to his Imitation of Horace's *Art of Poetry*,— a feeble echo of Pope and Johnson. This insipid performance he repeatedly designed to publish, and was withheld only by the solicitations of his friends. He has distinctly declared his approbation of the unities; the most absurd laws by which genius was ever held in servitude. In one of his works, we think in his Letter to Mr Bowles, he compares the poetry of the eighteenth century to the Parthenon, and that of the nineteenth to a Turkish mosque; and boasts that, though he had assisted his contemporaries in building their grotesque and barbarous edifice, he had never joined them in defacing the remains of a chaster and more graceful architecture. In another letter, he compares the change which had recently passed on English poetry, to the decay of Latin poetry after the Augustan age. In the time of Pope, he tells his friend, it was all Horace with us. It is all Claudian now.

For the great old masters of the art he had no very enthusiastic veneration. In his Letter to Mr Bowles he uses expressions which clearly indicate that he preferred Pope's *Iliad* to the original. Mr Moore confesses that his friend was no very fervent admirer of Shakspeare. Of all the poets of the first class, Lord Byron seems to have admired Dante and Milton most. Yet in the fourth canto of *Childe Harold* he places Tasso—a writer not merely inferior to them, but of quite a different order of mind—on at least a footing of equality with them. Mr Hunt is, we suspect, quite correct in saying, that Lord Byron could see little or no merit in Spenser.

But Lord Byron the critic, and Lord Byron the poet, were two very different men. The effects of his theory may indeed often be traced in his practice. But his disposition led him to accommodate himself to the literary taste of the age in which he lived; and his talents would have enabled him to accommodate himself to the taste of any age. Though he said much of his contempt for men, and though he boasted that amidst all the inconstancy of fortune and of fame he was all-sufficient to himself, his literary career indicated nothing of that lonely and unsocial pride which he affected. We cannot conceive him, like Milton or Wordsworth, defying the criticism of his contemporaries, retorting their scorn, and labouring on a poem in the full assurance that it would be unpopular, and in the full assurance that it would be immortal. He has said, by the mouth of one of his heroes, in speaking of political greatness, that 'he must serve who fain would sway,' and this he assigns as a reason for not entering into political life. He did not consider that the sway which he had exercised in literature had been purchased by servitude—by the sacrifice of his own taste to the taste of the public.

He was the creature of his age; and wherever he had lived, he would have been the creature of his age. Under Charles I he would have been more quaint than Donne. Under Charles II the rants of his rhyming plays would have pitted it, boxed it, and galleried it, with those of any Bayes or Bilboa. Under George I the monotonous smoothness of his versification, and the terseness of his expression, would have made Pope himself envious.

As it was, he was the man of the last thirteen years of the eighteenth century, and of the first twenty-three years of the nineteenth century. He belonged half to the old, and half to the new school of poetry. His personal taste led him to the former; his thirst of fame to the latter;—his talents were equally suited to both. His fame was a common ground on which the zealots of both sides—Gifford, for example, and Shelley—might meet. He was the representative, not of either literary party, but of both at once, and of their conflict, and of the victory by which that conflict was terminated. His poetry fills and measures the whole of the vast interval through which our literature has moved since the time of Johnson. It touches the *Essay on Man* at the one extremity, and *The Excursion* at the other.

There are several parallel instances in literary history. Voltaire, for example, was the connecting link between the France of Louis the Fourteenth, and the France of Louis the Sixteenth,—between Racine and Boileau on the one side, and Condorcet and Beaumarchais on the other. He, like Lord Byron, put himself at the head of an intellectual revolution,—dreading it all the time,—murmuring at it,—sneering at it,—yet choosing rather to move before his age in any direction, than to be left behind and forgotten. Dryden was the connecting link between the literature of the age of James the First, and the literature of the age of Anne. Oromandes and Arimanes fought for him—Arimanes carried him off. But his heart was to the last with Oromandes. Lord Byron was, in the same manner, the mediator between two generations—between two hostile poetical sects. Though always sneering at Mr Wordsworth, he was yet, though perhaps unconsciously, the interpreter between Mr Wordsworth and the multitude. In the *Lyrical Ballads* and *The Excursion*, Mr Wordsworth appeared as the high priest of a worship, of which Nature was the idol. No poems have ever indicated so exquisite a perception of the beauty of the outer world, or so passionate a love and reverence for that beauty. Yet they were not popular;—and it is not likely that they ever will be popular as the works of Sir Walter Scott are popular. The feeling which pervaded them was too deep for general sympathy. Their style was often too mysterious for general comprehension. They made a few esoteric disciples, and many scoffers. Lord Byron founded what may be called an exoteric Lake school of poetry; and all the readers of poetry in England, we might say in Europe, hastened to sit at his feet. What Mr Wordsworth had said like a recluse, Lord Byron said like a man of the world,—with less profound feeling, but with more perspicuity, energy, and conciseness. We would refer our readers to the last two cantos of *Childe Harold*, and to *Manfred*, in proof of these observations.

Lord Byron, like Mr Wordsworth, had nothing dramatic in his genius. He was indeed the reverse of a great dramatist; the very antithesis to a great dramatist. All his characters,—Harold looking back on the western sky, from which his country and the sun are receding together,—the Giaour, standing apart in the gloom of the side-aisle, and casting a haggard scowl from under his long hood at the crucifix and the censer,—Conrad, leaning on his sword by the watch-tower,—Lara, smiling on the dancers,—Alp, gazing steadily on the fatal cloud as it passes before the moon,—Manfred, wandering among the precipices of Berne,—Azzo, on the judgment-seat,—Ugo, at the bar,—Lambro, frowning on the siesta of his daughter and Juan,—Cain, presenting his unacceptable offering,—are all essentially the same. The varieties are varieties merely of age, situation, and costume. If ever Lord Byron attempted to exhibit men of a different kind, he always made them either insipid or unnatural. Selim is nothing. Bonnivart is nothing. Don Juan, in the first and best cantos, is a feeble copy of the Page in the *Marriage of Figaro*. Johnson, the man whom Juan meets in the slave-market, is a most striking failure. How differently would Sir Walter Scott have drawn a bluff, fearless Englishman, in such a situation! The portrait would have seemed to walk out of the canvass.

Sardanapalus is more hardly drawn than any dramatic personage that we can remember. His heroism and his effeminacy,—his contempt of death, and his dread of a weighty helmet,—his kingly resolution to be seen in the foremost ranks, and the anxiety with which he calls for a looking-glass, that he may be seen to advantage, are contrasted with all the point of Juvenal. Indeed the hint of the character seems to have been taken from what Juvenal says of Otho:

> Speculum civilis sarcina belli.
> Nimirum summi ducis est occidere Galbam,
> Et curare cutem summi constantia civis,
> Bebriaci in campo spolium affectare Palati,
> Et pressum in facie digitis extendere panem.[1]

These are excellent lines in a satire. But it is not the business of the dramatist to exhibit characters in this sharp antithetical way. It is not in this way that Shakspeare makes Prince Hal rise from the rake of East-cheap into the hero of Shrewsbury, and sink again into the rake of Eastcheap. It is not thus that Shakspeare has exhibited the union of effeminacy and valour in Antony. A dramatist cannot commit a greater error than that of following those pointed descriptions of character, in which satirists and historians indulge so much. It is by rejecting what is natural, that satirists and historians produce these striking characters. Their great object generally is to ascribe to every man as many contradictory qualities as possible: and this is an object easily attained. By judicious selection and judicious exaggeration, the intellect and the disposition of any human being might be described as being made up of nothing but startling contrasts. If the dramatist attempts to create a being answering to one of these descriptions, he fails, because he reverses an imperfect analytical process. He produces, not a man, but a personified epigram. Very eminent writers have fallen into this snare. Ben Jonson has given us a Hermogenes, taken from the lively lines of Horace; but the inconsistency which is so amusing in the satire, appears unnatural, and disgusts us, in the play. Sir Walter Scott has committed a far more glaring error of the same kind in the novel of *Peveril*. Admiring, as every reader must admire, the keen and vigorous lines in which Dryden satirized the Duke of Buckingham, he attempted to make a Duke of Buckingham to suit them,—a real living Zimri;—and he made, not a man, but the most grotesque of all monsters. A writer who should attempt to introduce into a play or a novel such a Wharton as the Wharton of Pope, or a Lord Hervey answering to Sporus, would fail in the same manner.

[1] [Juvenal, *Satire II*, ll. 103–7: '. . . a mirror among the kit of Civil War! It needed, in truth, a mighty general to slay Galba, and keep his own skin sleek; it needed a citizen of highest courage to ape the splendours of the Palace on the field of Bebriacum, and plaster his face with dough' (Loeb trans.).]

But to return to Lord Byron: his women, like his men, are all of one breed. Haidee is a half-savage and girlish Julia; Julia is a civilized and matronly Haidee. Leila is a wedded Zuleika—Zuleika a virgin Leila. Gulnare and Medora appear to have been intentionally opposed to each other. Yet the difference is a difference of situation only. A slight change of circumstances would, it should seem, have sent Gulnare to the lute of Medora, and armed Medora with the dagger of Gulnare.

It is hardly too much to say, that Lord Byron could exhibit only one man and only one woman,—a man proud, moody, cynical,—with defiance on his brow, and misery in his heart; a scorner of his kind, implacable in revenge, yet capable of deep and strong affection;—a woman all softness and gentleness, loving to caress and to be caressed, but capable of being transformed by love into a tigress.

Even these two characters, his only two characters, he could not exhibit dramatically. He exhibited them in the manner, not of Shakspeare, but of Clarendon. He analyzed them. He made them analyze themselves, but he did not make them show themselves. He tells us, for example, in many lines of great force and spirit, that the speech of Lara was bitterly sarcastic,—that he talked little of his travels,—that if much questioned about them, his answers became short, and his brow gloomy. But we have none of Lara's sarcastic speeches, or short answers. It is not thus that the great masters of human nature have pourtrayed human beings. Homer never tells us that Nestor loved to tell long stories about his youth; Shakspeare never tells us that in the mind of Iago every thing that is beautiful and endearing was associated with some filthy and debasing idea.

It is curious to observe the tendency which the dialogue of Lord Byron always has to lose its character of dialogue, and to become soliloquy. The scenes between Manfred and the Chamois-hunter,—between Manfred and the Witch of the Alps,—between Manfred and the Abbot, are instances of this tendency. Manfred, after a few un-important speeches, has all the talk to himself. The other interlocutors are nothing more than good listeners. They drop an occasional question, or ejaculation, which sets Manfred off again on the inexhaustible topic of his personal feelings. If we examine the fine passages in Lord Byron's dramas,—the description of Rome, for example, in *Manfred*,—the description of a Venetian revel in *Marino Faliero*,—the dying invective which the old Doge pronounces against Venice, we shall find there is nothing dramatic in them; that they derive none of their effect from the character or situation of the speaker; and that they would have been as fine, or finer, if they had been published as fragments of blank verse by Lord Byron. There is scarcely a speech in Shakspeare of which the same could be said. No skilful reader of the plays of Shakspeare can endure to see what are called the fine things taken out, under the name of 'Beauties' or of 'Elegant Extracts;' or to hear any single passage,— 'To be or not to be,' for example, quoted as a sample of the great poet. 'To be or not to be,' has merit undoubtedly as a composition. It would have merit if put into the mouth of a chorus. But its merit as a composition vanishes when compared with its merit as belonging to Hamlet. It is not too much to say that the great plays of Shakspeare would lose less by being deprived of all the passages which are commonly called the fine passages, than those passages lose by being read separately from the play. This is perhaps the highest praise which can be given to a dramatist.

On the other hand, it may be doubted whether there is, in all Lord Byron's plays, a single remarkable passage which owes any portion of its interest or effect to its connexion with the characters or the action. He has written only one scene, as far as we can recollect, which is dramatic even in manner—the scene between Lucifer and Cain. The conference in that scene is animated, and each of the interlocutors has a fair share of it. But this scene, when examined, will be found to be a confirmation of our remarks. It is a dialogue only in form. It is a soliloquy in essence. It is in reality a debate carried on within one single unquiet and sceptical mind. The questions and the answers, the objections and the solutions, all belong to the same character.

A writer who showed so little of dramatic skill in works professedly dramatic, was not likely to write narrative with dramatic effect. Nothing could indeed be more rude and careless than the structure of his narrative poems. He seems to have thought, with the hero of *The Rehearsal*, that the plot was good for nothing but to bring in fine things. His two longest works, *Childe Harold* and *Don Juan*, have no plan whatever. Either of them might have been extended to any length, or cut short at any point. The state in which *The Giaour* appears, illustrates the manner in which all his poems were constructed. They are all, like *The Giaour*, collections of fragments; and, though there may be no empty spaces marked by asterisks, it is still easy to perceive, by the clumsiness of the joining, where the parts, for the sake of which the whole was composed, end and begin.

It was in description and meditation that he excelled. 'Description,' as he said in *Don Juan*, 'was his *forte*.' His manner is indeed peculiar, and is almost unequalled,—rapid, sketchy, full of vigour; the selection happy; the strokes few and bold. In spite of the reverence which we feel for the genius of Mr Wordsworth, we cannot but think that the minuteness of his descriptions often diminishes their effect. He has accustomed himself to gaze on nature with the eye of a lover—to dwell on every feature—and to mark every change of aspect. Those beauties which strike the most negligent observer, and those which only a close attention discovers, are equally familiar to him, and are equally prominent in his poetry. The proverb of old Hesiod, that half is often more than the whole, is eminently applicable to description. The policy of the Dutch, who cut down most of the precious trees in the Spice Islands, in order to raise the value of what remained, was a policy which poets would do well to imitate. It was a policy which no poet understood better than Lord Byron. Whatever his faults might be, he was never, while his mind retained its vigour, accused of prolixity.

His descriptions, great as was their intrinsic merit, derived their principal interest from the feeling which always mingled with them. He was himself the beginning, the middle, and the end, of all his own poetry—the hero of every tale—the chief object in every landscape. Harold, Lara, Manfred, and a crowd of other characters, were universally considered merely as loose incognitos of Byron; and there is every reason to believe that he meant them to be so considered. The wonders of the outer world—the Tagus, with the mighty fleets of England riding on its bosom—the towers of Cintra overhanging the shaggy forest of cork-trees and willows—the glaring marble of Pentelicus—the banks of the Rhine—the glaciers of Clarens—the sweet Lake of Leman—the dell of Egeria, with its summer-birds and rustling lizzards—the shapeless ruins of Rome, overgrown with ivy and wall-flowers—the stars, the sea, the mountains;—all were mere accessories—the background to one dark and melancholy figure.

Never had any writer so vast a command of the whole eloquence of scorn, misanthropy, and despair. That Marah was never dry. No art could sweeten, no draughts could exhaust, its perennial waters of bitterness. Never was there such variety in monotony as that of Byron. From maniac laughter to piercing lamentation, there was not a single note of human anguish of which he was not master. Year after year, and month after month, he continued to repeat that to be wretched is the destiny of all; that to be eminently wretched, is the destiny of the eminent; that all the desires by which we are cursed lead alike to misery;—if they are not gratified, to the misery of disappointment—if they are gratified, to the misery of satiety. His principal heroes are men who have arrived by different roads at the same goal of despair—who are sick of life—who are at war with society—who are supported in their anguish only by an unconquerable pride, resembling that of Prometheus on the rock, or of Satan in the burning marl; who can master their agonies by the force of their will, and who, to the last, defy the whole power of earth and heaven. He always described himself as a man of the same kind with his favourite creations, as a man whose heart had been withered—whose capacity for happiness was gone, and could not be restored; but whose invincible spirit dared the worst that could befall him here or hereafter.

How much of this morbid feeling sprang from an original disease of the mind—how much from real misfortune—how much from the nervousness of dissipation—how much of it was fanciful—how much of it was merely affected—it is impossible for us, and would probably have been impossible for the most intimate friends of Lord Byron, to decide. Whether there ever existed, or can ever exist, a person answering to the description which he gave of himself, may be doubted: but that he was not such a person is beyond all doubt. It is ridiculous to imagine that a man, whose mind was really imbued with scorn of his fellow-creatures, would have published three or four books every year in order to tell them so; or that a man, who could say with truth that he neither sought sympathy nor needed it, would have admitted all Europe to hear his farewell to his wife, and his blessings on his child. In the second canto of *Childe Harold*, he tells us that he is insensible to fame and obloquy—

> Ill may such contest now the spirit move,
> Which heeds nor keen reproof nor partial praise.

Yet we know, on the best evidence, that, a day or two before he published these lines, he was greatly, indeed childishly, elated by the compliments paid to his maiden speech in the House of Lords.

We are far, however, from thinking that his sadness was altogether feigned. He was naturally a man of great sensibility—he had been ill educated—his feelings had been early exposed to sharp trials—he had been crossed in his boyish love—he had been mortified by the failure of his first literary efforts—he was straitened in pecuniary circumstances—he was unfortunate in his domestic relations—the public treated him with cruel injustice—his health and spirits suffered from his dissipated habits of life—he was, on the whole, an unhappy man. He early discovered that, by parading his unhappiness before the multitude, he excited an unrivalled interest. The world gave him every encouragement to talk about his mental sufferings. The effect which his first confessions produced, induced him to affect much that he did not feel; and the affectation probably reacted on his feelings. How far the character in which he exhibited himself was genuine, and how far theatrical, would probably have puzzled himself to say.

There can be no doubt that this remarkable man owed the vast influence which he exercised over his contemporaries, at least as much to his gloomy egotism as to the real power of his poetry. We never could very clearly understand how it is that egotism, so unpopular in conversation, should be so popular in writing; or how it is that men who affect in their compositions qualities and feelings which they have not, impose so much more easily on their contemporaries than on posterity. The interest which the loves of Petrarch excited in his own time, and the pitying fondness with which half Europe looked upon Rousseau, are well known. To readers of our time, the love of Petrarch seems to have been love of that kind which breaks no hearts; and the sufferings of Rousseau to have deserved laughter rather than pity—to have been partly counterfeited, and partly the consequences of his own perverseness and vanity.

What our grandchildren may think of the character of Lord Byron, as exhibited in his poetry, we will not pretend to guess. It is certain, that the interest which he excited during his life is without a parallel in literary history. The feeling with which young readers of poetry regarded him, can be conceived only by those who have experienced it. To people who are unacquainted with real calamity, 'nothing is so dainty sweet as lovely melancholy.' This faint image of sorrow has in all ages been considered by young gentlemen as an agreeable excitement. Old gentlemen, and middle-aged gentlemen, have so many real causes of sadness, that they are rarely inclined 'to be as sad as night only for wantonness.' Indeed they want the power almost as much as the inclination. We know very few persons engaged in active life, who, even if they were to procure stools to be melancholy upon, and were to sit down with all the premeditation of Master Stephen, would be able to enjoy much of what somebody calls the 'ecstasy of woe.'

Among that large class of young persons whose reading is almost entirely confined to works of imagination, the popularity of Lord Byron was unbounded. They bought pictures of him; they treasured up the smallest relics of him; they learned his poems by heart, and did their best to write like him, and to look like him. Many of them practised at the glass, in the hope of catching the curl of the upper lip, and the scowl of the brow, which appear in some of his portraits. A few discarded their neckcloths, in imitation of their great leader. For some years the Minerva press sent forth no novel without a mysterious, unhappy, Lara-like peer. The number of hopeful under-graduates and medical students who became things of dark imaginings,—on whom the freshness of the heart ceased to fall like dew,—whose passions had consumed themselves to dust, and to whom the relief of tears was denied, passes all calculation. This was not the worst. There was created in the minds of many of these enthusiasts, a pernicious and absurd association between intellectual power and moral depravity. From the poetry of Lord Byron they drew a system of ethics, compounded of misanthropy and voluptuousness; a system in which the two great commandments were, to hate your neighbour, and to love your neighbour's wife.

This affectation has passed away; and a few more years will destroy whatever yet remains of that magical potency which once belonged to the name of Byron. To us he is still a man, young, noble, and unhappy. To our children he will be merely a writer; and their impartial judgment will appoint his place among writers, without regard to his rank, or to his private history. That his poetry will undergo a severe sifting; that much of what has been admired by his contemporaries will be rejected as worthless, we have little doubt. But we have as little doubt, that, after the closest scrutiny, there will still remain much that can only perish with the English language.

48. Bulwer-Lytton on Byron's popularity

1833

Edward George Earle Lytton Bulwer-Lytton (1802–73), novelist, man of letters and politician. Extracts from his assessment of Byron in *England and the English*, 1833. Quoted here from 2nd edn., 1833, II, 67, 69–76, 89–96.

. . . It is in the poetry and the poetic prose of our time that we are chiefly to seek for that sympathy which always exists between the intellectual and the social changes in the prevalent character and sentiment of a People. . . .

Let us consider:—

In the earlier portion of this work, in attempting to trace the causes operating on the National Character of the English, I ascribed to the peculiar tone and cast of our aristocracy much of that reserved and unsocial spirit which proverbially pervades all classes of our countrymen. To the same causes, combined with the ostentation of commerce, I ascribed also much of that hollowness and glitter which belong to the occupations of the great world, and that fretfulness and pride, that uneasy and dissatisfied temper, which are engendered by a variety of small social distinctions, and the eternal *vying*, and consequent mortification, which those distinctions produce. These feelings, the slow growth of centuries, became more and more developed as the effects of civilization and wealth rendered the aristocratic influences more general upon the subordinate classes. In the indolent luxuries of a court, what more natural than satiety among the great, and a proud discontent among their emulators? The peace just concluded, and the pause in continental excitement, allowed these pampered, yet not unpoetical springs of sentiment, to be more deeply and sensibly felt; and the public, no longer compelled by War and the mighty career of Napoleon to turn their attention to the action of life, could give their sympathies undivided to the first who should represent their thoughts. And these very thoughts, these very sources of sentiment—this very satiety —this very discontent—this profound and melancholy temperament, the result of certain social systems—the first two cantos of *Childe Harold* suddenly appeared to represent. They touched the most sensitive chord in the public heart—they expressed what every one felt. The position of the author once attracting curiosity, was found singularly correspondent with the sentiment he embodied. His rank, his supposed melancholy, even his reputed beauty, added a natural interest to his genius. He became the Type, the Ideal of the state of mind he represented, and the world willingly associated his person with his works, because they thus seemed actually to incorporate, and in no undignified or ungraceful shape, the principle of their own long-nursed sentiments and most common emotions. Sir Philip Sidney represented the popular sentiment in Elizabeth's day—Byron that in our own. Each became the poetry of a particular age put into action—each, incorporated with the feelings he addressed, attracted towards himself an enthusiasm which his genius alone did not deserve. It is in vain, therefore, that we would now coolly criticise the merits of the first Cantos of *Childe Harold*, or those Eastern Tales by which they were succeeded, and in which another sentiment of the age was addressed, namely, that craving for adventure and wild incident which the habit of watching for many years the events of a portentous War, and the meteoric career of the modern Alexander, naturally engendered. We may wonder, when we now return to those poems, at our early admiration at their supposed philosophy of tone and grandeur of thought. In order to judge them fairly, we must recall the feelings they addressed. With nations, as with individuals, it is necessary to return to past emotions in order to judge of the merits of past appeals to them. We attributed truth and depth to Lord Byron's poetry in proportion as it expressed our own thoughts; just as in the affairs of life, or in the speeches of orators, we esteem those men the most sensible who agree the most with ourselves—embellishing and exalting only (not controverting) our own impressions. And in tracing the career of this remarkable poet, we may find that he became less and less popular in proportion, not as his genius waned, but as he addressed more feebly the prevalent sentiment of his times: for I suspect that future critics will agree that there is in his tragedies, which were never popular, a far higher order of genius than in his Eastern Tales or the *first* two cantos of *Childe Harold*. The highest order of poetical genius is usually evinced by the conception rather than the execution; and this often makes the main difference between Melodrame and Tragedy. There is in the early poems of Lord Byron scarcely any clear conception at all; there is no harmonious plan, comprising one great, consistent, systematic whole; no epic of events artfully wrought, progressing through a rich variety of character, and through the struggles of contending passions, to one mighty and inevitable end. If we take the most elaborate and most admired of his tales, *The Corsair*, we shall recognize in its conception an evident want of elevation. A pirate taken prisoner—released by a favourite of the harem—escaping—and finding his mistress dead; there is surely nothing beyond melodrame in the design of this story, nor do the incidents evince any great fertility of invention to counterbalance the want of greatness in the conception. In this too, as in all his tales, though full of passion—and this is worth considering, since it is for his delineations of passion that the vulgar laud him—we may observe that he describes a passion, not the *struggles* of passions. But it is in the last that a master is displayed: it is contending emotions, not the prevalence of one emotion, that call forth all the subtle comprehension, or deep research, or giant grasp of man's intricate nature, in which consists the highest order of that poetic genius which works out its result by character and fiction. Thus the struggles of Medea are more dread than the determination; the conflicting passions of Dido evince the most triumphant effect of Virgil's skill;—to describe a murder is the daily task of the melodramatist—the irresolution, the horror, the *struggle* of Macbeth, belong to Shakspeare alone. When Byron's heroes commit a crime, they march at once to it: we see not the pause—the self-counsel —the agony settling into resolve; he enters not into that delicate and subtile analysis of human motives which excites so absorbing a dread, and demands so exquisite a skill. Had Shakspeare conceived a Gulnare, he would probably have presented to us in terrible detail her pause over the couch of her sleeping lord: we should have seen the woman's weakness contesting with the bloody purpose; she would have re-membered, though even with loathing, that on the breast she was about to strike, her head had been pillowed;—she would have turned aside— shrunk from her design—again raised the dagger: you would have heard the sleeping man breathe—she would have quailed—and, quail-ing, struck! But the death-chamber—that would have been the scene in which, above all others, Shakspeare would have displayed himself— is barred and locked to Byron. He gives us the crime, but not all the wild and fearful preparation to it. So again in Parisina:—from what opportunities of exercising his art does the poet carefully exclude him-self! With what minute, and yet stern analysis, would Sophocles have exhibited the contest in the breast of the adulteress!—the love—the

honour—the grief—the dread—the horror of the incest, and the violence of the passion!—but Byron proceeds at once to the guilty meeting, and the tragic history is, as much as can be compatible with the
materials, merged into the amorous fragment. If Byron had, in his
early poems, conceived the history of Othello, he would have given us
the murder of Desdemona, but never the interviews with Iago. Thus,
neither in the conception of the plot, nor the fertile invention of incident, nor, above all, in the dissection of passions, can the early poems
of Lord Byron rank with the higher masterpieces of Poetical Art.

But at a later period of his life more exalted and thoughtful notions
of his calling were revealed to him, and I imagine that his acquaintance
with Shelley induced him to devote his meditative and brooding mind
to those metaphysical inquiries into the motives and actions of men
which lead to deep and hidden sources of character, and a more entire
comprehension of the science of poetical analysis.

Hence his tragedies evince a much higher order of conception, and a
much greater mastery in art than his more celebrated poems. What
more pure or more lofty than his character of Angiolina, in *The Doge of
Venice*! I know not in the circle of Shakspeare's women, one more
true, not only to nature—that is a slight merit—but to the highest and
rarest order of nature. Let us pause here for one moment—we are in
no hacknied ground. . . .

[He goes on to make a hyperbolic and exclamatory case for Byron's
plays, praising the dramatic genius, the nobility of conception, and the
superb characterization evidenced in *Marino Faliero, The Two Foscari*
and *Sardanapalus*.]

Nothing has been more constantly asserted of Byron than his want
of variety in character. Every criticism tells us that he never paints but
one person, in whatever costume; that the dress may vary, but the lay
figure remains the same. Never was any popular fallacy more absurd!
It is true that the dogma holds good with the early poems, but is entirely contradicted in the later plays. Where, in the whole range of
fiction, are there any characters more strongly contrasted, more
essentially various and dissimilar, than Sardanapalus, the Assyrian king,
and Marino Faliero, the Venetian Doge;—than Beleses, the rugged
priest, cut out of the marble of nature; and Jacopo Foscari, moulded
from the kindliest of the southern elements;—than the passionate
Marina, the delicate and queenly Angiolina, the heroic Myrrha—the
beautiful incarnation of her own mythology? To name these is sufficient

to refute an assertion hitherto so credulously believed, and which may serve as an illustration of the philosophy of popular criticism. From the first works of an author the standard is drawn by which he is compared; and in no instance are the sins of the parents more unfortunately visited on the children.

Yet why, since the tragedies evince so matured and profound a genius, are they so incalculably less popular than the early poems? It may be said, that the dramatic form itself is an obstacle to popularity; yet scarcely so, for I am just old enough distinctly to remember the intense and universal curiosity with which the public awaited the appearance of *The Doge of Venice*; the eagerness with which it was read, and the disappointment which it occasioned. Had the dramatic form been the cause of its unpopularity, it would have occasioned for it at the first a cool and lukewarm reception: the welcome which greeted its announcement is a proof that the disappointment was occasioned by the materials of the play, and not *because* it was a play. Besides, *Manfred*, one of the most admired of all Byron's works, was cast in the dramatic mould. One cause of the comparative unpopularity of the plays is, perhaps, that the *style* is less rich and musical than that of the poems; but the principal cause is *in that very versatility, that very coming out from self, the want of which has been so superficially complained of.* The characters were beautifully conceived; but they represented not that character which we expected, and yearned to see. That mystic and idealized shape, in which we beheld ourselves, had receded from the scene—we missed that touching egotism which was the expression of the Universal Heart—across the enchanted mirror new shadows passed, but it was our own likeness that we desired—the likeness of those deep and cherished feelings with which the poet had identified himself! True, that he still held the glass to human nature; but it was no longer to that aspect of nature which we most coveted to behold, and to which custom had not yet brought satiety. This was the true cause of our disappointment. Byron now addressed the passion, and the sentiment, and the thought, common to *all* time, but no longer those peculiar to the temper of the age—

> Our friend was to the dead,
> *To us he died when first he parted from us.*
>
>   *   *   *   *   *
>
> He stood beside us, like our youth,
> Transform'd for us the real to a dream,

Clothing the palpable and the familiar
With golden exhalations of the dawn.[1]

The disappointment we experienced when Byron departed from the one ideal image, in which alone our egotism loved to view him, is made yet more visible in examining his character than in analyzing his works. We grow indignant against him in proportion, not as we find him unworthy as a man, but departing from the attributes in which our imagination had clothed him. He was to the Public as a lover to his mistress, who forgives a crime more easily than a foible, and in whom the judgment becomes acute only in proportion as the imagination is undeceived. Had the lives, the sketches, the details, which have appeared subsequently to his early and poetical death, but sustained our own illusions—had they preserved 'the shadow and the majesty' with which we had enveloped him, they might have represented him as far more erring than he appears to have been, and we should have forgiven whatever crimes were consistent with the dark but lofty nature we ascribed to him. But weakness, insincerity, the petty caprice, the womanish passion, the vulgar pride, or even the coarse habit—these we forgave not, for they shocked and mocked our own self-love; they were as sardonic reproaches on the blind fallacy of our own judgment; they lowered the ideal in our own breasts; they humbled the vanity of our own nature; we had associated the poet with ourselves; we had felt *his* emotions as the refining, the exalted expression of *ours*, and whatever debased our likeness, debased ourselves! through his foibles our self-love was wounded: he was the great Representative of the Poetry of our own hearts; and, wherever he seemed unfaithful to his trust, we resented it as a treason to the majesty of our common cause.

But perhaps the hour in which we most deeply felt how entirely we had wound and wrapt our own poetry in himself, was that in which the news of his death reached this country. Never shall I forget the singular, the stunning sensation, which the intelligence produced. I was exactly at that age, half man and half boy, in which the poetical sympathies are most keen—among the youth of that day a growing diversion from Byron to Shelley and Wordsworth had just commenced—but the moment in which we heard he was no more, united him to us at once, without a rival. We could not believe that the bright race was run. So much of us died with him, that the notion of his death had something of the unnatural, of the impossible. It was as if a part of

[1] Coleridge's *Wallenstein*.

the mechanism of the very world stood still;—that we had ever questioned—that we had ever blamed him, was a thought of absolute remorse, and all our worship of his genius was not half so strongly felt as our love for himself.

When he went down to dust, it was as the abrupt close of some history of deep passion in our actual lives,—the interest—the excitement of years came to a gloomy pause—

> His last sigh
> Dissolved the charm—the disenchanted earth
> Lost all her lustre—Where her glittering towers,
> Her golden mountains, where? all darken'd down
> To naked waste—a dreary vale of years!
> THE GREAT MAGICIAN'S DEAD![1]

Exaggerated as this language may appear to our children, our contemporaries know that all words are feeble to express the universal feeling of England at that lonely death-bed in a foreign land, amidst wild and savage strangers, far from the sister, the wife, the child, whose names faltered on the lips of the dying man,—closing in desolation a career of sadness—rendering his latest sigh to the immemorial land which had received his earliest song, and where henceforth and for ever

> Shall Death and Glory a joint sabbath keep.

Even now, at this distance of time, all the feelings that then rushed upon us, melt upon me once more. Dissenting as I now do from much of the vague admiration his more popular works receive, and seeing in himself much that Virtue must lament and even Wisdom contemn, I cannot but think of him as of some early friend, associating with himself all the brightest reminiscences of youth, burying in his grave a poetry of existence that can never be restored, and of whom every harsh sentence, even while not unfaithful to truth, is dishonouring to the fidelity of love—

> 'THE BEAUTIFUL IS VANISHED AND RETURNS NOT.'

I have dwelt thus much upon Byron, partly because though the theme is hacknied, it is not exhausted[2]—partly because I perceive an

---

[1] Young.
[2] In advancing, too, the new doctrine, that his Dramas are better than his early poems, it was necessary to go somewhat into the conception of those Dramas.

unjust and indiscriminate spirit of depreciation springing up against that great poet (and I hold it the duty of a critic to oppose zealously the caprice and change of mere fashions in opinion)—and principally, because, in reviewing the intellectual spirit of the age, it is necessary to point out at some length the manner in which its most celebrated representative illustrated and identified it with himself.

49. Henry Taylor on Byron's deficiencies as a poet

1834

Henry Taylor (1800–86), civil servant and dramatist. Extract from the Preface to his play *Philip Van Artevelde*, 1834, I, ix–xxi.

... My views have not ... been founded upon any predisposition to depreciate the popular poetry of the times. It will always produce a powerful impression upon very young readers, and I scarcely think that it can have been more admired by any than by myself, when I was included in that category. I have not ceased to admire this poetry in its degree; ... but I am unable to concur in opinion with those who would place it in the foremost ranks of the art: nor does it seem to have been capable of sustaining itself quite firmly in the very high degree of public estimation in which it was held at its first appearance, and for some years afterwards. The poetical taste to which some of the popular poets of this century gave birth, appears at present to maintain a more unshaken dominion over the writers of poetry, than over its readers.

These poets were characterised by great sensibility and fervour, by a profusion of imagery, by force and beauty of language, and by a versification peculiarly easy and adroit, and abounding in that sort of melody, which, by its very obvious cadences, makes itself most pleasing to an unpractised ear. They exhibited, therefore, many of the most attractive graces and charms of poetry—its vital warmth not less than its external embellishments; and had not the admiration which they excited, tended to produce an indifference to higher, graver, and more various endowments, no one would have said that it was, in any evil sense, excessive. But from this unbounded indulgence in the mere luxuries of poetry, has there not ensued a want of adequate appreciation for its intellectual and immortal part? I confess, that such seems to me to have been both the actual and the natural result; and I can hardly believe the public taste to have been in a healthy state, whilst the most approved poetry of past times was almost unread. We may now, perhaps, be turning back to it; but it was not, as far as I can judge, till more than a quarter of a century had expired, that any signs of re-action could be discerned. Till then, the elder luminaries of our poetical literature were obscured, or little regarded; and we sate with dazzled eyes at a high festival of poetry, where, as at the funeral of Arvalan, the torch-light put out the star-light.

So keen was the sense of what the new poets possessed, that it never seemed to be felt that any thing was deficient in them. Yet their deficiencies were not unimportant. They wanted, in the first place, subject matter. A feeling came more easily to them than a reflection, and an image was always at hand when a thought was not forthcoming. Either they did not look upon mankind with observant eyes, or they did not feel it to be any part of their vocation to turn what they saw to account. It did not belong to poetry, in their apprehension, to thread the mazes of life in all its classes and under all its circumstances, common as well as romantic, and, seeing all things, to infer and to instruct: on the contrary, it was to stand aloof from every thing that is plain and true; to have little concern with what is rational or wise; it was to be, like music, a moving and enchanting art, acting upon the fancy, the affections, the passions, but scarcely connected with the exercise of the intellectual faculties. These writers had, indeed, adopted a tone of language which is hardly consistent with the state of mind in which a man makes use of his understanding. The realities of nature, and the truths which they suggest, would have seemed cold and incongruous, if suffered to mix with the strains of impassioned sentiment and glowing imagery in which they poured themselves forth. Spirit was not to be debased by any union with matter, in their effusions; dwelling, as they did, in a region of poetical sentiment which did not permit them to walk upon the common earth, or to breathe the common air.

Writers, however, whose appeal is made so exclusively to the excitabilities of mankind, will not find it possible to work upon them continuously without a diminishing effect. Poetry of which sense is not the basis, though it may be excellent of its kind, will not long be reputed to be poetry of the highest order. It may move the feelings and charm the fancy; but failing to satisfy the understanding, it will not take permanent possession of the strong-holds of fame. Lord Byron, in giving the most admirable example of this species of poetry, undoubtedly gave the strongest impulse to the appetite for it. Yet this impulse is losing its force, and even Lord Byron himself repudiated, in the latter years of his life, the poetical taste which he had espoused and propagated. The constitution of this writer's mind is not difficult to understand, and sufficiently explains the growth of his taste.

Had he united a philosophical intellect to his peculiarly poetical temperament, he would probably have been the greatest poet of his age. But no man can be a very great poet who is not also a great philosopher. Whatever Lord Byron's natural powers may have been, idleness and light reading, an early acquisition of popularity by the exercise of a single talent, and an absorbing and contracting self-love, confined the field of his operations within narrow limits. He was in knowledge merely a man of Belles-lettres; nor does he appear at any time to have betaken himself to such studies as would have tended to the cultivation and discipline of his reasoning powers, or the enlargement of his mind. He had, however, not only an ardent and brilliant imagination, but a clear understanding; and the signs both of what he had and of what he wanted, are apparent in his poetry. There is apparent in it a working and moulding spirit, with a want of material to work up,—a great command of language, with a want of any views or reflections which, if unembellished by imagery, or unassociated with passionate feelings, it would be very much worth while to express. Page after page throughout his earlier poems, there is the same uninformed energy at work upon the same old feelings; and when at last he became conscious that a theme was wanting, it was at a period of life when no man will consent to put himself to school; he could change his style and manner, but he could not change his moral and intellectual being, nor extend the sphere of his contemplations to subjects which were alien in *spirit* from those with which he had been hitherto, whether in life or in literature, exclusively conversant: in short, his mind was past the period of growth; there was (to use a phrase of Ben Jonson's) an *ingeni-stitium*, or wit-stand: he felt, apparently, that the food on which he had fed his mind had not been invigorating; but it could no longer bear a stronger diet, and he turned his genius loose to rove over the surface of society, content with such light observations upon life and manners as any acute man of the world might collect upon his travels, and conscious that he could recommend them to attention by such wit, brilliancy, dexterity of phrase, and versatility of fancy, as no one but himself could command.

His misanthropy was probably, like his tenderness, not practical, but merely matter of imagination, assumed for purposes of effect. But whilst his ignorance of the better elements of human nature may be believed to have been in a great measure affected, it is not to be supposed that he knew of them with a large and appreciating knowledge. Yet that knowledge of human nature which is exclusive of what is good in it, is, to say the least, as shallow and imperfect as that which is exclusive of what is evil. There is no such thing as philosophical misanthropy; and if a misanthropical spirit, be it genuine or affected, be found to pervade a man's writings, that spirit may be poetical as far as it goes, but being at fault in its philosophy, it will never, in the long run of time, approve itself equal to the institution of a poetical fame of the highest and most durable order.

These imperfections are especially observable in the portraitures of human character (if such it can be called) which are most prominent in Lord Byron's works. There is nothing in them of the mixture and modification,—nothing of the composite fabric which Nature has assigned to Man. They exhibit rather passions personified, than persons impassioned. But there is a yet worse defect in them. Lord Byron's conception of a hero is an evidence, not only of scanty materials of knowledge from which to construct the ideal of a human being, but also of a want of perception of what is great or noble in our nature. His heroes are creatures abandoned to their passions, and essentially, therefore, weak of mind. Strip them of the veil of mystery and the trappings of poetry, resolve them into their plain realities, and they are such beings as, in the eyes of a man of masculine judgment, would certainly excite no sentiment of admiration, even if they did not provoke contempt. When the conduct and feelings attributed to them are reduced into prose, and brought to the test of a rational consideration, they must be perceived to be beings in whom there is no strength, except that of their intensely selfish passions,—in whom all is vanity; their exertions being for vanity under the name of love, or revenge, and their sufferings for vanity under the name of pride. If such beings as these are to be regarded as heroical, where in human nature are we to look for what is low in sentiment, or infirm in character?

How nobly opposite to Lord Byron's, was Shakspeare's conception of a hero:

> Give me that man
> That is not passion's slave, and I will wear him
> In my heart's core; aye, in my heart of heart.

Lord Byron's genius, however, was powerful enough to cast a highly romantic colouring over these puerile creations, and to impart the charms of forcible expression, fervid feeling, and beautiful imagery, to thoughts in themselves not more remarkable for novelty than for soundness. The public required nothing more; and if he himself was brought latterly to a sense of his deficiencies of knowledge and general intellectual cultivation, it must have been more by the effect of time in so far maturing his very vigorous understanding, than by any correction from without. No writer of his age has had less of the benefits of adverse criticism. His own judgment, and that of his readers, have been left equally without check or guidance; and the decline in popular estimation which he has suffered for these last few years, may be rather attributed to a satiated appetite on the part of the public, than to a rectified taste: for those who have ceased to admire his poetry so ardently as they did, do not appear in general to have transferred their admiration to any worthier object.

Nor can it be said that anything better, or indeed anything half so good, has been subsequently produced. The poetry of the day, whilst it is greatly inferior in quality, continues to be like his in kind. It consists of little more than a poetical diction, an arrangement of words implying a sensitive state of mind, and therefore more or less calculated to excite corresponding associations, though, for the most part, not pertinently to any matter in hand; a diction which addresses itself to the sentient, not the percipient, properties of the mind, and displays merely symbols or types of feelings, which might exist with equal force in a being the most barren of understanding. . . .

50. Mazzini on Byron and Liberty

[1839] 1870

Giuseppe Mazzini (1805–72), the Italian patriot, revolutionary and man of letters, wrote his essay on 'Byron and Goethe' in 1839. It appeared anonymously in the *Morning Chronicle* for September 1839, in a version stigmatized as 'very incorrect' by his later translator. It is included in *The Life and Writings of Joseph Mazzini*, London, 1864–70, VI, 61–94. The following extract is from pp. 62, 66–74, 84–94.

... Byron and Goethe—the two names that predominate, and, come what may, ever will predominate, over our every recollection of the fifty years that have passed away. They rule;—the master-minds, I might almost say the tyrants, of a whole period of poetry; brilliant yet sad; glorious in youth and daring, yet cankered by the worm i' the bud, despair. They are the two Representative Poets of two great schools; and around them we are compelled to group all the lesser minds which contributed to render the era illustrious. The qualities which adorn, and distinguish their works, are to be found, although more thinly scattered, in other poets their contemporaries; still theirs are the names that involuntarily rise to our lips whenever we seek to characterise the tendencies of the age in which they lived. ...

Byron and Goethe summed up. This is at once the philosophical explanation of their works, and the secret of their popularity. The spirit of an entire epoch of the European world became incarnate in them ere its decease, even as—in the political sphere—the spirit of Greece and Rome became incarnate before death in Caesar and Alexander. They were the poetic expression of that principle, of which England was the economic, France the political, and Germany the philosophic expression: the last formula, effort, and result of a society founded on the principle of Individuality. That epoch, the mission of which had been, first through the labours of Greek philosophy, and afterwards through Christianity, to rehabilitate, emancipate, and develop individual man—appears to have concentrated in them, in

330

Fichte, in Adam Smith, and in the French school *des droits de l'homme*,[1] its whole energy and power, in order fully to represent and express all that it had achieved for mankind. It was much; but it was not the whole; and therefore it was doomed to pass away. The epoch of individuality was deemed near the goal; when lo! immense horizons were revealed; vast unknown lands in whose untrodden forests the principle of individuality was an insufficient guide. By the long and painful labours of that epoch, the human unknown quantity had been disengaged from the various quantities of different nature by which it had been surrounded; but only to be left weak, isolated, and recoiling in terror from the solitude in which it stood. The political schools of the epoch had proclaimed the sole basis of civil organization to be the right to liberty and equality (liberty for all), but they had encountered social anarchy by the way. The Philosophy of the Epoch had asserted the Sovereignty of the human *Ego*, and had ended in the mere adoration of *fact*, in *Hegelian* immobility. The Economy of the epoch imagined it had organized *free* competition, while it had but organized the oppression of the weak by the strong; of labour by capital; of poverty by wealth. The Poetry of the epoch had represented individuality in its every phase; had translated in sentiment what science had theoretically demonstrated; and it had encountered the void. But as society at last discovered that the destinies of the race were not contained in a mere problem of liberty, but rather in the harmonization of liberty with association;—so did poetry discover that the life it had hitherto drawn from individuality alone, was doomed to perish for want of aliment; and that its future existence depended on enlarging and transforming its sphere. Both society and poetry uttered a cry of despair: the death-agony of a form of society produced the agitation we have seen constantly increasing in Europe since 1815: the death-agony of a form of poetry evoked Byron and Goethe. I believe this point of view to be the only one that can lead us to a useful and impartial appreciation of these two great spirits.

There are two forms of Individuality; the expressions of its internal and external, or—as the Germans would say—of its subjective and objective life. Byron was the poet of the first, Goethe of the last. In Byron the *Ego* is revealed in all its pride of power, freedom, and desire, in the uncontrolled plenitude of all its faculties; inhaling existence at every pore, eager to seize 'the life of life.' The world around him neither rules nor tempers him. The Byronian Ego aspires to rule *it*;

[1] ['Of the rights of man.']

but solely for dominion's sake, to exercise upon it the Titanic force of his will. Accurately speaking, he cannot be said to derive from it either colour, tone, or image; for it is *he* who colours; he who sings; he whose image is everywhere reflected and reproduced. His poetry emanates from his own soul; to be thence diffused upon things external; he holds his state in the centre of the Universe, and from thence projects the light radiating from the depths of his own mind; as scorching and intense as the concentrated solar ray. Hence that terrible unity which only the superficial reader could mistake for monotony.

Byron appears at the close of one epoch, and before the dawn of the other; in the midst of a community based upon an aristocracy which has outlived the vigour of its prime; surrounded by a Europe containing nothing grand, unless it be Napoleon on one side and Pitt on the other, genius degraded to minister to egotism; intellect bound to the service of the past. No seer exists to foretell the future: belief is extinct; there is only its pretence: prayer is no more; there is only a movement of the lips at a fixed day or hour, for the sake of the family, or what is called *the people:* love is no more; desire has taken its place; the holy warfare of ideas is abandoned; the conflict is that of interests. The worship of great thoughts has passed away. That which *is*, raises the tattered banner of some corpse-like traditions; that which *would be*, hoists only the standard of physical wants, of material appetites: around him are ruins, beyond him the desert; the horizon is a blank. A long cry of suffering and indignation bursts from the heart of Byron; he is answered by anathemas. He departs; he hurries through Europe in search of an ideal to adore; he traverses it distracted, palpitating, like Mazeppa on the wild horse; borne onwards by a fierce desire; the wolves of envy and calumny follow in pursuit. He visits Greece; he visits Italy; if anywhere a lingering spark of the sacred fire, a ray of divine poetry, is preserved, it must be *there*. Nothing. A glorious past, a degraded present; none of life's poetry; no movement, save that of the sufferer turning on his couch to relieve his pain. Byron, from the solitude of his exile, turns his eyes again towards England; he sings. What does he sing? What springs from the mysterious and unique conception which rules, one would say in spite of himself, over all that escapes him in his sleepless vigil? The funeral hymn, the death-song, the epitaph of the aristocratic idea; we discovered it, we Continentalists; not his own countrymen. He takes his types from amongst those privileged by strength, beauty, and individual power. They are grand, poetical, heroic, but solitary; they hold no communion with the world around them, unless it be to rule over it; they defy alike the good and evil principle; they 'will bend to neither.' In life and in death 'they stand upon *their* strength;' they resist every power, for their own is all their own; it was purchased by

> —— Superior science—penance—daring—
> And length of watching—strength of mind—and skill
> In knowledge of our fathers.

Each of them is the personification, slightly modified, of a single type, a single idea—the *individual;* free, but nothing more than free; such as the epoch now closing has made him; Faust, but without the compact which submits him to the enemy; for the heroes of Byron make no such compact. Cain kneels not to Arimanes; and Manfred, about to die, exclaims—

> The mind, which is immortal, makes itself
> Requital for its good and evil thoughts—
> Is its own origin of ill, and end—
> And its own place and time, its innate sense,
> When stripped of this mortality, derives
> No colour from the fleeting things without,
> But is absorbed in sufferance or in joy;
> Born from the knowledge of its own desert.

They have no kindred: they live from their own life only: they repulse humanity, and regard the crowd with disdain. Each of them says: *I have faith in myself;* never, *I have faith in ourselves.* They all aspire to power or to happiness. The one and the other alike escape them; for they bear within them, untold, unacknowledged even to themselves, the presentiment of a life that mere liberty can never give them. Free they are; iron souls in iron frames, they climb the alps of the physical world as well as the alps of thought; still is their visage stamped with a gloomy and ineffaceable sadness; still is their soul—whether, as in Cain and Manfred it plunge into the abyss of the infinite, 'intoxicated with eternity,' or scour the vast plain and boundless ocean with the Corsair and Giaour—haunted by a secret and sleepless dread. It seems as if they were doomed to drag the broken links of the chain they have burst asunder, rivetted to their feet. Not only in the petty society against which they rebel, does their soul feel fettered and restrained; but even in the world of the spirit. Neither is it to the enmity of society that they succumb; but under the assaults of this nameless anguish; under the corroding action of potent faculties 'inferior still to their desires and their conceptions,' under the deception that comes from within. What can they do with the liberty so painfully won? On whom, on what, expend the exuberant vitality within them? *They are alone;* this is the secret of their wretchedness and impotence. They 'thirst for good'—Cain has said it for them all—but cannot achieve it; for they have no mission, no belief, no comprehension even of the world around them. They have never realized the conception of *Humanity* in the multitudes that have preceded, surround, and will follow after them; never thought on their own place between the past and future; on the continuity of labour that unites all the generations into one Whole; on the common end and aim, only to be realized by the common effort; on the spiritual post-sepulchral life even on earth of the individual, through the thoughts he transmits to his fellows; and, it may be—when he lives devoted and dies in faith—through the guardian agency he is allowed to exercise over the loved ones left on earth.

Gifted with a liberty they know not how to use; with a power and energy they know not how to apply; with a life whose purpose and aim they comprehend not;—they drag through their useless and convulsed existence. Byron destroys them one after the other, as if he were the executioner of a sentence decreed in heaven. They fall unwept, like a withered leaf into the stream of time.

> Nor earth nor sky shall yield a single tear,
> Nor cloud shall gather more, nor leaf shall fall,
> Nor gale breathe forth one sigh for thee, for all.

They die, as they have lived, alone; and a popular malediction hovers round their solitary tombs.

This, for those who can read with the soul's eyes, is what Byron sings; or rather what Humanity sings through him. The emptiness of the life and death of solitary individuality, has never been so powerfully and efficaciously summed up as in the pages of Byron. The crowd do not comprehend him: they listen; fascinated for an instant; then repent, and avenge their momentary transport by calumniating and insulting the poet. His intuition of the death of a form of society, they call wounded self-love; his sorrow for *all*, is misinterpreted as cowardly egotism. They credit not the traces of profound suffering revealed by his lineaments; they credit not the presentiment of a new life which from time to time escapes his trembling lips; they believe not in the despairing embrace in which he grasps the material universe

—stars, lakes, alps, and sea—and identifies himself with it, and through it with God, of whom—to him at least—it is a symbol. They do, however, take careful count of some unhappy moments, in which, wearied out by the emptiness of life, he has raised,—with remorse I am sure—the cup of ignoble pleasures to his lips, believing he might find forgetfulness there. How many times have not his accusers drained this cup, without redeeming the sin by a single virtue; without —I will not say bearing—but without having even the capacity of appreciating the burden which weighed on Byron! And did he not himself dash into fragments the ignoble cup, so soon as he beheld something worthy the devotion of his life?

[A discussion of Goethe follows, and a series of contrasts is drawn between his work and Byron's.]

And yet, notwithstanding all the contrasts, which I have only hinted at, but which might be far more elaborately displayed by extracts from their works; they arrived—Goethe, the poet of individuality in its objective life—at the egotism of indifference; Byron—the poet of individuality in its subjective life—at the egotism (I say it with regret, but *it*, too, is egotism) of despair: a double sentence upon the epoch which it was their mission to represent and to close!

Both of them—I am not speaking of their purely literary merits, incontestable and universally acknowledged—the one by the spirit of resistance that breathes through all his creations; the other by the spirit of sceptical irony that pervades his works, and by the independent sovereignty attributed to art over all social relations—greatly aided the cause of intellectual emancipation, and awakened in men's minds the sentiment of liberty. Both of them—the one, directly, by the implacable war he waged against the vices and absurdities of the privileged classes, and indirectly by investing his heroes with all the most brilliant qualities of the despot, and then dashing them to pieces as if in anger;—the other by the poetic rehabilitation of forms the most modest, and objects the most insignificant, as well as by the importance attributed to details—combated aristocratic prejudices, and developed in men's minds the sentiment of equality. And having by their artistic excellence exhausted both forms of the poetry of individuality, they have completed the cycle of its poets; thereby reducing all followers in the same sphere to the subaltern position of imitators, and creating the necessity of a new order of poetry; teaching us to recognise a *want* where before we felt only a desire. Together they have laid an era in the tomb; covering it with a pall that none may lift; and, as if to proclaim its death to the young generation, the poetry of Goethe has written its history, while that of Byron has graven its epitaph.

And now farewell to Goethe; farewell to Byron! farewell to the sorrows that crush but sanctify not—to the poetic flame that illumines but warms not—to the ironical philosophy that dissects without reconstructing—to all poetry which, in an age where there is so much to *do*, teaches us inactive contemplation; or which, in a world where there is so much need of devotedness, would instil despair. Farewell to all types of power without an aim; to all personifications of the solitary individuality which seeks an aim to find it not, and knows not how to apply the life stirring within it;—to all egotistic joys and griefs—

> Bastards of the soul;
> O'erweening slips of idleness: weeds;—no more—
> Self-springing here and there from the rank soil;
> O'erflowings of the lust of that same mind
> Whose proper issue and determinate end,
> When wedded to the love of things divine,
> Is peace, complacency, and happiness.

Farewell, a long farewell to the past! The dawn of the future is announced to such as can read its signs, and we owe ourselves wholly to it.

The duality of the middle ages, after having struggled for centuries under the banners of Emperor and Pope; after having left its trace and borne its fruit in every branch of intellectual development; has reascended to heaven—its mission accomplished—in the twin flames of poesy called Goethe and Byron. Two hitherto distinct formulae of life became incarnate in these two men. Byron is isolated man, representing only the internal aspect of life; Goethe isolated man, representing only the external.

Higher than these two incomplete existences; at the point of intersection between the two aspirations towards a heaven they were unable to reach, will be revealed the poetry of the future; of humanity; potent in new harmony, unity, and life.

But because, in our own day, we are beginning, though vaguely, to foresee this new social poetry, which will soothe the suffering soul by teaching it to rise towards God through Humanity; because we now stand on the threshold of a new epoch, which, but for them, we should not have reached;—shall we decry those who were unable to do more for us than cast their giant forms into the gulf that held us all doubting and dismayed on the other side? From the earliest times has genius been made the scapegoat of the generations. Society has never lacked men who have contented themselves with reproaching the Chattertons of their day with not being patterns of self-devotion, instead of physical or moral suicides; without ever asking themselves whether they had, during their lifetime, endeavoured to place aught within the reach of such but doubt and destitution. I feel the necessity of protesting earnestly against the reaction set on foot by certain thinkers against the mighty-souled, which serves as a cloak for the cavilling spirit of mediocrity. There is something hard, repulsive, and ungrateful, in the destructive instinct which so often forgets what *has* been done by the great men who preceded us, to demand of them merely an account of what more *might* have been done. Is the pillow of scepticism so soft to genius as to justify the conclusion that it is from egotism only that at times it rests its fevered brow thereon? Are we so free from the evil reflected in their verse as to have a right to condemn their memory? That evil was not introduced into the world by them. They saw it, felt it, respired it; it was around, about, on every side of them, and they were its greatest victims. How could they avoid reproducing it in their works? It is not by deposing Goethe or Byron, that we shall destroy either sceptical or anarchical indifference amongst us. It is by becoming believers and organizers ourselves. If we are such, we need fear nothing. As is the public, so will be the poet. If we revere enthusiasm, the fatherland, and humanity; if our hearts are pure, and our souls steadfast and patient, the genius inspired to interpret our aspirations, and bear to heaven our ideas and our sufferings, will not be wanting. Let these statues stand. The noble monuments of feudal times create no desire to return to the days of serfdom.

But I shall be told, there are imitators. I know it too well; but what lasting influence can be exerted on social life by those who have no real life of their own? They will but flutter in the void, so long as void there be. On the day when the *living* shall arise to take the place of the dead, they will vanish like ghosts at cock-crow. Shall we never be sufficiently firm in our own faith to dare to show fitting reverence for the grand typical figures of an anterior age? It would be idle to speak of social art at all, or of the comprehension of Humanity, if we could not raise altars to the new gods, without overthrowing the old. Those only should dare to utter the sacred name of Progress, whose souls possess intelligence enough to comprehend the past, and whose hearts possess sufficient poetic religion to reverence its greatness. The temple of the true believers in art is not the chapel of a sect; it is a vast Pantheon, in which the glorious images of Goethe and Byron will hold their honoured place, long after *Goethism* and *Byronism* shall have ceased to be.

When, purified alike from imitation and distrust, men learn to pay righteous reverence to the mighty fallen, I know not whether Goethe will obtain more of their admiration as an artist, but I am certain that Byron will inspire them with more love, both as man and poet—a love increased even by the fact of the great injustice hitherto shown to him. While Goethe held himself aloof from us, and from the height of his Olympian calm seemed to smile with disdain at our desires, our struggles, and our sufferings,—Byron wandered through the world, sad, gloomy, and unquiet; wounded, and bearing the arrow in the wound. Solitary and unfortunate in his infancy; unfortunate in his first love, and still more terribly so in his ill-advised marriage; attacked and calumniated both in his acts and intentions, without inquiry or defence; harassed by pecuniary difficulties; forced to quit his country, home, and child; friendless—we have seen it too clearly since his death—pursued even on the Continent by a thousand absurd and infamous falsehoods, and by the cold malignity of a world that twisted even his sorrows into a crime; he yet, in the midst of inevitable reaction, preserved his love for his sister and his Ada; his compassion for misfortune; his fidelity to the affections of his childhood and youth, from Lord Clare to his old servant Murray, and his nurse Mary Gray. He was generous with his money to all whom he could help or serve, from his literary friends down to the wretched libeller Ashe. Though impelled by the temper of his genius, by the period in which he lived, and by that fatality of his mission to which I have alluded, towards a poetic Individualism, the inevitable incompletness of which I have endeavoured to explain, he by no means set it up as a standard. That he presaged the future with the prevision of genius, is proved by his definition of poetry in his journal—a definition hitherto misunderstood, but yet the best I know: '*Poetry is the feeling of a former world and of a future.*' Poet as he was, he preferred activity for good, to all that his art could do. Surrounded by slaves and their oppressors; a traveller in countries where even remembrance seemed extinct; never did he desert the cause of the peoples; never was he false to human sympathies. A witness of the progress of the Restoration, and the triumph of the principles of the Holy Alliance, he never swerved from his courageous opposition; he preserved and publicly proclaimed his faith in the rights of the peoples and in the final[1] triumph of liberty. The following passage from his journal is the very abstract of the law governing the efforts of the true party of progress at the present day: 'Onwards! it is now the time to act; and what signifies self, if a single spark of that which would be worthy of the past[2] can be bequeathed unquenchably to the future? It is not one man, nor a million, but the *spirit* of liberty which must be spread. The waves which dash on the shore are, one by one, broken; but yet the *ocean* conquers nevertheless. It overwhelms the armada; it wears the rock; and if the Neptunians are to be believed, it has not only destroyed but made a world.' At Naples, in the Romagna, wherever he saw a spark of noble life stirring, he was ready for any exertion; or danger, to blow it into a flame. He stigmatized baseness, hypocrisy, and injustice, whencesoever they sprang.

Thus lived Byron, ceaselessly tempest-tossed between the ills of the present, and his yearnings after the future; often unequal; sometimes sceptical; but always suffering—often most so when he seemed to laugh;[3] and always loving, even when he seemed to curse.

Never did 'the eternal spirit of the chainless mind' make a brighter apparition amongst us. He seems at times a transformation of that immortal Prometheus, of whom he has written so nobly; whose cry of agony, yet of futurity, sounded above the cradle of the European world; and whose grand and mysterious form, transfigured by time, reappears from age to age, between the entombment of one epoch and the accession of another; to wail forth the lament of genius, tortured by the presentiment of things it will not see realized in its time. Byron, too, had the 'firm will' and the 'deep sense;' he, too, made of

---

[1] 'Yet, Freedom! yet, thy banner torn, but flying
    Streams, like the thunder-storm, *against* the wind:
    Thy trumpet voice, though broken now and dying,
    The loudest still the tempest leaves behind.
    The tree hath lost its blossoms, and the rind,
    Chopped by the axe, looks rough and little worth,
    But the sap lasts—and still the seed we find
    Sown deep, even in the bosom of the North,
So shall a better spring less bitter fruit bring forth.'

[2] Written in Italy.

[3] 'And if I laugh at any mortal thing,
   'Tis that I may not weep.'

his 'death a victory.' When he heard the cry of nationality and liberty burst forth in the land he had loved and sung in early youth, he broke his harp and set forth. While the *Christian* Powers were protocolizing or worse—while the *Christian* nations were doling forth the alms of a few piles of ball in aid of the *Cross* struggling with the Crescent; he, the poet and pretended sceptic, hastened to throw his fortune, his genius, and his life, at the feet of the first people that had arisen in the name of the nationality and liberty he loved.

I know no more beautiful symbol of the future destiny and mission of art than the death of Byron in Greece. The holy alliance of poetry with the cause of the peoples; the union—still so rare—of thought and action—which alone completes the human Word, and is destined to emancipate the world; the grand solidarity of all nations in the conquest of the rights ordained by God for all his children, and in the accomplishment of that mission for which alone such rights exist;—all that is now the religion and the hope of the party of progress throughout Europe, is gloriously typified in this image, which we, barbarians that we are, have already forgotten.

The day will come when Democracy will remember all that it owes to Byron. England too, will, I hope, one day remember the mission—so entirely English, yet hitherto overlooked by her—which Byron fulfilled on the Continent; the European rôle given by him to English literature, and the appreciation and sympathy for England which he awakened amongst us.

Before he came, all that was known of English literature was the French translation of Shakspeare, and the anathema hurled by Voltaire against the 'intoxicated barbarian.' It is since Byron that we Continentalists have learned to study Shakspeare and other English writers. From him dates the sympathy of all the true-hearted amongst us for this land of liberty, whose true vocation he so worthily represented among the oppressed. He led the genius of Britain on a pilgrimage throughout all Europe.

England will one day feel how ill it is—not for Byron but for herself —that the foreigner who lands upon her shores should search in vain in that Temple which should be her national Pantheon, for the Poet beloved and admired by all the nations of Europe, and for whose death Greece and Italy wept as it had been that of the noblest of their own sons.

In these few pages—unfortunately very hasty—my aim has been, not so much to criticize either Goethe or Byron, for which both time and space are wanting, as to suggest and if possible lead English criticism upon a broader, more impartial, and more useful path than the one generally followed. Certain travellers of the eleventh century relate that they saw at Teneriffe a prodigiously lofty tree, which from its immense extent of foliage, collected all the vapours of the atmosphere; to discharge them when its branches were shaken, in a shower of pure and refreshing water. Genius is like this tree, and the mission of criticism should be to shake the branches. At the present day it more resembles a savage striving to hew down the noble tree to the roots.

51. Thackeray on Byron's insincerity

1846

In June 1841 William Makepeace Thackeray (1811–63) had written dismissively of Byron in his 'Memorials of Gormandizing': 'You like your dinner, man; never be ashamed to say so. If you don't like your victuals, pass on to the next article; but remember that every man who has been worth a fig in this world, as poet, painter, or musician, has had a good appetite and a good taste. Ah, what a poet Byron would have been had he taken his meals properly, and allowed himself to grow fat—if nature intended him to grow fat—and not have physicked his intellect with wretched opium pills and acrid vinegar, that sent his principles to sleep, and turned his feelings sour! If that man had respected his dinner, he never would have written *Don Juan.*' (*Fraser's Magazine*, XXIII, 712–13.) In his *Notes of a Journey from Cornhill to Grand Cairo* (1st edn., 1846, pp. 74–6) he now reports from Athens.

. . . I have seen but two or three handsome women, and these had the great drawback which is common to the race—I mean, a sallow, greasy, coarse complexion, at which it was not advisable to look too closely.

And on this score I think we English may pride ourselves on possessing an advantage (by *we*, I mean the lovely ladies to whom this is addressed with the most respectful compliments) over the most classical country in the world. I don't care for beauty which will only bear to be looked at from a distance like a scene in a theatre. What is the most beautiful nose in the world, if it be covered with a skin of the texture and colour of coarse whity-brown paper; and if Nature has made it as slippery and shining as though it had been anointed with pomatum? They may talk about beauty, but would you wear a flower that had been dipped in a grease-pot? No; give me a fresh, dewy, healthy rose out of Somersetshire: not one of those superb, tawdry, unwholesome exotics, which are only good to make poems about. Lord Byron wrote more cant of this sort than any poet I know of. Think of 'the peasant girls with dark blue eyes' of the Rhine—the brown-faced, flat-nosed, thick-lipped, dirty wenches! Think of 'filling high a cup of Samian wine;' small beer is nectar compared to it, and Byron himself always drank gin. That man *never* wrote from his heart. He got up rapture and enthusiasm with an eye to the public;—but this is dangerous ground, even more dangerous than to look Athens full in the face, and say that your eyes are not dazzled by its beauty. The Great Public admires Greece and Byron; the public knows best. Murray's 'Guide Book' calls the latter 'our native bard.' Our native bard! *Mon Dieu! He* Shakspeare's, Milton's, Keats's, Scott's native bard! Well, woe be to the man who denies the public gods!

52. Poe on Byron's metrics

1848

Edgar Allan Poe (1809–49). Extract from 'The Rationale of Verse' (*Southern Literary Messenger*, October–November 1848), quoted here from *The Works of Edgar Allan Poe*, ed. J. H. Ingram, Edinburgh, 1875, III, 246–51.

Of this essay, in which Poe challenges traditional theories of scansion, Saintsbury wrote: ' "The Rationale of Verse", though there are faults in it, due to ignorance or carelessness in terminology, to haste, and to imperfect reading, is one of the best things ever written on English prosody, and quite astonishingly original.' (*A History of Criticism and Literary Taste*, 1900–4, III, 635.)

. . . I shall now best proceed in quoting the initial lines of Byron's *Bride of Abydos:*

> Know ye the land where the cypress and myrtle
>   Are emblems of deeds that are done in their clime—
> Where the rage of the vulture, the love of the turtle
>   Now melt into softness, now madden to crime?
> Know ye the land of the cedar and vine,
> Where the flowers ever blossom, the beams ever shine,
> And the light wings of Zephyr, oppressed with perfume,
> Wax faint o'er the gardens of Gul in their bloom?
> Where the citron and olive are fairest of fruit
> And the voice of the nightingale never is mute—
> Where the virgins are soft as the roses they twine,
> And all save the spirit of man is divine?
> 'Tis the land of the East—'tis the clime of the Sun—
> Can he smile on such deeds as his children have done?
> Oh, wild as the accents of lovers' farewell
> Are the hearts that they bear and the tales that they tell.

Now the flow of these lines (as times go) is very sweet and musical. They have been often admired, and justly—as times go—that is to say, it is a rare thing to find better versification of its kind. And where verse is pleasant to the ear, it is silly to find fault with it because it refuses to be scanned. Yet I have heard men, professing to be scholars, who made no scruple of abusing these lines of Byron's on the ground that they were musical in spite of *all law*. Other gentlemen, *not* scholars, abused 'all law' for the same reason—and it occurred neither to the one party nor to the other that the law about which they were disputing might possibly be no law at all—an ass of a law in the skin of a lion.

The Grammars said something about dactylic lines, and it was easily seen that *these* lines were at least meant for dactylic. The first one was, therefore, thus divided:

Knōw yĕ thĕ | lānd whĕre thĕ| cȳprĕss ănd | mȳrtlĕ. |

The concluding foot was a mystery; but the Prosodies said something about the dactylic 'measure' calling now and then for a double rhyme; and the court of inquiry were content to rest in the double rhyme, without exactly perceiving what a double rhyme had to do with the question of an irregular foot. Quitting the first line, the second was thus scanned:

Āre ĕmblĕms | ōf deĕds thăt | āre dōne ĭn | thĕir clīme. |

It was immediately seen, however, that *this* would not do—it was at war with the whole emphasis of the reading. It could not be supposed that Byron, or any one in his senses, intended to place stress upon such monosyllables as 'are,' 'of,' and 'their,' nor could 'their clime,' collated with 'to crime,' in the corresponding line below, be fairly twisted into anything like a 'double rhyme,' so as to bring everything within the category of the Grammars. But further these Grammars spoke not. The inquirers, therefore, in spite of their sense of harmony in the lines, when considered without reference to scansion, fell back upon the idea that the 'Are' was a blunder—an excess for which the poet should be sent to Coventry—and, striking it out, they scanned the remainder of the line as follows:

——ĕmblĕms ŏf | deĕds thăt ăre | dōne ĭn thĕir clīme. |

This answered pretty well; but the Grammars admitted no such foot as a foot of one syllable; and besides the rhythm was dactylic. In despair, the books are well searched, however, and at last the investigators are gratified by a full solution of the riddle in the profound

'Observation' quoted in the beginning of this article:—'When a syllable is wanting, the verse is said to be catalectic; when the measure is exact, the line is acatalectic; when there is a redundant syllable it forms hypermeter.' This is enough. The anomalous line is pronounced to be catalectic at the head and to form hypermeter at the tail—and so on, and so on; it being soon discovered that nearly all the remaining lines are in a similar predicament, and that what flows so smoothly to the ear, although so roughly to the eye, is, after all, a mere jumble of catalecticism, acatalecticism, and hypermeter—not to say worse.

Now, had this court of inquiry been in possession of even the shadow of the *philosophy* of Verse, they would have had no trouble in reconciling this oil and water of the eye and ear, by merely scanning the passage without reference to lines, and, continuously, thus:

Know ye the | land where the | cypress and | myrtle Are | emblems of | deeds that are | done in their | clime Where the | rage of the | vulture the | love of the | turtle Now | melt into | softness now | madden to | *crime* | Know ye the | land of the | cedar and | vine Where the | flowers ever | blossom the | beams ever | shine And the | light wings of | Zephyr op | pressed by per | *fume Wax* | faint o'er the | gardens of | Gul in their | bloom Where the | citron and | olive are | fairest of | fruit And the | voice of the | nightingale | never is | mute Where the | virgins are | soft as the | roses they | *twine And* | all save the | spirit of | man is di | vine 'Tis the | land of the | East 'tis the | clime of the | Sun Can he | smile on such | deeds as his | children have | *done Oh* | wild as the | accents of | lovers' fare | well Are the | hearts | that they | bear and the | tales that they | *tell.*

Here 'crime' and 'tell' (italicised) are caesuras, each having the value of a dactyl, four short syllables, while 'fume Wax,' 'twine and,' and 'done Oh,' are spondees which, of course, being composed of two long syllables are also equal to four short, and are the dactyl's natural equivalent. The nicety of Byron's ear has led him into a succession of feet which, with two trivial exceptions as regards melody, are absolutely accurate, a very rare occurrence this in dactylic or anapaestic rhythms. The exceptions are found in the spondee 'twine And,' and the dactyl, 'smile on such.' Both feet are false in point of melody. In 'twine And' to make out the rhyme we must force 'And' into a length which it will not naturally bear. We are called on to sacrifice either the proper length of the syllable as demanded by its position as a member of a spondee, or the customary accentuation of the word in conversation. There is no hesitation, and should be none. We at once give up the sound for the sense, and the rhythm is imperfect. In this instance it is *very* slightly so, not one person in ten thousand could by ear detect the inaccuracy. But the *perfection* of verse as regards melody, consists in its *never* demanding any such sacrifice as is here demanded. The rhythmical must agree *thoroughly* with the reading flow. This perfection has in no instance been attained, but is unquestionably attainable. '*Smile on such,*' the dactyl, is incorrect, because '*such,*' from the character of the two consonants *ch* cannot *easily* be enunciated in the ordinary time of a short syllable, which its position declares that it is. Almost every reader will be able to appreciate the slight difficulty here, and yet the error is by no means so important as that of the '*And*' in the spondee. By dexterity we *may* pronounce '*such*' in the true time, but the attempt to remedy the rhythmical deficiency of the *And* by drawing it out, merely aggravates the offence against natural enunciation by directing attention to the offence.

My main object, however, in quoting these lines is to show that in spite of the Prosodies, the length of a line is entirely an arbitrary matter. We might divide the commencement of Byron's poem thus:

Know ye the | land where the |

or thus:

Know ye the | land where the | cypress and |

or thus:

Know ye the | land where the | cypress and | myrtle are |

or thus:

Know ye the | land where the | cypress and | myrtle are | emblems of. |

In short, we may give it any division we please, and the lines will be good, provided we have at least *two* feet in a line. As in mathematics two units are required to form number, so rhythm (from the Greek αριθμος, number) demands for its formation at least two feet, Beyond doubt we often see such lines as

Know ye the—
Land where the—

lines of one foot, and our Prosodies admit such, but with impropriety, for common sense would dictate that every so obvious division of a poem as is made by a line, should include within itself all that is necessary for its own comprehension, but in a line of one foot we can have no appreciation of *rhythm*, which depends upon the equality between *two* or more pulsations. The false lines, consisting sometimes

347

of a single caesura, which are seen in mock Pindaric odes, are of course 'rhythmical' only in connection with some other line, and it is this want of independent rhythm which adapts them to the purposes of burlesque alone. Their effect is that of incongruity (the principle of mirth), for they include the blankness of prose amid the harmony of verse.

My second object in quoting Byron's lines was that of showing how absurd it often is to cite a single line from amid the body of a poem for the purpose of instancing the perfection or imperfection of the line's rhythm. Were we to see by itself

Know ye the land where the cypress and myrtle,

we might justly condemn it as defective in the final foot, which is equal to only three, instead of being equal to four short syllables.

In the foot (*flowers ever*) we shall find a further exemplification of the principle of the bastard iambus, bastard trochee, and quick trochee, as I have been at some pains in describing these feet above. All the Prosodies on English verse would insist upon making an elision in 'flowers,' thus (flow'rs), but this is nonsense. In the quick trochee (mānў ăre thĕ) occurring in Mr. Cranch's *trochaic* line,[1] we had to equalise the time of the three syllables (*ny, are, the*) to that of the one *short* syllable whose position they usurp. Accordingly each of these syllables is equal to the third of a short syllable, that is to say, the *sixth of a long*. But in Byron's *dactylic* rhythm, we have to equalise the time of the three syllables (*ers, ev, er*) to that of the one *long* syllable whose position they usurp, or (which is the same thing) of the *two short*. Therefore the value of each of the syllables (*ers, ev,* and *er*) is the *third of a long*. We enunciate them with only half the rapidity we employ in enunciating the three final syllables of the quick trochee—which latter is a rare foot. The '*flowers ever*,' on the contrary, is as common in the dactylic rhythm as is the *bastard* trochee in the trochaic, or the bastard iambus in the iambic. We may as well accent it with the curve of the crescent to the right and call it a *bastard dactyl*. A *bastard anapaest*, whose nature I now need be at no trouble in explaining, will of course occur now and then in an anapaestic rhythm.

In order to avoid any chance of that confusion which is apt to be

---

[1] [This line is one quoted by Poe from 'one of our finest poets, Mr. Christopher Pease Cranch':

'Many are the thoughts that come to me
In my lonely musing.']

introduced in an essay of this kind by too sudden and radical an alteration of the conventionalities to which the reader has been accustomed,
I have thought it right to suggest for the accent marks of the bastard
trochee, bastard iambus, etc. etc., certain characters which, in merely
varying the direction of the ordinary short accent (˘) should imply,
what is the fact, that the feet themselves are not *new* feet, in any proper
sense, but simply modifications of the feet, respectively, from which
they derive their names. Thus a bastard iambus is, in its essentiality,
that is to say, in its time an iambus. The variation lies only in the
distribution of this time. The time, for example, occupied by the one
short (or *half of long*) syllable in the ordinary iambus is in the bastard
spread equally over two syllables, which are accordingly the *fourth of
long*.

But this fact—the fact of the essentiality, or whole time, of the foot
being unchanged, is now so fully before the reader, that I may venture
to propose, finally, an accentuation which shall answer the real
purpose—that is to say, what should be the real purpose, of all accentuation—the purpose of expressing to the eye the exact relative value of
every syllable employed in Verse. . . .

53. Kingsley on Shelley and Byron

[1853] 1859

Charles Kingsley (1819–75), novelist, churchman and social reformer. His essay 'Thoughts on Shelley and Byron' appeared in *Fraser's Magazine*, November 1853, and was reprinted in his *Miscellanies*, 1859. Quoted here from 2nd edn., 1860, I, 304–24.

The poets, who forty years ago proclaimed their intention of working a revolution in English literature, and who have succeeded in their purpose, recommended especially a more simple and truthful view of nature. The established canons of poetry were to be discarded as artificial; as to the matter, the poet was to represent mere nature as he saw her; as to form, he was to be his own law. Freedom and nature were to be his watchwords.

No theory could be more in harmony with the spirit of the age, and the impulse which had been given to it by the burning words of Jean Jacques Rousseau. The school which arose expressed fairly the unrest and unruliness of the time, its weariness of artificial restraint and unmeaning laws, its craving after a nobler and a more earnest life, its sense of a glory and mystery in the physical universe, hidden from the poets of the two preceding centuries, and now revealed by science. So far all was hopeful. But it soon became apparent, that each poet's practical success in carrying out the theory was, paradoxically enough, in inverse proportion to his belief in it; that those who like Wordsworth, Southey, and Keats, talked most about naturalness and freedom, and most openly reprobated the school of Pope, were, after all, least natural and least free; that the balance of those excellences inclined much more to those who like Campbell, Rogers, Crabbe, and Moore, troubled their heads with no theories, but followed the best old models which they knew; and that the rightful sovereign of the new Parnassus, Lord Byron, protested against the new movement, while he followed it; upheld to the last the models which it was the fashion to decry, confest to the last, in poetry as in morals, '*Video meliora proboque, deteriora sequor,*[1] and uttered again and again prophecies of the downfall of English poetry and English taste, which seem to be on the eve of realization.

Now no one will, we presume, be silly enough to say that humanity has gained nothing by all the very beautiful poetry which has been poured out on it during the last thirty years in England. Nevertheless, when we see poetry dying down among us year by year, although the age is becoming year by year more marvellous and inspiring, we have a right to look for some false principle in a school which has had so little enduring vitality, which seems now to be able to perpetuate nothing of itself but its vices.

The answer so easy twenty years ago, that the new poetry was spoiled by an influx of German bad taste, will hardly hold good now, except with a very few very ignorant people. It is now known, of course, that whatsoever quarrel Lessing, Schiller, and Goethe may have had with Pope, it was not on account of his being too severe an artist, but too loose a one; not for being too classical, but not classical enough; that English poets borrowed from them nothing but their most boyish and immature types of thought, and that these were reproduced, and laughed at here, while the men themselves were writing works of a purity, and loftiness, and completeness, unknown to the world—except in the writings of Milton—for nearly two centuries. This feature, however, of the new German poetry, was exactly the one which no English poet deigned to imitate, save Byron alone; on whom, accordingly, Goethe always looked with admiration and affection. But the rest went their way unheeding; and if they have defects, those defects are their own; for when they did copy the German taste, they, for the most part, deliberately chose the evil, and refused the good; and have their reward in a fame which we believe will prove itself a very short-lived one.

But we cannot deny that, in spite of all faults, these men had a strength. They have exercised an influence. And they have done so by virtue of seeing a fact which more complete, and in some cases more manly poets, did not see. Strangely enough, Shelley, the man who was the greatest sinner of them all against the canons of good taste, was the man who saw that new fact, if not most clearly, still most intensely, and who proclaimed it most boldly. His influence, therefore, is outliving that of his compeers, and growing and spreading, for good and for evil; and will grow and spread for years to come, as

[1] ['I see and approve the better course, but pursue the worse.']

long as the present great unrest goes on smouldering in men's hearts, till the hollow settlement of 1815 is burst asunder anew, and men feel that they are no longer in the beginning of the end, but in the end itself, and that this long thirty years' prologue to the reconstruction of rotten Europe is played out at last, and the drama itself begun.

Such is the way of Providence; the race is not to the swift, nor the battle to the strong, nor the prophecy to the wise. The Spirit bloweth where He listeth, and sends on his errands—those who deny Him, rebel against Him—profligates, madmen; and hysterical Rousseaus, hysterical Shelleys, uttering words like the east wind. He uses strange tools in His cosmogony: but He does not use them in vain. By bad men if not by good, by fools if not by wise, His work is done, and done right well.

There was, then, a strength and a truth in all these men; and it was this—that more or less clearly, they all felt that they were standing between two worlds; amid the ruins of an older age; upon the threshold of a new one. To Byron's mind, the decay and rottenness of the old was, perhaps, the most palpable; to Shelley's, the possible glory of the new. Wordsworth declared—a little too noisily, we think, as if he had been the first to discover the truth,—the dignity and divineness of the most simple human facts and relationships. Coleridge declares that the new can only assume living form, by growing organically out of the old institutions. Keats gives a sad and yet a wholesome answer to them both, as, young and passionate, he goes down with Faust 'to the Mothers,'

> To the rich warm youth of the nations,
> Childlike in virtue and faith, though childlike in passion and pleasure,
> Childlike still, still near to the gods, while the sunset of Eden
> Lingered in rose-red rays on the peaks of Ionian mountains.

And there, amid the old classic forms, he cries—'These things, too, are eternal:

> A thing of beauty is a joy for ever.

These, or things even fairer than they, must have their place in the new world, if it is to be really a home for the human race.' So he sings, as best he can, the half-educated and consumptive stable-keeper's son, from his prison-house of London-brick, and in one mighty yearn after that beauty from which he is debarred, breaks his young heart, and dies, leaving a name not 'writ in water,' as he dreamed, but on all fair things, all lovers' hearts, for evermore.

Here then, to return, is the reason why the hearts of the present generation have been influenced so mightily by these men, rather than by those of whom Byron wrote, with perfect sincerity—

> Scott, Rogers, Campbell, Moore, and Crabbe, will try
> 'Gainst you the question with posterity.

These lines, written in 1818, were meant to apply only to Coleridge, Wordsworth, and Southey. Whether they be altogether just or unjust, is not now the question: yet it must seem somewhat strange to our young poets, that Shelley's name is not among those who are to try the question of immortality against the Lake School; and yet many of his most beautiful poems had been already written. Were, then, *The Revolt of Islam* and *Alastor*, it seems, not destined, in Byron's opinion, to live as long as *The Lady of the Lake*, and 'The Mariners of England?' Perhaps not. At least the omission of Shelley's name is noteworthy. But still more noteworthy are these words of his to Mr. Murray, dated January 23, 1819:—

'Read Pope—most of you don't—but do . . . and the inevitable consequence would be, that you would burn all that I have ever written, and all your other wretched Claudians of the day (except Scott and Crabbe) into the bargain.' . . .

And here arises a new question—Is Shelley, then, among the Claudians? It is a hard saying. The present generation will receive it with shouts of laughter. Some future one, which studies and imitates Shakspeare instead of anatomizing him, and which gradually awakens to the now forgotten fact, that a certain man named Edmund Spenser once wrote a poem, the like of which the earth never saw before, and perhaps may never see again, may be inclined to acquiesce in the verdict, and believe that Byron had a discrimination in this matter, as in a hundred more, far more acute than any of his compeers, and had not eaten in vain, poor fellow, of the tree of the knowledge of good and evil. In the meanwhile, we may perceive in the poetry of the two men deep and radical differences, indicating a spiritual difference between them even more deep, which may explain the little notice which Byron takes of Shelley's poetry, and the fact that the two men had no deep sympathy for each other, and could not in anywise 'pull together' during their sojourn in Italy. Doubtless, there were plain outward faults of temper and character on both sides; neither was in a state of mind which could trust itself, or be trusted by those who loved them best. Friendship can only consist with the calm and self-restraint and self-respect of moral and intellectual health; and both were diseased, fevered, ready to take offence, ready, unwittingly, to give it. But the diseases of the two were different, as their natures were; and Shelley's fever was not Byron's.

Now it is worth remarking, that it is Shelley's form of fever, rather than Byron's, which has been of late years the prevailing epidemic. Since Shelley's poems have become known in England, and a timid public, after approaching in fear and trembling the fountain which was understood to be poisoned, has begun first to sip, and then, finding the magic water at all events sweet enough, to quench its thirst with unlimited draughts, Byron's fiercer wine has lost favour. Well—at least the taste of the age is more refined, if that be matter of congratulation. And there is an excuse for preferring champagne to waterside porter, heady with grains of paradise and quassia, salt and cocculum indicum. Nevertheless, worse ingredients than oenanthic acid may lurk in the delicate draught, and the Devil's Elixir may be made fragrant, and sweet, and transparent enough, as French moralists well know, for the most fastidious palate. The private sipping of eau de Cologne, say the London physicians, has increased mightily of late: and so has the reading of Shelley. It is not surprising. Byron's Corsairs and Laras have been, on the whole, impossible during the thirty years' peace; and piracy and profligacy are at all times, and especially now-a-days, expensive amusements, and often require a good private fortune —rare among poets. They have, therefore, been wisely abandoned as ideals, except among a few young persons, who used to wear turn-down collars, and are now attempting mustachios and Mazzini hats. But even among them, and among their betters—rather their more-respectables—nine-tenths of the bad influence which is laid at Byron's door, really is owing to Shelley. Among the many good-going gentlemen and ladies, Byron is generally spoken of with horror—he is 'so wicked,' forsooth; while poor Shelley, 'poor dear Shelley,' is 'very wrong, of course,' but 'so refined,' 'so beautiful,' 'so tender,'— a fallen angel, while Byron is a satyr and a devil. We boldly deny the verdict. Neither of the two are devils: as for angels, when we have seen one, we shall be better able to give an opinion: at present, Shelley is in our eyes far less like one of those old Hebrew and Miltonic angels, fallen or unfallen, than Byron is. And as for the satyr; the less that is said for Shelley, on that point, the better. If Byron sinned more desperately and flagrantly than he, it was done under the temptations of rank, wealth, disappointed love, and under the impulses of an animal nature, to which Shelley's passions were

As moonlight unto sunlight, and as water unto wine.

And, at all events, Byron never set to work to consecrate his own sin into a religion, and proclaim the worship of uncleanness as the last and highest ethical development of 'pure' humanity. No—Byron may be brutal; but he never cants. If at moments he finds himself in hell, he never turns round to the world, and melodiously informs them that it is heaven, if they could but see it in its true light.

The truth is, that what has put Byron out of favour with the public of late, is not his faults, but his excellencies. His artistic good taste, his classical polish, his sound shrewd sense, his hatred of cant, his insight into humbug, above all, his shallow, pitiable habit of being always intelligible; these are the sins which condemn him in the eyes of a mesmerizing, table-turning, spirit-rapping, Spiritualizing, Romanizing generation, who read Shelley in secret, and delight in his bad taste, mysticism, extravagance, and vague and pompous sentimentalism. The age is an effeminate one; and it can well afford to pardon the lewdness of the gentle and sensitive vegetarian, while it has no mercy for that of the sturdy peer, proud of his bull-neck and his boxing, who kept bears and bull-dogs, drilled Greek ruffians at Missolonghi, and 'had no objection to a pot of beer,' and who might, if he had reformed, have made a gallant English gentleman; while Shelley, if once his intense self-opinion had deserted him, would have probably ended in Rome, as an Oratorian or a Passionist.

We would that it were only for this count that Byron has had to make way for Shelley. There is, as we said before, a deeper moral difference between the men, which makes the weaker, rather than the stronger, find favour in young men's eyes. For Byron has the most intense and awful sense of moral law—of law external to himself. Shelley has little or none; less, perhaps, than any known writer who has ever meddled with moral questions. Byron's cry is, I am miserable, because law exists; and I have broken it, broken it so habitually, that now I cannot help breaking it. I have tried to eradicate the sense of it by speculation, by action: but I cannot—

The tree of knowledge is not the tree of life.

There is a moral law independent of us, and yet the very marrow of our life, which punishes and rewards us by no arbitrary external penalties, but by our own conscience of being what we are.

> The mind which is immortal, makes itself
> Requital for its good or evil thoughts;
> Is its own origin of ill, and end—
> And its own place and time—its innate sense
> When stript of this mortality, derives
> No colour from the fleeting things about,
> But is absorbed in sufferance or in joy,
> Born from the knowledge of its own desert.

This idea, confused, intermitted, obscured by all forms of evil—for it was not discovered, but only in the process of discovery—is the one which comes out with greater and greater strength, through all *Corsairs*, *Laras*, and *Parasinas*, till it reaches its completion in *Cain* and in *Manfred*, of both of which we do boldly say, that if any sceptical poetry at all be right, which we often question, they are right and not wrong; that in *Cain*, as in *Manfred*, the awful problem which, perhaps, had better not have been put at all, is nevertheless fairly put, and the solution, as far as it is seen, fairly confessed; namely, that there is an absolute and eternal law in the heart of man, which sophistries of his own, or of other beings, may make him forget, deny, blaspheme; but which exists externally, and will assert itself. If this be not the meaning of *Manfred*, especially of that great scene in the chamois hunter's cottage, what is?—If this be not the meaning of Cain, and his awful awakening after the murder, not to any mere dread of external punishment, but to an overwhelming, instinctive, inarticulate sense of having done wrong, what is?

Yes; that law exists, let it never be forgotten, is the real meaning of Byron, down to that last terrible *Don Juan*, in which he sits himself down, in artificial calm, to trace the gradual rotting and degradation of a man without law, the slave of his own pleasures; a picture happily never finished, because he who painted it was taken away before he had learnt, perhaps when he was beginning to turn back from—the lower depth within the lowest deep.

Now to this whole form of consciousness, poor Shelley's mind is altogether antipodal. His whole life through was a denial of external law, and a substitution in its place of internal sentiment. Byron's cry is, There is a law, and therefore I am miserable. Why cannot I keep the law? Shelley's is, There is a law, and therefore I am miserable. Why should not the law be abolished?—Away with it, for it interferes with my sentiments—Away with marriage, 'custom and faith, the foulest birth of time.'—We do not wish to follow him down into the fearful sins which he defended with the small powers of reasoning—and they were peculiarly small—which he possessed. Let any one who wishes to satisfy himself of the real difference between Byron's mind and Shelley's, compare the writings in which each of them treats the same subject— namely, that frightful question about the relation of the sexes, which forms, evidently, Manfred's crime; and see if the result is not simply this, that Shelley glorifies, what Byron damns. 'Lawless love' is Shelley's expressed ideal of the relation of the sexes: and his justice, his benevolence, his pity, are all equally lawless. 'Follow your instincts,' is his one moral rule, confounding the very lowest animal instincts with those lofty ideas of right, which it was the will of Heaven that he should retain, ay, and love, to the very last, and so reducing them all to the level of sentiments. 'Follow your instincts'—But what if our instincts lead us to eat animal food? 'Then you must follow the instincts of me Percy Bysshe Shelley. I think it horrible, cruel; it offends my taste.' What if our instincts lead us to tyrannize over our fellow-men? 'Then you must repress those instincts. I Shelley think that, too, horrible and cruel.' Whether it be vegetarianism or liberty, the rule is practically the same,—sentiment; which, in his case, as in the case of all sentiment- alists, turns out to mean at last, not the sentiments of mankind in general, but the private sentiments of the writer. This is Shelley; a sentimentalist pure and simple: incapable of anything like inductive reasoning; unable to take cognizance of any facts but those which please his taste, or to draw any conclusion from them but such as also pleases his taste; as, for example, in that eighth stanza of the 'Ode to Liberty,' which, had it been written by any other man but Shelley, possessing the same knowledge as he, one would have called a wicked and deliberate lie—but in his case, is to be simply passed over with a sigh, like a young lady's proofs of table-turning and rapping spirits. She wished to see it so—and therefore so she saw it.

For Shelley's nature is utterly womanish. Not merely his weak points, but his strong ones, are those of a woman. Tender and pitiful as a woman; and yet, when angry, shrieking, railing, hysterical as a woman. The physical distaste for meat and fermented liquors, coupled with the hankering after physical horrors, are especially feminine. The nature of a woman looks out of that wild, beautiful, girlish face—the nature: but not the spirit; not

> The reason firm, the temperate will,
> Endurance, foresight, strength and skill.

The lawlessness of the man, with the sensibility of the woman. . . .

Alas for him! He, too, might have discovered what Byron did; for were not his errors avenged upon him within, more terribly even than without? His cries are like the wails of a child, inarticulate, peevish, irrational; and yet his pain fills his whole being, blackens the very face of nature to him: but he will not confess himself in the wrong—Once only, if we recollect rightly, the truth flashes across him for a moment, amid the clouds of selfish sorrow—

> Alas, I have nor hope nor health,
>   Nor peace within, nor calm around;
> Nor that content surpassing wealth
>   The sage in meditation found,
>   And walked with inward glory crowned.

'Nor'——alas for the spiritual bathos, which follows that short gleam of healthy feeling, and coming to himself—

> —fame nor power, nor love, nor leisure,
>   Others I see whom these surround,
>   Smiling they live and call life pleasure,
> To me that cup has been dealt in another measure!

Poor Shelley! As if the peace within, and the calm around, and the content surpassing wealth, were things which were to be put in the same category with fame, and power, and love, and leisure. As if they were things which could be 'dealt' to any man; instead of depending (as Byron, who, amid all his fearful sins, was a man, knew well enough) upon a man's self, a man's own will, and that will exerted to do a will exterior to itself, to know and to obey a law. But no, the cloud of sentiment must close over again, and

> Yet now despair itself is mild
>   Even as the winds and waters are;
> I could lie down like a tired child,
>   And weep away this life of care,
> Which I have borne, and still must bear,
>   Till death like sleep might seize on me,
> And I might feel in the warm air,
>   My cheek grow cold, and hear the sea
> Breathe o'er my dying brain its last monotony! . .

Too beautiful to laugh at, however empty and sentimental. True: but why beautiful? Because there is a certain sincerity in it, which breeds coherence and melody, which, in short, makes it poetry. But what if such a tone of mind be consciously encouraged, even insincerely affected as the ideal state for a poet's mind, as his followers have done?

The mischief which such a man would do is conceivable enough. He stands out, both by his excellencies and his defects, as the spokesman and ideal of all the unrest and unhealth of sensitive young men for many a year after. His unfulfilled prophecies only help to increase that unrest. Who shall blame either him for uttering those prophecies, or them for longing for their fulfilment? Must we not thank the man who gives us fresh hope that this earth will not be always as it is now? His notion of what it will be may be, as Shelley's was, vague, even in some things wrong and undesirable. Still, we must accept his hope and faith in the spirit, not in the letter. So have thousands of young men felt, who would have shrunk with disgust from some of poor Shelley's details of the 'good time coming.' And shame on him who should wish to rob them of such a hope, even if it interfered with his favourite 'scheme of unfulfilled prophecy.' So men have felt Shelley's spell a wondrous one—perhaps, they think, a life-giving, regenerative one. And yet what dream at once more shallow, and more impossible? Get rid of kings and priests; marriage may stay, pending discussions on the rights of women. Let the poet speak—what he is to say being, of course, a matter of utterly secondary import, provided only that he be a poet; and then the millennium will appear of itself, and the devil be exorcised with a kiss from all hearts—except, of course, those of 'pale priests,' and 'tyrants, with their sneer of cold command' (who, it seems, have not been got rid of after all), and the Cossacks and Croats whom they may choose to call to their rescue. . . . And on the appearance of the said Cossacks and Croats, the poet's vision stops short, and all is blank beyond.—A recipe for the production of millenniums which has this one advantage, that it is small enough to be comprehended by the very smallest minds, and reproduced thereby, with a difference, in such spasmodic melodies as seem to those small minds to be imitations of Shelley's nightingale notes.

For nightingale notes they truly are. In spite of all his faults—and there are few poetic faults in which he does not indulge, to their very highest power,—in spite of his 'interfluous' and 'innumerous,' and the rest of his bad English—in spite of bombast, horrors, maundering, sheer stuff and nonsense of all kinds, there is a plaintive natural melody about this man, such as no other English poet has ever uttered, except Shakspeare, in some few immortal songs. Who that has read Shelley does not recollect scraps worthy to stand by Ariel's song—chaste, simple, unutterably musical? Yes, when he will be himself—Shelley the scholar and the gentleman and the singer, and leave philosophy and politics, which he does not understand, and shriekings and cursings, which are unfit for any civilized and self-respecting man, he is perfect. Like the American mocking-bird, he is harsh only when aping other men's tunes—his true power lies in his own 'native wood-notes wild.'

But it is not this faculty of his which has been imitated by his scholars; for it is not this faculty which made him their ideal, however it may have attracted them. All which sensible men deplore in him, is that which poetasters have exalted in him. His morbidity and his doubt have become in their eyes his differential energy, because, too often, it was all in him with which they had wit to sympathize. They found it easy to curse and complain, instead of helping to mend. So had he. They found it pleasant to confound institutions with the abuses which defaced them. So had he. They found it pleasant to give way to their spleen. So had he. They found it pleasant to believe that the poet was to regenerate the world, without having settled with what he was to regenerate it. So had he. They found it more pleasant to obey sentiment than inductive laws. So had he. They found it more pleasant to hurl about enormous words and startling figures, than to examine reverently the awful depths of beauty which lie in the simplest words, and the severest figures. So had he.

And thus arose a spasmodic, vague, extravagant, effeminate, school of poetry, which has been too often hastily and unfairly fathered upon Byron. Doubtless Byron has helped to its formation; but only in as far as his poems possess, or rather seem to possess, elements in common with Shelley's. For that conscious struggle against law, by which law is discovered, may easily enough be confounded with the utter repudiation of it. Both forms of mind will discuss the same questions; both will discuss them freely, with a certain plainness and daring, which may range through all grades, from the bluntness of Socrates down to reckless immodesty and profaneness. The world will hardly distinguish between the two; it did not in Socrates' case, mistook his reverent irreverence for Atheism, and martyred him accordingly, as it has since martyred Luther's memory. Probably, too, if a living struggle is going on in the writer's mind, he will not have distinguished the two elements in himself; he will be profane when he fancies himself only arguing for truth; he will be only arguing for truth, where he seems to the respectable undoubting to be profane. And in the meanwhile, whether the respectable understand him or not, the young and the inquiring, much more the distempered, who would be glad to throw off moral law, will sympathize with him often more than he sympathizes with himself. Words thrown off in the heat of passion; shameful self-revealings which he has written with his very heart's blood: ay, even fallacies which he has put into the mouths of dramatic characters for the very purpose of refuting them, or at least of calling on all who read to help him to refute them, and to deliver him from the ugly dream, all these will, by the lazy, the frivolous, the feverish, the discontented, be taken for integral parts and noble traits of the man to whom they are attracted, by finding that he, too, has the same doubts and struggles as themselves, that he has a voice and art to be their spokesman. And hence arises confusion on confusion, misconception on misconception. The man is honoured for his dishonour. Chronic disease is taken for a new type of health; and Byron is admired and imitated for that which Byron is trying to tear out of his own heart, and trample under foot as his curse and bane, something which is not Byron's self, but Byron's house-fiend, and tyrant, and shame. And in the meanwhile that which calls itself respectability and orthodoxy, and is—unless Augustine lied—neither of them, stands by; and instead of echoing the voice of him who said, 'Come to me ye that are weary and heavy laden, and I will give you rest,' mumbles proudly to itself, with the Pharisees of old, 'This people, which knoweth not the law, is accursed.'

We do not seek to excuse Byron any more than we do Shelley. They both sinned. They both paid bitter penalty for their sin. How far they were guilty, or which of them was the more guilty, we know not. We can judge no man. It is as poets and teachers, not as men and responsible spirits; not in their inward beings, known only to Him who made them, not even to themselves, but in their outward utterance, that we have a right to compare them. Both have done harm. Neither have, we firmly believe, harmed any human being who had not already the harm within himself. It is not by introducing evil, but by calling into consciousness and more active life evil which was already lurking in the heart, that any writer makes men worse. Thousands doubtless have read Byron and Shelley, and worse books, and have risen from them as pure as when they sat down. In evil as well as in good, the eye only sees that which it brings with it the power of seeing—say rather, the wish to see. But it is because, in spite of all our self-glorifying paeans, our taste has become worse and not better, that Shelley, the man who conceitedly despises and denies law, is taking the place of Byron, the man who only struggles against it, and who shows his honesty and his greatness most by confessing that his struggles are ineffectual; that, Titan as he may look to the world, his strength is misdirected, a mere furious weakness, which proclaims him a slave in fetters, while prurient young gentlemen are fancying him heaping hills on hills, and scaling Olympus itself. They are tired of that notion, however, now. They have begun to suspect that Byron did not scale Olympus after all. How much more pleasant a leader, then, must Shelley be, who unquestionably did scale his little Olympus —having made it himself first to fit his own stature. The man who has built the hay-rick will doubtless climb it again, if need be, as often as desired, and whistle on the top, after the fashion of the rick-building guild, triumphantly enough. For after all Shelley's range of vision is very narrow, his subjects few, his reflections still fewer, when compared, not only with such a poet as Spenser, but with his own contemporaries; above all with Byron. He has a deep heart, but not a wide one; an intense eye, but not a catholic one. And, therefore, he never wrote a real drama; for in spite of all that has been said to the contrary, Beatrice Cenci is really none other than Percy Bysshe Shelley himself in petticoats.

But we will let them both be. Perhaps they know better now.

One very ugly superstition, nevertheless, we must mention, of which these two men have been, in England at least, the great hierophants; that namely, on which we touched in our last—the right of 'genius' to be 'eccentric.' Doubtless there are excuses for such a notion: but it is one against which every wise man must set his face like a flint, and at the risk of being called a 'Philister' and a 'flunkey,' take part boldly with respectability and this wicked world, and declare them to be for once utterly in the right. Still there are excuses for it. A poet, especially one who wishes to be not merely a describer of pretty things, but a 'Vates' and seer of new truth, must often say things which other people do not like to say, and do things which others do not like to do. And, moreover, he will be generally gifted, for the very purpose of enabling him to say and do these strange things, with a sensibility more delicate than common, often painful enough to himself. How easy for such a man to think that he has a right not to be as other men are; to despise little conventionalities, courtesies, even decencies; to offend boldly and carelessly, conscious that he has something right and valuable within himself, which not only atones for such defects, but allows him to indulge in them, as badges of his own superiority!

This has been the notion of artistic genius which has spread among us of late years, just in proportion as the real amount of artistic genius has diminished; till we see men, on the mere ground of being literary men, too refined to keep accounts, or pay their butchers' bills; affecting the pettiest absurdities in dress, in manner, in food; giving themselves credit for being unable to bear a noise, keep their temper, educate their own children, associate with their fellow men; and a thousand other paltry weaknesses, morosenesses, self-indulgences, fastidiousnesses, vulgarities—for all this is essentially vulgar, and demands, not honour and sympathy, but a chapter in Mr. Thackeray's *Book of Snobs*. *Non sic itur ad astra*.[1] Self-indulgence and exclusiveness can only be a proof of weakness. It may accompany talent, but it proves that talent to be partial and defective. The brain may be large, but the manhood, the 'virtus,' is small, where such things are allowed, much more where they are gloried in. A poet such a man may be, but a world-poet never. He is sectarian, a poetical Quaker, a Puritan, who, forgetting that the truth which he possesses is equally the right and inheritance of every man he meets, takes up a peculiar dress or phraseology, as symbols of his fancied difference from his human brothers. All great poets, till Shelley and Byron, as far as we can discern, have been men especially free from eccentricities; careful not merely of the chivalries and the respectabilities, but also of the courtesies and the petty convention-alties, of the age in which they lived; altogether well-bred men of the world. The answer, that they learnt the ways of courts, does not avail; for if they had had no innate good-breeding, reticence, respect for forms and customs, they would never have come near courts at all. It is not a question of rank and fashion, but of good feeling, common sense, unselfishness. Goethe, Milton, Spenser, Shakspeare, Rabelais, Ariosto, were none of them high-born men; several of them low-born, and only rose to the society of high-born men because they were themselves innately high-bred, polished, complete, without exaggera-tions, affectations, deformities, weaknesses of mind and taste, whatever may have been their weaknesses on certain points of morals. The man of all men most bepraised by the present generation of poets, is perhaps Wolfgang von Goethe. Why is it, then, that of all men he is the one whom they strive to be most unlike?

And if this be good counsel for the man who merely wishes—and no blame to him—to sing about beautiful things in a beautiful way, it applies with tenfold force to the poet who desires honestly to proclaim

[1] ['This is no way to immortality.']

great truths. If he has to offend the prejudices of the world in important things, that is all the more reason for his bowing to those prejudices in little things, and being content to be like his neighbours in outward matters, in order that he may make them like himself in inward ones. Shall such a man dare to hinder his own message, to drive away the very hearers to whom he believes himself to be sent, for the sake of his own nerves, laziness, antipathies, much more of his own vanity and pride? If he does so, he is unfaithful to that very genius on which he prides himself. He denies its divinity, by treating it as his own possession, to be displayed or hidden as he chooses, for his own enjoyment, his own self-glorification. Well for such a man if a day comes to him in which he will look back with shame and self-reproach, not merely on every scandal which he may have caused by breaking the moral and social laws of humanity, by neglecting to restrain his appetites, pay his bills, and keep his engagements; but also on every conceited word and look, every gaucherie and rudeness, every self-indulgent moroseness and fastidiousness, as sins against the sacred charge which has been committed to him; and determine with that Jew of old, who, to judge from his letter to Philemon, was one of the most perfect gentlemen of God's making who ever walked this earth, to become 'all things to all men, if by any means he may save some.'

54. Bagehot on the mere fashion for Byron

[1864] 1879

Walter Bagehot (1826–77), economist, political theorist, and critic. Extract from 'Wordsworth, Tennyson, and Browning; or Pure, Ornate, and Grotesque Art in English Poetry', *National Review*, November 1864. Reprinted in *Literary Studies*, ed. R. H. Hutton, 1879. Quoted here from that edn., II, 338–41.

. . . Neither English poetry nor English criticism have ever recovered the *eruption* which they both made at the beginning of this century into the fashionable world. The poems of Lord Byron were received with an avidity that resembles our present avidity for sensation novels, and were read by a class which at present reads little but such novels. Old men who remember those days may be heard to say, 'We hear nothing of poetry now-a-days; it seems quite down.' And 'down' it certainly is, if for poetry it be a descent to be no longer the favourite excitement of the more frivolous part of the 'upper' world. That stimulating poetry is now little read. A stray schoolboy may still be detected in a wild admiration for *The Giaour* or *The Corsair* (and it is suitable to his age, and he should not be reproached for it), but the *real* posterity—the quiet students of a past literature—never read them or think of them. A line or two linger on the memory; a few telling strokes of occasional and felicitous energy are quoted, but this is all. As wholes, these exaggerated stories were worthless; they taught nothing, and therefore they are forgotten. If now-a-days a dismal poet were, like Byron, to lament the fact of his birth, and to hint that he was too good for the world, the *Saturday Reviewers* would say that 'they doubted if he *was* too good; that a sulky poet was a questionable addition to a tolerable world; that he need not have been born, as far as they were concerned.' Doubtless, there is much in Byron besides his dismal exaggeration, which made 'the sensation,' which gave him a wild moment of dangerous fame. As so often happens, the cause of his momentary fashion is the cause also of his lasting oblivion. Moore's former reputation was less excessive, yet it has not been more permanent. The prettiness of a few songs preserves the memory of his name, but as a poet to *read* he is forgotten. There is nothing to read in him; no exquisite thought, no sublime feeling, no consummate description of true character. Almost the sole result of the poetry of that time is the harm which it has done. It degraded for a time the whole character of the art. It said by practice, by a most efficient and successful practice, that it was the aim, the *duty* of poets, to catch the attention of the passing, the fashionable, the busy world. If a poem 'fell dead,' it was nothing; it was composed to please the 'London' of the year, and if that London did not like it, why, it had failed. It fixed upon the minds of a whole generation, it engraved in popular memory and tradition, a vague conviction that poetry is but one of the many *amusements* for the enjoying classes, for the lighter hours of all classes. The mere notion, the bare idea, that poetry is a deep thing, a teaching thing, the most surely and wisely elevating of human things, is even now to the coarse public mind nearly unknown.

As was the fate of poetry, so inevitably was that of criticism. The science that expounds which poetry is good and which is bad is dependent for its popular reputation on the popular estimate of poetry itself. The critics of that day had *a* day, which is more than can be said for some since; they professed to tell the fashionable world in what books it would find new pleasure, and therefore they were read by the fashionable world. Byron counted the critic and poet equal. The *Edinburgh Review* penetrated among the young, and into places of female resort where it does not go now. As people ask 'Have you read *Henry Dunbar*? and what do you think of it?' so they then asked, 'Have you read *The Giaour*? and what do you think of it?' Lord Jeffrey, a shrewd judge of the world, employed himself in telling it what to think; not so much what it ought to think, as what at bottom it did think; and so by dexterous sympathy with current society he gained contemporary fame and power. Such fame no critic must hope for now. His articles will not penetrate where the poems themselves do not penetrate. When poetry was noisy, criticism was loud; now poetry is a still small voice, and criticism must be smaller and stiller. As the function of such criticism was limited, so was its subject. For the great and (as time now proves) the *permanent* part of the poetry of his time—for Shelley and for Wordsworth—Lord Jeffrey had but one word. He said 'It won't do'. And it will not do to amuse a drawing-room.

The doctrine that poetry is a light amusement for idle hours, a metrical species of sensational novel, did not indeed become popular without gainsayers. Thirty years ago, Mr. Carlyle most rudely contradicted it. But perhaps this is about all that he has done. He has denied, but he has not disproved. He has contradicted the floating paganism, but he has not founded the deep religion. All about and around us a *faith* in poetry struggles to be extricated, but it is not extricated. Some day, at the touch of the true word, the whole confusion will by magic cease; the broken and shapeless notions cohere and crystallise into a bright and true theory. But this cannot be yet.

But though no complete theory of the poetic art as yet be possible for us, though perhaps only our children's children will be able to speak on this subject with the assured confidence which belongs to accepted truth, yet something of some certainty may be stated on the easier elements. . . . But it will be necessary to assign reasons, and the assigning of reasons is a dry task. Years ago, when criticism only tried to show how poetry could be made a good amusement, it was not impossible that criticism itself should be amusing. But now it must at least be serious, for we believe that poetry is a serious and a deep thing.

55. Byron and working-class readers: three points of view

1845; 1869, 1866; 1887, 1900

(*a*) FRIEDRICH ENGELS (1820–95), social philosopher and major contributor to Marxist theory. Extract from *The Condition of the Working Class in England* (originally published, in German, in 1845), trans. and ed. W. O. Henderson and W. H. Chaloner, 1958, pp. 272–3: 'No better evidence of the extent to which the English workers have succeeded in educating themselves can be brought forward than the fact that the most important modern works in philosophy, poetry and politics are in practice read only by the proletariat. The middle classes, enslaved by the influences generated by their environment, are blinded by prejudice. They are horror-stricken at the very idea of reading anything of a really progressive nature. The working classes, on the other hand, have no such stupid inhibitions and devour such works with pleasure and profit. In this connection the Socialists have a wonderful record of achievement, for they have promoted the education of the workers by translating the works of such great French materialist philosophers as Helvetius, Holbach and Diderot. These books, as well as many standard English books have been widely circulated among the workers in cheap editions. Strauss's *Life of Jesus* and Proudhon's book on *Property* are also read in England only by the workers. Again it is the workers who are most familiar with the poetry of Shelley and Byron. Shelley's prophetic genius has caught their imagination, while Byron attracts their sympathy by his sensuous fire and by the virulence of his satire against the existing social order. The middle classes, on the other hand, have on their shelves only ruthlessly expurgated "family" editions of these writers. These editions have been prepared to suit the hypocritical moral standards of the bourgeoisie.'

(*b*) GEORGE ELIOT (1819–80) noted in a letter of 23 August 1869 that 'Byron and his poetry have become more and more repugnant to me of late years'; adding in a letter of 21 September that 'He seems to me the most *vulgar-minded* genius that ever produced a great effect in literature.' (*The George Eliot Letters*, ed. Gordon S. Haight, 1954–5,

V, 54, 57.) The eponymous hero of *Felix Holt, The Radical* (1866) expresses a similar contempt:

'In the act of rising, Felix pushed back his chair too suddenly against the rickety table close by him, and down went the blue-frilled work-basket, flying open, and dispersing on the floor reels, thimble, muslin work, a small sealed bottle of atta of rose, and something heavier than these—a duodecimo volume which fell close to him between the table and the fender.

"O my stars!" said Felix, "I beg your pardon." Esther had already started up, and with wonderful quickness had picked up half the small rolling things while Felix was lifting the basket and the book. This last had opened, and had its leaves crushed in falling; and, with the instinct of a bookish man, he saw nothing more pressing to be done than to flatten the corners of the leaves.

"Byron's Poems!" he said, in a tone of disgust, while Esther was recovering all the other articles. " 'The Dream'—he'd better have been asleep and snoring. What! do you stuff your memory with Byron, Miss Lyon?"

Felix, on his side, was led at last to look straight at Esther, but it was with a strong denunciatory and pedagogic intention. Of course he saw more clearly than ever that she was a fine lady.

She reddened, drew up her long neck, and said, as she retreated to her chair again,

"I have a great admiration for Byron."

Mr. Lyon had paused in the act of drawing his chair to the tea-table, and was looking on at this scene, wrinkling the corners of his eyes with a perplexed smile. Esther would not have wished him to know anything about the volume of Byron, but she was too proud to show any concern.

"He is a worldly and vain writer, I fear," said Mr. Lyon. He knew scarcely anything of the poet, whose books embodied the faith and ritual of many young ladies and gentlemen.

"A misanthropic debauchee," said Felix, lifting a chair with one hand, and holding the book open in the other, "whose notion of a hero was that he should disorder his stomach and despise mankind. His corsairs and renegades, his Alps and Manfreds, are the most paltry puppets that were ever pulled by the strings of lust and pride." (*Felix Holt, The Radical*, 1866, I, 123–5.)

(c) MARK RUTHERFORD (William Hale White, 1831–1913), dissenter, bookseller and novelist. Extract from *The Revolution in Tanner's Lane*, 1887, pp. 23–6, 144–5: 'In the evening Zachariah took up the book. Byron was not, indeed, in his line. He took no interest in him, although, like every other Englishman, he had heard much about him. He had passed on his way to Albemarle Street the entrance to the Albany. Byron was lying there asleep, but Zachariah, although he knew he was within fifty yards of him, felt no emotion whatever. This was remarkable, for Byron's influence, even in 1814, was singular, beyond that of all predecessors and successors, in the wideness of its range. He was read by everybody. Men and women who were accessible to no other poetry were accessible to his, and old sea-captains, merchants, tradesmen, clerks, tailors, milliners, as well as the best judges in the land, repeated his verses by the page.

Mrs. Coleman, having cleared away the tea-things, sat knitting till half-past six. It was prayer-meeting night, and she never missed going. Zachariah generally accompanied her, but he was not quite presentable, and stayed at home. He went on with *The Corsair*, and as he read his heart warmed, and he unconsciously found himself declaiming several of the most glowing and eloquent lines aloud. He was by nature a poet; essentially so, for he loved everything which lifted him above what is commonplace. Isaiah, Milton, a storm, a revolution, a great passion—with these he was at home; and his education, mainly on the Old Testament, contributed greatly to the development both of the strength and weakness of his character. For such as he are weak as well as strong; weak in the absence of the innumerable little sympathies and worldlinesses which make life delightful, and but too apt to despise and tread upon these gentle flowers which are as really here as the sun and the stars, and are nearer to us. Zachariah found in *The Corsair* exactly what answered to his own inmost self, down to its very depths. The lofty style, the scorn of what is mean and base, the courage—root of all virtue— that dares and evermore dares in the very last extremity, the love of the illimitable, of freedom, and the cadences like the fall of waves on a sea-shore were attractive to him beyond measure. More than this, there was Love. His own love was a failure, and yet it was impossible for him to indulge for a moment his imagination elsewhere. The difference between him and his wife might have risen to absolute aversion, and yet no wandering fancy would ever have been encouraged towards any woman living. But when he came to Medora's song—

Deep in my soul that tender secret dwells,
Lonely and lost to light for evermore,
Save when to thine my heart responsive swells,
Then trembles into silence as before.

and more particularly the second verse—

There, in its centre, a sepulchral lamp
Burns the slow flame, eternal—but unseen;
Which not the darkness of despair can damp,
Though vain its ray as it had never been.

love again asserted itself. It was not love for a person; perhaps it
was hardly love so much as the capacity for love. Whatever it may
be, henceforth this is what love will be in him, and it will be fully
maintained, though it knows no actual object. It will manifest itself
in suppressed force, seeking for exit in a thousand directions; sometimes grotesque perhaps, but always force. It will give energy to
expression, vitality to his admiration of the beautiful, devotion to
his worship, enthusiasm to his zeal for freedom. More than this,
it will *not* make his private life unbearable by contrast; rather the
reverse. The vision of Medora will not intensify the shadow over
Rosoman Street, Clerkenwell, but will soften it. . . .'

'. . . The relationship between himself and his wife during those two
years had become, not openly hostile, it is true, but it was neutral.
Long ago he had given up the habit of talking to her about politics,
the thing which lay nearest to his heart just then. The pumping
effort of bringing out a single sentence in her presence on any abstract
topic was incredible, and so he learned at last to come home, though
his heart and mind were full to bursting, and say nothing more to her
than that he had seen her friend Mrs. Sykes, or bought his tea at a
different shop. On the other hand, the revolutionary literature of the
time, and more particularly Byron, increasingly interested him.
The very wildness and remoteness of Byron's romance was just what
suited him. It is all very well for the happy and well-to-do to talk
scornfully of poetic sentimentality. Those to whom a natural outlet
for their affection is denied know better. They instinctively turn to
books which are the farthest removed from commonplace and are
in a sense unreal. Not to the prosperous man, a dweller in beautiful
scenery, well married to an intelligent wife, is Byron precious, but to
the poor wretch, say some City clerk, with an aspiration beyond his
desk, who has two rooms in Camberwell; and who before he knew

what he was doing made a marriage—well—which was a mistake, but who is able to turn to that island in the summer sea, where dwells Kaled, his mistress—Kaled, the Dark Page disguised as a man, who watches her beloved dying:—

> Who nothing fears, nor feels, nor heeds, nor sees,
> Save that damp brow which rests upon his knees;
> Save that pale aspect, where the eye, though dim,
> Held all the light that shone on earth for him.'

(Cf. the following extract from Mark Rutherford's essay, 'The Morality of Byron's Poetry. "The Corsair",' *Pages from a Journal*, 1900, pp. 131–2: 'A word as to Byron's hold upon the people. He was able to obtain a hearing from ordinary men and women, who knew nothing even of Shakespeare, save what they had seen at the theatre. Modern poetry is the luxury of a small cultivated class. We may say what we like of popularity, and if it be purchased by condescension to popular silliness it is nothing. But Byron secured access to thousands of readers in England and on the Continent by strength and loveliness, a feat seldom equalled and never perhaps surpassed. The present writer's father, a compositor in a dingy printing office, repeated verses from *Childe Harold* at the case. Still more remarkable, Byron reached one of this writer's friends, an officer in the Navy, of the ancient stamp; and the attraction, both to printer and lieutenant, lay in nothing lower than that which was best in him. It is surely a service sufficient to compensate for many more faults than can be charged against him that wherever there was any latent poetic dissatisfaction with the vulgarity and meanness of ordinary life he gave it expression, and that he has awakened in the *people* lofty emotions which, without him, would have slept. The cultivated critics, and the refined persons who have *schrecklich viel gelesen*,[1] are not competent to estimate the debt we owe to Byron.')

[1] ['Read a frightful lot.']

56. Swinburne's defence of Byron

[1866] 1875

Algernon Charles Swinburne (1837–1909) wrote this critique as a preface to his *Selection from the Works of Lord Byron* (1866). It is reprinted here, with some minor omissions, from the revised version in his *Essays and Studies*, 1875, pp. 238–58.

The most delicate and thoughtful of English critics has charged the present generation of Englishmen with forgetfulness of Byron.[1] It is not a light charge: and it is not ungrounded. Men born when this century was getting into its forties were baptized into another church than his with the rites of another creed. Upon their ears, first after the cadences of elder poets, fell the faultless and fervent melodies of Tennyson. To them, chief among the past heroes of the younger century, three men appeared as predominant in poetry; Coleridge, Keats, and Shelley. Behind these were effaced, on either hand, the two great opposing figures of Byron and Wordsworth. No man under twenty can just now be expected to appreciate these. The time was when all boys and girls who paddled in rhyme and dabbled in sentiment were wont to adore the presence or the memory of Byron with foolish faces of praise. It is of little moment to him or to us that they have long since ceased to cackle and begun to hiss. They have become used to better verse and carefuller workmen; and must be forgiven if after such training they cannot at once appreciate the splendid and imperishable excellence which covers all his offences and outweighs all his defects: the excellence of sincerity and strength. Without these no poet can live; but few have ever had so much of them as Byron. His sincerity indeed is difficult to discover and define; but it does in effect lie at the root of all his good works: deformed by pretension and defaced by assumption, masked by folly and veiled by affectation; but perceptible after all, and priceless. . . .

Thus much . . . we may safely assert: that no man's work was ever more influenced by his character; and that no man's character was

[1] [Matthew Arnold, at the close of his essay, 'Heinrich Heine'.]

ever more influenced by his circumstances. Rather from things without than from things within him did the spirit of Byron assume colour and shape. His noblest verse leapt on a sudden into life after the heaviest evils had fallen upon him which even he ever underwent. From the beginning indeed he had much to fight against; and three impediments hung about him at starting, the least of which would have weighed down a less strong man: youth, and genius, and an ancient name.[1] In spite of all three he made his way; and suffered for it. At the first chance given or taken, every obscure and obscene thing that lurks for pay or prey among the fouler shallows and thickets of literature flew against him; every hound and every hireling lavished upon him the loathsome tribute of their abuse; all nameless creatures that nibble and prowl, upon whom the serpent's curse has fallen, to go upon his belly and eat dust all the days of his life, assailed him with their foulest venom and their keenest fangs. And the promise given of old to their kind was now at least fulfilled: they did bruise his heel. But the heads of such creatures are so small that it is hard to bruise them in return; it would first be necessary to discern them.

That Byron was able to disregard and to outlive the bark and the bite of such curs as these is small praise enough: the man who cannot do as much is destructible, and therefore contemptible. He did far more than this; he withstood the weight of circumstances to the end; not always without complaint, but always without misgiving. His glorious courage, his excellent contempt for things contemptible, and hatred of hateful men, are enough of themselves to embalm and endear his memory in the eyes of all who are worthy to pass judgment upon him. And these qualities gave much of their own value to verse not otherwise or not always praiseworthy. Even at its best, the serious poetry of Byron is often so rough and loose, so weak in the screws and joints which hold together the framework of verse, that it is not easy to praise it enough without seeming to condone or to extenuate such faults as should not be overlooked or forgiven. No poet is so badly represented by a book of selections. It must show something of his weakness; it cannot show all of his strength. Often, after a noble overture, the last note struck is

That his youth and his rank were flung in his face with vulgar insolence on the publication of his first little book it can hardly be necessary to remind any reader of Byron; but possibly even these offences might have been condoned in a scribbler whose work had given no offensive promise of greatness yet to be. In the verses on Lochnagar at least an ominous threat or presage of something new and splendid must have been but too perceptible to the discerning eye of criticism.

either dissonant or ineffectual. His magnificent masterpiece, which must endure for ever among the precious relics of the world, will not bear dissection or extraction. The merit of *Don Juan* does not lie in any part, but in the whole. There is in that great poem an especial and exquisite balance and sustenance of alternate tones which cannot be expressed or explained by the utmost ingenuity of selection. Haidée is supplanted by Dudù, the shipwreck by the siege, the Russian court by the English household; and this perpetual change, this tidal variety of experience and emotion, gives to the poem something of the breadth and freshness of the sea. Much of the poet's earlier work is or seems unconsciously dishonest; this, if not always or wholly unaffected, is as honest as the sunlight, as frank as the sea-wind. Here, and here alone, the student of his work may recognise and enjoy the ebb and flow of actual life. Here the pulse of vital blood may be felt in tangible flesh, Here for the first time the style of Byron is beyond all praise or blame: a style at once swift and supple, light and strong, various and radiant. Between *Childe Harold* and *Don Juan* the same difference exists which a swimmer feels between lake-water and sea-water: the one is fluent, yielding, invariable; the other has in it a life and pulse, a sting and a swell, which touch and excite the nerves like fire or like music. Across the stanzas of *Don Juan* we swim forward as over 'the broad backs of the sea'; they break and glitter, hiss and laugh, murmur and move, like waves that sound or that subside. There is in them a delicious resistance, an elastic motion, which salt water has and fresh water has not. There is about them a wide wholesome air, full of vivid light and constant wind, which is only felt at sea. Life undulates and death palpitates in the splendid verse which resumes the evidence of a brave and clear-sighted man concerning life and death. Here, as at sea, there is enough and too much of fluctuation and intermission; the ripple flags and falls in loose and lazy lines: the foam flies wide of any mark, and the breakers collapse here and there in sudden ruin and violent failure. But the violence and weakness of the sea are preferable to the smooth sound and equable security of a lake: its buoyant and progressive impulse sustains and propels those who would sink through weariness in the flat and placid shallows. There are others whom it sickens, and others whom it chills; these will do well to steer inshore.

It is natural in writing of Byron to slide into remembrances of what is likest to his verse. His work and Shelley's, beyond that of all our other poets, recall or suggest the wide and high things of nature; the large likeness of the elements; the immeasurable liberty and the stormy strength of waters and winds. They are strongest when they touch upon these; and it is worth remark how few are the poets of whom this can be said. Here, as elsewhere, Shakespeare is supreme when it pleased him; but it pleased him rarely. No poetry of shipwreck and the sea has ever equalled the great scene of *Pericles*; no such note of music was ever struck out of the clash and contention of tempestuous elements. In Milton the sublimity is chiefly of sound; the majesty of melodies unsurpassed from all time wellnigh excludes and supplants all other motives of material beauty. In the minds of mediaeval poets there was no width or depth to receive and contain such emotion. In Spenser, despite his fertile and fluent ingenuity, his subtle and sleepy graces, the effeminacy of colour no less than the monotony of metre makes it hopeless to look for any trace of that passionate sense of power and delight in great outer things of which we speak here. Among later men, Coleridge and Keats used nature mainly as a stimulant or a sedative; Wordsworth as a vegetable fit to shred into his pot and pare down like the outer leaves of a lettuce for didactic and culinary purposes. All these doubtless in their own fashion loved her, for her beauties, for her uses, for her effects; hardly one for herself.

Turn now to Byron or to Shelley. These two at least were not content to play with her skirts and paddle in her shallows. Their passion is perfect, a fierce and blind desire which exalts and impels their verse into the high places of emotion and expression. They feed upon nature with a holy hunger, follow her with a divine lust as of gods chasing the daughters of men. Wind and fire, the cadences of thunder and the clamours of the sea, gave to them no less of sensual pleasure than of spiritual sustenance. These things they desired as others desire music or wine or the beauty of women. This outward and indifferent nature of things, cruel in the eyes of all but her lovers, and even in theirs not loving, became as pliant to their grasp and embrace as any Clymene or Leucothea to Apollo's. To them the large motions and the remote beauties of space were tangible and familiar as flowers. Of this poetry, where description melts into passion and contemplation takes fire from delight, the highest sample is Shelley's 'Ode to the West Wind.' An imperfect mastery of his materials keeps the best things of Byron some few degrees below an equal rank. One native and incurable defect grew up and strengthened side by side with his noblest qualities: a feeble and faulty sense of metre. No poet of equal or inferior rank ever had so bad an ear. His smoother cadences are often vulgar and facile; his fresher notes are often incomplete and inharmonious. His verse stumbles and jingles, stammers and halts, where there is most need for a swift and even pace of musical sound. The rough sonorous changes of the songs in the *Deformed Transformed* rise far higher in harmony and strike far deeper into the memory than the lax easy lines in which he at first indulged; but they slip too readily into notes as rude and weak as the rhymeless tuneless verse in which they are so loosely set, as in a cheap and casual frame. The magnificent lyric measures of *Heaven and Earth* are defaced by the coarse obtrusion of short lines with jagged edges: no small offence in a writer of verse. Otherwise these choral scenes are almost as blameless as they are brilliant. The poet who above others took delight in the sense of sounding storms and shaken waters could not but exult over the vision of deluge with all his strength and breadth of wing. Tempest and rebellion and the magnificence of anguish were as the natural food and fire to kindle and sustain his indomitable and sleepless spirit. The godless martyrdom of rebels; the passion that cannot redeem; the Thebaid whose first hermit was Cain, the Calvary whose first martyr was Satan; these, time after time, allured and inspired him. Here for once this inner and fiery passion of thought found outer clothing and expression in the ruin of a world. Both without and within, the subject was made for him, and lay ready shapen for the strong impressure of his hand. His love of wide and tempestuous waters fills his work throughout as with the broad breath of a sea-wind. Even the weakest of his poems, a thing still-born and shapeless, is redeemed and revived by one glorious verse:

When the Poles crashed, and water was the world.

This passion and power in dealing with the higher things of nature, with her large issues and remote sources, has been bestowed upon Victor Hugo alone among our contemporaries. He also can pass beyond the idyllic details of landscape, and put out from shore into the wide waste places of the sea. And this of course is the loftiest form of such poetry as deals with outward nature and depends upon the forms of things. In Byron the power given by this passion is the more conspicuous through his want of dramatic capacity. Except in the lighter and briefer scenes of *Don Juan*, he was never able to bring two speakers face to face and supply them with the right words. In structure as in metre his elaborate tragedies are wholly condemnable; filled as they are in spirit with the overflow of his fiery energy. *Cain* and *Manfred* are properly monologues decorated and set off by some slight appendage of ornament or explanation. In the later and loftier poem there is no difference perceptible, except in strength and knowledge, between Lucifer and Cain. Thus incompetent to handle the mysteries and varieties of character, Byron turns always with a fresh delight and a fresh confidence thither where he feels himself safe and strong. No part of his nature was more profound and sincere than the vigorous love of such inanimate things as were in tune with his own spirit and senses. His professions of contempt were too loud to express it; scorn is brief or silent; anger alone finds vent in violent iteration and clamorous appeal. He had too much of fury and not enough of contempt; he foams at things and creatures not worth a glance or a blow. But when once clear of men and confronted with elements, he casts the shell of pretence and drops the veil of habit; then, as in the last and highest passage of a poem which has suffered more from praise than any other from dispraise, his scorn of men caught in the nets of nature and necessity has no alloy of untruth; his spirit is mingled with the sea's, and overlooks with a superb delight the ruins and the prayers of men.

This loftiest passage in *Childe Harold* has been so often mouthed and mauled by vulgar admiration that it now can scarcely be relished. Like a royal robe worn out, or a royal wine grown sour, it seems the worse for having been so good. But in fact, allowing for one or two slips and blots, we must after all replace it among the choice and high possessions of poetry. After the first there is hardly a weak line; many have a wonderful vigour and melody; and the deep and glad disdain of the sea for men and the works of men passes into the verse in music and fills it with a weighty and sonorous harmony grave and sweet as the measured voice of heavy remote waves. No other passage in the fourth canto will bear to be torn out from the text; and this one suffers by extraction. The other three cantos are more loosely built and less compact of fabric; but in the first two there is little to remember or to praise. Much of the poem is written throughout in falsetto; there is a savour in many places as of something false and histrionic. This singular and deep defect, which defaces so much of Byron's work, seems also to have deformed his personal character, to have given a twist to his enmities and left a taint upon his friendships. He was really somewhat sombre and sad at heart, and it pleased him to seem sadder than he was. He was impressible and susceptible of pleasure, able to command and enjoy it; and of this also it pleased him to make the most in public. But in fact he was neither a Harold nor a Juan; he was better than these in his own way, and assumed their parts and others with a hypocrisy but half insincere. The fault was probably in great part unconscious, and transparent as a child's acting. To the keen eye and cool judgment of Stendhal it was at once perceptible. Byron's letter to him in defence of Scott was doubtless not insincere; yet it is evident that the writer felt himself to be playing a graceful part to advantage. This fretful and petulant appetite for applause, the proper apanage of small poets and lowly aspirants, had in Byron's case to wrestle with the just pride of place and dignity of genius; no man ever had more of these; yet they did not always support him; he fell even into follies and vulgarities unworthy of a meaner name than his. In effect, when his errors were gravest, he erred through humility and not through pride. Pride would have sustained him far above the remarks and reviews of his day, the praise or dispraise of his hour. As it was, he was vulnerable even by creeping things; and at times their small stings left a poison behind which turned his blood. The contagion of their touch infected him; and he strove under its influence to hiss and wound as they. Here and there in his letters and reflections, in the loose records of his talk and light fragments of his work, the traces of infection are flagrant.

But these defects were only as scars on the skin, superficial and removable; they are past and done with; while all of him that was true and good remains, as it will to all time. Justice cannot be done to it here or now. It is enough if after careful selection as little injustice be done as possible. His few sonnets, unlike Shelley's, are all good; the best is that on Bonnivard, one of his noblest and completest poems. The versified narratives which in their day were so admirable and famous have yielded hardly a stray sheaf to the gleaner. They have enough of vigour and elasticity to keep life in them yet; but once chipped or broken their fabric would crumble and collapse. The finest among them is certainly either *The Giaour* or *The Siege of Corinth*; the weakest is probably either *Parisina* or *The Bride of Abydos*. But in none of these is there even a glimpse of Byron's higher and rarer faculty. All that can be said for them is that they gave tokens of a talent singularly fertile, rapid and vivid; a certain power of action and motion which redeems them from the complete stagnation of dead verses; a command over words and rhymes never of the best and never of the worst. In *The Giaour*, indeed, there is something of a fiery sincerity which in its successors appears diluted and debased.

The change began in Byron when he first found out his comic power, and rose at once beyond sight or shot of any rival. His early satires are wholly devoid of humour, wit, or grace; the verse of *Beppo*, bright and soft and fluent, is full at once of all. The sweet light music of its few and low notes was perfect as a prelude to the higher harmonies of laughter and tears, of scorn and passion, which as yet lay silent in the future. It is mere folly to seek in English or Italian verse a precedent or a parallel. The scheme of metre is Byron's alone; no weaker hand than his could ever bend that bow, or ever will. Even the Italian poets, working in a language more flexible and ductile than ours, could never turn their native metre to such uses, could never handle their national weapon with such grace and strength. The *terza rima* remains their own, after all our efforts to adapt it; it bears here only forced flowers and crude fruits; but the *ottava rima* Byron has fairly conquered and wrested from them. Before the appearance of *Beppo* no one could foresee what a master's hand might make of the instrument; and no one could predict its further use and its dormant powers before the advent of *Don Juan*. In the *Vision of Judgment* it appears finally perfected; the metre fits the sense as with close and pliant armour, the perfect panoply of Achilles. A poem so short and hasty, based on a matter so worthy of brief contempt and long oblivion as the funeral and the fate of George III, bears about it at first sight no great sign or likelihood of life. But this poem which we have by us stands alone, not in Byron's work only, but in the work of the world. Satire in earlier times had changed her rags for robes; Juvenal had clothed with fire, and Dryden with majesty, that wandering and bastard Muse. Byron gave her wings to fly with, above the reach even of these. Others have had as much of passion and as much of humour; Dryden had perhaps as much of both combined. But here and not elsewhere a third quality is apparent: the sense of a high and clear imagination. The grave and great burlesque of King George and St. Peter is relieved and sustained by the figures of Michael and Satan. These two, confronted and corresponding as noon and night, lift and light up the background of satire, blood-red or black according to the point of view. Above all, the balance of thought and passion is admirable; human indignation and divine irony are alike understood and expressed: the pure and fiery anger of men at sight of wrong-doing, the tacit inscrutable derision of heaven. Upon this light and lofty poem a commentary might be written longer than the text and less worth reading; but here it shall not be. Those who read it with the due delight, not too gravely and not too lightly, will understand more than can now be set down; those who read it otherwise will not understand anything. Even these can hardly fail to admire the vigour and variety of scorn, the beauty and the bitterness of verse, which raise it beyond comparison with any other satire. There is enough and too much of violence and injustice in the lines on Southey; but it must be remembered that he was the first to strike, and with an unfair weapon. A poet by profession, he had assaulted with feeble fury another poet, not on the fair and open charge of bad verses, but under the impertinent and irrelevant plea that his work was an affliction or an offence to religion and morality—the most susceptible, as the most intangible, among the creatures of metaphor. A man less irritable and less powerful than Byron might be forgiven for any reprisals; and the excellence of his verses justifies their injustice. But that Southey, who could win and retain for life the love and the praise of Landor, was capable of conscious baseness or falsity, Byron himself in sober moments should hardly have believed. Between official adoration and not less official horror—between George deified and Byron denounced—the Laureate's position was grotesque enough. It was almost a good office to pelt him with the names of hireling and apostate; these charges he could reject and refute. The facts were surely sufficient: that, as to religion, his 'present Deity' was the paltriest maniac among kings and Caesars; as to morality, his feelings or his faith obliged him to decry as pernicious the greatest work of his opponent.

Side by side with the growth of his comic and satiric power, the graver genius of Byron increased and flourished. As the tree grew higher it grew shapelier; the branches it put forth on all sides were fairer of leaf and fuller of fruit than its earlier offshoots had promised. But from these hardly a stray bud or twig can be plucked off by way of sample. No detached morsel of *Don Juan*, no dismembered fragment of *Cain*, will serve to show or to suggest the excellence of either. These poems are coherent and complete as trees or flowers; they cannot be split up and parcelled out like a mosaic of artificial jewellery, which might be taken to pieces by the same artisan who put it together. It must then be remembered that any mere selection from the verse of Byron, however much of care and of goodwill be spent upon the task, must perforce either exclude or impair his very greatest work. Cancel or select a leaf from these poems, and you will injure the whole framework equally in either case. It is not without reluctance that I have given any extracts from *Don Juan*; it is not without a full sense of the damage done to these extracts by the very act of extraction. But I could only have left them untouched with a reluctance even greater; and this plea, if it can, must excuse me. As fragments they are exquisite and noble, like the broken hand or severed foot of a Greek statue; but here as much is lost as there. Taken with their context, they regain as much of beauty and of force as the sculptured foot or hand when, reunited to the perfect body, they resume their place and office among its vital and various limbs. This gift of life and variety is the supreme quality of Byron's chief poem; a quality which cannot be expressed by any system of extracts. Little can here be given beyond a sample or two of tragic and serious work. The buoyant beauty of surrounding verse, the 'innumerable laughter' and the profound murmur of its many measures, the fervent flow of stanzas now like the ripples and now like the gulfs of the sea, can no more be shown by process of selection than any shallow salt pool left in the sand for sunbeams to drain dry can show the depth and length of the receding tide.

It would be waste of words and time here to enlarge at all upon the excellence of the pure comedy of *Don Juan*. From the first canto to the sixteenth; from the defence of Julia, which is worthy of Congreve or Molière, to the study of Adeline, which is worthy of Laclos or Balzac; the elastic energy of humour never falters or flags. English criticism, with a mournful murmur of unanimous virtue, did at the time, and may yet if it please, appeal against the satire which strikes home and approve the satire that flies abroad. It was said, and perhaps is still said, that the poem falls off and runs low towards the end. Those who can discover where a change for the worse begins might at least indicate the landmark, imperceptible to duller eyes, which divides the good from the bad. Others meantime will retain their belief that this cry was only raised because in these latter cantos a certain due amount of satire fell upon the false and corrupt parts of English character, its mealy-mouthed vices and its unsound virtues. Had the scene been shifted to Italy or France, we might have heard little of the poet's failing power and perverse injustice.

It is just worth a word of notice that Byron, like Fielding before him, has caught up a well-known name and prefixed it to his work, without any attempt or desire to retain the likeness or follow the tradition attached to it. With him Don Juan is simply a man somewhat handsomer and luckier than others of his age. This hero is not even a reduced copy of the great and terrible figure with which he has nothing in common but a name. The Titan of embodied evil, the likeness of sin made flesh, which grew up in the grave and bitter imagination of a Spanish poet, steeped in the dyes and heated by the flames of hell, appears even in the hands of Molière diminished, and fallen as it were from Satan to Belial; but still splendid with intellect and courage that tower above the meaner minds and weaker wills of women and of men; still inflexible to human appeal and indomitable by divine anger. To crush him, heaven is compelled to use thunder and hell-fire; and by these, though stricken, he is not subdued. The sombre background of a funereal religion is not yet effaced; but it tasked the whole strength of Molière, gigantic as that strength was, to grapple with the shadow of this giant, to transfigure upon a new stage the tragic and enormous incarnation of supreme sin. As it is, even when playing with his debtors or his peasants, the hero of Molière retains always some feature of his first likeness, some shadow of his early shape. But further than France the terrible legend has never moved. Rigid criticism would therefore say that the title of Byron's masterpiece was properly a misnomer: which is no great matter after all, since the new Juan can never be confounded with the old.

Of Byron's smaller poems there is less to say, and less space to say it. Their splendid merits and their visible defects call neither for praise nor blame. Their place and his, in the literature of England, are fixed points: no critical astronomy of the future can lower or can raise them: they have their own station for all time among the greater and the lesser stars. As a poet, Byron was surpassed, beyond all question and all comparison, by three men at least of his own time; and matched, if not now and then overmatched, by one or two others. The verse of Wordsworth, at its highest, went higher than his; the verse of Landor flowed clearer. But his own ground, where none but he could set foot, was lofty enough, fertile and various. Nothing in Byron is so worthy of wonder and admiration as the scope and range of his power. New fields and ways of work, had he lived, might have given room for exercise and matter for triumph to 'that most fiery spirit.' As it is, his work was done at Missolonghi; all of his work for which the fates could spare him time. A little space was allowed him to show at least a heroic purpose, and attest a high design; then, with all things unfinished before him and behind, he fell asleep after many troubles and triumphs. Few can ever have gone wearier to the grave; none with less fear. He had done enough to earn his rest. Forgetful now and set free for ever from all faults and foes, he passed through the doorway of no ignoble death out of reach of time, out of sight of love, out of hearing of hatred, beyond the blame of England and the praise of Greece. In the full strength of spirit and of body his destiny overtook him, and made an end of all his labours. He had seen and borne and achieved more than most men on record. 'He was a great man, good at many things, and now he has attained this also, to be at rest.'

57. John Morley on Byron and the Revolution
[1870] 1871

John Morley (1838–1923), historian, politician, and man of
letters. His essay on Byron appeared in the *Fortnightly Review* (of
which he was editor) in December 1870, and was reprinted, with
some amplification, in his *Critical Miscellanies*, 1871, pp. 251–90.

It is one of the singular facts in the history of literature, that the most
rootedly conservative country in Europe should have produced the
poet of the Revolution. Nowhere is the antipathy to principles and
ideas so profound, nor the addiction to moderate compromise so inveterate, nor the reluctance to advance away from the past so unconquerable, as in England; and nowhere in England is there so settled an
indisposition to regard any thought or sentiment except in the light of
an existing social order, nor so firmly passive a hostility to generous
aspirations, as in the aristocracy. Yet it was precisely an English aristocrat who became the favourite poet of all the most high-minded
conspirators and socialists of continental Europe for half a century; of
the best of those, that is to say, who have borne the most unsparing
testimony against the present ordering of society, and against the
theological and moral conceptions which have guided and maintained
it. The rank and file of the army has been equally inspired by the same
fiery and rebellious strains against the order of God and the order of
man. 'The day will come,' wrote Mazzini, thirty years ago, 'when
Democracy will remember all that it owes to Byron. England, too,
will, I hope, one day remember the mission—so entirely English, yet
hitherto overlooked by her—which Byron fulfilled on the Continent;
the European rôle given by him to English literature, and the appreciation and sympathy for England which he awakened amongst us.
Before he came, all that was known of English literature was the
French translation of Shakespeare, and the anathema hurled by Voltaire
against the "intoxicated barbarian." It is since Byron that we Continentalists have learned to study Shakespeare and other English
writers. From him dates the sympathy of all the true-hearted amongst

us for this land of liberty, whose true vocation he so worthily represented among the oppressed. He led the genius of Britain on a pilgrimage throughout all Europe.'[1]

The day of recollection has not yet come. It is only in his own
country that Byron's influence has been a comparatively superficial
one, and its scope and gist dimly and imperfectly caught, because it is
only in England that the partisans of order hope to mitigate or avoid
the facts of the Revolution by pretending not to see them, while the
friends of progress suppose that all the fruits of change shall inevitably
fall, if only they keep the forces and processes and extent of the change
rigorously private and undeclared. That intense practicalness, which
seems to have done so many great things for us, and yet at the same
moment mysteriously to have robbed us of all, forbids us even to cast a
glance at what is no more than an aspiration. Englishmen like to be
able to answer about the Revolution as those ancients answered about
the symbol of another Revolution, when they said that they knew not
so much as whether there were a Holy Ghost or not. The same want of
kindling power in the national intelligence which made of the English
Reformation one of the most sluggish and tedious chapters in our
history, has made the still mightier advance of the moderns from the
social system and spiritual bases of the old state, in spite of our two
national achievements of punishing a king with death and emancipating our slaves, just as unimpressive and semi-efficacious a performance in this country, as the more affrontingly hollow and
halt-footed transactions of the sixteenth century.

Just because it was wonderful that England should have produced
Byron, it would have been wonderful if she had received any permanently deep impression from him, or preserved a lasting appreciation of his work, or cheerfully and intelligently recognised his immense
force. And accordingly we cannot help perceiving that generations are
arising who know not Byron. This is not to say that he goes unread;
but there is a vast gulf fixed between the author whom we read with
pleasure and even delight, and that other to whom we turn at all
moments for inspiration and encouragement, and whose words and
ideas spring up incessantly and animatingly within us, unbidden,
whether we turn to him or no.

For no Englishman now does Byron hold this highest place, and this

[1] ... The number of translations that have appeared in Germany since 1830
proves the coincidence of Byronic influence with revolutionary movement in
that country.

is not unnatural in any way, if we remember in what a different shape the Revolution has now by change of circumstance and occasion come to present itself to those who are most ardent in the search after new paths. An estimate of Byron would be in some sort a measure of the distance that we have travelled within the last half century in our appreciation of the conditions of social change. The modern rebel is at least half acquiescence. He has developed a historic sense. The most hearty aversion to the prolonged reign of some of the old gods does not hinder him from seeing, that what are now frigid and unlovely blocks were full of vitality and light in days before the era of their petrifaction. There is much less eagerness of praise or blame, and much less faith in knife and cautery, less confidence that new and right growth will naturally and necessarily follow upon demolition.

The Revolution has never had that long hold on the national imagination in England, either as an idol or a bugbear, which is essential to keep the poet who sings it in effective harmony with new generations of readers. More than this, the Byronic conception was as transitional and inadequate as the methods and ideas of the practical movers, who were to a man left stranded in every country in Europe, during the period of his poetic activity. A transitional and unstable movement of society inevitably fails to supply a propulsion powerful enough to make its poetic expression eternal. There is no better proof of the enormous force of Byron's genius than that it was able to produce so fine an expression, of elements so intrinsically unfavourable to high poetry as doubt, denial, antagonism, and weariness. But this force was no guarantee for perpetuity of influence. Bare rebellion cannot endure, and no succession of generations can continue nourishing themselves on the poetry of complaint, and the idealisation of revolt. If, however, it is impossible that Byron should be all to us that he was to a former generation, and if we find no direct guidance in his muse, this is no reason why criticism should pass him over, nor why there may not be something peculiarly valuable in the noble freedom and genuine modernism of his poetic spirit, to an age that is apparently only forsaking the clerical idyll of one school, for the reactionary mediaevalism or paganism, intrinsically meaningless and issueless, of another.

More attention is now paid to the mysteries of Byron's life than to the merits of his work, and criticism and morality are equally injured by the confusion between the worth of the verse he wrote, and the virtue or wickedness of the life he lived. The admirers of his poetry appear sensible of some obligation to be the champions of his conduct, while those who have diligently gathered together the details of an accurate knowledge of the unseemliness of his conduct, cannot bear to think that from this bramble, men have been able to gather figs. The result of the confusion has been that grave men and women have applied themselves to investigate and judge Byron's private life, as if the exact manner of it, the more or less of his outrages upon decorum, the degree of the deadness of his sense of moral responsibility, were matter of minute and profound interest to all ages. As if all this had anything to do with criticism proper. It is right that we should know the life and manners of one whom we choose for a friend, or of one who asks us to entrust him with the control of public interests. In either of these two cases, we need a guarantee for present and future. Art knows nothing of guarantees. The work is before us, its own warranty. What is it to us whether Turner had coarse orgies with the trulls of Wapping? We can judge his art without knowing or thinking of the artist. And in the same way, what are the stories of Byron's libertinism to us? They may have biographical interest, but of critical interest hardly the least. If the name of the author of *Manfred, Cain, Childe Harold*, were already lost, as it may be in remote times, the work abides, and its mark on European opinion.

There is a sense in which biographical detail gives light to criticism, but not the sense in which the prurient moralist uses or seeks it. The life of the poet may help to explain the growth and prominence of a characteristic sentiment or peculiar idea. Knowledge of this or that fact in his life may uncover the roots of something that strikes, or unravel something that perplexes us. Considering the relations between a man's character and circumstance, and what he produces, we can from this point of view hardly know too much as to the personality of a great writer. Only let us recollect that this personality manifests itself outwardly in two separate forms, in conduct, and in literary production, and that each of these manifestations is to be judged independently of the other. If one of them is wholly censurable, the other may still be the outcome of the better mind; and even from the purely biographical aspect, it is a plain injustice to insist on identifying a character with its worse expression only.

Poetry, and not only poetry, but every other channel of emotional expression and aesthetic culture, confessedly moves with the general march of the human mind, and art is only the transformation into ideal and imaginative shapes of a predominant system and philosophy of life. Minor verse-writers may fairly be consigned, without disrespect, to the region of the literature of taste; and criticism of their work takes the shape of a discussion of stray graces, of new turns, of little variations of shade and colour, of their conformity to the accepted rules that constitute the technics of poetry. The loftier masters, though their technical power and originality, their beauty of form, strength of flight, music and variousness of rhythm, are all full of interest and instruction, yet, besides these precious gifts, come to us with the size and quality of great historic forces, for they represent the hope and energies, the dreams and the consummation, of the human intelligence in its most enormous movements. To appreciate one of these, we need to survey it on every side. For these we need synthetic criticism, which, after analysis has done its work, and disclosed to us the peculiar qualities of form, conception, and treatment, shall collect the products of this first process, construct for us the poet's mental figure in its integrity and just coherence, and then finally, as the sum of its work, shall trace the relations of the poet's ideas, either direct or indirect, through the central currents of thought, to the visible tendencies of an existing age.

The greatest poets reflect beside all else the broad-bosomed haven of a perfect and positive faith, in which mankind has for some space found shelter, unsuspicious of the new and distant wayfarings that are ever in store. To this band of sacred bards few are called, while perhaps not more than four high names would fill the list of the chosen: Dante, the poet of Catholicism; Shakespeare, of Feudalism; Milton, of Protestantism; Goethe, of that new faith which is as yet without any universally recognised label, but whose heaven is an ever-closer harmony between the consciousness of man and all the natural forces of the universe; whose liturgy is culture, and whose deity is a certain high composure of the human heart.

The far-shining pre-eminence of Shakespeare, apart from the incomparable fertility and depth of his natural gifts, arises secondarily from the larger extent to which he transcended the special forming influences, and refreshed his fancy and widened his range of sympathy, by recourse to what was then the nearest possible approach to a historic or political method. To the poet, vision reveals a certain form of the truth, which the rest of men laboriously discover, and prove by the tardier methods of meditation and science. Shakespeare did not walk in imagination with the great warriors, monarchs, churchmen, and rulers of history, conceive their conduct, ideas, schemes, and throw himself into their words and actions, without strengthening that original taste which must have first drawn him to historical subjects, and without deepening both his feeling for the great progression of human affairs, and his sympathy for those relative moods of surveying and dealing with them, which are not more positive, scientific, and political, than they may be made truly poetic.

Again, while in Dante the inspiring force was spiritual, and in Goethe it was intellectual, we may say that both in Shakespeare and Milton it was political and social. In other words, with these two, the drama of the one and the epic of the other were each of them connected with ideas of government and the other external movements of men in society, and with the play of the sentiments which spring from them. We assuredly do not mean that in either of them, least of all in Shakespeare, there is an absence of the spiritual element. This would be at once to thrust them down into a lower place; for the spiritual is of the very essence of poetry. But with the spiritual there mixes in our Englishmen a most abundant leaven of recognition of the impressions and impulses of the outer forms of life, as well as of active sympathy with the every-day debate of the world. They are neither of them inferior to the highest in sense of the wide and unutterable things of the spirit; yet with both of them, more than with other poets of the same rank, the man with whose soul and circumstance they have to deal is the πολιτικὸν ζῷον,[1] no high abstraction of the race, but the creature with concrete relations and a full objective life. In Shakespeare the dramatic form helps partly to make this more prominent, though the poet's spirit shines forth thus, independently of the mould which it imposes on itself. Of Milton we may say, too, that, in spite of the supernatural machinery of his greatest poem, it bears strongly impressed on it the political mark, and that in those minor pieces, where he is avowedly in the political sphere, he still rises to the full height of his majestic harmony and noblest dignity.

Byron was touched by the same fire. The contemporary and friend of the most truly spiritual of all English poets, Shelley, he was himself among the most essentially political. Or perhaps one will be better understood, describing his quality as a quality of poetical *worldliness*, in its enlarged and generous sense of energetic interest in real transactions, and a capacity of being moved and raised by them into those lofty moods of emotion, which in more spiritual natures are only kindled by contemplation of the vast infinitudes that compass the human soul

[1] ['Political animal.']

round about. That Shelley was immeasurably superior to Byron in all the rarer qualities of the specially poetic mind appears to us so unmistakably assured a fact, that difference of opinion upon it can only spring from a more fundamental difference of opinion as to what it is that constitutes this specially poetic quality. If more than anything else it consists in the power of transfiguring action, character, and thought, in the serene radiance of the purest imaginative intelligence, and the gift of expressing these transformed products in the finest articulate vibration of emotional speech, then must we not confess that Byron has composed no piece which from this point may compare with *Prometheus* or the *Cenci*, any more than Rubens may take his place with Titian? We feel that Shelley transports the spirit to the highest bound and limit of the intelligible; and that with him thought passes through one superadded and more rarefying process than the other poet is master of. If it be true, as has been written, that 'Poetry is the breath and finer spirit of all knowledge,' we may say that Shelley teaches us to apprehend that further something, the breath and finer spirit of poetry itself. Contrasting, for example, Shelley's 'Ode to the West Wind' with the famous and truly noble stanzas on the eternal sea which close the fourth canto of *Childe Harold*, who does not feel that there is in the first a volatile and unseizable element that is quite distinct from the imagination and force and high impressiveness, or from any indefinable product of all of these united, which form the glory and power of the second? We may ask in the same way whether *Manfred*, where the spiritual element is as predominant as it ever is in Byron, is worth half a page of *Prometheus*.

To perceive and admit this is not to disparage Byron's achievements. To be most deeply penetrated with the differentiating quality of the poet, is not, after all, to contain the whole of that admixture of varying and moderating elements, which goes to the composition of the broadest and most effective work. Of these elements, Shelley, with all his rare gifts of spiritual imagination and winged melodiousness of verse, was markedly wanting in a keen and omnipresent feeling for the course of human events. All nature stirred him, except the consummating crown of natural growth.

We do not mean anything so untrue as that Shelley was wanting either in deep humanity or in active benevolence, or that social injustice was a thing indifferent to him. I do not forget the energetic political propagandism of his youth in Ireland and elsewhere. Many a furious stanza remains to show how deeply and bitterly the spectacle of this injustice burnt into his soul. But these pieces are accidents. They do not belong to the immortal part of his work. An American original, unconsciously bringing the revolutionary mind to the climax of all utterances possible to it, has said that 'men are degraded when considered as the members of a political organisation.'[1] Shelley's position was on a yet more remote pinnacle than this. Of mankind he was barely conscious, in his loftiest and divinest flights. His muse seeks the vague translucent spaces, where the care of man melts away in vision of the eternal forces, of which man may be but the fortuitous manifestation of an hour.

Byron, on the other hand, is never moved by the strength of his passion or the depth of his contemplation quite away from the round earth, and the civil animal who dwells upon it. Even his misanthropy is only an inverted form of social solicitude. His practical zeal for good and noble causes might teach us this. He never grudged either money or time or personal peril for the cause of Italian freedom, and his life was the measure and the cost of his interest in the liberty of Greece. Then again he was full not merely of wit, which is sometimes only an affair of the tongue, but of humour also, which goes much deeper; and it is of the essence of the humoristic nature, that whether sunny or saturnine, it binds the thoughts of him who possesses it to the wide medley of expressly human things. Byron did not misknow himself, nor misapprehend the most marked turn of his own character, when he wrote the lines:—

> I love not Man the less, but Nature more,
> From these our interviews, in which I steal
> From all I may be, or have been before,
> To mingle with the universe and feel
> What I can ne'er express, yet cannot all conceal.

It was this which made Byron a social force, a far greater force than Shelley either has been or can be. Men read in each page that he was one of like passions with themselves; that he had their own feet of clay, if he had other members of brass and gold and fine silver which they had none of; and that vehement sensibility, tenacious energy of imagination, a bounding swell of poetic fancy, had not obliterated, but had rather quickened, the sense of the highest kind of man of the world, which did not decay but waxed stronger in him with years. His openness to beauty and care for it were always inferior in keenness and in hold upon him to his sense of human interest, and the superiority in

[1] Thoreau.

certain respects of *Marino Faliero*, for example, where he handles a social theme in a worthy spirit, over *Manfred*, where he seeks a something tumultuously beautiful, is due to that subordination in his mind of aesthetic to social intention, which is one of the most strongly distinctive marks of the truly modern spirit. The admirable wit both of his letters, and of pieces like the *Vision of Judgment* and *Don Juan*, where wit reaches as high as any English writer has ever carried it, shows in another way the same vividness and reality of attraction, which every side of human affairs possessed for this glowing and incessantly animated spirit.

In spite of a good many surface affectations, which may have cheated the lighter heads, but which may now be easily seen through, and counted off for as much as they are worth, Byron possessed a bottom of plain sincerity and rational sobriety, which kept him substantially straight, real, and human, and made him the genuine exponent of that immense social movement which we sum up as the Revolution. If Keats's whole soul was absorbed by sensuous impressions of the outer world, and his art was the splendid and exquisite reproduction of these; if Shelley on the other hand distilled from the fine impressions of the senses by process of inmost meditation some thrice ethereal essence, 'the viewless spirit of a lovely sound'; we may say of Byron that, even in the moods when the mightiness and wonder of nature had most effectually possessed themselves of his imagination, his mind never moved for very long on these remote heights apart from the busy world of men, but returned again like the fabled dove from the desolate void of waters to the ark of mortal stress and human passion. Nature, in her most dazzling aspects or stupendous parts, is but the background and theatre of the tragedy of man.

We may find a secondary proof of this in the fewness of those fine descriptive strokes and subtle indirect touches of colour or sound, which arise with incessant spontaneity, where a mastering passion for nature steeps the mind in vigilant, accurate, yet half-unconscious, observation. It is amazing through how long a catalogue of natural objects Byron sometimes takes us, without affixing to one of them any but the most conventional term, or a single epithet which might show that in passing through his mind it had yielded to him a beauty or a savour that had been kept a secret from the common troop. Byron is certainly not wanting in commanding image, as when Manfred likens the lines of foaming light flung along from the Alpine cataract to 'the pale courser's tail, the Giant steed, to be bestrode by death.' But imaginative power of this kind is not the same thing as that susceptibility to the minutest properties and unseen qualities of natural objects, which reveals itself in chance epithet of telling felicity, or phrase that opens to us hidden lights. Our generation is more likely to think too much than too little of this; for its favourite poet, however narrow in subject and feeble in moral treatment, is without any peer in the exquisitely original, varied, and imaginative art of his landscape touches.

This treatment of nature was in exact harmony with the method of revolutionary thought, which, from the time of Rousseau downwards had appealed in its profound weariness of an existing social state to the solitude and seeming freedom of mountain and forest and ocean, as though the only cure for the woes of civilisation lay in annihilating it. This was an appeal less to nature than from man, just as we have said that Byron's was, and hence it was distinct from the single-eyed appreciation and love of nature for her own sake, for her beauty and terror and unnumbered moods, which has made of her the mistress and consoler of many men in these times. In the days of old faith, while the catholic gods sat yet firm upon their thrones, the loveliness of the universe shone to blind eyes. Saint Bernard in the twelfth century could ride for a whole day along the shore of the Lake of Geneva, and yet when in the evening his comrades spoke some word about the lake, he inquired, 'What lake?' It was not mere difference of temperament that made the preacher of one age pass by in this marvellous unconsciousness, and the singer of another burst forth into that tender invocation of 'clear, placid Leman,' whose 'contrasted lake with the wild world he dwelt in' moved him to the very depths. To Saint Bernard the world was as wild and confused as it was to Byron; but then he had gods many and saints many, and a holy church in this world, and a kingdom of heaven awaiting resplendent in the world to come. All this filled his soul with a settled certitude, too absorbing to leave any space for other than religious emotion. The seven centuries that flowed between the spiritual mind of Europe when Saint Bernard was its spokesman, and the spiritual mind of which Byron was the interpreter, had gradually dissolved these certitudes, and the faint lines of new belief and a more durable order were still invisible. The assurance of science was not yet rooted, nor had men as yet learned to turn back to the history of their own kind, to the long chronicle of its manifold experiences, for an adequate system of life and an inspiring social faith. So they fled, in spirit or in flesh, into unfamiliar scenes, and vanished from society, because society was not sufficiently social.

The feeling was abnormal and the method was fundamentally artificial. A sentimentalism arose, which is in art what the metaphysical method is in philosophy. Yet a literature was born of it, whose freshness, force, elevation, and, above all, a self-assertion and peculiar aspiring freedom that have never been surpassed, still exert an irresistible attraction, even over minds that are furthest removed from the moral storm and disorder, and the confused intellectual convictions, of that extraordinary group. Perhaps the fact that their active force is spent, and that men find in them now only a charm and no longer a gospel, explains the difference between the admiration which some of us permit ourselves to feel for them, and the impatient dislike which they stirred in our fathers. Then they were a danger, because they were a force, misleading amiable and highminded people into blind paths. Now this is at an end, and, apart from their historic interest, the permanent elements of beauty draw us to them with a delight that does not diminish, as we recede further and further from the impotence of the aspirations, which thus married themselves to lofty and stirring words. To say nothing of Rousseau, the father and founder of the nature-worship, which is the nearest approach to a positive side that the Revolution has ever possessed, how much fine colour and freshness of feeling there is in *Réné*, what a sense of air and space in *Paul et Virginie*, and what must they have been to a generation that had just emerged from the close parlours of Richardson, the best of the sentimentalists of the pre-revolutionary type? May we not say, too, in parenthesis, that the man is the votary, not of wisdom, but of a bald and shapeless asceticism, who is so excessively penetrated with the reality, the duties, the claims, and the constant hazards of civilisation, as to find in himself no chord responsive to that sombre pensiveness into which Obermann's unfathomable melancholy and impotence of will deepened, as he meditated on the mean shadows which men are content to chase for happiness, and on all the pigmy progeny of giant effort? *C'est peu de chose*, says Obermann, *de n'être point comme le vulgaire des hommes; mais c'est avoir fait un pas vers la sagesse, que de n'être plus comme le vulgaire des sages.*[1] This penetrating remark hits the difference between De Sénancourt himself and most of the school. He is absolutely free from the vulgarity of wisdom, and breathes the air of higher peaks, taking us through mysterious and fragrant pine-woods, where more than he may

[1] ['It is only a little thing not to be like the common herd, but one has taken a step towards wisdom by being different from the mass of wise men.']

find meditative repose amid the heat and stress of that practical day, of which he and his school can never bear the burden.

In that *vulgaire des sages*,[1] of which De Sénancourt had none, Byron abounded. His work is in much the glorification of revolutionary commonplace. Melodramatic individualism reaches its climax in that long series of Laras, Conrads, Manfreds, Harolds, who present the fatal trilogy, in which crime is middle term between debauch and satiety, that forms the natural development of an anti-social doctrine in a full-blooded temperament. It was this temperament which, blending with his gifts of intellect, gave Byron the amazing copiousness and force that makes him the dazzling master of revolutionary emotion, because it fills his work with such variety of figures, such free change of incident, such diversity of passion, such a constant movement and agitation. It was this never-ceasing stir, coupled with a striking concreteness and an unfailing directness, which rather than any markedly correct or wide intellectual apprehension of things, made him so much more than any one else an effective interpreter of the moral tumult of the epoch. If we look for psychological delicacy, for subtle moral traits, for opening glimpses into unobserved depths of character, behold, none of these things are there. These were no gifts of his, any more than the divine gift of music was his. There are some writers whose words but half express the indefinable thoughts that inspired them, and to whom we have to surrender our whole minds with a peculiar loyalty and fulness, independent of the letter and printed phrase, if we would liquefy the frozen speech and recover some portion of the imprisoned essence. This is seldom a necessity with Byron. His words tell us all that he means to say, and do not merely hint nor suggest. The matter with which he deals is gigantic, and he paints with violent colours and sweeping pencil.

Yet he is free from that declamation with which some of the French poets of the same age, and representing a portion of the same movement, blow out their cheeks. An angel of reasonableness seems to watch over him, even when he comes most dangerously near to an extravagance. He is equally free from a strained antithesis, which would have been inconsistent, not only with the breadth of effect required by Byron's art, but also with the peculiarly direct and forcible quality of his genius. In the preface of *Marino Faliero*, a composition that abounds in noble passages, and rests on a fine and original conception of

[1] [Used here, apparently, in the sense of 'the vulgarity of wise men'.]

character, he mentions his 'desire of preserving a nearer approach to unity, than the irregularity which is the reproach of the English theatre.' And this sound view of the importance of form, and of the barbarism to which our English genius is prone, from 'Goody Blake and Harry Gill' up to the clownish savagery which occasionally defaces even plays attributed to Shakespeare, is collateral proof of the sanity and balance, which marked the foundation of his character, and which at no point of his work ever entirely failed him. Byron's admiration for Pope was no mere eccentricity.

We may value this self-control the more, by remembering the nature of his subjects. We look out upon a wild revolutionary welter, of vehement activity without a purpose, boundless discontent without a hope, futile interrogation of nature in questions for which nature can have no answer, unbridled passion, despairing satiety, impotence. It is too easy, as the history of English opinion about Byron's poetic merit abundantly proves, to underrate the genius which mastered so tremendous a conflict, and rendered that amazing scene with the flow and energy and mingled tempest and forlorn calm, which belonged to the original reality. The essential futility of the many moods which went to make up all this, ought not to blind us to the enormous power that was needed for the reproduction of a turbulent and not quite aimless chaos of the soul, in which man seemed to be divorced alike from his brother men in the present, and from all the long succession and endeavour of men in the past. It was no small feat to rise to a height that should command so much, and to exhibit with all the force of life a world that had broken loose from its moorings.

It is idle to vituperate this anarchy, either from the point of view of a sour and precise Puritanism, or the more elevated point of a rational and large faith in progress. Wise men are like Burke, who did not know how to draw an indictment against a whole nation. They do not know how to think nothing but ill of a whole generation, that lifted up its voice in heartfelt complaint and wailing against the conceptions, forms, and rulers, human and divine, of a society that the inward faith had abandoned, but which clung to every outward ordinance; which only remembered that man had property, and forgot that he had a spirit. This is the complaint that rings through Byron's verse. It was this complaint that lay deep at the bottom of the Revolution, and took form in every possible kind of protest, from a dishevelled neckcloth up to a profession of atheism. Byron elaborated the common emotion, as the earliest modern poets elaborated the common speech. He gave it inflections, and distinguished its moods, and threw over it an air of system and coherency, and a certain goodly and far-reaching sonorousness. This is the usual function of the spiritual leader, who leaves in bulk no more in the minds of those whom he attracts than he found, but he leaves it articulate with many sounds, and vivid with the consciousness of a multitude of defined impressions.

That the whole movement, in spite of its energy, was crude, unscientific, virtually abortive, is most true. That it was presided over by a false conception of nature as a benign and purifying power, while she is in truth a stern force to be tamed and mastered, if society is to hold together, cannot be denied of the revolutionary movement then, any more than it can be denied of its sequels now. Nor need we overlook its fundamental error of tracing half the misfortunes and woes of the race to that social union, to which we are really indebted for all the happiness we know, including even this dignifying sensibility of the woes of the race; and the other half to a fictitious entity styled destiny, placed among the nethermost gods, which would be more rightly regarded as the infinitely modifiable influence exercised by one generation of ourselves upon those that follow.

Every one of these faults of thought is justly chargeable to Byron. They were deeply inherent in the Revolution. They coloured thoughts about government, about laws, about morals. They effected a transformation of religion, but, resting on no basis of philosophical acceptance of history, the transformation was only temporary. They spread a fantastic passion, of which Byron was himself an example and a victim, for extraordinary outbreaks of a peculiar kind of material activity, that met the exigencies of an imperious will, while it had not the irksomeness of the self-control which would have exercised the will to more permanent profit. They destroyed faith in order, natural or social, actual or potential, and substituted for it an enthusiastic assertion of the claims of the individual to make his passions, aspirations, and convictions, a final and decisive law.

Such was the moral state which Byron had to render and interpret. His relation to it was a relation of exact sympathy. He felt the force of each of the many currents that united in one destructive stream, wildly overflowing the fixed banks, and then, when it had overflowed, often, it must be confessed, stagnating in lazy, brackish pools, while new tributaries began to flow in together from far other quarters. The list of his poems is the catalogue of the elements of the revolutionary spirit. For of what manner is this spirit? Is it not a masterful and impatient yearning after many good things, unsubdued and uninformed either by a just knowledge of the time, and the means which are needed to bring men the fruits of their hope, or by a fit appreciation of orderly and tranquil activity for the common service, as the normal type of the individual life? And this is precisely the temper and the spirit of Byron. Nowhere else do we see drawn in such traits that colossal figure, which has haunted Europe these four-score years and more, with its new-born passion, its half-controlled will, its constant cry for a multitude of unknown blessings under the single name of freedom, the one known and unadulterated word of blessing. If only truth, which alone of words is essentially divine and sacrosanct, had been the chief talisman of the Revolution, the movement would have been very different from that which we know. But to claim this or that in the name of truth, would have been to borrow the language which priests and presbyters, Dominic and Calvin, had covered thick with hateful associations. Freedom, after all, was the next best thing, for it is an indispensable condition of the best of all; but it could not lead men until the spirit of truth, which means science in the intellectual order, and justice in the social order, had joined company with it.

So there was violent action in politics, and violent and excessive stimulation in literature, the positive effects of the force moved in each sphere being deplorably small in proportion to the intense moral energy which gave the impulse. In literature the straining for mental liberty was the more futile of the two, because it expressed the ardent and hopeless longing of the individual for a life, which we may perhaps best call life unconditioned. And this unconditioned life, which the Byronic hero vainly seeks, and not finding, he fills the world with stormy complaint, is least of all likely to offer itself in any approximate form to men penetrated with gross and egotistical passions to their inmost core. The Byronic hero went to clasp repose in a frenzy. All crimson and aflame with passion, he groaned for evening stillness. He insisted on being free, in the corroding fetters of resentment and scorn for men. Conrad sought balm for disappointment of spirit in vehement activity of body. Manfred represents the confusion common to the type, between thirst for the highest knowledge and proud violence of unbridled will. Harold is held in a middle way of poetic melancholy, equally far from a speechless despair and from gay and reckless licence, by contemplation of the loveliness of external nature, and the great exploits and perishing monuments of man in the past; but he, equally with the others, embodies the paradoxical hope that angry isolation and fretful estrangement from mankind are equivalent to emancipation from their pettiness, instead of being its very climax and demonstration. As if freedom of soul could exist without orderly relations of intelligence and partial acceptance between a man and the sum of surrounding circumstances. That universal protest which rings through Byron's work with a plangent resonance, very different from the whimperings of punier men, is a proof that so far from being free, one's whole being is invaded and laid waste. It is no ignoble mood, and it was a most inevitable product of the mental and social conditions of western Europe at the close of the eighteenth century. Everlasting protest, impetuous energy of will, melancholy and despondent reaction;—this is the revolutionary course. Cain and Conrad; then Manfred and Lara and Harold.

In studying that portion of the European movement, which burst forth into flames in France between the fall of the Bastille and those fatal days of Vendémiaire, Fructidor, Floréal, Brumaire, in which the explosion came convulsively to its end, we seem to see a microcosm of the Byronic epos. The succession of moods is identical. Overthrow, rage, intense material energy, crime, profound melancholy, half-cynical dejection. The Revolution was the battle of Will against the social forces of a dozen centuries. Men thought that they had only to will the freedom and happiness of a world, and all nature and society would be plastic before their daring, as clay in the hands of the potter. They could only conceive of failure as another expression for inadequate will. Is not this one of the notes of Byron's Ode on the fall of Bonaparte? *L'audace, l'audace, et toujours l'audace.*[1] If Danton could have read Byron, he would have felt as one in front of a magician's glass. Every passion and fit, from the bloody days of September down to the gloomy walks by the banks of the Aube, and the prison-cry that 'it were better to be a poor fisherman than to meddle with the governing of men,' would have found itself there. It is true that in Byron we miss the firmness of noble and generous hope. This makes him a more veritable embodiment of the Revolution than such a precursor as Rousseau, in whom were all the unclouded anticipations of a dawn, that opened to an obscured noon and a tempestuous night. Yet one knows not, in truth, how much of that violence of will and restless activity and resolute force was due less to confidence, than to the urgent necessity which every one of us has felt, at some season and under some

[1] ['Boldness, boldness—always boldness.']

influence, of filling up spiritual vacuity by energetic material activity. Was this the secret of the mysterious charm that scenes of violent strife and bloodshed always had for Byron's imagination, as it was perhaps the secret of the black transformation of the social faith of '89 into the worship of the Conqueror of '99? Nowhere does Byron's genius show so much of its own incomparable fire and energy, nor move with such sympathetic firmness and amplitude of pinion, as in *Lara*, *The Corsair*, *Harold*, and other poems, where 'Red Battle stamps his foot,' and where

> The Giant on the mountain stands,
> His blood-red tresses deep'ning in the sun,
> With death-shot glowing in his fiery hands,
> And eye that scorcheth all it glows upon.

Yet other and intrinsically nobler passages, where this splendid imaginative energy of the sensations is replaced by the calmer glow of social meditation, prove that Byron was penetrated with the distinctively modern scorn and aversion for the military spirit, and the distinctively modern conviction of its being the most deadly of anachronisms. Such indirect satisfaction to the physical energies was to him, as their direct satisfaction was to the disillusioned France of '99, the relief demanded by a powerful nature for the impotence of hope and vision.

However this may have been, it may be confessed that Byron presents less of the flame of his revolutionary prototypes, and too much of the ashes. He came at the end of the experiment. But it is only a question of proportion. The ashes belong as much and as necessarily to the methods of the Revolution, in that phase, as do the blaze, that first told men of possible light and warmth, and the fire, which yet smoulders with abundant life underneath the grey cinders. And we have to remember that Byron came in the midst of a reaction; a reaction of triumph for the partisans of darkness and obstruction, who were assured that the exploded fragments of the old order would speedily grow together again, and a reaction of despondency for those who had filled themselves with illimitable and peremptory hopes. Silly Byronical votaries, who only half understood their idol, and loved him for a gloom, that in their own case was nothing but a graceful veil for selfishness and mental indolence, saw and felt only the melancholy conclusion, and had not travelled a yard in the burning path that led to it. They hugged Conrad's haughty misery, but they would have trembled at the thought of Conrad's perilous expedition. They were proud despondent Laras after their manner, 'lords of themselves, that heritage of woe,' but the heritage would have been still more unbearable, if it had involved Lara's bodily danger.

This shallowness has no part in Byron himself. His weariness was a genuine outcome of the influence of the time upon a character consumed by passion. His lot was cast among spent forces, and, while it is no hyperbole to say that he was himself the most enormous force of his time, he was only half conscious of this, if indeed he did not always inwardly shrink from crediting his own power and strength, as so many strong men habitually do, in spite of noisy and perpetual self-assertion. Conceit and presumption have not been any more fatal to the world, than the waste which comes of great men failing in their hearts to recognise how great they are. Many a man whose affectations and assumptions are a proverb, has lost the magnificent virtue of simplicity, for no other reason than that he needed courage to take his own measure, and so finally confirm to himself the reality of his pretensions. With Byron, as with some of his prototypes among the men of action in France and elsewhere, theatrical ostentation, excessive self-consciousness, extravagant claims, cannot hide from us that their power was secretly drained by an ever-present distrust of their own aims, their own methods, even of the very results they seemed to have achieved.

This diffidence was an inseparable consequence of the vast predominance of exalted passion over reflection, which is one of the revolutionary marks. Byron was fundamentally and substantially, as has been already said, one of the most rational of men. Hence when the passionate fit grew cold, as it always does in temperaments so mixed, he wanted for perfect strength a justification in thought. There are men whose being is so universally possessed by phantasies, that they never feel this necessity of reconciling the visions of excited emotion with the ideas of ordered reason. Byron was more vigorously constituted, and his susceptibility to the necessity of this reconciliation combined, with his inability to achieve it, to produce that cynicism which the simple charity of vulgar opinion attributes to the possession of him by unclean devils. It was his refuge, as it sometimes is with smaller men, from the disquieting confusion which was caused by the disproportion between his visions and aspirations, and his intellectual means for satisfying himself seriously as to their true relations and substantive value. Only the man arrives at practical strength who is convinced, whether rightly or wrongly, that he knows all about his own ideas that needs to be known. Byron never did thus know himself, either morally or intellectually. The higher part of him was consciously dragged down by the degrading reminiscence of the brutishness of his youth and its connections and associations, which hung like miasma over his spirit. He could not rise to that sublimest height of moral fervour, when a man intrepidly chases from his memory past evil done, suppresses the recollection of old corruptions, declares that he no longer belongs to them nor they to him, and is not frightened by the past from a firm and lofty respect for present dignity and worth. It is a good thing thus to overthrow the tyranny of the memory, and to cast out the body of our dead selves. That Byron never attained this good, though he was not unlikely to have done so, if he had lived longer, does not prove that he was too gross to feel its need, but it explains a moral weakness, which has left a strange and touching mark on some of his later works.

So in the intellectual order, he knew too much in one sense, and in another too little. The strong man is not conscious of gaps and cataclysms in the structure of this belief, or else he would in so far instantly cease to be strong. One living, as Byron emphatically did, in the truly modern atmosphere, was bound by all the conditions of the atmosphere to have mastered what we may call the natural history of his own ideas and convictions; to know something of their position towards fact and outer circumstance and possibility; above all to have some trusty standard for testing their value, and assuring himself that they do really cover the field which he takes them to cover. People with a faith and people living in frenzy are equally under this law; but they take the completeness and coherency of their doctrine for granted. Byron was not the prey of habitual frenzy, and he was without a faith. That is to say, he had no firm basis for his conceptions, and he was aware that he had none. The same unrest which drove men of that epoch to Nature, haunted them to the end, because they had no systematic conception of her working, and of human relations with her. In a word, there was no science. Byron was a warm admirer of the genius and art of Goethe, yet he never found out the central secret of Goethe's greatness, his luminous and coherent positivity. This is the crowning glory of the modern spirit, and it was the lack of this, which went so far to neutralise Byron's hold of the other chief characteristics of that spirit, its freedom and spaciousness, its humaneness and wide sociality, its versatility and manysidedness, and passionate feeling for the great natural forces.

[Argues for the beneficent effect of scientific knowledge on the intellectual, emotional and spiritual life.]

In Byron's time the pretensions of the two possible answers to the great and eternally open questions of God, Immortality, and the like, were independent of that powerful host of inferences and analogies, which the advance of physical discovery, and the establishment of a historical order, have since then brought into men's minds. The direct aggressions of old are for the most part abandoned, because it is felt that no fiercest polemical cannonading can drive away the impalpable darkness of error, but only the slow and silent presence of the dawning truth. *Cain* remains, a stern and lofty statement of the case against that theological tradition, which so outrages, where it has not already too deeply depraved, the conscience of civilised man. Yet every one who is competent to judge, must feel how infinitely more free the mind of the poet would have been, if besides this just and holy rage, most laudable in its kind, his intellectual equipment had been ample enough and precise enough to have taught him, that all the conceptions that races of men have ever held, either about themselves or their deities, have had a source in the permanently useful instincts of human nature, are capable of explanation, and of a historical justification; that is to say, of the kind of justification which is, in itself and of its own force, the most instant destruction to what has grown to be an anachronism.

Byron's curiously marked predilection for dramatic composition, not merely for dramatic poems, as *Manfred* or *Cain*, but for genuine plays, as *Marino Faliero*, *Werner*, the *Two Foscari*, was the only sign of his approach to the historic or positive spirit. Dramatic art, in its purest modern conception, is genuinely positive; that is, it is the presentation of action, character, and motive, in a self-sufficing, and self-evolving order. There are no final causes, and the first moving elements are taken for granted to begin with. The dramatist creates, but it is the climax of his work to appear to stand absolutely apart and unseen, while the play unfolds itself to the spectator, just as the greater drama of physical phenomena unfolds itself to the scientific observer, or as the order of recorded history extends in natural process under the eye of the political philosopher. Partly, no doubt, the attraction which dramatic form had for Byron is to be explained by that revolutionary thirst for action, of which we have already spoken; but partly also it may well have been due to Byron's rudimentary and unsuspected affinity with the more constructive and scientific side of the modern spirit.

His idea of Nature, of which something has been already said, pointed in the same direction; for, although he made an abstraction and a goddess of her, and was in so far out of the right modern way of thinking about these outer forces, it is to be remembered, that, while this dominant conception of Nature as introduced by Rousseau and others into politics was most mischievous and destructive, its place and worth in poetry are very different; because here in the region of the imagination it had the effect, without any pernicious practical consequences, of giving shape and proportion to that great idea of Ensemble throughout the visible universe, which may be called the beginning and fountain of right knowledge. The conception of the relationship of the different parts and members of the vast cosmos was not accessible to Byron, as it is to a later generation, but his constant appeal, in season and out of season, to all the life and movement that surrounds man, implied and promoted the widest extension of consciousness of the wholeness and community of natural processes.

There was one very manifest evil consequence of the hold, which this idea in its cruder shape gained over Byron and his admirers. The vastness of the material universe, as they conceived and half adored it, entirely overshadowed the principle of moral duty and social obligation. The domestic sentiment, for example, almost disappears in those works which made Byron most popular, or else it only appears, to be banished with reproach. This is quite in accordance with the revolutionary spirit, which was in one of its most fundamental aspects a revolt on behalf of unconditioned individual rights, and against the family. If we accept what seems to be the fatal law of progress, that excess on one side is only moderated by a nearly corresponding excess of an opposite kind, the Byronic dissolution of domestic feeling was not entirely without justification. There is probably no uglier growth of time than that mean and poor form of domesticity, which has always been too apt to fascinate the English imagination, ever since the last great effort of the Rebellion, and which rose to the climax of its popularity when the mad and malignant George III won all hearts by living like a farmer. Instead of the fierce light beating about a throne, it played lambently upon a sty. And the nation who admired, imitated. When the Regent came, and with him that coarse profligacy which has alternated with cloudy insipidity in the annals of the line, the honest part of the world, out of antipathy to the son, was driven even further into domestic sentimentality of a greasy kind, than it had gone from affection for the sire.

Byron helped to clear the air of this. His fire, his lofty spaciousness of outlook, his spirited interest in great national causes, his romance, and the passion both of his animosity and his sympathy, acted for a while like an electric current, and every one within his influence became ashamed to barter the large heritage of manhood, with its many realms and illimitable interests, for the sordid ease of the hearth and the good word of the unworthy. He fills men with thoughts that shake down the unlovely temple of comfort. This was good, to force whoever was not already too far sunk into the mire, high up to the larger atmosphere, whence they could see how minute an atom is man, how infinite and blind and pitiless the might that encompasses his little life. Many feeble spirits ran back homewards from the horrid solitudes and abysses of *Manfred*, and the moral terrors of *Cain*, and even the despair of *Harold*, and, burying themselves in warm domestic places, were comforted by the familiar restoratives and appliances. Firmer souls were not only exhilarated, but intoxicated by the potent and unaccustomed air. They went too far. They made war on the family, and the idea of it. Everything human was mischievously dwarfed, and the difference between right and wrong, between gratification of appetite and its control for virtue's sake, between the acceptance and the evasion of clear obligation, all became invisible or of no account in the new light. That constancy and permanence, of which the family is the type, and which is the first condition alike of the stability and progress of society, was obliterated from thought. As if the wonders that have been wrought by this regulated constancy of the feeling of man for man in transforming human life, were not far more transcendently exalting, than the contemplation of those glories of brute nature, which are barbaric in comparison.

It would be unjust not to admit, that there are abundant passages in his poems of too manifest depth and sincerity of feeling, for us to suppose that Byron himself was dead to the beauty of domestic sentiment. The united tenderness and dignity of Faliero's words to Angiolina, before he goes to the meeting of the conspirators, would, if there were nothing else, be enough to show how rightly, in his better moods, the poet appreciated the conditions of the family. Unfortunately the better moods were not fixed, and we had *Don Juan*, where the wit and colour and power served to make an anti-social and licentious sentiment attractive to puny creatures, who were thankful to have their lasciviousness so gaily adorned. As for Great Britain, she deserved *Don Juan*. A nation, whose disrespect for all ideas and aspirations that cannot be supported by a text, nor circulated by a religious tract society, was systematic, and where consequently the understanding is least protected against sensual sophisms, received no more than a just chastisement in 'the literature of Satan.' Here again, in the licence of this literature, we see the finger of the Revolution, and of that egoism which makes the passions of the individual his own law. Let us condemn and pass on, homily undelivered. If Byron injured the domestic idea on this side, let us not fail to observe how vastly he elevated it on others, and how, above all, he pointed to the idea above and beyond it, in whose light only can that be worthy, the idea of a country and a public cause. A man may be sure that the comfort of the hearth has usurped too high a place, when he can read without response the lines declaring that domestic ties must yield in 'those who are called to the highest destinies, which purify corrupted commonwealths.'

> We must forget all feelings save the one,—
> We must resign all passions save our purpose,—
> We must behold no object save our country,—
> And only look on death as beautiful,
> So that the sacrifice ascend to heaven
> And draw down freedom on her evermore.
>   *Calendaro.* But if we fail——
>   *I. Bertuccio*   They never fail who die
> In a great cause: the block may soak their gore;
> Their heads may sodden in the sun; their limbs
> Be strung to city gates and castle walls—
> But still their spirit walks abroad. Though years
> Elapse, and others share as dark a doom,
> They but augment the deep and sweeping thoughts
> Which overpower all others, and conduct
> The world at last to freedom. What were we
> If Brutus had not lived? He died in giving
> Rome liberty, but left a deathless lesson—
> A name which is a virtue, and a soul
> Which multiplies itself throughout all time,
> When wicked men wax mighty, and a state
> Turns servile.

And the man who wrote this was worthy to play an even nobler part than the one he had thus nobly described; for it was not many years after, that Byron left all, and laid down his life, for the emancipation of a strange land, and 'Greece and Italy wept for his death, as it had been that of the noblest of their own sons.' Detractors have done their best to pare away the merit of this act of self-renunciation by attributing it to despair. That contemporaries of their own humour had done their

best to make his life a load to him is true, yet to this talk of despair we
may reply in the poet's own words,

> When we know
> All that can come, and how to meet it, our
> Resolves, if firm, may merit a more noble
> Word than this, to give it utterance.

There was an estimate of the value and purpose of a human life, which
our Age of Comfort may fruitfully ponder.

To fix upon violent will and incessant craving for movement as the
mark of a poet, whose contemporaries adored him for what they took
to be the musing sweetness of his melancholy, may seem a critical
perversity. There is, however, a momentous difference between that
melancholy, which is as the mere shadow projected by a man's
spiritual form, and that other melancholy, which itself is the reality and
substance of a character; between the soul to whom dejection brings
graceful relief after labour and effort, and the soul which by irresistible
habit and constitution dwells ever in Golgotha. This deep and penetrating subjective melancholy had no possession of Byron. His character
was essentially objective, stimulated by outward circumstance, moving
to outward harmonies, seeking colour and image and purpose from
without. Hence there is inevitably a certain liveliness and animation,
even when he is in the depths. We feel that we are watching clouds
sweep majestically across the sky, and, even when they are darkest, blue
interspaces are not far off. Contrast the moodiest parts of *Childe Harold*
or of *Cain*, with Novalis's *Night Hymns*. Byron's gloom is a mere
elegance in comparison. The one pipes to us with a graceful despondency on the edge of the gulf, while the other carries us actually down
into the black profound, with no rebellious cry nor shriek of woe, but
sombrely awaiting the deliverance of death, with soul absorbed and
consumed by weariness. Let the reader mark the note of mourning
struck in the opening stanzas, for instance, of Novalis's *Longing after
Death*, their simplicity, homeliness, transparent sincerity, and then turn
to any of the familiar passages, where Byron meditates on the good
things which the end brings to men. How artificial he seems, and un-
seasonably ornate, and how conscious of his public. In the first, we sit
sadly on the ground in some veritable Place of a Skull; in the second
we assist at tragical distress after the manner of the Italian opera. We
should be disposed to call the first a peculiarly German quality, until we
remember Pascal. With Novalis, or with Pascal, as with all those whom

character, or the outer fates, or the two together, have drawn to dwell in the valley of the shadow, gloom and despondency are the very stuff of their thoughts. Material energy could have done nothing for them. Their nerves and sinews were too nearly cut asunder. To know the quality of Byron's melancholy, and to recognise how little it was of the essence of his character, we have only to consider how far removed he was from this condition. In other words, in spite of morbid manifestations of one sort and another, he always preserved a salutary and vivid sympathy for action, and a marked capacity for it.

It was the same impetuous and indomitable spirit of effort which moved Byron to his last heroic exploit, that made the poetry inspired by it so powerful in Europe, from the deadly days of the Holy Alliance onwards. Cynical and misanthropical as he has been called, as though that were his sum and substance, he yet never ceased to glorify human freedom, in tones that stirred the hearts of men and quickened their hope and upheld their daring, as with the voice of some heavenly trumpet. You may, if you choose, find the splendour of the stanzas in the Fourth Canto on the Bourbon restoration, on Cromwell, and Washington, a theatrical splendour. But for all that, they touched the noblest parts of men. They are alive with an exalted and magnanimous generosity, the one high virtue which can never fail to touch a multitude. Subtlety may miss them, graces may miss them, and reason may fly over their heads, but the words of a generous humanity on the lips of poet or chief have never failed to kindle divine music in their breasts. The critic may censure, and culture may wave a disdainful hand. As has been said, all such words 'are open to criticism, and they are all above it.' The magic still works. It is as though some mysterious and potent word from the gods had gone abroad over the face of the earth.

This larger influence was not impaired by Byron's ethical poverty. The latter was an inevitable consequence of his defective discipline. The triteness of his moral climax is occasionally startling. When Sardanapalus, for instance, sees Zarina torn from him, and is stricken with profound anguish at the pain with which he has filled her life, he winds up with such a platitude as this:

> To what gulfs
> A single deviation from the track
> Of human duties leaves even those who claim
> The homage of mankind as their born due!

The baldest writer of hymns might work up passion enough for a consummation like this. Once more, Byron was insufficiently furnished with positive intellectual ideas, and for want of these his most exalted words were constantly left sterile of definite and pointed outcome.

More than this, Byron's passionate feeling for mankind was narrowed by his failure to include in his conception the long succession of generations, that stretch back into the past and lie far on in the misty distances of the future.[1] This was a defect that his conception shares in common with that religion, which, while sublimely bidding man to love his neighbour as himself, yet leaves him in the profundity of a concentrated regard for his own soul, to forget both sacred reverence for the unseen benefactors of old time, and direct endeavour to be more to the future, than even the benefactions of the past have been to him. No good man is without both these sentiments in germ. But to be fully effective, they need to be fused together into a single thought, completing that idea of humanity, which, when imperfectly held, so constantly misleads men into short-sighted action, effective only for the hour, and at the hour's end turning to something worse than ineffective. Only he stands aright, who from his little point of present possession ever meditates on the far-reaching lines, which pass through his point from one interminable starlight distance to another. Neither the stoic pagan, nor the disciple of the creed which has some of the peculiar weakness of stoicism and not all its peculiar strength, could find Manfred's latest word untrue to himself:

> The mind which is immortal makes itself
> Requital for its good or evil thoughts—
> Is its own origin of ill and end,
> And its own place and time: its innate sense,
> When stripped of this mortality, derives
> No colour from the fleeting things without:
> But is absorbed in sufferance or joy,
> Born from the knowledge of its own desert.

It is only when a man subordinates this absorption in individual sufferance and joy to the thought that his life is a trust for humanity, that he is sure of making it anything other than 'rain fallen on the sand.' In his own career Byron was loftier than the individualism of his creed, and for this reason, though he may have no place in our own Minster, he belongs to the band of far-shining men, of whom Pericles declared the whole world to be the tomb.

[1] [This judgment was reversed by Morley in a later revision of this essay (*Critical Miscellanies*, 1886, I, 250–1).]

58. John Addington Symonds on Byron

1880

John Addington Symonds (1840–93), historian and essayist. Preface to the selection of Byron's poems in *The English Poets*, ed. T. H. Ward, 1880, IV, 244–55.

The first thing that strikes a student of Byron's collected works is the quantity of poetry produced by him in a short lifetime. The second is the variety of forms attempted—the scope and range of intellectual power displayed. The third is the inequality of the performance, due apparently in certain cases to haste of composition, in others to imperfect sympathy with the subjects treated, or again to some contemptuous compliance with a fashion which the author only tolerated.

Byron's character is stamped upon his work in a remarkable degree; and his character was powerfully biassed by external circumstance. The critic cannot therefore neglect his biography. In early childhood he was left to the sole care of a violent and injudicious mother. Impressed with the importance of the title to which he succeeded at the age of ten, he yet had neither friends nor connections of his own rank, and but slender means for sustaining its dignity. Handsome, active, and ambitious, he was debarred from engaging in field-sports by the malformation of his ankle. Thus, from the first, he lived under conditions eminently unfavourable for the growth of an equable temperament or for the acquisition of just views about society. His mental powers were acute and vigorous; his emotions sincere and direct; the impressions made upon his sensitive nature by the persons with whom he came in contact were vivid and indelible. Yet his judgment of the world was prematurely warped, while his naturally earnest feelings were overlaid with affectations and prejudices which he never succeeded in shaking off. He was constitutionally shy, uncertain in society, preferring the solitude of hills and woods and water, to the men and women whom he learned to misconceive and misinterpret. Though he strove to conceal this shyness beneath

an assumption of off-handed ease, his manners to the last were awkward. It was his misfortune to be well-born but ill-bred, combining
the pride of a peer with the self-consciousness of a *parvenu*. He rarely
suffered his true opinions and emotions to be visible. What he proffered
his acquaintance in their stead was stamped with artificiality. Trelawny
thought that Byron was what London in the days of the Prince Regent
made him. But we must go further back, and recognise that from his
boyhood he began to construct and wear a masquerade costume that
could not be abandoned. When Shelley discerned the 'canker of
aristocracy' and 'perverse ideas' in one whom he admired but never
made his friend; when Goethe complained of his 'Empeiria' or
taint of worldliness, they laid their fingers on this radical blot. The
ostentation which repels us in Byron's correspondence and in the
records left of him by his associates, the swaggering tone that spoils
so much of his best work and makes it impossible to love the man
as we should like to do, may be ascribed to a habit early acquired of
self-sophistication. He veneered the true and noble self which gave
life to his poetry with a layer of imperfectly comprehended cynicism
and weak misanthropy, that passed with him for wordly wisdom.
There are two distinct Byrons, interpenetrative, blended in his life
and work. To disentangle them is wellnigh impossible; for he cherished
his inferior self, and mistook its weakness and its falsehood for strength
and sincerity of insight.

Byron began to write verse while still a boy. He published *Hours
of Idleness* at the age of nineteen. Though this collection of juvenile
lyrics did not deserve high commendation, it might have been spared
the mangling it received from the blunt tomahawk of the *Edinburgh
Review*. His next essay was the product of mere rage against his critics
and against the men of letters who, he thought, had neglected him.
English Bards and Scotch Reviewers is an imitation of Gifford's satirical
style, full of such stinging epigrams as proved that the poet of *Hours of
Idleness* had thenceforth to be reckoned with. At the present time it is
chiefly valuable for the light it throws on Byron's psychological
development. Being of an exceptionally retentive temperament, each
style that he essayed left something ineffaceable upon his habit of
composition. The satire in question was begotten by indignation,
and dealt in invective. We trace an element of indignation, not
seldom of a less than sterling alloy, in nearly all his subsequent poems,
which break too frequently into invectives against unworthy or
mistaken objects of his spleen. Byron, it may be said at once, was

destitute of critical insight. Therefore not only are the judgments of *English Bards and Scotch Reviewers* worthless, but his maturest works are marred by strictures on contemporaries which now appear ridiculous. If Byron desired fame, he achieved it in fair and full measure by his satire. But disappointed by his reception into London society, he resolved on leaving England. His genius received its first true awakening upon his travels. Greece made him a poet, and he returned to England with two Cantos of *Childe Harold* ready for publication. It is difficult to speak in measured terms of a poem which has suffered more from eulogy and popularity than any other poem of equal excellence from depreciation or neglect. The celebrated passages of *Childe Harold*, quoted, extracted, learned by heart at school, and incorporated into guide-books, have become a bye-word and a weariness to the present generation. We do not know how to render justice to the sonorous rhetoric and the often magnificent poetry of a masterpiece that has been subjected to processes so vulgarising. Some deductions, on sounder critical grounds, must also be made from the first enthusiasm that welcomed *Childe Harold*. The poem is written in a declamatory style, which savours of an age when Campbell's *Pleasures of Hope* was thought to soar above the level of prize poetry. The Pilgrim is a *rococo* creation, to whom Byron failed to communicate the breath of life. When this fictitious hero disappears from the scene, the stanzas invariably improve. Therefore the third and fourth Cantos, written in the plenitude of Byron's power, where Childe Harold has been all but forgotten, might pass for a separate composition. With the person of the Pilgrim, the affectation of Spenserian language, sparely but awkwardly employed in the first Canto, is dropped. The vein of meditation is richer, deeper, more dignified in utterance. The personal emotion of the poet, saddened and elevated by his cruel experience of life, finds vent in larger harmonies and more impassioned bursts of eloquence. His sympathy with the oppressed, and his sense of the world's past greatness, attain the altitude of lyrical inspiration in the apostrophe to Rome; while his enjoyment of nature in her grander aspects, and the consolation he received from her amid the solitudes of sea and lake and mountain, are expressed with sublimity in the passages upon the Ocean and the Jura thunderstorm.

After the publication of the first two Cantos, Byron woke in London and 'found himself famous.' What was far worse for him than fame, fashion claimed the new poet for her own. Though still isolated from true friends and family connections, he became the darling of society, poured forth for its amusement those Oriental tales, of which *The Giaour* alone retains sufficient vitality or perfume of true poetry to make its perusal at the present day desirable. Byron did not excel in the art of telling a simple story, unvaried by digressions, unassisted by contrasts of pathos and humour. One of his latest compositions in the narrative style, *The Island*, is a total failure. The best of his earlier tales, *The Prisoner of Chillon* and *Mazeppa*, were produced after the period of his fashionable fame, when, in the quietude of exile, he wrote with sobered feelings for himself. They owe, moreover, their greater purity of outline and sincerity of feeling to the form of monologue adopted. For the moment Byron becomes Bonnivard and Mazeppa, speaking through their lips of sufferings with which he felt the liveliest sympathy.

The life he led in London between 1812 and 1816, confirmed Byron's affectations and increased his tendency to cynicism. But while warping his character and enslaving his genius to trumpery standards of taste, it supplied him with much of the material which was to be wrought up into *Don Juan*. We have therefore no reason to deplore the fact that he lived through it. On the other hand we may perhaps be thankful that his uncongenial union with Lady Byron came to an abrupt conclusion at the beginning of 1816. His temper needed to be deepened by pain; nor was it till the blow of Lady Byron's separation struck him, that the gravest chords of his genius uttered a note. From that time forward, in the ennobled Cantos of *Childe Harold*, no less than in occasional lyrics, the sorrow which drove him into exile and flung him for repose and consolation upon Nature, formed one of the principal topics of his purest poetry. The public who raved about *Lara* and *The Corsair*, must have felt that there was yet a greater Byron to arise, when they read the *Domestic Pieces*, so indiscreetly committed by friends to the pages of the London newspapers. Even though we may condemn, on principles of taste, the self-revelation which from this time forward became one of Byron's habits, though we may fail to appreciate the professed scorn of the world which he mingled with a free recourse to its confidence and sympathy upon delicate matters of his private life, there is no disputing the energy communicated to his genius by these trials.

The formation of Shelley's friendship as this epoch must be reckoned one of the most fortunate and decisive events of Byron's life. The immediate result of their intercourse at Geneva was evident in the poems composed during 1816 and 1817; in the loftier inspiration of *Childe Harold*, in the lyrical gravity of *Prometheus*, and in the maturer reflections of *Manfred*. The reading of Goethe's *Faust* was not without its share of influence, manifest in the general conception of both *Manfred* and *The Deformed Transformed*. Yet neither of these plays can be said to have been modelled upon *Faust*. Byron's genius could not work upon the same lines as Goethe's; nor can dramas, hurriedly conceived and rapidly executed, without a distinct philosophical intention, be compared with the slowly elaborated masterpiece of a lifetime, which condenses and anticipates the profoundest thoughts of the nineteenth century. In *Manfred* the type of character which had previously been sketched by Byron in his romantic poems, receives more concentrated expression. Manfred is the incarnation of a defiant, guilty, self-reliant personality, preserved from despair by its disdainful pride, linked to the common joys and sorrows of humanity by the slender but still vital thread of a passion which is also an unforgotten and unforgivable crime. The egotism which is the source and secret of his vaunted strength, foredooms Manfred to destruction; yet at the close of his course, he does not flinch. Such self-sustained stubbornness was Byron's ideal. But he infected the type with something melo-dramatic, which lowered it below the defiance of the Greek Pro-metheus, and he prepared no reconciliation of opposing motives in his dramatic scheme. Tested by common experience, the character he created in Manfred was soon found wanting in the essential elements of reality.

Byron's removal to Venice in 1817 marks a no less important epoch in his career than the meeting with Shelley at Geneva. He now came into close contact with the Italian genius in its raciest expression. He studied the writers of burlesque, and fastened with partiality on Pulci, two books of whose *Morgante Maggiore* he after-wards translated. It must not be imagined that the new form he was about to invent for English literature was borrowed from the Italian. Hookham Frere, in the octave stanzas of *Whistlecraft*, had already naturalised the Tuscan humoristic style. But neither the example of Frere nor the far more powerful influence of the Italian poets will suffice to account for *Beppo* and *Don Juan*. The blending of satire with description, of realism with imagination, of drollery with ideal beauty, were Italian possessions before Byron seized on them. But he added something characteristically his own. In *Beppo* he treated the incidents of a Venetian *novella*. At the same time he stood so completely outside his subject, and informed it with humour at once so far more pungent and so far more universal than pervades the best work of his supposed models, that Europe received at his hands a species hitherto unguessed and undiscovered. *Beppo* seems to have revealed to Byron the power that had been latent in him from the earliest days of boyhood; but which, partly from modesty and partly from the misdirection of his faculties, due to critical incapacity, had lain dormant. He found that he possessed an unrivalled command of comedy. *Beppo* was but a prelude to the two great works, *Don Juan* and *The Vision of Judgment*, on which his fame will ultimately rest, and last as long as there are minds to comprehend their many-sided excellence.

In the year 1818 Byron began *Don Juan*. Until his death in 1824 he used it as the channel of expression for the varied reminiscences of past experience, and for the miscellaneous pictures of society and human life with which his mind was stored. It was a poem without a plan, and for this very reason well adapted to his purpose. Juan is a name: the fact that his parentage and earliest adventures are Spanish does not bring him into competition with the Don Juan of Spanish legend. He has but little in common with the hero of Molière's play or Mozart's opera. Juan's biography is the thread on which Byron hangs descriptions, episodes, satirical digressions, and reflective passages of brilliant audacity. That *Don Juan*, as Byron began it in the extant sixteen cantos, should have arrived at a conclusion, seems inconceivable. It was therefore scarcely a misfortune that death cut the poet short, when he had closed the fourth chapter of his hero's adventures. Byron, it may be observed, was essentially an occasional poet. He needed some substratum of fact or personal emotion for his imaginative edifices, and wrote best when he was least hampered by self-imposed theories of art. *Childe Harold* and *Don Juan* may therefore be regarded as continuous poetic journals. He used them as receptacles for the ideas that every passing day suggested. 'If things are farcical,' he once said to Trelawny, during their voyage to Greece, 'they will do for *Don Juan*; if heroical, you shall have another canto of *Childe Harold*.' This accounts for the defect of structure in both poems. But while the change of style and tone in *Childe Harold* has been already pointed out, no such failure can be indicated in *Don Juan*. Within itself, and judged by the laws of its own nature, it is vigorously organised. The flux and reflux of contrasted incidents,—the balance of emotions between pathos and comedy, humour and satire,—the correspondence of voluptuous and piquant, sensual and tender, touches,—the passage from Donna Julia to Haidee and Dudu,—the siege succeeding to the shipwreck,—the picture of St. Petersburgh under Catherine followed by that of England ruled by Whig and Tory peers;—this counterpoise of interests, this rapid modulation from key to key, gives to *Don Juan*, fragment as it is, a fine artistic coherence.

The Drama lies outside the scope of this book. It is not therefore necessary to speak in detail about the tragedies, which occupied much of Byron's time at Venice and Ravenna, but which, neither as acting plays nor as poems, can be reckoned among his masterpieces. *Cain* and *Heaven and Earth*, called 'Mysteries' by their author, detach themselves from the rest, because Byron's insufficiency as a dramatist was in both these cases covered by the peculiar piquancy of the subject-matter. *Cain*, on its first appearance, had a veritable success of scandal; but, since its day, our advance in religious toleration and freedom of speech has shorn its daring scenes of half their lustre. The case is very different with *The Vision of Judgment*. In this poem, composed upon an event of so ephemeral importance as George III's funeral, and inspired by so trivial a passion as spite against Southey, Byron displayed in short compass the range and scope of his peculiar powers. His humour, common sense, inventive faculty, and luminous imagination, are here, as nowhere else, combined in perfect fusion. We only miss the pathos and the sympathy with nature displayed in previous compositions of a different purpose. The octave stanza, which he had essayed in *Beppo*, and perfected in *Don Juan*, is used with unrivalled command of its resources. Like some elemental substance taking shape beneath a spirit-touch, the metre obeys his will, and from the slightest bias of his fancy assumes imperishable form. Satire, which at the outset of Byron's career crawled like a serpent, has here acquired the wings and mailed panoply of a dragon. The poetry of *The Vision of Judgment*, sustained by the companion pictures of Lucifer and Michael, is no less brilliant than its burlesque, expressed in St. Peter and the King.

Byron's best poetry admits of no selections being made from it. He was deficient in those qualities of ear and taste which are necessary for the production of studied perfection on a small scale. We must admire him for the sweep and strength of his genius, or not at all. With the exception of a few personal lyrics, characterised by simplicity of feeling and limpidity of style, his shorter pieces do not adequately represent him. He succeeded best in all the mixed specimens he attempted. But precisely because those poems blend so many qualities, contrasted and assimilated by the poet's power, they cannot be perused in fragments. We may reckon this impossibility of doing justice to Byron by selections among the reasons for his present comparative neglect. Yet the change of opinion which has taken place among cultivated people during the last half century in this respect, is so striking, that no critic of Byron can avoid discussing it. To do so is in fact the simplest way of ascertaining his place in literature. During his lifetime he enjoyed a renown which has rarely fallen to the lot of any living writer. At the present day it is common to hear people asserting that Byron was not a true poet. Some causes of this revolution are patent. In the first place he cannot be called a moral poet. His collected works are not of a kind to be recommended for family reading; and the poems in which his genius shines most clearly, are precisely those which lie open to the charges of cynicism, unorthodoxy, or licentiousness. Again, he suffers from the very range and versatility of his performance. Like the Roman Empire, *magnitudine laborat suâ.*[1] His masterpieces are long, and make considerable demands upon the reader's patience. Byron has suffered even more from the mixed quality of his work. Not only are his poems voluminous, but they are exceedingly unequal; nor is it so easy, as in the case of Wordsworth, to separate what is worthless from the imperishable creations of his genius. The sudden burst of glory which followed upon the publication of *Childe Harold,* and the indiscriminate enthusiasm of his admirers, injured Byron during his lifetime by establishing the certainty that whatever he wrote would be read. It has injured him still more with posterity by stirring a reaction against claims in some respects so obviously ill-founded. Instead of subjecting the whole mass of Byron's poetry to a careful criticism, the world has been contented lately to reckon it among the nine days' wonders of a previous age. This injustice would, however, have been impossible, unless a current of taste inimical to Byron had set in soon after his death. Students of literature in England began about that period to assimilate Wordsworth, Coleridge, Keats, Shelley, Landor—those very poets whom Byron, in his uncritical arrogance, had despised or neglected. Their ears became accustomed to versification more exquisite and careful, to harmonies deeper and more refined if less resonant and brilliant. They learned to demand a more patient and studied delineation of natural beauty, passion more reserved, artistic aims at once more sober and more earnest, and emotions of a less obtrusively personal type. Tennyson

[1] ['He struggles under his own greatness.']

and Browning, with all the poet-artists of the present generation, represent as sheer a departure from Byronian precedent as it is possible to take in literature. The very greatness of Byron has unfitted him for an audience educated in this different school of poetry. That greatness was his truth to fact, conceived as action, feeling, energy; not as the material for picture-painting, reflection, or analysis. Men nursed on the idyllic or the analytic kinds of poetry can hardly do him justice; not because he is exactly greater, or they indisputably less, but because he makes his best points in a region which is alien to their sympathy. The idyll was a species invented by the Greeks in their decline, when the passion, action and practical energy—the lyrical emotion and the dramatic fervour of their past literature—had become fit subjects for little pictures, jewels of verse, refracting the light cast on them by culture, and returning it to the eyes of the beholder in a prism of suggestive hues. Our age is in a somewhat similar sense idyllic. We are now accustomed to the art which appeals to educated sensibilities, by suggestions and reflections, by careful workmanship and attentive study of form, by artistically finished epitomes of feeling, by picturesquely blended reminiscences of realism, culture, and poetical idealism. Byron's work is too primitive, too like the raw material of poetry, in its crudity and inequality, to suit our Neo-Alexandrian taste. He wounds our sympathies; he violates our canons of correctness; he fails to satisfy our subtlest sense of art. He showers upon us in profusion what we do not want, and withholds the things for which we have been trained to crave. His personality inspires no love, like that which makes the devotees of Shelley as faithful to the man as they are loyal to the poet. His intellect, though robust and masculine, is not of the kind to which we willingly submit. As a man, as a thinker, as an artist, he is out of harmony with us. Nevertheless nothing can be more certain than Byron's commanding place in English literature. He is the only British poet of the nineteenth century who is also European; nor will the lapse of time fail to make his greatness clearer to his fellow-countrymen, when a just critical judgment finally dominates the fluctuations of fashion to which he has been subject.

It is desirable in all disputed cases to readjust the balance of criticism by reference to authorities who command attention. This disposes me to quote the opinions of Byron's most eminent contemporaries, not because they seem to represent the final truth about his poetry, but because their deliberate enthusiasm must force the reader to a reconsideration of his merits. Shelley, who was no mean critic, and who was certainly not blinded to Byron's faults by their close intimacy, wrote of him in private correspondence thus: 'He touched the chord to which a million hearts responded, and the coarse music which he produced to please them, disciplined him to the perfection to which he now approaches.' This was in 1822. Again, in an earlier letter of the same year: 'Space wondered less at the swift and fair creations of God when he grew weary of vacancy, than I at this spirit of an angel in the mortal paradise of a decaying body.' Goethe, in conversation with Eckermann, after death had removed the English peer and poet above all reach of flattery, said: 'The English may think of Byron as they please; but this is certain, that they can show no poet who is to be compared with him. He is different from all the others, and for the most part, greater.' That this was no hasty utterance, is proved by Euphorion's part, assigned to Byron, in *Faust*, as the typical modern poet, and by many parallel passages in Eckermann's book of *Table Talk*. Mazzini, to quote an authority of a different type, breaks, at the end of his essay on Goethe and Byron, into the following vindication of the poet's claim: 'The day will come when Democracy will remember all that it owes to Byron. England too will, I hope, one day remember the mission—so entirely English, yet hitherto overlooked by her—which Byron fulfilled on the continent; the European rôle given by him to English literature, and the appreciation and sympathy for England which he awakened amongst us. Before he came, all that was known of English literature was the French translation of Shakespeare, and the anathema hurled by Voltaire against the "intoxicated barbarian." It is since Byron that we Continentalists have learned to study Shakespeare and other English writers. From him dates the sympathy of all the true-hearted amongst us for this land of liberty, whose true vocation he so worthily represented among the oppressed. He led the genius of Britain on a pilgrimage throughout all Europe.'

The judgments I have cited are of value when we seek to discern Byron's merits with eyes unblinded by contemporary prejudice. If we measure him from the standpoint of British literature, where of absolute perfection in verse there is perhaps less than we desire, he will scarcely bear the test of niceness to which our present rules of taste expose him. But if we try him by the standards of universal literature, where of finish and exactitude in execution there is plenty, we shall find that he has qualities of strength and elasticity, of elemental sweep and energy, which condone all defects in technical achievement. Such power, sincerity and radiance, such directness of generous enthusiasm and disengagement from local or patriotic prepossessions, such sympathy with the forces of humanity in movement after freedom, such play of humour and passion, as Byron pours into the common stock, are no slight contributions. Europe does not need to make the discount upon Byron's claims to greatness that are made by his own country.

59. Ruskin on Byron

1841–86

John Ruskin (1819–1900) wrote an impassioned defence of Byron in an essay for his tutor in 1836, and throughout his life he continued to comment, often very perceptively, on Byron's poetry. The following specimens are quoted from *The Works of John Ruskin*, ed. E. T. Cook and Alexander Wedderburn, 1903–12.

(a) Extracts from *Praeterita* (1885–9). *Works*, XXXV, 141–3, 144–6, 148–51: '. . . I do not know when my father first began to read Byron to me, with any expectation of my liking him—all primary training, after the *Iliad*, having been in Scott; but it must have been about the beginning of the teen period, else I should recollect the first effect of it. *Manfred* evidently I had got at, like *Macbeth*, for the sake of the witches. Various questionable changes were made, however, at that 1831 turning of twelve, in the hermitage discipline of Herne Hill. I was allowed to taste wine; taken to the theatre; and, on festive days, even dined with my father and mother at four: and it was then generally at dessert that my father would read any otherwise suspected delight: the *Noctes Ambrosianae* regularly when they came out—without the least missing of the naughty words; and at last, the shipwreck in *Don Juan*,—of which, finding me rightly appreciative, my father went on with nearly all the rest. I recollect that he and my mother looked across the table at each other with something of alarm, when, on asking me, a few festas afterwards, what we should have for after-dinner reading, I instantly answered "Juan and Haidée." My selection was not adopted, and, feeling there was something wrong somewhere, I did not press it, attempting even some stutter of apology which made matters worse. Perhaps I was given a bit of *Childe Harold* instead, which I liked at that time nearly as well; and, indeed, the story of Haidée soon became too sad for me. But very certainly, by the end of this year 1834, I knew my Byron pretty well all through, all but *Cain*, *Werner*, the *Deformed Transformed*, and *Vision of Judgment*, none of which I could understand, nor did papa and mamma think it would be well I should try to.

The ingenuous reader may perhaps be so much surprised that mamma fell in with all this, that it becomes here needful to mark for him some peculiarities in my mother's prudery which he could not discover for himself, from anything hitherto told of her. He might indeed guess that, after taking me at least six times straight through the Bible, she was not afraid of plain words to, or for, me; but might not feel that in the energy and affectionateness of her character, she had as much sympathy with all that is noble and beautiful in Byron as my father himself; nor that her Puritanism was clear enough in common sense to see that, while Shakespeare and Burns lay open on the table all day, there was no reason for much mystery with Byron (though until later I was not allowed to read him for myself). She had trust in my disposition and education, and was no more afraid of my turning out a Corsair or a Giaour than a Richard III, or a—Solomon. And she was perfectly right, so far. I never got the slightest harm from Byron: what harm came to me was from the facts of life, and from books of a baser kind, including a wide range of the works of authors popularly considered extremely instructive—from Victor Hugo down to Doctor Watts. . . .'

'. . . There was a hearty, frank, and sometimes even irrepressible, laugh in my mother! Never sardonic, yet with a very definitely Smollettesque turn in it! so that, between themselves, she and my father enjoyed their *Humphry Clinker* extremely, long before *I* was able to understand either the jest or gist of it. Much more, she could exult in a harmless bit of Smollettesque reality. . . .

If, however, there was the least bitterness or irony in a jest, my mother did not like it; but my father and I liked it all the more, if it were just; and, so far as I could understand it, I rejoiced in all the sarcasm of *Don Juan*. But my firm decision, as soon as I got well into the later cantos of it, that Byron was to be my master in verse, as Turner in colour, was made of course in that gosling (or say cygnet) epoch of existence, without consciousness of the deeper instincts that prompted it: only two things I consciously recognized, that his truth of observation was the most exact, and his chosen expression the most concentrated, that I had yet found in literature. By that time my father had himself put me through the two first books of Livy, and I knew, therefore, what close-set language was; but I saw then that Livy, as afterwards that Horace and Tacitus, were studiously, often laboriously, and sometimes obscurely, concentrated: while Byron wrote, as easily as a hawk flies and as clearly as a lake reflects, the exact truth in the precisely narrowest terms; nor only the exact truth, but the most central and useful one.

Of course I could no more measure Byron's greater powers at that time than I could Turner's; but I saw that both were right in all things that *I* knew right from wrong in; and that they must thenceforth be my masters, each in his own domain. The modern reader, not to say also, modern scholar, is usually so ignorant of the essential qualities of Byron, that I cannot go farther in the story of my own novitiate under him without illustrating, by rapid example, the things which I saw to be unrivalled in his work.

For this purpose I take his common prose, rather than his verse, since his modes of rhythm involve other questions than those with which I am now concerned. Read, for chance-first, the sentence on Sheridan, in his letter to Thomas Moore, from Venice, June 1st (or dawn of June 2nd!), 1818:

The Whigs abuse him; however, he never left them, and such blunderers deserve neither credit nor compassion. As for his creditors—remember Sheridan never had a shilling, and was thrown, with great powers and passions, into the thick of the world, and placed upon the pinnacle of success, with no other external means to support him in his elevation. Did Fox pay *his* debts? or did Sheridan take a subscription? Was ——'s drunkenness more excusable than his? Were his intrigues more notorious than those of all his contemporaries? and is his memory to be blasted and theirs respected? Don't let yourself be led away by clamour, but compare him with the coalitioner Fox, and the pensioner Burke, as a man of principle; and with ten hundred thousand in personal views; and with none in talent, for he beat them all out and out. Without means, without connection, without character (which might be false at first, and drive him mad afterwards from desperation), he beat them all, in all he ever attempted. But, alas poor human nature! Good-night, or rather morning. It is four, and the dawn gleams over the Grand Canal, and unshadows the Rialto.

Now, observe, that passage is noble, primarily because it contains the utmost number that will come together into the space, of absolutely just, wise, and kind thoughts. But it is more than noble, it is *perfect*, because the quantity it holds is not artificially or intricately concentrated, but with the serene swiftness of a smith's hammer-strokes on hot iron; and with choice of terms which, each in its place, will convey far more than they mean in the dictionary. Thus, "however" is used instead of "yet," because it stands for "howsoever," or, in full, for "yet whatever they did." "Thick" of society, because it means, not merely the crowd, but the *fog* of it; "ten hundred thousand" instead of "a million," or "a thousand thousand," to take the sublimity out of the number, and make us feel that it is a number of nobodies. Then the sentence in parenthesis, "which might be false," etc., is indeed obscure, because it was impossible to clarify it without a regular pause, and much loss of time; and the reader's sense is therefore left to expand it for himself into "it was, perhaps, falsely said of him at first, that he had no character," etc. Finally, the dawn "unshadows"—lessens the shadow on—the Rialto, but does not *gleam* on that, as on the broad water. . . .'

'But neither the force and precision, nor the rhythm, of Byron's language, were at all the central reasons for my taking him for master. Knowing the Song of Moses and the Sermon on the Mount by heart, and half the Apocalypse besides, I was in no need of tutorship either in the majesty or simplicity of English words; and for their logical arrangement, I had Byron's own master, Pope, since I could lisp. But the thing wholly new and precious to me in Byron was his measured and living *truth*—measured, as compared with Homer; and living, as compared with everybody else. My own inexorable measuring wand,—not enchanter's, but cloth-worker's and builder's,—reduced to mere incredibility all the statements of the poets usually called sublime. It was of no use for Homer to tell me that Pelion was put on the top of Ossa. I knew perfectly well it wouldn't go on the top of Ossa. Of no use for Pope to tell me that trees where his mistress looked would crowd into a shade, because I was satisfied that they would do nothing of the sort. Nay, the whole world, as it was described to me either by poetry or theology, was every hour becoming more and more shadowy and impossible. I rejoiced in all stories of Pallas and Venus, of Achilles and Aeneas, of Elijah and St. John: but, without doubting in my heart that there were real spirits of wisdom and beauty, nor that there had been invincible heroes and inspired prophets, I felt already, with fatal and increasing sadness, that there was no clear utterance about any of them—that there were for *me* neither Goddess guides nor prophetic teachers; and that the poetical histories, whether of this world or the next, were to me as the words of Peter to the shut up disciples—"as idle tales; and they believed them not".

But here at last I had found a man who spoke only of what he had seen, and known; and spoke without exaggeration, without mystery, without enmity, and without mercy. "That *is* so;—make what you will of it!" Shakespeare said the Alps voided their rheum on the valleys, which indeed is precisely true . . .,—but it was told in a mythic manner, and with an unpleasant British bias to the nasty. But Byron, saying that "the glacier's cold and restless mass moved onward day by day," said plainly what he saw and knew,—no more. So also, the *Arabian Nights* had told me of thieves who lived in enchanted caves, and beauties who fought with genii in the air; but Byron told me of thieves with whom he had ridden on their own hills, and of the fair Persians or Greeks who lived and died under the very sun that rose over my visible Norwood hills.

And in this narrow, but sure, truth, to Byron, as already to me, it appeared that Love was a transient thing, and Death a dreadful one. He did not attempt to console me for Jessie's death, by saying she was happier in Heaven; or for Charles's, by saying it was a Providential dispensation to me on Earth.[1] He did not tell me that war was a just price for the glory of captains, or that the National command of murder diminished its guilt. Of all things within range of human thought he felt the facts, and discerned the natures with accurate justice.

But even all this he might have done, and yet been no master of mine, had not he sympathized with me in reverent love of beauty, and indignant recoil from ugliness. The witch of the Staubbach in her rainbow was a greatly more pleasant vision than Shakespeare's, like a rat without a tail, or Burns's, in her cutty sark. The sea-king Conrad had an immediate advantage with me over Coleridge's long, lank, brown, and ancient, mariner; and whatever Pope might have gracefully said, or honestly felt of Windsor woods and streams, was mere tinkling cymbal to me, compared with Byron's love of Lachin-y-Gair.

I must pause here, in tracing the sources of his influence over me, lest the reader should mistake the analysis which I am now able to give them, for a description of the feelings possible to me at fifteen. Most of these, however, were assuredly within the knot of my unfolding mind —as the saffron of the crocus yet beneath the earth; and Byron— though he could not teach me to love mountains or sea more than I did in childhood, first animated them for me with the sense of real human nobleness and grief. He taught me the meaning of Chillon

[1] [When Ruskin was still a child, his little cousin Jessie 'fell ill, and died very slowly, of water on the brain', and when he was in his early teens, his favourite cousin Charles was drowned at Spithead (*Praeterita*, pp. 70, 136–7).]

and of Meillerie, and bade me seek first in Venice—the ruined homes of Foscari and Falier.

And observe, the force with which he struck depended again on there being unquestionable reality of person in his stories, as of principle in his thoughts. Romance, enough and to spare, I had learnt from Scott —but his Lady of the Lake was as openly fictitious as his White Maid of Avenel: while Rogers was a mere dilettante, who felt no difference between landing "where Tell leaped ashore," or standing where "St. Preux has stood." Even Shakespeare's Venice was visionary; and Portia as impossible as Miranda. But Byron told me of, and reanimated for me, the real people whose feet had worn the marble I trod on.

One word only, though it trenches on a future subject, I must permit myself about his rhythm. Its natural flow in almost prosaic simplicity and tranquillity interested me extremely, in opposition alike to the symmetrical clauses of Pope's logical metre, and to the balanced strophes of classic and Hebrew verse. But though I followed his manner instantly in what verses I wrote for my own amusement, my respect for the structural, as opposed to fluent, force of the classic measures, supported as it was partly by Byron's contempt for his own work, and partly by my own architect's instinct for "the principle of the pyramid," made me long endeavour, in forming my prose style. to keep the cadences of Pope and Johnson for all serious statement. . . .'

(*b*) Extract from *Letters Addressed to a College Friend During the Years 1840–1845* (1894). *Works*, I, 441–3: 'The object in all *art* is not to *inform* but to *suggest*, not to add to the knowledge but to kindle the imagination. He is the best poet who can by the fewest words touch the greatest number of secret chords of thought in his reader's own mind, and set *them* to work in their own way. I will take a simple instance in epithet. Byron begins something or other—"Tis midnight: on the mountains brown—The pale round moon shines deeply down."[1] Now the first eleven words are not poetry, except by their measure and preparation for rhyme; they are simple information, which might just as well have been given in prose—it *is* prose, in fact: It is twelve o'clock—the moon is pale—it is round—it is shining on brown mountains. Any fool, who had seen it, could tell us that. At last comes the poetry, in the single epithet, "deeply". Had he said "softly" or "brightly" it would still have been simple information.

[1] [See *The Siege of Corinth*, ll. 242–3.]

But of all the readers of that couplet, probably not two received exactly the same impression from the "deeply", and yet received more from that than from all the rest together. Some will refer the expression to the fall of the steep beams, and plunge down with them from rock to rock into the woody darkness of the cloven ravines, down to the undermost pool of eddying black water, whose echo is lost among their leafage; others will think of the deep heaven, the silent sea, that is drinking the light into its infinity; others of the deep *feeling* of the pure light, of the thousand memories and emotions that rise out of their rest, and are seen white and cold in its rays. This is the reason of the power of the single epithet, and this is its *mystery*.

Where it is thus desired, as in almost all good poetry it is, that the reader should work out much for himself, it becomes necessary to keep his mind in a peculiar temper, adapted for the exercise of the imagination: to do this, rhyme and rhythm are introduced, as melody, to assist the fancy, and bring the whole mind into an elevated and yet soothed spirituality. Where nothing is to be left to the imagination, where all is to be told downright, this is totally unnecessary: we can receive plain facts in any temper.

Now, in all art, whatever is not useful is detrimental. Rhyme and rhythm are, therefore, thoroughly injurious where there is no mystery, when there is not some undermeaning, some repressed feeling; and thus, in five-sixths of Scott's poetry, as it is called, the metre is an absolute excrescence, the rhythm degenerates into childish jingle, and the rhyme into unseemly fetters to yoke the convicted verses together.

Rokeby, had it been written in his own noble prose style, would have been one of his very first-raters; at present, it is neglected even by his most ardent admirers. And thus, not only is obscurity necessary to poetry, it is the only apology for writing it.

My space is diminishing so fast that I cannot say what I would of particular men, or I think I could show you in any real poet, Shakespeare, Wordsworth, Coleridge, Shelley, Byron, Spenser, G. Herbert, Elizabeth Barrett—whom you choose—that their finest passages never can be fathomed in a minute, or in ten minutes, or exhausted in as many years.'

(c) Extract from *Lectures on Architecture and Painting* (1854). *Works*, XII, 54–6: '. . . The real and proper use of the word romantic is simply to characterise an improbable or unaccustomed degree of beauty, sublimity, or virtue. For instance, in matters of history, is not the Retreat of the Ten Thousand romantic? Is not the death of Leonidas? of the Horatii? On the other hand, you find nothing romantic, though much that is monstrous, in the excesses of Tiberius or Commodus. So again, the battle of Agincourt is romantic, and of Bannockburn, simply because there was an extraordinary display of human virtue in both these battles. But there is no romance in the battles of the last Italian campaign,[1] in which mere feebleness and distrust were on one side, mere physical force on the other. And even in fiction, the opponents of virtue, in order to be romantic, must have sublimity mingled with their vice. It is not the knave, not the ruffian, that are romantic, but the giant and the dragon; and these, not because they are false, but because they are majestic. So again as to beauty. You feel that armour is romantic, because it is a beautiful dress, and you are not used to it. You do not feel there is anything romantic in the paint and shells of a Sandwich Islander, for these are not beautiful.

So, then, observe, this feeling which you are accustomed to despise —this secret and poetical enthusiasm in all your hearts, which, as practical men, you try to restrain—is indeed one of the holiest parts of your being. It is the instinctive delight in, and admiration for, sublimity, beauty, and virtue, unusually manifested. And so far from being a dangerous guide, it is the truest part of your being. It is even truer than your consciences. A man's conscience may be utterly perverted and led astray; but so long as the feelings of romance endure within us, they are unerring,—they are as true to what is right and lovely as the needle to the north; and all that you have to do is to add to the enthusiastic sentiment, the majestic judgment—to mingle prudence and foresight with imagination and admiration, and you have the perfect human soul. But the great evil of these days is that we try to destroy the romantic feeling, instead of bridling and directing it. Mark what Young says of the men of the world:

> They, who think nought so strong of the romance,
> So rank knight-errant, as a real friend.

And they are right. True friendship is romantic, to the men of the world—true affection is romantic—true religion is romantic; and if you were to ask me who of all powerful and popular writers in the cause of error had wrought most harm to their race, I should hesitate

[1] ['The unsuccessful Italian war of independence against the Austrians, 1848–1849' (Cook and Wedderburn).]

in reply whether to name Voltaire, or Byron, or the last most ingenious and most venomous of the degraded philosophers of Germany,[1] or rather Cervantes, for he cast scorn upon the holiest principles of humanity—he, of all men, most helped forward the terrible change in the soldiers of Europe, from the spirit of Bayard to the spirit of Bona-parte, helped to change loyalty into license, protection into plunder, truth into treachery, chivalry into selfishness; and, since his time, the purest impulses and the noblest purposes have perhaps been oftener stayed by the devil, under the name of Quixotism, than under any other base name or false allegation.'

(*d*) Extract from *Modern Painters*, Vol. III (1856). *Works*, V, 334–5:
'. . . the mass of sentimental literature, concerned with the analysis and description of emotion, headed by the poetry of Byron, is alto-gether of lower rank than the literature which merely describes what it saw. The true Seer always feels as intensely as any one else; but he does not much describe his feelings. He tells you whom he met, and what they said; leaves you to make out, from that, what they feel, and what he feels, but goes into little detail. And, generally speaking, pathetic writing and careful explanation of passion are quite easy, compared with this plain recording of what people said and did, or with the right invention of what they are likely to say or do; for this reason, that to invent a story, or admirably and thoroughly tell any part of a story, it is necessary to grasp the entire mind of every personage concerned in it, and know precisely how they would be affected by what happens; which to do requires a colossal intellect: but to describe a separate emotion delicately, it is only needed that one should feel it oneself; and thousands of people are capable of feeling this or that noble emotion, for one who is able to enter into all the feelings of somebody sitting on the other side of the table. Even, therefore, where this sentimental literature is first-rate, as in passages of Byron, Tenny-son, and Keats, it ought not to be ranked so high as the Creative; and though perfection, even in narrow fields, is perhaps as rare as in the wider, and it may be as long before we have another *In Memoriam* as another *Guy Mannering*, I unhesitatingly receive as a greater mani-festation of power the right invention of a few sentences spoken by Pleydell and Mannering across their supper-table, than the most tender and passionate melodies of the self-examining verse.'

[1] [I.e. Schopenhauer.]

(*e*) Extract from commentary on Turner's painting 'Childe Harold's Pilgrimage', in *Notes on the Turner Collection* (1857). *Works*, XIII, 143–4: '. . . the illustration is imperfect, just because it misses the *manliest* characters of Byron's mind: Turner was fitter to paint Childe Harold when he himself could both mock and weep, than now, when he can only dream: and, beautiful as the dream may be, he but joins in the injustice too many have done to Byron, in dwelling rather on the passionate than the reflective and analytic elements of his intellect. I believe no great power is sent on earth to be wasted, but that it must, in some sort, do an appointed work: and Byron would not have done this work, if he had only given melody to the passions, and majesty to the pangs, of men. His clear insight into their foibles; his deep sympathy with justice, kindness, and courage; his intense reach of pity, never failing, however far he had to stoop to lay his hand on a human heart, have all been lost sight of, either in too fond admiration of his slighter gifts, or in narrow judgment of the errors which burst into all the more flagrant manifestation, just because they were inconsistent with half his soul, and could never become incarnate, accepted, silent sin, but had still to fight for their hold on him. Turner was strongly influenced, from this time forward, by Byron's love of nature; but it is curious how unaware he seems of the sterner war of his will and intellect; and how little this quiet and fair landscape, with its delicate ruin, and softened light, does in reality express the tones of thought into which Harold falls oftenest, in that watchful and weary pilgrimage.'

(*f*) Extracts from *Fiction, Fair and Foul* (1880–1). *Works*, XXXIV, 328–34, 341–4: '. . . He was the first great Englishman who felt the cruelty of war, and, in its cruelty, the shame. Its guilt had been known to George Fox—its folly shown practically by Penn. But the *compassion* of the pious world had still for the most part been shown only in keeping its stock of Barabbases unhanged if possible: and, till Byron came, neither Kunersdorf, Eylau, nor Waterloo, had taught the pity and the pride of men that

> The drying up a single tear has more
> Of honest fame than shedding seas of gore.

Such pacific verse would not indeed have been acceptable to the Edinburgh volunteers[1] on Portobello sands. But Byron can write a

---

[1] ['Which Scott had joined on the enrolment of the Edinburgh Light Horse in 1797' (Cook and Wedderburn).]

battle song too, when it is *his* cue to fight. If you look at the introduction to the "Isles of Greece," namely the 85th and 86th stanzas of
the 3rd canto of *Don Juan,* you will find—what will you *not* find, if
only you understand them! "He" in the first line, remember, means
the typical modern poet.

> Thus usually, when he was asked to sing,
>   He gave the different nations something national.
> 'Twas all the same to him—'God save the King'
>   Or 'Ça ira' according to the fashion all;
> His muse made increment of anything
>   From the high lyric down to the low rational:
> If Pindar sang horse-races, what should hinder
> Himself from being as pliable as Pindar?
>
> In France, for instance, he would write a chanson;
>   In England a six-canto quarto tale;
> In Spain, he'd make a ballad or romance on
>   The last war—much the same in Portugal;
> In Germany, the Pegasus he'd prance on
>   Would be old Goethe's—(see what says de Staël)
> In Italy, he'd ape the 'Trecentisti';
> In Greece, he'd sing some sort of hymn like this t' ye.

Note first here . . . the concentrating and foretelling power.
The "God save the Queen" in England, fallen hollow now, as the
"Ça ira" in France—not a man in France knowing where either
France or "that" (whatever "that" may be) is going to; nor the
Queen of England daring, for her life, to ask the tiniest Englishman
to do a single thing he doesn't like;—nor any salvation, either of
Queen or Realm, being any more possible to God, unless under the
direction of the Royal Society: then, note the estimate of height and
depth in poetry, swept in an instant, "high lyric to low rational."
Pindar to Pope (knowing Pope's height, too, all the while, no man
better); then, the poetic power of France—resumed in a word—
Béranger; then the cut at *Marmion,* entirely deserved, as we shall see,
yet kindly given, for everything he names in these two stanzas is the
best of its kind; then Romance in Spain on—the *last* war, (*present*
war not being to Spanish poetical taste); then, Goethe the real heart
of all Germany, and last, the aping of the Trecentisti which has since
consummated itself in Pre-Raphaelitism! that also being the best
thing Italy has done through England, whether in Rossetti's "blessed
damozels" or Burne-Jones's "days of creation." Lastly comes the

mock at himself—the modern English Greek—(followed up by the "degenerate into hands like mine" in the song itself); and then—to amazement, forth he thunders in his Achilles-voice. We have had one line of him in his clearness—five of him in his depth—sixteen of him in his play. Hear now but these, out of his whole heart:

> What,—silent yet? and silent *all?*
> Ah no, the voices of the dead
> Sound like a distant torrent's fall,
> And answer, 'Let *one* living head,
> But one, arise—we come—we come:'
> —'Tis but the living who are dumb.

Resurrection, this, you see like Bürger's; but not of death unto death.[1]

"Sound like a distant torrent's fall." I said the *whole* heart of Byron was in this passage. First its compassion, then its indignation, and the third element, not yet examined, that love of the beauty of this world in which the three—unholy—children, of its Fiery Furnace were like to each other; but Byron the widest-hearted. Scott and Burns love Scotland more than Nature itself: for Burns the moon must rise over Cumnock Hills,—for Scott, the Rymer's glen divide the Eildons; but, for Byron, Loch-na-Gar *with Ida*, looks o'er Troy, and the soft murmurs of the Dee and the Bruar change into voices of the dead on distant Marathon.

Yet take the parallel from Scott, by a field of homelier rest:

> And silence aids—though the steep hills
> Send to the lake a thousand rills;
> In summer tide, so soft they weep,
> The sound but lulls the ear asleep;
> Your horse's hoof-tread sounds too rude,
> So stilly is the solitude.
>
> Nought living meets the eye or ear,
> But well I ween the dead are near;
> For though, in feudal strife, a foe
> Hath laid our Lady's Chapel low,
> Yet still beneath the hallowed soil,
> The peasant rests him from his toil,
> And, dying, bids his bones be laid
> Where erst his simple fathers prayed.

[1] [A reference to the ballad of Leonora 'whose dead lover takes horse and rides with her to Death' (Cook and Wedderburn).]

And last take the same note of sorrow—with Burns's finger on the fall of it:

> Mourn, ilka grove the cushat kens,
> Ye hazly shaws and briery dens,
> Ye burnies, wimplin' down your glens
> > Wi' toddlin' din,
> Or foamin' strang wi' hasty stens
> > Frae lin to lin.

As you read, one after another, these fragments of chant by the great masters, does not a sense come upon you of some element in their passion, no less than in their sound, different, specifically, from that of "Parching summer hath no warrant"?[1] Is it more profane, think you—or more tender—nay, perhaps, in the core of it, more true?

For instance, when we are told that

> Wharfe, as he moved along,
> To matins joined a mournful voice,

is this disposition of the river's mind to pensive psalmody quite logically accounted for by the previous statement, (itself by no means rhythmically dulcet,) that

> The boy is in the arms of Wharfe,
> And strangled by a merciless force?

Or, when we are led into the improving reflection,

> How sweet were leisure, could it yield no more
> Than 'mid this wave-washed churchyard to recline,
> From pastoral graves extracting thoughts divine!

[1] [A quotation from one of Wordsworth's 'Inscriptions' (*The Poetical Works of Wordsworth*, Oxford Standard Authors, 1960, p. 431):

> 'Parching Summer hath no warrant
> To consume this crystal Well;
> Rains, that make each rill a torrent,
> Neither sully it nor swell.'

This passage, like the quotations which follow from 'The Force of Prayer' and one of the River Duddon Sonnets (*op. cit.*, pp. 387–8, 302), roused Ruskin's exasperation. He thought that the piety and peace of Wordsworth's poetic vision ignored much of the suffering and nobility in human life, and he found more true compassion in Burns and Byron. Wordsworth, he declared, 'often wrote verses that were not musical, and sometimes expressed opinions that were not profound' (*Works*, XXXIV, 350). These verses are cited as examples of false or foul fiction, as opposed to fair and true.]

—is the divinity of the extract assured to us by its being made at leisure, and in a reclining attitude—as compared with the meditations of otherwise active men, in an erect one? Or are we perchance, many of us, still erring somewhat in our notions alike of Divinity and Humanity, poetical extraction, and moral position?

On the chance of its being so, might I ask hearing for just a few words more of the school of Belial?

Their occasion, it must be confessed, is a quite unjustifiable one. Some very wicked people—mutineers, in fact—have retired, misanthropically, into an unfrequented part of the country, and there find themselves safe indeed, but extremely thirsty. Whereupon Byron thus gives them to drink:

> A little stream came tumbling from the height
> And straggling into ocean as it might.
> Its bounding crystal frolicked in the ray
> And gushed from cliff to crag with saltless spray,
> Close on the wild wide ocean,—yet as pure
> And fresh as Innocence; and more secure.
> Its silver torrent glittered o'er the deep
> As the shy chamois' eye o'erlooks the steep,
> While, far below, the vast and sullen swell
> Of ocean's Alpine azure rose and fell.[1]

Now, I beg, with such authority as an old workman may take concerning his trade, having also looked at a waterfall or two in my time, and not unfrequently at a wave, to assure the reader that here *is* entirely first-rate literary work. Though Lucifer himself had written it, the thing is itself good, and not only so, but unsurpassably good, the closing line being probably the best concerning the sea yet written by the race of the sea-kings.

But Lucifer himself *could* not have written it; neither any servant of Lucifer. I do not doubt but that most readers were surprised at my saying, in the close of my first paper, that Byron's "style" depended in any wise on his views respecting the Ten Commandments. That so all-important a thing as "style" should depend in the least upon so ridiculous a thing as moral sense: or that Allegra's father, watching her drive by in Count G.'s coach and six, had any remnant of so ridiculous a thing to guide,—or check,—his poetical passion, may alike seem more than questionable to the liberal and chaste philosophy of the existing British public. But, first of all, putting the question of

[1] [See *The Island*, Canto III, ll. 63–72.]

who writes or speaks aside, do you, good reader, *know* good "style" when you get it? Can you say, of half-a-dozen given lines taken anywhere out of a novel, or poem, or play, That is good, essentially, in style, or bad, essentially? and can you say why such half-dozen lines are good, or bad?

I imagine that in most cases, the reply would be given with hesitation; yet if you will give me a little patience, and take some accurate pains, I can show you the main tests of style in the space of a couple of pages.'

[There follows an analysis of two passages from Shakespeare, demonstrating 'the conditions of greatness' which Ruskin finds common to both: 'absolute command over all passion, however intense'; 'choice of the fewest and simplest words that can be found in the compass of the language, to express the thing meant'; 'perfectly emphatic and clear utterance of the chosen words'; 'absolute spontaneity in doing all this'; 'melody in the words, changeable with their passion, fitted to it exactly, and the utmost of which the language is capable'; 'utmost spiritual contents in the words; so that each carries not only its instant meaning, but a cloudy companionship of higher or darker meaning according to the passion—nearly always indicated by metaphor.' Ruskin then goes on to discuss the additional harmonies achieved by rhyme, and illustrates sweetness, simplicity and melody from passages from *The Shepherd's Calendar*, a poem by Herrick, and 'The Phoenix and Turtle'.]

'If now, with the echo of these perfect verses in your mind, you turn to Byron, and glance over, or recall to memory, enough of him to give means of exact comparison, you will, or should, recognize these following kinds of mischief in him. First, if any one offends him—as for instance Mr. Southey, or Lord Elgin—"his manner have not that repose that marks the caste," etc.[1] *This* defect in his Lordship's style, being myself scrupulously and even painfully reserved in the use of vituperative language, I need not say how deeply I deplore.

Secondly. In the best and most violet-bedded bits of his work there is yet, as compared with Elizabethan and earlier verse, a strange taint; and indefinable—evening flavour of Covent Garden, as it were;— not to say, escape of gas in the Strand. That is simply what it proclaims itself—London air. If he had lived all his life in Green-head Ghyll, things would of course have been different. But it was his fate to come

[1] [See Tennyson's 'Lady Clara Vere de Vere'.]

to town—modern town—like Michael's son; and modern London (and Venice) are answerable for the state of their drains, not Byron.

Thirdly. His melancholy is without any relief whatsoever; his jest sadder than his earnest; while, in Elizabethan work, all lament is full of hope, and all pain of balsam.

Of this evil he has himself told you the cause in a single line, prophetic of all things since and now. "Where *he* gazed, a gloom pervaded space."[1]

So that, for instance, while Mr. Wordsworth, on a visit to town, being an exemplary early riser, could walk, felicitous, on Westminster Bridge, remarking how the city now did like a garment wear the beauty of the morning; Byron, rising somewhat later, contemplated only the garment which the beauty of the morning had by that time received for wear from the city: and again, while Mr. Wordsworth, in irrepressible religious rapture, calls God to witness that the houses seem asleep, Byron, lame demon as he was, flying smoke-drifted, unroofs the houses at a glance, and sees what the mighty cockney heart of them contains in the still lying of it, and will stir up to purpose in the waking business of it,

> The sordor of civilization, mixed
> With all the passions which Man's fall hath fixed.[2]

Fourthly, with this steadiness of bitter melancholy, there is joined a sense of the material beauty, both of inanimate nature, the lower animals, and human beings, which in the iridescence, colour-depth, and morbid (I use the word deliberately) mystery and softness of it,— with other qualities indescribable by any single words, and only to be analysed by extreme care,—is found, to the full, only in five men that I know of in modern times; namely, Rousseau, Shelley, Byron, Turner, and myself,—differing totally and throughout the entire group of us, from the delight in clear-struck beauty of Angelico and

---

[1] 'He,'—Lucifer. . . . It is precisely because Byron was *not* his servant, that he could see the gloom. To the Devil's true servants, their Master's presence brings both cheerfulness and prosperity; with a delightful sense of their own wisdom and virtue; and of the "progress" of things in general;—in smooth sea and fair weather,—and with no need either of helm touch, or oar toil: as when once one is well within the edge of Maelstrom.

[2] . . . Perfectly orthodox theology, you observe; no denial of the fall,—nor substitution of Bacterian birth for it. Nay, nearly Evangelical theology, in contempt for the human heart; but with deeper than Evangelical humility, acknowledging also what is sordid in its civilization.

the Trecentisti; and separated, much more singularly, from the cheerful joys of Chaucer, Shakespeare, and Scott, by its unaccountable affection for "Rokkes blak" and other forms of terror and power, such as those of the ice-oceans, which to Shakespeare were only Alpine rheum; and the Via Malas and Diabolic Bridges which Dante would have condemned none but lost souls to climb, or cross;—all this love of impending mountains, coiled thunder-clouds, and dangerous sea, being joined in us with a sulky, almost ferine, love of retreat in valleys of Charmettes, gulphs of Spezzia, ravines of Olympus, low lodgings in Chelsea, and close brushwood at Coniston.

And, lastly, also in the whole group of us, glows volcanic instinct of Astraean justice returning not to, but up out of, the earth, which will not at all suffer us to rest any more in Pope's serene "whatever is, is right"; but holds, on the contrary, profound conviction that about ninety-nine hundredths of whatever at present is, is wrong: conviction making four of us, according to our several manners, leaders of revolution for the poor, and declarers of political doctrine monstrous to the ears of mercenary mankind; and driving the fifth, less sanguine, into mere painted-melody of lament over the fallacy of Hope and the implacableness of Fate.

In Byron the indignation, the sorrow, and the effort are joined to the death: and they are the parts of his nature (as of mine also in its feebler terms), which the selfishly comfortable public have, literally, no conception of whatever; and from which the piously sentimental public, offering up daily the pure oblation of divine tranquillity, shrink with anathema not unembittered by alarm.'

(g) Extract from MS draft of *Fiction, Fair and Foul. Works*, XXXIV, 395-7: 'You have first to ask of all poetry, Is it good song, to begin with; had the man who put it together an ear to his head, a measure in his mind? is there true music in him? is there true symmetry?

I take up, for example nearest my hand, a bit of verse which it is almost certain nowadays that every holiday tourist to the English lakes will have the privilege of reading, and, if of a conscientious turn of mind, will think it his duty to read—Mr. Southey's description of the Fall of Lodore.

I find that Mr. Southey opens it with the remark that "Here it comes sparkling," and I find also by the context that Mr. Southey supposes this observation to be metrical, and even to be equivalent to the proper dactyl and troche dimeter of "Little Jack—Horner—sat in

the—corner." But Little Jack was written by a bard who had song in
him; whereas I farther perceive that Mr. Southey, using "Here it
comes" for a dactyl in one line, to be answered by "There it lies" in
the next, is animated by no Muse, nor Musaean spirit but only by a
wildly blundering itch for clatter; which, proceeding to tell us that the
cataract

> In this rapid race
> On which it is bent
> [It] reaches the place
> Of its steep descent,

and collecting on that occasion every jingling word that can be gathered
out of the dictionary, shakes them all out as a scullery-maid her
dustpan, achieving a series of diabolic discords, almost prophetic of the
future arrival of the railway train and the subsequent clatter of the knives
and forks at the Keswick *table d'hote*, with which the verses in question
are hereafter for ever to be accompanied. But read a line or two farther
for the sake of feeling what the false gallop of verse is in its extremity:

> The cataract strong
> Then plunges along. . . .
> Collecting, projecting,
> Receding and speeding, . . .
> And dinning and spinning
> And dropping and hopping, etc., etc.

While every girl and boy of our young English travellers (such the
will of popular education) must have this piece of disgrace to their
language and landscape nailed into their tender memories,—how many
of them—how many even of our present scholars, know this,—the
loveliest description of a shore waterfall, probably in European
literature?

> A little stream came tumbling from the height
> And straggling into ocean as it might.
> Its bounding crystal frolicked in the ray
> And gushed from cliff to crag with saltless spray,
> Close on the wild wide ocean,—yet as pure
> And fresh as Innocence; and more secure.
> Its silver torrent glittered o'er the deep
> As the shy chamois' eye o'erlooks the steep,
> While, far below, the vast and sullen swell
> *Of ocean's Alpine azure rose and fell.*'[1]

[1] See above, p. 434.

I have italicised the last line; one of those which can never be sur-passed, never superseded; which are reached only in the perfect use of a great nation's language at its utmost power.

Now, observe, the perfectness of this metrical skill in this group of lines is shown by their reserves and irregularities, just as much as by their melodies. Byron will not put out his whole force till the last line, and for the noblest piece of his subject; restricting and partly thwarting the measure at first, he gives his closing diapason with the ease of one of those Atlantic waves itself. But through all the restriction his every word tells, in thought and accent together.

I know in a moment by his first couplet that he has watched the course of *high* waterfalls, and felt how their lost and far-thrown or far-wafted spray gathers itself, as if by half paralysed effort, together in tricklets here and runlets there, and "straggles"—(the sense of straggl-ing touched as it were at the edge of the word)—on "as it may":—no channel for it now, but channel to be found from where it fell.

"Its bounding crystal frolicked in the ray." The line breaks just as the stream does. Pope would have bounded or swung regularly to the end of his pentametre—"Its bounding crystal caught a livelier ray," or the like. But Byron breaks the cadence at its mid-instant and the line itself frolics—in cascade:

> Yet as pure
> And fresh as innocence—and more secure.

He cares for innocence, then, and fears for it, this immoral person.

"As the shy chamois' eye o'erlooks the steep."—Forced, this, you think? Well—yes; but forced by concentration. He has more in his mind than he can possibly get said—chiefly, the personification of the stream as a joyful and pure creature, that "down the rocks can leap along,"[1] like maid or chamois; and *with* this, the remembrance coming to him of the far-away star-like light of the flash of a cascade among really high mountains, seen as motionless. And I know at the glance from this line that he has been among high mountains, that he has seen chamois, that he has seen mountain-maids like Louisa, and that he cares for and loves them all, in their perfect life and purity—this immoral person. And he carries me back to many a glade, dashed with stream-let-dew, among the high pines;—but chiefly of all to a little hill garden above Lucerne where, after we had been (one of my chief friends with

[1] [A reference to Wordsworth's poem 'Louisa', the heroine of which 'is fleet and strong, | And down the rocks can leap along | Like rivulets in May'.]

439

me) all day among somewhat rough Swiss peasants, suddenly a tame fawn met us,—and at the same instant we both called out the name of a young Irish girl—so deeply, so tenderly it was the image of her.

Observe finally,—with all this lovely investing light of feeling, Byron never loses sight of the absolute fact. What qualities are in the stream *like* girl or fawn, he sees intensely; he never forgets that it is but a stream after all. He will by no means let it change into a White Lady[1] or an Undine; nor shall it speak for itself, like the Talking Oak, or talking rivulet. What it *is*, he perfectly feels, perfectly shows—no more. And in like manner what everything Is. He is the truest, the sternest, Seer of the Nineteenth Century. No imagination dazzles him, no terror daunts, and no interest betrays.'

[1] [See Scott's *Monastery*. Undine—the sylph or water spirit in a romance by Baron de la Motte Fouqué. 'The Talking Oak' is a poem by Tennyson, and the talking rivulet is the same author's 'Brook'.]

60. Arnold on Byron

1850–88

Matthew Arnold (1822–88) paid a not uncritical tribute to Byron in his 'Memorial Verses. April 27, 1850', published in *Fraser's Magazine*, XLI (June 1850), 630:

> . . . When Byron's eyes were shut in death,
> We bow'd our heads and held our breath.
> He taught us little; but our soul
> Had *felt* him like the thunder's roll.
> With shivering heart the strife we saw
> Of Passion with Eternal Law,
> And yet with reverential awe
> We watch'd the fount of fiery life
> Which flow'd for that Titanic strife . . .

In subsequent writings Arnold sought to define with greater precision the nature of Byron's strengths and limitations. In 'The Function of Criticism at the Present Time' (*National Review*, November 1864; reprinted *Essays in Criticism*, 1865), he argued that 'the English poetry of the first quarter of this century, with plenty of energy, plenty of creative force, did not know enough'; and he included Byron in his indictment: 'every one can see that a poet, for instance, ought to know life and the world before dealing with them in poetry; and life and the world being, in modern times, very complex things, the creation of a modern poet, to be worth much, implies a great critical effort behind it; else it must be a comparatively poor, barren, and short-lived affair. This is why Byron's poetry had so little endurance in it, and Goethe's so much; both Byron and Goethe had a great productive power, but Goethe's was nourished by a great critical effort providing the true materials for it, and Byron's was not; Goethe knew life and the world, the poet's necessary subjects, much more comprehensively and thoroughly than Byron. He knew a great deal more of them, and he knew them much more as they really are.' (*Essays in*

441

Criticism, 1865, pp. 6-7). In his essay 'Heinrich Heine' (*Cornhill Magazine*, August 1863; reprinted *Essays in Criticism*, 1865) he praised Byron for his attempt to express the modern spirit, to apply modern ideas to life in his poetry: 'In the literary movement of the beginning of the nineteenth century the signal attempt to apply freely the modern spirit was made in England by two members of the aristocratic class, Byron and Shelley. Aristocracies are, as such, naturally impenetrable by ideas; but their individual members have a high courage and a turn for breaking bounds; and a man of genius, who is the born child of the idea, happening to be born in the aristocratic ranks, chafes against the obstacles which prevent him from freely developing it. But Byron and Shelley did not succeed in their attempt freely to apply the modern spirit in English literature; they could not succeed in it; the resistance to baffle them, the want of intelligent sympathy to guide and uphold them, were too great. Their literary creation, compared with the literary creation of Shakespeare and Spenser, compared with the literary creation of Goethe and Heine, is a failure. The best literary creation of that time in England proceeded from men who did not make the same bold attempt as Byron and Shelley. What, in fact, was the career of the chief English men of letters, their contemporaries? The greatest of them, Wordsworth, retired (in Middle-Age phrase) into a monastery. I mean, he plunged himself in the inward life, he voluntarily cut himself off from the modern spirit. Coleridge took to opium. Scott became the historiographer royal of feudalism. Keats passionately gave himself up to a sensuous genius, to his faculty for interpreting nature; and he died of consumption at twenty-five. Wordsworth, Scott, and Keats have left admirable works; far more solid and complete works than those which Byron and Shelley have left. But their works have this defect;—they do not belong to that which is the main current of the literature of modern epochs, they do not apply modern ideas to life; they constitute, therefore, *minor currents*, and all other literary work of our day, however popular, which has the same defect, also constitutes but a minor current. Byron and Shelley will long be remembered, long after the inadequacy of their actual work is clearly recognised, for their passionate, their Titanic effort to flow in the main stream of modern literature; their names will be greater than their writings; *stat magni nominis umbra.*[1] (*Essays in Criticism*, 1865, pp. 170–1.)

Arnold's considered assessment of Byron was written as a preface to his volume of selections, *Poetry of Byron* (1881), and reprinted in *Essays in Criticism: Second Series*, 1888, pp. 163–204.

When at last I held in my hand the volume of poems which I had chosen from Wordsworth, and began to turn over its pages, there arose in me almost immediately the desire to see beside it, as a companion volume, a like collection of the best poetry of Byron. Alone amongst our poets of the earlier part of this century, Byron and Wordsworth not only furnish material enough for a volume of this kind, but also, as it seems to me, they both of them gain considerably by being thus exhibited. There are poems of Coleridge and of Keats equal, if not superior, to anything of Byron or Wordsworth; but a dozen pages or two will contain them, and the remaining poetry is of a quality much inferior. Scott never, I think, rises as a poet to the level of Byron and Wordsworth at all. On the other hand, he never falls below his own usual level very far; and by a volume of selections from him, therefore, his effectiveness is not increased. As to Shelley there will be more question; and indeed Mr. Stopford Brooke, whose accomplishments, eloquence, and love of poetry we must all recognise and admire, has actually given us Shelley in such a volume. But for my own part I cannot think that Shelley's poetry, except by snatches and fragments, has the value of the good work of Wordsworth and Byron; or that it is possible for even Mr. Stopford Brooke to make up a volume of selections from him which, for real substance, power, and worth, can at all take rank with a like volume from Byron or Wordsworth.

Shelley knew quite well the difference between the achievement of such a poet as Byron and his own. He praises Byron too unreservedly, but he sincerely felt, and he was right in feeling, that Byron was a greater poetical power than himself. As a man, Shelley is at a number of points immeasurably Byron's superior; he is a beautiful and enchanting spirit, whose vision, when we call it up, has far more loveliness, more charm for our soul, than the vision of Byron. But all the

---

[1] ['He stands a shadow of a mighty name.']

personal charm of Shelley cannot hinder us from at last discovering in his poetry the incurable want, in general, of a sound subject-matter, and the incurable fault, in consequence, of unsubstantiality. Those who extol him as the poet of clouds, the poet of sunsets, are only saying that he did not, in fact, lay hold upon the poet's right subject-matter; and in honest truth, with all his charm of soul and spirit, and with all his gift of musical diction and movement, he never, or hardly ever, did. Except, as I have said, for a few short things and single stanzas, his original poetry is less satisfactory than his translations, for in these the subject-matter was found for him. Nay, I doubt whether his delightful Essays and Letters, which deserve to be far more read than they are now, will not resist the wear and tear of time better, and finally come to stand higher, than his poetry.

There remain to be considered Byron and Wordsworth. That Wordsworth affords good material for a volume of selections, and that he gains by having his poetry thus presented, is an old belief of mine which led me lately to make up a volume of poems chosen out of Wordsworth, and to bring it before the public. By its kind reception of the volume, the public seems to show itself a partaker in my belief. Now Byron also supplies plenty of material for a like volume, and he too gains, I think, by being so presented. Mr. Swinburne urges, indeed, that 'Byron, who rarely wrote anything either worthless or faultless, can only be judged or appreciated in the mass; the greatest of his works was his whole work taken together.' It is quite true that Byron rarely wrote anything either worthless or faultless; it is quite true also that in the appreciation of Byron's power a sense of the amount and variety of his work, defective though much of his work is, enters justly into our estimate. But although there may be little in Byron's poetry which can be pronounced either worthless or faultless, there are portions of it which are far higher in worth and far more free from fault than others. And although, again, the abundance and variety of his production is undoubtedly a proof of his power, yet I question whether by reading everything which he gives us we are so likely to acquire an admiring sense even of his variety and abundance, as by reading what he gives us at his happier moments. Varied and abundant he amply proves himself even by this token alone. Receive him absolutely without omission or compression, follow his whole outpouring stanza by stanza and line by line from the very commencement to the very end, and he is capable of being tiresome.

Byron has told us himself that *The Giaour* 'is but a string of passages.'

444

He has made full confession of his own negligence. 'No one,' says he, 'has done more through negligence to corrupt the language.' This accusation brought by himself against his poems is not just; but when he goes on to say of them, that 'their faults, whatever they may be, are those of negligence and not of labour,' he says what is perfectly true. '*Lara*,' he declares, 'I wrote while undressing after coming home from balls and masquerades, in the year of revelry, 1814. *The Bride* was written in four, *The Corsair* in ten days.' He calls this 'a humiliating confession, as it proves my own want of judgment in publishing, and the public's in reading, things which cannot have stamina for permanence.' Again he does his poems injustice; the producer of such poems could not but publish them, the public could not but read them. Nor could Byron have produced his work in any other fashion; his poetic work could not have first grown and matured in his own mind, and then come forth as an organic whole; Byron had not enough of the artist in him for this, nor enough of self-command. He wrote, as he truly tells us, to relieve himself, and he went on writing because he found the relief become indispensable. But it was inevitable that works so produced should be, in general, 'a string of passages,' poured out, as he describes them, with rapidity and excitement, and with new passages constantly suggesting themselves, and added while his work was going through the press. It is evident that we have neither deliberate scientific construction, nor yet the instinctive artistic creation of poetic wholes; and that to take passages from work produced as Byron's was is a very different thing from taking passages out of the *Oedipus* or the *Tempest*, and deprives the poetry far less of its advantage.

Nay, it gives advantage to the poetry, instead of depriving it of any. Byron, I said, has not a great artist's profound and patient skill in combining an action or in developing a character,—a skill which we must watch and follow if we are to do justice to it. But he has a wonderful power of vividly conceiving a single incident, a single situation; of throwing himself upon it, grasping it as if it were real and he saw and felt it, and of making us see and feel it too. *The Giaour* is, as he truly called it, 'a string of passages,' not a work moving by a deep internal law of development to a necessary end; and our total impression from it cannot but receive from this, its inherent defect, a certain dimness and indistinctness. But the incidents of the journey and death of Hassan, in that poem, are conceived and presented with a vividness not to be surpassed; and our impression from them is correspondingly clear and powerful. In *Lara* again, there is no adequate development either of the character of the chief personage or of the action of the poem; our total impression from the work is a confused one. Yet such an incident as the disposal of the slain Ezzelin's body passes before our eyes as if we actually saw it. And in the same way as these bursts of incident, bursts of sentiment also, living and vigorous, often occur in the midst of poems which must be admitted to be but weakly-conceived and loosely-combined wholes. Byron cannot but be a gainer by having attention concentrated upon what is vivid, powerful, effective in his work, and withdrawn from what is not so.

Byron, I say, cannot but be a gainer by this, just as Wordsworth is a gainer by a like proceeding. I esteem Wordsworth's poetry so highly, and the world, in my opinion, has done it such scant justice, that I could not rest satisfied until I had fulfilled, on Wordsworth's behalf, a long-cherished desire;—had disengaged, to the best of my power, his good work from the inferior work joined with it, and had placed before the public the body of his good work by itself. To the poetry of Byron the world has ardently paid homage; full justice from his contemporaries, perhaps even more than justice, his torrent of poetry received. His poetry was admired, adored, 'with all its imperfections on its head,'—in spite of negligence, in spite of diffuseness, in spite of repetitions, in spite of whatever faults it possessed. His name is still great and brilliant. Nevertheless the hour of irresistible vogue has passed away for him; even for Byron it could not but pass away. The time has come for him, as it comes for all poets, when he must take his real and permanent place, no longer depending upon the vogue of his own day and upon the enthusiasm of his contemporaries. Whatever we may think of him, we shall not be subjugated by him as they were; for, as he cannot be for us what he was for them, we cannot admire him so hotly and indiscriminately as they. His faults of negligence, of diffuseness, of repetition, his faults of whatever kind, we shall abundantly feel and unsparingly criticise; the mere interval of time between us and him makes disillusion of this kind inevitable. But how then will Byron stand, if we relieve him too, so far as we can, of the encumbrance of his inferior and weakest work, and if we bring before us his best and strongest work in one body together? That is the question which I, who can even remember the latter years of Byron's vogue, and have myself felt the expiring wave of that mighty influence, but who certainly also regard him, and have long regarded him, without illusion, cannot but ask myself, cannot but seek to answer. The present volume is an attempt to provide adequate data for answering it.

Byron has been over-praised, no doubt. 'Byron is one of our French superstitions,' says M. Edmond Scherer; but where has Byron not been a superstition? He pays now the penalty of this exaggerated worship. 'Alone among the English poets his contemporaries, Byron,' said M. Taine, *'atteint à la cîme,*—gets to the top of the poetic mountain.' But the idol that M. Taine had thus adored M. Scherer is almost for burning. 'In Byron,' he declares, 'there is a remarkable inability ever to lift himself into the region of real poetic art,—art impersonal and disinterested,—at all. He has fecundity, eloquence, wit, but even these qualities themselves are confined within somewhat narrow limits. He has treated hardly any subject but one,—himself; now the man, in Byron, is of a nature even less sincere than the poet. This beautiful and blighted being is at bottom a coxcomb. He posed all his life long.'

Our poet could not well meet with more severe and unsympathetic criticism. However, the praise often given to Byron has been so exaggerated as to provoke, perhaps, a reaction in which he is unduly disparaged. 'As various in composition as Shakespeare himself, Lord Byron has embraced,' says Sir Walter Scott, 'every topic of human life, and sounded every string on the divine harp, from its slightest to its most powerful and heart-astounding tones.' It is not surprising that some one with a cool head should retaliate, on such provocation as this, by saying: 'He has treated hardly any subject but one, *himself.*' 'In the very grand and tremendous drama of *Cain*,' says Scott, 'Lord Byron has certainly matched Milton on his own ground.' And Lord Byron has done all this, Scott adds, 'while managing his pen with the careless and negligent ease of a man of quality.' Alas, 'managing his pen with the careless and negligent ease of a man of quality,' Byron wrote in his *Cain*—

> Souls that dare look the Omnipotent tyrant in
> His everlasting face, and tell him that
> His evil is not good;

or he wrote—

> . . . And *thou* would'st go on aspiring
> To the great double Mysteries! the *two Principles!* [1]

[1] The italics are in the original.

One has only to repeat to oneself a line from *Paradise Lost* in order to feel the difference.

Sainte-Beuve, speaking of that exquisite master of language, the Italian poet Leopardi, remarks how often we see the alliance, singular though it may at first sight appear, of the poetical genius with the genius for scholarship and philology. Dante and Milton are instances which will occur to every one's mind. Byron is so negligent in his poetical style, he is often, to say the truth, so slovenly, slipshod, and infelicitous, he is so little haunted by the true artist's fine passion for the correct use and consummate management of words, that he may be described as having for this artistic gift the insensibility of the barbarian; —which is perhaps only another and a less flattering way of saying, with Scott, that he 'manages his pen with the careless and negligent ease of a man of quality.' Just of a piece with the rhythm of

> Dare you await the event of a few minutes'
> Deliberation?

or of

> All shall be void—
> Destroy'd!

is the diction of

> Which now is painful to these eyes,
> Which have not seen the sun to rise;

or of

> . . . there let him lay!

or of the famous passage beginning

> He who hath bent him o'er the dead;

with those trailing relatives, that crying grammatical solecism, that inextricable anacolouthon! To class the work of the author of such things with the work of the authors of such verse as

> In the dark backward and abysm of time—

or as

> Presenting Thebes, or Pelops' line,
> Or the tale of Troy divine—

is ridiculous. Shakespeare and Milton, with their secret of consummate felicity in diction and movement, are of another and an altogether higher order from Byron, nay, for that matter, from Wordsworth also; from the author of such verse as

> Sol hath dropt into his harbour

or (if Mr. Ruskin pleases) as

> Parching summer hath no warrant—[1]

as from the author of

> All shall be void—
> Destroy'd!

With a poetical gift and a poetical performance of the very highest order, the slovenliness and tunelessness of much of Byron's production, the pompousness and ponderousness of much of Wordsworth's are incompatible. Let us admit this to the full.

Moreover, while we are harkening to M. Scherer, and going along with him in his fault-finding, let us admit, too, that the man in Byron is in many respects as unsatisfactory as the poet. And, putting aside all direct moral criticism of him,—with which we need not concern ourselves here,—we shall find that he is unsatisfactory in the same way. Some of Byron's most crying faults as a man,—his vulgarity, his affectation,—are really akin to the faults of commonness, of want of art, in his workmanship as a poet. The ideal nature for the poet and artist is that of the finely touched and finely gifted man, the εὐφυής of the Greeks; now, Byron's nature was in substance not that of the εὐφυής at all, but rather, as I have said, of the barbarian. The want of fine perception which made it possible for him to formulate either the comparison between himself and Rousseau, or his reason for getting Lord Delawarr excused from a 'licking' at Harrow, is exactly what made possible for him also his terrible dealings in, *An ye wool; I have redde thee; Sunburn me; Oons, and it is excellent well.* It is exactly, again, what made possible for him his precious dictum that Pope is a Greek temple, and a string of other criticisms of the like force; it is exactly, in fine, what deteriorated the quality of his poetic production. If we think of a good representative of that finely touched and exquisitely gifted nature which is the ideal nature for the poet and artist,—if we think of Raphael, for instance, who truly is εὐφυής just as Byron is not,—we shall bring into clearer light the connection in Byron between the faults of the man and the faults of the poet. With

[1] See above, p. 433.

449

Raphael's character Byron's sins of vulgarity and false criticism would have been impossible, just as with Raphael's art Byron's sins of common and bad workmanship.

Yes, all this is true, but it is not the whole truth about Byron nevertheless; very far from it. The severe criticism of M. Scherer by no means gives us the whole truth about Byron, and we have not yet got it in what has been added to that criticism here. The negative part of the true criticism of him we perhaps have; the positive part, by far the more important, we have not. Byron's admirers appeal eagerly to foreign testimonies in his favour. Some of these testimonies do not much move me; but one testimony there is among them which will always carry, with me at any rate, very great weight,—the testimony of Goethe. Goethe's sayings about Byron were uttered, it must however be remembered, at the height of Byron's vogue, when that puissant and splendid personality was exercising its full power of attraction. In Goethe's own household there was an atmosphere of glowing Byron-worship; his daughter-in-law was a passionate admirer of Byron, nay, she enjoyed and prized his poetry, as did Tieck and so many others in Germany at that time, much above the poetry of Goethe himself. Instead of being irritated and rendered jealous by this, a nature like Goethe's was inevitably led by it to heighten, not lower, the note of his praise. The Time-Spirit, or *Zeit-Geist*, he would himself have said, was working just then for Byron. This working of the *Zeit-Geist* in his favour was an advantage added to Byron's other advantages, an advantage of which he had a right to get the benefit. This is what Goethe would have thought and said to himself; and so he would have been led even to heighten somewhat his estimate of Byron, and to accentuate the emphasis of praise. Goethe speaking of Byron at that moment was not and could not be quite the same cool critic as Goethe speaking of Dante, or Molière, or Milton. This, I say, we ought to remember in reading Goethe's judgments on Byron and his poetry. Still, if we are careful to bear this in mind, and if we quote Goethe's praise correctly,—which is not always done by those who in this country quote it,—and if we add to it that great and due qualification added to it by Goethe himself,—which so far as I have seen has never yet been done by his quoters in this country at all,—then we shall have a judgment on Byron, which comes, I think, very near to the truth, and which may well command our adherence.

In his judicious and interesting Life of Byron,[1] Professor Nichol

[1] [John Nichol, *Byron* (English Men of Letters Series), 1880.]

quotes Goethe as saying that Byron 'is undoubtedly to be regarded as the greatest genius of our century.' What Goethe did really say was 'the greatest *talent*,' not 'the greatest *genius*.' The difference is important, because, while talent gives the notion of power in a man's performance, genius gives rather the notion of felicity and perfection in it; and this divine gift of consummate felicity by no means, as we have seen, belongs to Byron and to his poetry. Goethe said that Byron 'must unquestionably be regarded as the greatest talent of the century.'[1] He said of him moreover: 'The English may think of Byron what they please, but it is certain that they can point to no poet who is his like. He is different from all the rest, and in the main greater.' Here, again, Professor Nichol translates: 'They can show no (living) poet who is to be compared to him;'—inserting the word *living*, I suppose, to prevent its being thought that Goethe would have ranked Byron, as a poet, above Shakespeare and Milton. But Goethe did not use, or, I think, mean to imply, any limitation such as is added by Professor Nichol. Goethe said simply, and he meant to say, '*no* poet.' Only the words which follow[2] ought not, I think, to be rendered, 'who is to be compared to him,' that is to say, '*who is his equal as a poet.*' They mean rather, 'who may properly be compared with him,' '*who is his parallel.*' And when Goethe said that Byron was 'in the main greater' than all the rest of the English poets, he was not so much thinking of the strict rank, as poetry, of Byron's production; he was thinking of that wonderful personality of Byron which so enters into his poetry, and which Goethe called 'a personality such, for its eminence, as has never been yet, and such as is not likely to come again.' He was thinking of that 'daring, dash, and grandiosity,'[3] of Byron, which are indeed so splendid; and which were, so Goethe maintained, of a character to do good, because 'everything great is formative,' and what is thus formative does us good.

The faults which went with this greatness, and which impaired Byron's poetical work, Goethe saw very well. He saw the constant state of warfare and combat, the 'negative and polemical working,' which makes Byron's poetry a poetry in which we can so little find rest; he saw the *Hang zum Unbegrenzten*, the straining after the unlimited, which made it impossible for Byron to produce poetic wholes such as

[1] 'Der ohne Frage als das grösste Talent des Jahrhunderts anzusehen ist.'
[2] 'Der ihm zu vergleichen wäre.'
[3] 'Byron's Kühnheit, Keckheit und Grandiosität, ist das nicht alles bildend?—Alles Grosse bildet, sobald wir es gewahr werden.'

the *Tempest* or *Lear;* he saw the *zu viel Empirie*, the promiscuous adoption of all the matter offered to the poet by life, just as it was offered, without thought or patience for the mysterious transmutation to be operated on this matter by poetic form. But in a sentence which I cannot, as I say, remember to have yet seen quoted in any English criticism of Byron, Goethe lays his finger on the cause of all these defects in Byron, and on his real source of weakness both as a man and as a poet. 'The moment he reflects, he is a child,' says Goethe;— *sobald er reflectirt ist er ein Kind.'*

Now if we take the two parts of Goethe's criticism of Byron, the favourable and the unfavourable, and put them together, we shall have, I think, the truth. On the one hand, a splendid and puissant personality—a personality 'in eminence such as has never been yet, and is not likely to come again'; of which the like, therefore, is not to be found among the poets of our nation, by which Byron 'is different from all the rest, and in the main greater.' Byron is, moreover, 'the greatest talent of our century.' On the other hand, this splendid personality and unmatched talent, this unique Byron, 'is quite too much in the dark about himself;'[1] nay, 'the moment he begins to reflect, he is a child.' There we have, I think, Byron complete; and in estimating him and ranking him we have to strike a balance between the gain which accrues to his poetry, as compared with the productions of other poets, from his superiority, and the loss which accrues to it from his defects.

A balance of this kind has to be struck in the case of all poets except the few supreme masters in whom a profound criticism of life exhibits itself in indissoluble connection with the laws of poetic truth and beauty. I have seen it said that I allege poetry to have for its characteristic this: that it is a criticism of life; and that I make it to be thereby distinguished from prose, which is something else. So far from it, that when I first used this expression, *a criticism of life*, now many years ago, it was to literature in general that I applied it, and not to poetry in especial. 'The end and aim of all literature,' I said, 'is, if one considers it attentively, nothing but that: *a criticism of life.*' And so it surely is; the main end and aim of all our utterance, whether in prose or in verse, is surely a criticism of life. We are not brought much on our way, I admit, towards an adequate definition of poetry as distinguished from prose by that truth; still a truth it is, and poetry can never prosper if it is forgotten. In poetry, however, the criticism of life has

[1] 'Gar zu dunkel über sich selbst.'

to be made conformably to the laws of poetic truth and poetic beauty. Truth and seriousness of substance and matter, felicity and perfection of diction and manner, as these are exhibited in the best poets, are what constitute a criticism of life made in conformity with the laws of poetic truth and poetic beauty; and it is by knowing and feeling the work of those poets, that we learn to recognise the fulfilment and non-fulfilment of such conditions.

The moment, however, that we leave the small band of the very best poets, the true classics, and deal with poets of the next rank, we shall find that perfect truth and seriousness of matter, in close alliance with perfect truth and felicity of manner, is the rule no longer. We have now to take what we can get, to forego something here, to admit compensation for it there; to strike a balance, and to see how our poets stand in respect to one another when that balance has been struck. Let us observe how this is so.

We will take three poets, among the most considerable of our century: Leopardi, Byron, Wordsworth. Giacomo Leopardi was ten years younger than Byron, and he died thirteen years after him; both of them, therefore, died young—Byron at the age of thirty-six, Leopardi at the age of thirty-nine. Both of them were of noble birth, both of them suffered from physical defect, both of them were in revolt against the established facts and beliefs of their age; but here the likeness between them ends. The stricken poet of Recanati had no country, for an Italy in his day did not exist; he had no audience, no celebrity. The volume of his poems, published in the very year of Byron's death, hardly sold, I suppose, its tens, while the volumes of Byron's poetry were selling their tens of thousands. And yet Leopardi has the very qualities which we have found wanting to Byron; he has the sense for form and style, the passion for just expression, the sure and firm touch of the true artist. Nay, more, he has a grave fulness of knowledge, an insight into the real bearings of the questions which as a sceptical poet he raises, a power of seizing the real point, a lucidity, with which the author of *Cain* has nothing to compare. I can hardly imagine Leopardi reading the

> . . . And *thou* would'st go on aspiring
> To the great double Mysteries! the *two Principles!*

or following Byron in his theological controversy with Dr. Kennedy, without having his features overspread by a calm and fine smile, and remarking of his brilliant contemporary, as Goethe did, that 'the moment he begins to reflect, he is a child.' But indeed whoever wishes to feel the full superiority of Leopardi over Byron in philosophic thought, and in the expression of it, has only to read one paragraph of one poem, the paragraph of *La Ginestra*, beginning

Sovente in queste piagge,

and ending

Non so se il riso o la pietà prevale.

In like manner, Leopardi is at many points the poetic superior of Wordsworth too. He has a far wider culture than Wordsworth, more mental lucidity, more freedom from illusions as to the real character of the established fact and of reigning conventions; above all, this Italian, with his pure and sure touch, with his fineness of perception, is far more of the artist. Such a piece of pompous dulness as

O for the coming of that glorious time,

and all the rest of it, or such lumbering verse as Mr. Ruskin's enemy,

Parching summer hath no warrant—

would have been as impossible to Leopardi as to Dante. Where, then, is Wordsworth's superiority? for the worth of what he has given us in poetry I hold to be greater, on the whole, than the worth of what Leopardi has given us. It is in Wordsworth's sound and profound sense

Of joy in widest commonalty spread;

whereas Leopardi remains with his thoughts ever fixed upon the *essenza insanabile*, upon the *acerbo, indegno mistero delle cose.*[1] It is in the power with which Wordsworth feels the resources of joy offered to us in nature, offered to us in the primary human affections and duties, and in the power with which, in his moments of inspiration, he renders this joy, and makes us, too, feel it; a force greater than himself seeming to lift him and to prompt his tongue, so that he speaks in a style far above any style of which he has the constant command, and with a truth far beyond any philosophic truth of which he has the conscious and assured possession. Neither Leopardi nor Wordsworth are of the same order with the great poets who made such verse as

Τλητὸν γὰρ Μοῖραι θυμὸν θέσαν ἀνθρώποισιν.

[1] ['The incurable essence . . . the bitter, shameful mystery of things.']

or as
> *In la sua volontade e nostra pace;*

or as
> . . . Men must endure
> Their going hence, even as their coming hither;
> Ripeness is all.

But as compared with Leopardi, Wordsworth, though at many points less lucid, though far less a master of style, far less of an artist, gains so much by his criticism of life being, in certain matters of profound importance, healthful and true, whereas Leopardi's pessimism is not, that the value of Wordsworth's poetry, on the whole, stands higher for us than that of Leopardi's, as it stands higher for us, I think, than that of any modern poetry except Goethe's.

Byron's poetic value is also greater, on the whole, than Leopardi's; and his superiority turns in the same way upon the surpassing worth of something which he had and was, after all deduction has been made for his shortcomings. We talk of Byron's *personality*, 'a personality in eminence such as has never been yet, and is not likely to come again;' and we say that by this personality Byron is 'different from all the rest of English poets, and in the main greater.' But can we not be a little more circumstantial, and name that in which the wonderful power of this personality consisted? We can; with the instinct of a poet Mr. Swinburne has seized upon it and named it for us. The power of Byron's personality lies in 'the splendid and imperishable excellence which covers all his offences and outweighs all his defects: *the excellence of sincerity and strength.*'

Byron found our nation, after its long and victorious struggle with revolutionary France, fixed in a system of established facts and domin-ant ideas which revolted him. The mental bondage of the most power-ful part of our nation, of its strong middle-class, to a narrow and false system of this kind, is what we call British Philistinism. That bondage is unbroken to this hour, but in Byron's time it was even far more deep and dark than it is now. Byron was an aristocrat, and it is not difficult for an aristocrat to look on the prejudices and habits of the British Philistine with scepticism and disdain. Plenty of young men of his own class Byron met at Almack's or at Lady Jersey's, who regarded the established facts and reigning beliefs of the England of that day with as little reverence as he did. But these men, disbelievers in British Philistinism in private, entered English public life, the most con-ventional in the world, and at once they saluted with respect the habits and ideas of British Philistinism as if they were a part of the order of creation, and as if in public no sane man would think of warring against them. With Byron it was different. What he called the *cant* of the great middle part of the English nation, what we call its Philistinism, revolted him; but the cant of his own class, deferring to this Philistinism and profiting by it, while they disbelieved in it, revolted him even more. 'Come what may,' are his own words, 'I will never flatter the million's canting in any shape.' His class in general, on the other hand, shrugged their shoulders at this cant, laughed at it, pandered to it, and ruled by it. The falsehood, cynicism, insolence, misgovernment, oppression, with their consequent unfailing crop of human misery, which were produced by this state of things, roused Byron to irreconcilable revolt and battle. They made him indignant, they infuriated him; they were so strong, so defiant, so maleficent,— and yet he felt that they were doomed. 'You have seen every trampler down in turn,' he comforts himself with saying, 'from Buonaparte to the simplest individuals.' The old order, as after 1815 it stood victorious, with its ignorance and misery below, its cant, selfishness, and cynicism above, was at home and abroad equally hateful to him. 'I have simplified my politics,' he writes, 'into an utter detestation of all existing governments.' And again: 'Give me a republic. The king-times are fast finishing; there will be blood shed like water and tears like mist, but the peoples will conquer in the end. I shall not live to see it, but I foresee it.'

Byron himself gave the preference, he tells us, to politicians and doers, far above writers and singers. But the politics of his own day and of his own class,—even of the Liberals of his own class,—were impossible for him. Nature had not formed him for a Liberal peer, proper to move the Address in the House of Lords to pay compliments to the energy and self-reliance of British middle-class Liberalism, and to adapt his politics to suit it. Unfitted for such politics, he threw himself upon poetry as his organ; and in poetry his topics were not Queen Mab, and the Witch of Atlas, and the Sensitive Plant—they were the upholders of the old order, George the Third and Lord Castlereagh and the Duke of Wellington and Southey, and they were the canters and tramplers of the great world, and they were his enemies and himself.

Such was Byron's personality, by which 'he is different from all the rest of English poets, and in the main greater.' But he posed all his life, says M. Scherer. Let us distinguish. There is the Byron who posed,

there is the Byron with his affectations and silliness, the Byron whose
weakness Lady Blessington, with a woman's acuteness, so admirably
seized: 'His great defect is flippancy and a total want of self-possession.'
But when this theatrical and easily criticised personage betook himself
to poetry, and when he had fairly warmed to his work, then he
became another man; then the theatrical personage passed away;
then a higher power took possession of him and filled him; then at
last came forth into light that true and puissant personality, with its
direct strokes, its ever-welling force, its satire, its energy, and its
agony. This is the real Byron; whoever stops at the theatrical preluding
does not know him. And this real Byron may well be superior to the
stricken Leopardi, he may well be declared 'different from all the rest of
English poets, and in the main greater,' in so far as it is true of him,
as M. Taine well says, that 'all other souls, in comparison with his,
seem inert'; in so far as it is true of him that with superb, exhaustless
energy, he maintained, as Professor Nichol well says, 'the struggle that
keeps alive, if it does not save, the soul;' in so far, finally, as he deserves
(and he does deserve) the noble praise of him which I have already
quoted from Mr. Swinburne; the praise for 'the splendid and imperishable excellence which covers all his offences and outweighs all his
defects: *the excellence of sincerity and strength.*'

True, as a man, Byron could not manage himself, could not guide
his ways aright, but was all astray. True, he has no light, cannot lead us
from the past to the future; 'the moment he reflects, he is a child.'
The way out of the false state of things which enraged him he did not
see,—the slow and laborious way upward; he had not the patience,
knowledge, self-discipline, virtue, requisite for seeing it. True, also,
as a poet, he has no fine and exact sense for word and structure and
rhythm; he has not the artist's nature and gifts. Yet a personality of
Byron's force counts for so much in life, and a rhetorician of Byron's
force counts for so much in literature! But it would be most unjust to
label Byron, as M. Scherer is disposed to label him, as a rhetorician
only. Along with his astounding power and passion he had a strong and
deep sense for what is beautiful in nature, and for what is beautiful in
human action and suffering. When he warms to his work, when he is
inspired, Nature herself seems to take the pen from him as she took it
from Wordsworth, and to write for him as she wrote for Wordsworth,
though in a different fashion, with her own penetrating simplicity.
Goethe has well observed of Byron, that when he is at his happiest his
representation of things is as easy and real as if he were improvising.

It is so; and his verse then exhibits quite another and a higher quality from the rhetorical quality,—admirable as this also in its own kind of merit is,—of such verse as

Minions of splendour shrinking from distress,

and of so much more verse of Byron's of that stamp. Nature, I say, takes the pen for him; and then, assured master of a true poetic style though he is not, any more than Wordsworth, yet as from Wordsworth at his best there will come such verse as

Will no one tell me what she sings?

so from Byron, too, at his best, there will come such verse as

He heard it, but he heeded not; his eyes
Were with his heart, and that was far away.

Of verse of this high quality, Byron has much; of verse of a quality lower than this, of a quality rather rhetorical than truly poetic, yet still of extraordinary power and merit, he has still more. To separate, from the mass of poetry which Byron poured forth, all this higher portion, so superior to the mass, and still so considerable in quantity, and to present it in one body by itself, is to do a service, I believe, to Byron's reputation, and to the poetic glory of our country.

Such a service I have in the present volume attempted to perform. To Byron, after all the tributes which have been paid to him, here is yet one tribute more—

Among thy mightier offerings here are mine!

not a tribute of boundless homage certainly, but sincere; a tribute which consists not in covering the poet with eloquent eulogy of our own, but in letting him, at his best and greatest, speak for himself. Surely the critic who does most for his author is the critic who gains readers for his author himself, not for any lucubrations on his author;— gains more readers for him, and enables those readers to read him with more admiration.

And in spite of his prodigious vogue, Byron has never yet, perhaps, had the serious admiration which he deserves. Society read him and talked about him, as it reads and talks about *Endymion* to-day; and with the same sort of result. It looked in Byron's glass as it looks in Lord Beaconsfield's, and sees, or fancies that it sees, its own face there; and then it goes its way, and straightway forgets what manner of man it saw. Even of his passionate admirers, how many never got beyond the theatrical Byron, from whom they caught the fashion of deranging their hair, or of knotting their neck-handkerchief, or of leaving their shirt-collar unbuttoned; how few profoundly felt his vital influence, the influence of his splendid and imperishable excellence of sincerity and strength!

His own aristocratic class, whose cynical make-believe drove him to fury; the great middle-class, on whose impregnable Philistinism he shattered himself to pieces,—how little have either of these felt Byron's vital influence! As the inevitable break-up of the old order comes, as the English middle-class slowly awakens from its intellectual sleep of two centuries, as our actual present world, to which this sleep has condemned us, shows itself more clearly,—our world of an aristocracy materialised and null, a middle-class purblind and hideous, a lower class crude and brutal,—we shall turn our eyes again, and to more purpose, upon this passionate and dauntless soldier of a forlorn hope, who, ignorant of the future and unconsoled by its promises, nevertheless waged against the conservation of the old impossible world so fiery battle; waged it till he fell,—waged it with such splendid and imperishable excellence of sincerity and strength.

Wordsworth's value is of another kind. Wordsworth has an insight into permanent sources of joy and consolation for mankind which Byron has not; his poetry gives us more which we may rest upon than Byron's,—more which we can rest upon now, and which men may rest upon always. I place Wordsworth's poetry, therefore, above Byron's on the whole, although in some points he was greatly Byron's inferior, and although Byron's poetry will always, probably, find more readers than Wordsworth's, and will give pleasure more easily. But these two, Wordsworth and Byron, stand, it seems to me, first and pre-eminent in actual performance, a glorious pair, among the English poets of this century. Keats had probably, indeed, a more consummate poetic gift than either of them; but he died having produced too little and being as yet too immature to rival them. I for my part can never even think of equalling with them any other of their contemporaries;—either Coleridge, poet and philosopher wrecked in a mist of opium; or Shelley, beautiful and ineffectual angel, beating in the void his luminous wings in vain. Wordsworth and Byron stand out by themselves. When the year 1900 is turned, and our nation comes to recount her poetic glories in the century which has then just ended, the first names with her will be these.

61. W. E. Henley on Byron

[1881] 1890

W. E. Henley (1849–1903), poet, journalist and man of letters, reviewed Arnold's selection of the *Poetry of Byron* in the *Athenaeum*, 25 June 1881. This review was reprinted in revised form as an essay on Byron in *Views and Reviews*, 1890, pp. 56–62. (The original review included an approving comment on defences of Byron recently offered by Swinburne, Symonds and Ruskin, as well as Arnold; it criticized Arnold's selection for its scrappiness, and attacked as unfair his method of 'demonstrating' Byron's bad workmanship by contrasting admittedly poor lines of his with great lines by Wordsworth, Milton and Shakespeare.)

Two obvious reasons why Byron has long been a prophet more honoured abroad than at home are his life and his work. He is the most romantic figure in the literature of the century, and his romance is of that splendid and daring cast which the people of Britain—'an aristocracy materialised and null, a middle class purblind and hideous, a lower class crude and brutal'—prefers to regard with suspicion and disfavour. He is the type of them that prove in defiance of precept that the safest path is not always midway, and that the golden rule is sometimes unspeakably worthless: who set what seems a horrible example, create an apparently shameful precedent, and yet contrive to approve themselves an honour to their country and the race. To be a good Briton a man must trade profitably, marry respectably, live cleanly, avoid excess, revere the established order, and wear his heart in his breeches pocket or anywhere but on his sleeve. Byron did none of these things, though he was a public character, and ought for the example's sake to have done them all, and done them ostentatiously. He lived hard, and drank hard, and played hard. He was flippant in speech and eccentric in attire. He thought little of the sanctity of the conjugal tie, and said so; and he married but to divide from his wife—who was an incarnation of the national virtue of respectability—under circumstances too mysterious not to be discreditable. He was hooted into exile, and so far from reforming he did even worse than he had done before. After bewildering Venice with his wickedness and consorting with atheists like Shelley and conspirators like young Gamba, he went away on a sort of wild-goose chase to Greece, and died there with every circumstance of publicity. Also his work was every whit as abominable in the eyes of his countrymen as his life. It is said that the theory and practice of British art are subject to the influence of the British schoolgirl, and that he is unworthy the name of artist whose achievement is of a kind to call a blush to the cheek of youth. Byron was contemptuous of youth, and did not hesitate to write—in *Beppo* and in *Cain*, in *Manfred* and *Don Juan* and the *Vision*— exactly as he pleased. In three words, he made himself offensively conspicuous, and from being infinitely popular became utterly contemptible. Too long had people listened to the scream of this eagle in wonder and in perturbation, and the moment he disappeared they grew ashamed of their emotion and angry with its cause, and began to hearken to other and more melodious voices—to Shelley and Keats, to Wordsworth and Coleridge and the 'faultless and fervent melodies of Tennyson.' In course of time Byron was forgotten, or only remembered with disdain; and when Thackeray, the representative Briton, the artist Philistine, the foe of all that is excessive or abnormal or rebellious, took it upon himself to flout the author of *Don Juan* openly and to lift up his heavy hand against the fops and fanatics who had affected the master's humours, he did so amid general applause. Meanwhile, however, the genius and the personality of Byron had come to be vital influences all the world over, and his voice had been recognised as the most human and the least insular raised on English ground since Shakespeare's. In Russia he had created Pushkin and Lermontoff; in Germany he had awakened Heine, inspired Schumann, and been saluted as an equal by the poet of *Faust* himself; in Spain he had had a share in moulding the noisy and unequal talent of Espronceda; in Italy he had helped to develop and to shape the melancholy and daring genius of Leopardi; and in France he had been one of the presiding forces of a great aesthetic revolution. To the men of 1830 he was a special and peculiar hero. Hugo turned in his wake to Spain and Italy and the East for inspiration. Musset, as Mr. Swinburne has said—too bitterly and strongly said—became in a fashion a Kaled to his Lara, 'his female page or attendant dwarf.' He was in some sort the grandsire of the Buridan and the Antony of Dumas. Berlioz went to him for the material for his *Harold en Italie*, his *Corsaire* overture, and his *Épisode*. Delacroix painted the *Barque de Don Juan* from him, with the *Massacre de Scio*, the *Marino Faliero*, the *Combat du Giaour et du Pacha*, and many a notable picture more. Is it at all surprising that M. Taine should have found heart to say that alone among modern poets Byron '*atteint à la cime*'?[1] or that Mazzini should have reproached us with our unaccountable neglect of him and with our scandalous forgetfulness of the immense work done by him in giving a 'European *rôle* . . . to English literature' and in awakening all over the Continent so much 'appreciation and sympathy for England'?

He had his share in the work of making Matthew Arnold possible, but he is the antipodes of those men of culture and contemplation—those artists pensive and curious and sedately self-contained—whom Arnold best loved and of whom the nearest to hand is Wordsworth. Byron and Wordsworth are like the Lucifer and the Michael of *The Vision of Judgment*. Byron's was the genius of revolt, as Wordsworth's was the genius of dignified and useful submission; Byron preached the dogma of private revolution, Wordsworth the dogma of private apotheosis; Byron's theory of life was one of liberty and self-sacrifice, Wordsworth's one of self-restraint and self-improvement; Byron's practice was dictated by a vigorous and voluptuous egoism, Wordsworth's by a benign and lofty selfishness; Byron was the 'passionate and dauntless soldier of a forlorn hope,' Wordsworth a kind of inspired clergyman. Both were influences for good, and both are likely to be influences for good for some time to come. Which is the better and stronger is a question that can hardly be determined now. It is certain that Byron's star has waned, and that Wordsworth's has waxed; but it is also certain that there are moments in life when the 'Ode to Venice' is almost as refreshing and as precious as the 'Ode on the Intimations,' and when the epic mockery of *Don Juan* is to the full as beneficial as the chaste philosophy of *The Excursion* and the 'Ode to Duty.' Arnold was of course with Michael heart and soul, and was only interested in our Lucifer. He approached his subject in a spirit of undue deprecation. He thought it necessary to cite Scherer's opinion that Byron is but a coxcomb and a rhetorician: partly, it would appear, for the pleasure of seeming to agree with it in a kind of way and partly to have the satisfaction of distinguishing and of showing it to be a mistake. Then, he could not quote Goethe without apologising for the warmth of that consummate artist's expressions and explaining some of them away. Again, he was pitiful or disdainful, or both, of Scott's

[1] ['Reached the summit.']

462

estimate; and he did not care to discuss the sentiment which made that great and good man think *Cain* and *The Giaour* fit stuff for family reading on a Sunday after prayers, though as Mr. Ruskin has pointed out, in one of the wisest and subtlest bits of criticism I know, the sentiment is both natural and beautiful, and should assist us not a little in the task of judging Byron and of knowing him for what he was. That Arnold should institute a comparison between Leopardi and Byron was probably inevitable: Leopardi had culture and the philosophic mind, which Byron had not; he is incapable of influencing the general heart, as Byron can; he is a critics' poet, which Byron can never be; he was always an artist, which Byron was not; and—it were Arnoldian to take the comparison seriously. Byron was not interested in words and phrases but in the greater truths of destiny and emotion. His empire is over the imagination and the passions. His personality was many-sided enough to make his egoism representative. And as mankind is wont to feel first and to think afterwards, a single one of his heart-cries may prove to the world of greater value as a moral agency than all the intellectual reflections that Leopardi contrived to utter. After examining this and that opinion and doubting over and deprecating them all, Arnold touched firm ground at last in a dictum of Mr. Swinburne's, the most pertinent and profound since those of Goethe, to the effect that in Byron there is a 'splendid and imperishable excellence which covers all his offences and outweighs all his defects: the excellence of sincerity and strength.' With this 'noble praise' our critic agreed so vigorously that it became the keynote of the latter part of his summing up, and in the end you found him declaring Byron the equal of Wordsworth, and asserting of this 'glorious pair' that 'when the year 1900 is turned, and the nation comes to recount her poetic glories in the century which has just then ended, the first names with her will be these.' The prophecy is as little like to commend itself to the pious votary of Keats as to the ardent Shelleyite: there are familiars of the Tennysonian Muse, the Sibyl of 'Rizpah' and 'Vastness' and 'Lucretius' and 'The Voyage,' to whom it must seem impertinent beyond the prophet's wont; there are—(but *they* scarce count)—who grub (as for truffles) for meanings in Browning. But it was not uttered to please, and in truth it has enough of plausibility to infuriate whatever poet-sects there be. Especially the Wordsworthians.

62. Swinburne's attack on Byron

[1884] 1886

Swinburne's essay, 'Wordsworth and Byron', expressing his dissent from Arnold's estimate of these two poets, appeared in the *Nineteenth Century* for April and May 1884. It was reprinted in his *Miscellanies*, 1886, pp. 63–156. The following extract deals with Byron's defective artistry.

... Mr. Arnold has at once a passion and a genius for definitions. It is doubtless good to have such a genius, but it is surely dangerous to have such a passion. All sane men must be willing to concede the truth of an assertion which he seems to fling down as a challenge from the ethical critic to the aesthetic—that a school of poetry divorced from any moral idea is a school of poetry divorced from life. Even John Keats himself, except in his most hectic moments of sensuous or spiritual debility, would hardly, I should imagine, have undertaken to deny this. What may reasonably be maintained is a thesis very different from such a denial; namely, that a school of poetry subordinated to any school of doctrine, subjugated and shaped and utilized by any moral idea to the exclusion of native impulse and spiritual instinct, will produce work fit to live when the noblest specimens of humanity are produced by artificial incubation. However, when we come to consider the case of Byron, we must allow it to be wholly undeniable that some sort of claim to some other kind of merit than that of a gift for writing poetry must be discovered or devised for him, if any place among memorable men is to be reserved for him at all. ...

Before entering on the question, what criticism of life in any intelligible sense of the phrase may be derivable or deducible from the writings of Wordsworth or of Byron, I would venture to put forward, by no means a counter theory or a rival definition to Mr. Arnold's theory or definition of poetry, but a simple postulate, or at least a simple assumption, on which I would rest my argument. If it be not admitted, there is an end of the matter: it would be absolute waste of time, for one who assumes it as indisputable, to enter into controversy with one who regards it as disputable that the two primary and essential qualities of poetry are imagination and harmony: that where these qualities are wanting there can be no poetry, properly so called: and that where these qualities are perceptible in the highest degree, there, even though they should be unaccompanied and unsupported by any other great quality whatever—even though the ethical or critical faculty should be conspicuous by its absence—there, and only there, is the best and highest poetry. Now it is obviously impossible to supply any profitable or serviceable definition of these terms. All writers on the subject, from Mr. Arnold himself down to the smallest perceptible Byronite or Wordsworthian that ever wagged a tail or pricked an ear in the 'common cry of' critics, are compelled sooner or later to give expression to their views and their conclusions with as much implicit dogmatism as Mr. John Dennis or Dr. Samuel Johnson. If any one chooses to assert that Flatman or Sprat or Byron had the secret of harmony, it would be as profitable an expenditure of time and reason to argue against his proposition as to contend with a musical critic who should maintain that *Orphée aux Enfers* was a more sublime example of sacred music than *Israel in Egypt*. Byron is as fit to be considered the rival of Coleridge and Shelley as Offenbach to be considered a competitor with Handel and Beethoven. In other matters than those in which Coleridge and Shelley were supreme; on ground where they could not set a trespassing foot without being at once convicted of comparative if not absolute incompetence; Byron was supreme in his turn—a king by truly divine right; but in a province outside the proper domain of absolute poetry. He is undisputed suzerain of the debateable borderland to which Berni has given his name: the style called Bernesque might now be more properly called Byronic, after the greater master who seized and held it by right of the stronger hand. If to be great as a Bernesque writer is to be great as a poet, then was Byron assuredly a great poet: if it be not, then most assuredly he was nothing of the kind. On all other points, in all other capacities, he can only claim to be acknowledged as a poet of the third class who now and then rises into the second, but speedily relapses into the lower element where he was born. Nothing, I repeat, does so much credit to his intelligence as the fact that he should himself have seen this with more or less clearness: nothing does more discredit to his character than the effect produced by this consciousness on his bearing towards others, his contemporary superiors. Too clear-sighted—or his cleverness belies itself—not to know them for such, he was too vain, too envious, and too dishonest to acknowledge that he knew or even to abstain from denying it. And here we may not unprofitably observe the difference between the ever-itching vanity of such a writer as Byron and the candid pride of a great poet. When Dante Alighieri or William Shakespeare, when John Milton or when Victor Hugo may be pleased to speak as one not unconscious of his own greatness, such consciousness will be confounded with vanity by no man who does not bear as a birth-mark the sign of the tribe of Zoilus: it would show a certain degree of weakness and incompetence, if the greatest among men and writers should alone be doomed to share the incapacity of their meanest assailants to perceive or to acknowledge that they are not less than great. Far different from the high and haughty equity of such men's self-knowledge and self-reverence is the malevolent and cowardly self-conceit of a Byron, ever shuffling and swaggering and cringing and backbiting in a breath. The most remarkable point in his pretentious and restless egotism is that a man capable of writing such bad verse should ever have been capable of seeing, even in part, how very bad it was; how very hollow were its claims; how very ignorant, impudent, and foolish, was the rabble rout of its adorers. That his first admirers in foreign countries were men of a far different order is a curious and significant truth which throws a double light upon the question in hand. The greatest European poet of his day, the greatest European patriot of our own, united in opinion perhaps on this one point only, have left eloquent and enduring testimony to the greatness of their ideal Byron. The enthusiasm of Goethe on the one hand and Mazzini on the other should be ample and final witness to the forcible and genuine impression made by the best work of Byron upon some of the highest minds in Europe. But in the former case we have first of all to consider this: what was the worth of Herr von Goethe's opinion on any question of extra-German literature? Of French he presumably knew at least as much as of English: and his criticism of French literature, if it can hardly be matter of 'argument for a week,' may certainly afford 'laughter for a month, and a good jest for ever.' He rebuked the French for their injustice to so great a poet as Dubartas; he would doubtless have rebuked the English for their neglect of so great a poet as Quarles. He discerned among the rising Frenchmen of 1830 one genius of pre-eminent promise, one youth in whom he might hail his destined successor in the curule chair of European letters: and this favoured son of Apollo was none other—*si Musis placet!*[1]—than M.

[1] ['If it pleases the Muses!']

Prosper Mérimée. He might as rationally have remarked that England, in the age of Hume and Gibbon, Collins and Gray, Fielding and Richardson, Johnson and Goldsmith, Chatterton and Sterne, had produced one writer of absolutely unparalleled merit—in the person of Mr. Horace Walpole.

Taking these considerations into due account, it is not without amusement as well as regret, it is not without regret as well as amusement, that we find even in our own day two English writers of such distinction as Mr. Matthew Arnold and Mr. John Nichol debating and discussing as a matter of no small interest and moment to Englishmen, what it was that Goethe really said and what it was that Goethe really meant to say about the proper place of Byron among English poets. 'No array of terms,' protests Walt Whitman, 'can say how much I am at peace about God, and about death:' and consequently he counsels mankind, 'Be not curious about God.' No array of terms can say how much I am at peace about Goethe's opinions on modern poetry, after examination of such samples as have just been given: and if my voice had weight or authority enough to make itself heard, I would fain take leave to counsel even my elders and my betters, Be not curious to know whether, or in what sense, Goethe meant to say that Byron was the greatest of English poets—whether greater only than Coleridge and Shelley, or greater also than Shakespeare and Milton: for such questions, as St. Paul observes of genealogies, are unprofitable and vain.

The later tribute of Mazzini to Byron claims at our hands a very different degree of consideration. Not merely because, for all who knew and loved him, the name of the man who realized for them the ideal of selfless heroism—of infinite pity, helpfulness, love, zeal, and ardour as divine in the heat of wrath as in the glow of charity—set before us in the records of the life and character of Jesus is never to be lightly spoken, or cited without a sense of inward and infinite reverence: not merely because they feel and acknowledge that in him it was given them to see for once how divine a thing human nature may be when absolutely and finally divorced from all thought or sense of self; made perfect in heroism and devotion, even to the point, not merely unattainable but unimaginable for most men, of disregarding even the imputations of selfishness and cowardice; 'gentle, and just, and dreadless' as Shelley's ideal demigod, with the single-hearted tenderness and lovingkindness of a little child: not on any such inadequate and uncritical grounds as these, but simply because it seems to me that Mazzini alone has hit the mark which should be aimed at by all who undertake the apology or attempt the panegyric of Byron. 'That man *never* wrote from his heart,' says Thackeray, sweepingly and fiercely: 'he got up rapture and enthusiasm with an eye to the public.' The only answer to this is that on one single point, but that one a point of unsurpassed importance and significance, the imputation is insupportable and unjust. He wrote from his heart when he wrote of politics —using that sometimes ambiguous term in its widest and most accurate significance. A just and contemptuous hatred of Georgian government, combined with a fitful and theatrical admiration of the first Bonaparte, made him too often write and speak like a vilely bad Englishman—'the friend of every country but his own:' but his sympathy with the cause of justice during the blackest years of dynastic reaction on the continent makes him worthy even yet of a sympathy and respect which no other quality of his character or his work could now by any possibility command from any quarter worth a moment's consideration or regard. On the day when it shall become accepted as a canon of criticism that the political work and the political opinions of a poet are to weigh nothing in the balance which suspends his reputation—on that day the best part of the fame of Byron will fly up and vanish into air. Setting aside mere instances of passionately cynical burlesque, and perhaps one or two exceptional examples of apparently sincere though vehemently demonstrative personal feeling, we find little really living or really praiseworthy work of Byron's which has not in it some direct or indirect touch of political emotion.

But, without wishing to detract from the just honour which has been paid to him on this score, and paid at least in full if not with over-measure, we must not overlook, in common justice, the seamy side of his unique success among readers who did not read him in English. It is something, undoubtedly, to be set down to a man's credit, that his work—if his work be other than poetic—should lose nothing by translation: always assuming that it has anything to lose. But what shall be said of a poet whose work not only does not lose, but gains, by translation into foreign prose? and gains so greatly and indefinitely by that process as to assume a virtue which it has not? On taking up a fairly good version of *Childe Harold's Pilgrimage* in French or Italian prose, a reader whose eyes and ears are not hopelessly sealed against all distinction of good from bad in rhythm or in style will infallibly be struck by the vast improvement which the text has undergone in the course of translation. The blundering, floundering, lumbering and stumbling stanzas, transmuted into prose and transfigured into grammar, reveal the real and latent force of rhetorical energy that is in them: the gasping, ranting, wheezing, broken-winded verse has been transformed into really effective and fluent oratory. A ranter, of course, it is whose accents we hear in alternate moan and bellow from the trampled platform of theatrical misanthropy: but he rants no longer out of tune: and we are able to discern in the thick and troubled stream of his natural eloquence whatever of real value may be swept along in company with much drifting rubbish. It is impossible to express how much *Childe Harold* gains by being done out of wretchedly bad metre into decently good prose: the New Testament did not gain more by being translated out of canine Greek into divine English. Not that even under these improved conditions Byron's is comparable to the work of a first-rate orator or preacher; but one may perceive how men to whom English poetry was a strange tongue might mistake it for an impressive and effective example of English poetry.

It seems a trivial waste of time to insist repeatedly and in detail upon the rudiments of art: but when a man who can hardly ever attempt a picture on even the smallest scale without displaying his absolute ignorance of the veriest elements of painting is hailed as a master of his craft, those who respect as well as understand the conditions of its existence will not think a little time and trouble misspent in the reduction of such a thesis to its natural and demonstrable absurdity. But in writing on so absurd a subject it would be absurd to employ what Mr. Arnold calls the grand style. Let us rather take a handful of samples at random which may give some notion of Byron's; probably the finest example in all literature of that grandiose meanness which was often the leading note of the author's character and conduct. There are faults of style perceptible, no doubt, in poets of real greatness: Wordsworth's, for instance, are vexatious to the most loyal and thankful student in no small degree: but they are such faults as are possible to a great poet in moments of great perversity; Byron's, most distinctly, are not. His lava kisses and his baby earthquakes; his walls which have scalps, and pinnacle those scalps (was ever such jolter-headed jargon heard before, from Bedlam or Parnassus?) in cloud less thick than the confusion of such a chaos of false images; his stormy nights that are lovely in their strength as is—of all things on earth—the light of a woman's dark eye, or a dark eye in woman; his day that dies like a dolphin; his 'grocer's shop kept by one Nightingale'—as Landor ingeniously expounded the long insoluble conundrum with which *The Bride of Abydos* confronts all comers on the threshold: these and other such hideous absurdities as these oblige us to reconsider the question, whether the generation of our fathers may not have been right after all in deciding—as we know from so illustrious a spokesman as Thackeray that his young contemporaries, in the freshness of their enthusiasm for Wordsworth, Keats, and the rising star of Tennyson, did most unhesitatingly and vehemently decide—that this idol of our grandfathers or grandmothers could maintain no higher title to fame than one which is the appanage of every successful pressman or improvisatore—the title of a very clever man. One thing is very certain: no man with a touch of true spiritual instinct could have perpetrated such monstrous stupidities. The perpetrator had fancy, wit, fire natural and artificial, with very remarkable energy and versatility: but in all the composition of his highly composite nature there was neither a note of real music nor a gleam of real imagination. If these certainly rather considerable defects are held sufficient to deprive a man of all claim to the title of poet, then undoubtedly Byron is no more a poet than any one of the tribe of dunces decimated by Pope. But the same may be said of Pope himself; and the present writer at least is not Wordsworthian enough to insist, in the name of critical accuracy, that the title of poet—'with a difference'—may not be granted to the authors of *Don Juan* and *The Rape of the Lock*.'

This conjunction of names would be unjust to either poet if we should overlook the points in which either excelled the other. Pope could not have put such fiery fancy, such a force of impulse and emotion, into *The Vision of Judgment* or the successful parts of *Don Juan*, any more than he could have been guilty of such unspeakable abominations, such debauched excesses of bad taste run mad and foaming at the mouth, as the examples lately cited from *Childe Harold*; or than he could, in his critical aspect,—however captious his temper, and however limited his view—have been capable of such grotesque impertinence as theirs (if any such critics there be) who would defend such examples of poetic style by reminding objectors of the undisputed and indisputable facts that a dying dolphin does really exhibit a superb succession of colours, and that to a young lover the light of a dark eye in woman, or a woman's dark eye, is an object of equal and superior impressiveness and importance to the sight of a thunder-storm at midnight. Who in the name of Momus ever questioned it? Neither is it less unquestionable to any one who knows good work from bad that the fashion in which these facts have been expressed in verse and utilized for illustration by the author of *Childe Harold* is such as would have been simply impossible to a writer born with even an average allowance of imaginative perception or of instinctive taste. And this is the author placed almost at the head of modern poets by the eminent poet and critic who has so long, so loudly, and so justly preached to the world of letters the supreme necessity of 'distinction' as the note of genuine style which alone enables any sort of literary work to survive! Shakespeare and Hugo are not good enough for him: in *Macbeth* and in *Hernani* he finds damning faults of style, and a plentiful lack of distinction: the text of the latter he garbles and falsifies as Voltaire garbled and falsified the text of Shakespeare, and apparently for the same purpose—as unworthy of the one philosopher as of the other. But in Byron—of all remembered poets the most wanting in distinction of any kind, the most dependent for his effects on the most vulgar and violent resources of rant and cant and glare and splash and splutter—in Byron the apostle of culture, and the author of such nobly beautiful and blameless work as *Thyrsis* and the songs of Callicles, finds a seed of immortality more promising than in Coleridge or Shelley, the two coequal kings of English lyric poetry. . . .

Great as was Milton's influence on Wordsworth, it could no more affect the indomitable independence of his genius than the study of classic poets could affect that of Milton's own. When the impression of Milton's rhythmic majesty is most perceptible in the sublimest and most splendid verse of Wordsworth, it is always nevertheless the note of Wordsworth's own voice, not of Milton's as repeated and enfeebled by a dwindling echo, that we hear. Let us see how far the direct mimicry of a great poet's metrical inspiration could avail to give strength or sweetness to the naturally flaccid and untunable verse of Byron. This is the sort of stuff he has to offer in imitation of Coleridge's metre in *Christabel*—or rather in imitation of Scott's imitation of Coleridge's metre.

> Mount ye, spur ye, skirr the plain,
> That the fugitive may flee in vain, (*sic*)
> When he breaks from the town; and none escape,
> Aged or young, in the Christian shape.

This is a sample of Byron's choicer verse, as selected for our admiring notice by Mr. Arnold, in a volume designed to bear witness of his superiority as a poet to Coleridge and Shelley. The editor in his preface has done me the honour to cite, in a tone of courteous and generous cordiality which I am anxious to acknowledge, the phrase in which I have claimed for Byron at his best 'the excellence of sincerity and strength.' But surely he would not differ from me in thinking that this is not the broken gallop of rough vigour; it is the sickly stumble of drivelling debility. *Harold the Dauntless*—a poem not on the whole to be classed, any more than *The Field of Waterloo*, among the more justifiable claims of Scott to poetic immortality—has nothing in it of such pitiful incompetence. And I agree with Mr. Arnold that the passage in which it occurs is no unfair sample of one of the most animated and spirited among the serious poems of Byron. Let us try again—still following in the wake of the same distinguished critic. Here is another taste from the same platter, as served up on the select and studiously arranged board at which he invites us to sit down and partake of the chosen viands over which he has just said grace.

> Though her eye shone out, yet the lids were fix'd,
> And the glance that it gave was wild and unmix'd
> With aught of change, as the eyes may seem
> Of the restless who walk in a troubled dream;
> Like the figures on arras, that gloomily glare,
> Stirr'd by the breath of the wintry air,
> So seen by the dying lamp's fitful light, (!)
> Lifeless, but life-like, and awful to sight;
> As they seem, through the dimness, about to come down
> From the shadowy wall where their images frown;
> Fearfully flitting to and fro,
> As the gusts on the tapestry come and go.
>
> Now this, we feel, is the sort of thing
> That is easy for any boy to bring
> Up to any extent who has once
> Read Coleridge or Scott, and is not quite a dunce,
> Though he have but a blue-eyed cat's pretence
> To an ear—as needs no sort of evidence.
> It could hardly be easier even to spout
> Volumes of English hexameters out
> (With as much notion of music in rhythms
> As men seek in a column of logarithms)
> Than thus to perpetuate the simper and snivel
> Of those various Medoras, that dreadfully drivel;
> And, from all who have any conception what verse is,
> To provoke remarks that might sound like curses.

A very few years ago, it would have been no more necessary to offer such remarks as these than to suggest that Sir William Davenant was not equal to Milton as an epic poet, nor Sir Robert Stapylton superior to Shakespeare as a dramatist. And I really should almost as soon have expected to see Lord Tennyson take up the cudgels for *Gondibert*, or Sir Henry Taylor for *The Slighted Maid*, as to find Mr. Arnold throwing the shield of his authority over the deformed and impotent nakedness of such utterly unutterable rubbish. He has complained elsewhere, with perfect justice, that Byron is 'so empty of matter.' Is it then the charm of execution, the grace of language, the perfection of form, which attracts him in the author of *The Siege of Corinth*? Is it 'the fount of fiery life,' 'the thunder's roll,' perceptible in such productions as these? . . . Is it his dramatic or lyrical gift? There is certainly some very effective rhetoric in one or two of his shorter pieces: but 'the lyrical cry' which his panegyrist so properly requires—the pure note which can be breathed only from the pure element of lyric verse—is wanting alike in his earliest and his latest effusions, noble and impressive in sentiment and in style as a few—a very few of them—indisputably are. As to his dramatic faculty, it was grossly overpraised by Macaulay in the following sentence:—'It is hardly too much to say, that Lord Byron could exhibit only one man and only one woman.' On the contrary, I would venture to submit, but in a very different sense, it is greatly too much to say. He could exhibit only two squeaking and disjointed puppets: there is, as far as I can remember, just one passage in the whole range of his writings which shows any power of painting any phase of any kind of character at all: and this is no doubt a really admirable (if not wholly original) instance of the very broadest comedy—the harangue addressed by Donna Julia to her intruding husband. The famous letter addressed to her boy-lover on his departure . . . is an admirably eloquent and exceptionally finished piece of writing, but certainly, with its elaborate poise of rhetoric about the needle and the pole, is not an exceptional instance either of power to paint character and passion from the naked life, or of ability to clothe and crown them with the colour and the light of genuine imagination. A poet with any real insight into the depth of either comic or tragic nature could have desired no finer occasion for the display of his gift, though assuredly he could have chosen none more difficult and dangerous, than such a subject as is presented by history in the figure of Catherine the Great. Terror and humour would have been the twin keynotes of his work; as effective in their grotesque and lurid union as the harmony of terror and pity in the severer art of the ancient stage. . . . What has Byron made of the great, generous, fearless, shameless and pitiless woman of genius whom a far mightier artist was six years later to place before us in her habit as she lived, breathing lust and blood, craving fame and power, consumed and unsubdued by the higher and the lower ardours of a nature capable of the noblest and ignoblest ambition and desire? The Russian episode in *Don Juan* is a greater discredit to literature by its nerveless and stagnant stupidity than even by the effete vulgarity of its flat and stale uncleanliness. Haidée and Dudù are a lovely pair of lay-figures: but the one has only to be kissed, and to break a blood-vessel: the other—has even less to do. Lady Adeline promises better than any other study from the same hand, and Aurora Raby is a graceful sketch in sentimental mezzotint: what might have been made of them in time we can but guess: it is only certain that nothing very much worth making had been made of them, when the one poem in which Byron showed even a gleam of power to draw characters from life was dropped or cut short at a point of somewhat cynical promise. Further evidence would hardly have been requisite to display the author's incapacity for dramatic no less than for lyric poetry, even had his injudicious activity not impelled him to write plays beside which even Voltaire's look somewhat less wretchedly forlorn. For indeed nothing quite so villainously bad as Byron's tragedies is known to me as the work of any once eminent hand which ever gave proof of any poetic vigour or energy at all. As a dramatist, Voltaire stands nearer to Corneille—nay, Dryden stands nearer to Shakespeare—than Byron to Voltaire or to Dryden. In one only of his dramatic miscreations is there the dimmest glimpse of interest discoverable, even as regards the mere conduct of the story: and this play is the most impudent instance of barefaced theft to be found in the records of our literature. The single original thing in it, and the most original thing in its companion dramas, is of course the rhythm; and on this it would assuredly have seemed needless to waste a word or a smile, had not the author of some of the stateliest and purest blank verse ever written appeared as the most recent champion of Byron's claim to a place among the great representative poets of a language in which the metre of Marlowe and of Milton affords a crowning test of poetic power.

> The only way to criticise it is
> To write a sentence (which is easy to
> Do, and has been done once or twice before
> Now) in the metre of *Cain*, or of *The*
> *Two Foscari*, or *Heaven and Earth*, or *The*
> *Deformed Transformed*, *Sardanapalus*, or

> *Werner*—nay, *Faliero* (such is the
> Way the name is elongated in his
> Play—which is not agreeable to an
> Ear which has any sense of sound left). It
> Is hardly harder (as the bard might have
> Said) to write pages upon pages in
> This style—base beyond parody—than to
> Write as ill in Scott's usual metre: but
> All will allow that in both cases it
> Is an excruciating process for
> Persons accustomed to read or write verse.[1]

Imitation of Byron's 'mighty line'—parody of it, I repeat, is impossible—would not long since have been a weary, stale, flat and unprofitable jest: but it is a flatter and a staler jest yet to reclaim precedence for his drawling draggle-tailed drab of a Muse over Polymnia when she speaks through Coleridge, Euterpe when she speaks through Keats, Urania when she speaks through Shelley. Iynx it was—the screaming wryneck—that inspired the verse of Byron with its grace of movement and its charm of melody. And all the world knows what became of that songstress and her tuneful sisters when they challenged the Muses to a contest less unequal than would be the contest of the long since plume-plucked Byron with the least of the three poets just named. . . .

When the highest intelligence enlisted in the service of the higher criticism has done all it can ever aim at doing in exposition of the highest things in art, there remains always something unspoken and something undone which never in any way can be done or spoken. The full cause of the full effect achieved by poetry of the first order can be defined and expounded with exact precision and certitude of accuracy by no strength of argument or subtlety of definition. All that exists of good in the best work of a Byron or a Southey can be defined, expounded, justified and classified by judicious admiration, with no fear lest anything noticeable or laudable should evade the analytic apprehension of critical goodwill. No one can mistake what there is to admire, no one can want words to define what it is that he admires, in the forcible and fervent eloquence of a poem so composed of strong oratorical effects arranged in vigorous and telling succession as Byron's 'Isles of Greece.' There is not a single point missed that an orator on the subject would have aimed at making: there is not a touch of rhetoric

[1] The metre here is Byron's, 'every line:
For God's sake, reader! take it not for mine.'

that would not, if delivered under favourable circumstances, have brought down the house or shaken the platform with a thunder-peal of prolonged and merited applause. It is almost as effective, and as genuine in its effect, as anything in *Absalom and Achitophel*, or *The Medal*, or *The Hind and the Panther*. It is Dryden—and Dryden at his best—done out of couplets into stanzas. That is the very utmost that Byron could achieve; as the very utmost to which Southey could attain was the noble and pathetic epitome of history, with its rapid and vivid glimpses of tragic action and passion, cast into brief elegiac form in his monody on the Princess Charlotte. And the merits of either are as easily definable as they are obvious and unmistakable. The same thing may be said of Wordsworth's defects: it cannot be said of Wordsworth's merits. The test of the highest poetry is that it eludes all tests. Poetry in which there is no element at once perceptible and indefinable by any reader or hearer of any poetic instinct may have every other good quality; it may be as nobly ardent and invigorating as the best of Byron's, or as nobly mournful and contemplative as the best of Southey's: if all its properties can easily or can ever be gauged and named by their admirers, it is not poetry—above all, it is not lyric poetry—of the first water. There must be something in the mere progress and resonance of the words, some secret in the very motion and cadence of the lines, inexplicable by the most sympathetic acuteness of criticism. Analysis may be able to explain how the colours of this flower of poetry are created and combined, but never by what process its odour is produced. Witness the first casual instance that may be chosen from the wide high range of Wordsworth's.

> Will no one tell me what she sings?
> Perhaps the plaintive numbers flow
> For old, unhappy, far-off things,
> And battles long ago.

If not another word were left of the poem in which these two last lines occur, those two lines would suffice to show the hand of a poet differing not in degree but in kind from the tribe of Byron or of Southey. In the whole expanse of poetry there can hardly be two verses of more perfect and profound and exalted beauty. But if anybody does not happen to see this, no critic of all that ever criticized, from the days of Longinus to the days of Arnold, from the days of Zoilus to the days of Zola, could succeed in making visible the certainty of this truth to the mind's eye of that person. . . .

63. Saintsbury on Byron's second-rateness

1896

George E. B. Saintsbury (1845–1933), man of letters, Professor of Rhetoric and English Literature at Edinburgh University from 1895 to 1915. Extract from *A History of Nineteenth Century Literature (1780–1895)*, 1896, pp. 78–81.

... Although opinions about Byron differ very much, there is one point about him which does not admit of difference of opinion. No English poet, perhaps no English writer except Scott (or rather 'The Author of *Waverley*'), has ever equalled him in popularity at home; and no English writer, with Richardson and Scott again as seconds, and those not very close ones, has equalled him in contemporary popularity abroad. The vogue of Byron in England, though overpowering for the moment, was even at its height resisted by some good judges and more strait-laced moralists; and it ebbed, if not as rapidly as it flowed, with a much more enduring movement. But abroad he simply took possession of the Continent of Europe and kept it. He was one of the dominant influences and determining causes of the French Romantic movement; in Germany, though the failure of literary talent and activity of the first order in that country early in this century made his school less important, he had great power over Heine, its one towering genius; and he was almost the sole master of young Russia, young Italy, young Spain, in poetry. Nor, though his active and direct influence has of course been exhausted by time, can his reputation on the Continent be said to have ever waned.

These various facts, besides being certain in themselves, are also very valuable as guiding the inquirer in regions which are more of opinion. The rapidity of Byron's success everywhere, the extent of it abroad (where few English writers before him had had any at all), and the decline at home, are all easily connected with certain peculiarities of his work. That work is almost as fluent and facile as Scott's, to which, as has been said, it owes immense debts of scheme and manner; and it

477

is quite as faulty. Indeed Scott, with all his indifference to a strictly academic correctness, never permitted himself the bad rhymes, the bad grammar, the slip-shod phrase in which Byron unblushingly indulges. But Byron is much more monotonous than Scott, and it was this very monotony, assisted by an appearance of intensity, which for the time gave him power. The appeal of Byron consists very mainly, though no doubt not wholly, in two things: the lavish use of the foreign and then unfamiliar scenery, vocabulary, and manners of the Levant, and the installation, as principal character, of a personage who was speedily recognised as a sort of fancy portrait, a sketch in cap and yataghan, of Byron himself as he would like to be thought. This Byronic hero has an ostentatious indifference to moral laws, for the most part a mysterious past which inspires him with deep melancholy, great personal beauty, strength, and bravery, and he is an all-conquering lover. He is not quite so original as he seemed, for he is in effect very little more than the older Romantic villain-hero of Mrs. Radcliffe, the Germans, and Monk Lewis, costumed much more effectively, placed in scheme and companionship more picturesquely, and managed with infinitely greater genius. But it is a common experience in literary history that a type more or less familiar already, and presented with striking additions, is likely to be more popular than something absolutely new. And accordingly Byron's bastard and second-hand Romanticism, though it owed a great deal to the terrorists and a great deal more to Scott, for the moment altogether eclipsed the pure and original Romanticism of his elders Coleridge and Wordsworth, of his juniors Shelley and Keats.

But although the more extreme admirers of Byron would no doubt dissent strongly from even this judgment, it would probably be subscribed, with some reservations and guards, by not a few good critics from whom I am compelled to part company as to other parts of Byron's poetical claim. It is on the question how much of true poetry lies behind and independent of the scenery and properties of Byronism, that the great debate arises. Was the author of the poems from *Childe Harold* to *Don Juan* really gifted with the poetical 'sincerity and strength' which have been awarded him by a critic of leanings so little Byronic in the ordinary sense as Matthew Arnold? Is he a poetic star of the first magnitude, a poetic force of the first power, at all? There may seem to be rashness, there may even seem to be puerile insolence and absurdity, in denying or even doubting this in the face of such a European concert as has been described and admitted above. Yet the critical conscience admits of no transaction; and after all, as it was

478

doubted by a great thinker whether nations might not go mad like individuals, I do not know why it should be regarded as impossible that continents should go mad like nations.

At any rate the qualities of Byron are very much of a piece, and, even by the contention of his warmest reasonable admirers, not much varied or very subtle, not necessitating much analysis or disquisition. They can be fairly pronounced upon in a judgment of few words. Byron, then, seems to me a poet distinctly of the second class, and not even of the best kind of second, inasmuch as his greatness is chiefly derived from a sort of parody, a sort of imitation, of the qualities of the first. His verse is to the greatest poetry what melodrama is to tragedy, what plaster is to marble, what pinchbeck is to gold. He is not indeed an impostor; for his sense of the beauty of nature and of the unsatisfactoriness of life is real, and his power of conveying this sense to others is real also. He has great, though uncertain, and never very fine, command of poetic sound, and a considerable though less command of poetic vision. But in all this there is a singular touch of illusion, of what his contemporaries had learnt from Scott to call gramarye. The often cited parallel of the false and true Florimels in Spenser applies here also. The really great poets do not injure each other in the very least by comparison, different as they are. Milton does not 'kill' Wordsworth; Spenser does not injure Shelley; there is no danger in reading Keats immediately after Coleridge. But read Byron in close juxtaposition with any of these, or with not a few others, and the effect, to any good poetic taste, must surely be disastrous; to my own, whether good or bad, it is perfectly fatal. The light is not that which never was on land or sea; it is that which is habitually just in front of the stage: the roses are rouged, the cries of passion even sometimes (not always) ring false. I have read Byron again and again; I have sometimes, by reading Byron only and putting a strong constraint upon myself, got nearly into the mood to enjoy him. But let eye or ear once catch sight or sound of real poetry, and the enchantment vanishes. . . .

64. Paul Elmer More on Byron's classicism

1898

Paul Elmer More (1864–1937), the American philosopher and critic, and exponent of the New Humanism, wrote on 'The Wholesome Revival of Byron' in the *Atlantic Monthly* for December 1898 (LXXXII, 801–9). The classicism which he praises in Byron involves 'a certain predominance of the intellect over the emotions', a consequent 'simplicity and tangibility of general design', an interest in humanity rather than nature, and a concentration on 'the simple elemental passions' leading to 'an art which depends on broad effects instead of subtle and vague impressions'. The following extracts are from pp. 803–5, 807.

. . . Were the subject not too technical, the radical difference between these classes of poets [classical and romantic] might be shown by a study of their use of metaphor. Poetry hardly exists without metaphor. Besides the formal simile there is in verse the more pervasive use of metaphorical language, by which the whole world of animate and inanimate nature is brought into similarity and kinship with the human soul, so that our inner life is enlarged and exalted by a feeling of universal dominion. The classical metaphor is simple and intellectual; through its means the vague is fixed and presented clearly to the mind by comparison with the more definite, the complex by comparison with the simple, the abstract with the concrete, the emotional with the sensuous. Its rival, the romantic metaphor, appeals to the fancy by the very opposite method. It would be easy to take the *Prometheus Unbound* and show how Shelley persistently relaxes the mind by vague and abstract similes. The moments are said to crawl like '*death*-worms;' spring is compared with the 'memory of a dream,' with 'genius', or 'joy which riseth up as from the earth;' 'the rushing avalanche' is likened to 'thought by thought . . . piled up, till some great truth is loosened, and the nations echo round.' In the famous and exquisitely beautiful singing-metaphor of that poem we have in miniature a perfect picture of the romantic poet's art:

> Meanwhile thy spirit lifts its pinions
> In music's most serene dominions;
> Catching the winds that fan that happy heaven.
> And we sail on, away, afar
> Without a course, without a star,
> But by the instinct of sweet music driven.

Perhaps nowhere could a more perfect expression of this wayward and delicate spirit of romance be found, unless in that brief phrase of *A Winter's Tale*:

> A wild dedication of yourselves
> To unpathed waters, undreamed shores.

Take away this subtle and baffling overgrowth of the emotions, and the sturdier metaphor of the classical poets remains. Individual comparisons of this vague character may no doubt be cited from Byron (they are not altogether wanting even in Homer), but they are in him distinctly exceptions. In general the poetic medium in which he works has an intellectual solidity akin to the older masters.

Poetry is the most perfect instrument of expression granted us in our need of self-utterance, and it is something to have learned in what way this instrument is shaped to the hand of a strong poet. But this is not all. We desire to know further the material he chooses and how he treats it. How does he deal with the great themes of literature? How does he stand toward nature and man? And here too we shall find a real contrast between Byron and his contemporaries.

There is a scene in Mrs. Gaskell's *Cranford* which to me has always seemed to set forth the aim of the romantic nature-poet in a charming light. It is the bewitching chapter where the ladies visit old Mr. Holbrook, the bachelor, and he, musing after dinner in the garden, quotes and comments on Tennyson:

'The cedar spreads his dark-green layers of shade.'
'Capital term—layers! Wonderful man! . . . Why, when I saw the review of his poems in *Blackwood*, I set off within an hour, and walked seven miles to Misselton (for the horses were not in the way) and ordered them. Now, what colour are ash-buds in March?'
Is the man going mad? thought I. He is very like Don Quixote.
'What colour are they, I say?' repeated he vehemently.
'I am sure I don't know, sir,' said I, with the meekness of ignorance.
'I knew you didn't. No more did I—an old fool that I am!—till this young man comes and tells me. Black as ash-buds in March. And I've lived all my life

in the country; more shame for me not to know. Black: they are jet-black madam.'

Excellent botany, no doubt, and very dainty verse; and yet I cannot think the fame of the great masters of song depends on such trivialities as this. *Black as ash-buds in March,*—one might read all the famous epics of the past without acquiring this curious bit of information. Now it is perfectly sure that, practically, all the versemakers of the present day look to natural description for their main theme, and would clap their poetical hands as in the joy of a vast inspiration over one such novel bit of observation that chanced to fall in their way. And in this they have but carried to its extreme tenuity the disposition of the romantic poets, their forbears. There is a good deal of this petty, prying nature-cult in Keats and Shelley, along with inspiration of a more solid or mystical quality. And it is Wordsworth who chants over the small celandine:

> Since the day I found thee out,
> Little flower!—I'll make a stir,
> Like a great astronomer.

Some kinship of spirit, some haunting echo of the revolutionary cry, binds us very close to the singers of that age, and we are perforce influenced by their attitude toward the outer world. It would be a matter of curious inquiry to search out the advent of this nature-worship into poetry, and to trace it down through later writers. . . .

An eternal harmony did indeed spring from this new source of music; it was a substantial gain, a new-created idealism in poetry. But we should not shut our eyes to the concomitant danger and loss. In this flattering absorption into nature the poet was too apt to forget that, after all, the highest and noblest theme must forever be the struggle of the human soul; he was too ready to substitute vague reverie for honest thought, and to lose his higher sympathy with man in the eager pursuit of minute phenomena. We are all familiar with the travestied nature-cult to be seen especially in unattached women, who seek in this way an outlet for unemployed emotions such as formerly they found in religious enthusiasm. There is, alas, too much of this petty sentimentality in the verse of the day. We turn to the earlier bards of the century, the founders of this new religion, for guidance and inspiration, and too often we imitate their weakness instead of their strength. Wordsworth has made a stir over the small celandine, and Tennyson has discovered that ash-buds are black in March; the present generation must, for originality, examine the fields with a botanist's lens, while the poor reader, who retains any use of his mind, is too often reminded of the poet Gray's shrewd witticism, that he learnt botany to save himself the trouble of thinking. If for no other reason, we are justified in calling attention to Byron, who in his treatment of nature shows the same breadth and mental scope, the same human sympathy, which characterize his classical use of metaphor. . . .

At bottom Byron's sympathy is not with nature, but with man, and in the expression of this sympathy he displays the sturdy strength of classic art. Théophile Gautier, in his study of Villon, has a clever appeal for the minor bards. 'The most highly vaunted passages of the poets,' he says, 'are ordinarily commonplaces. Ten verses of Byron on love, on the brevity of life, or on some other subject equally as new will find more admirers than the strangest vision of Jean Paul or of Hoffmann: this is because very many have been or are in love, and a still greater number are fearful of death, but very few, even in dreams, have beheld the fantastic images of the German story-tellers pass before them.' Gautier himself, as one of the 'fantastics', may be prejudiced in their favor, but his characterization of Byron is eminently right. It is a fact that the great poets, the classic poets, deal very much with commonplaces, but Gautier should know his Horace well enough to remember that nothing is more difficult than the art of giving these commonplaces an individual stamp.

Here again it may be wise to turn for a while from the romantic poets who search out the wayward, obscure emotions of the heart to one who treated almost exclusively those simple, fundamental passions which are most compatible with predominance of intellect and breadth of expression. I hardly know where in English literature, outside of Shakespeare, one is to find the great passions of men set forth so directly and powerfully as in Byron, and on this must rest his final claim to serious consideration. . . .

65. Chesterton on Byron's optimism

1902

In his essay on 'The Optimism of Byron' (*Twelve Types*, 1902, pp. 31–44), G. K. Chesterton (1874–1936) draws an amusing contrast between Byron's pessimism and that of the *fin de siècle*: 'Byronism tended towards the desert; the new pessimism towards the restaurant.' But he argues that Byron's ostensible pessimism is evidence of his basic optimism (*op. cit.*, pp. 39, 41–4).

. . . Surely it is ridiculous to maintain seriously that Byron's love of the desolate and inhuman in nature was the mark of vital scepticism and depression. When a young man can elect deliberately to walk alone in winter by the side of the shattering sea, when he takes pleasure in storms and stricken peaks, and the lawless melancholy of the older earth, we may deduce with the certainty of logic that he is very young and very happy. . . .

It was so, indeed, with Byron himself; his really bitter moments were his frivolous moments. He went on year after year calling down fire upon mankind, summoning the deluge and the destructive sea and all the ultimate energies of nature to sweep away the cities of the spawn of man. But through all this his sub-conscious mind was not that of a despairer. . . . It was not until the time in which he wrote *Don Juan* that he really lost this inward warmth and geniality, and a sudden shout of hilarious laughter announced to the world that Lord Byron had really become a pessimist.

One of the best tests in the world of what a poet really means is his metre. He may be a hypocrite in his metaphysics, but he cannot be a hypocrite in his prosody. And all the time that Byron's language is of horror and emptiness, his metre is a bounding *pas de quatre*. He may arraign existence on the most deadly charges, he may condemn it with the most desolating verdict, but he cannot alter the fact that on some walk in a spring morning when all the limbs are swinging and all the blood alive in the body, the lips may be caught repeating:

Oh, there's not a joy the world can give like that it takes away,
When the glow of early youth declines in beauty's dull decay;
'Tis not upon the cheek of youth the blush that fades so fast,
But the tender bloom of heart is gone ere youth itself be past.

That automatic recitation is the answer to the whole pessimism of Byron.

The truth is that Byron was one of a class who may be called the unconscious optimists, who are very often, indeed, the most uncompromising conscious pessimists, because the exuberance of their nature demands for an adversary a dragon as big as the world. But the whole of his essential and unconscious being was spirited and confident, and that unconscious being, long disguised and buried under emotional artifices, suddenly sprang into prominence in the face of a cold, hard, political necessity. In Greece he heard the cry of reality, and at the time that he was dying, he began to live. He heard suddenly the call of that buried and sub-conscious happiness which is in all of us, and which may emerge suddenly at the sight of the grass of a meadow or the spears of the enemy.

66. J. Churton Collins on Byron's greatness

1905

John Churton Collins (1848–1908), as a passionate advocate of Literature as opposed to 'Language', was the stormy petrel of English studies in the eighties and nineties (see Stephen Potter, *The Muse in Chains*, 1937, pp. 183–201; and D. J. Palmer, *The Rise of English Studies*, 1965, pp. 65, 78–103). His essay 'The Collected Works of Lord Byron' (a review article on the *Letters and Journals*, ed. R. E. Prothero, and the *Poetical Works*, ed. E. H. Coleridge) appeared in the *Quarterly Review* for April 1905, and was reprinted with minor but significant revisions in his *Studies in Poetry and Criticism*, 1905, pp. 78–123. The following extract (*op. cit.*, pp. 116–23) deals with *Don Juan* and Byron's claims to greatness as a poet.

... To pass to his masterpieces; *Childe Harold* and *Don Juan*, regarded comprehensively, are perhaps the two most brilliant achievements in the poetry of the world,[1] and they are achievements which have nothing in common. Each moves in a sphere of its own, as each exhibits powers differing not in degree merely, but in kind. *Childe Harold* is a superb triumph partly of pure rhetoric and partly of rhetoric touched with inspired enthusiasm. In *Don Juan* we are in another world and under the spell of another genius. The sentimentalist has passed into the cynic, the moralist into the mocker. We are no longer in the temples and palaces of poetry, but in its profane places and meaner habitations. The theme now is not Nature in her glory, but humanity in its squalor; not the world as God made it, but as the devil rules it. For the series of splendid pageants, for the raptures and sublimities of its predecessor, has been substituted, in broad, free fresco, the tragic farce into which man's lusts and lawlessness, madness and follies, have perverted life. It was into this mock-heroic that Byron, disengaging himself from all

[1] [Cf. pp. 108, 116: 'In ... the sphere of satire and comedy his masterpiece—and here his power is sustained—is *The Vision of Judgment*'; 'As satire in mock-heroic, *The Vision of Judgment* has neither equal nor second in European literature.']

that vanity had induced him to affect, and from all that his cleverness and command of rhetoric had enabled him to assume, poured out his powers in sheer and absolute sincerity—the Titanism which was of the very essence of his genius, the scorn and mockery, the wit, the persiflage, the irony, 'the sense of tears in human things,' the brutal appetites, the more refined affections of which he was still, in some of his moods, susceptible.

Don Juan is admirable alike in conception, in range, in expression. To give unity to a work which blends all that amuses and entertains us in *Lazarillo de Tormes*, *Gil Blas*, the *Novelle Amorose*, and Horace Walpole's *Letters*, much of what impresses and charms us in the *Odyssey* and the *Aeneid*, which has all the cynicism of La Rochefoucauld and Swift, all the callous levity of the worst school of our comedy, and yet subdues us with a pathos which has now the note of Ecclesiastes and now the note of Catullus—this indeed required a master-hand. The unity of the poem is the unity impressed on it by truth, by truth to nature and truth to life, for Byron in writing it did but hold up the mirror to himself and his own experiences.

'What an antithetical mind!' (he himself wrote after reading certain letters of Burns)—'tenderness, roughness, delicacy, coarseness, sentiment, sensuality, soaring and grovelling, dirt and deity, all mixed up in that one compound of inspired clay.'

Such, in fact, was Byron himself, and such is this poem, the glory and the shame of our poetry. But if much is to be forgiven to one who loves greatly, something may be forgiven to one who hates rightly. The justification of *Don Juan* is its ruthless exposure of some of the most despicable characteristics of the English people: the ubiquity of hypocrisy, the ubiquity of cant; immorality masking as morality, and ceremony as religion, for the vilest purposes, the one to make capital out of the frailties and lapses of those who are at least sincere, the other as a means for dignifying almost every form which moral cowardice and moral vanity can assume.

In its execution *Don Juan* deserves all the praise which Byron's most extravagant admirers have heaped on it. Never was our language so completely clay in the moulder's hands. Whatever he has to express seems to embody itself spontaneously in the complicated form of verse which he has chosen. With a skill and ease which, in our literature at least, are unrivalled, he has blended every extreme in nature and life, in style and tone, without producing the effect either of incongruity or even of impropriety. *Don Juan* has little enough in common with the

Odyssey, and yet in some respects it recalls it. In both poems the similitude which at once suggests itself is the element so closely associated with the action of both—the sea. A freshness, a breeziness, a pungency as of the brine-laden air of beach or cliff seems to pervade it. Over the spacious expanse of its narrative, teeming with life and in ever-changing play, now in storm and now in calm, roll and break, wave after wave in endless succession, the incomparable stanzas on whose lilt and rush we are swept along.

The importance of Byron in English poetry is not to be estimated by ordinary critical tests; it is not by its quality that his work is to be judged. The application of perfectly legitimate criteria to his poetry would justify us in questioning whether he could be held to stand high even among the *Dii minores*[1] of his art; it would certainly result in assigning him a place very much below Wordsworth and Shelley, and even below Keats. Of many, nay, of most of the qualities essential in a poet of a high order, there is no indication in anything he has left us. Of spiritual insight he has nothing; of morality and the becoming, except in their coarser aspects, he has no sense. If the beautiful appealed to him, it appealed to him only in its material expression and sentimentally as it affected the passions. Of no poet could it be said with so much truth—and how much does that truth imply!—that he had not 'music in his soul.' Turn where we will in his work, there is no repose, no harmony; all is without balance, without measure, and, if we except *Don Juan* and *The Vision of Judgment,* without unity. At his worst he sinks below Peter Pindar; at his best his accent is never that of the great masters. A certain ingrained coarseness, both in taste and feeling, which became more emphasised as his powers matured, not only made him insensible of much which appeals to the poet as distinguished from the rhetorician, but is accountable for the jarring notes, the lapses into grossness, and the banalities which so often surprise and distress us in his poetry.

As an artist, his defects are equally conspicuous. In architectonic he is as deficient as Tennyson. *Childe Harold,* as well as all his minor narratives, simply resolve themselves into a series of pageants or episodes. Some, notably *The Giaour,* are little more than congeries of brilliant scraps. No eminent English poet, with the exception of Browning, had so bad an ear. His cacophanies are often horrible; his blank-verse is generally indistinguishable from prose; and his rhythm in rhymed verse is without delicacy, and full of discords. Every solecism in

[1] ['Lesser gods.']

grammar, every violation of syntax and of propriety of expression, might be illustrated from his diction and style. Nor is this all. His claim to originality can only be conceded with much modification in its important aspects, and with very much more modification in the less important.

These are large deductions to make; and yet Goethe placed Byron next to Shakespeare among the English poets; and in fame and popularity, by the consentient testimony of every nation in Europe, next to Shakespeare among Shakespeare's countrymen, he still stands. Such a verdict it is much more easy to understand than to justify. To his countrymen Byron's flaws and limitations will always be more perceptible and important than they will be to the people of the Continent; while, in all that appeals to humanity at large, his work will come more nearly home on the other side of the Channel than that of any other English poet except Shakespeare; and necessarily so. Byron's poetry originally was not so much an appeal to England as to Europe. His themes, his characters, his inspiration, his politics, his morals, were all derived from the Continent or from the East. England was little more than the incarnation of everything against which he reacted, at first with contempt and then in fury. The trumpet-voice of the world of the Revolution and of the revolt against the principles of the Holy Alliance, it was on the Continent that he found most response. And there indeed he can never cease to be popular. The laureate of its scenery, the rhapsodist of its traditions, the student and painter of almost every phase of its many-sided life, the poet of the passions which burn with fiercer fire in the South than in the colder regions of the North, he neither has nor is likely to have, with the single exception of Shakespeare, an English rival across the Channel.

The greatness of Byron lies in the immense body and mass of the work which he has informed and infused with life, in his almost unparalleled versatility, in the power and range of his influential achievement. Youth and mature age alike feel his spell, for of the passions he is the Orpheus, of reflection the Mephistopheles. There is not an emotion, there is scarcely a mood, to which he does not appeal, and to which he has not given expression. Of almost every side of life, of almost every phase of human activity, he has left us studies more or less brilliant and impressive. He had, in extraordinary measure, nearly every gift, intellectually speaking, which man can possess, from mere cleverness to rapt genius; and there was hardly any species of composition which he did not more or less successfully attempt. . . .

As Goethe and Wordsworth were the Olympians, so he was the Titan of the stormy and chaotic age in which he lived; and his most authentic poetry is typical of his temper and attitude. He has impressed on our literature the stamp of a most fascinating and commanding personality, and on the literature of every nation in Europe he has exercised an influence to which no other British writer except Shakespeare has even approximated. . . . Such is the intrinsic power and attraction of a great part of his poetry that he will always be a favourite —if not in the first rank of their favourites—with his countrymen; and, although no purely critical estimate would place him on a level with at least five, if not more, of our poets, yet it must be admitted that, next to Shakespeare, he would probably be most missed.

67. J. F. A. Pyre on Byron and modern taste

1907

Pyre (1871–1934) was an American academic. His essay 'Byron in our Day' appeared in the *Atlantic Monthly* for April 1907 (XCIX, 542–52). The following extract is from pp. 542–4, 548–9, 550–1.

. . . The truth is, that nothing less than a readjustment of the principles upon which poetry is produced and estimated will have to precede a just estimate of Byron's poetry, of Byron as a force in the society which speaks the language he wrote. An instance of the cocksureness of each provincial generation of men is our assumption, latterly, that our standards of taste have settled to a constant. The principle upon which poets, critics and cultivated readers now mostly proceed is about as follows: a certain very lovely group of emotions is set aside from others, and we are instructed that these are the emotions which are awakened by poetry; whatever awakens any other sensations may be all very well, but it is not poetry. 'It's clever, but is it art?' This standard of poetic emotion is accompanied by a standard of delicate craftsmanship, pertaining particularly to details, skill in versification and in verbal melody, preciosity or *simplesse* of diction. With these standards in full sway the subject-matter of the poet is naturally limited to what can be best treated in such a manner. The result we all know. Poetry—contemporary poetry—has ceased to have any sufficient relation to life. Its 'dead but sceptred sovereigns still rule us from their urns;' but the living voice is seldom heard. Meanwhile, our criticism has become flaccid and over-tolerant; we do not hear, so often as formerly, the sturdy protests of 'men who are competent to look, and who do look, with a jealous eye, to the honour of English Literature;' such men as Keats was so nobly willing to 'conciliate'. Rather, we adopt an elegiac tone; we set the seal upon the usefulness of poetry, regretfully owning that the world has changed and that the divinest of the arts has become the trivial pursuit of the esoteric and the delicate voluptuary; the poet is a meaningless ornament of society, 'the idle

singer of an empty day.' The world has changed! There is the old
Alexandrian cry. With a culture more widely disseminated than the
English-speaking peoples have ever enjoyed, we are without one single
writer of verse of the first magnitude.

The decadence of modern English poetry began from Keats. Pure
Romanticism attained its highest excellence in the *Christabel* of Coleridge and in Keats's *St. Agnes' Eve*. Cut off before his ardor for beauty
had time to ripen under a sound and adequate experience of life, Keats
left to his successors a vessel of art, full to overflowing with rich and
sensuous appeal, and upon the rim of the bowl which held the Circean
draught, he inscribed this motto:

> 'Beauty is truth, truth beauty,'—that is all
> Ye know on earth, and all ye need to know.

With this were the followers of Iacchus made drunk. In other words,
the influence of Keats determined the main direction of English poetry.
Tennyson in his early period owed too much to Shakespeare and
Milton, and to his own temperament, to be regarded as directly imitative of Coleridge and Keats; but he is like them in aesthetic method
and quality. No one else lamented Tennyson's abandonment of the
Lotus land so much as FitzGerald. Perhaps this was not an accident in
the critic who was also the poet of the Omar Quatrains,—lovely
verses, full of exquisite sensualism and unfaith. Some facts lie outside of
the movement, of course; but even Browning was not untouched by
aestheticism, and only his fullness of intellect and rugged individuality
preserved him strong and single.

Next, the Pre-Raphaelite Brothers, Rossetti in chief, made even
religion voluptuous, allied English poetry as never before with the
sister arts, searched with a new and morbid sensitiveness alike into the
sensuous elements of the Arthurian Legend and the Christian Myth,
and overlaid them with a filigree of rare detail. Mr. Swinburne, somewhat swayed by Shelley, and flushed by the eroticism of some of the
French Romantics, carried technique, particularly that of sound, to the
point where meaning merges into music. He was by no means lacking
in passion and ideas of his own; but from him the creed of poetry as a
verbal art received powerful and 'damnable' iteration. From this time
on, thin and quavering parodies innumerable fill the air. Tennysonian
maidens and Pre-Raphaelite damosels, and angels 'in bright aureoles,'
'gleam and glimmer in shimmering shoals.' Poetry begins to be confused with choir-stalls, organ-lofts, tapestry-hangings, peacock-

screens, and variegated backgrounds; deep chloral fumes settle over *The City of Dreadful Night*; we get farther and farther from normal human experience, into a region where white peacocks wander about in gas-lit gardens of green chrysanthemums and yellow carnations, and other perverted vegetables; finally, we have for gain the patchouli and *lingerie* of *London Nights*. One would like to hear at last the large laugh and primitive bestiality of Rabelais, or even the hearty blasphemies of *Don Juan*, clearing through this atmosphere of insipid and effeminate pruriency. But our revolt to the natural world finds us nothing more new than a plaintive little band of Gaelic minstrels 'sitting on a green knoll apart,' piping a slender Irishism, remotely reminiscent of the posy, 'Beauty is truth, that is all you know.'

> The gleam,
> The light that never was on sea or land,
> The consecration and the poet's dream,

appear, after all, to him who has his eyes upon life, not to him who turns from it. Those who pursue the vision of beauty and pleasure too deeply into the wilderness of dreams, grasp only the Dead Sea apples of inspiration, strain after the mirage of poetry, glimpse at last but the corpse-light above the place where it lies buried. Romanticism has run out. It has gone, not to seed, but to a seedless pod; and no out-crossing can regenerate the species. We require a new stock.

'Aestheticism,' said Ibsen, in a letter written as long ago as 1865, 'is as fatal to poetry, as theology is to religion.' In the recognition of that principle, there lay the promise of a *man* in literature, not a mere musician, or bundle of nerves, quivering tunefully to each wandering air and sighing tremulously after a 'land of heart's desire.' Here is promise of a poetic instrument, stretched with strings of iron, to be struck by a mighty hand. In our own poetry, only one manly voice has been heard for a generation; it is not a great voice, and yet how Mr. Kipling has called to the heart of his time, we all know, perfectly well! The health of poetic art, more than of any other, depends upon a close and nourishing connection with the society which gives it being, and when that relation ceases to exist the art is doomed to perish. . . .

It has been urged that [Byron's] genius was all destructive, that he had no constructive wisdom. But his sense of the unsatisfactoriness of life is in itself recreative. One does not hate the false, unless his eyes, however bandaged, have had some glimpse of the truth. Byron is allied to the great minds of tragedy and comedy by his alertness to the incongruities of life, the grand and the trivial. What conformed to true design he could set forth with noble eloquence, and, at times, with superb poetic beauty; but he was more at home in the passions of discontent. Over what seemed but splendid failures in the scheme of things, he grieved with incomparable melancholy; the trivial, he lashed with diabolic mockery and scorn. His flippancy arises out of those moods in which all things seem trivial,—moods to which a Shakespeare or a Goethe never succumbs. Yet when all is said and done, such is the effect of his delight in the exercise of his own force, his own 'boldness, dash, and daring,' that we are not depressed but exhilarated; the total effect is not that of despair but of defiant will. We come out of the tumult, the vastness, and the gloom, energized, lifted up, electrified, as he himself came from the embraces of the sea, the caress of the night and the storm.

But his eloquence lacks the sustained distinction, his comedy the light-heartedness, of the very greatest. 'The mind in creation is as a fading coal,' said Shelley. In Byron, the poetic fire often fades suddenly and leaves us staring at blackened spots in his creations. He was dependent upon his volleying passion for illumination, and this failing, he had no assured art of style, or lacked the patience, to patch up his transitions or overlay with conciliating decoration the blotches where inspiration cooled. And this grave defect is very unsatisfactorily remedied by representing him in extracts, such as those chosen by Arnold. One must feel the long sweep, the general buoyancy of Byron, in order to understand him. It is this which is exhilarating, which carries us triumphantly over many a flagrant delinquency of metre or of diction. The critic who comes 'to peep and botanize' will find nothing but misery in Byron's style, unless, indeed, he come, as many critics do, to gloat. There are few single lines of magical appeal, as in Keats and Coleridge. It is almost impossible to select a single stanza, even from the best parts of *Childe Harold*, that is not disappointing if examined too closely. And yet, somehow, we are sustained and swept onward. . . .

When Byron discovered himself in *Don Juan*, his mind had matured, his way of life had become more wholesome, his technical ability had reached its height; what was of particular importance, he had learned to write more slowly and with greater patience; his daily stint was two octaves of *Don Juan*. The scheme of the poem was such as to allow him to deploy all his powers. Flesh and blood narrative, description which *is* the thing, satire in all keys, sentiment, trenchant reflection, are woven together with a mastery and ease which continually astonish, and never tire, though they sometimes shock. He is, by turns, comical and savage, pathetic and terrible, romantic and burlesque, earnest and reckless, intellectual and voluptuous; he laughs and weeps, prays and blasphemes, sings, shouts, threatens, cajoles, caresses, stabs right and left. Half a dozen stanzas as cleverly keyed and turned as the one quoted above to illustrate his satire of the blue-stockings [1] would be sufficient to make the fame and determine the bent of a minor poet, such as Praed; and this represents only one of a thousand moods. And yet, *Don Juan* is not a series of passages; the narrative swims forward without effort; our eyes are continually on the hero; our heart aches with the meaning of it all. It is a shallow view of this poem which regards it as a mere string of studied disenchantments, lewdnesses, cynicisms, and blasphemies. It is the panorama of life as Byron saw it, 'with all its imperfections on its head,' a mixture of good and evil, which he was bound to render frankly as it appeared to him, and as he lived and judged it,—not well perhaps, but passionately, fearlessly, and as a citizen of the world. Byron's recent editor [2] is not wrong in calling *Don Juan* the 'epic of modern life.'

Byron's view of life was, after all, essentially moral. He was deeply and sincerely interested in the moral aspect of things; only, he laid the stress elsewhere than on the conventional morality of his day. That conventional morality—often a mere matter of appearances—he stigmatized as cant; he hated that cant, not comically, at bottom, but earnestly, savagely; and he assailed it with furious blows, shocked it without mercy or caution. There is no doubting his sincerity when he cries out in his letters, 'It is the most moral of poems;' his contempt is as genuine as it is bitter, when he says to the British nation,—

> You're not a moral people and you know it
> Without the need of too sincere a poet.

But he was less interested in private, domestic morality than in public, political morality. Nothing could more clearly present this contrast than his terrible arraignment of George III, in *The Vision of Judgment*. And herein, he took a large, a continental view,—not an insular, British view. Perhaps he was wrong, but he was sincere. Further, his treatment of this theme is essentially poetical. He creates a myth, a political myth. His assaults on individuals are not, for the most part, the result of

[1] [I.e. *Don Juan*, Canto IV, stanza CXI: 'Yet some of you are most seraphic creatures. . . .']

[2] [Paul Elmer More (in the Cambridge Standard Edn. of *Byron's Poetical Works*), echoing Henley. (See *The Works of W. E. Henley*, 1908, IV, 183.)]

personal rancor, though this sometimes added to the zest of his attack. He erected a mythus of political devildom, and its heroes were Castlereagh and Wellington and George III, and, most of all, Southey, the recalcitrant laureate, the idealization, in his mind, of pusillanimous time-serving, of scribbling, prosperous British cant.

There is no doubt that *Don Juan* is often shocking; perhaps the sum total of its impression is that of a terrible disorder of enormous and varied powers, often ill-directed. There is no mistaking the inferiority of Byron's force to that of Shelley, in attractiveness, in sweetness, radiance, and charm; but there is, likewise, no mistaking Byron's superiority in massiveness, in variety, and in effectiveness. Shelley, who understood Byron thoroughly, was not deceived on that point; he well knew which was the mightier spirit. Shelley, too, not being one of the canters, readily saw that in *Don Juan* the immense talent of his great contemporary had first found the means of freely rendering itself effective. . . .

68. Arthur Symons on Byron

1909

Arthur William Symons (1865–1945), poet, editor and critic, member of the Rhymers' Club and author of *The Symbolist Movement in Literature* (1899), wrote on Byron in his book *The Romantic Movement in English Poetry*, 1909. The following extracts are from pp. 239–40, 244–9, 253–6, 260–3.

The life of Byron was a masque in action, to which his poetry is but the moralising accompaniment of words. 'One whose dust was once all fire' (words which Byron used of Rousseau, and which may still more truthfully be used of himself), Byron still lives for us with such incomparable vividness because he was a man first and a poet afterwards. He became a poet for that reason, and that reason explains the imperfection of his poetry. Most of his life he was a personality looking out for its own formula, and his experiments upon that search were of precisely the kind to thrill the world. What poet ever had so splendid a legend in his lifetime? His whole life was lived in the eyes of men, and Byron had enough of the actor in him to delight in that version of 'all the world's a stage.' His beauty and his deformity, his 'tenderness, roughness, delicacy, coarseness, sentiment, sensuality, soaring and grovelling, dirt and deity, all mixed up in that one compound of inspired clay' (it is his own summary of Burns), worked together with circumstances to move every heart to admiration and pity. He was a poet, and he did what others only wrote; he seemed to write what others dared not think. . . .

. . . 'My qualities,' he tells us of his school-days at Harrow, 'were much more oratorical than poetical, and Dr. Drury, my grand patron, had a great notion that I should turn out an orator, from my fluency, my turbulence, my voice, my copiousness of declamation, and my action.' The criticism justified itself; Byron's qualities in verse are indeed 'much more oratorical than poetical'; and, in all his earlier work, theory accentuated this natural tendency so fatally that we have to scrape off a great deal of false glitter if we are to find the good metal

497

which is often enough to be found, even in the metrical romances, with their pseudo-romance, founded on direct observation, their pseudo-passion, doing injustice to a really passionate nature, their impossible heroes, not without certain touches of just self-portraiture, their impossible heroines, betraying after all a certain first-hand acquaintance with the 'dreadful heart of woman.' In narrative verse Byron finally made for himself a form of his own which exactly suited him, but in lyrical verse he never learnt to do much that he could not already do in the *Hours of Idleness*. His 'last lines' are firmer in measure, graver in substance, but they are written on exactly the same principle as the 'Well! thou art happy' of 1808. There is the same strained simplicity of feeling, in which a really moved directness comes through the traditional rhetoric of the form. Every stanza says something, and it says exactly what he means it to say, without any of the exquisite evasions of a more purely poetic style; without, too, any of the qualifying interruptions of a more subtle temperament. Byron's mind was without subtlety; whatever he felt he felt without reservation, or the least thinking about feeling: hence his immediate hold upon the average man or woman, who does not need to come to his verse, as the verse of most other poets must be approached, with a mind already prepared for that communion. There is force, clearness, but no atmosphere; everything is seen detached, a little bare, very distinct, in a strong light without shadows.

In studying Byron one is always face to face with the question: Can intention, in art, ever excuse performance? Can (one is tempted to say) the sum of a number of noughts arrive at an appreciable figure? Wordsworth wearies us by commonplace of thought and feeling, by nervelessness of rhythm, by a deliberate triviality; Coleridge offers us metaphysics for poetry; Browning offers us busy thinking about life for meditation; there is not a scene in Shakespeare which is perfect as a scene of Sophocles is perfect; but with Byron the failure is not exceptional, it is constant; it is like the speech of a man whose tongue is too large for his mouth. There are indeed individual good lines in Byron, a great number of quite splendid lines, though none indeed of the very finest order of poetry; but there is not a single poem, not a single passage of the length of 'Kubla Khan,' perhaps not a single stanza, which can be compared as poetry with a poem or passage or stanza of Keats or Shelley, such as any one will find by merely turning over the pages of those poets for five minutes at random. What is not there is precisely the magic which seems to make poetry its finer self, the perfume of the flower, that by which the flower is remembered, after its petals have dropped or withered. Even Browning abandons himself at times to the dream which floats, musically or in soft colour, through the senses of his mind. But Byron, when he meditates, meditates with fixed attention; if he dreams, he dreams with open eyes, to which the darkness is aglow with tumultuous action; he is at the mercy of none of those wandering sounds, delicate spirits of the air, which come entreating their liberty from the indefinite, in the releasing bondage of song. He has certain things to say, he has certain impulses to embody; he has, first, a certain type of character, then a view of the world which is more obviously the prose than the poetic view of the world, but certainly a wide view, to express; and it remains for him, in this rejection or lack of all the lesser graces, to be either Michael Angelo or Benjamin Haydon.

Or, at least, so it would seem; and yet, so it does not seem to be. Byron is not Michael Angelo, not merely because his conceptions were not as great as Michael Angelo's, but because he had not the same power of achieving his conceptions, because he had not the same technical skill. When Michael Angelo left great naked vestiges of the rock still clinging about the emerging bodies of his later sculpture, it was not because he could not finish them with the same ivory smoothness as the 'Pietà' in St. Peter's; it was because he had found out all the art of man's visible body, and had apprehended that deeper breathing of the spirit of life, which is in the body, yet which is not the body; and was caught in the agony of the last conflict with the last mystery. To leave an appealing or terrifying or lamentable incompleteness, where before there had been the clear joy of what is finished and finite: there, precisely, was the triumph of his technique. But Byron is not Haydon, because he is not a small man struggling to be a great man, painting large merely because he cannot paint small, and creating chaos on the canvas out of ambition rather than irresistible impulse. He is fundamentally sincere, which is the root of greatness; he has a firm hold on himself and on the world; he speaks to humanity in its own voice, heightened to a pitch which carries across Europe. No poet had ever seemed to speak to men so directly, and it was through this directness of his vision of the world, and of his speech about it, that he became a poet, that he made a new thing of poetry.

Look, for instance, at his epithets and at his statements, and you will find, whenever he is at his best, an unparalleled justness of expression, a perfect hitting of the mark, which will sometimes seem rather the vigour of prose than the more celestial energy of poetry, but not always. When, in *The Vision of Judgment*, George III is brought pompously to the gate of Heaven and is seen to be nothing but

> An old man
> With an old soul, and both extremely blind;

when, in *Childe Harold*, Napoleon is seen

> With a deaf heart that never seemed to be
> A listener to itself;

when

> France gets drunk with blood to vomit crime;

when Cromwell

> Hewed the throne down to a block;

when history is defined as 'the Devil's scripture,' Rome as 'the Niobe of nations,' ivy as 'the garland of eternity'; when Castlereagh's speeches are summed up:

> Nor even a sprightly blunder's spark can blaze
> From that Ixion grindstone's ceaseless toil,
> That turns and turns to give the world a notion
> Of endless torment and perpetual motion;

there is at least, in all these vivid and unforgettable phrases, a heat of truth which has kindled speech into a really imaginative fervour. Seen in the form which perhaps more immediately impressed the world, as being liker to the world's notion of poetry—

> Admire—exult—despise—laugh—weep—for here
> There is such matter for all feeling: Man!

it is sheer rhetoric, and, for all its measure of personal sincerity, becomes false through over-emphasis. The closer Byron's writing seems to come to prose the nearer it really comes to poetry, because it comes nearer to humanity and to the world, his subject-matter, which appears to take him for its voice, rather than to be chosen by him with any conscious selection.

Byron loved the world for its own sake and for good and evil. His quality of humanity was genius to him, and stood to him in the place of imagination. Whatever is best in his work is full of this kind of raw or naked humanity. It is the solid part of his rhetoric, and is what holds us still in the apparently somewhat theatrical addresses to the Dying

Gladiator and the like. Speaking straight, in *Don Juan* and *The Vision of Judgment*, it creates almost a new kind of poetry, the poetry of the world, written rebelliously, but on its own level, by a man to whom the world was the one reality. Only Byron, and not Shelley, could lead the revolt against custom and convention, against the insular spirit of England, because to Byron custom and convention and the insular spirit were so much more actual things. . . .

Byron was at once the victim and the master of the world. Two enemies, always in fierce grapple with one another, yet neither of them ever thrown, Byron and the world seem to touch at all points, and to maintain a kind of equilibrium by the equality of their strength. To Byron life itself was imaginative, not the mere raw stuff out of which imagination could shape something quite different, something far more beautiful, but itself, its common hours, the places he passed on the way, a kind of poem in action. All his verse is an attempt to make his own poetry out of fragments of this great poem of life, as it came to him on his heedful way through the midst of it. . . .

Byron has power without wisdom, power which is sanity, and human at heart, but without that vision which is wisdom. His passion is without joy, the resurrection, or that sorrow deeper than any known unhappiness, which is the death by which we attain life. He has never known what it is to be at peace, with himself or with outward things. There is a certain haste in his temper, which does not allow him to wait patiently upon any of the spiritual guests who only come unbidden, and to those who await them. His mind is always full of busy little activities, with which a more disinterested thinker would not be concerned. Himself the centre, he sees the world revolving about him, seemingly as conscious of him as he of it. It is not only that he never forgets himself, but he never forgets that he is a lord, and that one of his feet is not perfect.

In his letters, with their brilliant common sense, their wit, their clear and defiant intellect, their intolerant sincerity, as in his poems, it is not what we call the poet who speaks, it is what we call the natural man. Byron is the supreme incarnation of the natural man. . . .

And . . . not so very long before it was too late, he discovered how he was meant to write in verse, 'with common words in their common places,' as Jeffrey defined it; and then, for the first time, his verse became as good as his prose, and a stanza of his rhyme could be matched as mere writing against a paragraph from one of his letters. Neither Keats nor Shelley, not even Wordsworth, much less Coleridge, was content with our language as we have it; all, on theory or against theory, used inversions, and wrote otherwise than they would speak; it was Byron, with his boisterous contempt for rules, his headlong way of getting to the journey's end, who discovered that poetry, which is speech as well as song, and speech not least when it is most song, can be written not only with the words we use in talking, but in exactly the same order and construction. And, besides realising this truth for other people who were to come later and make a different use of the discovery, he realised for himself that he could make poetry entirely conversational, thus getting closer to that world which was 'too much with him.' Who in English poetry before Byron has ever talked in verse? Taking a hint from Frere, who had nothing to say, and did but show how things might be said, Byron gave up oratory and came nearer than he had yet come to poetry by merely talking. 'I have broken down the poetry as nearly as I could to common language,' he says in a letter, referring to *Sardanapalus*; but in such attempts to be 'as simple and severe as Alfieri,' the lamentable attempts of the dramas, there is only too thorough a 'breaking down' of poetry to a level which is not even that of good prose. In *Beppo*, in *The Vision of Judgment*, and in *Don Juan*, words, style, language, subject, are at one; the colloquial manner is used for what is really talk, extraordinarily brilliant talk, and at the same time, as Goethe saw, a 'classically elegant comic style'; the natural man is at last wholly himself, all of himself, himself not even exaggerated for effect.

Never, in English verse, has a man been seen who was so much a man and so much an Englishman. It is not man in the elemental sense, so much as the man of the world, whom we find reflected, in a magnificent way, in this poet for whom (like the novelists, and unlike all other poets) society exists as well as human nature. No man of the world would feel ashamed of himself for writing poetry like *Don Juan*, if he could write it; and not only because the poet himself seems conscious of all there is ridiculous in the mere fact of writing in rhyme, when everything can be so well said in prose. It is the poetry of middle age (premature with Byron, '*ennuyé* at nineteen,' as he assures us), and it condenses all the temporary wisdom, old enough to be a little sour and not old enough to have recovered sweetness, of perhaps the least profitable period of life. It is sad and cynical with experience, and is at the stage between storm and peace; it doubts everything, as everything must be doubted before it can be understood rightly and rightly apprehended; it regrets youth, which lies behind it, and hates the thought of age, which lies before it, with a kind of passionate self-pity; it has knowledge rather than wisdom, and is a little mirror of the world, turned away from the sky, so that only the earth is visible in it. Shakespeare has put all the world's motley into his picture; but is not the world, to Shakespeare, that 'insubstantial pageant' which is always about to fade, and which fades into nothingness whenever Hamlet gets alone with his soul, or Macbeth with his conscience, or even Othello with his honour? Byron's thought, which embraced Europe as another man's thought might have embraced the village from which he had risen, was too conscious of politics, nations, events, Napoleon, George III, and other trifles in eternity, to be quite free to overlook the edge of the globe, and bring back news, or at least a significant silence, from that ultimate inspection. He taught poetry to be vividly interested in all earthly things, and for their own sake; and if any one had reminded him with Calderon that 'Life's a dream, and dreams themselves are a dream,' he would have replied that, at all events, the dream is a real thing, and the only reality, to the dreamer, and that he was not yet through with his sleep. . . .

The melancholy of Childe Harold, of Byron himself, which has been so often associated with the deeper and more thoughtful melancholy of René, of Obermann, is that discontent with the world which comes from too great love of the world, and not properly an intellectual dissatisfaction at all. It gave birth to a whole literature of pessimism, in which what had been in Byron an acute personal ache became an imagined travailing of the whole world in a vast disgust at its own existence. Where Byron, as he admitted, 'deviated into the gloomy vanity of "drawing from self,"' less energetic and more contemplative writers spoke for humanity, as they conceived it, and found everything grey with their own old age of soul, which had never been young. It was only Byron who could say, after a visit to the opera, on which he comments with the most cheerful malice: 'How I do delight in observing life as it really is!' And it is just here that he distinguishes himself from his followers, in his right to say, as he said:

> But I have lived, and have not lived in vain.

Byron is a moralist, and a moralist of great simplicity. He had

> That just habitual scorn, which could contemn
> Men and their thoughts,

at the same time that he was conscious of his own most human weaknesses; and, in a fragment not included in *Don Juan*, he cries very sincerely:

> I would to heaven that I were so much clay,
> As I am blood, bone, marrow, passion, feeling.

He speaks his impressive epitaph over human greatness and the wrecks of great cities, because it is the natural impulse of the natural man; and his moralisings, always so personal, are generally what would seem to most people the obvious thought under the circumstances. When he is most moved, by some indignation, which in verse and prose always made him write best, he seems to resign himself to what was noblest in him: the passion for liberty (a passion strong enough to die for, as he proved), the passion against injustice, the passion of the will to live and the will to know, fretting against the limits of death and ignorance. It was then that 'thoughts which should call down thunder' came to him, calling down thunder indeed, on the wrongs and hypocrisies of his time and country, as a moralist more intellectually disinterested, further aloof from the consequences of his words, could not have done.

Byron had no philosophy; he saw no remedy or alternative for any evil, least of all in his own mind, itself more tossed than the world without him. He had flaming doubts, stormy denials; he had the idealism of revolt, and fought instead of dreaming. His idolatry of good is shown by his remorseful consciousness of evil, morbid, as it has seemed to those who have not realised that every form of spiritual energy has something of the divine in it, and is on its way to become divine. *Cain* is a long, restless, proud, and helpless questioning of the powers of good and evil, by one who can say:

> I will have nought to do with happiness
> Which humbles me and mine,

with a pride equal to Lucifer's; and can say also, in all the humility of admitted defeat:

> Were I quiet earth,
> That were no evil.

'Obstinate questionings,' resolving themselves into nothing except that pride and that humility of despair, form the whole drama in which Byron has come nearest to abstracting thinking, in his 'gay metaphysical style,' as he called it. 'Think and endure' is Lucifer's last counsel to Cain. 'Why art thou wretched?' he has already asked him; and been answered: 'Why do I exist?' Cain's arraignment of God, which has nothing startling to us, who have read Nietzsche, raised all England in a kind of panic; religion itself seemed to be tottering. But Byron went no further in that direction; his greater strength lay elsewhere. Dropping heroics, he concludes, at the time that he is writing *Don Juan*, that man 'has always been and always will be an unlucky rascal,' with a tragic acquiescence in that summary settlement of the enigma, laughingly. Humour was given us that we might disguise from ourselves the consciousness of our common misery. Humour turned by thought into irony, which is humour thinking about itself, is the world's substitute for philosophy, perhaps the only weapon that can be turned against it with success. Byron used the world's irony to condemn the world. He had conquered its attention by the vast clamour of his revolt; he had lulled it asleep by an apparent acceptance of its terms; now, like a treacherous friend, treacherous with the sublime treachery of the intellect, he drove the nail into its sleeping forehead.

And so we see Byron ending, after all the 'daring, dash, and grandiosity' (to use Goethe's words, as they are rendered by Matthew Arnold) of his earlier work, a tired and melancholy jester, still fierce at heart. Byron gives us, in an overwhelming way, the desire of life, the enjoyment of life, and the sense of life's deceit, as it vanishes from between our hands, and slips from under our feet, and is a voice and no more. In his own way he preaches 'vanity of vanities,' and not less cogently because he has been drunk with life, like Solomon himself, and has not yet lost the sense of what is intoxicating in it. He has given up the declamation of despair, as after all an effect, however sincere, of rhetoric; his jesting is more sorrowful than his outcries, for it shows him to have surrendered.

> We live and die,
> But which is best, you know no more than I.

All his wisdom (experience, love of nature, passion, tenderness, pride, the thirst for knowledge) comes to that in the end, not even a negation.

Bibliography

This short select bibliography is of works listing or describing nineteenth-century criticism of Byron, or providing evidence of his reactions to it.

BUTLER, E. M., *Byron and Goethe*, 1956.

CHEW, S. C., *Byron in England: His Fame and After-Fame*, 1924.

COLERIDGE, E. H., ed., *The Works of Lord Byron: Poetry*, 2nd edn., 1904–5.

ESCARPIT, ROBERT, *Lord Byron: un tempérament littéraire*, 1955–7.

ESTÈVE, EDMOND, *Byron et le romantisme français*, 1907.

HAYDEN, J. O., *Th Romantic Reviewers 1802–1824*, 1969.

JACK, IAN, *English Literature 1815–1832*, 1963.

JOHNSON, E. D. H., 'Don Juan in England,' *ELH* (*A Journal of English Literary History*), XI, 1944.

LEONARD, W. E., *Byron and Byronism in America*, 1905.

MARCHAND, L. A., *Byron: A Biography*, 1957.

MURRAY, JOHN, ed., *Lord Byron's Correspondence*, 1922.

PROTHERO, R. E., ed., *The Works of Lord Byron: Letters and Journals*, 1898–1901.

RUTHERFORD, A., *Byron: A Critical Study*, 1961.

SMILES, SAMUEL, *A Publisher and His Friends: Memoir and Correspondence of the Late John Murray*, 1891.

STEFFAN, T. G., *Lord Byron's 'Cain': Twelve Essays and a Text*, 1969.

STEFFAN, T. G. and PRATT, W. W., eds., *Byron's 'Don Juan'* (see in particular the Appendix to Vol. IV, 'A Survey of Commentary on *Don Juan*').

STROUT, A. L., ed., *John Bull's Letter to Lord Byron*, 1947.

TRUEBLOOD, P. G., *The Flowering of Byron's Genius*, 1945.

WARD, W S., 'Byron's "Hours of Idleness" and Other than Scotch Reviewers,' *Modern Language Notes*, LIX, 1944.

Select Index

1: *Poems by Byron*

2: Periodicals and Anonymous Works

3: Writers, Artists and Others Quoted, Cited, or Compared with Byron